New York City

THE ROUGH GUIDE

There are more than one hundred and fifty Rough Guide titles
covering destinations from Amsterdam to Zimbabwe

Forthcoming titles include
Argentina • Croatia • Ecuador • Southeast Asia

Rough Guide Reference Series
Classical Music • Drum'n'Bass • English Football • European Football
House • The Internet • Jazz • Music USA • Opera • Reggae
Rock Music • Techno • Unexplained Phenomena • World Music

Rough Guide Phrasebooks
Czech • Dutch • Egyptian Arabic • European Languages • French
German • Greek • Hindi & Urdu • Hungarian • Indonesian
Italian • Japanese • Mandarin Chinese • Mexican Spanish • Polish
Portuguese • Russian • Spanish • Swahili • Thai • Turkish • Vietnamese

Rough Guides on the Internet
www.roughguides.com

Rough Guide Credits

Text Editor:	Mary Beth Maioli
Series Editor:	Mark Ellingham
Editorial:	Martin Dunford, Jonathan Buckley, Jo Mead, Kate Berens, Amanda Tomlin, Ann-Marie Shaw, Paul Gray, Helena Smith, Judith Bamber, Kieran Falconer, Orla Duane, Olivia Eccleshall, Ruth Blackmore, Sophie Martin, Geoff Howard, Claire Saunders, Gavin Thomas, Alexander Mark Rogers, Polly Thomas, Joe Staines, Lisa Nellis, Andrew Tomičíc (UK); Andrew Rosenberg (US)
Online Editors:	Kelly Cross (US)
Production:	Susanne Hillen, Andy Hilliard, Link Hall, Helen Ostick, Julia Bovis, Michelle Draycott, Anna Wray, Katie Pringle, Robert Evers
Cartography:	Melissa Baker, Maxine Burke, Nichola Goodliffe, Ed Wright
Picture Research:	Louise Boulton
Finance:	John Fisher, Gary Singh, Ed Downey, Catherine Robertson
Marketing & Publicity:	Richard Trillo, Niki Smith, David Wearn, Jemima Broadbridge (UK); Jean-Marie Kelly, Myra Campolo, Simon Carloss (US)
Administration:	Tania Hummel, Charlotte Marriott, Demelza Dallow

Acknowledgments

Biggest thanks on this new edition goes to everyone at both Rough Guide offices, especially Andrew Rosenberg for knowing everything about everything; Jean-Marie Kelly for laughs and support; Myra Campolo for nightlife suggestions; Kelly Cross for Mac crisis control; Martin Dunford for brilliance and patience; Melissa Flack for terrific mapmaking; Susanne Hillen and Katie Pringle for seamless production; Chris Hume, Mary Kent Hearon and Sonja Kenney for tips, advice and late-night life saving; Antonia Hebbert and Silke Kerwick for Basics; and Russell Walton for proofreading. Special thanks to the inimitable Darren Colby for all the usual things.

Diana Wells would like to thank Larry Lustig for his Brooklyn restaurant recommendations, Heather Pasante at the Museum of Modern Art and Craig Pospisil for his architectural expertise. Most of all thanks to Mary Beth Maioli for being such a helpful and supportive editor.

Rebecca Hirschfield would like to thank Paul Lawsky; Jack Putnam; Madeline Rogers; Diane Dallal; JoAnne Meyers; Nestor Danyluk; Richard and Carol Lentz; Doris Quinones; Neal Shoemaker; Keith Forest; Seth Kamil and Thoran Tritter; Matt Postal; Angela Russo; Cynthia Lee; Carolyn Stone; Adrian Gonzalez; Ted and Rosalyn Gottlieb; Alexander Wood; Lisa Robb and Lourdes Silva; Lloyd Ultan; and Robert Sinclair Jr.

Nick Thomson thanks Rob Lubeck and Tim Joyce for hanging in the pubs and talking sports.

Many thanks are also due to those who wrote in with comments and corrections for the sixth edition – see the list on p.iv. Keep the letters coming!

This seventh edition published January 2000 by Rough Guides Ltd, 62–70 Shorts Gardens, London WC2H 9AH .Reprinted August 2000
Distributed by the Penguin Group:
Penguin Books Ltd, 27 Wrights Lane, London W8 5TZ.
Penguin Books USA Inc, 375 Hudson Street, New York, NY 10014, USA.
Penguin Books Australia Ltd, 487 Maroondah Highway, PO Box 257, Ringwood, Victoria 3134, Australia.
Penguin Books Canada Ltd, 10 Alcorn Avenue, Toronto, Ontario M4V 1E4, Canada.
Penguin Books (NZ) Ltd, 182–190 Wairau Road, Auckland 10, New Zealand.

Printed in England by Clays Ltd, St Ives PLC
Typography and **original design** by Jonathan Dear and The Crowd Roars.
Illustrations throughout by Edward Briant.

© Martin Dunford and Jack Holland 2000
560pp. Includes index.

A catalogue record for this book is available from the British Library.
ISBN 1-85828-507-0

New York City

THE ROUGH GUIDE

Written and researched by
Martin Dunford and Jack Holland

With additional contributions by
Adrian Curry, Rebecca Hirschfield, Nick Thomson
and Diana Wells

THE ROUGH GUIDES

Help us update

We've gone to a lot of effort to ensure that this edition of the *Rough Guide to New York City* is completely up-to-date and accurate. However, things do change – in New York more rapidly than anywhere – and if you feel that there's something we've missed, or that you'd like to see included, please write and let us know. We'll credit all contributions, and send a copy of the new book (or any other *Rough Guide*, if you prefer) for the best letters.

Please mark letters "Rough Guide to New York City" and send to: Rough Guides, 62–70 Shorts Gardens, London WC2H 9AH or Rough Guides, 375 Hudson St, 3rd floor, New York, NY 10014.

Email should be sent to:
mail@roughguides.co.uk

Online updates about Rough Guide titles can be found on our Web site at *www.roughguides.com*

The Authors

Martin Dunford and **Jack Holland** first met at the University of Kent at Canterbury. Following jobs as diverse as insurance collection, beer-barrel rolling and EFL teaching in Greece, they co-founded the Rough Guides in the early 1980s. After co-authoring several other titles, Martin is now editorial director of Rough Guides while Jack recently escaped from Berlin, where he lived for four years.

Readers' letters

We'd like to thank all the readers who wrote in with comments and updates to the sixth edition: Lydia Porter, David Marrinan, Steve Brailey, Ervin Matik, Maree Glasson, Xanthe Craddock, Daniel Harris, Pete Davies, Rosemary Behan, Tim Galhgan, Lee Williams, S.H. Fahy, Geert van Loo, Slu Trigger, Jenny Mitchell, G. Ferguson, Morag Robertson, Steve Fleming, Claire Thompson, Rebecca Hogg, Sharon Edmead, Ron Rocco, Carol Burgess, Clare Ellis, Karen Yair, Livia Ratcliffe, Moyra Orgill, Pamela Tully, Christine Walter, Joe Stubley, Lai Chong-Siltola, Sanja Cvetnić, Noel O'Connor and all the folks who contacted us via email but preferred to remain anonymous.

Our apologies to anyone whose name has been omitted or misspelt.

Rough Guides

Travel Guides • Phrasebooks • Music and Reference Guides

We set out to do something different when the first *Rough Guide* was published in 1982. Mark Ellingham, just out of university, was traveling in Greece. He brought along the popular guidebooks of the day, but found they were all lacking in some way. They were either strong on ruins and museums but went on for pages without mentioning a beach or taverna. Or they were so conscious of the need to save money that they lost sight of Greece's cultural and historical significance. Also, none of the books told him anything about Greece's contemporary life – its politics, its culture, its people and how they lived.

So with no job in prospect, Mark decided to write his own guidebook, one which aimed to provide practical information that was second to none, detailing the best beaches and the hottest clubs and restaurants, while also giving hard-hitting accounts of every sight, both famous and obscure, and providing up-to-the-minute information on contemporary culture. It was a guide that encouraged independent travelers to find the best of Greece, and was a great success, getting shortlisted for the Thomas Cook travel guide award, and encouraging Mark, along with three friends, to expand the series.

The Rough Guide list grew rapidly and the letters flooded in, indicating a much broader readership than had been anticipated, but one which uniformly appreciated the Rough Guides' mix of practical detail and humor, irreverence and enthusiasm. Things haven't changed. The same four friends who began the series are still the caretakers of the Rough Guide mission today: to provide the most reliable, up-to-date and entertaining information to independent-minded travelers of all ages, on all budgets.

We now publish 150 titles and have offices in London and New York. The travel guides are written and researched by a dedicated team of more than 100 authors, based in Britain, Europe, the USA and Australia. We have also created a unique series of phrasebooks to accompany the travel series, along with the acclaimed series of music guides, and a best-selling pocket guide to the Internet and World Wide Web. We also publish comprehensive travel information on our Web site: *www.roughguides.com*

Contents

Part Three Listings   311

Part Four Contexts   489

Index   525

List of maps

MAP SYMBOLS

〔80〕	Interstate	Ⓜ	Subway Station
〔30〕	U.S. Highway	ⓘ	Information Centre
〔1〕	State Highway	✉	Post Office
▓▓▓	Tunnel	✡	Synagogue
— —	Ferry route	✝	Buddhist Temple
▬ ▬ ▬	State border	■	Building
-----	Borough/county boundary	✚	Church
— — —	Chapter division boundary	▨	Wildlife Refuge
———	River	▨	Park
✈	Airport		

Introduction

New York City is the most beguiling place there is. You may not think so at first – for the city is admittedly mad, the epitome in many ways of all that is wrong in modern America. But spend even a week here and it happens – the pace, the adrenaline take hold, and the shock gives way to myth. Walking through the city streets is an experience, the buildings like icons to the modern age, and above all to the power of money. Despite all the hype, the movie-image sentimentalism, **Manhattan** – the central island and the city's real core – has massive romance: whether it's the flickering lights of the Midtown skyscrapers as you speed across the Queensboro Bridge, the 4am half-life Downtown, or just wasting the morning on the Staten Island ferry, you really would have to be made of stone not to be moved by it all.

None of which is to suggest that New York is a conventionally pleasing city. Take a walk in Manhattan beside Central Park, notably its east side, past the city's richest apartments and best museums, and keep walking: within a dozen or so blocks you find yourself in the lower reaches of Spanish Harlem. The shock could hardly be more extreme. The city is constantly like this, with glaring, in-your-face wealth juxtaposed with urban problems – poverty, the drug trade, homelessness – that have a predictably high profile. Things definitely changed during the Nineties, especially in the Mayor Giuliani years. Crime figures are at their lowest in years and are still dropping (statistically, New York is now one of the country's safest big cities), and renewal plans have finally begun to undo years of urban neglect. But for all its new clean-cut image New York remains a unique place – one you'll want to return to again and again.

The city also has more straightforward pleasures. There are the different **ethnic neighborhoods** of Lower Manhattan, from Chinatown to the Jewish Lower East Side and ever-diminishing Little Italy; and the artsy concentrations in SoHo, TriBeCa, and the East and West Village. There is the **architecture** of corporate

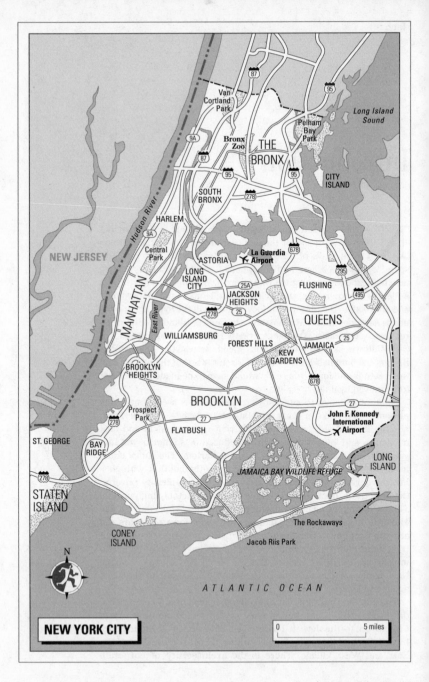

NEW YORK CITY

0   5 miles

Manhattan and the more residential Upper East and West Side districts (the whole city reads like an illustrated history of modern design); and there is the **art**, which affords weeks of wandering in the Metropolitan and Modern Art museums and countless smaller collections. You can eat anything, at any time, cooked in any style; **drink** in any kind of company; sit through any number of obscure **movies**. The established arts – **dance, theater, music** – are superbly catered for, and although the contemporary **music scene** is perhaps not as vital or original as in, say, London or Los Angeles, New York's **clubs** are varied and exciting, if rarely inexpensive. And for the avid consumer, the choice of **shops** is vast, almost numbingly exhaustive in this heartland of the great capitalist dream.

Costs

Perhaps your biggest single problem in New York is going to be **money**, or rather how to hold on to what you have. The exchange rate for foreign visitors is fairly good these days – around $1.60 to the pound sterling at time of writing – and the city (as long as you're not renting an apartment) is generally as cheap as it has been for some time. Still, it's an expensive place to spend time, and far pricier than most of the rest of the US. **Accommodation** will be your biggest day-to-day expense, with rock-bottom double hotel rooms in Manhattan costing around $100, much more for anywhere in the mid-range, and even a basic YMCA double room going for over $50 – though there are options that work out cheaper (see our recommendations in Chapter 16). The **bottom line** for staying alive – after this – is around $30 a day, a figure which will of course skyrocket the more you dine out and party, although it is possible to eat out both well and inexpensively. There are bargain **restaurants** – see Chapter 17 for listings – where you'll be well-fed for $10 or less, while the all-American breakfast will set you up for the day, and ubiquitous delis, pizza places and falafel stands provide the cheapest snacks for just a couple of dollars.

Climate and when to go

New York's **climate** ranges from the stickily hot and humid in midsummer to well below freezing in January and February: winter and high summer (most people claim the city is unbearable in July and

Average New York Temperatures											
	Jan	Feb	Mar	Apr	May	Jun	Jul	Aug	Sep	Oct	Nov	Dec
Max °F	38	40	49	61	72	80	85	84	77	66	54	42
Max °C	3	4	9	16	22	27	29	29	25	19	12	6
Min °F	26	27	34	44	53	63	68	67	60	50	41	31
Min °C	-3	-3	1	7	12	17	20	19	16	10	5	-1

August) are much the worst time you could come. Spring is gentle, if unpredictable, and usually wet, while fall is perhaps the best season: come at either time and you'll find it easier to get things done and the people more welcoming. Whatever time of year you come, dress in layers: buildings tend to be overheated during winter months and air-conditioned to the point of iciness in summer. Also bring comfortable and sturdy shoes – you're going to be doing a lot of walking.

Basics

Getting there from Britain and Ireland

Unless you're in no hurry and can afford the *QE2*, the only way to get to New York from Britain and Ireland is to fly. A wide range of airlines serve the London–New York route, so competition is intense, and the choice of tickets and fares can be bewildering. For the best offers, it pays to shop around. Use the Net: *www.cheapflights.co.uk* and *www.lastminute.co.uk*. Check the travel ads in the Sunday papers – and, in London, *Time Out* and the *Evening Standard* – or consult one of the agents detailed overleaf. Treat our comments as a general guide only, and one that's likely to have undergone at least subtle alterations by the time you read it.

From Britain

Flights tend to **leave** Britain in the morning or afternoon and **arrive** in New York in the afternoon or evening; flying time is seven to eight hours. Coming back, most flights depart in the evening to arrive in Britain early next morning; flying time, due to the prevailing winds, is shorter – six to seven hours.

Airlines

Of the nine airlines that currently fly between Britain and New York, the major operators are British Airways, who offer five nonstop services each day from London Heathrow to JFK, another from Heathrow to Newark, and one daily flight to JFK from London Gatwick and Manchester. American Airlines has six daily flights from Heathrow to JFK, Continental has two daily flights to Newark from Gatwick, and one each from Manchester and Birmingham, and United has four daily flights from Heathrow, of which three go to JFK and one to Newark. Virgin Atlantic flies twice daily Heathrow to Newark and once from Gatwick to Newark, while Delta has two daily flights from Gatwick via Brussels to JFK, plus one daily service between Manchester and JFK. Air India flies once daily from Heathrow to JFK, Kuwait Airways flies the same route three times weekly, and finally El Al flies two or three times weekly between London Stansted and Newark.

Fares and agents

Fares vary according to season, availability and the current level of inter-airline competition. There are three main fare seasons: low season (October to March, excluding Christmas and New Year); mid season (April to mid-June); and high season (mid-June to September and three weeks or so around Christmas and New Year). If you contact any of the airlines directly, you may learn of some special cut-price deal (particularly in winter), but they're more likely to offer you an **Apex ticket**. The conditions on these are pretty standard whoever you fly with: seats must be booked 21 days or more in advance, and you must stay for a minimum of seven nights, a maximum of one month; they're also usually nonrefundable and can't be changed without incurring a hefty penalty fee. Prices are pretty much the same across the board: low-season midweek rates start at around £250 return, rising to around £350 in spring, and over £400 in high season. Tax of £52.40 is added to all fares, and flying at

To choose whether you'd rather fly into JFK or Newark airports, and details on **how to reach Manhattan** from either, see "Points of arrival" on p.14.

AIRLINES IN BRITAIN

Air India	☎ 020/8745 1000	**Delta Airlines**	☎ 0800/414767
www.airindia.com		**El Al**	☎ 020/7957 4100
American Airlines	☎ 0345/789789	**Kuwait Airways**	☎ 020/7412 0007
www.aa.com		**United Airlines**	☎ 0845/844 4777
British Airways	☎ 0345/222111	*www.ual.com*	
www.british-airways.com		**Virgin Atlantic**	☎ 01293/747747
Continental Airlines	☎ 0800/776464	*www.fly.virgin.com*	

TRAVEL AGENTS IN BRITAIN

STA Travel		Manchester	☎ 0161/721 4000
London	☎ 020/7361 6262	*www.flynow.com*	
Bristol	☎ 0117/929 4399	**Usit Campus**	
Cambridge	☎ 01223/366966	National call center	☎ 0870/240 1010
Leeds	☎ 0113/244 9212	London	☎ 020/7730 2101
Manchester	☎ 0161/834 0668	Birmingham	☎ 0121/414 1848
Newcastle-upon-Tyne	☎ 0191/233 2111	Brighton	☎ 01273/570226
Oxford	☎ 01865/792800	Bristol	☎ 0117/929 2494
www.statravel.co.uk		Cambridge	☎ 01223/324283
		Edinburgh	☎ 0131/668 3303
Trailfinders		Manchester	☎ 0161/833 2046
London	☎ 020/7938 3366	Oxford	☎ 01865/242067
Birmingham	☎ 0121/236 1234	*www.usitcampus.co.uk*	
Bristol	☎ 0117/929 9000		
Glasgow	☎ 0141/353 2224	**Usit Council**	
Manchester	☎ 0161/839 6969	London	☎ 020/7437 7767
		www.usitcouncil.co.uk	
Travel Bug			
London	☎ 020/7835 2000		

TOUR OPERATORS IN BRITAIN

BonVoyage		**Trans Atlantic Vacations**	
Southampton	☎ 023/8024 8248	Horley	☎ 01293/774441
British Airways Holidays		**United Vacations**	
Crawley	☎ 0870/242 4243	Heathrow Airport	☎ 020/8313 0999
www.baholidays.co.uk		**Virgin Holidays**	
Destination USA		Crawley	☎ 01293/617181
London	☎ 020/7400 7000		
www.destination-group.com			

the weekend costs extra. A fully flexible economy fare may cost £1000 more. If you're keen to find the cheapest possible fare, it makes more sense to contact an agent that specializes in low-cost flights, as listed above. Especially if you're under 26 or a student, these can knock up to fifty percent off the fares quoted by the airlines, bringing prices down to under £200 return. Your flight may not be direct, however, and there may be other drawbacks. The best deals are generally with the less popular airlines like

Kuwait Airways or Air India. You might also call one of the American specialists we've listed, who often have access to the very cheapest transatlantic seats as well as summer charters. Their brochures are available in most High Street travel agents, or you can contact them direct at the numbers given above.

If you're on a really tight budget you may want to consider flying as a **courier**, although during the off season at least you may find it's not worth the hassle given the variety of low fares available. Courier flights can be arranged with Flight Masters, 83 Mortimer St, London W1 (020/7462 0022) or Bridges Worldwide, Old Mill Road House, West Drayton, Middlesex TW3 (01895/465065). The flights involve a package being checked through with your luggage, in return for a cheaper flight. Call up armed with the date you'd like to travel and how long you plan to stay, and they can advise whether flights are available; however, you will find return times and luggage are very restricted. Another option for a small membership fee, is to join the International Association of Air Travel Couriers, c/o International Features, 1 Kings Rd, Dorchester, Dorset DT1 (01305/264564; www.courier.org or the British branch's Web site, www.aircourier.co.uk) who are agents for lots of courier companies.

From Ireland

The only nonstop scheduled services to New York from Ireland are provided by Aer Lingus, which flies once to JFK and twice to Newark from Dublin each day, and also once daily from Shannon to JFK, at a cost of up to IR£500 for an **Apex ticket**. As usual, though, the best plan is to **approach an agent** direct, preferably one specializing in under-26 or student travel, which can

bring the price down to as little as IR£315 for a round-trip ticket in low season, around IR£50 more during the summer.

Inclusive tours

All-in deals – flights plus hotel accommodation in New York City – can be a good idea if you're only planning a short stay. Low-season prices per person for a return flight plus three nights staying in a middle-range midtown hotel start at £400–500 and rise to more like £600–700 at peak periods; seven nights would cost from £600 up to around £900 per person, again depending on the time of year. Most High Street travel agents have the full range of brochures and can advise on the best deals.

Entry requirements

Citizens of Britain and Ireland do not require visas for visits to the United States of less than ninety days. You must have a full **passport** (valid for at least ninety days from the date on which you enter the US), and your flight ticket must be a return ticket (or onward ticket, but not to a neighbor of the US, such as the Caribbean). You also have to fill in the **visa waiver form** handed out on incoming planes.

AIRLINES IN IRELAND			
Aer Lingus www.aerlingus.ie	☎ 01/844 4777	**Delta Airlines**	☎ 01/676 8080 toll free 1800-768080
British Airways www.british-airways.com	☎ 1-800/626747	**Virgin Atlantic** www.fly.virgin.com	☎ 01/873 3388

TRAVEL AGENTS IN IRELAND			
Joe Walsh Tours Dublin	☎ 01/676 3053	**Usit NOW** Belfast	☎ 028/9032 7111
Student & Group Travel Dublin	☎ 01/677 7834	Cork Dublin	☎ 021/270900 ☎ 01/602 1600
Thomas Cook Belfast Dublin	☎ 028/9088 3900 ☎ 01/677 1721	**Williames** Belfast	☎ 028/9023 0714
Twohigs Dublin	☎ 01/677 2666 or 670 9750		

TOUR OPERATORS IN IRELAND			
American Holidays Belfast	☎ 028/9023 8762	Dublin	☎ 01/679 8800

Immigration control takes place on arrival in New York, when you're expected to provide details of where you are staying on your first night.

For further details, contact the American embassies in Britain (24–31 Grosvenor Square, London W1A 1AE; ☎020/7499 9000); 0891/200290, recorded information, calls charged at 60p per minute) or Ireland (42 Elgin Rd, Ballsbridge, Dublin; ☎01/668 7122). The best way to get information is through the embassy Web site: *www.usembassy.org.uk*. British and Irish consulates in New York are listed on p.485.

For advice on staying on in New York, see p.50.

Travel insurance

Though not compulsory, **travel insurance** including medical coverage is essential in view of the high costs of health care in the US. Credit cards (particularly American Express) often have certain levels of medical or other insurance

included, especially if you use them to pay for your trip; in addition, if you have a good "all risks" home insurance policy it may well cover your possessions against loss or theft even when overseas, and many private medical schemes also cover you while abroad. If you plan to participate in potentially dangerous activities such as watersports or skiing, you'll almost certainly have to pay an extra premium; check carefully that your policy will cover you in case of an accident.

Most travel agents and tour operators sell travel insurance policies offered by Usit Campus or STA in the UK and Usit NOW in Ireland are usually reasonable value. If you feel the cover is inadequate, or you want to compare prices, any insurance broker, bank or specialist travel insurance company should be able to help: call Columbus Direct Insurance (☎020/7375 0011), Endsleigh Insurance (☎020/7436 4451), or Frizzell Insurance (☎01202/292333). Two weeks' coverage for a trip to the US might cost around £30, a month more like £50.

Getting there from Australia and New Zealand

The high season for airfares to the US is mid-May to August and mid-December to mid-January; low season is mid-January through February, and October through November; shoulder season is the rest of the year. Tickets purchased directly

from the airlines tend to be expensive, and travel agents offer much better deals on fares and have the latest information on fly-drive packages and stopover specials. The best discounts are through Flight Centres and STA, who can also advise on visa regulations. Fares from eastern Australian capitals are generally the same (airlines offer a free connecting service between these cities), whereas fares from Perth and Darwin are about AUS$400 more.

Not surprisingly, given the distances involved, there are no direct scheduled flights and packages to New York from **Australia** or **New Zealand**, and most people reach the eastern United States by way of the West Coast gateway cities of Los Angeles and San Francisco. You can do this by either buying an **all-in ticket** via LA or San Francisco, or simply flying to LA and using one of the **domestic flight coupons** you can buy with your international ticket (these must be

AIRLINES AND AGENTS IN AUSTRALIA AND NEW ZEALAND

Air New Zealand, 5 Elizabeth St, Sydney ☎ 02/9223 4666; corner of Customs and Queen streets, Auckland ☎ 09/357 3000.

Anywhere Travel, 345 Anzac Parade, Kingsford, Sydney ☎ 02/663 0411.

Budget Travel, 16 Fort St, Auckland plus branches around the city ☎ 09/366 0061 or 0800/808 040.

Canada & America Travel Specialists, 342 Pacific Highway, Crows Nest, Sydney ☎ 02/9922 4600.

Flight Centres, Australia: 82 Elizabeth St, Sydney plus branches nationwide ☎ 13 1600. New Zealand: National Bank Towers, 205–225 Queen St, Auckland ☎ 09/309 6171; other branches countrywide.

Japan Airlines, Floor 14, Darlington Park, 201 Sussex St, Sydney ☎ 02/9272 1111; Floor 12, Westpac Tower, 120 Albert St, Auckland ☎ 09/379 9906.

Korean Airlines, 36 Carrington St, Sydney ☎ 02/9262 6000; 7–9 Falcon St, Parnell, Auckland ☎ 09/307 3687.

Qantas, International Square, Jamison St, Sydney ☎ 13 1313; Qantas House, 154 Queen St, Auckland ☎ 09/357 8900 or 0800/808 767.

STA Travel, Australia: 702 Harris St, Ultimo, Sydney; 256 Flinders St, Melbourne; other offices in state capitals and major universities; nearest branch ☎ 13 1776, fastfare telesales 1300/360 960. New Zealand: Traveler's Centre, 10 High St, Auckland ☎ 09/309 4058, fastfare telesales 09/366 6673, plus branches in Wellington, Christchurch, Dunedin, Palmerston North, Hamilton and at major universities; *traveller@statravelaus.com.au*.

Student Uni Travel, 92 Pitt St, Sydney ☎ 02/9232 8444; plus branches in Melbourne, Darwin, Perth, Cairns and Brisbane.

Trailfinders, 8 Spring St, Sydney ☎ 02/9247 7666.

Travel.com.au, 80 Clarence St, Sydney ☎ 02/9290 1500; *consultant@travel.com.au*.

United Airlines, 10 Barrack St, Sydney ☎ 13 1777; 7 City Rd, Auckland ☎ 09/379 3800.

Usit Beyond, corner of Shortland St and Jean Batten Place, Auckland; plus branches in Palmerston North, Christchurch, Hamilton and Wellington ☎ 09/379 4224, 0800/788 336 or 0800-STUDENT; *www.usitbeyond.co.nz*.

bought before you leave your home country). The latter can work out to be cheaper than opting for a straight-through fare, especially if you intend to take in other US cities besides New York. For example, a low-season straight return ticket to LA costs around AUS$1599/NZ$1999 with Air New Zealand, with domestic flight coupons costing around AUS$610 (for a minimum of three), making it one of the cheapest ways to get to New York. In comparison an add-on return fare will cost you in the region of AUS$470/NZ$550. Another option worth consideration if New York is part of a wider US trip – and you have plenty of time – is to travel overland by car, train or bus from your West Coast point of entry.

Traveling from Australia and New Zealand, the best onward flight connections, via LA or San Francisco, are with United Airlines, Air New Zealand and Qantas, all of which have daily services from Sydney, Melbourne and Auckland via LA or San Francisco for around AUS$1975/NZ$2375 in low season up to AUS$2699/NZ$2999 in high season. The lowest fares to New York, however, are via Asia. Japan Airlines has daily flights from Sydney, Brisbane and Cairns via Tokyo or Osaka for around AUS$1700–2150, based on the season, and several times a week from Auckland, NZ$2040–3000, also based on season. Korean Airlines flies from Sydney and Brisbane via Seoul several times a week from AUS$1835–2275 and from Auckland and Christchurch for NZ$2039–2500.

Round-the-world and air passes

If you intend to take in New York as part of a world trip a **round-the-world** ticket offers the best value for money, working out just a little more than an all-in ticket. Qantas–British Airways' "Global Explorer" and "One World" tickets, in conjunction with American Airlines, offer six stopovers worldwide, limited backtracking, and additional stopovers (around $150 each), from AUS$2299/$2999–NZ$2699/$3699. Air New Zealand and Ansett Australia are part of the "Star Alliance" with United Airlines, and offer various routings which include New York on a mileage basis, from AUS$2699/NZ$3239–AUS$3209/NZ$3850.

Air passes or coupons valid for single flights in continental US are offered by various domestic airlines. These can only be purchased with your international ticket and all cost about AUS$610 for a minimum of three with each additional coupon costing around AUS$100.

Entry requirements

Australian and New Zealand **passport** holders staying less than ninety days do not require a visa, providing they arrive on a commercial flight with an onward or return ticket. For longer stays a US multiple-entry visa costs AUS$78. You'll need an application form, available from the US visa information service (☎1902/262 682), one signed passport photo and your passport. You must either mail it or personally lodge it at one of the American embassy or consulate addresses – in Australia, 21 Moonah Place, Canberra, ACT 2600 (☎02/6214 5600), and in New Zealand,

29 Fitzherbert Terrace, Thorndon, Wellington (☎04/472 2068). For postal applications in Australia, payment can be made at any post office; you'll also need to include the receipt of payment and an SAE. Processing takes about ten working days for postal applications; personal lodgements take two days – but check details with the consulate first. Restrictions still apply to communists and communist sympathizers. Visas are denied to convicted criminals.

Travel insurance

Travel insurance is definitely recommended and is available from most travel agents or direct from insurance companies. Most policies are fairly similar in premium and coverage. A typical policy covering New York will cost around AUS$100/NZ$120 for two weeks; AUS$160/NZ$200 for one month; and AUS$320/NZ$400 for three months, depending on the excess amount covered. Companies worth trying are Cover More (in Sydney ☎02/9202 8000 or freecall 1800/251 881; in Auckland ☎09/377 5958 or 0800/657 744) and Ready Plan (in Melbourne ☎03/9791 5077 or 1300/555 017; in Auckland ☎09/300 5333).

Getting there from the United States and Canada

By air

From most places in North America, flying is the fastest and easiest way to reach New York. It can also be the cheapest – but finding that cheap fare won't always be easy. Fares fluctuate so wildly that it doesn't make sense to try to quote them here. Even the shuttles – flights used mainly by business people during the week – from nearby Boston and Washington, DC, can vary from month to month.

New York is the hub of most North American traffic so fares are very competitive. Prices depend more on passenger volume than anything else, so you'll do better (if you have a

For information on how to reach Manhattan from its three **airports** (although most domestic flights come into La Guardia), see "Points of arrival" on p.14. All **Amtrak services**, including trains from Canada, arrive at **Penn Station** at 32nd Street and Seventh and Eighth avenues; only local Metro-North commuter trains use Grand Central Station at 42nd St and Park Avenue. By **bus**, you arrive in New York at the **Port Authority Bus Terminal**, Eighth Avenue and 42nd Street.

choice) flying from one of the larger cities. Your best bet is to start calling the major airlines (see the box overleaf for toll-free numbers) as early as possible – even earlier if you'll be traveling at Thanksgiving or Christmas – because cheap fares usually account for only a portion of the seats available on a given flight, and they fill up fast. It's not impossible to get a last-minute deal, but on the major airlines cheapest fares usually require you to purchase your ticket 14 or 21 days in advance and stay a Saturday night. You should also keep an eye open for any special promotional fares the major airlines may be advertising in the newspapers. Try the smaller airlines, too, since they often pitch in with cheaper deals. Travel agents won't necessarily find you a better fare so much as save you the trouble of making the phone calls yourself. As a guideline, round-trip **fares** from the West Coast average $450, from Chicago it's about $250 and roughly $180 from Miami. From Canada, reckon on paying CAN$340 or so from Toronto or Montréal and around CAN$840 from Vancouver.

You might be able to cut costs further by going through a **specialist flight agent** – either a **consolidator**, who buys up blocks of tickets from the airlines and sells them at a discount, or a **discount agent**, who in addition to dealing with discounted flights may also offer special student and youth fares and a range of other travel-related services such as travel insurance, rail passes, car rentals, tours and the like. Look for these services in small ads in the backs of newspapers, they can be the best place to find last-minute options; they're also good for **one-way tickets**, which can be ridiculously expensive on the big airlines. The drawbacks are that penalties for changing your plans can be stiff and these companies make their money by dealing in bulk – so

don't expect them to answer lots of questions. And if you're a nervous flier, bear in mind that these agents often book flights on small, no-name airlines; that's how they get them so cheap.

Inclusive tours

Many operators run **all-inclusive vacations**, combining plane tickets and hotel accommodation with (for example) sightseeing, wining and dining, or admission to Broadway shows. Even if the "package" aspect doesn't thrill you to pieces, these deals can still be more convenient and sometimes even more economical than arranging the same thing yourself, providing you don't mind losing a little flexibility. With such a vast range of packages available, it's impossible to give an overview – major travel agents will have brochures detailing what's on offer.

By train

For those heading to New York City from within the same radius as the shuttle flights noted opposite, travel **by train** is a viable alternative, though not likely to be much cheaper. The most frequent services are along the New England–New York–Washington DC corridor; fares from Washington and Boston are around $125 round-trip, $185 for Metroliner (which is faster and guarantees you a seat). There is also one daily train linking Montréal and Toronto with New York. Round-trip fares on these services start at around CAN$145 (from Montréal) or CAN$190 (from Toronto). Train fares are often based on availability; book as early as possible to get the cheapest rates.

Although in theory it's possible to haul yourself **long-distance** from the West Coast, the Midwest or the South, it's an exhausting trip (three days plus from California) and fares are downright expensive as well. A much better deal, allowing you to stagger the journey over up to 45 days with up to 3 **stopoffs** is the "Explore America Pass" that costs $399 in the high season (June through mid-September) or $339 in the low season. There's also a "North America Rail Pass" that's sold in conjunction with "Via" the Canadian Rail network, but can be booked through Amtrak (☎1-800/722-6137). This allows you 30 days travel in Canada and the US with 3 stopovers for $645, CAN$895 (high season is from June 1 to Oct 16) or $450, CAN$625 (low season). For non-US citizens only,

MAJOR AIRLINE TOLL-FREE NUMBERS

Air Canada in US ☎ 1-800/776-3000; in Canada ☎ 1-888/247-2262; *www.aircanada.ca*

America West Airlines ☎ 1-800/235-9292; *www.americawest.com*

American Airlines ☎ 1-800/433-7300; *www.americanair.com*

Canadian Airlines in US ☎ 1-800/426-7000; in Canada ☎ 1-800/665-1177; *www.cdnair.ca*

Continental Airlines ☎ 1-800/525-0280; *www.flycontinental.com*

Delta Airlines ☎ 1-800/221-1212; *www.delta-air.com*

Hawaiian Airlines ☎ 1-800/367-5320; *www.hawaiianair.com*

Northwest Airlines ☎ 1-800/225-2525; *www.nwa.com*

Southwest Airlines ☎ 1-800/435-9792; *www.iflyswa.com*

Tower Air ☎ 1-800/221-2500 or 718/553-8500; *www.towerair.com*

TWA ☎ 1-800/221-2000; *www.twa.com*

United Airlines ☎ 1-800/241-6522; *www.ual.com*

US Airways ☎ 1-800/428-4322; *www.usairways.com*

DISCOUNT FLIGHT AGENTS

Council Travel, 205 E 42nd St, New York, NY 10017, and branches in many other US cities ☎ 1-888/COUNCIL or 212/822-2700; *www.counciltravel.com*. Student/budget travel agency.

Now Voyager, 74 Varick St, Suite 307, New York, NY 10016 ☎ 212/431-1616; *www.nowvoyagertravel.com*, Lesbian and gay-friendly consolidator.

STA Travel, 5900 Wilshire Blvd, Suite 2110, Los Angeles, CA 90036, and other branches in the Los Angeles, San Francisco and Boston, Miami, Chicago, Seattle, Washington DC areas. ☎ 1-800/777-0112 or 212/627-3111; *www.sta-travel.com*. Worldwide discount travel firm specializing in student/youth fares; also student IDs, travel insurance, car rental, rail passes, etc.

Travel Avenue, 10 S Riverside, Suite 1404, Chicago, IL 60606 ☎ 1-800/333-3335 or 312/876-6866; *www.tipc.com*. Full-service travel agent that offers discounts in the form of rebates.

Travel Cuts, 187 College St, Toronto, ON M5T 1P7 ☎ 1-800/667-2887 or 416/979-2406; *www.travelcuts.com*. Branches in Montréal, Vancouver, Calgary, Winnipeg, etc. Canadian discount travel organization.

UniTravel, 11737 Administration Drive, Suite 120, St Louis, MO 63146 ☎ 1-800/325-2222 or 314/569-2501. Consolidator. Worth calling for last-minute bookings or to avoid such restrictions as Saturday night stay requirements.

TOUR OPERATORS

American Airlines Vacations ☎ 1-800/321-2121; *www.aavacations.com*

American Express Vacations ☎ 1-800/241-1700; *www.americanexpress.com/travel*

Amtrak Vacations ☎ 1-800/321-8684; *www.amtrak.com*

Broadway Theatours, 1350 Broadway, New York, NY 10018 ☎ 1-800/843-7469; *www.manhattanconcierge.com*

Delta Vacations, ☎ 1-800/872-7786; *www.deltavacations.com*

Globus and Cosmos, 5301 S Federal Circle, Littleton, CO 80123; *www.globusandcosmos.com*

International Gay and Lesbian Travel Association ☎ 1-800/448-8550; *www.iglta.org*. Trade group with lists of gay-owned or gay-friendly travel agents, accommodations and other travel businesses.

Smithsonian Study Tours & Seminars, 1100 Jefferson Drive SW, Room 3077, Washington, DC 20560 ☎ 202/357-7000; *www.si.edu/tsa/sst*

there's a National USA Rail Pass which allows you unlimited 15-day travel for $425 (high season)/$285 (low) or 30 days for $535 (high) or $375 (low). Ask your travel agent for more information, or call Amtrak's information and reservations number: ☎ 1-800/USA-RAIL.

By bus

This is the most time-consuming and least comfortable mode of travel, and by the time you've kept yourself alive on the trip it's never the most economical. The only way in which buses are more useful than trains is that they generally run more frequently and serve a much larger portion of the country – so if New York is just one stop on an eclectic backcountry tour, check out **Greyhound's** Ameripass, though it is (like Amtrak's USA Railpass) open to foreign citizens only and as such can only be bought overseas or in New York. It offers unlimited travel on the network for 4 days ($119), 7 days ($179), 15 days ($269), 30 days ($369) or 60 days ($539). Otherwise, Greyhound has a similar pass available to all, offering 7 days unlimited travel ($199), 15 days ($299), 30 days ($409) or 60 days ($599). Greyhound's regular maximum fare for any distance with no advance booking is $120 (one-way)/$195 (round-trip). Buy your ticket 7 days in advance and the price drops to $79/$158, 14 days in advance $59/$118, and 21 days in advance gets you a flat round-trip rate of $99. Call ☎ 1-800/231-2222 for more information on the regular fares or ☎ 1-888/454-7277 for the passes.

You can also find bus bargains within the northeast corridor; in this busy region, bus competition can be as fierce as airline competition, sending prices up and down within days, if not hours. One-way from either DC or Boston to New York can go for as little as $20, though it is usually closer to $30. Bonanza (☎ 1-800/556-3815), for instance, runs a service connecting New England to New York City and currently have a Boston–New York round-trip fare of $55.

One alternative to bus hell is the famous, slightly alternative **Green Tortoise** bus, which connects **San Francisco** with New York every couple of weeks between May and October. Not the best choice if your idea of hell tends towards Sartre (the Tortoise is full of "other people"), but more gregarious types can look forward to a laid-back journey with generally like-minded souls through some of America's most beautiful spots. There are plenty of stops for hiking, river-rafting, hot springs and more, and the buses themselves are comfortable and congenial, with tape-deck systems and ample mattresses to sack out on.

The 10-day **northern route** (via Reno, Idaho, Montana, Wyoming, South Dakota, Minnesota, Chicago, Indiana and Pennsylvania) runs mostly in the hottest part of the summer and costs around $349 plus $111 for food, while the 14-day **southern route** (generally via Los Angeles, the Mojave Desert, Arizona, New Mexico, Texas, New Orleans and Appalachia) costs $389 plus $121 for food. From outside the San Francisco Bay area call ☎ 1-800/TORTOIS for more information (☎ 415/956-7500 if you're local), or write to 494 Broadway, San Francisco, CA 94133.

Driveaways

Potentially the cheapest legitimate way of getting to New York is to arrange for a **driveaway**, in which you deliver a car cross-country for its owner, paying only fuel costs. Look in your local Yellow Pages under "Automobile Transporters." Cars are not always available – especially to a popular destination like New York – so it helps if you have some flexibility and time to hang around and wait for one.

The usual **requirements** stipulate that you have to be 21 or over, have a valid driver's license (and sometimes a clean record printout from your local DMV) plus some other form of ID and have around $300 as a deposit, which may be required in cash or travelers' checks. This should be refundable on arrival and theoretically there's nothing to pay on the way except gas and motel bills. But keep in mind that while it's accepted that you may want to see a bit of the country on the way, there are generally tight delivery deadlines – 2 to 3 weeks coast to coast or 400 miles a day, for example – and if you're late without good reason you'll forfeit the deposit. Try to hit the company up for extra days and mileage when you take the job: if on a journey from Chicago to New York you invent a sick auntie who needs to be visited in Atlanta, you might get an official extension right off the bat . . . although you could alternatively find yourself en route to Atlanta and no further while some other eager driver takes your car on to New York.

Entry requirements for Canadians

For a brief excursion, **Canadian citizens** need only proof of their citizenship (such as a passport or a birth certificate or baptismal certificate in conjunction with a **photo ID**) to enter the US. The US embassy in Canada is located at 100 Wellington St, Ottawa, ON K1P 5A1 (☎613/238-5335), if you have any questions about visitor status. Other US consulates are in Calgary (☎403/266-8962); Halifax (☎902/429-2485); Montréal (☎514/398-9695); Quebec City (☎418/692-2095); Toronto (☎416/595-1700); and Vancouver (☎604/685-4311). For visits of longer than 90 days, a visa is required. If you plan to work or study in the US, then you should call ☎716/849-6760.

Travel insurance

American travelers should find that their health insurance covers any charges or costs – but certain insurers require you to notify them in advance of your travel plans. Several of the major **credit cards** (particularly American Express) offer automatic coverage for various aspects of traveling, and they may also offer their own additional policies; while **Canadians** are covered for medical mishaps abroad by their provincial health plans. In addition, homeowners' or renters' insurance often covers theft or loss of documents, money and valuables while overseas.

After exhausting the possibilities above, you might want to contact a **specialist travel insurance company**; your travel agent can usually recommend one, or see the list below. Travel insurance policies vary: some are comprehensive while others cover only certain risks (accidents, illnesses, delayed or lost luggage, canceled flights, etc). In particular, ask whether the policy pays medical costs up front or reimburses you later, and whether it provides for medical evacuation to your home country. For policies that include lost or stolen luggage, check exactly what is and isn't covered, and make sure the per-article limit will cover your most valuable possession. The best premiums are usually to be had through student/youth travel agencies – the current rates for STA policies for example, are $55 for 8–15 days or $115 for 1 month. If you're planning to do any "dangerous sports" (such as skiing or mountaineering) be sure to ask whether these activities are covered: some companies levy a surcharge.

Some **travel insurance companies in North America** are **Access America** ☎1-800/284-8300; **Carefree Travel Insurance** ☎1-800/323-3149; **Desjardins Travel Insurance** (Canadian citizens only) ☎1-800/463-7830; **STA Travel Insurance** ☎1-800/777-0112; **Travel Guard** ☎1-800/826-1300.

Health

Coming from Europe, you don't require any inoculations to enter the States. What you do need is insurance (see p.6), as medical bills for the most minor accident can be astronomical – and there's no way they can be escaped.

If you need to see a **doctor**, lists can be found in the Yellow Pages under "Clinics" or "Physicians and Surgeons." Your consulate (see p.485 for listings) will also have selected names. A basic consultation fee can be upwards of $250 before you even start talking, and medicines – either prescribed or over the counter – don't come cheap either; keep receipts for all you spend and claim on your insurance when you return.

Minor ailments can be remedied at a **drugstore**. These sell a fabulous array of lotions and potions designed to allay the fears of the most neurotic New Yorkers, but foreign visitors should bear in mind that many pills available over the counter at home are by **prescription only** here (for example, any codeine-based painkillers) and brand names can be confusing. Also note that many brand-name drugs are distributed under generic names and are much cheaper. When in doubt, ask at a pharmacy, where prescription drugs are dispensed (for addresses, see pp.477–478).

Should you be in an accident, don't worry about dying on the sidewalk – medical services will pick you up and charge later. For minor accidents, there are emergency rooms, open 24 hours, at the following Manhattan hospitals: Bellevue Hospital, First Avenue and E 27th Street (☎562-4141); St Vincent's Hospital, Seventh Avenue and W 11th Street (☎604-7996); New York Hospital, Cornell Medical Center E 70th Street at York

Avenue (☎746-5050); Mount Sinai Hospital, Madison Avenue at 100th Street (☎241-7171). If you need emergency dental treatment, the Dental Referral Service (☎1-800/577-7317) will recommend a dentist in your area.

Alternative and natural medicine

If alternatives to conventional medicine are what you're after, you'll find plenty – just don't expect them to be any cheaper than the standard kind. C.O. Bigelow Apothecaries at 414 Sixth Avenue between Eighth and Ninth streets (☎473-7324) has the largest selection of **homeopathic products** in the city, with a knowledgeable staff who can assist you or recommend a naturopathic doctor. The New York Open Center, 83 Spring St, between Broadway and Crosby (☎219-2527) has a small bookstore and a good selection of free publications having to do with (among other things) health and natural living; you'll be able to find acupuncture, massage therapy, Chinese herbology, Bach flower remedies and a whole range of other options through them. You'll also find listings in the Yellow Pages and on the bulletin boards of health food stores and natural food restaurants. Keep in mind, however, that many insurers are reluctant to recognize alternative treatments; check your policy carefully before you open your wallet.

Playing safe

HIV/AIDS is one health risk which unfortunately needs its own mention. While much of the hysteria that surrounded the early years of AIDS awareness has died down, the dangers are as real as ever, and not just within the gay community. New York City has one of the highest concentrations of HIV-positive people in the world. You've heard it all before, but we make no apologies for saying it all again: take the obvious precautions. If you choose to use drugs intravenously, on no account share needles; it's best if you bring your own. If you choose to have penetrative sex of any kind, use condoms, which you'll find readily available at supermarkets, 24-hour delis and drugstores. For more information and advice about HIV and AIDS, call the **GMHC Hotline** (run by Gay Men's Health Crisis, an organization not exclusively for gay men) at ☎807-6655.

Points of arrival

Airports

Three major airports serve New York. **International and domestic flights** are handled at **John F Kennedy (JFK)** (☎718/244-4444), in the borough of Queens, and **Newark** (☎973/961-6000), in northern New Jersey; **La Guardia** (☎718/533-3400), also in Queens, handles **domestic flights** only.

Wherever you arrive, the cheapest way into Manhattan is **by bus**. In the following sections we've outlined the bus connections from each airport, along with their public transit alternatives. The two Manhattan **bus terminals**, used by all airport buses, are Grand Central Station and the Port Authority Bus Terminal. For most hotels, **Grand Central** (at Park Ave and 42nd St) is the more convenient: well poised for taxis to midtown Manhattan and with a subway station for routes towards the east of the city. Bear in mind also that some of the larger Midtown hotels – the *Marriott Marquis*, *Hilton*, etc – operate a free shuttle service to and from Grand Central. The **Port Authority Terminal** at Eighth Avenue at 42nd Street (☎564-8484) isn't as good a bet for Manhattan (there's a lot of humping luggage from bus to street level), though you may find it handy if you're heading for the west side of the city (via the #A, #C or #E trains) or out to New Jersey (by bus). Some airport buses also stop off at **Penn Station** at 34th Street between Seventh and Eighth avenues where you can catch Amtrak long-distance trains on to other parts of America, and at the **World Trade Center** at the bottom of Manhattan – good for Downtown/Brooklyn subways and connections to New Jersey.

Taxis are the easiest option if you are in a group or are arriving at an antisocial hour, but otherwise you may consider them an unnecessary expense: reckon on paying roughly $16–22 from La Guardia, a flat rate of $30 from JFK and $35–55 from Newark; and you'll be responsible for paying the turnpike and tunnel tolls – an extra $5 or so. And don't forget – a tip of fifteen to twenty percent is expected. If you do decide to splurge on a cab, ignore the individual drivers vying for your attention as you exit the baggage claim; these **"gypsy cab"** operators are notorious

> For general information on getting to and from the airports, call ☎1-800/AIR-RIDE.

for ripping off tourists. Ask any airport official to direct you to the taxi stand, where you'll be sure to get into an official New York City yellow taxi. There are also a few **car services**, which have direct phones near the exits; they're competitive in price with taxis (they charge set rates), sometimes even lower.

A newer option is the Gray Line Air Shuttle, a minibus you can pick up at any of the three airports (check with the ground transportation desk or the courtesy phone in the baggage area) or arrange by phone (☎1-800/451-0455 or 212/315-3006). These shuttles are giving the older airport buses (see below) a run for their money, since for only a few dollars more they'll take you straight to your hotel – at least if you're staying in Midtown. The shuttles operate from the airport between 7am and 11.30pm, and from the hotels between 6am and 7pm; the cost (one-way) if you buy your ticket at the airport is $13 per person to La Guardia, $14 to JFK or Newark; otherwise it's $16 to La Guardia, $19 to JFK or Newark. Round-trip fares are double those for one-way. Super Shuttle (☎1-800/258-3826 or 212/258-3826) is a new service operating to and from Manhattan only, 24 hours daily. Representatives are present in the baggage claim areas, and courtesy phones are also available. One-way fares are $13 from La Guardia, $14 from JFK and $17 from Newark and, in the opposite direction, $14 to La Guardia, $15 to JFK and $17 to Newark. Reservations are necessary from Manhattan to the airport at least 1–2 days ahead of time.

JFK

New York Airport Service. Buses leave JFK for Grand Central Station, Port Authority Bus Terminal, Penn Station and Midtown hotels every 15 to 20 minutes between 6am and midnight. In the other direction, they run from the same locations every 15 to 30 minutes between 5am and 10pm.

When you come to catch your flight home, remember that JFK is large and very spread out: if your terminal is last on the bus route (like British Airways) you should allow a further fifteen minutes or so to get there.

Journeys take from 45 to 60 minutes, depending on time of day and traffic conditions; the fare is $13 (students $6) one-way, discounts are also available to senior citizens, the disabled and children when you travel from (not to) Grand Central Station. For details on services, discounts, etc call ☎718/706-9658.

Public transit. Free shuttle buses run from all terminals at JFK to the Howard Beach subway stop on the #A train; from there, one subway token ($1.50) will take you anywhere in the city you want to go. Late at night, this might not be your best choice, since trains run infrequently and can be rather deserted, but in the daytime or early evening, it's a very viable, if tedious (travel time is at least an hour to Howard Beach) option. Alternatively, you can take the #Q10 green bus (subway token or $1.50, exact change and no paper money) to its last stop, right by the subway in Kew Gardens, Queens, and pick up the #E or #F train (for an additional token) to Manhattan. Travel time is about the same, but avoid this route like the plague at rush hour, since it's the most overcrowded line in the whole transit system. See the subway map (color map at back) to determine which is the most convenient route to your particular destination. For more information on subway and bus options, call ☎718/330-1234, 24 hours any day of the week.

Newark

Olympia Airport Express. Buses leave for Manhattan every twenty to thirty minutes (6.15am to midnight), stopping at the World Trade Center, Grand Central and Penn Station; going the other way, they run just as frequently (5.10am to 11.10pm); service to and from Port Authority runs 24 hours a day. In either direction, the journey takes roughly 30 to 45 minutes depending on the traffic, and the fare is $10. There's a connecting service available to certain Midtown hotels for an extra $5. Buses are also available from Newark to JFK for $23, to La Guardia for $20 but there is a connection at Port Authority or Grand Central Station. Buses for each airport run from 6am to midnight every 20 minutes. Details on ☎964-6233 or 908/354-3330.

PATH Rapid Transit. Involves a shuttle bus (AIRLINK #302) to Newark's Penn Station, where PATH trains run to stations in Manhattan; the fare is $4 for the bus, $1 for the train. Note that while the PATH train runs 24 hours a day, the Airlink buses only run from approximately 6.15am to 1.40am. The bus service runs every 20 to 30 minutes Mon–Fri and every 30 minutes Sat–Sun. Tickets are sold at the bus's point of departure. Call ☎1-800/234-PATH.

AIRLINE OFFICES IN NEW YORK CITY

Many of these airlines have additional offices throughout the city.

Air Canada ☎1-800/776-3000 125 Park Ave (at 42nd St)	**El Al** ☎852-0600 120 W 45th St (between 6th and 7th aves)
Air India ☎751-6200 or 407-1460 15th Floor, 570 Lexington Ave (at 51st St)	**Kuwait** ☎308-5454 350 Park Ave
American ☎1-800/433-7300 2nd Floor, 125 Park Ave (at 42nd St)	**Northwest/KLM** ☎1-800/225-2525 100 E 42nd St (at Park Ave)
Continental ☎319-9494 Airline Lobby, One World Trade Center	**United** ☎1-800/241-6522 1 E 59th St (at 5th Ave)
Delta ☎1-800/221-1212 100 E 42nd St (at Park Ave)	**Virgin Atlantic** ☎1-800/862-8621 125 Park Ave (at 42nd St) /319-9494

LaGuardia

New York Airport Service. Buses run between Manhattan (Grand Central Station and the Port Authority Bus Terminal) and La Guardia every 15 to 30 minutes either way. The service operates 6am to midnight (to Grand Central and Port Authority), 5am to 10pm (from Grand Central), 6.40am to 9pm (from Port Authority). Buses also run to Penn Station from 6.40am to 11.40pm every 30 minutes, 10 and 40 after the hour; from Penn Station, 7.40am to 8.10pm same time-scale as above. Journey time is 45 to 60 minutes, depending on traffic and the fare is $10 (students $6) each way. For details on services, discounts etc call ☎718/706-9658.

Public transit. The best (and least-known) bargain in New York airport transit is the #M60 bus, which for $1.50 will take you into Manhattan, across 125th Street, and down Broadway to 106th Street. Ask the driver for a transfer when you get on the bus and you can get practically anywhere (for an explanation of transfers, see p.19). If you're heading for *Hosteling International* (p.315), it's an easy four-block walk from the #M60's last stop. Journey time can range from 20 minutes late at night to an hour in rush-hour traffic.

If the Upper West Side is not your destination, you might want to consider taking the #Q33 or #Q47 bus ($1.50/$1 off-peak and weekends) from La Guardia to the Roosevelt Avenue subway stop in Jackson Heights, Queens, where for another $1.50 you can get the #7, #E, #F or #R train to Manhattan. Total travel time is approximately 40 minutes to Midtown.

LaGuardia to JFK

Manhattan Airport Service. There's a service that links JFK and La Guardia airports between 5.40am and 11pm. Buses leave on average, every thirty minutes (though it varies depending on your direction and the time of day) and take 45 minutes to 60 minutes; at select times they make one stop along the way. The fare is $11 one way. Call ☎718/706-9658.

Arriving by bus or train

If you're coming to New York by Greyhound, Trailways, Bonanza or any of the other long-distance **bus lines**, you'll arrive at the Port Authority Bus Terminal at 42nd Street and Eighth Avenue (see p.14 for details of both terminals). By Amtrak **train**, you'll be coming in at Penn Station, 32nd Street and Seventh and Eighth avenues.

Getting around the city

The subway

The New York subway is dirty, noisy, intimidating and initially incomprehensible. It's also the fastest and most efficient method of getting from A to B throughout Manhattan and the Outer Boroughs, and it is a great deal safer and more user-friendly than it used to be. Put aside your qualms: an estimated 6 million people ride the subway every day, quite a few for the very first time.

One way to make yourself feel better right at the start is to familiarize yourself with the system when you first arrive. Read over the map inserted at the back of this book, or pick up a free subway plan at any subway station (also at the information booth on the concourse at Grand Central, the New York Convention and Visitors Bureau, or any of the Visitors Information Centers listed on p.22). The following basic guidelines will make more sense when you combine them with visual information.

The basics

• Broadly speaking, train routes in Manhattan run uptown or downtown, following the great avenues and converging, as the island itself does, in the downtown financial district. Crosstown routes are limited.

• Trains and their routes are generally identified by a number or letter. Though the subway is open 24 hours a day, some routes operate at certain times of day only; read your map carefully for the details. Also, in the interest of safety, some entrances to stations are only open during certain hours. The green globe outside the sub-

way entrance is to identify the open station from a distance.

• There are two types of train: the **express**, which stops only at major stations, and the **local**, which stops at every station. If your destination is an express stop, the quickest way to get there is to change from local to express at the first express station, either by walking across the platform or taking the stairs to another level.

• Any subway journey costs a **flat fare of $1.50**. One way to pay your fare is with a **subway token**, available from any token booth and some check cashing stores. Stocking up means no waiting in line, and they can be used for buses too.

• The **MetroCard**, a multitrip card with an electronic strip which allows you to transfer (for free) from subway to bus, bus to subway or bus to bus within a period of 2 hours, is the most convenient and economical way to pay for your trip. It's available, from all token booths and some check cashing stores, in several forms: cards can be bought for $3 to $80; $15 purchases allow 11 rides for the cost of 10, and $30 purchases allow 22 rides for the cost of 20. Unlimited-ride cards allow unlimited travel for a certain period of time: a 7-day pass for $17, a 30-day pass for $63 and a daily "Fun Pass" for $4. Unfortunately, the "Fun Pass," valid for 24 hours, is not available from token booths, but can be found at most major hotels and grocery stores (look for "fun pass" advert stickers on the door) such as Gristedes or call ☎638-7622 to find out the closest location to purchase a fun pass.

• Service changes due to track repairs and other maintenance work are frequent (especially after midnight and on weekends) and confusing even to the most proficient subway rider. To keep abreast of the situation, read every Service Notice you see – they're the red-and-white posters plastered on bulletin boards and posts throughout the system – and don't be afraid to ask other passengers what's going on. **Listen** closely to all announcements (they are in English despite what it may sound like), occasionally express trains run on local tracks, if you see people board the train, listen to an announcement and immediately get back off, you can bet the train is not running its scheduled course, again, ask other passengers if you're uncertain.

• Don't be afraid to **ask directions** or **look at a map** on the train or in the station. You may draw attention, but not the threatening kind you're thinking of – you're more likely to get ten people all talking at once, offering contradictory advice. Obviously, if you're traveling late at night you should be sure of your route before you set out – knowing it will enable you to travel much easier and with more confidence. But, if you follow commonsense safety rules (see the box opposite and the "Police and trouble" section, p.41), there's nothing wrong with admitting you're new at any of this.

• If you're starting to panic, or are lost, phone ☎718/330-1234. State your location and your destination and the operator will tell you the most direct route by subway or bus.

Fun on the subway

A special treat on the subway is to stand right at the front of the train next to the driver's cabin and watch as stations hurtle by and rats flee along the track. The #A train from 125th Street to 59th Street is best for this.

A challenge is to watch for the "ghost stations" as you go by. These are stations that have closed for various reasons over the years and remain intact underground though no longer visible or accessible from the street. A slow-moving #6 train will sometimes give you a glimpse of one at 18th Street and Park Avenue South; on the #1 or #9 you might catch sight of another at 91st Street and Broadway. One ghost station that is open to visitors, however, is the old Court Street station in Brooklyn; abandoned in 1946, it is now the site of the New York Transit Museum. (For details, see p.299)

"Stand clear of the doors… I said, stand clear of the doors. You – yes, you in the green jacket! In or out? Look, I got all day…" New York's subway conductors are known for their accents, their sense of humor, and above all their attitude. New trains with computerized announcements are starting to creep in, so listen to the real thing while you still can.

Lines and directions

Perhaps the main source of confusion for visitors is the multiplicity of **line/train names**. The letters and numbers on the subway map will be recognized by everyone, but the old line names – the IRT, the IND and the BMT – are still very much in use (even though they ceased to exist as separate companies in 1940), as are popular "direction names." Just to give one example: the West Side IRT, Broadway Local, 7th Avenue Local and Number 1 train are all the same thing. One way in which New Yorkers do *not* refer to trains is by color: if you're looking for the #2 or #3 and ask for the red line, you'll probably be met with a blank stare.

The main lines and directions in Manhattan are outlined below.

• The local #1 and #9 and express #2 and #3 trains run north and south along Broadway and Seventh Avenue. This is the West Side IRT (for Interborough Rapid Transit, the company that opened New York's first subway line) and is also known as the Broadway line or the 7th Avenue line. Pay close attention north of 96th Street and south of Chambers Street, where the local and express trains diverge.

• The local #6 and express #4 and #5 trains run north and south along Lexington and Park avenues, diverging north of 125th Street and south of Brooklyn Bridge. This is the East Side IRT, and is often called the Lexington Avenue line.

• The #7 train runs east and west along 42nd Street from Times Square (Broadway/7th Ave) to Grand Central (Park Ave) and then out to Queens. This is also an IRT train, known commonly as the Flushing line.

• The express #A and local #C and #E trains run north and south along Eighth Avenue in midtown Manhattan, with the #E branching off south of Canal Street (to go to the World Trade Center) and north of 50th Street (where it heads crosstown out to Queens). The #C terminates at Washington Heights while the #A continues on to Inwood at the northern tip of Manhattan. These IND trains (named after the Independent subway line, the first to be owned by the city rather than a private company) are often known collectively as the 8th Avenue line.

• The local #F and express #B, #D and #Q trains run north and south along Sixth Avenue in Midtown, turning east at West Fourth Street North of the 47–50 Street stop (Rockefeller Center), the #F, the #Q, and sometimes the #B branch off to go

Safety on the subway

Everyone has different views on **subway safety**, and everyone, too, has their horror stories. Many are exaggerated – and the subway definitely feels more dangerous than it actually is – but it's as well to follow a few established rules.

At night, always try to use the **center cars**, since they are more crowded. Yellow signs on the platform saying "During off hours train stops here" indicate where the conductor's car will stop. While you're waiting, keep to the "**Off-Hour Waiting Area**" (marked in yellow), where you can be seen by the token booth attendants; in cases where this area is on a different level, there will be a sign (accompanied by a chirping or whistling sound) to let you know a train is arriving, so don't worry about missing your train.

By day the whole train is theoretically safe, but don't go into empty cars if you can help it. If you do find yourself in an empty or nearly empty car, move into a fuller one at the next station. Some trains have doors that connect between cars, but do not use them other than in an emergency, since this is both dangerous and illegal. You should also, at all times, **avoid** standing near the edge of the platform.

Keep an eye on **bags** at all times, especially when sitting or standing near the doors. With all the jostling in the crowds near the doors, this is a favorite snatching spot.

For more information on safety, see "Police and trouble," p.41.

---

crosstown to Queens; check your map for details, since this line can be confusing. IND trains all, they're collectively known as the 6th Avenue line.

• The #N and #R trains run along Broadway from lower Manhattan to 57th Street connecting with Brooklyn at Whitehall Street and with Queens via the Queensboro Bridge. These were originally BMT (Brooklyn–Manhattan Transit) trains, and may still be referred to as such.

• The **Grand Central–Times Square Shuttle** connects the east and west sides of the IRT by running under 42nd Street. It's marked on maps as the #S train.

• The #L is another useful crosstown line, running east and west along 14th Street between Eighth and First avenues. East of First Avenue, the #L (a BMT train) runs out to Brooklyn.

Buses

New York's **bus system** is a lot simpler than the subway, and you can also see where you're going and hop off if you pass anything interesting. It also features many more crosstown routes, which are especially useful if you're going from the Upper West Side to the Upper East Side or vice versa. The major disadvantage of the bus system is that it can be extremely **slow** – in peak hours almost down to walking pace. **Bus maps**, like subway maps, can be obtained from the main concourse of Grand Central or the Convention and Visitors Bureau at 53rd Street and Seventh Avenue. We've printed a small Manhattan bus map, located at the back of the book, to tide you over.

A quick glance at the **routes** will reveal that they run along all the avenues and across major streets. There are three **types of bus**: **regular**, which stop every two or three blocks at five- to ten-minute intervals; **limited stop**, which travel the same routes, though stop at only about a quarter of the regular stops; and **express**, which cost extra and stop hardly anywhere, shuttling commuters in and out of the Outer Boroughs and suburbs. In addition, you'll find small private buses running in from New Jersey. Buses display their **number, origin and destination** up front.

Bus stops are marked by yellow curbstones and a blue, white and red sign that often (but by no means always) indicates which buses stop there. In addition, there will sometimes be a sign showing routes, times (rarely accurate) and intersections. To signal that you want **to get off** a bus, press the black strip on the wall. The "Stop Requested" sign at the front of the bus will come on, and the driver will stop at the next official bus stop. After midnight, you can request to get off on any block along the route the bus travels, regardless of whether it's a regular stop or not.

Fares and transfers

Anywhere in Manhattan the **fare** is $1.50, payable on entry with either a subway token, a MetroCard (the most convenient way) or with the correct change – no bills.

If you're going to be using buses a lot, it pays to understand the **transfer system**. Transfers were designed to let a single fare take you, one way, anywhere in Manhattan. Since few buses go both up and down *and* across, you can transfer from any bus to almost any other that continues your trip. (You can't use transfers for return trips.) They're given free on demand when you pay your fare, although if you use a transfer to get on a bus, you can't then ask for another one. The top of the transfer will tell you how much time you have in which to use it – usually around two hours. If you're not sure of where to get off to transfer, just ask the driver for some help. If you use a MetroCard, you can automatically transfer for free within two hours from swiping the card.

Private bus companies

The lack (and disruption) of bus services in lower-income areas both in and out of Manhattan has been a major source of controversy over the years. It seems that whenever the city feels the need to cut back on services, those who need them the most end up losing out. In Queens, **private bus companies** pick up the slack (you'll find them listed, without additional information, on the regular Queens Bus Map), and in outer regions of most of the Outer Boroughs, small vans (known as "Dollar Vans") pick up and drop off passengers along old bus routes, generally for $1 or $1.50. While some of these vans are not strictly legal, they serve a definite purpose, and if you ask the driver or another passenger, you may be able to figure out how to use them.

Taxis

Taxis are always worth considering, but especially if you're in a hurry, in a group, or if it's late at night.

In Manhattan, there are two types: **medallion cabs**, immediately recognizable by their yellow paintwork and medallion up top, and **gypsy cabs**, unlicensed, uninsured operators who tout for business wherever tourists arrive. Avoid gypsy cabs like the plague as they're rip-off merchants – their main hunting grounds are outside usual tourist arrival points like Grand Central.

Up to **four people** can travel in an ordinary medallion cab or, if you're lucky enough to find it, the last-remaining, old-fashioned Checker cab. **Fares** are $2 for the first fifth of a mile, 30¢ for each fifth of a mile thereafter or for each 90 seconds in stopped or slow traffic. The basic charge rises by 50¢ from 8pm to 6am, and by 100 percent if you take a cab outside the New York City limits (eg to Newark airport). Trips outside Manhattan can additionally incur toll fees; not all of the crossings cost money, however, and the driver should ask you which route you wish to take.

The **tip** should be fifteen to twenty percent of the fare; you'll get a dirty look if you offer less. Also likely to cause a problem is change: drivers don't like splitting anything bigger than a $10 bill and are in their rights to refuse a bill over $20.

Before you hail a cab, it's always a good idea to work out exactly where you're going and if possible the quickest route there – a surprising number of cabbies are new to the job and some speak little English. If you feel the driver doesn't seem to know your destination, don't hesitate to point it out on a map. An **illuminated sign** on top of the taxi indicates its availability. However, if the **words** "Off Duty" are lit, it means what it says and the driver won't pick you up.

Officially there are certain **regulations** governing taxi operators. A driver can ask your destination only when you're seated – and must transport you (within the five boroughs), however undesirable your destination may be. You may face some problems, though, if it's late and you want to go to an outer borough. Also, if you request it, a driver must pick up or drop off other passengers, open or close the windows, and stop smoking (they can also ask you to stop). If you have any **problems** with a driver, get the license number from the right-hand side of the dashboard, or medallion number from the rooftop sign or from the print-out receipt for the fare, and phone the NYC Taxis and Limousine Commission on ☎ 302-8294. This is also the number to call if you realize you've **left something** in a cab.

Driving

In a word, don't. Even if you're brave enough to take responsibility for dodging lunatic cab drivers, car rental is expensive, parking lots almost laughably so, and street parking hard to find. There's not much else to compare it to in the States, and if you're from abroad, better to keep your American driving fantasies to upstate excursions.

If you do need to drive, bear in mind a number of **rules**. **Seatbelts** are compulsory for everyone in front and for children in back. The **speed limit** is 35mph within the city, and you can be pulled over and given a breathalyzer test (known as the alcotest) at a police officer's discretion. (You're within your rights to refuse, but you'll then have to go to police headquarters.) Unlike most of the rest of the country, within city limits it's illegal to make a **right turn** at a red light.

Read signs carefully to figure out where to **park** – if the sign says "No Standing," "No Stopping," or "Don't Even THINK of Parking Here" (yes, really), that's a no. Also watch for street-cleaning hours (when an entire side of a street will be off-limits for parking), and don't park in a bus stop or in front of a fire hydrant. Private parking is expensive, extremely so at peak periods, but it makes sense to leave your car somewhere legitimate: if it's towed away you'll need to liberate it from the **car pound** (☎ 971-0770) – expect to pay around $150 in cash ($15 for each additional day they store it for you) and waste the best part of a day.

Car **theft and vandalism** are also problems, although more so in less-traveled parts of the city where vandals won't be seen working on your car. If you're going to have a car in the city for a while you should utilize some form of obvious deterrent to would-be thieves – the long yellow bars that lock between steering wheel and windscreen are a popular choice, as is the "Club." Avoid leaving valuables in your car at any time.

Cycling

Pulling away from the lights on a bike in Manhattan can mean a replay of the Monaco Grand Prix, and it's just about as dangerous. To enjoy it – and it can be a viable form of transportation once you're confident enough – do as the locals do and go for all possible rentable safety equipment: pads, a **helmet** (by law, you must wear a helmet), goggles and a whistle to move straying pedestrians. When you stop, be sure to chain, lock, and chain again your machine to something totally immovable if you'd like it to be there when you return.

Bike **rental** starts at about $7 an hour or $35 a day – which means opening to closing (9.30am to 6.30pm for instance) so ask about

The Yellow Pages have full listings of **bike rental firms** but among good-value, central suppliers are:

Bikes in the Park, Loeb Boathouse, Central Park (☎ 861-4137). The best place to rent bikes to tour the park. You can even rent a tandem for $14 an hour.

Metro Bicycles, 1311 Lexington Ave at 88th St (☎ 427-4450); 546 6th Ave at 15th St (☎ 255-5100); and other branches in Manhattan. One of the city's largest bike stores.

Midtown Bicycles, 360 W 47th St at 9th Ave (☎ 581-4500). Standard at $7 an hour and $35 a day or $40 if you return the bike within an hour of the store opening next morning.

West Side Bikes, 231 W 96th St between Broadway and Amsterdam (☎ 663-7531). Upper West Side store, again handy for Central Park.

24-hour rates. You'll need one or two pieces of ID (passport and credit card will be sufficient) and, in some cases, a deposit (around $200), though most firms will be satisfied with a credit card imprint. Rates and deposits are generally more for racing models and mountain bikes.

Walking

Few cities equal New York for sheer street-level stimulation, and getting around **on foot** is often the most exciting – and exhausting – method of exploring. Count on around fifteen minutes to walk ten north–south blocks – rather more at rush hour. And keep in mind that however you plan your wanderings you're going to spend much of your time slogging it out on the streets. **Footwear** is important (sneakers are good for spring/summer; winter needs something waterproof). So is **safety**: a lot more people are injured in New York carelessly crossing the road than are mugged. In fact the city now has a law against jaywalking. Pedestrian crossings don't give you automatic right of way unless the WALK sign is on – and, even then, cars may be turning, so be prudent. A good rule of thumb is to make eye contact with the driver, giving him or her your best "don't mess with me" New York look; if you can't make eye contact, run.

Rollerblading

While **rollerblading** is still a popular form of recreation, more and more people are using it as a speedy way to get around the city. If you're not proficient, the streets of Manhattan aren't really the place to learn; get some practice in Central Park or one of the other traffic-free blading spots (see "Sports and Outdoor activities", p.418 for details), though, and you're away. You'll find rentals, once again, in the Yellow Pages, or try one of the popular Blades stores (120 W 72nd St between Central Park West and Columbus, ☎787-3911; 1414 2nd Ave between 73rd and 74th streets, ☎249-3178). A credit card should be deposit enough, and prices run the gamut, ranging from $16 for 2 hours or $27 for 24 hours on weekends to $16 for 24 hours during the week. If after a day or two you find that you're hooked, some places give you a discount off the purchase price for having rented first.

Information, maps and tours

Once in New York, the best place to head for all kinds of information is the New York Convention and Visitors Bureau at 810 Seventh Avenue at 53rd Street (Mon–Fri 8.30am–6pm, weekends and holidays 9am–5pm; or call to speak with one of their counselors at ☎484-1222; *www.nycvisit.com*). Going to the office is worthwhile: they have up-to-date leaflets on what's going on in the arts and elsewhere plus bus and subway maps and information on hotels and accommodation – though they can't actually book anything for you. Their quarterly *Official NYC Guide* is good too, though the kind of information it gives – on restaurants, hotels, shopping and sights – is also available in the various free tourist magazines and guidettes you'll find in hotels and elsewhere. These include complete (if superficial) rundowns on what's on in the (more mainstream) arts, eating out, shops, etc and a host of ads that might just point you in the right direction.

The state-run **I Love New York** organization also has a good stock of free booklets and maps available by post from 1 Empire State Plaza, Albany,

---

You'll find other small **tourist information centers** and kiosks all over the city, starting with the airports, Grand Central and Penn stations, and Port Authority Bus Terminal. You'll probably come across others without trying, but the following list should help:

Bloomingdale's International Visitors' Center, Lexington Ave (at 59th St) ☎705-2098.

Harlem Visitors' Bureau, 219 W 135th St (between 7th and 8th Ave) Call first ☎283-3315.

NYU Information Center, Shimkin Hall, 50 W 4th St (at Greene St/Washington Square) ☎998-4636.

Saks Fifth Avenue Ambassador Concierge Desk, 611 5th Ave (at 49th St) ☎940-4141.

Times Square Visitor and Transit Information Center, 1560 Broadway (between 46th and 47th sts) Open every day 8am–8pm. ☎869-1890.

New York on the Internet

There are countless **Web sites** that contain travel information about New York; if you have access to the **Internet**, you may want to do some extra research before (or during) your trip. What follows is a short list of both fun and informative sites for travelers. Here you'll find what's on around town, a sampling of local media and Woody Allen's given name (Allen Konigsberg). Be sure, too, to check out our own Web site at *www.roughguides.com*

CitySearch NY
www.citysearchnyc.com/nyc/index/html
A solid search engine, weekly updated listings and tame features all on this comprehensive site.

Data Lounge
www.datalounge.com/
Where gay travelers can peruse community news, glance at the city's social calendar, or simply test the matchmaking skills of Edwina.

NYC Beer Guide
www.nycbeer.org/toc.html
The Beer Guide serves up the suds, from micro-breweries to well-stocked bodegas.

NYC Visitors Bureau
www.nycvisit.com
Official Web site of the New York Convention and Visitors Bureau.

PaperMag
www.papermag.com/
Updated daily and covering the cultural gamut, this hip guide has been on the cutting-edge of every trend to hit the streets.

Parks Department
www.nycparks.org
The official word on all of the events in the city's parks.

Sidewalk.Com
www.newyork.sidewalk.com
Sidewalk offers extensive listings with reliable recommendations and a search engine that can find you everything from "dive bars" to "hot spots" in seconds.

Total NY
www.totalny.com/
One of the few guides sporting real New York attitude, Total's quirky features and eclectic listings will tell you where to go and what to do.

The Village Voice
www.villagevoice.com/
The best thing here, from the elder (some say out-of-touch) alternative weekly, is the paper's witty listings section, "Choices."

Webtunes
webtunes.com/
Loaded with RealAudio samples and venue listings, this site has the lowdown on the city's music scene.

Woody Allen
www.media.uio.no/studentene/
ragnhild.paalsrud/woody/Woody.html
Everything you ever wanted to know about Woody but were afraid to ask.

NY 12223 (☎518/474-4116). Much of their information concentrates on New York State, though; if you're at all interested in exploring beyond the five boroughs, it's worth getting their comprehensive statewide map and regional guides. They do also have specifically New York City-oriented information, not least restaurant and hotel lists and maps.

Maps

We reckon our maps of the city should be fine for most purposes; **commercial maps**, like the Rand McNally *Plan of the City and all Five Boroughs* ($3.95), fill in the gaps. Others include the tiny laminated Streetwise maps – neatly laid-out and not expensive at around $6 from most bookstores. Street atlases of all five boroughs cost around $13; if you're after a map of one of the individual Outer Boroughs, try those produced by Geographia or Hagstrom at about $3.50, again on sale in bookstores. For fun, try the *New York Pop-Up Map* which covers Manhattan and costs $5.95. For more options, or if you have trouble finding any of these, the Complete Traveler is a good map and guide shop; see p.472 for details.

Tours

One way of getting a hold on New York is simply to climb up to the **observation deck** of one of its tallest buildings, most obviously the Empire State Building or the World Trade Center. Of the two, the Empire State's position in the heart of Manhattan gives it the edge; see p.135 for more details. You can enjoy the view of lower Manhattan for free by simply walking across the Brooklyn Bridge (see p.78), or almost for free by taking the Staten Island Ferry (see opposite and p.252). However, if you want more detailed background than this, or you have a specific interest in the city, there are all kinds of **tours** you can join, taking in the city from just about every angle and by just about every means available.

Big Apple Greeter

If you're at all nervous about exploring New York, or even just overwhelmed by the possibilities the city offers, look into **Big Apple Greeter**. One of the best – and certainly cheapest – ways to see the city from a native's viewpoint, it's a nonprofit organization that matches up visitors with trained, volunteer "greeters." You can specify the part of the city you'd like to see, indicate an aspect of New York life you'd like to explore, or plead for general orientation – whatever your interests, the chances are that they will find someone to take you around. Visits have a friendly, informal feel, and generally last a few hours (although some have been known to go on all day). Best of all, the service is free. While you can call once you're in New York, it's strongly recommended that you contact the organization as far in advance as possible to ensure greeter availability. Write to: Big Apple Greeter, 1 Centre St, NY 10007 (☎669-8159, fax 669-3685; *cstone@bigapplegreeter.org*; *www.bigapplegreeter.com*).

Bus tours

Apart from equipping yourself with a decent map, perhaps the most obvious way of orienting yourself to the city is to take a **bus tour** – something that's extremely popular, though frankly you'll find yourself swept around so quickly as to scarcely see anything. Still, the tops of double deckers are a great place to figure out what's where for later explorations – and in recent years, there has been an explosion of these, with the deals getting better (and the routes more

---

Double decker bus tours

Gray Line Sightseeing Terminal
Port Authority at 42nd St and 8th Ave,
NY 10019
☎1-800/669-0051 for tickets and locations

New York Apple Tours
1040 6th Ave
NY 10018
☎1-800/876-9868 for tickets and locations.
Terminal: 8th Ave and 53rd St

New York Double Decker Tours
Empire State Building
350 5th Ave, #4721
NY 10118
☎1-800/692-2870 for tickets and locations

---

comprehensive) each year as the three biggest companies – Gray Line, New York Apple and NY Double Decker – clamor for your business. In all three cases, the basics are the same: you purchase a ticket from any number of locations including the bus terminal, your hotel, or the bus itself at one of its many stops, and you can hop on and off the bus anywhere along its route. The more you spend, the more of the city you're entitled to see, and the longer time you have for seeing it – in general, an all-city tour over two days will cost under $40, while you can also have two-hour or half-day tours for around $25. All tours have discounts for children under 12. Buses run seven days a week, from (approximately) 9am to 6pm, with special rates and times for evening tours.

NY Double Decker tends to be cheaper and a bit more flexible while *Gray Line* and *New York Apple* offer a wider range of tours – stop by their terminals or pick up their leaflets at a Visitor Center or your hotel for up-to-date specifics.

Helicopter tours

If you have the money, a better and certainly more exciting option is to take a look at the city from the air, by taking a ride in a **helicopter**. This is expensive, but it's an experience you won't easily forget. Liberty Helicopter Tours, at the western end of 30th Street or from the Wall Street heliport at Pier 6 (☎967-4550), offer flights ranging from $46 (for four-and-a-half minutes) to $149 (15 minutes) – buy your ticket ahead of time (at a hotel or tour operator) to avoid a $5 surcharge. If you're leaving from 30th Street the best seat for photos is on the right-hand side in the back of the helicopter; you may have to be a bit pushy to get back there but it's worth it. Helicopters take off regularly between 9am and 9pm, every day unless winds and visibility are too bad; you don't need to make a reservation but in high season (and nice weather) you may have quite a wait if you just show up. One decision to make is whether to go by day or night; after doing one, you'll probably want to do the other.

Tours on water

New York is an island city, and a great way to see it from that standpoint is to take the **Circle Line ferry** (☎563-3200; *www.circleline.com*). Departing from **Pier 83** at West 42nd Street and Twelfth Avenue, it sails all the way around Manhattan, taking in everything from the classic soaring views of downtown Manhattan to the bleaker stretches of Harlem and the industrially blighted Bronx – complete with a live wisecracking commentary; the three-hour tour is $22 ($12 for children under 12). The evening Harbor Lights Cruises offer dramatic views of the skyline while the Harlem Spirituals Gospel Cruise will make a believer out of you; these two-hour tours are $18 ($10 for children under 12). Boats departing from Pier 16 at **South Street Seaport** feature a one-hour downtown skyline cruise plus two-hour live music tours (offering a choice of Blues, Jazz or Gospel) with prices ranging from $25–40, and if you're feeling really sporty try *The Beast*, a bright red speedboat which will throw you around for thirty minutes at a dashing 45 miles per hour. Boats run between late March and mid-December, running roughly twice a day in low season, almost hourly in midsummer.

An alternative is to check out tours offered by **NY Waterway** (☎1-800/533-3779; *www.nywaterway.com*), with 90-minute tours leaving the far west end of 38th Street four times daily; $18 for adults, $9 for children 3–12, $16 for seniors. NY Waterway also offers Hudson Valley tours to historic spots further up the river.

The bargain that still can't be beaten, even more so now that the fare has been obliterated, is the free **Staten Island Ferry** (☎718/390-5253), which leaves from its own terminal in lower Manhattan's Battery Park. It's a commuter boat, so avoid crowded rush hours if you can; at other times, grab a spot at the back (going out) and watch the skyline shrink away. Departures are every 15–20 minutes at rush hours, every 30

minutes mid-day and evenings, and every hour late at night – weekend services are less frequent. (Few visitors spend any time on Staten Island itself; it's easy to just turn around and get back on the ferry. For information on what's outside the terminal, see p.251.)

Walking tours

Options for **walking tours** of parts of Manhattan or the Outer Boroughs are many and varied. Usually led by experts, these tours offer fact-filled wanders through particular areas or focus on particular subjects. You'll find fliers for some of them at the various Visitor Centers; for what's happening in a particular week, check the *New York Times* (Friday or Sunday), the weekly *Village Voice* or *NY Press* (both out on Wednesdays), or any of the free weekly papers around town. Detailed below are some of the more interesting tours we've encountered: note that they don't all operate year-round, the more esoteric only setting up for a couple of outings at specific times of year. If you're interested, phone ahead for the full schedules.

Art Tours of Manhattan (☎609/921-2647). Much the best people to go with if you're interested in first-hand accounts of the city's art scene, establishment and fringe. The custom-designed tours include the galleries of SoHo, Chelsea, 57th St and Madison Ave, as well as "hospitality" visits to an artist's studio, all guided by qualified – and entertaining – art historians. All this individual attention doesn't come cheap. Tours for up to four people cost around $225.

Big Onion Walking Tours (☎439-1090; *www.bigonion.com*). Founded by two Columbia University graduate students, Big Onion specializes in tours with an ethnic and historical focus: pick one particular group, or take the "Immigrant New York" tour and learn about everyone. Cost is $10 or $8 for students and seniors; $11–13 for the food-included "Multi-Ethnic Eating Tour."

Braggin' About Brooklyn (☎718/297-5107). General and specifically African-American themed Brooklyn tours. Tours are $15 and tour times change daily. Call for details.

Bronx County Historical Society, 3309 Bainbridge Ave, Bronx (☎718/881-8900; *www.bronxhistoricalsociety.org*). Neighborhood tours range from strolls through suburban Riverdale to hikes across the desolate wastes of the South Bronx. Excellent value at $10 per person ($5 for society members), though the least frequent of any of the tours listed here.

Brooklyn Center for the Urban Environment, Tennis House, Prospect Park, Brooklyn (☎718/788-8500; www.bcue.com). Focusing on the architectural as well as the natural environment, this organization specializes in summertime neighborhood "noshing" tours that give you a flavor – literally – of Brooklyn's distinct ethnic neighborhoods. Other frequent tours focus on historic Green-Wood Cemetery (see p.227); all walking tours cost $8, $5 for students and seniors. Ask about $35 ($30 for members, students and seniors) ecology boat tours around the oddly fluorescent Gowanus Canal, too.

Greenwich Village Literary Pub Crawl (☎212/613-5796). A two-and-a-half-hour tour guided by actors from the New Ensemble Theater Company, who lead you to some of the most prominent pubs in literary history and read from associated works. Tours meet at the White Horse Tavern, 567 Hudson St, at 2pm every Saturday. Reservations are highly recommended; price is $12, $9 for students and senior citizens.

Harlem Heritage Tours, 230 W 116th St, Suite #5C (☎280-7888; loveharlem@aol.com). Cultural tours of Harlem, general and specific (such as "Harlem Jazz Clubs"), are led mid-day and evening for $15–20, reservations are recommended. Call for details. Very helpful tour guides.

Harlem Spirituals Gospel and Jazz Tours, 890 8th Ave, 2nd floor (☎757-0425; www.harlemspiritual.com). Various tours of Harlem, the Bronx, and Brooklyn, ranging from Sunday-morning church visits to nighttime affairs taking in dinner and a club. Professionally run and excellent value, with prices in the range of $15–75 per person (discounts for children).

Hassidic Discovery Welcome Center, 305 Kingston Ave, Brooklyn (☎1-800/838-TOUR; www.jewishtours.com). Four-hour tours on Sundays of Hassidic Crown Heights conducted by Rabbi Beryl Epstein. Transport from midtown Manhattan available. Reservations required.

Lower East Side Tenement Museum, 97 Orchard St (☎431-0233). This museum organizes Saturday and Sunday walking tours of the Lower East Side in the Spring and Fall months, focusing on the heritage of the various ethnic groups present, community rebuilding, and relations among different groups. Prices are $10 or

$8 for students and seniors, and tickets are available) for museum admission and a tour combined ($11–13).

Municipal Arts Society, 457 Madison Ave, between 50th and 51st sts (☎439-1049 or 935-3960; www.mas.org). Opinionated tours taking a look at New York neighborhoods from an architectural, cultural, historical and often political perspective. On occasion, these tours visit spots not otherwise open to the public – look out for "hard hat" jaunts around construction sites – so it's worth calling for a schedule. Free (donations requested) Wednesday lunchtime tours of Grand Central Station start at 12.30pm from the information booth. Most other tours also start at 12.30pm, last for 90 minutes, and cost from $10 to $15, with discounts for students and seniors (weekend and day-long tours cost more).

The 92nd Street Y, 1395 Lexington Ave, between 91st and 92nd sts (☎996-1100; www.92ndsty.org). None better, offering a mixed bag of walking tours ranging from straight explorations of specific New York neighborhoods to art tours, walking tours of political New York, or a pre-dawn visit to the city's wholesale meat and fish markets. Average costs are $20–55 per person, and specific tours can be organized to accommodate groups with special interests. Look out, too, for the Y's day excursions by bus to accessible parts of the Tri-State area: New York, New Jersey and Connecticut. Commentary is almost always guaranteed to be erudite and informative, and the organization, which sponsors concerts, readings and other events, is well worth checking out in any case.

Queens Historical Society, 143-35 37th Ave, Flushing, Queens (☎718/939-0647; www.preserve.org/queens). No actual guided walking tours, but if you stop by their headquarters in Kingsland Homestead (see p.241 for more information), they'll give you a free do-it-yourself walking tour of the Flushing Freedom Mile.

Radical Walking Tours (☎718/492-0069). 15 different $10 tours of "alternative" Manhattan from a distinctly left-wing perspective. Tours focus on political and social history of Manhattan, such as "Central Park – Trees, Grass and the Working Class"; no reservations required; call for schedule information.

River to River Downtown Tours, 375 South End Ave (☎321-2823). Individual and small group tours of lower Manhattan by New York aficionado Ruth Alscher-Green. Individual prices are $35, or $50 for two people, for a unique two-hour tour spiced with gossip and anecdotal tidbits.

Street Smarts NY (☎212/969-8262). Lively weekend tours, with favorites such as "SoHo Ghosts," "Pubs and Poltergeists" and "Manhattan Murder Mysteries." All tours are $10 and general-

ly begin around 2pm, no reservations needed, call for meeting place and information.

The Urban Park Rangers. A varied selection of free educational walks in all five boroughs throughout the year, focusing on nature and sometimes history in the city's parks. (For walks and information on other parks' events ☎1-888/NY-PARKS; *www.nyparks.org*).

The media

Newspapers and magazines

The 1990s have not been good to the New York print media, and the days are gone when New York could support twenty different **daily newspapers**. Today, only three remain: the broadsheet *The New York Times* and the tabloids *The Daily News* and *The New York Post* – with the recent demise of a fourth, the semi-tabloid *Newsday* (still available in the city, but in Queens and Long Island editions), reminding both readers and publishers of the precarious standing of the rest. The tabloids, especially, seem to take turns battling for survival: in 1990, the *Daily News* became embroiled in a dispute that saw the circulation of the paper drop by two-thirds, as it was boycotted by newsstands and sold by homeless hawkers on the subway. In July 1993 the *New York Post* almost closed down after a succession of owners and a deal in which the staff accepted a pay cut of twenty percent to recover debts of some $25 million. Only by bending the federal anti-trust laws was the paper's future secured. The general feeling is that New York's readership won't be able to support two such similar papers indefinitely, but for now both are managing to hold steady.

The **New York Times** (60¢) is an American institution: it prides itself on being the "paper of record" and is the closest thing America's got to a quality national paper. It has solid, sometimes stolid, international coverage, and places much emphasis on its news analysis; significant recent improvements in its coverage of local issues are largely a legacy of the fierce competition offered by its defunct rival *Newsday*. Each weekday there are "Metro," "Business Day," "Sports" and "Arts"

sections in addition to the main paper plus rotating special sections – "Dining In," "House and Home," "Science Times" etc and separate Weekend sections devoted to "Movies and Performing Arts" and "Fine Arts and Leisure" on Fridays. The Sunday edition ($2.50), available from early Saturday night in most parts of the city, is a thumping bundle of newsprint divided into an ever expanding number of different supplements that could take you the whole day (or the whole week) to read. The paper's legendary crossword puzzles, which increase in difficulty throughout the week, culminate in Sunday's *New York Times Magazine*'s puzzle, which should keep you occupied all weekend.

It takes serious coordination to read the *Times* on the subway (just watch the way the commuters fold it), one reason (but a minor one) why many turn to the *Post* and the *Daily News*. Tabloids in format and style, these arch-rivals concentrate on local news, usually screamed out in banner headlines. Pre-strike, the **Daily News** (50¢) was far and away the better of the two, renowned as a picture newspaper but with a fresh, energetic – and serious – style that put its British equivalents to shame, with intelligent features and many racy headlines, most famous of which was its succinct summary of the president's attitude to New York during the crisis of the mid-1970s: "FORD TO CITY – DROP DEAD." Five months after the strike began, the paper's owners, the *Chicago Tribune*, paid Robert Maxwell $60 million to take the paper (with all its pension and severance liabilities) off their hands, and the unions agreed to return to work. However, crippled by enormous debts and having lost most of its star writers, the general feeling was that "New York's Hometown Newspaper," as it likes to call itself, was about to go down the pan. After Maxwell's death, one Mortimer Zuckerman stepped in as the new owner, but the *News* still can't seem to get back on the rails – as the 1997 departure of respected editor Pete Hamill attested.

The **New York Post** (50¢) is the city's oldest newspaper, started in 1801 by Alexander Hamilton, though it's been in decline for the last twenty years. Known for its solid city news reporting, not to mention consistent conservative-slanted sermonizing, it's perhaps renowned most for its sensational approach to stories: "HEADLESS WOMAN FOUND IN TOPLESS BAR" was one of its more memorable headlines from the 1980s. The *Post* came close to ceasing publication after a sorry series of long-running wrangles that came to a head when real-estate broker Abraham Hirschfeld attempted a takeover of the paper early in 1993. The *Post* devoted four extraordinary issues to vilifying Hirschfeld, dishing the dirt on his business affairs. This had the desired effect, and he backed off, letting News International mogul Rupert Murdoch into the bidding: his company has run the paper from March 1993, but has had problems concerning his ownership of other areas of the media. Rather than force the *Post* into bankruptcy, the laws governing media monopolies were relaxed in Murdoch's favor – and since then, the paper has managed to continue its precarious existence.

The other New York–based daily newspaper is the **Wall Street Journal** (75¢), in fact a national financial paper that also has strong national and international news coverage (with a decidedly conservative bent) – despite an old-fashioned design that eschews the use of photographs. The USA's only other national daily newspaper is **USA Today** (50¢), a color broadsheet that places its emphasis on weather and news roundups rather than in-depth reporting. It was the original model for the now defunct British tabloid *Today*, and you'll see it on sale throughout New York – though it's less frequently read than the local papers.

The weeklies and monthlies

Of the **weekly papers**, the **Village Voice** (Wednesdays, free in Manhattan, $1.25 elsewhere) is the most widely read, mainly for its comprehensive arts coverage and investigative features. Originating in Greenwich Village, it made its name as a youthful, intelligent, vaguely left-leaning journal – the nearest the city ever got to "alternative" journalism. After a brief flirtation in the 1980s with Rupert Murdoch's News International group, the paper is now owned by pet-food mogul Leonard Stern, and many would say its decline into the mainstream is just a matter of time. In 1995 the *Voice* saw the controversial firing of some of its longest-standing and most popular columnists (including the entire sports department) – despite vocal criticism from their colleagues who remained. Nonetheless, the *Voice* is still a good read, offering vocal and opinionated news stories with sharp focus on the media, gay issues and civil rights. It's also one of the best pointers to what's on around town (although movie listings can be unreliable). Catch it early enough on Wednesday morning (or late Tuesday night at the newsstand on Astor Place) and you could grab yourself a free pass to a new movie the following week; look out for the full-page ad that tells you where and when to wait in line. Its competitor, the **New York Press**, is an edgier alternative to the *Voice*; angrier and not afraid to offend just about everyone reading it. The listings are also quite good and look out for its "Best of Manhattan" special edition, published each September: along with superlatives in the fields of eating, drinking and entertainment, it will assist you in your quest for the Best Out-of-Town Spiritual Retreat and the Best Colonic. Other free weeklies include, **Edge NY**, a magazine for independent theater, the satirical **Rotten Apple**, which promises "all the news the others are afraid to print'" and **Literal Latte**, a bimonthly journal of evocative prose, poetry and art.

The other leading weeklies include glossy **New York** magazine ($2.99), which has reasonably comprehensive listings and is more of an entertainment journal than the harder-hitting *Voice*, and **Time Out New York** ($1.95) – a clone of its London original, combining the city's most comprehensive what's on listings with New York-slanted new stories and entertainment and lifestyle features. Then there's the long-established **New Yorker** ($2.95), still the most prominent journal to feature poetry and short fiction alongside its much-loved cartoons. British editor Tina Brown was brought in to rid the magazine of its conservative, fuddy-duddy image, and although she was initially decried by fans, the general consensus seems to be that Brown has taken the magazine back to its smart, sophisticated, irreverent and urbane roots of the 1930s; certainly the theatre and gallery reviews remain the best available. Brown has since been replaced by David Remnick, and the magazine, with no significant change of direction in sight, continues its highbrow crusade. The late Andy Warhol's **Interview** ($2.95) is, as the name suggests, mainly given over to interviews, as well as fashion. Ike Ude's quarterly **aRUDE** ($5) looks very much like *Interview* in its halcyon days; while the new **Soho Style** ($5) claims to define the Downtown Experience. Perhaps the best, certainly the wackiest, most downtown-oriented alternative to the *Voice* is **Paper** magazine ($3.50), a monthly that carries witty and well-written rundowns on New York City nightlife and restaurants and all the current news and gossip. Finally, if you want a weekly with more of a political edge, there's the ironic, pink **New York Observer** ($1) and the earnest, black **Amsterdam News** (75¢).

International publications

British and European newspapers are widely available throughout the city, usually the day after publication – except for the *Financial Times*, which is printed (via satellite) in the US and sold on most newsstands. If you're after a specific paper or magazine, there are a number of outlets worth trying: The Magazine Store, 30 Lincoln Plaza, at 63rd Street and Broadway (☎246-4766), where you can also pick up most UK periodicals; another Magazine Store, (no relation) at 20 Park Ave S between 17th and 18th streets (☎598-9406); Hotalings, 142 W 42nd between Broadway and Sixth Avenue (☎840-1868), Hudson News, 753 Broadway at Eighth Street or Nico's, on the corner of Sixth Avenue and 11th Street (☎255-9175) – one of the best sources in the city of general and specialist magazines, with a huge worldwide stock. In addition, the Barnes & Noble Superstores (see Chapter 24 for addresses) and Borders stock a wide selection of magazines and some international newspapers, which you can peruse for free over coffee.

Television

For foreign travelers to understand the many facets of the American psyche, they should find TV with cable and surf through the 70-plus sta-

tions. Chaos reigns, and it's easy to get addicted – morbid curiosity about home shopping networks, psychic hotlines, Spanish soap operas, and public access proselytizing can get the best of even the most devout television snob. Even if your hotel only gets the regular broadcast stations, start watching the morning line-up of tabloid talk shows or the evening run of sitcoms and you're in danger of forgetting to see the New York sights altogether. In almost all cases, programs are interrupted by frequent, blaring commercials, which you may find fascinating until they become downright annoying.

If after this warning you're still brave enough to take the plunge, here's a brief guide to help you sort through some of what's available: for more **complete listings**, grab a copy of *TV Guide* ($1.49) or check the newspaper listings.

Broadcast TV

Broadcast TV is what you automatically get (with reception variations, of course) when you plug a TV into the wall; on most hotel TV sets, you'll be able to get some or all of the channels listed below.

Perhaps the most noticeable trend in American broadcast TV in recent years has been the explosion of **daytime talk shows**, which have all but obliterated the game shows that once dominated the mornings. Generally devoted to exploring and exploiting the more bizarre weaknesses of everyday people, these shows feature confrontational and/or sympathetic hosts who interrogate on-stage guests with the help of vocal audience par-

Broadcast TV channels
2 WCBS (CBS)
4 WNBC (NBC)
5 WNYW (Fox)
7 WABC (ABC)
9 WWOR (Independent)
11 WPIX/WB11 (Independent)
13 WNET (PBS)
21 WLIW (PBS)
25 WNYE (Educational)
31 WNYC (PBS)
41 WXTV (Spanish language)
47 WNJU (Spanish language)
55 WLIG (Independent)

TICKETS TO TV SHOW TAPINGS

If you want to experience the excitement, horror, boredom and surprise of American TV up close, there are always free tickets on offer for various shows. While some of the more popular require written requests months in advance, almost all have standby lines where you can try your luck on a particular day. Keep in mind that for most shows you must be over 16 and sometimes 18 to be in the audience; if you're underage or traveling with children, call ahead to be sure. Listed here are some of the more popular shows:

Late-night shows

David Letterman. Still everyone's top choice even after his move to CBS and the Ed Sullivan Theater. Send a postcard request as far in advance as possible to Letterman Tickets, 1697 Broadway, New York, NY 10019. The limit is two tickets per postcard. Alternatively, standby tickets are given away at noon at the same address (between 53rd and 54th sts); get there no later than 9.30am or forget it. Information: ☎ 975-1003.

Late Night with Conan O'Brien. Letterman's replacement on NBC is fun in a harmless sort

of way. Write to NBC Tickets, "Late Night with Conan O'Brien," 30 Rockefeller Plaza, New York, NY 10112. Pick-up is at 4pm on the day of the show from the Page Desk at the same address. For standby tickets go to the same place before 9.00am, Monday to Friday. Information: ☎ 664-4000.

Saturday Night Live. Despite this comedy show's decline, audience members keep coming, so the policy of an annual ticket lottery still stands. Not very convenient unless you're willing to plan your trip around the date they give you, but you can send a postcard – which must arrive in August – to NBC Tickets, "Saturday Night Live," 30 Rockefeller Plaza, New York, NY 10112, and see what happens. Tickets are issued to either the dress-rehearsal or the actual show. They hand out standby tickets (these are one per person and do not guarantee admission) at the 49th St side of the GE Building at 30 Rockefeller Plaza at 9.15am any Saturday that there's a show (call ☎ 664-4000 to make sure, since some Saturdays are reruns), and you might get lucky if you get there early enough.

---

ticipants. Competition has seen the topics of each show become more and more sensational, and it's become common practice to tell guests they're on stage for one reason and then spring the real topic on them. The frenzy came to a terrible – and some would say inevitable – conclusion in 1995, when one guest on the *Jenny Jones Show*, outraged at discovering on national TV that the person who had a secret crush on him was, in fact, a *man*, went out after the show and shot his unfortunate admirer dead.

Something else you'll probably notice is the amount of **scheduled news** shown every evening. Despite all the offerings, you can still find yourself uninformed, since most of the news is local, much time is devoted to sports and weather, and sensational stories dominate as the various networks battle for the attention of the talk-show-happy public. The only truly **national news coverage** is at 6.30pm on ABC, CBS and NBC. *Sixty Minutes* (CBS, Sunday at 7pm) is prob-

ably the best news analysis show, and an American institution, with top-quality investigative reporting. *Nightline* (ABC, 11.30pm Monday to Friday), anchored by leading journalist Ted Koppel, is also worth catching, a decent forum for debate on the major stories that day.

As for entertainment, the wittiest, most inventive TV series since Pee Wee Herman was banished from his Playhouse, remains Matt Groening's animated *Simpsons*. And in the same genre, *King of the Hill*, from Mike "*Beavis and Butthead*" Judge, are well worth a look. While the networks scramble to attract ever younger – and whiter – audiences (the target groups most valuable to advertisers) they seem unable to stop the mass defection of viewers to cable – witness the success of the 1998–99 season's quirky Mafia series on *The Sopranos* on HBO.

Channels 13, 21 and 31 are given over to PBS (Public Broadcasting Service), which earned itself the nickname "Purely British Station" for its fond-

Daytime shows

Montel Williams. His show is aimed at both young and old, focusing on finding resolutions to problems – particularly interracial obstacles. Call the Montel Williams Show ☎ 830-0300 for the most up-to-date information on getting into a taping.

Regis and Kathie Lee. The show itself is almost a throwback to the earlier days of American talk TV with a variety of topics aimed at a family audience. Kathie Lee Gifford is equally well known for her problems with the tabloids. There's more than a year's wait, but if you want to try, send a postcard with your name, address and telephone number to Live Tickets, PO Box 777 Ansonia Station, New York, NY 10023-777, or stop by the ABC studios at 67th St and Columbus Ave no later than 8am to pick up a standby number which might get you in. More information ☎ 456-1000.

Ricki Lake. The younger, fresher face of talk; her shows are known for being fun and much less likely to make you feel like you're spying on the miseries of people less fortunate than you. Write to Ricki Lake, 226 W 26th St, 4th floor, New York, NY 10001 as far in advance as possible or go to 221 W 26th St at least 2 hours before a taping (Mon–Thurs 3pm and

5pm or Fri noon and 3pm) for standby. More information: ☎ 352-3322.

Rosie O'Donnell. Rising above the morning sludge, Rosie's show has become immensely popular; expect guests to be big Hollywood stars, but also expect a year's waiting list. You could try writing to: NBC Tickets, "The Rosie O'Donnell Show", 30 Rockefeller Plaza, New York, NY 10112. Tapings are Monday to Thursday at 10am with an additional show on Wednesday at 2pm. Standby tickets (which do not guarantee admission) are available from the Page Desk at 30 Rockefeller Plaza. More information: ☎ 664-4000.

Sally Jessy Raphael. Another big name who tackles the trashy; her shows tend to be more sedate, however, than some. Tapings are Monday to Wednesday and you can make reservations up to a day in advance by calling ☎ 1-800/411-7941 ext 7470. For same-day standby tickets go to the *Hotel Pennsylvania* at 33rd St (between 7th and Broadway) by 9am.

Judge Mills Lane. The famous Nevada District Judge and World Champion Boxing referee whose "Let's get it on!" inspired Mike Tyson to bite off Evander Holyfield's ear, now holds court on WB11/WPIX. For tickets call ☎ 691-3129 one month in advance.

---

ness for BBC drama series. Where it excels, however, is with its wonderfully evocative historical documentaries, surveying the "American Experience" with epics such as Ken Burns' *The Civil War* and *Baseball*, along with the *American Presidents* series – all of which have been deservedly praised. Of the PBS channels available in the city, WNET offers the better programming, while the others often seem like a poor man's Channel 13, spicing up their reruns of WNET's better shows with the worst that British TV has to export. If you missed the best episodes of *Fawlty Towers* or *Are You Being Served?*, now is the chance to make up for it.

Cable TV

Cable TV is also available in many hotels: the number of channels received depends on how much the subscriber pays; to watch a recently released film on one of the pay-per-view channels usually adds about $5 to your hotel bill. Cable net-

works appear on different channels in different parts of New York; if the back of the remote control (a fixture no cable box is without) doesn't list them, ask the hotel desk or simply channel-surf.

The most striking thing you'll notice about the scores of different stations (with, literally, hundreds more on the way) is the lack of variety. Some of the highlights include **HBO** (Home Box Office) which produces its own programming plus recently released movies; endless sports channels showcasing international as well as American games (look for British Premier League soccer on Sunday nights on **Fox Sports Network**); and again plenty of news. **CNN** (Cable News Network) already well known in Europe, offers around-the-clock news; **C-SPAN** does much the same but concentrates on news from Congress and the Supreme Court, including live sessions from both, as well as the British House of Commons. **A&E** (Arts and Entertainment) and **Bravo** offer intelligent coverage of the arts while the **Independent**

FM RADIO STATIONS

88.3 (WBGO) Jazz*

89.9 (WKCR) Columbia University

90.7 (WFUV) Contemporary folk/Celtic/international*

91.5 (WNYE) Educational/community/children

92.3 (WXRK) "K Rock" Classic rock/Howard Stern in the morning

92.7 (WLIR) "Modern" rock (alternative/80s new wave)

93.1 (WPAT) Spanish

93.9 (WNYC) Classical*

95.5 (WPLJ) Top 40

96.3 (WQXR) Classical

97.1 (WBLS) "Hot 97" Hip-hop, R&B

97.5 (WALK) Adult contemporary

97.9 (WSKQ) Spanish

98.7 (WRKS) "Kiss" Urban classics

99.5 (WBAI) Varied/ethnic

99.9 (WEZN) Adult contemporary

100.3 (WHTZ) "Z100" Top 40

101.1 (WCBS) Oldies

101.9 (WQCD) Smooth Jazz

102.7 (WNEW) Rock

103.5 (WKTU) Pop/Disco

104.3 (WAXQ) Classic rock

105.1 (WMXV) Adult contemporary

105.9 (WNWK) Multiethnic

106.7 (WLTW) Light rock

107.5 (WBLS) Urban contemporary

AM RADIO STATIONS

570 (WMCA) Christian/talk

620 (WJWR) Sports

660 (WFAN) Sports/Imus in the Morning

710 (WWOR) News/talk

770 (WABC) Talk/news/Rush Limbaugh

820 (WNYC) News/talk*

880 (WCBS) News

930 (WPAT) Contemporary

970 (WWDJ) Christian music

1010 (WINS) News

1050 (WEVD) News/talk

1130 (WBBR) News

1190 (WLIB) Afro-Caribbean news/talk

1280 (WADO) Spanish

1380 (WKDM) Multiethnic

1560 (WQEW) Children's programming

1600 (WWRL) Gospel/soul/talk

*Indicates national public radio (NPR), often with syndicated programs

---

Film Channel offers some of the strangest films recently released. If you're looking for something more idiosyncratic, you might want to check out the **public access** channels, which will show anything from harmless amateur video-diaries to the vilest hate rant imaginable. And then there's always Channel 35, where, alongside *Holy Mass* and the *Chicks With Dicks* hotline, you'll find *The Box* – a video jukebox which used to have a channel of its own until Time Warner (who controls cable in the city) felt compelled to distance itself from its mostly hip-hop programming.

Radio

The **FM** dial is crammed with local stations of highly varying quality and content. If you possess a Walkman radio, bring it, as skipping through the channels is a pleasure. Stations are constantly chopping and changing formats, opening up and closing down, but we've tried to give a current listing of some of what's on offer. Whereas you'll find mostly music on FM, **AM** stations tend to be more talk oriented. The *New York Times* lists highlights on a daily basis; explore on your own, however, and you're sure to come across something interesting.

Incidentally, it's possible to tune into the **BBC World Service** on the 49-meter shortwave band, or just the World Service news, broadcast on a number of the public radio stations.

Money and banks

New York is an expensive place to visit pretty much any way you slice it. Though there's plenty to do and see that's fairly inexpensive, or even free, inevitably the costs will catch up to you – most likely in the form of accommodation and food and drink. See the Introduction (p.xi), for an overview of costs.

Taking, changing and accessing money

Expect to pay most of your major expenses by **credit card**; hotels and car rental agencies usually demand a credit card imprint as security, even if you intend to settle the bill in cash, and you'll be at a serious disadvantage if you don't have one. Visa, MasterCard, Diners Club, American Express and Discover are the most widely used.

You'll also need to carry a certain amount of **cash**. If you have a MasterCard or Visa, or a cash-dispensing card linked to an international network such as **Cirrus** or **Plus** – check with your home bank before you set off – you can withdraw cash from appropriate **automatic teller machines** (ATMs). For both American and foreign visitors, US dollar **travelers' checks** are a better way to carry money than ordinary bills; they offer the great security of knowing that lost or stolen checks will be replaced. Checks such as American Express, Visa and Thomas Cook are universally accepted as cash in stores, restaurants and gas stations. You'll get your change in dollars, so remember to order a good number of $10 and $20 checks: few places like to hand over all their spare change in return for a check.

Finally, it's possible that your local 24-hour Korean deli will cash a small check for you – this could be a lifesaver if you run out of cash at 4am. Foreign travelers should not bring travelers' checks issued in their own currencies; it can be hard to find a bank prepared to change them, no other business is likely to accept them, and you will probably lose some money in exchange fees to the bank if they do choose to help you out.

Emergencies

All else has failed. You're broke and 3500 miles from home. Before you jump off the Brooklyn Bridge, weigh up the alternatives.

Assuming you know someone who is prepared to send you money in a crisis, the quickest way is to have them take the cash to the nearest Travelers Express Moneygram (☎1-800/543-4080) office and have it instantaneously wired to the office nearest you. This process should take five to ten minutes. They charge according to the country involved and the amount sent: From the US the rate for wiring $100 is $12 while $1000 will incur a fee of $66; from Canada the rates for the equivalent amounts are CAN$18/CAN$85; from Europe $20/$60; from Australia or New Zealand $12/$50. The option of using a credit card is available only when wiring money in the US. There's a maximum of $500 and an additional fee of $12. Western Union offers a similar service, at slightly higher rates (US ☎1-800/325-6000; UK ☎0800/833833).

If you have a fair amount of leeway, you might consider a postal money order, which is exchangeable at any post office. Whether this works out cheaper will depend on the type of mail service you use – priority, express, etc. The equivalent for foreign travelers is the international money order, for which you need to allow up to seven days in the mail before arrival. Estimates as to how long an ordinary check sent from overseas takes to clear range from a maximum of 4 to 8 weeks.

Should you have literally no cash nor access to any, the alternatives include selling blood or working illegally (see "Staying on," p.50). Foreign travelers have the final option of throwing themselves on the mercy of their nearest national consulate (see p.485), who will – in worst cases only – repatriate you, but will never, under any circumstances, lend money.

Banks and exchange

Banking hours are usually (with some variation) Monday–Friday 9am–3pm: some banks stay open later on Thursdays or Fridays, and a few have limited Saturday hours. Major banks – such as **Citibank** and **Chemical** – will exchange travelers' checks and currency at a standard rate. Outside banking hours, you're dependent on a limited number of private exchange offices in Manhattan (listed below), as well as offices at the international airports. All will change travelers' checks and exchange currency, although they may have disadvantageous rates and/or commission charges, the cost of which it's wise to ask about first.

Money:
a note for foreign travelers

US currency comes in bills of $1, $5, $10, $20, $50 and $100, plus various larger (and rarer) denominations. All are the same size and same green color, making it necessary to check each bill carefully. The dollar is made up of 100 cents (¢) in coins of 1 cent (known as a penny), 5 cents (a nickel), 10 cents (a dime) and 25 cents (a quarter). Change – especially quarters – is needed for buses, vending machines and telephones, so always carry plenty.

Generally speaking, one pound sterling will buy roughly $1.60; one Canadian dollar is worth approximately 65¢; one Australian dollar is worth around 65¢; and one New Zealand dollar will get you roughly 55¢.

EXCHANGE OFFICES

The following offices are all open outside banking hours, and handle wire transfers and money orders as well as straightforward transactions.

Avis Currency Exchange, 200 Park Ave at 45th St (Met Life Building, formerly the PanAm Building), Third Floor East, Room 332 (Mon–Fri 8am–5pm; ☎1-800/258-0456 or 661-0826). Also on the main concourse at Grand Central (Mon–Fri 7am–7pm, Sat & Sun 8am–3pm; ☎661-0826); at 1451 Broadway between 41st and 42nd sts (Mon–Fri 10am–8pm, Sat & Sun noon–8pm; ☎944-7600); and in Stern's Department Store, 33rd St and 6th Ave (Mon–Sat 10am–6pm, Sun 11am–6pm; ☎268-8517).

Thomas Cook, 317 Madison Ave at 42nd St (Mon–Sat 9am–7pm, Sun 9am–5pm; ☎883-0401). Also 511 Madison Ave at 53rd St (Mon–Sun 9am–5pm; ☎753-0117); 1590 Broadway at 48th St at Times Square (Mon–Sat 9am–7pm, Sun 9am–5pm; ☎265-6063); 1271 Broadway at 32nd St (Mon–Sat 9am–6.30pm, Sun 9am–5pm; ☎679-4877); and at 29 Broadway at Morris St (Mon–Fri 8.30am–4.30pm; ☎363-6206).

NUMBERS TO RING FOR LOST CREDIT CARDS OR TRAVELERS' CHECKS

American Express checks	☎1-800/221-7282	Thomas Cook/	
American Express cards	☎1-800/528-4800	MasterCard checks	☎1-800/223-9920
Citicorp/Citibank	☎1-800/645-6556	Visa cards	☎1-800/336-8472
Diners Club	☎1-800/234-6377	Visa checks	☎1-800/227-6811
MasterCard cards	☎1-800/826-2181		

Communications: telephones and the post

The New York telephone system is reliable if expensive, especially when dialing long distance, though the postal system doesn't quite match the efficiency European visitors may expect.

Phone calls

Public telephones are easily found – you'll see them on street corners as well as in hotel lobbies, bars and restaurants, although you may have to look for one that actually works. With the decentralization of the American phone system, rival phone companies are free to set up pay phones; they all look alike at first glance, but most New Yorkers will tell you to look for the more reliable **Bell Atlantic** phones, since the others don't always give the same value for money. All pay phones take 25¢, 10¢ and 5¢ coins, and the cost of a local call – ie one within the 212 and 718 area codes covering the five boroughs

Rasps, squeaks and blips

If it's your first time in the USA, the various tones used by the phone system need a little explanation. The dial tone is a low, continuous rasp or a single low drone; the ringing tone a long nasal squawk with short gaps; the busy signal (engaged tone) a series of rapid blips; number unobtainable is a single high-pitched squeak or an extremely rapid busy signal.

– is 25¢ (slightly more to or from really remote parts of 718). If your pay phone won't accept your quarter, it means the change box is full. It's nothing personal, you'll just have to keep trying other phones. On a Bell Atlantic phone, the local rate is 25¢ for the first 3 minutes. When your time is up, a voice should instruct you to put in more money at a rate of 5¢ for each extra 2 minutes. If you fail to do this, then you'll be cut off.

Making **telephone calls from your hotel room** will cost considerably more than from a pay phone and should be avoided if possible (you'll usually find pay phones in the lobby). On the other hand, some budget hotels offer free local calls from rooms – ask when you check in.

Long-distance and international calls

All **long-distance** and **international calls** can be dialed direct from any private or public phone. If it's the latter, just dial the number and an operator will tell you the rate for the first 3 minutes; the problem has always been coming up with the copious amounts of change necessary to call anywhere for any length of time. To solve this problem, you might want to consider a **prepaid phone card**, which you can purchase at most grocery stores and newsstands. These are issued by the major phone companies as well as countless others (who may charge exorbitant rates – so beware!) and give you a prepaid dollar amount of long-distance time, which you access by punching in numbers (instructions are on the card) at any public phone.

All phones accept **credit cards** – an operator or recorded message will tell you to either read out or punch in the number; international rates are usually competitive. Beware of using your BT or Mercury **charge cards** – their international rates can be staggeringly expensive. **Reverse-charge** calls (or "collect calls") can also prove costly: it's always best to use a collect call to give your number to the person you are calling – and then get them to call you back. To make a collect call through a US phone company you can dial ☎0 followed by the number you wish to call

AREA CODES AROUND NEW YORK

Bronx, Brooklyn, Queens and Staten Island (1) **718**

Long Island (1) **516**

Other nearby areas of New York State (1) **914**

New Jersey (1) **201, 973, 908, 609** or **732**

To phone into Manhattan from these areas or anywhere else (1) **212**

SERVICE NUMBERS

Emergencies **911** for police, ambulance and fire

Operator **0**

Directory assistance **411** (New York City); **1 + (area code) + 555-1212** (numbers in other area codes)

USEFUL TELEPHONE CODES

The telephone code to dial **to the US** from the outside world is **1**.

To make international calls **from the US**, dial **011** followed by the country code:

Australia 61

Denmark 45

Germany 49

Ireland 353

Netherlands 31

New Zealand 64

Sweden 46

United Kingdom 44

For codes not listed here, dial the operator or check the front of the local White Pages.

OVERSEAS OPERATOR NUMBERS

To call an operator in your own country in order to make a collect call from the US, dial the following numbers:

Australia ☎1-800/682-2878, 1-800/937-6822 or 1-800/676-0061 (☎008/032 032 in Australia for information).

Ireland ☎1-800/562-6262 (☎1800/250 250 in Ireland for information).

New Zealand ☎1-800/248-0064 (☎123 or 126 in New Zealand for information).

United Kingdom ☎1-800/445-5667 (☎0800/345144 in the UK for information).

TELEPHONE SERVICES AND HELPLINES

AIDS Hotline ☎447-8200; for counseling and information ☎1-800/590-2437

Al-Anon (for families of alcoholics) ☎254-7230

Alateen (for teenage drinkers) ☎254-7230

Alcoholics Anonymous ☎647-1680

Crime Victims Hotline ☎577-7777 (24 hours)

Herpes Advice Line ☎213-6150; 24hr recorded info ☎540-0540

Missing Persons Bureau- New York City Police Department ☎374-0319

Movies ☎777-FILM

Narcotics Anonymous ☎929-6262

New York City On Stage ☎768-1818

New York Council on Problem Gambling ☎1-800/437-1611

NYC Gay and Lesbian Anti-Violence Project ☎807-0197

Pills Anonymous ☎874-0700

Sex Crimes Report Hotline (N.Y.C.P.D.) ☎267-7273

Sex Crimes Victim Services Agency ☎577-7777 (24 hours)

Suicide Hotline (24 hours) ☎1-800/543-3638; ☎673-3000 (The Samaritans)

Suicide Prevention Hotline ☎718/389-9608.

Any number with **800** or **888** in place of the area code is "toll-free," which means it costs nothing to call. Many national firms, government agencies, inquiry numbers, hotels and car rental firms have a central toll-free number. To find it look in the Yellow Pages or dial ☎1-800/555-1212 for toll-free directory inquiries.

A so-far purely American phenomenon is using **letters** as part of a phone number – the idea is that it'll be easier for you to remember that way, and whether it's a toll-free information number (such as ☎1-800/AIR RIDE for airport transport) or a chicken delivery service (in Brooklyn's Cobble Hill, a sign says simply "DIAL HOT BIRD"), it actually seems to work. Take a look at the keypad of any push-button phone and you'll get the hang of it in no time.

and an operator will take it from there. Otherwise you can dial ☎1-800/COLLECT or 1-800/CALLATT – these last two numbers both claim to be the cheapest options. It's also possible to make a collect call by **calling an operator** in your own country: see the box opposite for the relevant numbers.

Within the US, **rates** are generally cheapest between 11pm and 8am weekdays, all day on weekends; the next cheapest time is between 6pm and 11pm weekdays. For overseas, the best times vary depending on the time difference; a general rule is that if it's a convenient time for the person you're trying to reach, it's an expensive time for you to make the call. Another factor making it difficult to predict the cost of your call is that the three big long-distance companies – AT&T, Sprint and MCI – are constantly warring to offer the better deal to customers. Their rates are generally within a penny of each other – if they're not, they will be when you call back an hour later. But before you make a call using any of the options listed above – and this includes collect calls – it pays to dial the operator to check the rate.

By dialing ☎411 at any NY area pay phone you can get free directory assistance to find phone numbers, addresses or even just a cross street.

Yellow Pages

Unbelievably useful (if hardly the sort of things you'll want to lug around) are the **Bell Atlantic White** and **Yellow Pages** phone books. The first is an alphabetical list of private numbers and businesses (with blue-edged pages sandwiched between the two sections containing listings for New York City, State and Federal government agencies); the second details every consumer-oriented business and service in the city, listing delicatessens, grocers, liquor stores, pharmacies, physicians and surgeons by location, and restaurants by location and cuisine. It's also handy for finding bike and car rental firms – and just about anything legal that can be paid for. Look for it in most bars, hotel rooms and lobbies and the larger post offices.

Area codes

Normally, **telephone numbers** are in the form of ☎123/456-7890. The first three digits are the area code and are needed only when dialing a different area. In New York City, the **212** code covers Manhattan; the **718** code covers the Outer Boroughs of Brooklyn, the Bronx, Queens, and Staten Island. Phoning within any area code, simply dial the last seven digits of the number. Outside the area, dial **1** first, then the **area code** and **number**.

Where we've given phone numbers for places outside Manhattan, you'll find codes are included. To check codes elsewhere, consult the phone book or call the operator (see box opposite).

Letters and poste restante

In terms of efficiency the New York (and American) **postal service** comes a very poor second to its phone system. New Yorkers will tell you stories about postcards arriving thirty years after they were sent – legends, mostly, but ones with a basis in truth. The service is rarely atrocious, but it is unpredictable and unreliable – even within Manhattan mail can take a few days to arrive, and a letter to LA might take a week. Overseas airmail can take anything between five and fourteen days, and sending mail abroad by surface post consigns it to anywhere from four to eight weeks' disappearance.

Letters

Ordinary mail **within the US** costs 33¢ for letters weighing up to an ounce, 20¢ for postcards. Any "G" stamps you come across are left over from the previous rates; you can purchase "make up" stamps to bring these in line with the current rates from the post office. Letters to Canada are 48¢ for the first half-ounce or 54¢ for up to an ounce; for Mexico, they're 40¢ for the first half-ounce and 46¢ for up to an ounce. Postcards to Canada are 45¢ and to Mexico 40¢.

Airmail service is the same price for anywhere else in the world. Postcards are 55¢ and aerograms 60¢; letters are also 60¢ for the first half-ounce and rise steeply after that. If you're a long-winded letter-writer, buy your stamps from the post office window to make sure you put enough postage on – the US postal service doesn't take kindly to being shortchanged.

Envelopes in the US must include the sender's address and the recipient's zip code: without the code, letters can end up terminally lost, and certainly delayed. If you're unsure of a Manhattan zip use the guide we've printed opposite or phone ☎967-8585; elsewhere ask for the relevant zip-code directory at the post office.

You can **buy stamps** in shops, some supermarkets and delis, though these may cost considerably more than the face value. The best place is, unsurprisingly, a **post office**: although the hours vary (you're unlikely to find the Wall St branch open on Saturdays) they are, roughly, Monday–Friday 9am–5pm, Saturday 9am–noon, and there are a lot around. In Manhattan, the massive main **General Post Office** at Eighth Avenue between West 31st and West 33rd streets is open seven days a week, around-the-clock, for important services; see for yourself by going there at 11.30pm on April 15 (tax day in the US), when the television news crews gather to capture the procrastinators' frantic last-minute rush. Letters posted from this or other large post offices seem to arrive soonest, whereas the blue bin-like **mailboxes** on street corners tend to take a while.

Packages

Packages cost a lot to send however you decide to do it, with the price increasing in direct proportion to the size of the package, the distance of the location, and the speed of the service. The post office sells boxes in different sizes, or you can come up with your own by scouring the streets; just make sure it's clean enough for your writing to be read when you address it. Seal your box well with tape, but don't tie it with string, which can cause disaster in automated postal equipment. Mark both the address it's going to and your return address (General Delivery is OK) on the same side of the package, clearly indicating (with "TO" and "FROM") which is which. If the package is headed overseas, once you're at the

---

MANHATTAN POST OFFICES

Ansonia, 178 Columbus Ave off 68th St, NY 10023.

Bowling Green, 25 Broadway between State and Morris sts, NY 10004.

Canal Street, 350 Canal St between Broadway and Church St, NY 10013.

Cathedral, 215 W 104th St between Broadway and Amsterdam Ave, NY 10025.

Church, 90 Church St between Vesey and Barkley sts, NY 10007.

Cooper, 93 4th Ave at 11th St, NY 10003.

Franklin D Roosevelt, 909 3rd Ave between 54th and 55th sts, NY 10022.

Gracie, 229 E 85th St between 2nd and 3rd aves, NY 10028.

Grand Central, 450 Lexington Ave at 45th St, NY 10017.

JAF Building, 421 8th Ave at 33rd St, NY 10001.

Knickerbocker, 128 E Broadway between Pike and Essex sts, NY 10002.

Lenox Hill, 217 E 70th St between 2nd and 3rd aves, NY 10021.

Madison Square, 149 E 23rd St between Lexington and 3rd aves, NY 10010.

Manhattanville, 365 W 125th St between St Nicholas and Morningside aves, NY 10027.

Midtown, 223 W 38th St between 7th and 8th aves, NY 10018.

Morningside, 232 W 116th St between 7th and 8th aves, NY 10026.

Murray Hill, 115 E 34th St between Park and Lexington aves, NY 10016.

Old Chelsea, 217 W 18th St between 7th and 8th aves, NY 10011.

Peck Slip, 1 Peck Slip between Pearl and Water sts, NY 10038.

Peter Stuyvesant, 432 E 14th St between Ave A and 1st Ave, NY 10009.

Planetarium, 127 W 83rd St between Columbus and Amsterdam aves, NY 10024.

Prince, 103 Prince St between Greene and Mercer sts, NY 10012.

Radio City, 322 W 52nd St between 8th and 9th aves, NY 10019.

Rockefeller Center, 610 5th Ave at 49th St, NY 10020.

Times Square, 340 W 42nd St between 8th and 9th aves, NY 10036.

Village, 201 Varick St at W Houston St, NY 10014.

Wall Street, 73 Pine St between Williams and Pearl sts, NY 10005.

Yorkville, 1619 3rd Ave between 90th and 91st sts, NY 10128.

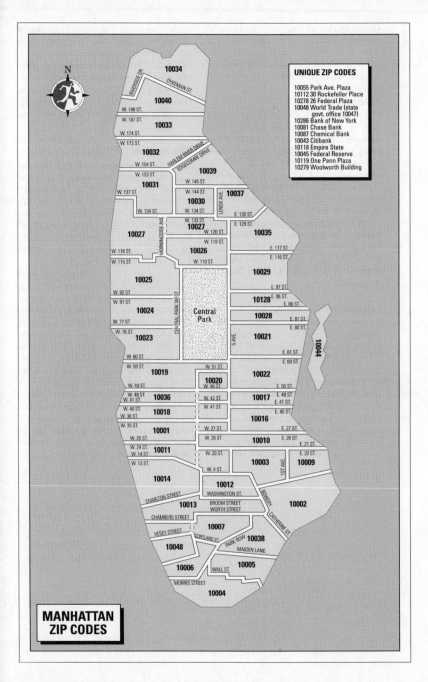

window the clerk will have you fill out a Customs Declaration form, which is straightforward – if all you're sending home is smelly old clothes, it's fine to put NCV (No Commercial Value) instead of a dollar amount on the form.

Telegrams

To send a **telegram** – also called a cable – you'll need to go to a telegraph company office, addresses of which can be found in the Yellow Pages. With a credit card you can simply phone up (Western Union ☎1-800/325-6000 or Globalcomm ☎1-800/835-4723) and dictate. Prices for international telegrams are expensive (around $15 for the first 7 words, then about $1 for each extra word) and, assuming the cooperation of the postal service in the country to which they are sent, they should take 2–3 days. For domestic service you can either send a telegram (delivered by hand the same day) or a **mailgram** (delivered by mail, taking 12 to 48 hours but costing less).

Poste restante

You can receive International mail **poste restante** by having it addressed to you c/o Poste Restante, General Post Office, 421 Eighth Ave, NY 10001. To collect letters, go to the window (☎330-3099) between 8am and 6pm Monday to Saturday; you'll need to show your passport or some other photo ID. Check regularly, as mail is kept for only thirty days before being returned to sender – so tell your correspondents to make sure there's a return address on the envelope. The Post Office will not forward mail to a new address once you leave. For domestic mail the routine is slightly dif-

ferent: The correct address is c/o General Delivery, the window hours are between 10am and 1pm Monday to Saturday and the mail is held for only 10 days. **Receiving mail at someone else's address**, be sure your correspondent puts "c/o" that person's name on the envelope, since without that you risk your mail being returned to sender by an overzealous letter carrier.

The Internet

If you're traveling without your own computer and modem, accessing the Internet is possible at a couple of locations, such as the **cybercafe**, 273A Lafayette St at Prince St (☎334-5140); 250 W 49th St between Broadway and Eighth Ave (☎333-4109); *www.cyber-cafe.com*; and **alt.coffee**, 139 Ave A between Ninth St and St Marks (☎529-2233; *www.altdotcoffee.com*). These places usually charge an average of $10 per hour, during which you can telnet to your email account back home, enabling you to pick up and send mail as if you'd never left. You can also surf the net to your heart's content, fiddle around with CD-ROMs, scan, print, or just drink coffee; if you're new at this whole game, the staff will gladly help you figure things out. Another alternative is to stop by a branch of the New York City Public Library where **free** Internet use is available during library hours. Each branch has their own set of rules so just ask a librarian how to get online.

You can also send your findings about New York to us: **our email address** is *newyork@ roughguides.co.uk;* or visit **our Web site** at *www.roughguides.com* as a starting point for travel information (and many other resources).

Police and trouble

The New York City Police – the NYPD, aka "New York's Finest" – are for the most part approachable, helpful and overworked. This means that asking directions gets a friendly response, reporting a theft a weary "Whaddya want me to do about it" – and any smile is greatly appreciated. Unfortunately, in this realm of New York life as in others, race can play a part in the response you get, especially in light of recent media attention (here as elsewhere in the US). Wary of strained relations between police and minority communities, officers – even those from minority communities themselves – may be a little more reserved with you if your skin is any color but white. This is not to say that they'll refrain from helping you if you're in trouble, however.

Each area of New York has its own **police precinct**; to find the nearest station to you, call ☎374-5000 (during business hours only) or check the phone book or directory inquiries (☎411). In **emergencies** phone ☎**911** or use one of the outdoor posts that give you a direct line to the emergency services. Out of the city you may have to tangle with the **State Police**, who operate the Highway Patrol – and do so quite ruthlessly.

Staying out of trouble

Irrespective of how dangerous New York really is – and it is considerably safer than it was, say, a decade ago – it can sometimes *feel* dangerous. Perhaps more than in any other city in the world, a sense of nervy self-preservation is rife here:

people make studied efforts to avoid eye contact, and any unusual behavior clears a space immediately: the atmosphere of impending violence is sometimes sniffable.

The reality is somewhat different. There is a great deal of crime in New York, some of it violent. But keep in mind that more than eight million people live in the city, and, as far as per capita crime rates go, Boston is more dangerous, as are New Orleans, Dallas, Washington DC, and, believe it or not, one hundred and some odd other US cities. Even considering New York on its own, it's pleasing (and not misleading) to note that in 1997 the city boasted its lowest crime rate – violent crimes included – since 1968. And it's still on its way down. This is due in part to periodic gun amnesties and increased gun confiscation: anyone taken into custody for even the most petty crime can be searched for weapons, so the police have simply started cracking down on the minor offenses, like jaywalking, shoplifting, even public urination, which they used to overlook. A less inspiring contributing factor is the shift in focus of the criminal drug culture; where crack, a stimulant that inspired violence in its addicts, once ruled, heroin, a depressant that causes sluggishness more than anything, is now much more prevalent.

New York's tension doesn't automatically mean violence; it's largely due to the frenetic pace at which most of the city operates. Take several million people, pump them full of caffeine, make them believe that they have to get where they're going five minutes faster than is actually humanly possible, and pack them onto a tiny island – there's bound to be an edge in the air. Which is not to say you should discount the possibility of danger altogether. Do as the locals do and keep it in the back of your consciousness, not at the forefront. As with any big city, the main thing is to walk with confidence and remember the few places and/or times that you really should avoid. Throughout the guide, we've outlined places where you should be careful and those few best skirted altogether, but really it's a case of using your common sense; it doesn't take long to figure out that you're somewhere unsavory.

The hard and fast rule that will best enable you to travel around New York safely and confidently is simple to remember: **be aware of your surroundings at all times**. Contrary to the warnings of the folks back home, it's OK to let on you're a visitor – if you follow rules of paranoia and never look up, you'll miss a lot of what's striking about New York. Looking up and around, reading this guidebook, and pulling out your camera can make you more of a target, but only because the assumption is that tourists are careless. You are much more likely to have your pocket picked while you're looking at your map than you are to encounter something more violent. So carry bags closed and across your body, don't let cameras dangle, keep wallets in front – not back – pockets, and don't flash money or your Oyster Rolex around. Avoid crowds, especially around rip-off merchants like street gamblers, where half the con is played on the participants and the other half on the spectators. Never be afraid to move away if you feel someone is standing too close to you.

It is, of course, the murders that make the headlines: reassure yourself that ninety percent of victims are known to their killers, which is to say most killings are personal disputes rather than random attacks. **Mugging**, on the other hand, can and does happen. It's impossible to give hard and fast rules on what to do should you meet up with a mugger: whether to run or scream or fight depends on you and the situation. Most New Yorkers would hand over the money every time, and that's probably what you should do – in fact, some people always carry a spare $20 or so as "mug money," lest their attacker turn nasty at finding empty pockets. Having a spare $20 should be your common

Victim services

If you are unlucky enough to be mugged, the city's Victim Services 24-hour hotline (☎577-7777) offers telephone advice and will direct anyone who has suffered a crime against their person to where they can receive one-to-one counseling.

practice anyway; if you find yourself somewhere you'd rather not be, you want to be able to jump in a cab.

Of course the best tactic is to **avoid being mugged**, and following the "awareness" rules outlined above is a good start. Some good late-night points are worth adding to that: even if you are terrified, or drunk (or both), don't appear so; never walk down a dark side street, especially one you can't see the end of, or through a deserted park; walk in the street itself, stick to the roadside edge of the sidewalk or where it's easier for you to run into the road if necessary and attract the attention that muggers hate.

If the worst happens and your assailant is toting a gun or a knife, play it calmly. Remember that he (for this is generally a male pursuit) is probably almost as scared as you and just as jumpy; keep still, don't make any sudden movements – and do what he says. When he has run off, hail a cab and ask to be taken to the nearest police station: taxis rarely charge for this, but if they do the police are supposed to pay. Standing around on the street in a shocked condition is inviting more trouble, though you'd be pleasantly surprised at the number of people who would sincerely come to your aid. At the station, you'll get sympathy and little else; file the theft and take the reference to claim your insurance back home.

Women's New York:
problems and contacts

Newcomers to the city, whether male or female, face the fact that New York is a huge, overwhelming and potentially violent place. On a first visit, it will probably take a few days to mentally adjust to the city and its culture, and this is the time when you'll be feeling (and appearing) at your most vulnerable. Affecting an attitude of knowing where you're going (even if you don't) protects you from trouble, as will some basic tips in survival psychology.

The first – and fundamental – step is to avoid being seen as an easy target: female New Yorkers project a tough, streetwise image through their body language and dress, even when they're all glammed up and ready to party. If this play-acting sounds exhausting, the pay-off is that there's nothing unusual in women traveling in the city alone or with other women, at pretty much any time of day or night, so you won't be the focus of attention that you might be in other parts of the world. People gravitate to New York from the rest of America whether to study, further their careers or just hang out – so it's easy to move around, make friends and plug into New York's networks. Also on the positive side, the women's movement of the 1960s and 1970s has had a much more dynamic effect in New York (indeed throughout East and West Coast America) than in Europe. Women are much more visible in business, politics and the professions than you may be used to, and the attitudes around can equally well be more progressive and sophisticated.

All this progress has had a somewhat paradoxical effect, however, with successful mainstreaming eliminating the impetus, if not the need, for a strong women's community. New York's last feminist bookstore closed its doors in 1994, and while women's work still flourishes in all aspects of the arts, there's no central source for information on what's going on. Nowadays, most if not all feminist activism centers around reproductive rights, which you'll find to be one of the most volatile issues in American politics. If

you want to see the political side of New York feminism, you'll find it outside an abortion clinic. In addition, check out the lesbian listings in "Gay and lesbian New York", on p.47 and throughout the guide.

Feeling safe

It must be safe to travel around New York; American women do it all the time. So runs the thinking, but New York does throw up unique and definite problems for women – and especially for women traveling alone and just getting to know the city. If you feel and look like a visitor, not quite knowing which direction to ride the subway, for instance, it's little comfort to know that New York women routinely use it on their own and late in the evening. What follows are a few points to bear in mind when beginning your explorations of the city: if they duplicate, in part, the comments in "Staying out of trouble" p.41, no apologies.

The truth is you're more likely to feel unsafe than be unsafe – something that can lead to problems in itself, for part of the technique in surviving (and enjoying) New York is to look as if you know what you're doing and where you're going. Maintain the facade and you should find a lot of the aggravation fades away, though bear in mind that for Americans subtle hints aren't the order of the day: if someone's bugging you, let them know your feelings loudly and firmly. Some women carry whistles; many more carry their keys between their fingers when walking home at night. These tactics, while not much good in the event of real trouble, can lend you confidence, which in turn wards off creeps. Much more powerful are **chemical repellents** such as pepper sprays, available from sporting goods stores. If you do carry one of these, make sure you know how and when to use it, and what its effects will be. Properly used they are extremely effective at disabling your attacker long enough for you to make good your escape, and they do not cause any lasting injury to the attacker.

Harassment in the city is certainly worse for women than men – and it can be a lot scarier. But it's not always that different, at least in intent. You're far, far less likely to be raped than you are **mugged**. For a few ground rules on lessening chances of mugging, see p.42, but above all be wary about any display of wealth in the wrong place – if you wear jewelry (or a flash-looking watch), think about where you're walking before setting out for the day; in general, it's a good idea to tuck necklaces inside your clothing and turn rings around so the stones don't show, at least when you're out on the street or riding the subway. If you are **being followed**, turn around and look at the person following you, and step off the sidewalk and into the street; attackers hate the open, and they'll lose confidence knowing you've seen them. Never let yourself be pushed into a building or alley and never turn off down an unlit, empty-looking street; listen to your instincts when they tell you to take the long way around. If you're unsure about the area where you're staying, don't hold back from asking other women's advice. They'll tell you when they walk and when they take a bus so as to avoid walking more than a block; which bars and parks they feel free to walk in with confidence; and what times they don't go anywhere without a cab. Listen to this advice and merge it into your own experience. However, don't avoid parts of the city just through hearsay – you might miss out on what's most of interest – and learn to expect New Yorkers (Manhattanites in particular) to sound alarmist; it's part of the culture.

If you don't have much money, **accommodation** is important: it can be very unnerving to end up in a hotel with a bottom-of-the-heap clientele. Make sure that your hotel has a lobby that's well lit, the door locks on your room are secure and the night porters seem reliable. If you feel uneasy, move. If you're staying for a couple of weeks or more, you might try one of the city's women-only long-term residences; for addresses of these, see "Staying on," p.52.

Crisis/support centers

There are competent and solid **support systems** for women in crisis, or in need of medical or emotional support. At the following you can be assured of finding skilled, compassionate staff.

Sex Crimes Hotline ☎267-7273 or 267-RAPE. Staffed by specially trained female detectives of the New York City Police Department who will take your statement and conduct an investigation, referring you to counseling organizations if you wish. If you don't want to go to the police, then the **Bellevue Hospital Rape Crisis Program**, 1st Ave and 27th St; ☎562-3755 or 562-3435. Provides free and confidential counseling, medical treatment and follow-up counseling and referral as necessary. See also the Victim Services phone line, p.42.

Women's Healthline ☎230-1111. Provides a broad range of information on women's health problems (such as birth control, abortion, sexually transmitted diseases) and can refer callers to state licensed clinics and hospitals.

Other contacts

Barnard College Women's Center, Barnard College, 117th St and Broadway; ☎854-2067. A friendly but primarily academic resource which maintains an extensive research library collection of books, articles and periodicals.

Ceres, 584 Broadway (between Prince and Houston sts), Suite 306; ☎226-4725. Art gallery run by an all-women cooperative. Exhibits mainly – though not exclusively – women's work.

Enchantments, 341 E 9th St; ☎228-4394. Lesbian-friendly center for spiritual enlightenment. Useful bulletin board.

Eve's Garden, 119 W 57th St (between 6th and 7th aves), Suite 1201; ☎757-8651. This "sexuality boutique for women and their partners" stocks erotic accessories, books and videos. Mon–Sat 11am–7pm.

NARAL (New York affiliate of the National Abortion & Reproductive Rights Action League), 462 Broadway (between Grand and Broome), Suite 540; ☎343-0114. A good source of information on current legal issues; they'll also refer you to reliable providers of reproductive services.

National Council of Jewish Women, 9 E 69th St (between Madison and 5th aves); ☎535-5900. Organization focused primarily on community service. Occasionally sponsors lectures, discussion groups and other events.

See also the lesbian listings in "Gay and lesbian New York" on pp.46–47, and the women's/lesbian bars and clubs fully detailed in Chapters 18 and 19.

National Organization for Women, 150 W 28th St (at 7th Ave), Room 304; ☎627-9895. The largest feminist organization in the US.

Planned Parenthood of New York City Inc, Margaret Sanger Center, 26 Bleecker St (at Mott St); ☎274-7200; *www.ppnyc.org*. Sexual and reproductive health services.

Refuse and Resist ☎385-9303. Activist group defending reproductive rights and fighting against hate crimes.

WOW Cafe (Women's One World Theater), 59 E 4th St (between 2nd and 3rd aves); ☎777-4280. Feminist/lesbian theater collective with meetings open to all women on Tuesdays at 6.30pm. Call for information on upcoming events.

Gay and lesbian New York

There are few places in America – indeed in the world – where gay culture thrives as it does in New York. A glance at the pages of the *Village Voice*, where gay theater, gossip and politics share space with more mainstream goings-on, is enough to show how proudly the gay and lesbian community shows its many faces. It's estimated that around twenty percent of New Yorkers are lesbian or gay; and when you extend that category to include bisexuals and transgender individuals, the numbers climb even further – as they do when you take into account the numbers of gay-identified newcomers who come to New York each day for the welcome refuge the city can offer them.

Until recently, the liberal face of New York politics has been good to the gay community, with tremendous strides having been made for gay rights since the catalyst of the Stonewall Riots 25 years ago. The passage of the **Gay Rights Bill** contributed significantly to the high visibility of lesbians and gay men in local government; until recently, the New York State governor, the mayor, the City Council president and controller, and the Manhattan borough president all employed full-time liaison officers to work with gay and lesbian groups. Unfortunately, the election of both a Republican governor and a Republican mayor have seen cutbacks in this area and a move away from officially sanctioned support for gay-oriented initiatives. While the gay community has enough of a widespread political base to resist any onslaught on the battles already won, negative effects are definitely being felt in the most time-sensitive areas of gay activism: HIV/AIDS

legislation and research. The urgency of this devastating epidemic – which still affects the gay community more than any other – is one reason the outspoken New York gay community will not lapse into complacency.

Socially, lesbians and gay men are fairly visible, and while it's not recommended that you and your partner hold hands in public before checking out the territory, there are **neighborhoods** in the city where you'll find yourself in a comfortable majority. Chelsea (centered around 8th Ave between 14th and 23rd sts) and the East Village are the largest of these, and have largely replaced the West Village as the hub of gay New York. There's still a strong presence centered around Christopher Street, but it's in Chelsea that gay socializing is most out and open. The other haven is Brooklyn's Park Slope, though perhaps more for women than for men; it's primarily a residential area and so a little harder to get to know, but talk to enough of the Chelsea regulars and you're bound to find a bunch who call Park Slope home.

There are several **free newspapers** that serve New York's gay community: *Blade*, *Next* and *HX* are all published weekly, while *LGNY News* is bi-weekly. You'll find these available at the Center (see overleaf), at bars, cafés, lesbian and gay bookshops, and occasionally at newsstands along with glossy national mags such as *Out*, *The Advocate*, *Girlfriends*, *Diva*, etc, and the useful quarterly *Metro Source*. Overleaf are some of the other resources we think you'll find helpful. In addition, we've listed gay-run (and gay-friendly) hotels on p.47; and gay bars and nightclubs in Chapters 18 and 19 respectively.

Lesbian and gay resources

The **Lesbian and Gay Community Services Center**, 1 Little West 12th St, NY 10014 (corner of Hudson and Gansevoort sts); ☎620-7310; *www.gaycenter.org*. The Center's free paper, *Center Voice*, is mailed to more than 55,000 households, which should give you an idea of how it's grown in the fifteen years since it opened in an abandoned school. At the time of writing it is in the midst of a multimillion-dollar renovation, after which it will move back to its home at 208 W 13th St. The Center, which houses countless diverse organizations (including ACT UP and the Metro Gay Wrestling Alliance) also sponsors workshops, dances, movie nights, guest speakers, youth services, programs for parents and kids, an archive and library, the annual Center Garden Party and lots more that we don't have room to list here. Even the bulletin boards are fascinating. All in all, you really can't beat it as a place to start.

Brooklyn AIDS Task Force, 502 Bergen St (Carlton St at 6th Ave), Brooklyn, NY 11217; ☎718/622-2910. Counseling available on gay and lesbian issues.

Gay and Lesbian National Hotline ☎1-888/THE GLNH or 989-0999 (Mon–Fri 6pm–10pm; Sat noon–5pm). Information, help and referrals.

GLAAD-NY (Gay and Lesbian Alliance Against Defamation), 150 W 26th St at 7th Ave, Suite 503; ☎807-1700; *www.glaad.org*. Monitors the portrayal of gays, lesbians and bisexuals in the media, and organizes caucuses and discussion groups on media topics. Volunteers and visitors welcome.

Lambda Legal Defense and Education Fund, 120 Wall St, 15th floor, NY 10005; ☎809-8585; *www.lambdalegal.org*. Active against discrimination affecting people with AIDS and the lesbian, gay, bisexual and transgender community. Publications, speakers and newsletter.

New York Area Bisexual Network ☎459-4784. Call for information on bisexual support groups, discussions, social events and other activities.

Shades of Lavender ☎718/622-2910 ext 103. Division of the Brooklyn AIDS Task Force. Regular events, social and support groups. A small but friendly operation popular with the Park Slope crowd.

Bookshops

A Different Light, 151 W 19th St (between 6th & 7th aves); ☎989-4850; *www.adlbooks.com*. Excellent selections of books and publications from around the country. Open 7 days a week 11am–11pm. Hosts regular book signings and readings.

The Oscar Wilde Bookshop, 15 Christopher St (between 6th & 7th aves); ☎255-8097; *www.oscarwildebooks.com*. The world's first gay and lesbian bookstore. Unbeatable.

Health and well-being

Callen-Lorde Community Health Center, 356 W 18th St (between 8th and 9th aves); ☎675-3559; *www.callen/lorde.org*. Clinic with sliding pay-scale based on income which can either treat or refer you. Mon–Thurs 9am–8pm (closed Wed 1–5pm).

Center for Mental Health and Social Services, at the Center, 1 Little West 12th St; ☎620-7310. Free confidential counseling and referrals.

Gay Men's Health Crisis (GMHC), 119 W 24th St (between 6th and 7th aves); ☎807-6664; *www.gmhc.org*. Despite the name, this organization – the oldest and largest not-for-profit AIDS organization in the world – provides information and referrals to everyone.

Identity House, 39 W 14th St, Suite 205 (between 5th and 6th aves); ☎243-8181. Psychological counseling, referrals, groups and workshops for the lesbian, gay, bisexual and transgender community.

SAGE: Senior Action in a Gay Environment, 305 7th Ave (at 27th St); ☎741-2247. Also at the Center, 1 Little West 12th St. Advice and numerous activities for gay seniors.

Arts and media

There's always a fair amount of gay theater going on in New York: check the listings in the *Village Voice* and the free papers noted above.

Dyke TV, PO Box 55, Prince St Station, NY 10012; ☎343-9335; *www.dyketv.org*. Media and arts center with half-hour show Tuesday nights at 8pm on Manhattan Cable Channel 34 covering news, arts, politics, sports and other features – including current issues in lesbian activism. Also offers training for lesbians in video and computer technologies.

Gay Cable Network ☎727-8825; *www. gcntv.com*. A variety of programs featuring news, interviews, entertainment reviews and more, mainly for men. Broadcast on Manhattan Cable Channel 35 and on other cable networks in the city.

Heritage of Pride, 154 Christopher St, Suite 1D, NY 10014; ☎80-PRIDE; *www.nycpride.org*. The group that organizes the bulk of citywide events for June, Gay Pride Month.

Leslie-Loman Gay Art Foundation, 127 Prince St between Wooster and W Broadway (in the basement); ☎673-7007; *www.planet.net/ corp/leslie_loman*. The foundation maintains an archive and permanent collection of lesbian and gay art, with galleries open to the public from September to June.

New Festival (aka New York Lesbian and Gay Film Festival) ☎727-8825; *www. newfestival.org*. The festival takes place each June.

Accommodation

A few suggestions if you're looking for a place to rest your head that is specifically friendly to gays and lesbians and convenient for the scene.

Chelsea Mews Guest House, 344 W 15th St, NY 10011 (between 8th and 9th aves) ☎255-9174. All male gay guesthouse. Local calls are included.

Chelsea Pines Inn, 317 W 14th St; ☎929-1023. Well-priced hotel, whose guests are mostly gay, housed in an old brownstone on the Greenwich Village/Chelsea border that offers clean, comfortable, attractively furnished rooms. Best to book in advance.

Colonial House Inn, 318 W 22nd St, NY 10011 (between 8th and 9th aves); ☎243-9669. Economical, 20-room bed-and-breakfast in the heart of Chelsea. Also welcomes straight guests. Boasts a clothing-optional roofdeck.

Incentra Village House, 32 8th Ave between 12th and Jane sts; ☎206-0007. Twelve-room town house, some rooms with kitchenette. Three-night minimum stay at weekends. Also welcomes straight guests.

Religion

There are numerous gay religious organizations in New York.

Congregation Beth Simchat Torah, 57 Bethune St, NY 10014; ☎929-9498. Lesbian and gay synagogue with Friday night services at 8.30pm.

Dignity/Big Apple ☎818-1309. Catholic liturgy and social each Saturday at 8pm at the Center.

Metropolitan Community Church, 446 W 36th St, NY 10018 (between 9th and 10th aves); ☎629-7440. Services each Sunday at 10.30am, 12.30am (in Spanish) and 7pm.

Exclusively for women

Astraea, 116 E 16th, 7th floor, NY 10003, #520 (between Park Ave S and Irving Place); ☎529-8021; *www.astraea.org*. National lesbian foundation offering financial support, education and networking to lesbian organizations and projects.

Lesbian Herstory Archives, PO Box 1258, NY 10116; ☎718/768-DYKE, fax 768-4663; *www.datalounge.com/lha*. Celebrated and unmissable. Call or write for an appointment or for schedule of events.

Lesbian Switchboard ☎741-2610 Mon–Fri 6–10pm. Because no lesbian organizations receive any centralized funding, the community relies on the commitment of small groups of volunteers. One such group is the Switchboard – the place to phone for information on events, happenings and contacts in the New York community.

See also "Women's New York," p.43.

Disabled access in the city

Knowing the rolling topography of New York City under my wheels is like downloading some ancient guidebook directly into the soul.

John Hockenberry in *The New York Times*, August 26, 1995.

With an introduction like that, how could you miss it? For disabled travelers, New York presents challenges, to be sure, but the rewards almost always outweigh the difficulties.

New York City has had recent, wide-ranging disabled access regulations imposed on an aggressively disabled-unfriendly system. The Americans with Disabilities Act, a landmark achievement essentially guaranteeing the rights of the disabled in the US, stipulated that public buildings (and this includes hotels) built after 1993 must be accessible. Buildings built before that time must be modified – to the extent that this is possible – although this is open to some interpretation. The reality in New York is that there are wide variations in accessibility, making navigation a tricky business. At the same time, you'll find New Yorkers surprisingly willing to go out of their way to help you. If you're having trouble and you feel that passersby are ignoring you, it's most likely out of respect for your privacy – if you need assistance, never hesitate to ask.

In an effort to make up for the limitations to the city's accessibility, city agencies offer a considerable amount of information and advice. New York is also home to many of the country's largest disabled services and advocacy groups, so you can be almost certain to find the support you need to overcome initial obstacles. The key is to be informed before you arrive. To that end, we've listed the most useful contacts below.

Getting around

For wheelchair users, getting around on the **subway** is next to impossible without someone to help you, and extremely difficult at most stations even then. The New York City Mass Transit Authority is working to make the majority of stations accessible, but at the rate they're going (and

the state the subway is in), it won't happen soon. **Buses** are another story, and are the first choice of many disabled New Yorkers themselves. (For a detailed explanation of the bus system, see "Getting around the city," p.19.) All MTA buses are equipped with wheelchair lifts and locks. To get on a bus, wait at the bus stop to signal the driver you need to board; when he or she has seen you, move to the back door, where he or she will assist you. For travelers with other mobility difficulties, the driver will "kneel" the bus to allow you easier access. Wheelchair users may also be eligible for the MTA's Access-a-Ride bus service, though probably not if you're staying a very short time. For more information, including a Braille subway map, contact the MTA by calling the Accessible Line ☎718/596-8585; TDD ☎718/596-8273; or writing to 370 Jay St, Brooklyn, NY 11201. A free publication, *Accessible Travel*, is available from Michael Levy at ☎373-5616.

Taxis are a viable option for visitors with visual and hearing impairments and minor mobility difficulties; for wheelchair users, however, the disappearance of all but one of the big Checker cabs has made taxi travel pretty impossible. If you have a collapsible wheelchair, drivers are required to store it and assist you; the unfortunate reality is that most drivers won't stop if they see you waiting. If you're refused, try to get the cab's medallion number and report the driver to the Taxi and Limousine Commission at ☎221-8294.

Aside from the bus, the best way to travel New York by wheelchair is still the **sidewalk**. Watch out for uneven curbs and cobblestones, especially on smaller streets, but overall you shouldn't have a problem.

General advice and information

Big Apple Greeter, 1 Center St, NY 10007 (accessibility info on ☎669-3602, fax 669-3685, TTY 669-8273; *big applegreeter.org*; *www.bigapplegreeter. org*). Big Apple Greeter, who employ a full-time access coordinator, is accepted by many as the main authority on New York accessibility. The free service (described in more detail on p.24) matches you with a volunteer who spends a few hours showing you the city. Big Apple Greeter has also compiled a resource list especially for travelers with disabilities, and they'll be happy to supply you with this on request.

The Lighthouse, 111 E 59th St, NY 10022 (☎821-9200). General services for the visually impaired. They also have Braille and large-print guides to New York.

The Mayor's Office for People with Disabilities, 100 Gold St, 2nd floor, NY 10038 (between Frankfort and Spruce) (☎788-2830; TDD 788-2838). General information.

New York Society for the Deaf, 817 Broadway, 7th floor, NY 10003 (☎ and TTY 777-3900). A good source of information on interpreter services.

The New York State Travel Information Center, 1 Commercial Plaza, Albany, NY 12245 (☎1-800/225-5697). Write or call for the *I Love New York Travel Guide*, a general booklet to the state and city that includes accessibility ratings.

Upward Mobility (☎718/645-7774). Lift-equipped, wheelchair accessible limousine service.

Wheelchair Workshop (☎718/472-5500). Wheelchair repairs and rental.

Finally, **Access for All** is a comprehensive guide to cultural resources for the disabled. A copy is available for $5; write to Hospital Audiences, Inc, 546–548 Broadway, 3rd Floor, NY 10012 (☎1-888/424-4685 or 575-7663; TDD 575-7673).

Staying on

Nobody ever says it's easy to live and work in New York City, New Yorkers especially – most of whom, when you broach the subject of prolonged residence, will talk obsessively about their jobs and salaries (assuming they have them), and where they live, or will live, or won't be living any more. When the movie *Single White Female* came out, New Yorkers didn't question its credibility on artistic levels: they knew it was make-believe because there was no way Bridget Fonda could have found, let alone afforded, that apartment in the Ansonia building. You know you're somebody if you've got access to the *New York Times* real estate section before it hits the newsstands; everyone else can be found lining up in Cooper Square to pick up the *Voice* the minute it comes out on Tuesday night – even though the new listings are available on their Web site earlier in the day (see p.23). Basically, finding a place to live that's safe, clean and affordable is a challenge at best and torture at worst. And once you've got that, you still have to get a job to pay for it.

If you're a **foreigner**, you naturally start at a disadvantage, at least as far as contacts go. If you have an English accent it may help, but don't count too heavily on it. The British Consulate claims that each year an alarming number of Britons wind up in New York City in need of shelter, sustenance and sympathy. Both work and rooms, however, are there, if you've got the energy, imagination or plain foolhardiness to pursue them. Below are the basic ground rules and those matters of bureaucracy which, even if you

choose to ignore them, you should certainly be aware of.

Legal (and illegal) work: information for foreigners

For **extended, legal stays** in the US it helps if you have relatives (parents, or children over 21) who can sponsor you. Alternatively, a firm offer of work from a US company or, less promisingly, an individual, will do. Armed with a letter specifying this you can apply for a **special working visa** from any American embassy or consulate abroad *before* you set off for the States.

There are a whole range of these visas, depending on your skills, projected length of stay, etc – but with a couple of exceptions they're extremely hard to get. The **easiest** tend to be for academic posts or other jobs (in the computer field, for instance) which the US feels it particularly needs to fill. For **students** (and occasionally non-students) there are a limited number of Exchange Visitor Programs (EVPs), whose participants are given a **J-1** visa that entitles them to accept paid summer employment and to apply for a **social security number** (an identification for tax purposes which virtually no American citizen is without). Most J-1 visas are issued for positions in American summer camps through schemes like BUNAC: information is available from their office at 16 Bowling Green Lane, London EC1R 0BD (☎020/7251 3472).

Should all this seem too far-fetched, you could, like thousands of others each year, forget regulations completely and hunt out **work on your own**. To do this you'll have to pound the streets, check the bulletin boards (see the "Directory" on p.485) and the media, and in most cases lie about your social security number to satisfy your prospective boss. If you're already in New York and decide you want to stay and work, this will most likely be your only choice: employment visas can't realistically be obtained in the city. Be advised, though, that for anyone with only a standard tourist visa, **any kind of work is totally illegal**. If you're caught, you could be liable for deportation, and your employer for a

Overstaying your welcome: advice for foreign travelers

For visitors granted admission to the US under the visa waiver scheme (see p.5), the date stamped in your passport is the latest you're legally entitled to stay. Leaving a few days after may not matter, especially if you're heading home, but more than a week or so can result in a protracted – and generally unpleasant – interrogation from officials: it's been known for immigration control to question overstayers deliberately long enough to miss their flights. Additionally, you may well find that you are denied entry to the US in the future and that your American hosts and/or employers face legal proceedings. In fact, exceeding your time limit by more than 180 days can subject you to a ban of up to 10 years!

If you do want to stay on, the best option is to get an **extension** before your time is up. You do this by applying to the US Immigration and Naturalization Service for an Issuance or Extension of Permit to Re-Enter the USA. In New York you'll find the office at **26 Federal Plaza** (at Worth St between Lafayette and Centre sts), open for in-person visits Monday to Friday between 7.30am and 3.30pm; you can also speak to an officer by phone (☎1-800/375-5283 or 1-800/870-3676 to order forms) between 8am and 5.30pm. Brace yourself – you're plunging, voluntarily, into a side of American bureaucracy that's known for being frustrating,

unpleasant and, above all, suspicious. Your application (on form I 539) must be submitted before your I 94 (the card you are issued at the point of entry) expires or no fewer than 15 and not more than 90 days before your visa expires and it costs a hefty – and nonrefundable – $120, so think carefully about what you're doing. Think, too, about how you'll answer any questions, as it will automatically be assumed that you are working illegally; it's up to you to furnish convincing proof that you can support yourself financially. Taking along an upstanding US citizen to vouch for you is a good idea. You'll also need to think up a good reason to explain why you didn't allow the extra time initially: well-worn but effective excuses include saying your money lasted longer than you planned, or that your parents/husband/wife have decided to come over for a while. Should you need a further extension, apply for it at a different office, and keep your fingers crossed.

Your only other option, and this is by no means infallible, is to **leave the country** and **come back** in. From New York, Montréal is a short flight or a long train/bus ride away; and you don't need a visa to get in. You can apply for a new visa there, or, if you came in on a visa waiver, just turn around and come back. Keep in mind that the longer you spend in Canada, the less obvious your return to New York State will be.

---

substantial fine – something that has virtually destroyed the market for casual labor.

Of more immediate concern for temporary workers is the business of finding out exactly what people do in New York – and how you can fit in. For ideas (and positions) check the employment ads in *The New York Times*, *NY Press*, *Village Voice* and in the plethora of smaller, free neighborhood tabloids available throughout the city. Other papers to try are the ethnic weeklies that crowd every newsstand: the *Irish Voice* and *Irish Echo* can be particularly useful for Irish travelers if you want to get in touch with the large immigrant population who came before you.

Possibilities obviously depend on your own personal skills and inventiveness, but among the more general or obvious you might look at some of the following suggestions.

• **Restaurant and bar work**. With more than 25,000 restaurants in the city, this is perhaps the best bet, especially since 15% of the bill (see "Tipping" p.488) can add up to a lot of extra take-home pay at the end of the night. For the reasons mentioned above, however, restaurateurs are much more wary than they were about taking on someone who doesn't have (or who has obviously made up) a social security number, and jobs are no longer assured in this field. Experience helps, as does dropping by in person, since most restaurants won't deal with you over the phone. This is one area in which a "refined" British accent is a plus, since many owners and managers will appreciate the positive effect it may have on customers.

• **Child-care, house-cleaning, dog-walking, cat-sitting**. New Yorkers frequently advertise these tasks on notices posted in supermarkets, corner drugstores, health food shops, pet stores, bus shelters, and on university and college bulletin boards.

• **Telemarketing/market research**. Often not too choosy about whom they employ – and sometimes impressed (especially the market research people) with very English English.

• **Music teacher.** If you can teach guitar, saxophone or keyboards there's lots of scope among wannabe band members in the East Village.

• **Painting and decorating.** Hard work but good rates. Some agencies offer this kind of work – or you can hunt privately through friends.

• **Foreign language lessons.** If you've a language or two, try advertising on a bulletin board or in the weeklies. Rates can be good.

• **Artist's model.** Pass your name and a contact number around to the various independent studios or artist hangouts in SoHo or TriBeCa. Or try to reach the model-booking directors at the art schools themselves.

• **Nightclub bouncer.** For those with physique – and a liking for the hours.

• **Blood donation**. A final, if slightly desperate, option for quick emergency cash. Check Yellow Pages for agencies or hospitals.

If you're fortunate enough to get by on your own funds for a while, you might want to consider getting an **internship**, basically offering your services for free in return for contacts, experience or possible sponsorship. In fields like publishing and the arts, it's a great way to get your foot in the door.

Whatever you do (or try to do), proceed with caution at all times. Remember, as an illegal worker you have *no* rights, and some potential employers will be eager to exploit this. Be selective, if you can. And don't enter into any slave labor type set-up if you're at all suspicious.

Finding an apartment or long-stay room

If work can be hard to find, wait till you start **apartment hunting**. Costs are outrageous. A studio apartment – one room with bathroom and kitchenette – in a reasonably safe Manhattan neighborhood can rent for upwards of $1000 a month, and even in traditionally undesirable parts of the city – **the Lower East Side** and **Hell's**

Kitchen being the most recent and extreme examples – gentrification (and property rentals) are proceeding apace. Many newcomers to the city settle for sharing studios and one-bedrooms among far too many people; the alternative, not a bad one, is to look in the Outer Boroughs or the nearby New Jersey towns of Jersey City or Hoboken. With everyone else following that example, however, even those neighborhoods are becoming expensive, and to find a real deal you have to hunt hard and check out even the most unlikely possibilities.

The best source for actually hearing about an apartment or room is, as anywhere, word of mouth. On the media front, keep an eye on the ads in the *Voice, The New York Times* and the smaller ethnic papers mentioned overleaf; and if you're reading this before setting out for New York, consider advertising yourself, particularly if you have a flat in London to exchange. Try **commercial and campus bulletin boards** too, where you might secure a temporary apartment or sublet while the regular tenant is away.

Some of the city's many **universities and colleges** also provide vacancies, especially in the summertime. For instance, Barnard College (write to Summer Housing at Barnard, Columbia University, 3009 Broadway, NY 10027; ☎854-8021) offers a variety of dormitory facilities from the end of May to mid-August for between $600 and $1000 a month with a 7-night minimum stay: write well in advance, as they're "selective" about who gets a room, and be prepared to show that you've got a temporary job, internship, or course of study that requires you to be in the city. New York University Summer Housing (14A Washington Place, NY 10003; ☎998-4621; *www.nyu.edu/summer/housing*), charges a weekly rate that varies according to the room's amenities and your enrollment status (if you are not a student, plan on paying between $150 and $210 per week, with mandatory and optional meal plan). There's a three-week minimum stay, and priority is given to students in NYU programs; once again, write well in advance.

Less satisfactory perhaps, but still a fallback option are **long-stay hotels**. A dwindling number of these cater specifically to single women on long stays: *Webster Apartments,* 419 W 34th St, NY 10001 (☎967-9000); *Parkside Evangeline Residence,* 18 Gramercy Park S, NY 10003 (☎677-6200); and *Katherine House,* 118 W 13th St, NY 10011 (☎242-6566). The last two are situated in a much nicer part of the city, though each usually has a long waiting list – call ahead. It's even harder to find a cheap, long-stay accommodation open to both women and men; most hostel style establishments have strict limits on the number of days they will allow you to stay. One exception is the *International Student Hostel*, 154 E 33rd St, NY 10016 (☎228-7470, fax 228-4689) – though this is open to students only. However, you should bear in mind that most of the cheaper hotels offer reduced weekly rates. Contact the respective reservations managers for full details.

The **New York Convention and Visitors Bureau**, 810 Seventh Ave between 52nd and 53rd sts (☎484-1222; *www.nycvisit.com*), can also be worth a call. They dole out a leaflet listing hotel rates. As a last resort, you could call **Victim Services** ☎577-7700 or 577-3899. Although they've officially assumed the duties of the "Traveller's Aid" booth that used to be in Times Square, their concern is more with crime victims and US teens stranded without funds. So don't expect much sympathy unless you fall into either of those categories. However, they may be able to refer you to low-budget (or even free) temporary accommodation. One piece of advice – city shelters are notoriously dangerous and unsavory, so don't end up there if you can at all avoid it.

Just possibly (and only if you can afford the fee), you might find it to your advantage to resort to one of the city's several roommate-finding agencies. Oldest and most reliable is **Roommate Finders**, 250 W 57th St (☎489-6942), a nondiscriminatory but discriminating company who charge a flat rate, all-inclusive rate of $250. If you use one of the other agencies – the *Voice* carries all their names, numbers and descriptions – make sure you read the contract before money changes hands or papers are signed.

Lastly, for the really organized, other viable accommodation alternatives include **homesteading, co-op** and **mutual housing associations**. These revolve around low-rent group occupation and renovation of often abandoned, city-owned buildings. It's the group element – and the commitment this entails – that mark this system as different from squatting. Each individual tenant contributes the particular skills at his or her disposal, as well as monthly dues that collectively support normal operating, maintenance and repair costs. Various agencies designed to assist and protect co-op groups and tenant associations have sprung up, providing legal assistance, rehabilitation and repair loan pools, architectural services, tool lending, training, technical assistance and so on: all very urban grass roots, community-oriented stuff. As for getting involved: in the words of one young British homesteader, it's a matter of "being in the street and seeing what's happening." Sound advice in any case, but for more direct information call the Urban Homestead Assistance Board at 120 Wall St, NY 10005 (☎479-3300). And good luck.

The City

Chapter 1

Introducing the City

N ew York City comprises the central island of Manhattan along with four Outer Boroughs – Brooklyn, Queens, the Bronx and Staten Island. Manhattan, to many, is New York. Certainly, whatever your interest in the city it's here that you'll spend the most time, and, unless you have friends elsewhere, are likely to stay. Understanding the intricacies of Manhattan's layout, and above all getting some grasp on its subway and bus system (for which see Basics), should be your first priority. If at all possible, try to master at least some of the following before arrival – on your flight, train trip or bus ride if need be.

A guide to the Guide

New York is very much a city of **neighborhoods**, and the chapters of our guide reflect this: each chapter covers a large area, and even the shortest will require at least a day of wandering, even if you intend to take in only the salient parts of what there is to see. The neighborhoods may be ethnic, geographic or historic: in some cases the name is more of a convenient label than an accurate description. For an overview of each neighborhood, turn to the introduction of each chapter.

The chapters

The guide starts at the southern tip of the island and moves north: **Chapter 2**, "The Harbor Islands," comprises the first parts of New York (and America) that nineteenth-century immigrants would have seen – the Statue of Liberty and Ellis Island, the latter recalling its history in an excellent Museum of Immigration. **Chapter 3**, "The Financial District and the Civic Center," takes in the skyscrapers and historic buildings of Manhattan's southern reaches – the famous silhouette seen on a thousand and one posters, with icons like the World Trade Center and the Woolworth Building prominent.

North of the Civic Center are the first of the ethnic neighborhoods: Chinatown is perhaps the city's most homogeneous ethnic area, a

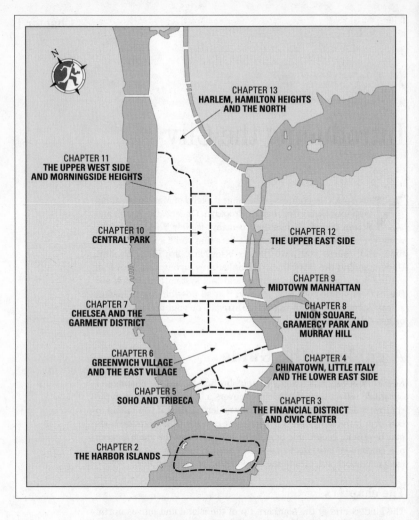

CHAPTER 13
HARLEM, HAMILTON HEIGHTS
AND THE NORTH

CHAPTER 11
THE UPPER WEST SIDE
AND MORNINGSIDE HEIGHTS

CHAPTER 10
CENTRAL PARK

CHAPTER 12
THE UPPER EAST SIDE

CHAPTER 9
MIDTOWN MANHATTAN

CHAPTER 7
CHELSEA AND THE
GARMENT DISTRICT

CHAPTER 8
UNION SQUARE,
GRAMERCY PARK AND
MURRAY HILL

CHAPTER 6
GREENWICH VILLAGE
AND THE EAST VILLAGE

CHAPTER 4
CHINATOWN, LITTLE ITALY
AND THE LOWER EAST SIDE

CHAPTER 5
SOHO AND TRIBECA

CHAPTER 3
THE FINANCIAL DISTRICT
AND CIVIC CENTER

CHAPTER 2
THE HARBOR ISLANDS

vibrant locale that's great for Chinese food and ethnic shopping; Little Italy, on the other hand, has few traces of the once-strong immigrant presence. These two, along with the Lower East Side, a traditionally Jewish – though now strongly Hispanic as well – neighborhood that's scattered with some interesting lowlife bars and clubs, plus a few trendy ones, form **Chapter 4**. SoHo was once an area of light industry and office buildings, but when the industry went into decline, artists moved into the buildings: their open-plan design made them perfect for studios, and SoHo is now the number-one district for galleries and the commercial art scene. TriBeCa is catching some of the fallout of SoHo's art dealing and is now similarly happening; read about both neighborhoods in **Chapter 5**. Greenwich Village has long been a cool place to hang out (at least in name), the jazz clubs and cafés forming a focus for the area's students and would-be bohemians. In the East Village the radicalism is a little more real; you'll find both described in **Chapter 6**. **Chapter 7** covers Chelsea and the Garment District: Chelsea is a mostly residential neighborhood, but it has been working hard to redefine itself via a growing arts scene, a vibrant shopping strip and some tourist attractions; the Garment District gets its name from the clothes production that goes on here, and can be a bargain shopper's paradise. **Chapter 8**, "Union Square, Gramercy Park and Murray Hill," covers an area that was once the most fashionable in town, the birthplace of presidents and home to the Morgan banking dynasty. Also here is that enduring symbol of the city and skyscraper extraordinaire, the Empire State Building.

Chapter 9, "Midtown Manhattan," covers the stretch that runs from 42nd Street to Central Park. Here the great avenues – Fifth, Park and Madison – become the domain of New York's rich and powerful: for years this has been a showcase for corporate building, and you'll find some of New York's most awe-inspiring, neck-cricking architecture here (the Chrysler Building, Rockefeller Center), along with some superb museums (the Museum of Modern Art, the Museum of TV and Radio) and opulent stores. **Chapter 10** covers Central Park, a supreme piece of nineteenth-century landscaping without which life in Manhattan would be unthinkable – and certainly unliveable. Flanking the park, the Upper West Side – **Chapter 11** – is mostly residential and extremely affluent, boasting Lincoln Center, Manhattan's temple to the performing arts, the American Museum of Natural History, and beautiful Riverside Park on the Hudson. This chapter also contains descriptions of Columbia University, Morningside Heights and the Cathedral of St John the Divine, the largest Gothic building in the world. On the other side of the park, the Upper East Side (**Chapter 12**) is decidedly more grandiose, the nineteenth-century millionaires' mansions now transformed into a string of magnificent museums known as the "Museum Mile." Alongside is a patrician residential neighborhood that boasts some of the swankiest addresses in Manhattan.

Above Central Park lie several distinct neighborhoods: Harlem, the historic black city-within-a-city whose name was for a long time synonymous with racial tension and urban deprivation, but today has a healthy sense of an improving go-ahead community; Hamilton Heights, a comparatively affluent area that feels too rural to be part of Manhattan; and Washington Heights, a mixed neighborhood far from the Downtown attractions, one that few visitors ever venture to visit. Inwood, at the very northern tip of Manhattan Island, has an unusual draw in the Cloisters, a nineteenth-century mock-up of a medieval monastery, packed with great European Romanesque and

Gothic art and (transplanted) architecture. These areas are all described in **Chapter 13**.

It's a fact that few visitors, especially those with limited time, bother to venture off Manhattan Island and out to the Outer Boroughs – covered in **Chapter 14**. This is a pity, because each of the Boroughs – Brooklyn, the Bronx, Queens and Staten Island – has points of great interest, both from an historical and a contemporary point of view, and revitalization in areas such as the South Bronx is remarkable to see (as well as being way off the beaten track). More frequented destinations include the picturesque streets of Brooklyn Heights and the atmospheric charm of Coney Island and nearby Brighton Beach, the nature sanctuaries of Queens and the Bronx, and the suburban-pastoral landscape of near-autonomous Staten Island. Chapter 15 explores the city's museums and galleries – covering everything from the giant New York institutions uptown to the tiny side street galleries downtown.

Transport, terminology and the layout of the city

As mentioned above, each of the chapters covers a large area: you'll need to have at least a basic knowledge of New York's public transit system in order to get around what are often distances too long to tackle on foot. For a complete guide to the city's transit networks, see "Getting around the city" in Basics.

Despite its grid-pattern arrangement, Manhattan can seem a wearyingly complicated place to get around: blocks of streets and avenues, apparently straightforward on the map, can be uniquely confusing on foot, and too many subway lines just don't meet up where you would expect them to (as well as being poorly marked underground). Don't let subways and buses overawe you, though, since with a little know-how you'll find them efficient and fast. And if you're at all unsure, just ask – New Yorkers are the most helpful and accurate of direction givers and have a seemingly infinite interest in initiating visitors into the great mysteries of their city.

You should also bear in mind that you'll hear the terms "Lower Manhattan," "Midtown" and "Upper Manhattan." Roughly speaking, **Lower Manhattan** runs from the southern tip of the island to around 14th Street; **Midtown Manhattan** stretches from about 34th Street to the southern tip of Central Park; and **Upper Manhattan** contains the Park itself, the neighborhoods on either side of it, and the whole area to the north.

From north to south the island of Manhattan is about thirteen miles long and from east to west around two miles wide. Whatever is north of where you're standing is **uptown**; whatever south, **downtown**. East or west is **crosstown** (hence "crosstown buses"). The **southern (downtown) part of Manhattan** was first to be settled, which means that its streets have names and that they're somewhat randomly arranged; similarly, the tangle of Greenwich Village is difficult to navigate, and you can waste much time wondering how West 4th and West 11th streets could possibly intersect. **Uptown, above Houston Street on the East Side, 14th Street on the West,** the streets are numbered and follow a strict grid pattern. The numbers of these streets increase as you move north. Downtown, the main **points of reference** are buildings: the World Trade Center and the Woolworth Building are unmistakeable landmarks. Uptown, just look for the big north–south **avenues. Fifth Avenue**, the greatest of these, cuts along the east side of Central Park and serves as a dividing line between east streets (the **"East Side"**) and west streets (the **"West Side"**) – but only once you're south of Central Park, which does Fifth's job for about fifty blocks and separates the Upper West and Upper East Sides. **House numbers** increase as you walk away from either side of Fifth Avenue; numbers on avenues increase as you move north.

Chapter 2

The Harbor Islands

The tip of Manhattan Island and the enclosing shores of New Jersey, Staten Island and Brooklyn form the broad expanse of New York Harbor, one of the finest natural harbors in the world and one of the things that persuaded the first immigrants to settle here several centuries ago. The harbor is an almost landlocked body of water, divided into the Upper and Lower Bay, some hundred miles square in total and stretching as far as the Verrazano Narrows – the narrow neck of land between Staten Island and Long Island. It's possible to appreciate Manhattan by simply gazing out from the promenade on Battery Park. But to get a proper sense of New York's specialness, and to get the best views of the classic skyline, you

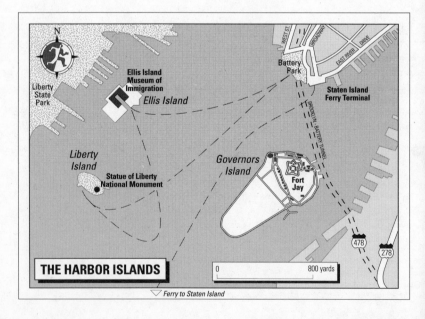

should really take to the water. You can do this either by taking a ride on the Staten Island ferry, or by taking the Circle Line ferry out to the Statue of Liberty and Ellis Island: two far more compelling targets for a trip.

Practicalities

Ferries, run by Circle Line, go to both the Statue of Liberty and Ellis Island and leave from the pier in Battery Park, every twenty minutes in summer roughly between 8.30am and 4.30pm. The fare is $7 for the full round-trip, and half that price for children (tickets from Castle Clinton in Battery Park). If you take the last ferry, it won't be possible to see both islands, so it's best to try and leave as early as possible, thereby avoiding the lines (which can be long in high season, especially on weekends) and giving yourself enough time to explore both islands thoroughly. Liberty Island needs a good couple of hours, especially if the weather's fine and there aren't too many people; Ellis Island, too, demands at least two hours if you want to see everything. There are no admission fees for either Ellis Island or the Statue of Liberty. Visitor information for both sites is available from The Statue of Liberty-Ellis Island Foundation: ☎883-1986; 52 Vanderbilt Ave, NY 10017-3898; *www.ellisisland.org*.

The Statue of Liberty

Out of all of America's symbols, none has proved more enduring or evocative than the **Statue of Liberty**. This giant figure, torch in hand and clutching a stone tablet, has for a century acted as a figurehead for the American Dream; indeed there is probably no more immediately recognizable profile in existence. It's worth remembering that the statue is – for Americans at least – a potent reminder that the USA is a land of immigrants: it was New York Harbor where the first big waves of European immigrants arrived, their ships entering through the Verrazano Narrows to round the bend of the bay and catch a first glimpse of "Liberty Enlightening the World" – an end of their journey into the unknown, and the symbolic beginning of a new life.

These days, although only the very wealthy can afford to arrive here by sea, and a would-be immigrant's first (and possibly last) view of the States is more likely to be the customs check at JFK Airport, Liberty remains a stirring sight, with Emma Lazarus's poem, *The New Colossus*, written originally to raise funds for the statue's base, no less quotable than when it was written . . .

> *Here at our sea-washed, sunset gates shall stand*
> *A mighty woman with a torch, whose flame*
> *Is the imprisoned lightning, and her name*
> *Mother of Exiles. From her beacon-hand*

The Statue of Liberty

Glows world-wide welcome; her mild eyes command
The air-bridged harbor that twin cities frame.
'Keep ancient lands, your storied pomp!' cries she
With silent lips. 'Give me your tired, your poor,
Your huddled masses yearning to breathe free,
The wretched refuse to your teeming shore.
Send these, the homeless, tempest-tost to me,
I lift my lamp beside the golden door.'

The statue, which depicts Liberty throwing off her shackles and holding a beacon to light the world, was the creation of the French sculptor Frédéric Auguste Bartholdi, who crafted it a hundred years after the American Revolution in recognition of solidarity between the French and American people (though it's fair to add that Bartholdi originally intended the statue for Alexandria in Egypt). Bartholdi built Liberty in Paris between 1874 and 1884, starting with a terra-cotta model and enlarging it through four successive versions to its present size, a construction of thin copper sheets bolted together and supported by an iron framework designed by Gustave Eiffel. The arm carrying the torch was exhibited in Madison Square Park for seven years, but the whole statue wasn't officially accepted on behalf of the American people until 1884, after which it was taken apart, crated up and shipped to New York.

It was to be another two years before it could be properly unveiled: money had to be collected to fund the construction of the base, and for some reason Americans were unwilling – or unable – to dip into their pockets. Only through the campaigning efforts of newspaper magnate Joseph Pulitzer, a keen supporter of the statue, did it all come together in the end. Richard Morris Hunt built a pedestal around the existing star-shaped Fort Wood, and Liberty was formally dedicated by President Cleveland on October 28, 1886, in a flag-waving shindig that has never really stopped. The statue was closed for a few years in the mid-1980s for extensive renovation and, in 1986, fifteen million people descended on Manhattan for the statue's centennial celebrations.

Today you can climb steps up to the crown, but the cramped stairway though the torch sadly remains closed to the public. Don't be surprised if there's an hour-long wait to ascend. Even if there is, Liberty Park's views of the lower Manhattan skyline, the twin towers of the World Trade Center lording it over the jutting teeth of New York's financial quarter, are spectacular enough.

Ellis Island

Just across the water, and just a few minutes on by ferry, sits **Ellis Island,** the first stop for over twelve million immigrants hoping to settle in the USA. The island, originally known as Gibbet Island by the English (who used it for punishing unfortunate pirates), became an immigration station in 1892, a necessary processing point for the massive influx of mostly southern and eastern European immigrants. It remained open until 1954, when it was abandoned and left to fall into atmospheric ruin.

The immigration process

Up until the 1850s, there was no official **immigration process** in New York. Then, the surge of Irish, German and Scandinavian immigrants escaping the great famines of 1846 and failed revolutions of 1848 forced authorities to open an immigration center at Castle Clinton in Battery Park. By the 1880s, widespread hardship in eastern and southern Europe, the pogroms in Russia and the massive economic failure in southern Italy forced thousands to flee the Continent. At the same time, America was experiencing the first successes of its industrial revolution, and more and more people started to move to the cities from the country. Ellis Island opened in 1892, just as America came out of a depression and began to assert itself as a world power. News spread through Europe of the opportunities in the New World, and immigrants left their homelands by the thousands.

The immigrants who arrived at Ellis Island were all steerage-class passengers; richer immigrants were processed at their leisure onboard ship. The scenes on the island were horribly confused: most families arrived hungry, filthy and penniless, rarely speaking English and invariably awed by the beckoning metropolis across the water. Immigrants were numbered and forced to wait for up to a day while Ellis Island officials frantically tried to process them; the center had been designed to accommodate 500,000 immigrants a year, but double that number came during the early part of the century. Con men preyed from all sides, stealing immigrants' baggage as it was checked and offering rip-off exchange rates for whatever money they had managed to bring. Each family was split up – men sent to one area, women and children to another – while a series of checks took place to weed out the undesirables and the infirm. The latter were taken to the second floor, where doctors would check for "loathsome and contagious diseases" as well as signs of insanity. Those who failed medical tests were marked with a white cross on their backs and either sent to the hospital or put back on the boat. Steamship carriers had an obligation to return any immigrants not accepted to their original port, though according to official records, only two percent were ever rejected, and many of those jumped into the sea and tried to swim to Manhattan, or committed suicide, rather than face going home.

There was also a legal test, which checked nationality and, very important, political affiliations. The majority of the immigrants were processed in a matter of hours and then headed either to New Jersey and trains to the West, or into New York City to settle in one of the rapidly expanding ethnic neighborhoods.

Ellis Island Museum of Immigration

By the time of its closure, Ellis Island was a formidable complex. The first building burned down in 1897, the present one was built in 1903, and there were various additions built in the ensuing years – hospitals, outhouses and the like, usually on bits of landfill that were added to the island in an attempt to contend with the swelling numbers passing through. The buildings were derelict until the mid-1980s, since when the main, four-turreted central building has been completely renovated, reopening in 1990 as the **Ellis Island Museum of Immigration** (see p.296 for times and admission prices). This is an ambitious museum that eloquently recaptures the spirit of the place, with films, exhibits and tapes documenting the celebration of America as the immigrant nation. It also is surprisingly well-done and uncommercial, considering how easy it would be to pull at heartstrings and make the place a sugary tourist trap. All the same, you can't help but feel that it might have been more memorable before the authorities got their hands on the place.

Some 100 million Americans can trace their roots back through Ellis Island and, for them especially, the museum is an engaging display. On the first floor, located in the old railroad ticket office, is the excellent "Peopling of America," which chronicles four centuries of American immigration, offering a statistical portrait of those who arrived – who they were, where they came from, why they came.

The huge, vaulted Registry Room on the second floor, scene of so much trepidation, elation and despair, has been left bare, with just a couple of inspectors' desks and American flags. In the side hall, a series of interview rooms re-create step by step the process that immigrants passed through on their way to being naturalized; the white-tiled rooms are soberingly bureaucratic. Each is illustrated by the recorded voices of those who passed through Ellis Island, recalling their experience, along with photographs, thoughtful and informative explanatory text, and small artifacts – train timetables and familiar items brought from home. There are descriptions of arrival and the subsequent interviews, and examples of questions asked and medical tests given. One of the dormitories, used by those kept overnight for further examination, has been left almost intact. On the top floor, there are evocative photographs of the building before it was restored, along with items rescued from the building and rooms devoted to the peak years of immigration. In the museum's theater, the Hypothetical Theater Company puts on "Ellis Island Stories," re-enactments of immigrant oral histories from the museum archive, several times daily (see p.296 for specific times).

Outside, the museum has an eerie, unfinished feel, heightened by the empty shell of what was once the center's hospital. On the fortified spurs of the island, names of immigrant families who passed through the building over the years are engraved in copper; paid for by a minimum donation of $100 from their descendants. This "American Immigrant Wall of Honor" helped fund the restoration and now features the names of over 500,000 individuals and families. The museum is currently accepting submissions for the "New Millennium Edition" of the wall. These names will be engraved and listed in a computer register by April 2000. Proceeds will go towards funding the new American Family Immigration History Center – an interactive research facility whose database will contain information from the ship's manifests or passenger lists and other information about over 17 million immigrants who passed through New York Harbor from 1892 to 1924.

Governor's Island

Until recently, **Governor's Island**, the last of the three small islands that lie just south of Manhattan, was the largest and most expensively-run Coast Guard installation in the world, housing some 3800 service personnel and their families. It was also the oldest military installation in continuous service in the US, active since 1637. The annual upkeep – estimated at $30 million – was too much to justify in light of budget cuts and the end of the Cold War, so in 1995 Governor's Island was handed over to the General Services Administration of the Federal Government. The Coast Guard was moved to Homeport, Staten Island, and rumors now abound about the picturesque spot's uncertain future. As part of the Balanced Budget Act, the government is trying to sell the island at market value (an estimated $500 million), but will require a guarantee of how the island will be used before making the sale official. Possibilities include an extension of Columbia University's campus or mixed public and private housing. President Clinton offered to persuade Congress to turn the island over to New York for $1 – contingent on its redevelopment to include park space accessible to the public – but Mayor Giuliani and Governor Pataki balked at the gesture. For now, no one knows what its future will be, and, at the time of writing, tours are not available to the public. However, it could be worth a try to call the **New York Convention and Visitors Bureau** (☎484-1222), or the **General Services Administration** (☎264-2573), to find out more about visitor (and owner) status.

For a preview of what you're missing, Jan Morris wrote of Governor's Island, "nowhere in New York is more pastoral"; indeed, what the new owner will procure with the purchase of the 172-acre tract of land, is unobstructed views of lower Manhattan and New York Harbor, a handful of colonial and nineteenth-century houses, as

Governor's Island

well as **Fort Jay** and **Castle Williams** – the latter, the complement to Castle Clinton, put up in 1789 by zealous and ever vigilant volunteers in the Revolution. The buyer will also have to decide the fate of the services that flourished on the island during the Coast Guard's occupation, including a bank, golf course, bowling alley, school, *Super 8* motel and library.

Chapter 3

The Financial District and the Civic Center

The skyline of Manhattan's two most southerly neighborhoods – the **Financial District** and **Civic Center** – is the one you see in all the movies, dramatic skyscrapers pushed into the narrow tip of the island and framed by the monumental elegance of the Brooklyn Bridge. Despite its emphasis on business, it's perhaps Manhattan's most historic locale and as such makes for a neat wander after (or before) visiting the Harbor Islands.

The Financial District

The heart of the nation's – and the world's – wheeler-dealing, the **Financial District** is where Manhattan (and indeed America) began. Unfortunately, precious few buildings remain from those days, having been shunted out by big business eager to boost corporate image with headquarters in the right place. A nascent residential community – housed in converted office space and formerly abandoned buildings along the waterfront – and the accompanying increase in local cultural events have helped the Financial District begin to shed its nine-to-five existence. Still, don't expect too much down here outside of business hours.

Wall Street and the New York Stock Exchange

The Dutch arrived here first, building a wooden wall at the edge of their small settlement to protect themselves from pro-British settlers to the north: hence the narrow canyon of today's **Wall Street** gained its name. It's here, behind the Neoclassical facade of the **New York Stock Exchange**, that the purse strings of the capitalist world are pulled. Take a long look at the mythological figures on the building's pediment: they represent Progress overseeing Agriculture and Industry. When the original stone figures began deteriorating in the

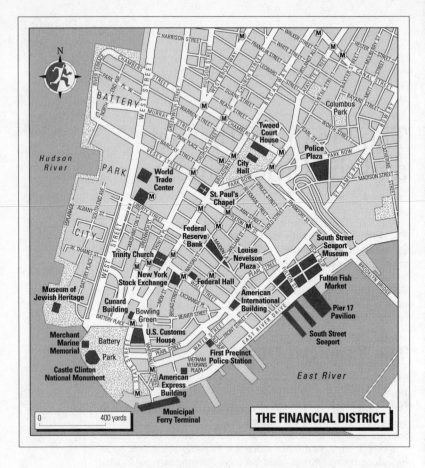

The Financial District

Manhattan air, the Exchange clandestinely replaced them with these virtually indestructible sheet-metal copies, for under no circumstances was any aspect of vulnerability to be associated with the Exchange.

From the Visitors' Gallery (Mon–Fri 9am–4.30pm; free, but come before noon for the best chance of getting in), the Exchange floor appears a melee of brokers and buyers, all scrambling for the elusive fractional cent on which to make a megabuck. Sit through the glib introductory film, though, and the hectic scurrying and constantly moving hieroglyphs of the stock prices make more sense. Along with the film, there's a small exhibition on the history of the Exchange – notably quiet on the more spectacular screwups. The most disastrous, the notorious "Black Tuesday" of 1929, is mentioned almost in passing, perhaps because it was so obviously caused by the greed and short-sightedness of the money men themselves. In those days, shares could be bought "on margin," which meant the buyer needed to pay only a small part of their total cost, borrowing the rest and using the shares as security. This worked fine as long as the market kept rising – as share dividends came in to pay off the loans, investors' money bought more shares. But it was, as Alistair Cooke put it, "a mountain of credit on a mole-hill of actual money," and only a small scare was needed to start the avalanche. When the market investors had to find more cash to service their debts and make up for the fall in value of their stocks, they sold off their shares cheaply. A panicked chain reaction ensued, and on October 24, sixteen million shares were traded; five days later, the whole Exchange collapsed as $125 million was wiped off stock values. Fortunes disappeared overnight: millions lost their life savings; banks, businesses and industries shut their doors; and unemployment spiraled helplessly. The Great Depression began. It says much for the safety nets that surround the market's operations today that the equally tumultuous crash of October 1987 caused comparatively negligible reverberations.

Federal Hall and Trinity Church

The **Federal Hall National Memorial**, at Wall Street's canyon-like head, can't help but look a little foolish: an Ionic temple that woke up one morning and found itself surrounded by skyscrapers. The building was built by Town and Davis as the Customs House in the 1830s and served briefly as the first capital of the United States. An exhibition inside (Mon–Fri 9am–5pm; free) relates the heady days of 1789 when George Washington was sworn in as America's first president from a balcony on this site. It was a showy affair for a great, if rather pompous, man: "I fear we may have exchanged George III for George I," commented one senator after observing Washington's affectations. Washington's pretensions notwithstanding, democracy got its start here some sixty years earlier when printer John Peter Zenger was acquitted of libel in 1735, setting an important precedent for freedom of speech in America. The documents and models inside repay a wander, as does the hall with its elegant rotunda and Cretan maidens worked into the decorative railings. Washington's statue stands, very properly, on the steps.

At Wall Street's far end, **Trinity Church** (guided tours daily at 2pm) waits darkly in the wings, an ironic onlooker to the street's dealings. There's been a church here since the end of the seventeenth century, but this knobby neo-Gothic one – the third model – went up in 1846, and for fifty years was the city's tallest building, a reminder of just how recently high-rise Manhattan has sprung up. It has the air of an English church (Richard Upjohn, its architect, came from Dorset in southern England), especially in the sheltered **grave-yard**, resting place of early Manhattanites and lunching office workers.

A search around the old tombstones rewards with such luminaries as the first secretary to the Treasury, Alexander Hamilton.

Around Wall Street

Trinity Church is an oddity amid its office-building neighbors, several of which are worth nosing into. **One Wall Street**, immediately opposite the church, is among the best, with an Art Deco lobby in red and gold that naggingly suggests a bankers' bordello. East down Wall Street, the **Morgan Guaranty Trust Building**, at no. 23, bears the scars of a weird happening on September 16, 1920: a horse-drawn cart pulled up outside and its driver jumped off and disappeared down a side street. A few seconds later, the cart blew up in a devastating explosion, knocking out windows half a mile away. Thirty-three people were killed and hundreds injured, but the explosion remains unexplained. One theory holds that it was a premeditated attack on Morgan and his vast financial empire; another claims that the cart belonged to an explosives company and was illegally traveling through the city. Recent research has more or less concluded that the blast was the doing of an Italian anarchist in retribution for the executions of Sacco and Vanzetti. Curiously, or perhaps deliberately, the pockmark scars on the building's wall have never been repaired.

A most impressive leftover of the confident days before the Wall Street Crash is the old **Cunard Building** at 25 Broadway. Its marble walls and high dome once housed a steamship's booking office – hence the elaborate, whimsical murals of variegated ships and nautical mythology splashed around the ceiling. As the large liners gave way to jet travel, Cunard could no longer afford such an extravagant shop window. Today, its fate is to house a post office – one that's been fitted out with little feeling for the exuberant space it occupies – while on the second floor is the **New York City Police Museum**, the largest and oldest collection of memorabilia and NYPD firepower in the country. In front of the Cunard Building, rearing on the street partition, is a sculpture of a **bull** – not, as one might imagine, the symbol of an eternally bullish market but rather, so the legend goes, the contribution of a hapless artist who had nowhere else to store his colossal creation. Across the street at 26 Broadway, located in the former headquarters of John D. Rockefeller's Standard Oil Company, is the **Museum of American Financial History**, the largest public museum archive of financial documents and artifacts in the world.

For details on the New York City Police Museum and the Museum of American Financial History see pp. 298 & 297.

Bowling Green and around

Broadway comes to a gentle end at the **Bowling Green**, an oval of turf used for the game by eighteenth-century colonial Brits on a lease of "one peppercorn per year." The encircling iron fence is an original of 1771, though the crowns that once topped the stakes were removed in later revolutionary fervor, as was a statue of George III, which was melted into musket balls – little bits of the monarch that were fired at his troops during the Revolutionary War. In 1783, the green was one of the last areas to be evacuated by the British, and it was the site of celebration when New York ratified the Constitution in 1788.

Earlier, the green was the location of one of Manhattan's more memorable business deals, when Peter Minuit, first director general of the Dutch colony of New Amsterdam, bought the whole island from the Indians for a bucket of trade goods worth sixty guilders (about $24). The other side of the story (the part you never hear) was that these Indians didn't actually own the island; no doubt both parties went home smiling. Today, the green is a spot for office people picnicking in the shadow of Cass Gilbert's **US Customs House**, an heroic monument to the Port of New York and home of the **Smithsonian National Museum of the American Indian**. The House, built in 1907, was intended to pay homage to the booming maritime market, and the four statues (sculpted by Daniel Chester French, who also created the Lincoln Memorial in Washington, DC) at the front of the building represent the four continents; the twelve scenes on the facade personify the world's commercial centers; and the head of Mercury – Roman god of commerce – adorns the top of each exterior column for good measure. As if French foresaw the House's current use, the sculptor blatantly comments on the mistreatment of Indians in his statues: most striking is the work on the left side of the front main staircase, which depicts a Native American in full headdress timidly peering over the shoulder of "America," who sits grandly on her throne and holds an oversized sheaf of corn on her lap – a symbol of Indian prosperity and contribution to world culture. Equally telling is the sculpture on the opposite side of the stairs, in which "America," this time her throne decorated with Mayan glyphs, has her foot on the head of Quetzalcoatl, the plumed serpent.

For an account of the National Museum of the American Indian see pp.303

Inside the House, on the rotunda, are blue, gray and brown murals of bustling ships, painted by Reginald Marsh. In these renditions, steamers bring cargo, people and prosperity to the New York harborside, all under the approving eye of Liberty herself. Portraits of explorers who played a critical role in establishing the US's frontiers – Cabot, Hudson, Columbus, Gomez – are interspersed between the scenes. Considering how the adjacent Indian Museum reminds one how poorly indigenous people on "discovered" lands were treated, these homages read, ironically, like a rogues' gallery.

Battery Park and Castle Clinton

Beyond the Customs House, lower Manhattan lets out its breath in **Battery Park**, a bright and breezy space overlooking the panorama of the Statue of Liberty, Ellis Island and Governor's Island, all dotting

America's largest harbor. Before landfill closed the gap, **Castle Clinton**, the 1811 fort on the west side of the park, was on an island, one of several forts defending New York Harbor, with its battery of cannons providing its name. Later, it found new life as a prestigious concert venue – in 1850, the enterprising P.T. Barnum threw a hugely hyped concert by soprano Jenny Lind, the "Swedish Nightingale," with tickets at $225 a throw – before doing service (pre-Ellis Island) as the dropoff point for arriving immigrants. Today, the squat castle isn't that interesting, though if you're curious it's open to the public (daily 8.30am–5pm); bear in mind that it's also the place to buy tickets for and board ferries to the Statue of Liberty and Ellis Island.

South of Castle Clinton stands the **East Coast Memorial**, a series of granite slabs inscribed with the names of all the American seamen who were killed in World War II; to the castle's north, perched ten feet into the harbor, is the American Merchant Mariners' Memorial, an eerie depiction of a marine futilely reaching for the hand of a man sinking underneath the waves. Fittingly, both these memorials look out across New York Harbor; they also offer tremendous views of the Statue of Liberty and Ellis Island.

Along the curve of State Street, just across from Battery Park, a rounded dark, red-brick Georgian facade, no. 7, identifies the **Shrine of Elizabeth Ann Seton**, the first native-born American to be canonized. St Elizabeth lived here briefly before moving to found a religious community in Maryland. The shrine – small, hushed and illustrated by pious and tearful pictures of the saint's life – is one of a few old houses that have survived the modern onslaught.

See p.300 for details on New York Unearthed.

Behind the Seton Shrine at 6 Pearl St/17 State St is **New York Unearthed** (Mon–Fri noon–6pm; free), the South Street Seaport Museum's tiny, hands-on, annex devoted to the city's archeology. Built on the site of Herman Melville's 1819 birthplace, the building's upper floor consists of artifacts excavated from different periods of New York's history. There's a "Pitt and Liberty" plate commemorating William Pitt's opposition to the Stamp Act, Britain's first attempt to tax the colonies; a selection of personal items from Brooklyn's Weeksville, the first free African-American community in New York State after the 1827 abolition of slavery; and even 1950s-era luncheonette ware. In the basement, relics from an 1835 fire that ravaged Lower Manhattan are also on display.

For perspective on the eighteenth-century appearance of Manhattan's then-heart, the **Fraunces Tavern Block Historic District**, which escaped the 1835 fire, retains eleven 1830s-era buildings. The ochre-and-red-brick **Fraunces Tavern** itself, located on the corner of Pearl and Broad streets, claims to be a colonial inn, although in truth it is more of an expert fake. Having survived extensive modification, several fires and nineteenth-century use as a hotel, the three-story Georgian brick house was almost totally reconstructed by the Sons of the Revolution in the early part of the century to mimic its appearance on December 4, 1783 – complete with period interiors and furnishings. It was then, after the British had been conclusively beaten, that a weeping George Washington took leave of his assembled officers, intent on returning to rural life in Virginia: "I am not only retiring from all public employments," he wrote, "but am retiring within myself." With hindsight, it was a hasty statement, for six years later he was to return as the new nation's president. The Tavern's second floor re-creates the site's history with a series of illustrated panels; the cozy restaurant is an unusually stately tourist draw (Mon–Fri 10am–4.45pm, Sat and Sun noon–4pm; $2.50, $1 students and seniors).

Along Water Street

Turn a corner by the Tavern and you're on **Water Street**, in its southern reaches an attenuated agglomeration of skyscrapers developed in the early 1960s. At that time, the powers-that-were thought that Manhattan's economy was stagnating because of lack of room for growth, so they widened throughways like Water Street by razing many of the Victorian brownstones and warehouses that lined the waterfront. By doing so, they missed a vital chance to allow the old to give context to the new; ironically, a decent chunk of the office buildings they ambitiously built have since been converted to condos. With their streamline steel, glass and concrete facades, the buildings are rather faceless: if you stand in the barren plaza of the nearby **American Express Building** at 2 New York Plaza and look up, it's hard to feel anything but dwarfed and insignificant.

Not all of Water Street's development is so depressing: turn east down Old Slip and a pocket-size palazzo that was once the **First Precinct Police Station** slots good-naturedly into the narrow strip, a cheerful throwback to a different era. A little to the south, off Water Street, is the **Vietnam Veterans' Memorial**, an assembly of glass blocks etched with troops' letters home. The mementos are sad and often haunting, but the memorial is disrespectfully shabby.

Cross Water Street, take the next left to Pine St and you'll find one of Manhattan's most joyful skyscrapers. In 1916, the authorities became worried that the massive buildings looming up around town would shield light from the streets, and turn the Lower and Midtown areas into grim passages between soaring monoliths. The result of their fears was the first zoning ordinance, which ruled that a building's total floor space couldn't be any more than twelve times the area of its site. This led to the "setback" style of skyscraper, and the **American International Building** at 70 Pine St is the ultimate wedge of Art Deco wedding cake: a chocolate-and-black marble base leads into a level of sandstone and then brick, with aluminum lattice-work patterns and curlicue-tipped "shoots" gracing the facade. Additionally, it has one of the best Art Deco lobbies in town and as with other lobbies, no one minds you going in; plus, from inside you

can get a good view of the whole building – which might have been
as well known as the Empire State or Chrysler buildings had it been
more visible. Almost opposite, I.M. Pei's gridiron **88 Pine St** stands
coolly formal in white: a self-contained and confident modern
descendant.

Around the South Street Seaport

At the eastern end of Fulton Street the **South Street Seaport** comes
girded with the sort of praise and publicity that generally augurs a
commercial bland-out. In reality it's a mixed bag: a fair slice of commercial gentrification was necessary to woo developers and tourists,
but the presence of a centuries-old working fish market has kept
things real in a way that should be a lesson for the likes of London's
Covent Garden. Unfortunately, like so much of bona fide New York,
the market is now under threat from Mayor Giuliani: rumor has it
that since fish truckers find the Hunt's Point wholesale market in the
Bronx more convenient, plans to develop the waterfront are underway, thus taking the seafood out of the seaport.

For a hundred years, this stretch of the waterside was New York's
sailship port: it began when Robert Fulton started a ferry service
from here to Brooklyn and left his name on the street and then its
market. The harbor lapped up the trade brought by the opening of
the Erie Canal and by the end of the nineteenth century was sending
cargo ships on regular runs to California, Japan and Liverpool. When
the balance of shipping shifted to the Hudson River and the FDR
Drive was constructed in the 1950's, however, decline was rapid. A
private initiative beginning in 1967 rescued the remaining warehouses and saved the historic seaport just in time.

Regular guided tours of the Seaport run from the **Visitors'
Center**, an immaculate brick-terraced house located at 12–14
Fulton St. An assemblage of upmarket chain shops like Ann Taylor,
Coach, and Abercrombie & Fitch, line Fulton and the adjacent Front
Street: such bland boutiques are a typical element of US waterfront
refurbishment projects. However, keep your eyes peeled for the
many beautiful and unusual buildings preserved down here. 203
Front St – now a store for clothing giant J. Crew – is worth a look:
in the 1880s, the building was a hotel that catered to unmarried
laborers on the dock.

Nestled among this shopping district is the **New Fulton Market**,
constructed in 1983. Recently refurbished, it's essentially a craft
emporium, with a few cafés and fast-food eateries on the second
floor. Across the way, the cleaned-up **Schermerhorn Row**, a unique
ensemble of Georgian-Federal-style early warehouses, dating to
about 1811 houses the "English" *North Star Pub* at one end and the
pricey *Sloppy Louie's* at the other; for food, it's better to wander
down Front Street past the formerly derelict residences, to *Jeremy's
Ale House* (254 Front St at Dover St). *Jeremy's* is a silver-painted

brick warehouse that serves tasty yet inexpensive fried clams, calamari and oysters, and offers the local dockworkers half-price beer
from 8 to 10am. (Ask owner Jeremy to tell you about the countless
trophy ties and bras hanging from the walls.)

Even more evocative is the *Paris Café* at 119 South St, located in
the **Meyer's Hotel** at the end of **Peck Slip**, which played host in the
late 1880s to a panoply of luminaries. Thomas Edison used the café
as a second office while designing the first electric power station in
the world on Pearl Street; the opening of the Brooklyn Bridge was
celebrated on the roof with Annie Oakley and Buffalo Bill Cody as
guests; Teddy Roosevelt broke bread here; and journalist John Reed
and other members of the Communist Party of America met secretly
here in 1921 to found the organization. These days, sans presidents
and communists, the elegant square bar and tempting seafood specials still pull in a lively crowd.

The Fish Market and South Street Seaport Museum
The elevated East Side Highway forms a suitably grimy gateway to
the **Fulton Fish Market**, a tatty building that wears its eighty
years as the city's wholesale outlet with no pretensions. This
enclave generates over a billion dollars in revenues annually, and
is a place where one's word of honor still seals business dealings;
however, it has recently come under the jurisdiction of municipal
authorities, intent upon stemming the corruption and mafia influence in the area. These backroom dealings are of no threat to
casual visitors, and by no means should they stop you from touring the site.

If you can manage it, the time to be here is around 5am when buyers' trucks park up beneath the highway to collect the catches, the
air reeks of salt and scale and there's lots of nasty things to step in.
It's invigorating stuff, a twilight world that probably won't be around
much longer – the city's regulation of the area, along with the adjacent **Pier 17 Pavilion**, a hypercomplex of restaurants and shops,
may be nails in its coffin.

Housed in a series of painstakingly restored 1830s warehouses at
207–211 Water St is the **South Street Seaport Museum** (April
1–Sept 30 daily 10am–6pm, Thurs 10am–8pm; Oct 1–March 31
Wed–Mon 10am–5pm; $6, $4 students, admission includes all tours,
films, galleries and museum-owned ships, as well as New York
Unearthed). The Seaport offers a collection of refitted ships and
chubby tugboats, plus a handful of maritime art and trades exhibits.
In the summer, the 1885 schooner *Pioneer*, the 1893 fishing
schooner *Lettie G. Howard* and the tug *W.O. Decker*, will coast you
around the harbor for an additional consideration; call the museum
for schedules. Unless sailing is your passion, it's better to skip the
ships and freeload at the numerous **outdoor concerts**, held almost
nightly throughout the warmer months.

The Brooklyn Bridge

From just about anywhere in the Seaport you can see one of New
York's most celebrated delights, the **Brooklyn Bridge**. One of several spans across the East River (the Manhattan and Williamsburg
bridges, respectively, are in sight behind it), the bridge's Gothic gate-
ways are dwarfed by lower Manhattan's skyscrapers. But in its day,
the Brooklyn Bridge was a technological quantum leap: it towered
over the low brick structures around it and, for twenty years, was the
world's largest suspension bridge, the first to use steel cables and –
for many more – the longest single span. To New Yorkers it was an
object of awe, the massively concrete symbol of the Great American
Dream: "All modern New York, heroic New York, started with the
Brooklyn Bridge," wrote Kenneth Clark, and indeed its meeting of art
and function, of romantic Gothic and daring practicality, became a
sort of spiritual model for the next generation's skyscrapers.

It didn't go up without difficulties: John Augustus Roebling, its
architect and engineer, crushed his foot taking measurements for the
piers and died of gangrene three weeks later; his son Washington
took over only to be crippled by the bends from working in an inse-
cure underwater caisson, and subsequently directed the work from
his sickbed overlooking the site. Twenty workers died during the
construction and, a week after the opening day in 1883, twelve people were crushed to death in a panicked rush on the bridge's foot-
path. Despite this (and innumerable suicides), New Yorkers still look
to the bridge with affection: for the 1983 centennial it was festooned
with decorations – "Happy Birthday Brooklyn Bridge" ran the signs
– and the city organized a party, replete with shiploads of fireworks.

Whether the bridge has a similar effect on you or not, the view
from it is undeniably spectacular. Walk across its wooden planks
from City Hall Park and don't look back till you're midway:
the Financial District's giants clutter shoulder to shoulder through
the spidery latticework, the East River pulses below and cars scream
to and from Brooklyn. It's a glimpse of the 1990s metropolis, and on
no account to be missed.

The Federal Reserve Bank

Back on the island, Fulton Street arcs right across lower Manhattan
with **Maiden Lane** as its southern parallel, an august and anonymous
rollercoaster of finance houses with **Nassau Street** linking the two in
a downbeat area of discount goods and fast food. Where Nassau and
Maiden Lane meet, Johnson and Burgee's castle of **Federal Reserve
Plaza**, a Lego fortress and cavernous arched hall, which complements the original 1924 **Federal Reserve Bank**. The Federal
Reserve Plaza proved to be one of Philip Johnson's last projects with
John Burgee: he split with the architect soon after, leaving Burgee
broke and in the architectural wilderness.

There's good reason for the Reserve Bank proper's iron-barred exterior: stashed eighty feet below the somber neo-Gothic interior are most of the "free" world's **gold reserves** – 9000 tons of them, occasionally shifted from vault to vault as wars break out or international debts are settled. It is possible – but tricky – to tour the piles of gleaming bricks; write to the Public Information Department, Federal Reserve Bank, 33 Liberty St, NY 10045 or check out their Web site at *www.ny.frb.org* or phone ☎720-6130 at least a week ahead, since tickets have to be mailed.

Upstairs, in the Bank, dirty money and counterfeit currency are weeded out of circulation by automated checkers which shuffle dollar bills like endless packs of cards. Assistants wheelbarrow loads of cash around ("How much there?" I asked one; "$8.5 million," he replied), and, as you'd imagine, the security is just like in the movies.

Around the Federal Reserve Bank

When you've unboggled your mind of high finance's gold, you can see some of its glitter at **1 Chase Manhattan Plaza**, immediately to the south on Pine Street. This, the prestigious New York headquarters of the bank, boasts a boxy international-style tower that was the first of its kind in lower Manhattan, and which brought to downtown the concept of a plaza entrance. Unfortunately, Chase Manhattan's plaza has all the charm of a parking lot, and even Dubuffet's *Four Trees* sculpture can't get things going.

Continue to the end of Cedar Street, and you'll find the **Marine Midland Bank** at 140 Broadway: a smaller, more successful tower by the same design team and decorated with a tiptoeing sculpture by Isamu Noguchi. More sculpture worth catching lies behind Chase Manhattan Plaza on **Louise Nevelson Plaza**, which divides Maiden Lane and Liberty Street. Here, a clutch of Nevelson's works perch like a mass of shrapnel on an island of land: a striking ploy of sculpture that works well in the urban environment. The mural painting of Seurat's *A Sunday Afternoon on the Grande Jatte*, to one side of the plaza was a backdrop for the film Die Hard: With A Vengeance.

Go back down Liberty Street to Church Street and at **1 Liberty Plaza** stands the **US Steel Building**, a threatening black mass all the more offensive since the famed **Singer Building** was demolished to make way for it. Ernest Flagg's 1908 construction was one of the most delicate on the New York skyline, a graceful Renaissance-style tower of metal and glass destroyed in 1968 and replaced with what has justly been called a "gloomy, cadaverous hulk." But before you conclude that modern monoliths seem to be all size and no style, double back down John Street to **no. 127**, where you'll see a most playful creation, a bit cutesy but cheekily out of synch with its surroundings. Designed by Emery Roth and Sons, the building struts a blue and red neon exterior that is the antithesis of the Financial District's staid and streamlined facades; its interior, featuring brightly colored ducts and pipes wrapped in twinkling Christmas lights, are enough to induce heart attacks in the area's conservative populace. The restaurant adjacent to the property refused to sell to the developer, so architects made its side wall into a giant-size digital clock which keeps accurate time, even down to the second.

The World Trade Center

Wherever you are in lower Manhattan, two buildings dominate the landscape. Critics say the twin Ronson lighters of the **World Trade Center towers** don't relate to their surroundings and aren't especially pleasing in design – and, spirited down to a tenth of their size, they certainly wouldn't get a second glance. But the fact is that they're big, undeniably and frighteningly so, and a walk across the plaza in summer months (closed in winter, as icicles falling from the towers can kill) can make your head reel.

Perhaps the idea of so huge a project similarly affected the judgment of the Port Authority of New York and New Jersey, the Center's chief financier, which for several years found itself expensively stuck with two half-empty white elephants – which were quickly surpassed as the world's tallest building by the Sears Tower in Chicago. Now the Center, whose towers are the best part of a five-building development, is full and successful, and the building has become one of the emblems of the city itself. With courage, a trip to the 107th floor **observation deck** of 2 World Trade Center (daily: June–Sept 9.30am–11.30pm; Oct–May 9.30am–9.30pm; $12.50) gives a mind-blowing view from a height of 1350 feet – over a quarter of a mile. From the open-air rooftop promenade (closed during bad weather), the silent panorama is more dramatic still: everything in New York is below you, including the planes gliding into the airports. Even Jersey City looks exciting. As you timidly edge your way around, ponder the fact that one Philippe Petit once walked a tightrope between the two towers: nerve indeed. Best time to ascend is toward sunset, when the tourist crowds thin and Manhattan slowly turns itself into the most spectacular light show this side of the Apocalypse. If you're hungry

---

The bombing of the World Trade Center

On February 26, 1993, the World Trade Center complex was rocked by an **explosive device** left in one of the underground parking lots; six people were killed and over a thousand injured. For a moment, the nightmare scenario of the destruction of one of the world's largest office buildings seemed possible, but apart from some minor structural damage, the building held fast. The evacuation of over 50,000 office workers was swiftly and safely carried out, and the biggest headache for the companies in the Trade Center was the fact that the towers were closed for weeks while structural examinations took place. Blame for the bomb fell upon an Arab terrorist group led by the radical Muslim cleric Shaikh Omar Abdel-Rahman, who was found guilty of involvement by a NYC court in summer 1995.

or thirsty – and willing to shell out – you could also get the view by visiting the refurbished *Windows on the World* restaurant (1 World Trade Center, 107th floor), and its accompanying bar, modestly titled *The Greatest Bar on Earth*.

The TKTS booth on the mezzanine level sells discounted same-day tickets for Broadway shows as well as tickets for Wed, Sat and Sun matinees the day before the performance (Mon–Fri 11am–5.30pm, Sat 11am–3.30pm).

St Paul's Chapel

Straight across from the World Trade Center, yet coming from a very different order of things, is **St Paul's Chapel**. It's the oldest church in Manhattan, dating from 1766 – eighty years earlier than Trinity Church and almost prehistoric by New York standards. Though the building seems quite American in feel, its architect was from London, and he used St Martin-in-the-Fields in London as his model for this unfussy eighteenth-century space of soap-bar blues and pinks. George Washington worshipped here and his pew, zealously treasured, is much on show.

Battery Park City

The hole dug for the foundations of the World Trade Center's towers threw up a million cubic yards of earth and rock; these excavations were dumped into the Hudson to form the 23-acre base of **Battery Park City**. The Park, a self-sufficient island of office blocks, luxury apartments and chain boutiques bordered by an esplanade over a mile long landscaped as a park, is a paradigm for the Financial District: here the Big Boys and Girls can be in the heart of things but work in a climate that's less frantic and more nature-oriented than most in Manhattan.

The centerpiece of the Park is the **World Financial Center**, coordinated by Olympia and York Co, the Toronto team that was also responsible for London's Canary Wharf disaster. The buildings – four chunky, interconnected granite and glass towers with geometrically shaped tops – look like piles of building blocks. Their interiors are more refined: six acres of marble were used for their lobby floors and walls, while jacquard fabric lines the elevators. The **Winter Garden**, a huge, glass-ceilinged public plaza, brings light and life into the mall of shops and restaurants. Decorated by sixteen palm trees transplanted from the Mojave Desert, the plaza is an oasis; bask here for a bit, have some lunch, and take in a view of the swanky private boats docked in North Cove. There are often free concerts here.

A couple of new **museums** are starting to transform the Battery Park City landscape, with the distinctive Mayan pyramid of the 1997 **Museum of Jewish Heritage**, on the water at Battery Park Plaza. The building's six sides and tiered roof symbolize the six million

*See pp.302 &
300 for a
detailed
account of the
Museum of
Jewish
Heritage and
the Skyscraper
Museum.*

Jews who perished in the Holocaust. In 2001, if all goes as planned, the Museum of Jewish Heritage will have **The Skyscraper Museum** as its neighbor. The museum, moving from its temporary Wall Street location to the ground floor of the new *Ritz Carlton Hotel*, will have more space to feature exhibits about New York's high-rise legacy.

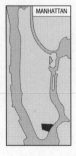

City Hall Park and the Civic Center

Broadway and Park Row form the apex of **City Hall Park**, a noisy, pigeon-splattered triangle of green with the **Woolworth Building** as a venerable and venerated onlooker. Some think this is New York's definitive skyscraper, and it's hard to disagree – money, ornament and prestige mingle in Cass Gilbert's 1913 "Cathedral of Commerce," whose soaring, graceful lines are fringed with Gothic decoration more for fun than any portentous allusion: if the World Trade Center towers railroad you into wonder by sheer size, then the Woolworth charms with good nature. Frank Woolworth made his fortune from his "five and dime" stores – everything cost either 5¢ or 10¢, strictly no credit. True to his philosophy, he paid cash for his skyscraper, and the whimsical reliefs at each corner of the lobby show him doing just that: counting out the money in nickels and dimes. Facing him in caricature are the architect (medievally clutching a model of his building), renting agent and builder. Within, vaulted ceilings ooze honey-gold mosaics and even the mailboxes are magnificent. The whole building has a well-humored panache more or less extinct in today's architecture – have a look at the Citibank next door to see what recent years have come up with.

The Civic Center and City Hall

At the top of the park, marking the beginning of the **Civic Center** and its incoherent jumble of municipal offices and courts, stands **City Hall** (Mon–Fri 10am–4pm). Finished in 1812 to a good-looking design that's a marriage of French Chateau and American Georgian, its first sorry moment of fame came in 1865 when Abraham Lincoln's body lay in state for 120,000 New Yorkers to file past. Later, after the city's 1927 feting of the returned aviator Charles Lindbergh, it became the traditional finishing point for Broadway tickertape parades given for astronauts, returned hostages and, recently, the city's triumphant baseball team – the NY Yankees. Inside, it's an elegant meeting of arrogance and authority, with the sweeping spiral staircase delivering you to the precise geometry of the Governor's Room and the self-important rooms that formerly contained the **Board of Estimates Chamber**.

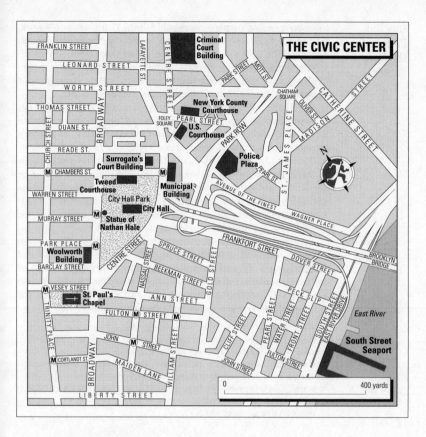

The following text labels appear on the map:

THE CIVIC CENTER

FRANKLIN STREET
LEONARD STREET
WORTH STREET
THOMAS STREET
DUANE ST.
READE ST.
CHAMBERS ST. Ⓜ
WARREN STREET
MURRAY STREET
PARK PLACE
BARCLAY STREET
VESEY STREET
FULTON Ⓜ STREET Ⓜ
JOHN Ⓜ STREET
CORTLANDT ST. Ⓜ
LIBERTY STREET

LAFAYETTE ST.
CENTRE STREET
BROADWAY
CHURCH STREET
TRINITY PLACE

Criminal Court Building
PARK STREET
MOTT ST.
CHATHAM SQUARE
CATHERINE STREET
OLIVER ST.
MADISON STREET
ST. JAMES PLACE

New York County Courthouse
FOLEY SQUARE
PEARL STREET
U.S. Courthouse
PARK ROW
PEARL ST.
Police Plaza

Surrogate's Court Building
Tweed Courthouse
City Hall Park
Municipal Building
City Hall
AVENUE OF THE FINEST
WAGNER PLACE

Statue of Nathan Hale

FRANKFORT STREET
BROOKLYN BRIDGE
DOVER STREET

Woolworth Building
CENTRE STREET
SPRUCE STREET
NASSAU STREET
BEEKMAN STREET
GOLD STREET
PECK SLIP
SOUTH STREET
EAST RIVER DRIVE

St. Paul's Chapel
ANN STREET
CLIFF STREET
PEARL STREET
WATER STREET
FRONT STREET
FULTON STREET

East River

JOHN STREET
MAIDEN LANE
WILLIAM STREET

South Street Seaport

N

0   400 yards

The Tweed Courthouse

If City Hall is the acceptable face of municipal bureaucracy, the **Tweed Courthouse** is a reminder of its corruption. Located directly behind City Hall, William Marcy "Boss" Tweed's monument to greed looks more like a genteel mansion than a municipal building: its long windows and sparse ornamentation are, ironically, far less grandiose or ostentatious than those of many of its peers. The man behind its construction, Boss Tweed, had worked his way from nowhere to become chairman of the Democratic Central Committee at Tammany Hall in 1856 and, by a series of adroit and illegal moves, had manipulated the city's revenues into both his own and his supporters' pockets. He consolidated his position by registering thousands of immigrants as Democrats in return for a low-level welfare system, and then paid off the queues of critics.

For a while Tweed's grip strangled all dissent (even over the courthouse's budget, which rolled up from $3 million to $12 million, possibly because one carpenter was paid $360,747 for a month's work, a plasterer $2,870,464 for nine) until a political cartoonist, Thomas Nast, and the editor of the *New York Times* (who'd refused a half-million-dollar bribe to keep quiet) turned public opinion against him. With suitable irony Tweed died in 1878 in Ludlow Street jail – a prison he'd had built when Commissioner of Public Works.

City Hall Park is dotted with statues of worthier characters, not least of whom is Horace Greeley, founder of the *New York Tribune* newspaper, and in front of whose bronzed countenance a farmer's market – fresh fruits, vegetables and bread – is held each Tuesday and Friday (April–Dec 8am–6pm). Poll position in the worthy patriot statue league goes to **Nathan Hale**. In 1776 Hale was captured by the British and hanged for spying, but not before he'd spat out his gloriously and memorably famous last words: "I regret that I only have but one life to lose for my country." Those words, and his swashbuckling statue, were to be his epithet.

The same year and at this same place, **George Washington** ordered the first reading in the city of the Declaration of Independencé. Thomas Jefferson's eloquent, stirring statement of the new nation's rights had just been adopted by the Second Continental Congress in Philadelphia, and it no doubt fired the hearts and minds of the troops and people assembled.

> *We hold these truths to be self-evident, that all men are created equal, that they are endowed by their creator with certain unalienable rights, that among these are Life, Liberty and the pursuit of Happiness; that to secure these rights Governments are instituted among Men, deriving their just powers from the consent of the governed; that whenever any form of Government becomes destructive of these ends, it is the Right of the People to alter or abolish it, and to institute new Government . . .*

The Municipal Building and around

Back on Centre Street, the **Municipal Building** stands like an oversized chest of drawers, its shoulders straddling Chambers Street in an attempt to either embrace or engulf City Hall. Atop, an extravagant pile of columns and pinnacles signals a frivolous conclusion to a no-nonsense building; below, though not apparent, subway cars travel through its foundation. Walk through the building's arch and you'll reach **Police Plaza**, a concrete space with the russet-hued Police Headquarters at one end and a rusty-colored sculpture at its center. One side of the plaza runs down past the anachronistic neo-Georgian Church of St Andrew's to the pompous **United States Courthouse**, and stops at the glum-gray Foley Square, named after the sheriff and saloonkeeper Thomas "Big Tom" Foley. On the northeast edge of the square resides the **New York County courthouse**, a grand though underwhelming building that's much more interesting and accessible, its rotunda decorated with storybook WPA murals illustrating the history of justice. If there's time, take a look too at the Art Deco **Criminal Courts Building** (known as "The Tombs," from a funereal Egyptian-style building that once stood on this site located on Centre Street), and the fortress-like **Family Court**, a Rubik's cube that's been partially twisted, facing it across the way. All courts are open to the public (Mon–Fri 9am–5pm); the Criminal Courts are your best bet for viewing pleasure.

By and large, civic dignity begins to fade north of here, as ramshackle electrical stores and signs offering "Immigrant fingerprinting and photo ID" mark the edge of Chinatown.

Chapter 4

Chinatown, Little Italy
and the Lower East Side

With more than 200,000 residents (125,000 of them
Chinese and the rest other Asian ethnicities), 7 Chinese
newspapers, 12 Buddhist temples, around 150 restaurants
and over 300 garment factories, Chinatown is Manhattan's largest
ethnic neighborhood. Over recent years, it has pushed its boundaries
north across Canal Street into Little Italy, now sprawling east into the
nether fringes of the Lower East Side.

On the surface, Chinatown is prosperous – a "model slum," some
have called it – with the lowest crime rate, highest employment and
least juvenile delinquency of any city district. Walk through its
crowded streets at any time of day, and every shop is doing a brisk
and businesslike trade: restaurant after restaurant is booming; there
are storefront displays of shiny squids, clawing crabs and clambering
lobster; and street markets offer overflowing piles of exotic green
vegetables, garlic and ginger root. Chinatown has the feel of a land
of plenty, and the reason why lies with the Chinese themselves: even
here, in the very core of downtown Manhattan, they have been careful to preserve their own way of dealing with things, preferring to
keep affairs close to the bond of the family and allowing few intru-
sions into a still-insular culture. There have been several concessions
to Westerners – storefront signs now offer English translations, and
there's a *Häagen Dazs* ice-cream store on lower Mott Street that
can't help but seem incongruous. The one time of the year when
Chinatown bursts open is during the **Chinese New Year festival**,
held each year on the first full moon after January 19, when a giant
dragon runs down Mott Street (formerly to the accompaniment of
firecrackers, now banned by the city as a fire hazard), and the gut-
ters run with ceremonial dyes.

*For more on
Chinese New
Year, see p.432*

Beneath the neighborhood's blithely prosperous facade, however,
there is a darker underbelly. Sharp practices continue to flourish, with
traditional extortion and protection rackets still in business. Non-

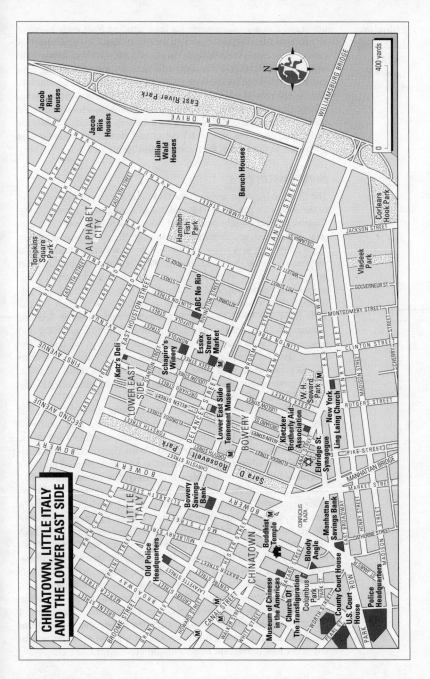

CHINATOWN, LITTLE ITALY AND THE LOWER EAST SIDE

union sweatshops – their assembly lines grinding from early morning to late into the evening – are still visited by the US Department of Labor, who come to investigate workers' testimonies of being paid below minimum wage for seventy-plus-hour work weeks. Living conditions are abysmal for the poorer Chinese – mostly recent immigrants and the elderly – who reside in small rooms in overcrowded tenements ill-kept by landlords. Yet, because the community has been cloistered for so long and has only just begun to seek help from city officials for its internal problems, you won't detect any hint of difficulties unless you reside in Chinatown for a considerable length of time.

Some history

The Chinese began to arrive in the mid-nineteenth century, following in the wake of a trickle of Irish and Italian immigrants. Most of these Chinese had previously worked out West, building railways and digging gold mines, and few intended to stay: their idea was simply to make a nest egg and retire to a life of leisure with their families (99 percent were men) back in China. Some, a few hundred perhaps, did go back, but on the whole the big money took rather longer to accumulate than expected, and so Chinatown became a permanent settlement. The residences were not particularly welcomed by the authorities: the Mafia-like Tongs' protection rackets which doubled as municipal aid societies and dabbled in prostitution, gambling and opium dens on the side, gave the neighborhood a bad rap and by the end of the nineteenth century, made the quarter's violence notorious, as far as white observers were concerned. As a result, in 1882, the US government passed the Exclusion Act forbidding entry to any further Chinese workers for ten years.

After the 1965 Immigration Act did away with the 1924 "National Origins" provision, a large number of new immigrants, many of whom were women, began arriving in Chinatown; within a few years, the area's massive male majority had been displaced. Local businessmen took advantage of the declining Midtown garment business and made use of the new, large and unskilled female workforce: they opened garment factories and paid their workers low wages. Entrepreneurial activity suited Chinese immigrant labor: opening a hand (or, as they came to be known, "Chinese") laundry, for example, required neither a high level of English nor winning the respect of a white employer. At the same time, many small restaurants opened up, spurred by the early 1970s Western interest in Chinese food and by the plight of working Chinese women, who, no longer having time to cook, took food from these restaurants home to feed their families. When the Wall Street crowd became interested in the area, fancier restaurants, more money and greater investment flowed into the quarter; that capital soon attracted more Asian money from overseas. In little time, Chinatown had an internal economy unlike any other new immigrant neighborhood in New York.

In the early 1990s, waves of illegal immigrants from the Fujian province of China began to arrive in New York, upsetting the power structure in Chinatown. Unlike the established Cantonese, who had dominated Chinatown's politics for a century or so, these were largely uneducated laborers who spoke Mandarin. The cultural and linguistic differences made it difficult for the Fujianese to find work in Chinatown, and a large number turned to more desperate means. Fujianese-on-Fujianese violence comprised the majority of Chinatown's crime in 1994, prompting local Fujianese leaders to break Chinatown's traditional bond of silence and call in city officials for help. They also began to construct a network of social agencies and political groups to improve the immigrants' plight. Aided by this, and by the fact that many well-off Cantonese have moved to Queens and the suburbs, the Fujianese have now become the controlling force in Chinatown.

Exploring Chinatown

Most New Yorkers come to Chinatown not to get the lowdown on Chinese politics but to eat. Nowhere in this city can you eat so well, and so much, for so little. **Mott Street** is the area's main thoroughfare, and along with the streets around – Canal, Pell, Bayard, Doyers and Bowery – hosts a glut of restaurants, tea and rice shops and grocers. The food is dotted all over; Cantonese cuisine predominates, but there are also many restaurants that specialize in the spicier Szechuan and Hunan cuisines, along with Fukien, Soochow and the spicy Chowchou dishes. Anywhere you walk into is likely to be good, but if you're looking for specific recommendations (especially for lunchtime dim sum), some of the best are detailed in Chapter 17, "Eating".

Besides eating, the lure of Chinatown lies in wandering amid the exotica of the shops and absorbing the neighborhood's vigorous street life. Be forewarned: population density and congestion make this area among New York's hottest (in temperature) on a summer's day. There are a few interesting routes if you want to set structure to your explorations. Mott Street, again, is the obvious starting point: follow it from Worth Street and there's the **Chinatown Museum** at the far end, on the site of the district's first Chinese shop – unfortunately, its more of a tacky video arcade than a bona fide museum. **The Museum of Chinese in the Americas** is a more dedicated place to learn about the history of Chinese immigrants (see p.302 for details on both of the above mentioned museums). Further up, a rare building predates the Chinese intake, the early nineteenth-century green-domed Catholic school and **Church of the Transfiguration** at the corner of Mott Street, off of Mosco Street. To the right is picturesquely crooked Doyers Street, once known as "Bloody Angle," so named for its miserable reputation as a dumping ground for dead bodies – the underside of relations between the Tongs. Around the Angle there is a lattice of streets and alleys where you'll find shops stocked with Old World trinkets and plastic tourist goods.

Returning to Mott, take a left down Bayard Street and you've arrived at **Columbus Park**, a shady haunt favored by the neighborhood's elderly. At the Park's northernmost tip is an open-air concert hall, topped by a pagoda roof and decorated with fading pictures of a bird and a dragon. Continue on north and you'll arrive at **Canal Street,** at all hours a crowded thoroughfare crammed with jewelry shops and kiosks hawking sunglasses, T-shirts and fake Rolexes. Two shopping institutions on Canal are not to be missed: one, the **Pearl River Department Store**, at no. 277 (the corner of Canal and the Bowery), is the closest you'll ever get to a Shanghai bazaar without going to China. Specialities here include all sorts of embroidered slippers and silk clothing, rice cookers, pottery, and beautiful lacquered paper umbrellas – much sought after by interior decorators pinching a few pennies. Across the street at no. 308, housed in an imposing red-and-white-painted turn-of-the-century warehouse, are the many levels of **Pearl Paint**, which claims to be the largest art supply store in the world. As you approach **Grand Street** – which used to be the city's Main Street in the mid-1800s – outdoor fruit, vegetable and live seafood stands line the curbs – offering snow peas, bean curd, fungi, oriental cabbage and dried sea cucumbers to the passersby. Ribs, whole chickens and Peking ducks glisten in the storefront windows nearby: the sight of them can put more than a vegetarian off his food. Perhaps even more fascinating are the Chinese herbalists. The roots and powders in their boxes, drawers and glass are century-old remedies, but, to those accustomed to Western medicine, may seem like voodoo potions.

Once you've traveled this circuit (or at least a rough approximation of it), you've seen Chinatown's nucleus. Moving on, stroll over to the **Bowery** and wander the streets leading down to the housing projects that flank the East River, most of which are nowadays inhabited by Fujianese Chinese. On your way you'll pass **Confucius Plaza** at the intersection of Bowery and Division streets; guarded by a statue of **Confucius**, this housing complex, built in the 1970s, was and still is considered the best living quarters in Chinatown. Make a point as well of crossing Chatham Square, where proud Fujianese civic organizations recently erected a statue of **Lin Zexu**, a Fujian Province official who helped start the Opium Wars of the nineteenth century by banning the drug. Lin used opium as an excuse to fight the British, but the Fujianese, stereotyped as Chinatown's drug lords, have made a point of casting their hero as anti-substance: inscribed in English and Chinese at the statue's base are the words Say No to Drugs. Opposite Chatham Square and slightly to the south, on Park Row between James and Oliver streets, is the anomalous

first **cemetery** of the Spanish and Portuguese Synagogue, congregation Shearith Israel, the oldest Jewish congregation in New York
(now located in a synagogue at 70th Street and Central Park West).
It was in use from 1656 to 1833, and the pleasure of the rare sight of
eroded seventeenth-century headstones in Manhattan is only dampened by the fact that the site cannot be visited.

Double back by way of East Broadway or Henry Street to where
the **Manhattan Bridge**, with its grand Beaux Arts entrance out of
place amid the neon signs and Chinese cinemas, crosses the East
River. From here you could head north up Chrystie Street, which
forms the nominal border between Chinatown and the Lower East
Side, or west down Canal Street, past the hubbub and into the area
known as Little Italy, long the center of the city's considerable Italian
community.

Little Italy

Signs made out of red, green and white tinsel effusively welcome visitors to **Little Italy**, a signal perhaps that Little Italy is light years
away from the solid ethnic enclave of old. It's a lot smaller and more
commercial than it was, and the area settled by New York's huge
nineteenth-century influx of Italian immigrants – who (like their
Jewish and Chinese counterparts) cut themselves off clannishly to
re-create the Old Country – is being encroached upon a little more
each year by Chinatown. Few Italians still live here and the surfeit of
restaurants – some of which pipe the music of NY's favorite Italian
son, Frank Sinatra, onto the street – tend to have valet-parking and
high prices. In fact, it is this quantity of restaurants, more than anything else, that gives Little Italy away: go to the city's true Italian
areas, Belmont in the Bronx or Carroll Gardens in Brooklyn, and
you'll find very few genuine Italian eateries, since Italians prefer to
consume their native food at home. It's significant, too, that when
Martin Scorsese came to make *Mean Streets* it was in Belmont that
he decided to shoot it, even though the film was about Little Italy.

But that's not to advise missing out on Little Italy altogether. Some
original bakeries and *salumerias* (Italian specialty food stores) do
survive, and there, amid the imported cheeses, sausages and salamis
hanging from the ceiling, you can buy sandwiches made with slabs of
mozzarella or eat slices of homemade focaccia. In addition, there still
are plenty of places to indulge yourself with a cappuccino and pricey
pastry, not least *Ferrara's* on Grand Street, the oldest and most
popular.

If you're here in September, the **Festa di San Gennaro** is a wild,
tacky and typically Italian splurge to celebrate the saint's day, when
Italians from all over the city converge on Mulberry Street, Little
Italy's main strip, and the area is transformed by street stalls and
numerous Italian fast-snack outlets. None of the restaurants around

Little Italy here really stands out, but the former site of *Umberto's Clam House*, on the corner of Mulberry and Hester streets, was quite notorious in its time: it was the scene of a vicious gangland murder in 1972, when Joe "Crazy Joey" Gallo was shot dead while celebrating his birthday with his wife and daughter. Gallo, a big talker and ruthless businessman, was keen to protect his business interests in Brooklyn; he was alleged to have offended a rival family and so paid the price. *Umberto's Clam House* has since relocated to 129 Mulberry St where things are a bit quieter.

In striking counterpoint to the clandestine lawlessness of the Italian underworld, the old **Police Headquarters**, a palatial Neoclassical confection meant to cow would-be criminals into obedience with its high-rise dome and lavish ornamentation, is located at the corner of Centre and Broome streets. The police headquarters moved to a bland modern building in the Civic Center in 1973, and the overbearing palace has been converted into upmarket condominiums, some of which Steffi Graf, Winona Ryder and Christy Turlington have all called home. Walk beyond Broadway and you're already in **SoHo**, which, like Chinatown, is a booming district bursting its borders from the further side of Broadway (see Chapter 5).

In fact, east of Broadway and south of Houston, fashion and style have found new breeding ground. Lining the streets are fresh, creative and independent designer boutiques, coffeehouses and cafés, establishing this area as the latest in chic. Referred to (by relators and editors determined to label every block in the city) as **NoLita**, this section *No*rth of *Li*ttle *Ita*ly, which extends east from Lafayette, Mott and Elizabeth streets between Prince and Houston, is great to stroll by for hip shopping and to catch self-expression spilling into the streets as the young and the restless loiter around the scene.

The Lower East Side

I don't wanna be buried in Puerto Rico
I don't wanna rest in Long Island cemetery
I wanna be near the stabbing shooting
gambling fighting and unnatural dying
and new birth crying
So please when I die . . .
Keep me nearby
Take my ashes and scatter them thru out
the Lower East Side . . .

Miguel Piñero, *A Lower East Side* Poem

The **Lower East Side** is one of Manhattan's least changed and most evocative Downtown neighborhoods, a little-known quarter which began to attract humanitarian attention worldwide toward the end of the last century when it became an insular slum for over half a million Jewish immigrants – and the most densely populated spot in the world. Coming here from Eastern Europe via Ellis Island, these refugees were in search of a better life, scratching out a living in a free-for-all of crowded competition centered around sweatshops, piecework and pushcarts. Since then, the area has become considerably depopulated and better maintained, and the inhabitants are now largely working-class Puerto Rican or Chinese rather than Jewish; but otherwise, at least on the surface, little has visibly changed.

The area's lank brick tenements (a term which comes from the Latin *tenare*, to hold, and literally denotes a human holding-tank), ribbed with blackened fire escapes, must have seemed a bleak destiny for those who arrived here, crammed into a district which daily became more densely populated and where low standards of hygiene and abysmal housing made disease rife and life expectancy low: in 1875, there was 40 percent infant mortality, mainly due to cholera. It was conditions like these that spurred local residents like Jacob Riis and, later, Stephen Crane to record the plight of the city's immigrants in their writings and photographs, thereby spawning not only a whole school of realistic writing but also some notable social reforms. Not for nothing – and not without some degree of success – did the Lower East Side become known as a neighborhood where political battles were fought. The Lower East Side of today, split neatly by Houston Street, is wholesomely seedy but definitely a bit trendy, with new nightspots popping up almost weekly.

South of Houston

This is the most readily explored part of the Lower East Side – and the most rewarding. It began as Kleine Deutschland (Little Germany) in the first half of the nineteenth century, a home to relatively well-off Jewish merchants, but as they moved onward and upward a more desperate group of Jewish immigrants, fleeing poverty in Eastern Europe, flooded in. On the streets south of Houston, Jewish immigrants indelibly stamped their character with their own shops, delis, restaurants, synagogues and, later, community centers. Even now, with the runover of immigrants from Chinatown having settled in the neighborhood, it still holds the remnants of its Jewish past, such as the area's homemade kosher cuisine and the Orthodox bathhouse. Some outsiders are drawn to the area for the **bargain shopping**. You can get just about anything at cut-price in the stores: clothes on **Orchard Street**, lamps and shades on the **Bowery**, ties and shirts on Allen Street, underwear and hosiery on **Grand Street**, textiles on Eldridge. And, whatever you're buying, people will if necessary haggle down to the last cent. The time to come is Sunday morning, for the **Orchard Street Market**, when you'll catch the vibrancy of the Lower East Side at its best. Weekdays the stores are still there, but far fewer people come to shop and the streets can have a forbidding, desolate feel.

The Lower East Side

If you haven't got the time to tour the Lower East Side extensively, make sure to visit the **Lower East Side Tenement Museum** at 90 Orchard St, which does a brilliantly imaginative job of bringing to life the neighborhood's immigrant past and present. This will probably be your only chance to see the crumbling, claustrophobic interior of an 1864 tenement (purchased by the museum in 1992 and the first tenement ever to be landmarked), with its deceptively elegant, though ghostly, entry hall and two communal toilets for every four families (see p.301 for museum details).

Around East Broadway

Although the southern half of **East Broadway** is now almost exclusively Chinese, the street used to be the hub of the Jewish Lower East Side. For the old feel of the quarter – where the synagogues remain active (many in the area have become churches for the Puerto Ricans) – best explore north of here (and north of the Manhattan Bridge access ramp), starting with **Canal Street. The Eldridge Street Synagogue** in its day was one of the neighborhood's most grand with its brick and terra-cotta hybrid of Moorish arches and Gothic rose window. Currently, the building is being completely restored, and only the basement is left open to the public for the sporadic get-togethers of a much-dwindled congregation, but tours of the majestic interior are offered on Sundays (hourly noon–4pm; $5). Across the street, the dingy tenement at **no. 19** was home to vaudeville and film star Eddie Cantor.

Carry on east down Canal Street and, at nos. 54–58, look above the row of food and electrical stores and you'll see the stately facade of **Sender Jarmulowsky's Bank**, dwarfing the buildings around it. The bank was founded in 1873 by a peddler who made his fortune reselling ship tickets, to cater to the financial needs of the influx of non-English-speaking immigrants. Around the turn of the century, as the bank's assets accrued, rumors began circulating about its insolvency. As World War I became an imminent reality, the bank was plagued by runs and riots when panicked patrons tried to withdraw their money to send to relatives back in Europe. Finally, in 1914, the bank collapsed; with its closure, thousands lost what little savings they had.

At the corner of Canal and Ludlow streets, no. 5, prominently marked with a Star of David and the year 1892, is the **Kletzker Brotherly Aid Association** building, a vestige of a time when Jewish towns set up their own lodges (in this case, the town was Kletzk in Belarus) to provide community health care and Jewish burials, assistance for widows, and the like. The tradition has been schizophrenically preserved by an Italian funeral parlor at the front of the building and a Chinese funeral home at the side.

Continue on east, past the junction of Canal Street and East Broadway, and at 175 East Broadway you'll come to the dilapidated brick office tower now occupied by the **New York Ling Laing Church**, the building that once housed the editorial offices of the *Forward*, New York's foremost left-leaning Yiddish-language newspaper. Nowadays, the Hebrew characters on the facade have been covered over by signs in Chinese, a testament to how each wave of immigrants salvages the precious space and makes it their own by painting over predecessors' history. Move along further, to the intersection of East Broadway and Grand, where, adjacent to the Puerto Rican *bodegas* (grocery stores) and the concrete and glass eyesore Public School 134, proudly stands a cultural anachronism: an operating *mikveh*, or ritual bathhouse, where Orthodox Jewish women must bathe prior to marriage and monthly thereafter.

East Broadway, Essex and Grand streets frame the pie slice-shaped complex which comprises **Seward Park** and its neighboring apartment blocks. Constructed by the city to provide a bit of green space in the overburdened precincts of the Lower East Side, the park boasted the first public playground in New York and is still surrounded by benevolent institutions set up for the benefit of ambitious immigrants.

East down Grand leads through housing projects to the messy **East River Park** – not one of the city's most attractive open spaces. It's better to skip that area and double back up Grand, toward Essex Street, where you'll find more stores and activity. A few blocks on your way you'll pass the **Church of St Mary**, the third-oldest Catholic church (1832) in the city. The Church is a favorite resting spot of elderly Jewish couples, who sit on the benches outside and watch the world go by.

Essex Street and around

Essex Street leads to **Delancey Street**, the horizontal axis of the Jewish Lower East Side, now a tacky boulevard, and to the **Williamsburg Bridge**, which once served as a shelter for New York's homeless and now doubles as a makeshift parking lot. On either side of Delancey sprawls the **Essex Street Market**, erected under the aegis of Mayor LaGuardia in the 1930s, when pushcarts were made illegal (ostensibly because they clogged the streets, but mainly because they competed with established businesses). Look for the neon signs of *Ratner's Dairy Restaurant*, one of the Lower East Side's most famous dairy restaurants, nearby at 138 Delancey. Incongruously, the back room of *Ratner's* has been converted into a fashionable, somewhat hidden nightspot, *Lansky's Lounge* (the barely marked alley entrance is at 104 Norfolk St; look for murals of various desserts on the building's walls). Back on Essex, at no. 35, is *The Essex Street (Guss') Pickle Products*, where people line up outside the storefront to buy homemade pickles taken fresh from barrels of garlicky brine.

East of Essex Street, the atmosphere changes abruptly. Here the inhabitants are mainly Latino, mostly Puerto Ricans but with a fair

For more on Jewish food in the Lower East Side – and elsewhere in New York – see Chapter 17, "Eating," and Chapter 18, "Drinking."

smattering of immigrants from other Latin and South American countries. Most of the Jews who got richer long ago moved into middle-income housing further uptown or in the other boroughs, and there's little love lost between those who remain and the new inhabitants. Today, much of the area east of Essex has lost the traditional Sunday bustle of Jewish market shopping and has been replaced by the Saturday afternoon Spanish chatter of the new residents shopping for records, inexpensive clothes and electrical goods. **Clinton Street** – a mass of cheap Latino retailers, restaurants and travel agents – is in many ways the central thoroughfare of the Puerto Rican Lower East Side.

One stalwart from bygone times, decorated with old casks and bottles, is **Schapiro's Winery**, which has been at 124 Rivington St since 1899 and is still run by the Schapiro family (try to have a chat with the owners). If you are here on a Sunday, check out the free 2pm wine tours. There are tastings hosted hourly, Mon–Thurs 11am–5pm and Fridays after 3pm, at this, the city's only kosher wine and spirits warehouse, where customary sweet wine (a Jewish tradition, for a sweet life) is made on the premises. Further east, at 156 Rivington, a welded gate composed of old gears and scrap metal identifies **ABC No Rio**, a community arts center whose grafittied entryway exemplifies this and other Downtown neighborhoods' struggle between a dodgy past and a rapidly upmarket future. In 1980, the space was given to a group of artists who had put on a notable exhibit concerning skyrocketing rents; it has gone on to host gallery shows, concerts, installations and the like. The Housing and Preservation Department (HPD) attempted to reclaim the space in June 1995, saying it was a neighborhood blight. It was indeed shabby. Since then, however, a deal has been struck for ABC to keep the building, as long as they put in $75,000 worth of improvements (which it certainly doesn't look like they've gotten around to yet).

Ludlow and Orchard streets
Ludlow Street sparked the hipster migration south of the East Village where a half-dozen or so bars, such as the popular *Local 138* at 138 Ludlow and *Max Fish* at 178 Ludlow, dot the block. There are also a number of secondhand stores offering kitsch items and slightly worn treasures. Around the intersection of Allen and Stanton streets are several bar/performance spaces. For comedy try *Surf Reality*, hidden behind a massive welded door at 172 Allen St and for great local music check out *Baby Jupiter* at 170 Orchard St and *Arlene Grocery* at 95 Stanton St.

On the corner of Ludlow and East Houston you'll find *Katz's Deli*, a joint-like delicatessen famous for its assembly-line counter service and lauded by locals as one of the best in New York. If it looks familiar, don't be surprised: this was the scene of Meg Ryan's faked orgasm in *When Harry Met Sally*. There are a variety of Jewish del-

See Chapter 19, "Nightlife," for more details.

icacies available on East Houston: *Russ & Daughters*, at no. 179, specializes in smoked fish, herring and caviar, and *Yonah Schimmel*, further down at no. 137, has been making some of New York's best knishes since 1910.

Continue west on Houston and you'll arrive at **Orchard Street**, center of the so-called Bargain District, and best on Sundays when it is filled with stalls and storefronts hawking discounted designer clothes and bags. The rooms above the stores here used to house sweatshops, named so because whatever the weather, a stove had to be kept warm for pressing the clothes that were made there. The garment industry moved uptown ages ago, and the rooms are a bit more salubrious now – often home to pricey apartments.

The Bowery

Walk east from here and it's for the most part burned-out tenements interspersed with a scattering of Spanish-style grocery stores; to the west things aren't much better. **Bowery** spears north out of Chinatown as far as Cooper Square on the edge of the East Village. This wide thoroughfare has gone through many changes over the years: it took its name from "Bouwerie," the Dutch word for farm, when it was the city's main agricultural supplier; later, in the closing decades of the last century, it was flanked by music halls, theaters, hotels and middle-market restaurants, drawing people from all parts of Manhattan. Though in some sections it is still a skid row for the city's drunk and derelict, such days are limited; as the demand for apartments continues, the tide of gentrification is slowly sweeping its way south through the Lower East Side.

The one – bizarre – focus, certainly a must for any Lower East Side wanderings, is the **Bowery Savings Bank** on the corner of Grand Street. Designed by Stanford White in 1894, it rises out of the neighborhood's debris like a god, as does its sister bank on 42nd Street, a shrine to the virtue of saving money. Inside, the original carved check-writing stands are still in place, and the coffered ceiling, together with White's great gilded fake marble columns, couldn't create a more potent feeling of security. An inscription above the door as you exit leaves you in no doubt: "Your financial welfare is the business of this bank." Quite so, but back on the Bowery, moving between the panhandlers and shabby new businesses, you wonder whose interests they have in mind.

Chapter 5

SoHo and TriBeCa

Since the mid-1960s, SoHo, the grid of streets that runs South of Houston Street, has meant art. The midland between the Financial District and Greenwich Village, it had been, for most of the twentieth century, a raggedy, gray wasteland of manufacturers and wholesalers. But as the Village increased in price and declined in hipness, artists moved into the loft spaces and cheap-rental studios. Galleries were established, which quickly attracted the city's art crowd, as well as boutiques and restaurants. Like in the Village, gentrification soon followed, and what remains is a mix of chichi antique, art and clothes shops, earthy industry and high living. Yet although SoHo now carries the veneer of the establishment – a loft in the area means money (and lots of it) – no amount of gloss can cover up SoHo's quintessential appearance, its dark alleys of paint-peeled former garment factories fronted by some of the best cast-iron facades in the country.

Some history

Even up to the late 1960s, SoHo was a slum. It had experienced a bit of a vogue in the mid-nineteenth century when it fringed New York's then-liveliest and most fashionable street, Broadway, but quickly became a seamier backdrop of industrial and red-light areas – cheerfully known as "Hell's Hundred Acres" – when 14th Street replaced Broadway as New York's commercial and entertainment center. At the turn of the century, SoHo – now nicknamed "The Valley" because of its low industrial buildings – was scandalized by the **Triangle Shirtwaist Factory Fire** of 1911, when a sweatshop's young, mostly immigrant female workforce burned to death because they were locked inside the building during their shift hours and had no means of escape when fire broke out.

In the 1940s, costs drove artists from Greenwich Village: they began moving into SoHo, converting the large, cheap and light-filled factories into lofts and work spaces. One hindrance plagued them, however: the buildings were zoned exclusively for small industry,

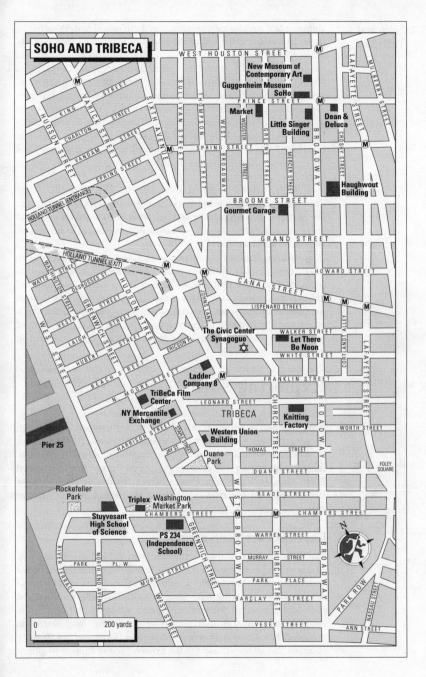

SOHO AND TRIBECA

WEST HOUSTON STREET

New Museum of
Contemporary Art

Guggenheim Museum
SoHo

PRINCE STREET

Market

Little Singer
Building

Dean &
Deluca

Haughwout
Building

BROOME STREET

Gourmet Garage

GRAND STREET

HOWARD STREET

CANAL STREET

LISPENARD STREET

WALKER STREET

The Civic Center
Synagogue

Let There
Be Neon

WHITE STREET

Ladder
Company 8

FRANKLIN STREET

TriBeCa Film
Center

LEONARD STREET

TRIBECA

Knitting
Factory

NY Mercantile
Exchange

WORTH STREET

Western Union
Building

THOMAS STREET

Pier 25

Duane
Park

FOLEY
SQUARE

DUANE STREET

READE STREET

Rockefeller
Park

Triplex   Washington
Market Park

CHAMBERS STREET

CHAMBERS STREET

Stuyvesant
High School
of Science

PS 234
(Independence
School)

WARREN STREET

MURRAY STREET

PARK PLACE

PARK PL. W.

BARCLAY STREET

VESEY STREET

N

0   200 yards

ANN STREET

HUDSON STREET
KING STREET
CHARLTON STREET
VANDAM STREET
SPRING STREET
VARICK STREET
SIXTH AVENUE
SULLIVAN STREET
THOMPSON STREET
WEST BROADWAY
WOOSTER STREET
GREENE STREET
MERCER STREET
BROADWAY
CROSBY STREET
LAFAYETTE STREET
MULBERRY STREET
HOLLAND TUNNEL (ENTRANCE)
HOLLAND TUNNEL (EXIT)
WATTS STREET
DESBROSSES ST.
VESTRY STREET
LAIGHT STREET
HUBERT STREET
BEACH STREET
WASHINGTON STREET
GREENWICH STREET
HUDSON STREET
ST. JOHN'S LANE
ERICSON PL.
MOORE STREET
STAPLE STREET
JAY ST.
HARRISON STREET
CHURCH STREET
BROADWAY
CORTLAND ALLEY
LAFAYETTE STREET
WEST STREET
RIVER TERRACE
NORTH END AVENUE
GREENWICH STREET
WEST STREET
WEST BROADWAY
CHURCH STREET
BROADWAY
PARK ROW
NASSAU STREET

SoHo and TriBeCa

shipping and warehouses; residence in them was illegal. Pestered by these lawbreakers, the city government attempted to raze parts of SoHo in the early 1960s. Joining forces with the conservationist movement, the wily artists trumpeted SoHo's formidable cast-iron architecture – indeed, some of the most impressive in America – and saved the quarter (and their accommodation) by having the area declared an **historic district**. The mayor of New York, still faced with the problem of this (albeit historic) slum, revised the building codes in the late 1960s to allow industrial spaces to be open to "artists in residence." Three thousand artists moved in, in the first year, and contemporary New York's full-scale intertwining of industry and art began.

In 1970, several major uptown galleries (Leo Castelli, Andre Emmerich and John Weber) moved to SoHo and injected money into the scene. The Guggenheim marked Downtown's arrival – several years after the fact, though – when it opened its SoHo branch on Broadway at Prince Street in 1992.

Nowadays, despite how SoHo was won, few artists or experimental galleries are left in the area: the late-1980s art boom drove up rents, and only the more established or consciously "commercial" galleries can afford to stay. Although SoHo still has the city's densest population of galleries, the risk-takers have moved elsewhere – either south to TriBeCa or, more recently, north to Chelsea, both of which are undergoing the same transformation that occurred in SoHo in the late 1960s.

Exploring SoHo

Houston Street (pronounced *How*ston rather than *Hew*ston) marks the top of SoHo's trellis of streets, any exploration of which necessarily means crisscrossing and doubling back. **Greene Street** is as good a place to start as any, highlighted all along by the nineteenth-century cast-iron facades that, in part if not in whole, saved SoHo from the bulldozers. **Prince Street**, **Spring Street** and **West Broadway** hold the best selection of shops and galleries in the area.

Cast-iron architecture

The technique of cast-iron architecture was utilized simply as a way of assembling buildings quickly and cheaply, with iron beams rather than heavy walls carrying the weight of the floors. The result was the removal of load-bearing walls, greater space for windows and, most noticeably, remarkably decorative facades. Almost any style or whim could be cast in iron and pinned to a building, and architects indulged themselves in Baroque balustrades, forests of Renaissance columns and all the effusion of the French Second Empire to glorify

SoHo's sweatshops. Have a look at **72–76 Greene St**, an extrava-
gance whose Corinthian portico stretches the whole five stories, all
in painted metal, and at the strongly composed elaborations of its
sister building at **no. 28–30**. These are the best, but from Broome to
Canal streets, most of the fronts on Greene Street's west side are
either real (or mock) cast iron.

Ironically, what began as an engineering trait turned into a purely
decorative one as stone copies of cast iron (you'd need a magnet to
tell the real from the replicas) came into fashion. At the northeast
corner of Broome Street and Broadway is the magnificent
Haughwout Building, perhaps the ultimate in the cast-iron genre.
Rhythmically repeated motifs of colonnaded arches are framed
behind taller columns in a thin sliver of a Venetian palace – and it was
the first building ever to boast a steam-powered Otis elevator. In
1904, Ernest Flagg took the possibilities of cast iron to their conclusion in his "**Little Singer**" **Building** at 561 Broadway (at Prince St),
a design whose use of wide window frames points the way to the
glass curtain wall of the 1950s.

Markets and galleries

SoHo celebrates its architecture in Richard Haas's smirky **mural** at
114 Prince St (corner of Greene St), also the venue of one of
SoHo's affordable **markets** (there's another at the meeting of
Spring and Wooster streets). Many of the clothes and antique
shops around are beyond reasonable budgets, although the Stussy
store at 104 Prince is a favorite haunt of clubbers from the
Continent. Bargain treasures and pure bric-a-brac can also be
found at the **Antique Flea Market**, held every weekend on the corner of Grand Street and Broadway. See Chapter 24, "Shops and
Markets," for other suggestions.

What you'll find in the innumerable **galleries** is similarly overpriced but makes for fascinating browsing, with just about every
variety of contemporary artistic expression on view. No one minds
you looking in for a while, and doing this is also a sure way of bumping into the more visible eccentrics of the area. Most of the **galleries**
are concentrated on West Broadway and Prince Street, in a patch
that fancies itself as an alternative Madison Avenue (though certainly not lower in price). They're generally open from Labor Day to
Memorial Day, Tuesday–Saturday 10/11am–6pm, Saturdays being
most lively; for listings of galleries (and details of gallery tours) see
p.304 and pick up a copy of *Time Out New York* or the more in-
depth *Gallery Guide*, the latter available free at galleries upon
request. For a view of recent art outside the confines of SoHo, drop
in on the **New Museum of Contemporary Art** at 583 Broadway
between Prince and Houston streets (see p.294).

*For something
slightly less
contemporary,
visit the
Guggenheim
SoHo, p.291.*

South to Canal Street

Loosely speaking, SoHo's diversions get grottier as you drop south. Still, **Broome** and **Grand** streets, formerly full of dilapidated storefronts and dusty windows, have recently become home to a small band of boutiques, galleries, cafés and French restaurants. The new development is particularly concentrated around Sixth Avenue, where old warehouses still offer some cheap – though increasingly rare – loft space. Most people come down this way for the chic and vintage clothes places like **Canal Jean Co** at 504 Broadway (between Spring and Broome streets), or to buy a homemade lunch at *Gourmet Garage* (Broome at Mercer St). Just south is **Canal Street**, which links the Holland Tunnel with the Manhattan Bridge and forms a main thoroughfare between New Jersey and Brooklyn. On the edge of Chinatown is SoHo's open bazaar: brash storefronts loaded with fake designer watches, electrical gear, leather goods, sneakers, and some porn video shops. Sadly, as TriBeCa – SoHo's other southern neighbor – skips up the social ladder, Canal Street is becoming increasingly "cleaned up."

TriBeCa

TriBeCa, the *Tri*angle *Be*low *Ca*nal Street, has caught the fallout of SoHo artists, and is rapidly changing from a wholesale garment district to an upscale community that mixes commercial establishments with loft residences, studios, galleries and chic eateries. Less a triangle than a crumpled rectangle – the area bounded by Canal and Murray streets, Broadway and the Hudson River – it takes in spacious industrial buildings whose upper layers sprout plants and cats behind tidy glazing: the apartments of TriBeCa's new gentry.

Like "SoHo," the name TriBeCa was a semiotic rehaul more suited to the increasingly trendy neighborhood than its former moniker, Washington Market — the mid-1970s invention of an entrepreneurial realtor. The late 1970s saw the first residential reworkings of industrial buildings, encouraged by tax abatements and the convenient dovetailing of three subway lines, the #1/9, A/C and the N/R. In the late 1980s, when the East Village became gentrified and SoHo properties skyrocketed in value, there was a scramble for TriBeCa's warehouses. Today, however, living space in TriBeCa is approaching SoHo's in status and price, and a zoning loophole allowing for the addition of penthouses is being exploited at breakneck speed. Although pockets of the area are still enclaves for blue-collar folk, the neighborhood is attracting the media elite. John F. Kennedy, Jr. and, Carolyn Bessette Kennedy, lived here, until their tragic death in July 1999; supermodel Naomi Campbell and actor Harvey Keitel – as well as upper-middle-class families. Most of the new residents are smitten by the neighborhood's slower pace – indeed, because it is on the edge of the island, it's not well traveled – and by its sense of community.

Despite rising rents, commercial space in TriBeCa is still cheaper than any of the other "artistic" neighborhoods, so creative industries have been moving to the area en masse. Galleries, recording studios, computer graphics companies and photo labs are setting up shop in old garment warehouses; avant-garde performance venues like The Knitting Factory at 74 Leonard St are bringing art out of the closet and into public space. The film industry is also making TriBeCa home, with the **TriBeCa Film Center** – a film production company owned by, among others, Robert De Niro – paving the way. The Center is located in a converted red-brick warehouse at 375 Greenwich St, along with one of Mr De Niro's restaurants, the *TriBeCa Grill*, whose clientele often includes well-known names and faces from the film world.

In the evening, TriBeCa isn't as deserted as it used to be: as little as five years ago, come nightfall, the sound of footsteps would echo off the cobbled streets and against the cast-iron buildings. TriBeCa used to shut when the Wall Street crowd went home, but the growth of **Battery Park City** has brought smart restaurants into the neighborhood, and some of the traditional after-work bars – like *Puffy's*, an old Prohibition speakeasy at 81 Hudson St – now stay open much later.

For more on TriBeCa restaurants and nightlife, see Chapters 17 and 19.

Exploring TriBeCa

To get a feel for TriBeCa's mix of old and new, go to **Duane Park**, a sliver of green between Hudson and Greenwich streets. Around the Park's picturesque perimeter you'll see the old depots of New York's egg, butter and cheese distribution center (now regrouped with other wholesale markets at Hunt's Point in the Bronx) wedged between new residential apartments. The orange Art Deco facade of the **Western Union Building** is at the edge of the block, while the World Trade Center and Woolworth and Municipal buildings guard the skyline like soldiers.

Walk a few blocks south on Hudson Street to hit **Chambers Street**, home to much of the evidence of the neighborhood's upswing. Freshly scrubbed brick buildings have replaced many of the discount shops, along with bookstores and restaurants, and at West Broadway and Chambers Street is a tiny new park named for James Bogardus, an ironmonger who put up the city's first cast-iron facade in 1849. A new public elementary school – **PS 234,** also known as **Independence School** – sits at the intersection of Greenwich and Chambers; built in 1988, it sports a fanciful exterior, with images of boats and ships worked into its iron gates. Across from the school is the verdant and expansive **Washington Market Park**, built on the site where the city's first major fruit and vegetable market was located.

TriBeCa

Continuing down Chambers toward West Street, you'll pass the **Triplex** at the Borough of Manhattan Community College (the largest performing arts center in lower Manhattan, it stages over 200 – poorly advertised – events a year), and finally arrive at the **TriBeCa Bridge**, a futuristic walkway across West Street made of silver steel tubes, white girders and glass. The bridge leads to the new orange-brick **Stuyvesant High School of Science**, long-awaited by the school's competitively-selected students. Along the river from the bridge to 13th Street, eventually to be extended up to 59th Street, is a jogging and cycling promenade which passes by **Pier 25**, a public recreation center boasting three beach volleyball courts – built atop 540 cubic yards of sand trucked in from New Jersey – and a miniature golf course. If you head straight out behind the high school, you'll find yourself in **Rockefeller Park**, a promenade jutting into the Hudson. Don't miss the bronze dog, attached to the water fountain at the far end of the park, straining his leash to get at a bronze cat which is about to pounce on a bronze bird. Reminiscent of the way New York often feels.

To get a sense of the area's new clientele, take a left out of Duane Park and follow Greenwich toward Canal Street. In this main strip restaurants from the affordable (*Yaffa's*) to the outrageously expensive (*TriBeCa Grill*) line the street. Because the road is so wide, traffic moves at highway speed, an irksome development that has spurred a plan to reduce the street's lanes from six to two by planting trees where there is now tarmac.

Parallel to Greenwich is Hudson Street, which catches the overflow of fancy restaurants then, in sharp contrast, peters out into still-active warehouses, whose denizens do the same work they have for decades. Instead of heading down there, walk east along to White St where it meets Church Street. Located at 49 White St is **The Civic Center Synagogue**, a 1967 temple whose curving, wave-like facade, covered in marble tiles, is quite striking, while at no. 38 is Rudi Stern's Let There Be Neon, a gallery boasting signs, chairs, household goods and stage sets all in – you guessed it – neon. At the corner of White Street and West Broadway is a rare remaining Federal-era store, in continuous use since 1809, now home to the stylish yet wholly unpretentious, *Liquor Store Bar*. One block farther west, between Varick and North Moore streets, is **Ladder Company 8**, a turn-of-the-century brick-and-stone firehouse dotted with white stars and used as the haunted headquarters of the *Ghostbusters*.

Chapter 6

Greenwich Village and the East Village

C leanly bordered by Houston Street to the south and 14th Street to the north, Greenwich Village and its grungier sister, the East Village, continue to serve, if in name only, as the Bohemia of New York City. On the west side, Greenwich Village proper makes for a great day of walking through a grid of streets that doesn't even attempt to conform to the rest of the city's established numbered pattern. At least you'll never be bored since, despite a commercialization that has sanitized the neighborhood, there is still a quaintness to Greenwich Village that is genuine and enjoyable. Across the divide of Broadway is the East Village, which despite the encroachment of chain stores like the Gap and K-Mart, retains its decidedly ethnic mix, down and dirty demeanor, and – much more so than Greenwich Village – a political and anti-establishment edge that continues today.

Greenwich Village

If you're a New Yorker, it's fashionable to dismiss **Greenwich Village** (or "the Village" as it's most widely known) as *passé*. And it's true that, while the nonconformist image of Greenwich Village survives well enough if you don't actually live in New York, it's a tag that has long since ceased to hold genuine currency. The only writers who can afford to live here nowadays are copywriters, the only actors those who are starring regularly on Broadway, and as for politics – the average Village resident long since scrapped them for the more serious pursuit of making money. Greenwich Village is firmly for those who have Arrived. Not that the Village doesn't have appeal: to a great extent the neighborhood still sports the attractions that brought people here in the first place, and people still clamor for a Greenwich Village address: quaint side streets and stunning historic brownstones that can't be rivaled elsewhere in town. It's quiet, resi-

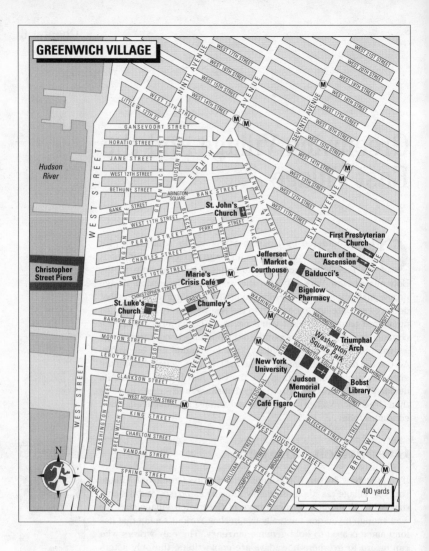

GREENWICH VILLAGE

Hudson
River

Christopher
Street Piers

St. John's
Church

Jefferson
Market
Courthouse

First Presbyterian
Church

Church of the
Ascension

Balducci's

Marie's
Crisis Café

Bigelow
Pharmacy

St. Luke's
Church

Chumley's

Washington
Square Park

Triumphal
Arch

New York
University

Judson
Memorial
Church

Bobst
Library

Café Figaro

N

0   400 yards

dential, but with a busy streetlife that lasts later than in many other
parts of the city; there are more restaurants per head than anywhere
else; and bars, while never cheap, clutter every corner. If interesting
people no longer live in the Village, they do hang out here –
Washington Square is a hub of aimless activity throughout the year –
and as long as you have no illusions about the "alternativeness" of the
place there are few better initiations into the city's life, especially at
night.

Some history

Greenwich Village grew up as a rural retreat from the early and frenetic nucleus of New York City, first becoming sought after during
the yellow fever epidemic of 1822 as a refuge from the infected
streets downtown. When the fever was at its height the idea was
mooted of moving the entire city center here. It was spared that dubious fate, and left to grow into a wealthy residential neighborhood
that sprouted elegant Federal and Greek Revival terraces and lured
some of the city's highest society names. Later, once the rich had
moved uptown and built themselves a palace or two on Fifth Avenue,
these large houses were to prove a fertile hunting ground for struggling artists and intellectuals on the lookout for cheap rents. By the
turn of the century, Greenwich Village was well on its way to becoming New York's Left Bank; at the very least it has always been seen
this way by outsiders – gentrification actually set in rather quickly.
Of early Village characters, one Mabel Dodge was perhaps most
influential. Wealthy and radical, she threw parties for the literary and
political cognoscenti – parties to which everyone hoped, sooner or
later, to be invited. Just about all of the well-known names who lived
here during the first two decades of the century spent some time at
her house at 23 Fifth Ave, a little north of Washington Square. Emma
Goldman discussed anarchism with Gertrude Stein and Margaret
Sanger; Conrad Aiken and T.S. Eliot dropped in from time to time;
and John Reed – who went on to write *Ten Days That Shook the
World*, the official record of the Russian Revolution – was a frequent
guest.

The Village
Voice, *NYC's
most venerable
listings/com-
ment/investiga-
tive magazine,
began life as a
chronicler of
Greenwich
Village nightlife
in the 1960s –*
see p.28.

Washington Square and around

The best way to see the Village is to walk, and by far the best place
to start is its natural center, **Washington Square**, commemorated as
a novel title by Henry James and haunted by most of the Village's
illustrious past names. It is not an elegant-looking place – too large
to be a square, too small to be a park. But it does retain its northern
edging of red-brick row houses – the "solid, honorable dwellings" of
Henry James's novel and now home to mostly administrative offices
for New York University (NYU) – and more imposingly, Stanford
White's famous **Triumphal Arch**, built in 1892 to commemorate the
centenary of George Washington's inauguration as president. Marcel
Duchamp, along with an agitator going by the name of "Woe,"
climbed to the top of the arch in 1913 to declare the Free Republic
of Greenwich Village. Don't plan on repeating that stunt; the arch
has been cordoned off around its perimeter in an effort to ward off
graffiti. James wouldn't, however, recognize the south side of the
square now: only the fussy **Judson Memorial Church** stands out
amid a messy blend of modern architecture, its interior given over
these days to a mixture of theater and local focus for a wide array of
community-based programs.

Most importantly, though, Washington Square remains the symbolic heart of the Village and its radicalism – so much so that when Robert Moses, the tarmacker of great chunks of New York City, wanted to plow a four-lane roadway through the center of the square there was a storm of protest that resulted not only in the stopping of the road but also the banning of all traffic from the park, then used as a turnaround point by buses. And that's how it has stayed ever since, notwithstanding some battles in the 1960s when the authorities decided to purge the park of folk singers and nearly had a riot on their hands. Today, in a recent and (mildly) successful effort to clear drug dealers from the park, the city has installed hidden security cameras, and undercover cops now mingle inconspicuously with the crowds. The park itself is closed after 11pm, a curfew that is strictly enforced. But, frankly, nothing's likely to happen to you in this part of town and if things look at all hazardous it's just as easy to walk around. As soon as the weather gets warm, the park becomes running track, performance venue, chess tournament and social club, boiling over with life as skateboards flip, dogs run, and acoustic guitar notes crash through the urgent cries of performers calling for the crowd's attention. At times like this, there's no better square in the city.

Exploring Washington Square

Eugene O'Neill, one of the Village's most acclaimed residents, lived (and wrote *The Iceman Cometh*) at 38 Washington Square S and consumed vast quantities of ale at **The Golden Swan Bar**, which once stood on the corner of Sixth Avenue and West 4th Street. *The Golden Swan* (variously called *The Hell Hole*, *Bucket of Blood* and other enticing nicknames) was best known in O'Neill's day for the dubious morals of its clientele – a gang of Irish hoodlums known as the Hudson Dusters – and for the pig in the basement that ate the customers' trash. O'Neill was great pals with this crowd and drew many of his characters from the personalities in this bar. It was nearby, also, that he got his first dramatic break, with a company called the Provincetown Players who, on the advice of John Reed, had moved down here from Massachusetts and set up shop on Macdougal Street, in a theater which still stands. A basketball court now fronts the block joining West 4th and West 3rd streets on Sixth Avenue. Here, some of the best and toughest street basketball you'll ever see is played out to often large crowds of spectators and the occasional TV crew.

At Washington Square South and La Guardia Place, where the **NYU Student Center** now stands, was once the boarding house known as Madame Katherine Blanchard's **House of Genius** – Willa Cather, Theodore Dreiser and O. Henry all called it home at one time or other. Back at the southwest corner of the park, follow **Macdougal Street** south, pausing for a detour down Minetta Lane

(once one of the city's most prodigious slums) and you hit **Bleecker
Street** – Main Street, Greenwich Village in many ways, with a
greater concentration of shops, bars, people and restaurants than
any other Village thoroughfare. This junction is also a vibrant corner with mock-European sidewalk cafés that have been literary
hangouts since the beginning of this century. The **Café Figaro**,
made famous by the Beat writers in the 1950s, is always thronged
throughout the day: far from cheap, though still worth the price of
a cappuccino to people-watch for an hour or so. Afterwards, you can
follow Bleecker Street one of two ways – east toward the solid towers of Washington Square Village, built with typical disregard for
history by NYU in 1958, or west right through the hubbub of
Greenwich Village life.

West of Sixth Avenue

Sixth Avenue itself is mainly tawdry stores and plastic eating houses, but on the other side, across Father Demo Square and up
Bleecker Street (until the 1970s there was an Italian open marketplace on this stretch, and it's still lined by a few Italian stores), are
some of the Village's prettiest residential streets. Turn left on **Leroy
Street** and cross over Seventh Avenue, where, confusingly, Leroy
Street becomes St Luke's Place for a block. The houses here, dating
from the 1850s, are among the city's most graceful, one of them
(recognizable by the two lamps of honor at the bottom of the steps)
is the ex-residence of **Jimmy Walker**, mayor of New York in the
1920s. Walker was for a time the most popular of mayors, a big-
spending, wisecracking man who gave up his work as a songwriter
for the world of politics and lived an extravagant lifestyle that rarely
kept him out of the gossip columns. Nothing if not shrewd, at a time
when America had never been so prosperous, he for a time reflected
people's most glamorous, big-living aspirations. He was, however,
no match for the hard times to come, and once the 1930s Depression
had taken hold he lost touch, and – with it – office.

*The excellent
White Horse
Tavern, 567
Hudson at West
11th St, is
where Dylan
Thomas had his
last drink. See
p.390 for
details.*

   South of Leroy Street, the Village fades slowly into the warehouse districts of SoHo and TriBeCa, a bleak area where nothing
much stirs outside working hours and the buildings are an odd mixture of Federal facades juxtaposed against grubby-gray rolldown-
entranced packing houses. There's a neatly preserved row from the
1820s on Charlton Street between Sixth Avenue and Varick; the area
just to its north, **Richmond Hill**, was George Washington's headquarters during the Revolution, later the home of Aaron Burr and
John Jacob Astor. But those apart, you may just as well continue on
Hudson Street up to **St Luke's in the Fields Church** at Barrow
Street. The church dates back to 1821 and the row of Federal-style
brick houses next door, housing for school and church administra-
tors, went up a few years later. Look behind the church for **St Luke's
Gardens**, a labyrinthine patchwork of garden, grass and benches

open to the public during the day and accessible through the gate
between church and school.

Hudson Street north of the church and up to Abington Square
(where Hudson bends to become Eighth Avenue and heads for
Chelsea) is a good avenue for meandering, with a bevy of unique
stores, coffee bars and restaurants. Fans of TV's *Taxi* will notice the
garage that posed as the "Sunshine Cab Company" (actually the
Dover Cab Company) at West 10th Street.

Around Bedford Street

Directly facing St Luke's, **Grove Street** runs into **Bedford Street**. If
you have time, peer into **Grove Court**, one of the neighborhood's
most typical and secluded little mews. Along with Barrow and
Commerce streets nearby, Bedford Street is one of the quietest and
most desirable Village addresses – Edna St Vincent Millay, the young
poet and playwright who did much work with the Provincetown
Playhouse, lived at no. 75 1/2 – said to be the narrowest house in the
city, nine feet wide and topped with a tiny gable. Another superlative:
the clapboard structure next door claims fame as the oldest house in
the Village, built in 1799 but much renovated since and probably
worth a considerable fortune now.

Further down Bedford Street, the former speakeasy **Chumley's**
(see p.389) is recognizable only by the metal grille on its door – a low
profile useful in Prohibition years that makes it hard to find today.
Back on Seventh Avenue look out for **Marie's Crisis Café** (see
p.395), now a gay bar but once home to Thomas Paine, English by
birth but perhaps *the* most important and radical thinker of the
American Revolutionary era, and from whose *Crisis Papers* the café
takes its name. Paine was significantly involved in the Revolution,
though afterwards regarded with suspicion by the government, especially after his active support for the French Revolution. By the time
of his death here, in 1809, he had been condemned as an atheist and
stripped of citizenship of the country he helped to found. Grove
Street meets Seventh Avenue at one of the Village's busiest junctions,
Sheridan Square – not in fact a square at all unless you count
Christopher Park's slim strip of green, but simply a wide and hazardous meeting ("the Mousetrap," some call it) of several busy
streets.

Christopher Street

Christopher Street, the main artery of the West Village, leads off
from here – traditional heartland of the city's gay community. The
square was named after one General Sheridan, cavalry commander
in the Civil War, and holds a pompous-looking statue to his memory,
but it's better known as scene of one of the worst and bloodiest of
New York's Draft Riots, when a marauding mob assembled here in
1863 and attacked members of the black community. It's said that if

it hadn't been for the protestations of local people they would have strung them up and worse; as it was they made off after sating the worst of their blood lust.

Not dissimilar scenes occurred in 1969, when the gay community wasn't as established as it is now. The violence on this occasion was down to the police, who raided the **Stonewall gay bar** and started arresting its occupants – for the local gay community the latest in a long line of harassments from the police. Spontaneously they decided to do something about it: word went around to other bars in the area, and before long the *Stonewall* was surrounded, resulting in a siege that lasted the better part of the night and sparked up again the next two nights. The riot ended with several arrests and a number of injured policemen. Though hardly a victory for their rights, it was the first time that gay men had stood up en masse to the persecutions of the police and, as such, represents a turning point in their struggle, formally instigating the gay rights movement and honored still by the annual **Gay Pride march** (held on the last Sunday in June).

Nowadays the gay community is much more a part of Greenwich Village life, indeed for most the Village would seem odd without it, and from here down to the Hudson is a tight-knit enclave – focusing on Christopher Street – of bars, restaurants and bookstores used specifically, but not exclusively, by gay men. The scene along the Hudson River itself, along and around West Street and the river piers, is considerably raunchier at night. By day, an attractive pedestrian walkway links Battery Park City up to the top of the Village and is bustling with bikers, runners and bladers who come for the river breezes and the view. Once the sun goes down, though, only the really committed or curious should venture (native New Yorkers, gay ones included, warn against going there at all). But on this far east stretch of Christopher, things crack off with the accent less on sex, more on a camp kind of humor. Among the more accessible gay bars, if you're strolling this quarter, are *The Monster* on Sheridan Square itself and *Marie's Crisis* on Grove Street (see opposite); for full gay listings, see p.394.

For more on gay New York, see p.45, Basics.

North of Washington Square

At the eastern end of Christopher Street is another of those car-buzzing, life-risking Village junctions where Sixth Avenue is met by **Greenwich Avenue**, one of the neighborhood's major shopping streets. Hover for a while at the romantic Victorian bulk of the **Jefferson Market Courthouse**, voted fifth most beautiful building in America in 1885, and built with all the characteristic vigor of the age. It hasn't actually served as a courthouse since 1946; indeed, at one time – like so many buildings in this city – it was branded for demolition. It was saved thanks to the efforts of a few determined Villagers, including e. e. cummings, and now lives out its days as the local library. Walk around behind for a better look, perhaps ponder-

ing for a moment on the fact that the adjacent well-tended allotment
was, until 1971, the **Women's House of Detention**, a prison known
for its abysmal conditions and numbering Angela Davis among its
inmates. Look out, also, for **Patchin Place,** a tiny mews whose neat,
gray rowhouses are yet another Village literary landmark, home to
the reclusive Djuna Barnes for more than forty years. Barnes's long-
time neighbor e. e. cummings used to call her "Just to see if she was
still alive." Patchin Place was at various times also home to Marlon
Brando, John Masefield, the ubiquitous Dreiser and O'Neill, and
John Reed (who wrote *Ten Days that Shook the World* here).

Across the road, **Balducci's** forms a Downtown alternative to its
Upper West Side rival, *Zabar's,* its stomach-tingling smells pricey but
hard to resist. Nearby, **Bigelow's Pharmacy** is possibly the city's oldest
drugstore and apparently little has changed; and, south a block and left,
West 8th Street is an occasionally rewarding strip of brash shoe stores,
tattoo parlors, and cut-price clothes stores. Up **West 10th Street** are
some of the best-preserved early nineteenth-century townhouses in the
Village, and one of particular interest at **no. 18**. The facade of this
house, which juts into the street, had to be rebuilt after the terrorist
Weathermen had been using the house as a bomb factory and one of
their devices exploded. Three of the group were killed in the blast, but
two others escaped and remained on the run until a few years ago.

For anyone not yet sated on architecture, a couple of imposing
churches are to be found by following 10th Street down as far as the
Fifth Avenue stretch of the Village, where the neighborhood's low-
slung residential streets lead to some eminently desirable apartment
buildings. On the corner stands the nineteenth-century **Church of the
Ascension**, a small, light church built by Richard Upjohn (the Trinity
Church architect), later redecorated by Stanford White and recently
restored outside and in, where a gracefully toned La Farge altarpiece
and some fine stained glass are on view. A block away, Joseph Wells's
bulky, chocolatey-brown Gothic revival **First Presbyterian Church** is
decidedly less attractive than Upjohn's structure, less soaring, heav-
ier, and in every way more sober, with a tower said to have been modeled on the one at Magdalen College Oxford, England. To look inside,
you need to enter through the discreetly added Church House (ring
the bell for attention if the door's locked). Afterwards you're just a few
steps away from the pin-neat prettiness of **Washington Mews**.

The East Village

The **East Village** is quite different in look, feel and tempo from its
western counterpart, Greenwich Village. Once, like the Lower East
Side proper which it abuts, a refuge of immigrants and always a
solidly working-class area, it became home to New York's nonconformist fringe in the earlier part of the twentieth century when, dis-
enchanted and impoverished by rising rents and encroaching

MANHATTAN

tourism, they left the city's traditional Bohemia and set up house here. Today the differences persist: where Greenwich Village is the home of Off-Broadway, the East Village plays stage to Off-Off; and rents, while rising fast, are still for the most part less than what you'll pay further west.

Over the years the East Village has hosted its share of famous artists, politicos and literati: W.H. Auden lived at 77 **St Mark's Place**, the neighborhood's main artery, and from the same building the Communist journal *Novy Mir* was run, numbering among its more historic contributors Leon Trotsky, who lived for a brief time in New York. Much later the East Village became the New York haunt of the Beats – Kerouac, Burroughs, Ginsberg et al – who, when not jumping trains across the rest of the country, would get together at Allen Ginsberg's house on East 7th Street for declamatory poetry readings and drunken shareouts of experience. Later, Andy Warhol debuted the Velvet Underground at the *Fillmore East*, which played host to just about every band you've ever heard of – and forgotten about – then became *The Saint* (also now-defunct), a gay disco known for its three-day parties. Still thriving, however, is the infamous club **CBGB** down on the Bowery – an atmospheric black hole with ratty chairs and tables, plastered with posters, and virtually unchanged in the twenty years and more since it hosted the then-relatively obscure likes of Patti Smith, Blondie, the Ramones, Talking Heads and the Police. Perhaps inevitably, a lot has changed over the last decade or so. Escalating rents have forced many people out, and the East Village isn't the hotbed of dissidence and creativity it once was; but the area remains one of downtown Manhattan's most vibrant neighborhoods, with boutiques, thrift stores, record shops, bars and restaurants, populated by a mix of old-world Ukrainians, students, punks, artists, skaters and burn-outs feeding continuous energy through the veins of the village streets 24 hours a day.

Around Cooper Square

To explore the East Village, it's best to use **St Mark's Place** as a base and branch out from there. Start at the western end, between Second and Third avenues, where radical bookstores and discount record shops compete for space with offbeat clothiers. **Seventh Street** boasts even more used clothing shops, while **6th Street** or "Indian Row" offers endless choices of all things curry. Countless, self-proclaimed priests of funky Manhattan chic mill around wolfing down pizzas or gazing lazily at the mildewed items for sale at the unofficial flea market across the road on **Cooper Square**, a busy crossroads formed by the intersection of the Bowery, Third Avenue and Lafayette Street. This is dominated by the seven-story brownstone mass of **Cooper Union**, erected in 1859 by a wealthy industrialist as a college for the poor, and the first New York structure to be hung on a frame of iron girders. It's best known as the place where, in 1860,

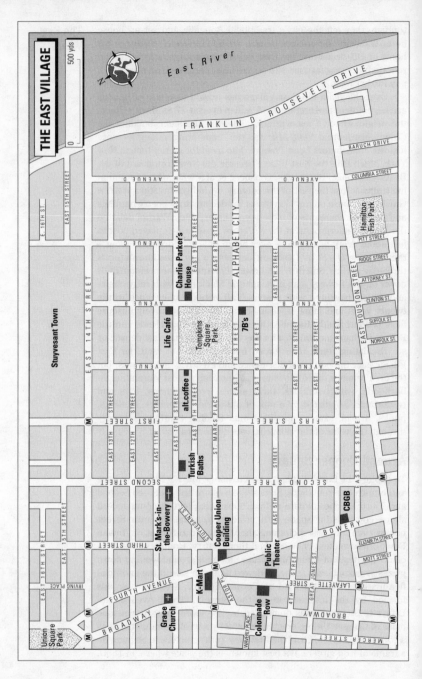

THE EAST VILLAGE

500 yds

0

East River

FRANKLIN D. ROOSEVELT DRIVE

BARUCH DRIVE

COLUMBIA STREET

E. 16TH ST

EAST 15TH STREET

AVENUE D

EAST 10TH STREET

Hamilton
Fish Park

PITT STREET

RIDGE STREET

Charlie Parker's
House

EAST 9TH STREET

AVENUE C

EAST 8TH STREET

EAST 5TH STREET

ATTORNEY ST

ALPHABET CITY

CLINTON ST

Stuyvesant Town

EAST 14TH STREET

AVENUE B

Life Café

Tompkins
Square
Park

7B's

EAST 7TH STREET

EAST 6TH STREET

AVENUE B

SUFFOLK ST

NORFOLK ST

EAST HOUSTON STREET

AVENUE A

EAST 5TH STREET

EAST 4TH STREET

EAST 3RD STREET

EAST 2ND STREET

EAST 13TH STREET

EAST 12TH STREET

EAST 11TH STREET

alt.coffee

EAST 10TH STREET

FIRST STREET

EAST 9TH STREET

ST. MARKS PLACE

FIRST STREET

AVENUE A

EAST 1ST STREET

Turkish
Baths

SECOND STREET

SECOND STREET

EAST 1ST STREET

St. Mark's-in-
the-Bowery

Cooper Union
Building

STUYVESANT ST

CBGB

BOWERY

ELIZABETH STREET

MOTT STREET

EAST 15TH STREET

THIRD STREET

Public
Theater

EAST 5TH STREET

ST STREET

JONES ST

EAST 16TH STREET

IRVING PLACE

FOURTH AVENUE

K-Mart

ASTOR PL

LAFAYETTE STREET

Grace
Church

BROADWAY

Colonnade
Row

WAVERLY PLACE

4TH STREET

GREAT JONES STREET

Union
Square
Park

BROADWAY

MERCER STREET

Abraham Lincoln wowed an audience of top New Yorkers with his so-called "might makes right" speech, in which he boldly criticized the pro-slavery policies of the southern states and helped propel himself to the White House later that year. Today, Cooper Union remains a working and prestigious art and architecture school, and has recently and sensitively been restored to nineteenth-century glory with a statue of the benevolent Cooper just in front.

Astor Place and around

Just beyond, feeding through to Broadway, is **Astor Place**, named after John Jacob Astor and, for a very brief few years, just before high society moved west to Washington Square, one of the city's most desirable neighborhoods. In the 1830s Lafayette Street in particular was home to the city's wealthiest names, not least John Jacob, one of New York's most hideously greedy tycoons, notorious for having won his enormous fortune by deceiving everybody right up to the president. It's said that when he was old and sick in his house here – no mean affair by all accounts but long since destroyed – although so weak he could accept no nourishment except a mother's milk and so fat he had to be tossed up and down in a blanket for exercise, his greed for money was such that he lay and dispatched servants daily to collect his rents. The old-fashioned kiosk of the Astor Place **subway station,** bang in the middle of the junction, discreetly remembers the man on the platforms, its colored reliefs of beavers recalling Astor's first big killings – in the fur trade. The orange-brick Astor Building (inhabited on its lower level by a *Starbucks Cafe*), with arched windows, is where John Jacob Astor III conducted business and warehoused textiles. It's now being converted into $1 million loft apartments, despite intense neighborhood resistance – one indication of just how fast the East Village is gentrifying. The giant cube just south of the subway station is the spinnable steel sculpture "Alamo" (by Bernard Rosenthal), in place since 1967. Get some mates to help you spin it around, if you can wade past the skateboarders who congregate there. More recently, this intersection has been developed not unlike a mall: on the northwest corner, **K-Mart,** discount retailer nonpareil, opened its doors in 1997 to the general horror of locals. The *K Café*, on the second floor, behind the underwear, has a great view of Astor Place and hosts occasional poetry readings. Really.

Today it's hard to believe that Astor Place was once home to wealth and influence. **Lafayette Street** is an undistinguished sort of thoroughfare, steering a grimy route between the East Village and, further down, SoHo, and all that's left to hint that this might once have been more than a down-at-heel gathering of industrial buildings is **Colonnade Row**, a strip of four 1832 Greek Revival houses with a Corinthian colonnade, now home to the Colonnade Theater. Opposite, the stocky brownstone and brick building was the Astor

**The East
Village**

Library, built with a bequest from John Jacob Astor starting in the 1850s and the first public library in New York. In 1965 the late Joseph Papp established here his **Public Theater**, something of a legend as forerunner of Off-Broadway theater and original venue of hit musicals like *Hair* and *A Chorus Line* and for years run by the man who pioneered *Shakespeare in the Park* (see p.408). On the ground floor, the newly opened, but definitely arrived, performance space/restaurant/bar, *Joe's Pub*, plays host to concerts, readings, and celebrity-studded private parties. The strip is also home to a number of expensive furniture shops, a fashion designer or two, and the *Village Voice*.

From the Public Theater you can either follow Lafayette Street down to Chinatown, or cut down Astor Place and turn right into Broadway. Two minutes away, **the corner of Washington Place and Greene Street** is significant. It was here in 1911 that one of the city's most notorious sweatshops burned to the ground, killing 125 women workers and spurring the State to institute laws forcing employers to take account of their workers' safety. Even now, though, there are sweatshops in New York in which safety conditions are probably little better. Back on Broadway, look north: filling a bend in the street is the lacy marble of **Grace Church**, built and designed in 1846 by James Renwick (of St Patrick's Cathedral fame) in a delicate neo-Gothic style. Dark and aisled, with a flattened, web-vaulted ceiling, it's one of the city's most successful churches – and, in many ways, one of its most secretive escapes.

Heading east

Walk east from here, cross back over Third Avenue and you come to another, quite different church – **St Mark's-in-the-Bowery**, a box-like structure originally built in 1799 but with a Neoclassical portico added half a century later. In the 1950s the Beat poets gave readings here, and it remains an important literary rendezvous with regular readings, dance performances and music recitals, as well as a traditional gathering point for the city's down-and-outs, desperately hanging on to their can collections (passport to a frugal meal that night) or slumped half-dead on drugs. Cross Second, on this stretch lined with Polish and Ukrainian restaurants, and you're on **10th Street,** formerly the heart of the East Village art scene, though nowadays local designers and antique shops dominate the street. Follow 10th Street east, past the old red-brick **Tenth Street Turkish Baths**, its steam and massage services active back into the last century. Make sure to take the time to wander through these streets where new shops and old treasures meld without effort. Just north at **11th Street** and 1st Avenue is *Veniero's*, a beloved village institution tempting the neighborhood with heavenly pastries since 1894. And further east you'll catch up with Avenue A, which now buzzes with cool thrift stores and trendy bars, Tompkins Square Park begins at 10th Street and further east is Alphabet City.

See p.488 for the lowdown on visiting the Tenth Street Turkish Baths.

Tompkins Square Park

Tompkins Square Park, isn't one of the city's most inviting spaces,
but has long acted as focus for the Lower East Side/East Village community and has a reputation as the city's center for political demonstrations and home of radical thought. It was here in 1874 that the
police massacred a crowd of workers protesting against unemployment, and here too in the 1960s that protests were organized and
made themselves heard. The late Yippie leader Abbie Hoffman lived
nearby, and residents like him, along with many incidents in the
square and on St Mark's Place (which joins the square on its western
side), have given the East Village its maverick name.

A few years back Tompkins Square Park became the focus of dissent against the gentrification of the East Village and Lower East
Side. From the mid-1980s, large chunks of real estate were bought
up, renovated and turned into condominiums, co-ops or high-rent
apartments for the new professional classes, much to the derision of
the old squatters and new activists. Until the early 1990s, the Square
was more or less a shantytown (known locally as "**Tent City**") for the
homeless, who slept on benches or under makeshift shelters on the
patches of green between the paths. In the winter, only the really
hardy or really desperate lived here, but when the weather got
warmer the numbers swelled, as activists, anarchists and all manner
of statement-makers descended upon the former army barracks from
around the country, hoping to rekindle the spirit of 1988. That was
the year of the Tompkins Square **riots**, when in August massive
demonstrations led to the police, badge numbers covered up and
nightsticks drawn, attempting to clear the park of people. In the
ensuing battle, many demonstrators were hurt, including a large
number of bystanders, and in the investigation that followed the
police were heavily criticized for the violence that had occurred. In
the summer of 1995 another riot erupted as police tried to evict a
group of squatters who had set up house in an empty apartment
building. This time, protesters were armed with video cameras and,
though heated, the riot never reached the proportions of the 1988
violence.

Despite this resistance, the park was overhauled, its winding pathways and playground restored: an 11pm lock-up and police surveil-
lance have secured the changes, though a mix of homeless people
still congregate on the benches and around the chessboards, and left-
overs from last night's parties can be found at most hours of the day.
One of the few things to see on the Square is a small **relief** just inside
the brick enclosure on the northern side, which shows a woman and
child gazing forlornly out to sea. It's a commemoration of a disaster
of 1904, when the local community, then mostly made up of German
immigrants, was decimated by the sinking of a cruise ship, the
General Slocum, in Long Island Sound, with the death of around a
thousand people. At no. 151 Avenue B, on the eastern side of the

park, is **Charlie Parker's house**, a simple whitewashed 1849 structure with a Gothic doorway. The Bird lived here from 1950 until
1954, when he died of a heroin overdose.

Alphabet City

East Houston Street divides the Lower East Side from the East
Village and from **Alphabet City**, one of the most dramatically revitalized areas of Manhattan. Here the island bulges out beyond the
city's grid structure, the extra avenues being named A to D. For
decades, Puerto Rican inhabitants have called this area *Loisaida*, a
hybrid bastardization of the words "Lower East Side" and the name
of a Puerto Rican town. Not many years ago this was a notoriously
unsafe corner of town, run by drug pushers and gangsters. People
told of cars lining up for fixes in the street, and the burned-out buildings were well-known safehouses for the brisk heroin trade. Most of
this was brought to a halt in 1983 with "Operation Pressure Point," a
massive police campaign to clean up the area and make it a place
where people would want to live. This has been achieved, with crime
down, bland brick housing going up all over, and the streets have
become the haunt of well-heeled young bohemians. Go beyond
Avenue C and you may get hassled, but – during the day at least –
you're unlikely to be mugged. It's worth a quick circuit around this
part of town just to see some of the murals and public art (like the
church decorated with mosaics and mirrors on Fifth Street between
avenues C and D). As on the Lower East Side, Hispanic residents
have recycled their predecessors' institutions: have a look at 638 E
6th St (between Avenues C and B), a synagogue converted into a colorful community center and Catholic church.

Walking down **Avenue A** away from Tompkins Square Park and
toward Houston Street, there are a number of hip thrift and clothes
shops, as well as a few trendy boutiques. However, the main attraction on Avenue A are the tons of great bars, restaurants, and bohemian cafés. Framing the park, there is *7B's* (7th St at Ave B), *Life Café*
(10th St at Ave B) and *alt.coffee* (9th St at Ave A). Meanwhile, on
Avenue B, a new selection of chic restaurants and bars have opened
up, and even further east on **Avenue C** there are a few eateries
emerging and students moving in, however, many blocks remain
home to many of the Latinos in the area, and *salsa* and *merengue*
boom from open windows, and old men gather in storefront social
clubs to sip drinks and play dominos. Further over, past **Avenue D**,
are the East River housing projects – a good bet if you are a drug
dealer, but not recommended otherwise.

Chapter 7

Chelsea and the Garment District

ew visitors bother with Chelsea and the Garment District, though the driving reason behind this – that there's nothing to do – has now been rendered obsolete. Chelsea is a low-built, sometimes seedy grid of tenements, rowhouses, and warehouses of very mixed character, with its heart between 14th and 23rd streets west of Broadway. It's here that the neighborhood has become a commercial player, mostly boosted by spillover from SoHo and the Village: stores, restaurants and a few notable tourist attractions pepper the scene, along with increasingly upmarket real estate. It then meanders – somewhat uninterestingly – up to 30th Street or so, leading to the Garment District, which muscles in between Sixth and Eighth avenues on 34th to 42nd streets and takes in the twin modern monsters of Penn Station and Madison Square Garden. The majority of people who come here do so for a specific reason – to catch a train or bus, to watch wrestling or basketball, or to work, and it's only a wedge of stores between Herald and Greeley Squares that attracts the out-of-towner.

Chelsea

Chelsea – named after the London neighborhood – took shape in 1830 thanks to its visionary owner, Clement Clarke Moore, better known as the author of the surprise poetic hit *A Visit from St Nick* (popularly known as *The Night before Christmas*). Anticipating New York's movement uptown, Moore laid out his land for sale in broad lots. Today, its historic districts are filled with affluent townhouse-dwellers though in fact the area never quite made it onto the short list of desirable places to be. Stuck as it was between Fifth Avenue and Hell's Kitchen and caught between the ritziness of the one and the poverty of the other, Manhattan's chic residential focus leapfrogged Chelsea, to the East 40s and 50s. The arrival of the slaughterhouses

CHELSEA & THE
GARMENT DISTRICT

and working-class poor who came to people the area sealed Chelsea's fate as a rough-and-tumble no-go area for decades. For years dreary facades and neglected buildings gave Chelsea its atmosphere of run-down residentialism, with the grid plan seeming too wide, the streets too bare to encourage visitors to linger.

The last few years, however, have seen a new Chelsea emerge and, with it, good reason to visit. This regeneration has been shaped by many forces, not the least of which has been the arrival of a large new gay community, seeking alternatives to the Village's soaring rents. The area's cafés, clubs and gyms teem with so-called "Chelsea Boys": neatly groomed and hypermuscled gay men, often in T-shirts and 501s. Also influential here is New York's peripatetic art scene. In the late 1980s and early 1990s, a number of respected galleries began making use of the large spaces available in the low-rise warehouses of Chelsea's western reaches, bringing a new cultural edge to

For more on the Chelsea gay scene see p.45.

the once down-and-out west side. And, taking advantage of large buildings that had fallen into disuse through the years, a retail boom of superstores along Sixth and Seventh avenues has brought many new shoppers into the neighborhood. Along the Hudson River, Chelsea Piers, an ultra-expensive sports complex development, is playing its part in the Chelsea boom. Despite the encroachment of these moneyed forces, many of the long-entrenched Hispanic families are staying put in their rent-controlled apartments, making today's Chelsea a good mix of the old world and the new, as fashionable restaurants, bars and shops catering to all persuasions grow up alongside leftover thrift stores, *bodegas* and grungy liquor stores.

Eighth Avenue and around

If Chelsea has a main drag it's **Eighth Avenue**, where the transformation of the neighborhood is most pronounced. A perfect route to wind your way up from the Village into the heart of Chelsea, Eighth Avenue between 14th and 23rd has a new retail energy to rival the fast-moving traffic in the street. A spate of new bars, restaurants, health food stores, gyms, bookstores and clothes shops have opened in the last five years in response to the new population. Eighth Avenue at 19th Street is home to one of the more important dance theaters in New York, the **Joyce**. The accomplished Feld Ballet is in residence here and a host of other touring companies keep this Art Deco style theater (complete with garish pink and purple neon signs) doing brisk business (see p.411). Even the Salvation Army store at 21st Street seems to have gotten into the act, with spruced up interiors and a fresh paint job.

If you detour west from Eighth Avenue, the cross streets between Ninth and Tenth avenues, specifically 20th, 21st and 22nd streets, constitute the **Chelsea Historic District** (although the label "district" is a bit grand for an area of three blocks), and boast a great variety of predominantly Italianate and Greek Revival rowhouses in brick and various shades of brownstone. Dating from the 1830s to the 1890s, they demonstrate the faith some early developers had in Chelsea as an up-and-coming New York neighborhood. Of particular historic note is 41 W 22nd St, where the area's first real estate developer, James Wells, resided. At 404 W 20th, the oldest house in the neighborhood stands out with its 1829 wooden-sided structure, predating Wells' all-brick constructions. The ornate iron fencing along this block heading west is original, and spectacular. However, the nineteenth century meets the modern era at the corner of West 22nd Street and Tenth Avenue in the Flash Gordonesque aluminium-sided **Empire Diner**, built in the 1930s.

Between Ninth and Tenth avenues, the block bounded by 20th and 21st streets contains one of Chelsea's oddities, the **General Theological Seminary** on Chelsea Square. Clement Clarke Moore donated an island of land to the institute in which he formerly taught, and today the harmonious assembly of ivy-clad Gothicisms surrounding a restive green feels like part of an Ivy League college campus. Though the buildings still house a working seminary, it's possible to explore the park on weekdays and Saturday at lunchtime, as long as you sign in and keep quiet (the entrance is via the modern building on Ninth Avenue). When Eighth Avenue reaches West 23rd Street, take a right toward Seventh Avenue to find one of the neighborhood's major claims to fame – the *Chelsea Hotel*.

The Chelsea Hotel

Chelsea has had several incarnations since its early nineteenth century development, the most colorful of which was arguably its heyday as Manhattan's Theater District in the 1870s and 1880s, before the scene moved uptown. Little remains of the theaters now, but the hotel that put up all the actors, writers and bohemian hangers-on was the first building in New York to be landmarked for both architectural and historical interest, in 1966. Originally built as a luxury cooperative apartment house, with New York's first penthouses and duplexes, in 1882, the building never attracted many affluent tenants, who still scorned cooperative living: but its soundproofed walls would eventually make it ideal for rock bands.

Since its conversion in 1905, the **Chelsea Hotel** has been the undisputed watering hole of the city's harder-up literati. Mark Twain and Tennessee Williams lived here and Brendan Behan and Dylan Thomas staggered in and out during their New York visits. Actresses Sarah Bernhardt and Lilly Langtry resided here around the turn of the century. Thomas Wolfe assembled *You Can't Go Home Again* from thousands of pages of manuscript he had stacked in his room, and in 1951 Jack Kerouac, armed with a specially adapted typewriter (and a lot of Benzedrine), typed the first draft of *On the Road* nonstop onto a 120-foot roll of paper. William Burroughs (in a presumably more relaxed state) completed *Naked Lunch* here, and Arthur C. Clarke wrote *2001: A Space Odyssey* while in residence. Arthur Miller (who was sick of having to put on a tie just to pick up his mail at the stylish *Plaza*), Paul Bowles and controversial artist Robert Mapplethorpe were also guests.

In the 1960s the *Chelsea* entered a wilder phase. Andy Warhol and his doomed protégés Edie Sedgwick and Candy Darling walled up here and made the film *Chelsea Girls* in (sort of) homage. Nico, Hendrix, Zappa, Pink Floyd, Patti Smith and various members of the Greatful Dead passed through, Bob Dylan wrote songs in and about it, and more recently, Sid Vicious stabbed Nancy Spungen to death in their suite, a few months before his own pathetic life ended with an overdose of heroin. The owner, in fact, had to divide their room into several smaller ones as visitors began to leave wreaths and candles outside the door. On a more cheerful note, the hotel inspired Joni Mitchell to write her song *Chelsea Morning* – a song that twanged the heartstrings of the young Bill and Hillary Clinton, who named their daughter after it (though there's no record of Chelsea ever having stayed in her eponymous hotel).

With a pedigree like this it's easy to forget the hotel itself, which has a down-at-heel Edwardian grandeur all of its own, and, incidentally is also an affordable place to stay (don't be surprised if you find yourself sharing the elevator with Didi Ramone); (see p.321).

West Chelsea

Further west along 23rd Street is one of New York's premier residences for those who believe in understated opulence. The **London Terrace Apartments**, two rows of apartment buildings a full city block long surrounding a private interior garden, had the misfortune of being completed in 1930 at the height of the Great Depression. Despite a swimming pool and doormen dolled out in London police uniforms, London Terrace stood empty for several years. Today, though, it's home to some of New York's trendier names, especially those from the fashion, art and music worlds. It was nicknamed "The Fashion Projects" by the *New York Times*, as much for its retinue of big-time designer, photographer and model residents (including Isaac Mizrahi, Annie Leibovitz and Deborah Harry) as for its ironic proximity to Chelsea's real housing projects just to the south and east.

Continue along 23rd Street and brave crossing the West Side Highway, and you'll reach one of Manhattan's most ambitious waterfront projects, **Chelsea Piers**, a $100 million, 1.7-million-square-foot development along four historic piers on the Hudson River. Opened in 1910 and designed by Warren and Whetmore (who were also at work on Grand Central Terminal at the time), this was the place where the great transatlantic liners would disembark their passengers (it was en route to the Chelsea Piers in 1912 that the *Titanic* sank). By the 1950s, however, the newer passenger ships were docking uptown at larger terminals, and the Piers were only used for freight. In the 1960s, the Piers fell into disuse and decay, and it is only recently that the area has been revived. The heart of the development is a huge sports complex, with two enclosed ice rinks and two open-air roller rinks, and a landscaped golf driving range, all open to the public (see Chapter 21, *Sports and Outdoor Activities*). There is also an impressive (though membership-only) indoor sports center, with basketball courts, batting cages, a rock-climbing wall, and more. Perhaps the best part of the development, though, is its emphasis on **public spaces**, including a waterfront walkway of over a mile and a pleasant water's edge park at the end of Pier 62. There's also Chelsea Brewing – a microbrewery – along with a few outdoor restaurants along the water. All feel somewhat contrived, but they still offer an away-from-the-city atmosphere and put you as close to the Hudson River as you can (or would want to) get.

Chelsea

The Chelsea Art Scene

Back over the West Side Highway and along 22nd Street are the galleries and warehouse spaces that house one of New York's most vibrant **art scenes**. The New York commercial art scene is in constant motion, always in search of better rents and the ultimate "cool" place to be and be seen. Galleries and exhibition spaces are already here, and more are on the way: nearly a dozen galleries have opened recently with an especially strong presence along West 22nd Street between Tenth and Eleventh avenues. The **Dia Center for the Arts**, a Chelsea pioneer, with space here since 1987, has its main exhibition gallery at 548 W 22nd St, featuring a dramatic **open-air** space on top where the *Rooftop Urban Park* opened in 1991. The effect of the two-way glass mirror pavilion is remarkable, its impact in constant flux as it works with the changing light and visual effects of the sky. More on the galleries of Chelsea in Chapter 15.

East Chelsea

The eastern edge of Chelsea has become a busy strip of commerce, concentrated mostly along **Sixth Avenue**, where a crush of moderately priced clothing stores, such as Old Navy and Today's Man, have driven the likes of local institution Barney's to bankruptcy – although places like Barney's seem to have a habit of surviving (see "Macy's" opposite). A neighborhood giant that's doing just fine is the obligatory Barnes & Noble superstore, between 21st and 22nd streets, though more interesting is A Different Light, around the corner on 19th Street, the country's largest gay and lesbian bookstore. Heading north above 23rd Street, away from Chelsea's heart, the city's largest **antiques market** (and surrounding junk sales) takes place on weekends in a few open-air parking lots centered around Sixth Avenue and 26th Street (see Chapter 24, "Shops and Markets"). The area around 28th Street is Manhattan's **Flower Market**: not really a market as such, more the warehouses where potted plants and cut flowers are stored before brightening offices and atriums across the city. Nothing marks the strip, and you come across it by chance, the greenery bursting out of drab blocks, blooms spangling storefronts and providing a welcome touch of life to a decidedly industrial neighborhood. For the record, West 28th Street was the original **Tin Pan Alley**, where music publishers would peddle songs to artists and producers from the nearby theaters. When the theaters moved, so did the publishers.

MANHATTAN

The Garment District and around

A few streets north, Sixth Avenue collides with Broadway at **Greeley Square**, an overblown name for what is a trashy triangle celebrating Horace Greeley, founder of the *Tribune* newspaper. Perhaps he deserves better: known for his rallying call to the youth of the nineteenth century to explore the continent ("Go West, young man!"), he also supported the rights of women and trade unions, commissioned a weekly column from Karl Marx and denounced slavery and capital punishment. His paper no longer exists (though one of its descendants is the bored traveler's last resort, the *International Herald Tribune*) and the square named after him is one of those bits of Manhattan that looks ready to disintegrate at any moment.

Herald Square

Herald Square faces Greeley Square in a headlong replay of the battles between the *Herald* newspaper and its arch rival Horace Greeley's *Tribune*. During the 1890s this was the Tenderloin area, with dance halls, brothels and rough bars like *Satan's Circus* and the *Burnt Rag* thriving beside the elevated railway that ran up Sixth Avenue. When the *Herald* arrived in 1895 it gave the square a new name and dignity, but it's perhaps best recognized as the square George M. Cohan asked to be remembered to in the famous song. These days it wouldn't fire anyone to sing about it, saved only from unkempt sleaziness by Macy's on the corner below.

Macy's

Macy's is the all-American superstore. Until the mid-1970s it contented itself by being the world's largest store (which it remains); then, in response to the needs of the high-rolling 1980s yuppie lifestyle it went fashionably and safely upmarket. When the economy went into a tailspin in 1990 Macy's fortunes declined dramatically, burdened by overexpansion and debt: New Yorkers were stunned when word went around that it was near to closure, and the ensuing media coverage was about as intense as if the mayor had sold the Statue of Liberty to Iraq. Fortunately Macy's scrambled out of bankruptcy by the skin of its teeth, with a debt restructuring plan that allowed it to continue financing its famed annual Thanksgiving Day Parade, one of the most famous and best-attended Manhattan parades, marked by its giant cartoon-character balloons and the arrival of Santa. Like all great stores Macy's is worth exploring – there's an amazing food emporium plus a reconstruction of P.J. Clarke's bar in the basement – though it may be wise to leave all forms of spending power at home. Next door, the tacky glitz of the **Manhattan Mall** can't hold a candle to Macy's.

Exploring the Garment District

In a way this part of Broadway is the shopfront to the **Garment District**, a loosely defined pool between 34th and 42nd streets and Sixth and Eighth avenues. From this patch three-quarters of all the women's and children's clothes in America are made, though you'd never believe it: outlets are strictly wholesale with no need to woo customers, and the only clues to the industry inside are the racks of clothes shunted around on the street and occasional bins of offcuts that give the area its look of an open-air rummage sale. Every imaginable button, bow, boa and bangle is on display – ideal if you like looking at things you can hardly believe are still manufactured. Anti-fur zealots should steer clear of West 30th Street (though a few blocks down, it's more Garment District than Chelsea), where peeking from industrial-sized barrels in cooled storefronts are the heads and tails of whole minks and foxes, waiting their turn to become winter coats.

One of the benefits of walking through this part of town is to take advantage of the designer's "**sample sales**," where floor samples and models' used castoffs are sold to the public at cheap prices, though if you can't afford a $750 Donna Karan dress, you probably still can't afford it at $450 (more on sample sales in Chapter 24). The Garment District is another New York neighborhood that has undergone a recent resurgence. An energetic Business Improvement District partnership has gone out of its way to splash up a revitalized Garment District that has seen more and more of its industry coming back to New York from overseas for local manufacturing. Brighter street lighting and better security help make the area safer for walking through, especially at night – which, despite the clean-up, is still all you're likely to be doing here.

Madison Square Garden and around

The Garment District is something to see in passing: the most prominent landmark in this part of town is the **Pennsylvania Station and Madison Square Garden complex**, a combined box and drum structure that swallows up millions of commuters in its train station below and accommodates the Knicks basketball and Rangers hockey teams (along with their fans) above. There's nothing memorable about Penn Station: its subterranean levels seem to have all the grime and just about everything else that's wrong with the subway, and to add insult to injury the original Penn Station, demolished to make way for this, is now hailed as a lost masterpiece, one that brought an air of dignity to the neighborhood and created the stage for the ornate **Post Office** and other elaborate Belle Epoque structures that followed. One of McKim, Mead and White's greatest designs, the original Penn Station reworked the ideas of the Roman Baths of Caracalla to awesome effect, its grand arcade lavishly covered with floors of pink marble and walls of pink granite. Glass tiles in its main waiting room allowed the light from the glass roof to flow through to the trains and platforms below: "Through it one entered the city like a god . . . One scuttles in now like a rat," mourned an observer.

For details of how to get tickets for the Knicks and Rangers games, see p.426.

Photos of the older building can be seen in the Amtrak waiting area of the new Penn Station. And you can walk back in time at the new entryway to the Long Island Railroad ticketing area on 34th

---

Old Penn Station and the Landmarks Preservation Law

When, in 1963, the old Penn Station was demolished in order to expand the Madison Square Garden sports complex, the notion of conservation was about ten years away from crystallizing into the broad-based middle-class power group that was to wield so much force in New York through the 1970s and 1980s. Despite the vocal complaints of a few, the forces of "modernization" were then all-powerful – so much so that hardly anything was saved of the original building: even a number of its carefully crafted statues and interiors became landfill for New Jersey's Meadowlands complex just across the Hudson River.

It was public disgust with the destruction of the station – along with the Singer Building, an early, graceful skyscraper in the Financial District that was demolished around the same time – that brought about the passing of the Landmarks Preservation Law. It ensures that buildings granted landmark status – for their aesthetic value, historical importance or associations – cannot be destroyed or even altered.

Street at Seventh Avenue: one of the old station's four-faced time pieces now hangs from the tall steel-framed glass structure which is itself reminiscent of the original building. Andrew Leicester's *Ghost Series* was commissioned in 1994 and lines the walls of the new corridor: terra cotta wall murals saluting the Corinthian and Ionic columns of the old Penn Station, as well as a rendering of *Day & Night*, an ornate statue surrounding a clock that once welcomed passengers at the old station's entrance. Also of note in the Long Island Railroad ticketing area: look above your head for a Maya Lin sculpture depicting the immeasurability of time in a subtly crafted ellipsis with random number patterns.

One further, more whimsical reminder of the old days is the **Pennsylvania Hotel** on the corner of Seventh Avenue and 33rd Street: a main venue for Glenn Miller and other big swing bands of the 1940s, it keeps the phone number that made it famous – 736-5000: under the old system, PENNsylvania 6-5000, the title of Miller's affectionate hit.

The General Post Office

Immediately behind Penn Station, the **General Post Office** is a McKim, Mead and White structure that survived, a relic from an era when municipal pride was all about making statements – though to say that the Post Office is monumental in the grandest manner still seems to underplay it. The old joke is that it had to be this big to fit in the sonorous inscription above the columns – "Neither snow nor rain nor heat nor gloom of night stays these couriers from the swift completion of their appointed rounds" – a claim about as believable as the official one that the Manhattan postal district handles more mail than Britain, France and Belgium combined. There's still a working post office branch here, though the main sorting stations

For full practical details on the Port Authority Terminal see p.14.

have moved into more modern space further west. For the last five years a plan has been bandied around to utilize the building as a new entrance to Penn Station, perhaps as some sort of expiation for the destruction of the original station. Whether the scheme will come to anything, time will tell – bureaucracy and money troubles seem to have tied this plan up indefinitely.

The **Port Authority Terminal Building** at 40th Street and Eighth Avenue is another sink for the area, though its poor reputation as a haven for down-and-outs is belied by its appearance these days as a spruced-up and efficiently run modern bus station. Greyhound leaves from here, as do regional services out to the boroughs, and (should you arrive in the early hours) it's a remarkably safe place, station staff keeping the winos and weirdos in check. Harder to believe is that the station holds an exceptional **bowling alley**, should you immediately have the urge upon arrival (see p.430 for more details). To the west of Port Authority, at no. 330 42nd St, is the **McGraw-Hill Building**, a greeny-blue radiator that architects raved over: "proto-jukebox modern," Vincent Scully called it. The lobby should definitely be seen.

Chapter 8

Union Square, Gramercy Park and Murray Hill

B roadway forms a dividing line between Chelsea and the
Garment District to the west and the area that comprises
Union Square, Gramercy Park and Murray Hill to the east,
bounded by 14th Street to the south and 42nd Street to the north. It
is here, between the great avenues – Third, Park and Fifth – that midtown Manhattan's skyscrapers begin to rise from the low-lying buildings, with perhaps the greatest of them all, the Empire State
Building, marking the junction of 34th Street and Fifth Avenue.

Union Square and around

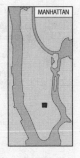

Union Square, where Broadway, Fourth and Park avenues meet, was
once the elegant center of the city's theatrical and shopping scene,
but has been better known more recently as gathering point for political demonstrations and, up until the mid-1980s, a seedy haunt of
dope pushing and street violence. It's much more inviting now, the
spill of shallow steps enticing you in to stroll the paths, feed the
squirrels and gaze at its array of statuary – something no one would
have dared to a few years back. As for the statues, they include an
equestrian figure of George Washington, a Lafayette by Bartholdi
(more famous for the Statue of Liberty), and, at the center of the
park, a massive flagstaff base whose bas-reliefs symbolize the forces
of Good and Evil in the Revolution.

On Mondays, Wednesdays, Fridays and Saturdays, the park plays
host to the city's best and most popular **greenmarket** on its northern
edge. Farmers and other food producers from upstate New York,
Long Island, New Jersey and even from Pennsylvania Dutch country
sell fresh fruit and vegetables, baked goods, cheeses, eggs, meats,
plants and flowers, all of very high quality (an advisory committee
sets up and enforces stringent rules on the growers and keeps out
wholesalers and brokers). During the warmer months (mid-April to

Union Square and around

mid-Oct), the *Luna Park Café* sets up shop in the beautifully refurbished **Pavilion** at the park's north end. Run by the trendy *Coffee Shop* business across the road, the all-outdoors restaurant makes Union Square nights a touch more swanky with music and twinkling white lights elegantly setting off the darkness.

The square itself is flanked by some good cafés and restaurants and quite a mixture of buildings, not least the **American Savings Bank** on the eastern edge, of which only the grandiose columned exterior survives. The pedimented building just south of here is the former **Tammany Hall**, the once notorious headquarters of the Democratic Party, decorated with a Native American headdress, while the narrow building almost opposite was Andy Warhol's original Factory. The **Consolidated Edison** (or ConEd) building, off the southeast corner, the headquarters of the company responsible for providing the city with energy and those famous steaming sewer

access holes, is, with its campanile, an odd premonition of the Metropolitan Life Building a few blocks further north.

North of Union Square

North and east of Union Square, walk the six blocks of **Irving Place** toward Gramercy Park. Irving Place was named for Washington Irving, the early-nineteenth century American writer whose creepy tale of the Headless Horseman, *The Legend of Sleepy Hollow*, has itself passed into legend. Although he never actually lived here, this seven-block strip bears his name and a bust of Irving, the first American writer to earn a living from his craft, stands in front of the turn-of-the-century Washington Irving High School across the street.

Pulitzer Prize winning short-story writer, O. Henry did in fact live along this stretch, at what was once no. 55, and there's also the landmark *Pete's Tavern* (18th St and Irving Place) – one of New York's oldest bars, in business since 1864. The bar promotes itself as the place where O. Henry dreamed up and wrote *Gift of the Magi*. Though that fact is in dispute, the legend serves the place and its atmosphere well.

The stretch of **Broadway** north and west of here was part of "Ladies' Mile," a line of fancy stores and boutiques whose heyday was the mid-nineteenth century. High-end shopping jumped over to Fifth Avenue around the turn of the century, but a few sculpted facades and curvy lintels remain, including Lord & Taylor's Victorian wedding-cake of a building with several exterior balcony levels, standing catercorner at 901 Broadway. Nearby on East 20th Street is **Theodore Roosevelt's birthplace** at no.28 (Wed–Sun 9am–5pm; $2), or at least a reconstruction of it: a rather sober 1858 mansion containing many original furnishings, some of Teddy's hunting trophies and a small gallery documenting the president's life, viewable on an obligatory guided tour.

Gramercy Park

Cross dingy Park Avenue South and Manhattan's clutter breaks into the ordered open space of **Gramercy Park**, a former swamp reclaimed in 1831. Residential London in spirit, this is one of the city's best squares, its center beautifully planted and, most noticeably, completely empty for much of the day – principally because the only people who can gain access are those rich or fortunate enough to live here. Still, stroll around the edge for a walk through a place that was once the center of New York's theater scene. Inside the gates is a statue of the actor Edwin Booth (brother of Lincoln's assassin, John Wilkes Booth) in the guise of Hamlet, one of his most famous roles. (Ironically, Edwin rescued Lincoln's son, Robert, from a train accident years before his brother's fateful action.) In 1888,

Booth turned his parkside home – 16 Gramercy Park S – into **The Players**, a private club with additions by architect (and Gramercy Park resident) Stanford White. Back then, actors and theater types were not accepted into regular society, so Booth created the club for play and socializing – neglecting, however, to admit women, who were only allowed in at the shockingly late date of 1989. At the same time, Booth established a Theater Library in the club to chronicle the history of the American stage. Later members included the Barrymores, Irving Berlin, Frank Sinatra, and (oddly) Sir Winston Churchill. Tours are given now by appointment only (☎228-7610; $5 adults, $3.50 students and seniors).

Next door to The Players is the equally patrician **National Arts Club**, which moved in 1906 to this location, Victorianized in the 1870s by Central Park designer Calvert Vaux at the request of owner Governor Samuel Tilden, and studded with terra-cotta busts of Shakespeare, Milton and Franklin among others. Collectors Henry Frick, J.P. Morgan and Teddy Roosevelt were prominent members of this institution, which was founded to support American artists at home. Unfortunately, the priceless members' dining room, with its vaulted glass dome and stained-glass window panels, is off-limits to the public, but rotating exhibitions can be viewed.

Have a walk around the square to get a look at the many early-nineteenth century townhouses and later buildings which housed celebrated figures too numerous to mention here. The **School of Visual Arts**, no. 17 Gramercy Park S, occupies the former home of Joseph Pulitzer; while at the northeastern corner of the square, **no. 38**, is the mock Tudor building in which John Steinbeck, then a struggling reporter for the now-defunct *New York World*, lived from 1925 to 1926 (it took getting fired from that job to plunge him into fiction). At 52 Gramercy Park N, the starting point of Lexington Avenue, is the imposing 1920s bulk of the old-fashioned **Gramercy Park Hotel**, whose staff is strangely unaware that Mary McCarthy, a very young John F. Kennedy and Humphrey Bogart with first wife Mayo Methot have been among its elite residents. Lining Gramercy Park West is a splendid row of brick Greek Revival **townhouses** from the 1840s whose ornate wrought-iron work is reminiscent of New Orleans' French Quarter; James Harper, of the publishing house, Harper & Row, lived at no. 4.

For details on the Gramercy Park Hotel *see p.322.*

To the east of Gramercy Park, **Peter Cooper Village** and **Stuyvesant Town** are perhaps the city's most successful examples of densely-packed urban housing, their tall, angled apartment buildings siding peaceful, tree-lined walkways. It's worth knowing, though, that this is private not public housing, and the owners, Metropolitan Life, were accused of operating a color-bar when the projects first opened. Certainly, the contrast with the immigrant slums a little way downtown isn't hard to detect. At the northeast corner of Peter Cooper Village stands **the Asser Levy Recreation Center**, named after the country's first Jewish citizen and kosher butcher, who arrived in 1654. The most notable of the many city-run athletic centers, the Asser Levy building was originally constructed in 1908 as a bathhouse – modeled on the Roman public baths – for the huddled, unwashed masses (the tenements of the East Side supposedly had but one bath for every 79 families). Abandoned in the 1970s, it was reopened as a city gym in 1990; the indoor skylit pool is anchored by a marble dolphin statue that doubles as a fountain. As with all city gyms, membership costs $25 a year (see p.430).

A few blocks west, the land that makes up **Stuyvesant Square** was a gift to the city from its governor and, like Gramercy Park, the park space in the middle was modeled on the squares of London's Bloomsbury. Though partially framed by the buildings of **Beth Israel Medical Center** and cut down the middle by the bustle of Second Avenue, it still retains something of its secluded quality, especially on the western side. Here there's a smatter of elegant terrace, the strangely colonial-looking **Friends' Meeting House**, and, next door, the weighty brownstone **Church of St George** – best known as the place where financier J.P. Morgan used to worship.

Lexington Avenue begins its long journey north at Gramercy Park: if you're heading uptown on the East Side from here, you'll pass the lumbering **69th Regiment Armory** at 25th Street – site in 1913 of the notorious Armory Show which brought modern art to New York for the first time (see "Twentieth-century American art" in *Contexts*) – to Manhattan's most condensed ethnic enclave, **Little India**. Blink, and you might miss this altogether: most of New York's 100,000 Indians live in Queens, yet there's still a sizeable handful of restaurants and fast-food places – far outnumbered by those down on East 6th Street – and a pocket of sweet and spice shops.

Madison Square

To the north and west of Gramercy Park, where Broadway and Fifth Avenue meet, is **Madison Square**, by day a maelstrom of dodging cars and cabs, buses and pedestrians but, mainly because of the quality of the buildings and the clever park-space in the middle, possessing a monumentality and neat seclusion that Union Square has long since lost. The **Flatiron Building** (originally the Fuller Construction Company, later renamed in honor of its distinctive shape), set cheekily on a triangular plot of land on the square's southern side, is one of the city's most famous buildings, evoking images of Edwardian New York. Its thin, tapered structure creates unusual wind currents at ground level, and years ago policemen were posted to prevent men gathering to watch the wind raise the skirts of women passing on 23rd Street. The cry they gave to warn off voyeurs – "23 Skidoo!" – has passed into the language. It's hard to believe that this was the city's first true skyscraper (although this is hotly debated), hung on a steel frame in 1902 with its full twenty stories dwarfing all the other structures around. Not for long though: the **Metropolitan Life Company** soon erected its clock tower, in 1902, on the eastern side of the square which, height-wise at least, put the Flatiron to shame.

Next door is the Corinthian-columned marble facade of the **Appellate Division** of the New York State Supreme Court, reso lutely righteous with its statues of Justice, Wisdom and Peace turning their weary backs on the ugly, black-glass New York Life Annex behind. The grand structure behind that, the **New York Life Building** proper, was the work of Cass Gilbert, creator of the Woolworth Tower downtown. It went up in 1928 on the site of the original **Madison Square Garden** – renowned scene of drunken and debauched revels of high and Broadway society. This was the heart of the theater district in those days and the place where the Garden's architect, **Stanford White**, was murdered by Harry Thaw. White, a partner in the illustrious architectural team of McKim, Mead and White, who designed many of the city's great Beaux Arts buildings, such as the General Post Office, the old Penn Station and Columbia University, was something of a rake by all accounts, with a reputation for womanizing and fast living. His romance with Thaw's future-wife Evelyn Nesbit, a Broadway showgirl (who was still unattached at the time), had been well publicized – even to the extent that the naked statue of the goddess Diana on the top of the building was said to have been modeled on her. Millionaire Thaw was so humiliated by this that one night he burst into the roof garden, found White, surrounded as usual by doting women and admirers, and shot him through the head. Thaw was carted away to spend the rest of his life in mental institutions, and his wife's showbusiness career took a tumble: she resorted to drugs and prostitution, dying in 1961 in Los Angeles.

So ended one of Madison Square's more dramatic episodes. Madison Square Garden has moved twice since then, first to a site on Eighth Avenue and 50th Street, finally to its present location in a hideous drum-shaped eyesore on the corner of 32nd Street and Seventh Avenue. There is, however, one reminder of the time when this was New York's theaterland – the **Episcopal Church of the Transfiguration** just off Fifth Avenue on 29th Street. This, a dinky rusticated church set back from the street, brown brick and topped with copper roofs, has since 1870 been the traditional place of worship of showbiz people. It was tagged with the name "The Little Church Around the Corner" after a devout but under-standing priest from a nearby church had refused to marry a theatrical couple and sent them here. It's an intimate building, furnished throughout in warm wood and with the figures of famous actors (most notably Edwin Booth as Hamlet) memorialized in the stained glass.

The Empire State Building

MANHATTAN

Further up Fifth Avenue is New York's prime **shopping territory**, home to most of the city's heavyweight department stores. Macy's is just a short stroll away on Herald Square; filling the space between 38th and 39th streets are the lavish headquarters of Lord & Taylor (see p.454). The **Empire State Building** – overshadowing by far the lure of such consumer items – occupies what has always been a prime site. Before it appeared this was home to the first *Waldorf Astoria Hotel*, built by William Waldorf Astor as a ruse to humiliate his formidable aunt, Caroline Schermerhorn, into moving Uptown. The hotel opened in 1893 and immediately became a focus for the city's rich – in an era, the "Gay Nineties," when "Meet me at the *Waldorf*" was the catchphrase to conjure with.* However, though the reputation of the *Waldorf* – at least for its prices – endures to this day, it didn't remain in its initial premises for very long, moving in 1929 to its current Art Deco home on Park Avenue.

Few would dispute the elegance of what took its place. The Empire State Building remains easily the most potent and evocative symbol of New York, and has done since its completion in 1931. The ground-breaking took place just three weeks before the stock market crash in October 1929, but despite the Depression, the building proceeded full steam ahead and came in well under budget after just fourteen months in the making. Soon after, King Kong clung to it and dis-tressed squealing damsels while grabbing at passing planes; in 1945 a plane crashed into the building's 79th story (see overleaf); while in 1979, two Englishmen parachuted from its summit to the ground, only to be carted off by the NY Police Department for disturbing the peace. More recently came the darkest moment in the building's his-tory: in February 1997 a man opened gunfire on the observation deck, killing one tourist and injuring seven others; as a result there is tighter security upon entrance, with metal detectors, package scan-ners and the like.

Its 103 stories and 1472 feet – toe to TV mast – make it the world's third tallest building, but the height is deceptive, rising in stately tiers with steady panache. Inside, its basement serves as an underground marbled shopping mall, lined with newsstands, beauty parlors, cafés, even a post office, and is finished everywhere with delicate Deco touches. After wandering around you can visit the **Guinness World of Records Exhibition** – though, frankly, you'd be better advised to save your money for the assault on the top of the tower. Also worth miss-ing is the **New York Skyride** on the second floor. The ten-minute sim-

*It was the consort of Mrs Schermerhorn Astor, Ward Macallister, who coined the label "The Four Hundred" to describe this crowd. "There are only about four hundred people in fashionable New York society," he asserted. "If you go outside that number you strike people who are either not at ease in a ballroom or else make other people not at ease. See the point?"

The plane that hit the Empire State Building

On the morning of Saturday, July 28, 1945, Lieutenant Colonel William Franklin Smith Jr was flying a B-25 bomber in thick fog above the Hudson River. A veteran of 34 bombing missions over Germany, he was impatient to get his plane on the ground. Having been told he would have to wait three hours for a landing slot at Newark airport, he falsely declared having "official business" at La Guardia – with the intention of diverting to Newark once he'd been cleared. He'd already strayed into La Guardia's busy airspace, so he was given immediate clearance to land at Newark to get the aircraft out of the way. Realizing this meant his flying across Manhattan, La Guardia air control sent out a warning message: *"At present we can't see the top of the Empire State Building..."*.

Neither could Smith. At 9.49am his twelve-ton plane smashed into the side of the 79th floor of the building, killing Smith, his co-pilot and a 20-year-old sailor who had been given permission to fly home on the plane to console his parents, who had learned that his brother had been killed in the Pacific. The Empire State swung back and forth in a two-foot arc as the plane smashed a twenty-foot hole in the wall. Fuel from the ruptured tanks flooded out and set two floors on fire. The port engine smashed straight through the building, exited the south wall and tumbled down to demolish a penthouse apartment on 34th Street. The other engine fell into the Empire State's elevator shaft, severing the cables and plunging the elevator and its attendant, Betty Lou Oliver, 1000 feet down to a subcellar: despite a broken back and legs, she survived. Ten others in the building were killed; had the accident happened on an ordinary working day, many more would undoubtedly have died.

ulated flight (daily: 10am–10pm; $11.50, $8.50 kids and seniors; ☎279-9777) soars above the skyscrapers, through Times Square, down Coney Island's Cyclone, and among other New York landmarks, but will leave the weak-hearted merely dizzy and the strong-willed wondering why they spent their money on this.

Getting to the top

The first elevators, alarmingly old and rickety if you've previously zoomed to the top of the World Trade Center, take you to the 86th floor, summit of the building before the radio and TV mast was added. The **views** from the outside walkways here are as stunning as you'd expect – better than those from the World Trade Center since Manhattan spreads on all sides. On a clear day visibility is up to eighty miles, but, given the city's pollution, on most it's more likely to be between ten and twenty. If you're feeling brave, and can stand the wait for the tight squeeze in the single elevator, you can go up to the Empire State's last reachable zenith, a small cylinder at the foot of the TV mast which was added as part of a harebrained scheme to erect a mooring post for airships – a plan subsequently abandoned after some local VIPs almost got swept away by the wind, and a second attempt at mooring, made by a Navy blimp, resulted in the

Skyscrapers

Along with Chicago and Hong Kong, Manhattan is one of the best places in the world in which to see **skyscrapers**, its puckered, almost medieval skyline of towers the city's most familiar and striking image. In fact there are only two main clusters of skyscrapers, but they set the tone for the city – the Financial District, where the combination of narrow streets and tall buildings forms slender, lightless canyons, and midtown Manhattan, where the big skyscrapers, flanking the wide central avenues between the 30s and the 60s, have long competed for height and prestige.

The term "skyscraper" was coined in 1890 by one John J. Flinn, describing the evolving style of building in turn-of-the-century Chicago, since when the two cities have always been battling to produce the tallest building. It's uncertain which city actually built the first real skyscraper, but the first generally recognized instance in New York was the Flatiron Building on Madison Square, designed in 1902, not least for the obvious way its triangular shape made the most of the new iron-frame technique of construction that had made such structures possible. A few years later, in 1913, New York clinched the title of the world's tallest building with the sixty-story Woolworth Building on Broadway, later going on to produce such landmarks as the Chrysler and Empire State buildings, and, more recently, the World Trade Center – though the latter's status as world's tallest building has since been usurped.

Styles have changed over the years and have perhaps been most influenced by the stringency of the city's zoning laws, which early in the century placed restrictions on the types of building permitted. At first skyscrapers were sheer vertical monsters, maximizing the floor space possible from any given site but with no regard to how this affected the neighboring buildings, which more often than not were thrown into shade by the new arrival. In order to stop this happening the city authorities invented the concept of "air rights," putting a restriction on how high a building could be before it had to be set back from its base. This forced skyscrapers to be designed in a series of steps – a law most elegantly adhered to by the Empire State Building, which has no less than ten steps in all, but it's a pattern you will see repeated all over the city.

Due to the pressure on space in Manhattan's narrow confines and the price of real estate, which makes speculatively constructing office buildings so lucrative, the skyscrapers continue to rise, and it's always possible to see some slowly rising steel frame somewhere in the city. Traditionally the workers who brave the heights to work on the skyscrapers, lifting the girders into place and bolting them together, often bent into impossible positions, squatting or balancing on thin planks, are Native Americans, due to a supposedly remarkable head for heights. They still make up forty percent of such workers in New York, and even eighty floors up don't wear any kind of safety harness, claiming it restricts their movements too much.

As for the future, there seems to be almost no limit to the heights that are envisaged, the most notable plan being Donald Trump's bid to reclaim the tallest-building title for New York with a new structure on the Upper West Side well over a hundred stories high. Whether or not this comes off, it's certain that even in times of recession skyscrapers remain the "machines for making money" that Le Corbusier originally claimed they were.

The Empire State Building

flooding of 34th Street. Once the wind got a hold of the Navy blimp, they had to drop the water used as ballast to balance, and the "blimp port" was permanently closed. You can't go outside and the extra sixteen stories don't really add much to the view, but you will have been to the top. The building's management has decided to close the 102nd floor observatory on weekends during the summer, because the crowds make the smallish space unmanageable, so go during the week if you want to hit the very top (daily 9.30am–midnight; $6, $3 for under 12s and seniors; ☎ 736-3100).

Murray Hill

Back down to earth, Fifth Avenue carves its way up the island. East down 34th Street lies **Murray Hill**, a tenuously tagged residential area of statuesque canopy-fronted apartment buildings, but with little apart from its WASPish anonymity to mark it out from the rest of midtown Manhattan. Built on one of the few remaining actual hills in the lower part of Manhattan island, Murray Hill is residential by design – no commercial building was allowed until the 1920s, when greedy real estate interests successfully challenged the rule in court. Like Chelsea further west, it lacks any real center, any sense of community and, unless you work, live or are staying in Murray Hill, there's little reason to go there at all; indeed you're more likely to pass through without even realizing it. Its boundaries are indistinct, but lie somewhere between Fifth Avenue and Third and, very roughly, 32nd to 40th streets, where begins the rather brasher commercialism of the Midtown business district.

When Madison Avenue was on a par with Fifth as the place to live, Murray Hill came to be dominated by the **Morgan family**, the crusty old financier J.P. and his offspring, who at one time owned a clutch of property here. Morgan junior lived in the **brownstone** on the corner of 37th Street and Madison (now headquarters of the American Lutheran Church), his father in a house that was later pulled down to make way for an extension to his **library** next door, the mock but tastefully simple Roman villa that still stands and is commonly mistaken for the old man's house. (If you've read the book or seen the film *Ragtime*, you'll remember that Coalhouse Walker made this fundamental mistake when attempting to hold Pierpoint Morgan hostage.) In fact, Morgan would simply come here to languish among the art treasures he had bought up wholesale on his trips to Europe: manuscripts, paintings, prints and furniture. Here, during a crisis of confidence in the city's banking system in 1907, he entertained New York's richest and most influential men night after night until they agreed to put up the money to save what could have been the entire country from bankruptcy, giving up $30 million himself as an act of good faith. You can visit the library's splendid interior and priceless collection; see p.294.

As you continue up Madison Avenue the influence of the Morgans rears its head again in the shape (or at least the name) of **Morgan's Hotel** between 37th and 38th streets – the last word in ostentatious discretion, not even bothering to proclaim its presence with the vulgarity of a sign. Stop in at its elegant bar for a drink if you've got the cash, and for details on how much it costs to sleep here, see p.323.

Chapter 9

Midtown Manhattan

You're likely to spend a fair amount of time in midtown Manhattan. It's here that most of the city's hotels are situated, here too that you'll most likely arrive – at Penn Station or Grand Central Station, or the Port Authority Bus Terminal. And the area is in many ways the city's center. Cutting through its heart is Fifth Avenue, New York's most glamorous (and most expensive) street, with the theater strip of Broadway and the cleaned-up razzle-dazzle of Times Square to the west and the fashionable Madison Avenue to the east.

On either side of Fifth Avenue are corporate headquarters of various kinds, a skyward wave that creates Manhattan's rollercoaster appearance. If you have any interest in architecture (or simply sensation) you'll want to stroll this sector, looking in and up at such delights as the **Chrysler**, **Citicorp** and **Seagram** buildings and the magnificent **Rockefeller Center**. Fifth Avenue itself is where to check out New York's most venerable sites of conspicuous consumption. And of course this is also a major museum strip, with the **Museum of Modern Art** and a host of lesser collections (like the **American Craft Museum** across the street) grouped together around 53rd Street (see the individual museum accounts in Chapter 15 for more on these).

West of Fifth Avenue, in particular west of Broadway, the area has a distinctly different appeal. It's not in the least classy, but **Times Square** and diagonal **Broadway**, framed by colorful theatres and cinemas, does feel like the city's nerve center. Unfortunately or fortunately, depending on how you look at it, Times Square and **42nd Street** heading west, previously the city's sleaze center, is now a jumble of 24-hour neon, old theaters and new megastores much rehabilitated by Disney, whose efforts have been met with a mixed reception. Further west is Clinton, better known as **Hell's Kitchen**, a bit bereft attraction-wise but with a welcome edge, at least around its main strips, that the Broadway area has now lost.

East along 42nd Street

42nd Street is one of the few streets in the world to have an entire musical named after it. With good reason, too, for you *can* do anything on 42nd Street, highbrow or low, and it's also home to some of the city's most characteristic buildings, ranging from great Beaux Arts palaces like **Grand Central Station**, to charge-card traps like the **Grand Hyatt Hotel**. Surrounded by superb architecture and breathtaking views down the great avenues, this section of New York is one of the most characterful – and by extension characteristic – parts of the city.

The New York Public Library

The New York Public Library (Center for the Humanities) on the corner of 42nd and Fifth Avenue is the first notable building on 42nd Street's eastern reaches: Beaux Arts in style and faced with white marble, it is the headquarters of what is arguably the largest public library system in the world. Its steps, framed by the majestic reclining lions which are the symbol of the NYPL, act as a meeting point and general hangout for pockets of people throughout the year. To tour the library either walk around yourself or take one of the tours (Mon–Sat 11am & 2pm; free), which last an hour and give a good all-round picture of the building. The traditional highlight of such a tour, or just poking around by yourself, is the large coffered **Reading Room** at the back of the building. Trotsky worked here on and off during his brief sojourn in New York just prior to the 1917 Revolution, introduced to the place by his friend Bukharin, who was bowled over by a library you could use so late in the evening. The opening times are considerably less impressive now, but the library still boasts a collection among the five largest in the world: 88 miles of books stored in eight levels of stacks beneath this room and running the length of Bryant Park (behind the library), which alone covers half an acre.

Grand Central Terminal

Back outside, push through the crush crossing Fifth Avenue and walk east down 42nd Street to where Park Avenue lifts off the ground at Pershing Square to weave its way around the solid bulk of **Grand Central Terminal**. This, for its day, was a masterful piece of urban planning: after the electrification of the railways made it possible to reroute trains underground, the rail lanes behind the existing station were sold off to developers and the profits went towards the building of a new terminal – constructed around a basic iron frame but clothed with a Beaux Arts skin. Since then Grand Central has taken on an almost mythical significance, even if today its major traffic is mainly commuters speeding out no further than Connecticut or

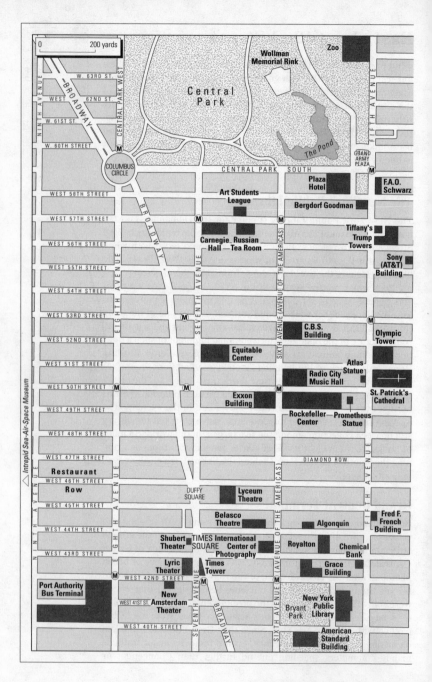

Westchester County, it remains in essence what it was in the nine-teenth century – symbolic gateway to an undiscovered continent.

You can either explore Grand Central on your own or take one of the excellent free **tours** run by the Municipal Arts Society (see p.26). But for the efforts of a few dedicated New Yorkers (and the late Jackie Onassis, whose voice was no doubt a godsend), Grand Central would-n't be here at all, or at least it would be much uglified. It was only deemed a National Landmark in 1978, after the railroad's plan to cap the whole thing with an office building was quashed. The most spectac-ular aspect of the building is its size, now cowed by the soaring airplane wing of the **Met Life Building** (formerly known as the Pan Am building, headquarters of the now-defunct airline) behind, but still no less impressive in the main station concourse. This is one of the world's finest and most imposing open spaces, 470 feet long and 150 feet high, the barrel-vaulted ceiling speckled like a Baroque church with a paint-ed representation of the winter night sky, its 2500 stars shown back to front: "As God would have seen them," the painter is reputed to have remarked. Stand in the middle and you realize that Grand Central rep-resents a time when stations were seen as appropriately dwarfing pre-ludes to great cities – "a city within a city," as it has been called. Walking around the resounding marble corridors is an elegant experience.

In 1995 the MTA (Metropolitan Transit Association) embarked on a massive renovation of Grand Central, cleaning the ceiling and restoring faded treasures, such as the massive chandeliers. The plans were not without commercial thrust – they included four new restau-rants overlooking the main concourse – but the terminal's more eso-teric reaches remain (thankfully) intact, and the main concourse has even been improved with the addition of a second sweeping staircase to counterbalance the first (both staircases were in the original plans but only one was built due to lack of funds). The restoration still isn't finished; the opening of the main dining concourse has been delayed while the experts work out how to ventilate the kitchens. But it is undeniably a success and makes wandering around Grand Central more of a pleasure than ever. Search out the **Tennis Club** on the third floor, which used to be a CBS studio but now offers up court-time for a membership fee of several thousand dollars a year; and the **Oyster Bar** (see also p.369) in the vaulted bowels of the station is one of the city's most highly regarded seafood restaurants, serving something like a dozen varieties of oyster and cram-packed every lunchtime with the Midtown office crowd. Just outside is something that explains why the *Oyster Bar*'s babble is not solely the result of the big-mouthed business people who eat there: you can stand on opposite sides of any of the vaulted spaces and hold a conversation just by whispering, an acoustic fluke that makes this the loudest eatery in town.

Around the Chrysler Building

Across the street, the former **Bowery Savings Bank** echoes Grand Central's grandeur – like its sister branch downtown, extravagantly

lauding the twin shibboleths of sound investment and savings. A
Roman-style basilica, it has a floor paved with mosaics, the columns
are each fashioned from a different kind of marble and, if you take a
look at the elevator doors (through a door on the right), you'll see
bronze bas-reliefs of bank employees hard at various tasks. But then,
this kind of lavish expenditure is typical of the buildings on this
stretch of 42nd Street, which is full of lobbies worth popping inside
for a glimpse. Start with the **Philip Morris Building**, across from
Grand Central on the corner of Park Avenue and 42nd, which contains a small offshoot of the Whitney Museum of American Art (see
box p.282); the immense vaulted-glass atrium-cum-sculpture court
is a bit showy but impressive nonetheless. The **Grand Hyatt Hotel**
back on the north side of 42nd Street is another notable instance of
excess, perhaps the best example in the city of all that is truly vulgar
about contemporary American interior design, its slushing water-
falls, lurking palms and gliding escalators representing plush-carpet-
ed bad taste at its most meretricious.

The **Chrysler Building**, across Lexington Avenue, is a different
story, dating from a time (1930) when architects carried off prestige
with grace and style. This was for a fleeting moment the world's
tallest building – until it was surpassed by the Empire State in 1931
– and, since the rediscovery of Art Deco a decade or so ago, has
become easily Manhattan's best loved. Its car-motif friezes, jutting
gargoyles, stainless steel pinnacle and crown bring the Manhattan
skyline as close as it comes to Fritz Lang's, 1926 sci-fi thriller,
Metropolis. Its designer, William Van Alen, indulged in a feud with
an erstwhile partner who was designing a building at 40 Wall St at
the same time. Each were determined to have the higher skyscraper:
Alen secretly built a stainless steel spire inside the Chrysler's crown;
when 40 Wall St was finally topped out a few feet higher than the
Chrysler, Alen popped the 185-foot spire out through the top of the
building, and won the day.

The Chrysler corporation moved out some time ago, and for a
while the building was left to degenerate by a company that didn't
wholly appreciate its spirit, but now a new owner has pledged to
keep it lovingly intact. The **lobby**, once a car showroom, is for the
moment all you can see (there's no observation deck), but that's
enough in itself, with opulently inlaid elevators, walls covered in
African marble and on the ceiling a realistic, if rather faded, study of
work and endeavor, showing airplanes, machines and brawny
builders who worked on the tower.

Beyond the Chrysler Building

Flanking each side of Lexington Avenue on the southern side of 42nd
Street are two more buildings worthy of a studied walk past. The
Chanin Building on the right is another Art Deco monument, cut
with terra-cotta carvings of leaves, tendrils and sea creatures. More

interestingly, the design on the outside of the weighty **Mobil Building** across the street is deliberately folded so as to be cleaned automatically by the movement of the wind.

East of here is the somber yet elegant former **Daily News Building**, whose stone facade fronts a surprising Deco interior – bastardized somewhat in the 1950s, when white marble replaced the original golden marble, an annex was added to the building, and the bronze elevator doors were replaced with stainless steel ones. The most impressive remnant of the original 1923 decor is a large globe encased in a lighted circular frame (with updated geography), made famous by *Superman*, in which the Daily News Building appropriately housed the Daily Planet. Various bronze meteorological devices are displayed on the walls, which were once connected to a weather station on the roof. The marble floor is inlaid with a system of intersecting bronze lines that detail the distances between NY and other major cities. The tabloid paper after which the building is named has recently moved its headquarters downtown to West 33rd Street. Take note that the building is not open on weekends.

Further east still, 42nd Street grows more tranquil. And on the left, between Second and First avenues, is one of the city's most peaceful (if surreal) spaces of all – the **Ford Foundation Building**. Built in 1967, this was the first of the atriums that are now commonplace across Manhattan, and it is certainly the most lush. Structurally, it's a giant greenhouse, gracefully supported by soaring granite columns and edged with two walls of offices visible through the windows. Workers, in turn, can look down on the subtropical garden, which changes naturally with the seasons. This was one of the first attempts at creating a "natural" environment, and it's astonishingly quiet. 42nd Street is no more than a murmur outside, and all you can hear is the burble of water, the echo of voices and the clipped crack of feet on the brick walkways, mingled with the ripe smell of the atrium's considerable vegetation. The indoor/outdoor experience here is one of New York City's great architectural coups.

East to the United Nations

At the east end of 42nd Street, steps lead up to the 1925 ensemble of **Tudor City**, which rises behind a tree-filled parklet. With its coats of arms, leaded glass and neat neighborhood shops, it is the very picture of self-contained residential respectability, and an official historic district. Trip down the steps from here and you're plum opposite the **United Nations** building, which rose up after World War II. Some see the United Nations complex as one of the major sights of New York; others, usually those who've been there, are not so complimentary. For, whatever the symbolism of the UN, there can be few buildings that are quite so dull to walk around. What's more, as if to rationalize the years of UN impotence in war and hunger zones worldwide, the (obligatory) guided tours emphasize that the

UN's main purpose is to promote dialogue and awareness rather than enforcement. So the organization itself moves at a snail's pace – bogged down by regulations and a lack of funds – which is the general feel of the tour as well.

For the determined, the complex consists of three main buildings – the thin glass-curtained slab of the **Secretariat**, the sweeping curve of the **General Assembly Building** and, just between, the low-rise connecting **Conference Wing**. It went up immediately after World War II and was finished in 1963, the product of a suitably international team of architects which included Le Corbusier – though he pulled out before the building was completed. Daily **tours** leave from the monumental General Assembly lobby (First Avenue at 46th Street; tours leave every 20min, 9.15am–4.45pm, and last an hour; $7.50, $4.50 students; ☎963-7539) and take in the main conference chambers of the UN and its constituent parts, the foremost of which is the General Assembly Chamber itself, expanded a few years back to accommodate up to 179 members' delegations (though there are at present only 159). It's certainly impressive, even given (or perhaps due to) its 1960s feel, though it does seem wasted on a body that meets only three months each year. Other council chambers situated in the Conference Building include the Security Council, the Economic and Social Council and the Trusteeship Council – all similarly retro (note the clunky machinery of the journalists' areas) and sporting some intriguing Marxist murals.

Once you've been whisked around all these, with the odd stop for examples of the many artifacts that have been donated to the UN by its various member states – rugs, sculptures, a garishly colored mosaic based on a Norman Rockwell painting (courtesy of Nancy Reagan) – the tour is more or less over and will leave you in the basement of the General Assembly Building. Here a couple of shops sell ethnic items from around the world and a **post office** will make you a UN postage stamp to prove that you've been here – though bear in mind it's only valid on mail posted from the UN. There's also a **restaurant** that serves a daily lunch buffet with dishes from different UN member countries, but the food, like the tour, is fairly taste-free.

Where the UN has real class is in its beautiful **gardens**, with their river view and modern sculpture. Carpets of daffodils and flowering cherry trees in spring and an extensive rose garden in summer make them worth a visit.

Fifth Avenue

Fifth Avenue bowls ahead from 42nd Street with all the confidence of the material world. It's been a great strip for as long as New York has been a great city and its name is an automatic image of wealth and opulence. Here that image is very real: all that considers itself suave and cosmopolitan ends up on Fifth, and the shops showcase New York's most opulent consumerism. Fifth rewards with some of

MANHATTAN

the city's best architecture: the boutiques and stores are just the icing on the cake.

In its lower Midtown reaches **Fifth Avenue** isn't really as alluring as the streets off. The only eye-catcher is the **Chemical Bank** on the southwest corner of 43rd, an early glass 'n' gloss box that teasingly displays its vault (no longer used) to passersby, a reaction against the fortress palaces of earlier banks. Around the next corner, West 44th Street contains several old guard New York institutions. The Georgian-style **Harvard Club** at no. 27, easily spotted of an evening by the paparazzi hanging around outside, has interiors so lavish that lesser mortals aren't allowed to enter. But it's still possible to enjoy the **New York Yacht Club**, its playfully eccentric exterior of bay windows molded as ships' sterns, and with waves and dolphins completing the effect of tipsy Beaux Arts fun. For years this was home of the Americas' Cup, a yachting trophy first won by the schooner *America* in 1851 and held here (indeed bolted to the table) until lost to the Australians amid much loss of face in 1984. Now though, for the time being at least, it's back in its place.

"Dammit, it was the twenties and we had to be smarty." So said Dorothy Parker of the group known as the Round Table, whose members hung out at the recently renovated **Algonquin Hotel** at no. 59 and gave it a name as the place for literary visitors to New York – a name that to some extent still endures. The Round Table used to meet regularly here, a kind of American-style Bloomsbury Group of the city's sharpest-tongued wits, and the club had a reputation for being as egotistical as it was exclusive. Times have changed considerably, but over the years the *Algonquin* has continued to attract a steady stream of famous guests, most with some kind of literary bent, not least Noel Coward (whose table someone will point out to you if you ask nicely), Bernard Shaw, Irving Berlin and Boris Karloff. The bar is one of the most civilized in town.

Taking over from the *Algonquin* as the lunch and supper spot for the literary set in the 1990s is the **Royalton** (44 W 44th St), a Philippe Starck-designed hotel whose design, style and Deco atmosphere bring the word "trendy" to new heights. Step into the nearly unmarked hotel for a peek at the lobby, keeping an eye out for Armani-clad doormen, whose snappy appearance belies the fact that behind the padded doors is a hotel, not a private club.

West 47th Street, or Diamond Row (described more fully on p.160), is another surprise off Fifth Avenue, but before hitting that, duck into the **Fred F. French Building** at 551 Fifth Ave. The colorfully tiled mosaics on its outside are a mere prelude to the combination of Art Deco and Near Eastern imagery ranged on the vaulted ceiling and bronze doors of the lobby. Also striking (and indicative of another era on Fifth) is the facade of what was once **Charles Scribner's Sons bookstore** at 597 Fifth Ave. The black and gold iron-and-glass storefront that seems to have fallen from an

Edwardian engraving has been given historic landmark status. All the more anachronistic, then, that the building now houses a United Colors of Benetton; the lone remnant of its literary history is a basement café-cum-salon that hosts frequent readings.

Fifth
Avenue

Rockefeller Center

Central to this stretch of Fifth is a complex of buildings that, more than any other in the city, succeeds in being utterly self-contained and at the same time in complete agreement with its surroundings. Built between 1932 and 1940 by John D. Rockefeller, son of the oil magnate, **Rockefeller Center** is one of the finest pieces of urban planning anywhere: office space with cafés, a theater, underground concourses and rooftop gardens work together with an intelligence and grace rare in any building then or now. It was a combination that shows every other city-center shopping mall the way, leaving you thinking that Cyril Connolly's snide description – "that sinister Stonehenge of Economic Man" – was way off the mark.

You're lured into the Center from Fifth Avenue down the gentle slope of the **Channel Gardens** (whimsically named because they divide La Maison Française and the British Empire Building) to the **GE Building** (formerly the RCA Building, but renamed when General Electric took it over a decade ago), focus of the Center. Rising 850 feet, its monumental lines match the scale of Manhattan itself, though softened by symmetrical setbacks to prevent an overpowering expanse of wall. At its foot the **Lower Plaza** holds a sunken restaurant in the summer months, linked visually to the downward flow of the building by Paul Manship's sparkling *Prometheus*; in winter it becomes an ice rink, giving skaters a chance to show off their skills to passing shoppers. More ponderously, a panel on the eastern side relates John D. Rockefeller's priggish credo in gold and black.

Inside, the GE Building is no less impressive. In the lobby José Maria Sert's murals, *American Progress* and *Time*, are faded but eagerly in tune with the 1930s Deco ambience – presumably more so than the original paintings by Diego Rivera, which were removed by John D.'s son Nelson when the artist refused to scrap a panel glorifying Lenin. A leaflet available from the lobby desk details a **self-guided tour** of the Center.

Among the many office ensembles in the GE Building is **NBC Studios**, home of the network's 25-year-old late-night comedy show *Saturday Night Live* (which simply refuses to die) among other programs, and it's possible to tour these (one-hour tours leave every fifteen minutes, Mon–Sat 8am–7pm, Sun 9.30am–4pm, tours leave from The NBC Experience Store on 49th St between 5th and 6th aves; $17.50 adults, $15 for children; ☎664-4000). For an early-morning TV thrill, gawk at NBC's *Today Show*, which broadcasts live from 7am to 9am weekday mornings from glass-enclosed studios

*See pp.30–31
for the full
story on TV
show tapings.*

in the new NBC News Building on the southwest corner of 49th and
Rockefeller Plaza. The TV studios here also hand out free tickets for
TV show recordings, which can be a great way of seeing the best and
tacky worst of the nation's television.

Radio City Music Hall

Just northwest of Rockefeller Center, at Sixth Avenue and 50th
Street, is **Radio City Music Hall**, an Art Deco jewel box that represents the last word in 1930s luxury. The staircase is regally resplendent with the world's largest chandeliers, the Stuart Davis murals
from the men's toilets are now in the Museum of Modern Art, and the
huge auditorium looks like an extravagant scalloped shell or a vast
sunset: "Art Deco's true shrine," as Paul Goldberger (former architecture critic of the *New York Times*) rightly called it. Believe it or
not, Radio City was nearly demolished in 1970: the outcry this
caused resulted in its being designated a National Landmark. To
explore, take a tour from the lobby (Mon–Sat 10am–5pm, Sun
11am–5pm; $13.75; ☎632-4041 or Madison Square Garden's
administrative offices, ☎465-6000).

North toward Central Park

A further bit of sumptuous Deco is the **International Building** on
Fifth Avenue, whose black marble and gold leaf give the lobby a
sleek, classy feel dramatized by the ritz of escalators and the view
across Lee Lawrie's bronze *Atlas* out to **St Patrick's Cathedral**.
Designed by James Renwick and completed in 1888, St Patrick's sits
bone-white among the glitz like a misplaced bit of moral imperative,
and seems the result of a painstaking academic tour of the Gothic
cathedrals of Europe: perfect in detail, lifeless in spirit. Holiness can
be found however, in the peaceful **Lady Chapel** at the back of the
Cathedral; here the graceful, simple, altar captures the mysticism
that its big sister lacks. Nevertheless, St Patrick's is an essential part
of the Midtown landscape, and one of the most important churches
(perhaps the most important Catholic church) in America. The
Gothic details are perfect and the Cathedral is certainly striking –
and made all the more so by the backing of the sunglass-black
Olympic Tower. Across the street, at 611 Fifth Ave (the corner of
50th St), are the striped awnings of **Saks Fifth Avenue**, one of the
last of New York's premier department stores to relocate in Midtown
(from Herald Square). With its columns on the ground floor and yellow brick road-like pathways through fashion collections, Saks is
every bit as glamorous as it was in 1922.

North of 52nd Street, Fifth Avenue's ground floors quickly shift
from airline offices to all-out glitz, with Cartier, Gucci, and Tiffany
and Co. among many gilt-edged names. If you're keen to do more
than merely window-shop, Tiffany's is worth a perusal, its sooth-

ing green marble and weathered wood interior best described by
Truman Capote's fictional Holly Golightly: "It calms me down
right away . . . nothing very bad could happen to you there."
Notable too are Steuben Glass, 715 Fifth Ave at 56th Street, a
showcase of delicate glass and crystalware perfectly displayed;
and Japan's largest department store chain, Takashimaya, at no.
683, where East meets West, expensively (try the authentic tea
room). Further along, the famed rich man's department store
Bergdorf Goodman, at no. 754, offers a wedding-cake interior, all
glossy pastels, chandeliers, pink curtains and the like. Just next
door are the glittering (and virtually priceless) window displays of
Harry Winston Jewelers, beloved of Princess Di and countless others. Newcomers to this prestigious area are the hardly-needed-but-
here-anyway Coca-Cola Store at 711 Fifth Ave, and on the northeast corner of Fifth and 57th, a three-story Warner Brothers paraphernalia store.

*For listings of
all Fifth
Avenue's best
stores, see
Chapter 24,
"Shops and
Markets."*

Just when you thought the glitter had gone about as far as it could
there's **Trump Tower** at 57th Street, whose outrageously overdone
atrium is just short of repellent – perhaps in tune with those who frequent the glamorous designer boutiques here. Perfumed air, polished marble paneling and a five-story waterfall are calculated to
knock you senseless with expensive "good" taste: it's all very entertaining. But the building is clever, a neat little outdoor garden is
squeezed high in a corner, and each of the 230 apartments above the
atrium gets views in three directions. Donald Trump, the property
developer all New York liberals love to hate, lives here, along with
other worthies of the hyper-rich crowd.

Topping all of this off is **F.A.O. Schwarz**, a block north at 745
Fifth Ave at 58th Street, a colossal emporium of children's toys
which welcomes visitors with an animatronics-like clock endlessly
repeating the frustratingly catchy jingle *welcome to our world of
toys*. Fight the kids off and there's some great stuff to play with –
once again, the best (and biggest, including gas-powered cars, life-
sized stuffed animals and Lego creations) that money can buy.

Across 58th Street, Fifth Avenue broadens to **Grand Army Plaza** and
the fringes of Central Park. Looming impressively on the plaza is,
aptly enough, the copper-edged **Plaza Hotel**, recognizable from its
many film appearances. Have a wander around to soak in the (slightly faded) gilt-and-brocade grandeur; the inside, including the snazzy
Oak Room bar, is worth a snoop too. The hotel's reputation was built
not just on looks, but on lore: it boasts its own historian, keeper of
such bits as when legendary tenor Enrico Caruso, enraged with the

---

The other great attractions as you walk north toward the park are the muse-
ums – chiefly the Museum of Modern Art (11 W 53rd St), American Craft
Museum (40 W 53rd St) and the nearby Museum of TV & Radio (25 W 52nd
St). For full accounts of each, see pp.273, 288 and 293 respectively.

loud ticking of the hotel's clocks, stopped them all by throwing a shoe at one (they were calibrated to function together). The Plaza apologized with a magnum of champagne.

To continue on, go back down to **57th Street** and head east toward Madison – going northward, it's an elegant stretch of exclusive shops and art galleries, albeit with the odd superstore. One dubious, though unmissable, attraction at no. 6 is **Nike Town**, an unrestrained celebration of the sneaker that needs to be seen to be believed. The overly earnest attempt at a museum, laden with sound-effects, space-age visuals and exhibits inlaid into the floor, walls and special display cases – including one that holds a custom-designed gold-plated athletic shoe worn by Michael Jordan – can't mask the commercialism.

MANHATTAN

Midtown East

If there is a stretch that is immediately and unmistakably New York it is the area that runs east from Fifth Avenue in the 40s and 50s. The great avenues of **Madison**, **Park**, **Lexington** and **Third** reach their richest heights as the skyscrapers line up in neck-cricking vistas, the streets choke with yellow cabs and office workers, and Con Edison vents belch steam from old heating systems. More than anything else it's buildings that define this part of town, the majority of them housing anonymous corporations and supplying excitement to the skyline in a 1960s build-'em-high glass-box bonanza. Others, like the Sony Building and the Citicorp Center, don't play that game; and enough remains from the pre-box days to maintain variety.

Madison Avenue

Madison Avenue shadows Fifth with some of its sweep but less of the excitement. A few good stores – notably several specialized in men's haberdashery, shoes and cigars – sit behind the scenes here, like Brooks Brothers, on the corner of East 44th Street, traditional clothiers to the Ivy League and inventors of the button-down collar. Between 50th and 51st streets the **Villard Houses** merit more than a passing glance, a replay of an Italian palazzo (one that didn't quite make it to Fifth Avenue) by McKim, Mead and White. The houses have been surgically incorporated into the *Helmsley Palace Hotel* and the interiors polished up to their original splendor.

Madison's most interesting buildings come in a four-block strip above 53rd Street: **Paley Park**, on the north side of East 53rd between Madison and Fifth, is a tiny vest-pocket park complete with mini-waterfall and a transparent tunnel through whose sides water pours. Around the corner the **Continental Illinois Center** looks like a cross between a space rocket and a grain silo. But it's the **Sony Building** (formerly the AT&T Building), between 55th and 56th

streets, that grabbed all the headlines. A Johnson–Burgee collabora-
tion, it followed the postmodernist theory of eclectic borrowing from
historical styles: a modernist skyscraper sandwiched between a
Chippendale top and a Renaissance base – the idea being to quote
from great public buildings and simultaneously return to the fantasy
of the early part of this century. The building has its fans, but in popular opinion the tower doesn't work, and it's unlikely to stand the test
of time. Perhaps Johnson should have followed the advice of his
teacher, Mies van der Rohe: "It's better to build a good building than
an original one." The first floor is well worth ducking into to soak in
the brute grandeur. It now houses a music store and a spate of interactive exhibits on record production and video-game production
(ceremoniously named the Sony Wonder Technology Lab). There is
also the requisite coffee bar and deli abutting a rather somber public
seating area.

The **IBM Building** next door at 590 Madison has a far more user-
friendly plaza. In the calm glass-enclosed atrium, tinkling music,
tropical foliage, the ubiquitous coffee bar and comfortable seating
area make for a far less ponderous experience. Across 57th Street, as
the first of Madison's boutiques appear, the **Fuller Building** is worth
catching – black-and-white Art Deco, with a fine entrance and tiled
floor. Cut east down 57th Street to find the **Four Seasons Hotel**,
notable for its I.M. Pei-designed foyer and lobby, ostentatious in its
sweeping marble.

Park Avenue

"Where wealth is so swollen that it almost bursts," wrote Collinson
Owen of **Park Avenue** in 1929, and things aren't much changed: corporate headquarters jostle for prominence in a triumphal procession
to capitalism, pushed apart by Park's broad avenue that was built to
cover elevated rail tracks. Whatever your feelings, it's one of the city's
most awesome sights. Looking south, everything progresses to the
high altar of the New York Central Building (now rechristened the
Helmsley Building), a delicate, energetic construction with a lewdly
excessive rococo lobby. In its day it formed a skilled punctuation
mark to the avenue, but had its thunder stolen in 1963 by the Met Life
Building, see p.144, (formerly the Pan Am Building) that looms
behind and above (with Grand Central on the other side). Bauhaus
guru Walter Gropius had a hand in designing this, and the critical con-
sensus is that he should have done better. As the headquarters of the
now-defunct international airline, the building's profile meant to suggest an aircraft wing, and the blue-gray mass certainly adds drama to
the cityscape; though whatever success the Met Life scores, it robs
Park Avenue of the views south it deserves and needs, sealing 44th
Street and drawing much of the vigor from the buildings all around.
Another black mark was the building's rooftop helipad, closed in the
1970s after a helicopter undercarriage collapsed shortly after land-

ing, causing a rotor to sheer off and kill four passengers who had just got off, as well as injuring several people on the ground.

Despite Park Avenue's power, an individual look at most of the skyscrapers reveals the familiar glass box, and the first few buildings to stand out do so exactly because that's what they're not. Wherever you placed the solid mass of the **Waldorf Astoria Hotel** (between 49th and 50th) it would hold its own, a resplendent statement of Art Deco elegance. Duck inside to stroll through a block of vintage Deco grandeur, sweeping marble and hushed plushness. If you're tempted, it's a smidgen cheaper than the comparable competition, with double rooms between $200 and $300. Crouching across the street, **St Bartholomew's Church** is a low-slung Byzantine hybrid that by contrast adds immeasurably to the street, giving the lumbering skyscrapers a much-needed sense of scale. That hasn't stopped the church fathers from wanting to sell the valuable air rights to real estate developers; so far landmark preservationists have prevented them from wrecking one of the few remaining bits of individuality in this part of the city. The spiky-topped **General Electric Building** behind seems like a wild extension of the church, its slender shaft rising to a meshed crown of abstract sparks and lightning strokes that symbolizes the radio waves used by its original occupier, RCA. The lobby (entrance at 570 Lexington) is yet another Deco delight.

Among all this it's difficult at first to see the originality of the **Seagram Building** between 52nd and 53rd streets. Designed by Mies van der Rohe with Philip Johnson, and built in 1958, this was the seminal curtain-wall skyscraper, the floors supported internally rather than by the building's walls, allowing a skin of smoky glass and whiskey-bronze metal (Seagram is a distiller), now weathered to a dull black. In keeping with the era's vision, every interior detail down to the fixtures and lettering on the mailboxes was specially designed. It was the supreme example of modernist reason, deceptively simple and cleverly detailed, and its opening caused a wave of approval. The **plaza**, an open forecourt designed to set the building apart from its neighbors and display it to advantage, was such a success as a public space that the city revised the zoning laws to encourage other high-rise builders to supply plazas. The result was the windswept anti-people places now found all over down- and midtown Manhattan, and a lot of pallid Mies copies, boxes that alienated many people from "faceless" modern architecture. Forty years on, the city is revamping its regulations to forestall the construction of any more of these buildings, and the idea of allowing architects to build higher in exchange for public plazas may soon be a thing of the past.

Across Park Avenue McKim, Mead and White's **Racquet and Squash Club** seems like a classical continuation of the Seagram Plaza. More interesting is **Lever House** situated across the avenue between 53rd and 54th, the building that set the modernist ball rolling on Park Avenue in 1952. Then, the two right-angled slabs that form a steel and glass bookend seemed revolutionary compared to the traditional buildings that surrounded it. Nowadays it's over-looked and not a little dingy.

Lexington Avenue and east

Lexington Avenue is always active, especially around the mid-40s, where commuters swarm around Grand Central and a well-placed **post office** on the corner of 50th Street. Just as the Chrysler Building dominates these lower stretches, the chisel-topped **Citicorp Center** (between 53rd and 54th streets) has taken the north end as its domain. Finished in 1979, the graph-paper design sheathed in alu-minum is architecture mathematics, and the building is now one of New York's most conspicuous landmarks. A story goes that a student of the building's engineer was playing with some of the equations of the just-finished tower's design when he discovered a flaw which placed it, as built, in danger from very strong winds. Though the force of wind required to topple the building was an unlikely occur-rence, a secretive mission to reinforce the structure was undertaken. Before the project was completed, the drama of a hurricane warning was played out with not a few architects, engineers and lawyers hav-ing a (thankfully unwarranted) sleepless night.

The slanted roof was designed to house solar panels and provide power, but the idea was ahead of the technology and Citicorp had to content itself with adopting the distinctive top as a corporate logo. The atrium of stores known as **The Market** is pleasant enough, recently redone, with some food options.

Hiding under the Center's skirts is **St Peter's**, known as "the Jazz Church" for being the venue of many a jazz musician's funeral. The tiny church was built to replace the one demolished to make way for Citicorp and part of the deal was that the church had to stand out from the Center – which explains the granite material. Thoroughly modern inside, it's worth peering in for sculptor **Louise Nevelson's Erol Beaker Chapel**, venue for Wednesday lunchtime jazz concerts (and evening concerts as well). More black angular Nevelson sculp-ture can be seen on the partition running down Park Avenue.

The Citicorp provided a spur for the development of Third Avenue, though things really took off when the old elevated railway that ran here was dismantled in 1955. Until then Third had been a strip of earthy bars and run-down tenements, in effect a border to the more salubrious Midtown district. After the Citicorp gave it an "official" stamp of approval, office buildings sprouted, revitalizing the flagging fortunes of midtown Manhattan in the late 1970s. The best section is between 44th and 50th streets – look out for the sheer marble mon-ument of the **Wang Building** between 48th and 49th, whose cross-patterns reveal the structure within.

All this office space hasn't totally removed interest from the street (there are a few good bars here, notably *P.J. Clarke's* at 55th, a New

York institution – see p.392), but most life, especially at nighttime, seems to have shifted across to **Second Avenue** – on the whole lower, quieter, more residential and with any number of singles/Irish bars to crawl between. The area from Third to the East River in the upper 40s is known as **Turtle Bay**, and there's a scattering of brownstones alongside chirpier shops and industry that disappear as you head north. Of course, the UN Headquarters Building (see p.146) has had a knock-on effect, producing buildings like 1 UN Plaza at 44th and First, a futurisitic chess piece of a hotel that takes its design hints from the UN Building itself. Inside, its marbled, chrome lobby is about as uninviting as any other modern American luxury hotel. Should this be your cup of tea, a double room will set you back a few hundred dollars; if not, just pray that all New York hotels don't end up like this.

First Avenue has a certain raggy looseness that's a relief after the concrete claustrophobia of Midtown, and **Beekman Place** (49th to 51st streets between First Avenue and the river) is quieter still, a beguiling enclave of garbled styles. Similar, though not quite as intimate, is **Sutton Place**, a long stretch running from 53rd to 59th between First and the river. Originally built for the lordly Morgans and Vanderbilts in 1875, Sutton increases in elegance as you move north and, for today's crème de la crème, **Riverview Terrace** (off 58th St) is a (very) private enclave of five brownstones. The Secretary-General of the UN has a place here and the locals are choosy who they let in: late, disgraced ex-President Richard Nixon was refused on the grounds he would be a security risk. There are a couple of small public parks here, affording fine views of the river and Queens' crumbling industrial waterfront.

Midtown West

The area **west of Fifth Avenue** in midtown Manhattan takes Times Square as its center, an exploded version of the East Side's more tight-lipped monuments to capitalism. Though it can't claim to compete with the avenues to the east, the area around this stretch of "naughty, bawdy 42nd Street" is still well worth exploring. Most of the pornography and crime are gone, replaced by products of Disney's imagination. For seediness, keep heading west to Eighth Avenue and beyond – but hurry: gentrification is fast approaching. There aren't many tourist attractions in this direction, which may be reason enough to go, though all the way over on the West Side Highway sits the massive Intrepid Sea-Air-Space Museum (for an account of which see p.297).

Bryant Park

The restoration of Bryant Park (6th Ave between W 40th–42nd streets) is one of the new 42nd Street's resounding success stories:

until recently a seedy spot, it is now a beautiful, grassy, square block
filled with slender trees, flowerbeds and inviting green chairs (the
fact that they aren't chained to the ground is proof enough of revitalization). Forming the backyard of the New York Public Library on
42nd Street, Bryant Park is, like Greeley Square to its south, named
after a newspaper editor – William Cullen Bryant of the *New York
Post*, also famed as a poet and instigator of Central Park. The park
has a rich history – it was the site of the first American World's Fair
in 1853, with a Crystal Palace, modeled on the famed London Crystal
Palace, on its grounds. Sitting here in the warmer months, you can
imagine yourself in Paris's Jardins de Luxembourg while the corporate lunch crowd is just grateful for a pleasant place to eat.
Summertime brings a lively scene to the park, as it hosts free jazz and
various performers throughout the week, and free outdoor movies on
Monday evenings; there's also a rather aggressive singles' scene at
the outdoor *Bryant Park Cafe* (which travels indoors to the *Bryant
Park Grill* for the remaining seasons).

Rising to the south of the park is the **American Radiator Building**
(now the American Standard Building) at 40 West 40th, its black
Gothic tower topped with honey-colored terra cotta that lights up to
resemble glowing coal – appropriate enough for the headquarters of
a heating company. To the north is the **Grace Building** which
swoops down on 42nd Street, breaking the rules by stepping out of
line with its neighbors.

Times Square

West from Bryant Park, 42nd Street meets Broadway at **Times
Square**, the center of the theater district, where the pulsating neon
suggests a heart for the city itself. Since the major cleanup launched
by the city and by business interests like Disney, the ambience here
has changed dramatically. Traditionally a melting pot of debauch,
depravity and fun, the area became increasingly edgy, a place where
out-of-towners supplied easy pickings for petty criminals, drug dealers and prostitutes (always, seemingly, a companion to theater districts). Most of the peep shows and sex shops have been pushed out,
and Times Square is now a largely sanitized universe of consumption. The neon signs seem to multiply at the same rate as coffee bars,
and Disney rules the roost on the stretch of 42nd between Seventh
and Eighth, home to the remaining palatial Broadway "houses" and
movie palaces.

Like Greeley and Herald squares, Times Square took its name
from a newspaper connection when the *New York Times* built
offices here in 1904. While the *Herald* and *Tribune* fought each
other in ever more vicious circulation battles, the *NYT* took the sober
middle ground under the banner "All the news that's fit to print," a
policy that enabled the paper to survive and become one of the country's most respected voices. **Times Tower** at the southernmost edge

of the square was its headquarters, originally an elegant building modeled on Giotto's *Campanile* in Florence. In 1928, the famous zipper sign displaying the news of the world was added; the building was "skinned" in 1965 and covered with the lifeless marble slabs visible today. It's also here where the alcohol-sozzled masses gather for New Year's Eve, to witness the giant sparkling ball dropping at the top of the Tower. The paper itself has long since crept off around a corner to a handsome building with globe lamps on 43rd Street, and today most of the printing is done in New Jersey.

Dotted around here are most of New York's great **theaters** (see Chapter 20, "The Performing Arts and Film"), though many have been destroyed (like the Vaudeville palaces that preceded *them*) to make way for office buildings – as was the original Paramount Theater, making way for the majestic 1927 clock-and-globe-topped **Paramount Building** at 1501 Broadway, between 43rd and 44th streets. The **New Amsterdam** and the **New Victory**, both on 42nd Street between Seventh and Eighth avenues, have been refurbished by Disney to their original splendor, one of the truly welcome results of the massive changes here. The **Lyceum** and **Lyric** theaters each have their original facades while the **Shubert** theater, which hosted *A Chorus Line* during its twenty-odd year run, still occupies its own small space and walkway. At 432 44th St is the former Presbyterian Church that became **The Actors Studio** in 1947, where Lee Strasberg, America's leading proponent of Stanislavski's Method acting technique, taught his students. Among the oldest is the **Belasco**, on 44th Street between Sixth and Seventh avenues, which was also the first of Broadway's theaters to incorporate machinery into its stagings. The neon, so much a signature of the square, originally accompanied the building of the theaters and spawned the term "the Great White Way"; in 1922, its lights moved G.K. Chesterton to remark, "What a glorious garden of wonder this would be, to anyone who was lucky enough to be unable to read." Today, businesses that rent offices here are actually required to allow signage on their walls – the city's attempt to retain the square's traditional feel. The displays, of course, have modernized – note the steaming Cup of Noodles at the southern end – and even the **Port Authority Bus Terminal** on 42nd and Eighth, a former sink of depravity, is to be covered with a skin of metal for ad displays.

Duffy Square is the northernmost island in the heart of Times Square and offers an excellent panoramic view of the square's lights, megahotels, theme-stores and theme-restaurants metastasizing daily. The nifty canvas-and-frame stand of the **TKTS booth**, modest in comparison, sells half-price, same-day tickets for Broadway shows (whose exorbitant prices these days make a visit to TKTS a near necessity). A lifelike statue of Broadway's doyen **George M. Cohan** looks on – though if you've ever seen the film *Yankee Doodle Dandy* it's impossible to think of him other than as a swaggering Jimmy

Cagney. Last word on the scene to Henry Miller from *Tropic of Capricorn*:

> It's only a stretch of a few blocks from Times Square to Fiftieth Street, and when one says Broadway that's all that's really meant and it's really nothing, just a chicken run and a lousy one at that, but even at seven in the evening when everyone's rushing for a table there's a sort of electric crackle in the air and your hair stands on end like an antenna and if you're receptive you not only get every bash and flicker but you get the statistical itch, the quid pro quo of the interactive, interstitial, ectoplasmic quantum of bodies jostling in space like the stars which compose the Milky Way, only this is the Gay White Way, the top of the world with no roof and not even a crack or a hole under your feet to fall through and say it's a lie. The absolute impersonality of it brings you to a pitch of warm human delirium which makes you run forward like a blind nag and wag your delirious ears.

Hell's Kitchen

To the west of Times Square lies **Clinton**, more famously known as **Hell's Kitchen**, an area centered on the engaging slash of restaurants, bars and ethnic delis of **Ninth Avenue**. Extending down to the Garment District (which makes for a nice, dumb joke, since together the two neighborhoods could be called "Chelsea Clinton") and up to the low 50s, this was once one of New York's most violent and lurid neighborhoods. Named after a tenement at 54th Street and Tenth Avenue (but a nineteenth-century term for *any* dismal situation), Hell's Kitchen was originally an area of soap and glue factories, slaughterhouses and the like, with sections named "Misery Lane" and "Poverty Row." Irish immigrants were the first inhabitants, soon joined by Greeks, Latinos, Italians and blacks – amidst the overcrowding, tensions rapidly developed between (and within) ethnic groups. Gangs roamed the streets, and though their rule ended in 1910 after a major police counteroffensive, the area remained dangerous until fairly recently (and in truth, it still pays to be wary). The neighborhood was rechristened Clinton in 1959 to hide its notorious past, but the name hasn't really stuck, though the district has attracted a new population, mostly musicians and Broadway types, and is moving up in a similar way to the East Village.

Head to it from Eighth Avenue (which now houses the porn businesses expelled from the square) down 46th Street – the so-called **Restaurant Row** that is the area's preferred haunt for pre- and post-theater dining. Here you can begin to detect a more pastoral feel, which only increases on many of the side streets around Ninth and Tenth avenues. Also check out the unstuffy **St Clements Episcopal Church** at 423 West 46th: it doubles as a community theater and in its foyer is a picture of Elvis Presley and Jesus, with the caption, "There seems to be a little confusion as to which one of them actually rose from the dead."

Continuing west, there's not too much to see. Ragged Eleventh Avenue is home to the automobile warehouses that used to spice up Times Square's Automobile Row, and past that is the sleazy West Side Highway. These streets are undistinguished, only highlighted by two well-preserved, old-timey restaurants on Eleventh, the *Landmark Tavern* (46th St) and the *Market Diner* (44th St).

North of Times Square

Heading north from Times Square, the **West 50s** between Sixth and Eighth avenues are emphatically tourist territory. Edged by Central Park in the north and the Theater District to the south, and with Fifth Avenue and Rockefeller Center in easy striking distance, the area has been invaded by overpriced restaurants and cheapo souvenir stores: should you wish to stock up on "I Love New York" underwear, this could be the place.

One sight worth searching out is the **Equitable Center** at 757 Seventh Ave. The building itself is dapper if not a little self-important, with Roy Lichtenstein's 68-foot *Mural with Blue Brush Stroke* poking you in the eye as you enter: best of all, look out for Thomas Hart Benton's *America Today* murals (in the left-hand corridor), which dynamically and magnificently portray ordinary American life in the days before the Depression.

Sixth Avenue

Sixth Avenue is properly named **Avenue of the Americas**, though no New Yorker ever calls it this: guidebooks and maps labor the convention, but the only manifestation of the tag are lamppost flags of Central and South American countries which serve as useful landmarks. If nothing else Sixth's distinction is its width, a result of the elevated railway that once ran along here, now replaced by the Sixth Avenue subway. In its day the Sixth Avenue "El" marked the border between respectability to the east and dodgier areas to the west, and in a way it's still a dividing line separating the glamorous strips of Fifth, Madison and Park avenues from the brasher western districts. At 1133 Sixth Ave (43rd St) is the Midtown branch of the **International Center of Photography**, whose glassy confines always advertise an interesting photo exhibit.

Diamond Row

One of the best things about New York City is the small hidden pockets abruptly discovered when you least expect them. West 47th Street between Fifth and Sixth avenues is a perfect example: **Diamond Row** (you'll know it by the brand new, Disneyesque diamond-shaped lamps mounted on pylons at the Fifth Avenue end) is a strip of shops chock-full of gems and jewelry, largely managed by Hasidic Jews who seem only to exist in the confines of the street. The Hasidim are Orthodox Jews – the name means "Pious Ones" – and

traditionally wear beards, sidelocks and dark, old-fashioned suits.
Large contingents live in Williamsburg and Crown Heights in
Brooklyn. Maybe they are what gives the street its workaday feel –
Diamond Row seems more like the Garment District than Fifth
Avenue, and the conversations you overhear on the street or in the
nearby delicatessens are memorably Jewish. This is also the place to
go to get jewelry fixed at reasonable prices.

Around the Rockefeller Extension

By the time Sixth Avenue reaches midtown Manhattan, it has become
a dazzling showcase of corporate wealth. True, there's little of the
ground-floor glitter of Fifth or the razzmatazz of Broadway, but what
is here, and in a way what defines the stretch from 47th to 51st
streets, is the **Rockefeller Center Extension**. Following the earlier
Time & Life Building at 50th Street (with its refreshing, if basic, rectangular fountain – the only water around on a hot summer's day),
three near-identical blocks went up in the 1970s, and if they don't
have the romance of their predecessor they at least possess some of
its monumentality. Backing on to Rockefeller Center proper, by day
and especially by night, the repeated statement of each block comes
over with some power, giving the wide path of Sixth Avenue much of
its visual excitement. At street level things can be just as interesting:
the broad sidewalks allow peddlers of food and handbills, street
musicians, mimics and actors to do their thing.

Across the avenue at 49th Street **Radio City Music Hall** has far
greater rewards (for a description, see p.150). Keep an eye open too
for the **CBS Building** on the corner of 52nd Street: dark and
inscrutable, this has been compared to the monolith from the film
2001 and, like it or not, it certainly forces a mysterious presence on
this segment of Sixth Avenue.

57th Street and Central Park South

West of Fifth Avenue, an impressive block, which has recently over-
taken SoHo as the center for upmarket art sales, is 57th Street.
Galleries here are noticeably snootier than their Downtown relations,
often requiring an appointment for viewing. A couple that usually
don't are the **Marlborough Gallery** (2nd floor, 40 W 57th), specializing in famous names both American and European, and the
Kennedy Gallery (same building, 5th floor), which deals in nine-
teenth- and twentieth-century American painting. Also noteworthy is
the **Art Students League** at no. 215, built in 1892 by Henry J.
Hardenbergh (who later built the *Plaza Hotel*) to mimic Francois I's
hunting lodge at Fontainebleau. Today this art school provides inexpensive art classes to the public.

At 154 W 57th St, is stately **Carnegie Hall**, one of the world's
greatest concert venues, revered by musicians and audiences alike.
The Renaissance-inspired structure was built in the 1890s by steel

magnate and self-styled "improver of mankind" Andrew Carnegie, and the superb acoustics ensure full houses most of the year. Tchaikovsky conducted the program on opening night and Mahler, Rachmaninov, Toscanini, Frank Sinatra and Judy Garland all played here. If you don't want, or can't afford, to attend a performance, sneak in through the stage door on 56th Street for a look – no one minds as long as there's not a rehearsal in progress. Alternatively, catch one of the tours (Mon, Tues, Thurs & Fri, except Summer, 11.30am, 2pm & 3pm; $6, $5 students; ☎247-7800 for more details).

A few doors down at no. 150, the **Russian Tea Room** (see p.375) reigns as one of those places to see and be seen at, ever popular with "in" names from the entertainment business. It was famously used in *Tootsie* as the restaurant where Dustin Hoffman chats up his agent in female guise. Recently, it has reopened after much speculation that it never would. Still, its formed revolving doors continue to usher in a well-heeled crowd, as would be expected in this posh part of town.

Chapter 10

Central Park

" **A** ll radiant in the magic atmosphere of art and taste." So raved *Harper's* magazine on the opening of **Central Park** in 1876, and though that was a slight overstatement, today few New Yorkers could imagine life without it. The park is devotedly used by locals: Midtown suits walk up to grab hot dogs by the Maine Monument; Latino families come down from El Barrio to picnic by the waters of Harlem Meer; bikini-clad sunbathers work on their tans in Sheep Meadow; and joggers, rollerbladers, bikers and nature lovers fill the park year-round. Over the years the park has seen some hard times, from official neglect to some truly horrible crime waves, but in recent years it has benefited from a major renovation project and is cleaner, safer and more user-friendly than ever. In bad times and good New Yorkers still treasure it more than any other city institution. Certainly life in New York would be a lot poorer without it.

Some history

Central Park came close to never happening at all. It was the poet and newspaper editor **William Cullen Bryant** who had the idea for an open public space back in 1844. He spent seven years trying to persuade City Hall to carry it out, while developers leaned heavily on the authorities not to give up any valuable land. But eventually the city agreed, and an 840-acre space north of the (then) city limits was set aside, a desolate swampy area occupied at the time by a shantytown of squatters. The two architects commissioned to design the landscape, **Frederick Law Olmsted** and **Calvert Vaux**, planned to create a rural paradise, "Greensward" as they called it, an illusion of the countryside smack in the heart of Manhattan. Greensward was to bring nature to an increasingly congested city thought to be badly in need of its edifying virtues.

The sparseness of the terrain provided Olmsted and Vaux with the perfect opportunity to design the park according to the precepts of English landscape gardening. They designed elegant bridges, each unique, and planned a revolutionary system of sunken transverse roads to segregate different kinds of traffic. Finally, after the nearly twenty years required for its construction, Central Park was unveiled in 1876. It opened to such acclaim that Olmsted and Vaux were soon in demand as park architects all over the States. Locally they went on to design Riverside and Morningside parks in Manhattan, and Prospect Park in Brooklyn. Working alone, Olmsted laid out the campuses of Berkeley and Stanford in California, and had a major hand in that most televised of American sights, Capitol Hill in Washington, DC.

At its opening, Central Park was declared a "people's park" – though most of the impoverished masses it was allegedly built to serve had neither the time nor the carfare to come up from their Downtown slums to 59th Street and enjoy it. But as New York grew and workers' leisure time increased, people started flooding in, and the park began to live up to its mission, sometimes in ways that might have scandalized its original builders.

Robert Moses, a relentless urban planner and parks commissioner who was for decades the power behind the city's biggest building projects, tried hard to put his permanent imprint on Central Park. Thankfully public opinion kept damage to a minimum; he only managed to pave over a small portion of the park, mostly in the form of unnecessary parking lots (since reconverted to green space). Moses was brought to bay by outraged citizens when in 1956 he tried to tear down a park playground to build a parking lot for *Tavern on the Green* – mothers and their young children stood in the way of the bulldozers, and the city sheepishly backed off. Today a nonprofit group called the Central Park Conservancy looks out for the park, and the city government has earmarked large funds to maintain it, increase its policing, and (benignly) renovate large areas, such as the Great Lawn, where renovations were completed in 1998. Today, in spite of the advent of motorized traffic, the sense of disorderly nature Olmsted and Vaux intended largely survives, with cars and buses cutting through the park in the sheltered, sunken transverses originally meant for horse-drawn carriages, mostly unseen from the park itself. The skyline, of course, has changed, and buildings thrust their way into view, sometimes detracting from the park's original pastoral intention, but at the same time adding to the sense of being on a green island in the center of a magnificent city.

Getting around the park

Central Park is so enormous (840 acres) that it's almost impossible to miss and nearly as impossible to cover in one visit. Nevertheless, the intricate **footpaths** that meander with no discernible organization through the park are one of its greatest successes; after all, the point here is to lose yourself . . . or at least to *feel* like you can. Legend has it that you can use the New York City skyline as your guiding compass, but only dyed-in-the-wool New Yorkers are completely comfortable with this method. That said, you can never stray too far from the footpaths, landmarks, or the more route-savvy regulars that blanket the park. **To figure out exactly where you are**, find the nearest **lamppost**: the first two digits on the post signify the number of the nearest cross street. It is also helpful to stop by one of the visitor's centers to pick up a free park map (see the box on p.171).

As for **safety**, you should be fine during the day, though always be alert to your surroundings and try to avoid being alone in an isolated part of the park. After dark, it's safer than it used to be but still not advisable to walk around, so if you want to look at the buildings of Central Park West lit up, à la Woody Allen's film *Manhattan*, the best option you have is to fork out for a buggy ride. The exception to the rule is in the case of a public evening event such as a concert or Shakespeare in the Park; these events are very safe, just make sure you leave with the rest of the crowds.

Bicycle rental and buggy rides

One of the best ways to see the park is to **rent a bicycle** from either the Loeb Boathouse (see p.168) or Metro Bicycles (Lexington at 88th St – see p.21). Bikes from the Boathouse are $8 an hour and from Metro $6 an hour; both require a $100 cash or credit card refundable deposit; that's a much better deal than the famed romantic buggy rides ($34 for a 20min trot and $10 for every additional 15min after that; ☎246-0520 for more information). Bear in mind that there has been longstanding vocal opposition to the buggy practice being allowed at all, with claims that the incompetence and greed of the buggy drivers lead to great cruelty to the horses used. Care has been improved though; according to a law enacted in 1994, the horses must get fifteen-minute rest breaks every two hours and cannot work more than nine hours a day. They're also not supposed to work at all when the temperature goes above 90° F. Buggy drivers can get their licenses suspended or revoked for disobedience.

For more on bicycle rental, see p.429.

Exploring the park

The **Reservoir** divides Central Park neatly in two. The larger and more familiar **southern part** holds most of the attractions (and people), but the **northern part** (above 86th St) is well worth a visit for its wilder natural setting and its dramatically different ambience. Organized walking tours are available from a number of sources including the Urban Park Rangers and the Visitors Centers (see the box on p.171), but almost any stroll (formal or informal) will invariably lead to something interesting. To visit Central Park is to begin to understand New York City and its residents – not to mention the fact that the park offers some of the city's most enjoyable and most reasonably priced, if not altogether free, activities.

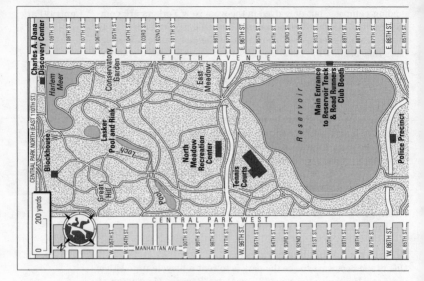

The southern park

Entering at the most southeasterly point of the park, **Grand Army Plaza,** at Fifth Avenue and 59th Street, to your left lies the **Pond** and a little further north you'll find the **Wollman Memorial Rink** (63rd St at mid-park; in summer Thurs & Fri 11am–6pm, Sat & Sun 11am–8pm, in winter open daily for ice skating; ☎396-1010). Sit or stand above the rink to watch skaters and contemplate the view of Central Park South's skyline emerging above the trees. Or **rent skates** of your own: $3 for roller skates and $6 (with credit-card deposit) for rollerblades, the most versatile (and popular) mode of park transportation.

See p.428 for information on ice-skating in Central Park.

East of the skating rink, at 64th Street and Fifth Avenue, is the small **Central Park Zoo** (Mon–Fri 10am–5pm, Sat, Sun & holidays 10.30am–5.30pm; $3.50 adults, 50¢ children aged 3–12, free for children under 3; ☎439-6500), whose collection is based on three climatic regions – the Tropic Zone, the Temperate Territory and the Polar Circle. Remodeled a decade ago at a cost of over $35 million and now officially called the Central Park Wildlife Conservation Center, the zoo has over 100 species on view in mostly natural-looking homes with the animals as close to the viewer as possible: the penguins, for example, swim around at eye-level in plexiglass pools. Other top attractions include polar bears, monkeys, a nocturnal exhibit, and sea lions cavorting in a pool right by the zoo entrance. This complex also boasts the recently opened **Tisch Children's Zoo,** with a petting zoo and interactive displays. Still, for a more extensive look at wildlife, you're better off heading to the **Bronx Zoo** (p.247).

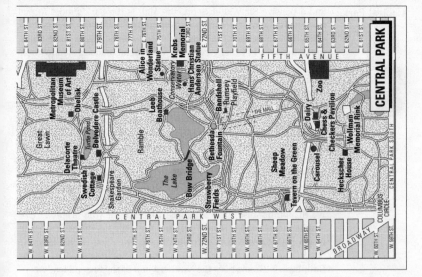

Unless you're attracted to a game of chess at the **Chess and Checkers Pavilion** (playing pieces are available at the Dairy Visitor Center), the next point to head for is the **Dairy** (65th St at mid-park), a kind of Gothic toy ranch building built in 1870 and originally stocked with cows (and milkmaids) for the purpose of selling milk and other dairy products to mothers with young children. It now houses one of the Park's **Visitor Centers** (Tues–Sun 10am–5pm; ☎ 794-6564), a worthwhile rest stop that distributes free leaflets and maps (and sells better ones), sells books on the history and development of the park and puts on sporadic exhibitions. Weekend walking tours often leave from here; call for times.

Just west of the Dairy, you will see the octagonal brick building that houses the **Carousel**. Built in 1903 and moved to the park from Coney Island in 1951, this is one of the park's little gems (64th St at mid-park; open Mon–Fri 10am–6pm, Sat & Sun 10am–6.30pm, weather permitting; ☎ 879-0244). One of fewer than 150 left in the country (one of the others is at Coney Island), the Carousel offers a ride on still-magical, hand-carved jumping horses accompanied by the music of a military band organ for only $1 a pop or six tickets for $5. (You can also book it for birthday parties; Wollman Rink handles its special events, call ☎ 396-1010 ext 13).

If you continue straight ahead and north past the Dairy and through the **Mall**, you will witness every manner of street performer. A recent landmark ruling allows minstrels to electronically amplify their music outside of the park's "quiet zones," which the Mall certainly is not. Flanked by statues of an ecstatic-looking Robert Burns

Central Park and a pensive Sir Walter Scott, the Mall is the park's most formal stretch. To the west lies the **Sheep Meadow** (66th–69th streets, west side), fifteen acres of commons where sheep grazed until 1934; today the area is usually crowded with picnic blankets, sunbathers and frisbee players. Two lawn-bowling and croquet grass courts are maintained on a hill near the Meadow's northwest corner; to the southeast are a number of very popular volleyball courts (call ☎360-8133 for information on lawn bowling; call ☎408-0201 for volleyball and other ball field permit information). On warm weekends, an area between the Sheep Meadow and the north end of the Mall is filled with colorfully-attired rollerbladers dancing to loud funk, disco and hip-hop music – one of the best free shows around. Just west of the Sheep Meadow is the once-exclusive, still-expensive, but now tacky landmark restaurant and finishing point of the annual New York City Marathon, **Tavern on the Green** (65th St and Central Park W). If nothing else, take a look at the exterior (the original 1870 building used to be a sheepfold) and the huge fake topiary trees in front of the Crystal Room (you'll know it when you see it). If you're not in the mood for pretension, grab a hot dog instead at the **Ballplayer's House** near the southern end of the Sheep Meadow.

At the northernmost point of the Mall lie the **Bandshell**, **Rumsey Playfield**, site of the free SummerStage performance series (see box, p.170), and the **Bethesda Terrace and Fountain** (72nd St at mid-park). Bethesda Terrace, the only formal element of the original Olmsted and Vaux plan, overlooks the lake; beneath it is an **Arcade** whose tiled floors and elaborate decoration are currently being restored. The crowning centerpiece of the Bethesda Fountain is the nineteenth-century **Angel of the Waters** sculpture; its earnest puritanical angels (Purity, Health, Peace and Temperance) continue to watch disappointedly over their wicked city (theater fans may remember that the last scene of the Pulitzer Prize-winning play *Angels in America* is set at this fountain). You can go for a Venetian gondola ride or rent a rowboat from the **Loeb Boathouse** on the lake's eastern bank (March–Nov daily 10am–6pm, weather permitting; rowboats are $10 for the first hour, $2.50 per each hour after, with a $30 refundable deposit; gondola rides are given 5–10pm for $30 per 30min per group and require reservations; ☎517-2233 for more information).

Across the water, at the narrowest point on the lake, is the elegant cast-iron and wood **Bow Bridge**, designed by park architect Calvert Vaux. Directly over the bridge you will find yourself in the unruly woods of **The Ramble**, a 37-acre area filled with narrow winding paths, rock outcroppings, streams and an array of native plant life. Once a favorite address for drug dealing and anonymous sex (a police crackdown and the AIDS epidemic lessened both) it is now a great place for bird-watching or a quiet stroll (though still not advisable if you're alone at night).

To the west of Bethesda Terrace, along the 72nd Street Drive, is the **Cherry Hill Fountain**, originally a turnaround point for carriages that was designed to have excellent views of the lake, the mall and the ramble. One of the pretty areas paved over by Parks Commissioner Robert Moses in 1934 for use as a parking lot, it was restored to its natural state in the early 1980s.

West of here, across the Park Drive, is **Strawberry Fields** (72nd St and Central Park W), a peaceful region of the park dedicated to the memory of John Lennon, who in 1980 was murdered in front of his home at the **Dakota Building**, across the street on Central Park West. Strawberry Fields is invariably crowded with those here to remember Lennon, as well as picnickers and seniors resting on the comfortable park benches. Near the West 72nd Street entrance to the area is a round Italian mosaic with the word "Imagine" at its center, donated by Yoko Ono and invariably covered with flowers. Every year without fail on December 8th, the anniversary of Lennon's murder, Strawberry Fields is packed with his fans, singing Beatles songs and sharing their grief, even after all these years.

See p.180 for more on the death of John Lennon.

Back to the east of Bethesda Terrace is the **Boat Pond** (72nd St and 5th Ave), officially named the **Conservatory Water** though New Yorkers never call it that, a small man-made pond where you can watch model boat races and regattas every Saturday in the summer (or participate by renting a craft from the cart in front of the **Krebs Memorial Boathouse**, just east of the water; $10 per hour). The fanciful *Alice in Wonderland* statue at the northern end of the pond was donated by publisher George Delacorte and is a favorite climbing spot for kids. During the summer the New York Public Library sponsors Wednesday morning (11am) storytelling sessions for children at the Hans Christian Andersen Statue on the west side of the pond (☎340-0906 for more information). A storyteller from the Central Park Conservancy also appears here at 11am on Saturdays throughout the summer.

If you continue north you will reach the backyard of the **Metropolitan Museum of Art** to the east at 81st Street (see p.259) and the **Obelisk** (nicknamed Cleopatra's Needle by locals) to the west, an 1881 gift from Egypt that dates back to 1450 BC. Also nearby is the **Great Lawn** (81st St at mid-park), recently reopened after a massive two-year, $18.5 million reconstruction. Originally the site of a reservoir from 1842 until 1931, it was drained and made into a playing field in the Thirties. It became a popular site for free concerts (Simon and Garfunkel, Diana Ross and others often attracted half a million people or more) and political rallies, but was badly overused and had serious drainage problems. Now rebuilt, reseeded and renewed, it will try to stay that way by only hosting the more sedate free New York Philharmonic and Metropolitan Opera concerts (see box overleaf). The lawn features eight softball fields and, at its northern end, new basketball and

Central Park volleyball courts, and a 1/8-mile running track. The refurbished **Turtle Pond** is at the southern end of the Lawn, with a new wooden dock and nature blind for better viewing of the aquatic wildlife (yes, there actually is wildlife here, including ducks, fish and frogs). What's not new, on the southeast corner of the pond, is a massive statue of fourteenth-century Polish king **Wladyslaw Jagiello**, a gift of the Polish government and the occasional site of Polish folk dancing.

Southwest of the Lawn is the **Delacorte Theater**, the venue of the annual free Shakespeare in the Park festivals. Next door, the tranquil **Shakespeare Garden** holds, they say, every species of plant or flower mentioned in the Bard's plays. East of the garden is **Belvedere Castle**, a mock medieval citadel first erected atop **Vista Rock** in 1869 as a lookout, but now the home of the Urban Park Rangers and a **Visitor Center** (Tues–Sun 10am–5pm; ☎772-0210; walking tours, bird-watching excursions and educational programs).

Seasonal events and activities

• SummerStage and Shakespeare in the Park are two of the most popular urban summertime programs. Both activities are free and help to take the sting out of New York's infamous hazy, hot and humid summers. In 1986 **SummerStage** presented its inaugural Central Park concert with Sun Ra performing to an audience of fifty people, but by the time he returned with Sonic Youth six years later, the audience had grown to ten thousand. Located at the Rumsey Playing Field near 72nd St and 5th Ave, a concert here is an invariably crowded, sticky but somehow bonding experience; in other words, well worth the free admission. Call the SummerStage hotline (☎360-2777) for more information.

Shakespeare in the Park takes place at the open-air Delacorte Theater, located near the W 81st St entrance to the park, where tickets are distributed daily at 1pm for that evening's performance, but you'll probably have to get in line well before. If you are Downtown, tickets are also distributed at the Public Theater (425 Lafayette) between 1pm and 3pm the day of the performance. Two plays are performed each summer (mid-June through early Sept, Tues–Sun at 8pm; free); Shakespeare is the Festival's meat, but having just completed the entire cycle of his plays over the course of more than twenty years, other works are being produced as well. Call the Shakespeare Festival (☎539-8750) for more information.

• **New York Philharmonic in the Park** (☎875-5709) and Metropolitan Opera in the Park (☎362-6000) hold several evenings of classical music in the summer.

• **Claremont Riding Academy**, 175 W 89th St (☎724-5100). Open Mon–Fri, 6.30am–10pm, Sat & Sun 6.30am–5pm. Horseback riding lessons are available, as are rentals for riders experienced in the English saddle. $42 for 30min lesson, $35 for a ride on Central Park's bridlepaths.

The highest point in the park, and as such a splendid viewpoint, the Castle also houses the New York Meteorological Observatory's weather center, responsible for providing the daily official Central Park temperature readings, and makes a lovely background prop for the Delacorte's Shakespeare performances. The **Swedish Cottage Marionette Theater** (mid-park at 79th St) at the base of Vista Rock holds puppet shows such as *The True Story of Rumpelstiltskin* or *Gulliver's Travels* for children (☎988-9093 for reservations and information)

The northern park

There are fewer attractions, but more open space, above the Great Lawn. Much of it is taken up by the **Reservoir** (86th–87th streets at mid-park, main entrance at 90th St and 5th Ave), a 107-acre, billion-gallon reservoir that was originally designed in 1862 as part of the

---

• **The Harlem Meer Festival**, 110th St between 5th and Lenox aves (☎860-1370). Fairly intimate and enjoyable free performances of jazz and salsa music outside the Dana Discovery Center on Sundays from 4–6pm throughout the summer.

General information

• **General Park Information** ☎360-3444. Also☎1-888/NYPARKS for special events information.

• Founded in 1980, the Central Park Conservancy is a nonprofit organization dedicated to preserving and managing the park. The Conservancy runs four Visitor Centers, with free maps and other helpful literature, as well as special events. All are open Tues–Sun, 10am–5pm: The Dairy (mid-park at 65th St; ☎794-6564); Belvedere Castle (mid-park at 79th St; ☎772-0210); North Meadow Recreation Center (mid-park at 97th St; ☎348-4867; also open Monday); and The Charles A. Dana Discovery Center (110th St off 5th Ave; ☎860-1370).

• **Manhattan Urban Park Rangers** ☎628-2345 (activities information); The rangers are there to help; they lead walking tours, give directions and provide first aid in emergencies.

• **Restrooms** are available at Hecksher Playground, the Boat Pond (Conservatory Water), Mineral Springs House (northwest end of Sheep's Meadow), Loeb Boathouse, the Delacorte Theater, the North Meadow Recreation Center, The Conservatory Garden and the Charles A. Dana Discovery Center.

• **Traffic**: the East and West Drives run just inside the periphery of the park and are closed to automobile traffic on weekdays, 10am–3pm and 7–10pm; weekends, 7pm Friday to 6am Monday; and holidays, 7pm the night before until 6am the day after.

• In case of emergency, use the **emergency call boxes** located throughout the park and along the Park Drives (they provide a direct connection to the Central Park Precinct), or dial 911 at any pay phone.

Croton Water System. No longer an active reservoir, but still referred to as one, it's unofficially called the Jacqueline Bouvier Kennedy Onassis Memorial Reservoir, after the area's most famous resident (Onassis lived nearby on 5th Ave and was frequently seen in the park). The reservoir is encircled by a running track, around which disciplined New Yorkers faithfully jog (the New York Road Runner's Club has a booth at the main entrance at 90th St). The raised track is a great place to get breathtaking 360-degree views of the skyline; just don't block any jogger's path or there will be hell to pay. Due north of the reservoir are a tennis court complex and the newly refurbished soccer fields of the **North Meadow Recreation Center** (97th St at mid-park; ☎348-4867). If you see nothing else above 86th Street in the park, don't miss the **Conservatory Garden**, between East 103rd and 106th streets, along Fifth Avenue, a pleasing, six-acre space made up of three formal, terraced gardens filled with flowering trees and shrubs, planted flower beds, fanciful fountains, and shaded benches. The main iron-gated entrance at 104th Street and Fifth Avenue is a favorite spot for weekend wedding party photographs, and the Garden itself is frequented by families, lovers of all ages, painters and sketch artists. Just north of the Garden is the **Robert Bendleim Playground** for disabled children, at 108th Street near Fifth Avenue. Here physically challenged youngsters play in "accessible" sandboxes and swings, or work out their upper bodies on balance beams, all very much in keeping with the inclusive nature of Central Park.

At the top of the park is the **Charles A. Dana Discovery Center** (110th St, between 5th and Lenox aves; Tues–Sun 10am–5pm, 4pm in winter; ☎860-1370), an environmental education center and Visitor Center, with free literature, changing visual exhibits, bird walks every Saturday at 11am in July and August, and multicultural performances (see box overleaf). Crowds of locals fish in the adjacent **Harlem Meer**, an eleven-acre pond created in 1864 and recently restored to its original, natural state (once again undoing the determined cement work of Parks Commissioner Robert Moses) and stocked with more than 50,000 fish. The Discovery Center provides bamboo poles and bait free of charge, though you'll have to release your catch of the day.

Chapter 11

The Upper West Side and Morningside Heights

T
hough dominated by some dazzling turn-of-the-century apartment buildings and the city's most prestigious performance space, the Upper West Side has always had a more unbuttoned vibe than its counterpart across the park. Rather than a stage for old wealth – mostly because the area was late to develop – it has seen its share of struggling actors, writers, opera singers and the like move into its spaces over the years, somewhat tempered by recent waves of gentrification. This isn't to say it lacks glamour: there is plenty of money in evidence, especially along the lower stretches of Central Park West and Riverside Drive, and at Lincoln Center, New York's palace of culture, but this is considerably less true as you move north. At its top end, marked at the edge by the monolithic Cathedral of St John the Divine, is Morningside Heights, an area that is the last gasp of Manhattan's wealth before Harlem.

The Upper West Side

North of 59th Street, paralleling the spread of Central Park, midtown Manhattan's somewhat tawdry West Side becomes decidedly less commercial, less garish, and, above Lincoln Center, more of a residential and shopping neighborhood. The Upper West Side is one of the city's most desirable addresses, and tends to attract what you might call New York's cultural elite and new-money types – musicians, writers, journalists, curators and the like – though there is also a small but jarringly visible homeless presence.

First some **orientation**. The Upper West Side is bordered by Central Park to the east, the Hudson River to the west, Columbus Circle at 59th Street to the south, and 110th Street (the northernmost point of Central Park and beginning of Morningside Heights) to the north. The main artery is Broadway and, generally speaking, the further you stray east or west the wealthier things become, until you

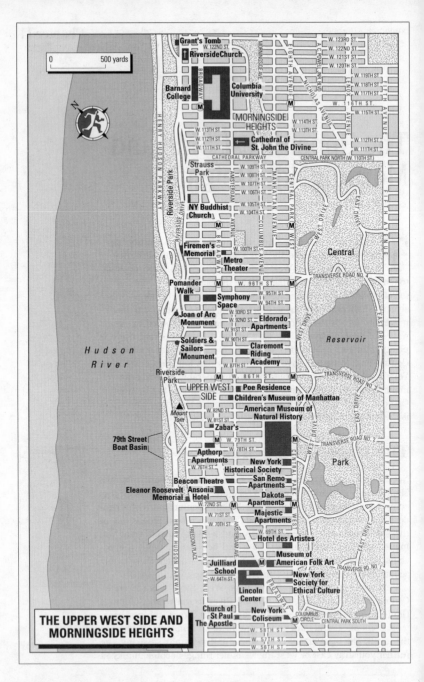

Grant's Tomb
W. 122ND ST.
Riverside Church
W. 123RD ST.
W. 122ND ST.
W. 121ST ST.
W. 120TH ST.
W. 119TH ST.
W. 118TH ST.
W. 117TH ST.
W. 116TH ST.
W. 115TH ST.

Barnard College
Columbia University

MORNINGSIDE HEIGHTS
W. 114TH ST.
W. 113TH ST.
W. 113TH ST.
W. 112TH ST.
W. 111TH ST.
Cathedral of St. John the Divine
W. 112TH ST.
W. 111TH ST.

CATHEDRAL PARKWAY
Central Park North (W. 110TH ST.)

Strauss Park
W. 109TH ST.
W. 108TH ST.
W. 107TH ST.
W. 106TH ST.
W. 105TH ST.
W. 104TH ST.

NY Buddhist Church

Firemen's Memorial
W. 100TH ST.
Metro Theater

Pomander Walk
W. 96TH ST.
W. 95TH ST.
W. 94TH ST.
Symphony Space
W. 93RD ST.
W. 92ND ST.
W. 91ST ST.
Eldorado Apartments
W. 90TH ST.
Joan of Arc Monument
Soldiers & Sailors Monument
Claremont Riding Academy
W. 87TH ST.

Riverside Park
W. 86TH ST.

UPPER WEST SIDE
Poe Residence
Children's Museum of Manhattan
W. 82ND ST.
W. 81ST ST.
American Museum of Natural History

Mount Tom
Zabar's
W. 79TH ST.
W. 78TH ST.

79th Street Boat Basin

Apthorp Apartments
W. 76TH ST.
New York Historical Society
San Remo Apartments
Beacon Theatre
Eleanor Roosevelt Memorial
Ansonia Hotel
W. 72ND ST.
Dakota Apartments
W. 71ST ST.
W. 70TH ST.
Majestic Apartments
W. 69TH ST.
Hotel des Artistes

Museum of American Folk Art
Juilliard School
W. 64TH ST.
New York Society for Ethical Culture
Lincoln Center

Church of St Paul The Apostle
New York Coliseum
COLUMBUS CIRCLE
CENTRAL PARK SOUTH
W. 58TH ST.
W. 57TH ST.
W. 56TH ST.

Hudson River

Henry Hudson Parkway
Riverside Park
Riverside Drive
Broadway
Amsterdam Avenue
Columbus Avenue
Central Park West
West End Avenue
Freedom Place

Central Park
Reservoir
West Drive
East Drive
Transverse Road No. 4
Transverse Road No. 3
Transverse Road No. 2
Transverse Rd. No. 1

Morningside Avenue
Manhattan Avenue
Eighth Avenue
Lenox Avenue
Fifth Avenue
A. C. Powell Jr. Blvd.
Nicholas Avenue

0   500 yards

THE UPPER WEST SIDE AND MORNINGSIDE HEIGHTS

reach the pinnacle of prosperity, the historic apartment houses of Central Park West and Riverside Drive. Sandwiched between these most prestigious of Manhattan addresses are modern high-rise apartment buildings and historic brownstones, dozens of restaurants, outdoor cafés and bars, clothing stores, gourmet food emporiums and a casual mix of people. Above 90th Street, particularly along Amsterdam Avenue and Columbus Avenue (streets that in the blocks around the 70s have become irreparably yuppified) you will still find enclaves of public housing, some shabby SRO ("single room occupancy") hotels, and downbeat street hustle that increase the further north you go, until the 100s where you'll find mostly poor Latino neighborhoods. However, even these areas have started to gentrify lately, with middle-class families moving into areas further north that they previously would have shunned.

Columbus Circle and around

Columbus Circle is located at the intersection of Broadway, Central Park West and 59th Street: a pedestrian's worst nightmare but a good place to start investigating the Upper West Side nonetheless. Christopher Columbus stands uncomfortably atop a lone column (a recent target for anti-imperialist graffiti) in the center of this odd cast of buildings grouped around a hazardous traffic circle. At the southern end stands an odd, white, vaguely Moorish, building that is one of the city's grand *folies*; when it went up in 1965, it was said to resemble a Persian brothel. It used to house the New York City Department of Cultural Affairs and a NY Conventions and Visitors Bureau, but now stands empty awaiting a new tenant.

To the west is the **Coliseum**, an exhibition hall with a dismal white concrete facade, built in 1956. Opposite the circle, on the park side, stands the **Maine Monument**, a large stone edifice with the prow of a ship jutting out from its base, crowned by a newly gilded and polished victory statue that shines proudly above the entrance to the park. Erected in 1912, it is dedicated to the "valiant seamen who perished in the Maine" during the turn-of-the-century Spanish–American War. Across the street, at the junction of Broadway and Central Park West, is the glittering **Trump International Hotel** (1 Central Park W), a new luxury hotel and residential condo, that during its recent renovation was touted as "The World's Most Prestigious Address" – just the most recent example of Trump's extraordinary hubris. A large silver globe sits on the plaza in front of the hotel, a glitzy and completely unnecessary replica of the Unisphere that is on display at the 1964 World's Fair site in Queens.

For relief, go west a few blocks and contemplate the **Church of St Paul the Apostle** (9th Avenue between 59th and 60th streets), a beautiful Old Gothic structure housing Byzantine basilica features, such as Stanford White's High Altar. A few steps further north the nearby **New York Society for Ethical Culture** (2 W 64th St at

The NY Conventions and Visitors Bureau has moved to 810 Seventh Ave, between 52nd and 53rd streets. See p.22 for details.

Central Park West; ☎874-5210), "a haven for those who want to share the high adventure of integrating ethical ideals into daily life." Founded in 1876 (though the building wasn't built until 1902), this distinguished organization also helped to found the National Association for the Advancement of Colored Peoples and the American Civil Liberties Union. It holds regular Sunday meetings, and organizes occasional recitals and lectures on social responsibility, politics and other related topics. It also runs an elementary school here where J. Robert Oppenheimer, who directed the development of the first atomic bomb, among other notable people, was a student.

Lincoln Center

Broadway continues north from Columbus Circle to the **Lincoln Center for the Performing Arts**, an imposing group of white-marble and glass buildings arranged around a large plaza and fountain, on the west side between 63rd and 66th streets. Robert Moses came up with the idea of creating a cultural center on the west side in the 1950s as a way of "encouraging" gentrification of the area, an exercise in urban renewal that has been extremely successful. A number of architects worked on the plans and the complex was finally built in the mid-1960s on a site that formerly held some of the city's poorest slums. After the slums were emptied (and the residents sent to ghettos further Uptown), but before construction actually started, the run-down lots served as the open-air set for the 1960 filming of *West Side Story*.

Home to the Metropolitan Opera and the New York Philharmonic, as well as a host of other smaller companies, Lincoln Center is worth seeing even if you're not into catching a performance; the best way is to go on an **organized tour**, otherwise you'll only be allowed to peak into the ornate lobbies of the buildings. Tours leave daily at 10.30am, 12.30pm, 2.30pm and 4.30pm from the ticket booth at the Met, and take in the main part of the Center at a cost of $9.50 ($8 for students) for an hour-long tour. Be warned that they can get very booked up; best phone ahead (☎875-5350) to be sure of a place. Backstage tours of the Met are also available; see opposite for more information.

You could also stop by for **free entertainment**: there's the Autumn Crafts Fair in early September, folk and jazz bands at lunchtime throughout the summer, and dazzling fountain and light displays each evening. In addition, Lincoln Center hosts a variety of affordable summertime events, including Mostly Mozart, the country's first and most popular indoor summer chamber music series, and Midsummer Night Swing, a summertime dance series that allows you to swing, salsa, hustle and ballroom dance on an outdoor bandstand at the Lincoln Center Plaza Fountain. Call **Lincoln Center Information** ☎875-5000 for specifics.

The New York State Theater and Avery Fisher Hall

Philip Johnson's spare and elegant **New York State Theater**, on the south side of the plaza, is home to the New York City Ballet, the New York City Opera and the famed annual December performances of *The Nutcracker Suite*. Its foyer is ringed with balconies embellished with delicately worked bronze grilles and boasts an imposing, four-story high ceiling finished in gold leaf. The ballet season runs from late November through February, and from early April through June; the opera season starts in July and runs through mid-November. Call ☎870-5570 for ticket information.

Johnson also had a hand in the **Avery Fisher Hall** opposite, on the north side of the plaza; he was called in to refashion the interior after its acoustics were found to be below par. The seating space here, though, does not possess the magnificence of his glittery horseshoe-shaped auditorium across the way, and the most exciting thing about Avery Fisher Hall is its foyer, dominated by a huge hanging sculpture by Richard Lippold, whose distinctive style you may recognize from an atrium or two Downtown. The New York Philharmonic performs here from September though May; the less expensive Mostly Mozart concerts take place here in July and August. Call ☎875-5030 for performance information.

The Metropolitan Opera House

The Metropolitan Opera House (aka "the Met"), the focal point of the plaza, is by contrast ornate, with enormous crystal chandeliers and red-carpeted staircases designed for grand entrances in gliding evening wear. Behind two of the higharched windows hang **murals** by Marc Chagall. The artist wanted stained glass, but it was felt at the time these wouldn't last long in an area still less than reverential toward the arts, so paintings were hung behind square-paned glass to give a similar effect. These days they're covered for part of the day to protect them from the morning sun; the rest of the time they're best viewed from the plaza outside. The mural on the left, *Le Triomphe de la Musique*, is cast with a variety of well-known performers, landmarks snipped from the New York skyline and a portrait of Sir Rudolph Bing, the man who ran the Met for more than three decades – here garbed as a gypsy. The other mural, *Les Sources de la Musique*, is reminiscent of Chagall's renowned Met production of *The Magic Flute*: the god of music strums a lyre while a Tree of Life, Verdi and Wagner all float down the Hudson River.

The opera house, with its elegant interior of African rosewood and red velvety chairs, says opulence, pure and simple. The acoustics and the singers make the music here; there is no electronic voice enhancement whatsoever (though the new multilingual titling and translation system is definitely state-of-the-art). **Backstage Tours** of the Met cost $8 and are given on Monday, Tuesday, Thursday, Friday and Sunday at 3.45pm and 10am on Saturday. As for performances, you'll find full details of what you can listen to and how to do it in Chapter 20, *The Performing Arts and Film* or call ☎362-6000.

The rest of Lincoln Center

Two piazzas flank the Met; to the south there is Damrosch Park, a large space with rows of chairs facing the **Guggenheim Bandshell**, where you can catch free summer lunchtime concerts and various performances. To the north you will find a lovely, smaller plaza facing the **Vivian Beaumont Theater** designed by Eero Saarinen in 1965 and home to the smaller **Mitzi E. Newhouse Theater** in its basement. This square is mostly taken up by a rectangular reflecting pool, around which Manhattan office workers munch their lunch while mid-pond reclines a lazy **Henry Moore** figure, given counterpoint at the edge by a spidery sculpture by **Alexander Calder**.

The **New York Public Library for the Performing Arts** (☎870-1630) is located behind the theater and holds over eight million items, and a museum that exhibits costumes, set designs and music scores. However, the library is under renovation until 2001, so it's best to call ahead as exhibits and times are constantly changing. Across 66th Street is **Alice Tully Hall**, a recital hall that houses the Chamber Music Society of Lincoln Center, and the **Walter E. Reade Theater**, which features foreign films and retrospectives and, together with the Avery Fisher and Alice Tully Halls, hosts the annual **New York Film Festival** in September. The famed **Juilliard School of Music** is in an adjacent building. **Dante Park**, a small triangular island on Broadway, across from the main Lincoln Center Plaza, is home to a statue designed in 1921 to commemorate the 600th anniversary of the poet's death. But that is no longer its greatest claim to fame; Movado (the Swiss watch designers) has just erected *TimeSculpture* there, a stone sculpture with a series of large brass clocks designed by Philip Johnson, dedicated in May 1999 to the patrons of Lincoln Center.

West 66th Street to 72nd Street

North of here, Broadway curves west and Ninth Avenue becomes chic **Columbus Avenue**, home to a multitude of outdoor cafés and eclectic boutiques, many of which are unfortunately being replaced by national chain stores, part of a citywide trend. In a clash of old meets new, the **Museum of American Folk Art** (see p.293) on Columbus Avenue between 65th and 66th streets is just one block south of the **American Broadcast Company** (ABC) television studios and the Capital Cities/ABC corporate headquarters, an imposing postmodern building that overwhelms some of its less intrusive neighbors (and now features a Disney store, stocked with unattractive ABC logo-identified materials).

One 67th Street, closer to Central Park West, is the **Hotel des Artistes**, built specially for artists in 1918, and the one-time

Manhattan address of the likes of Noel Coward, Norman Rockwell, Isadora Duncan and Alexander Woollcott. It's now a swanky co-op apartment building. On the ground floor is the famous **Café des Artistes**, one of Manhattan's most romantic, and pricey, restaurants. If you can't afford to eat here, take a peek inside or have a drink at the famous bar (but make sure you are dressed for it), just to absorb the ambience and see the nude-nymph wall murals by Howard Chandler Christy. The streets in the upper 60s and 70s between Columbus and Central Park West are quiet tree-lined blocks filled with beautifully renovated brownstones, many of which are one-family homes, this neighborhood is one of the most sought-after in the city.

Nearby, smack at the self-avowed forefront of cutting-edge technology, is the imposing **Sony Theaters** (Broadway at 68th St), with its huge IMAX 3D screen. This movie multiplex makes a nod to the Golden Age of Hollywood in the form of twelve large theaters that bear the names and design motifs from prestigious movie houses of the past. Not surprisingly, Sony's highly publicized 3D movies so far have been more impressive for their effects than for their plots, though *Everest* by David Brashears, who was filming in 1996 during the storm immortalized by Jon Krakauer's *Into Thin Air*, has been highly acclaimed.

On Central Park West, taking up the entire block between 71st and 72nd streets, is the **Majestic**, a mammoth pale yellow, Art Deco apartment house built in 1930 and best known for its twin towers and avant-garde brickwork (its sister building, the Century, is located at 25 Central Park W, between 62nd and 63rd streets). Across 72nd Street is the more famous **Dakota Building** (1 W 72nd St), so called because at the time of its construction in 1884 its Uptown location was considered to be as remote as the Dakota Territory. The grandiose German Renaissance-style mansion, with turrets, gables and other odd details, was built to persuade wealthy New Yorkers that life in an apartment could be just as luxurious as in a private house. Over the years there have been few residents here not publicly known in some way: big-time tenants included Lauren Bacall and Leonard Bernstein, and in the 1960s the building was used as the setting for Roman Polanski's film *Rosemary's Baby*. But the most famous recent resident of the Dakota was **John Lennon** (see box, overleaf). If you enter Central Park across the street you can see **Strawberry Fields**, and the mosaic dedicated to Lennon (for more on that, turn to p.169).

West 72nd Street to 86th Street

A good place to start your exploration of this historic neighborhood is at the western edge of 72nd Street, where Riverside Park and Riverside Drive begin and you're as close to the **Hudson River** as you can get before bumping into the West Side Highway. Just south of

The death of John Lennon

Today most people know the Dakota Building as the former home of **John
Lennon** – and present home of his wife Yoko Ono, who owns a number of
the apartments. It was outside the Dakota, on the night of December 8,
1980, that Lennon was murdered – shot by a man who professed to be one
of his greatest admirers.

His murderer, Mark David Chapman, had been hanging around outside
the building all day, clutching a copy of his hero's latest album, *Double
Fantasy*, and accosting Lennon for his autograph – which he got. This was
nothing unusual in itself – fans often used to loiter outside and hustle for
a glimpse of Lennon – but Chapman was still there when the couple
returned from a late-night recording session, and he pumped five .38 bullets into Lennon as he walked through the Dakota's 72nd Street entrance.
Lennon was picked up by the doorman and rushed to the hospital in a taxi,
but he died on the way from a massive loss of blood. A distraught Yoko
issued a statement immediately: "John loved and prayed for the human
race. Please do the same for him."

Why Chapman did this to John Lennon no one really knows; suffice it to
say his obsession with the man had obviously unhinged him. Fans may want
to light a stick of incense for Lennon across the road in Strawberry Fields,
a section of Central Park that has been restored and maintained in his memory through an endowment by Yoko Ono; trees and shrubs were donated by
a number of countries as a gesture toward world peace. The gardens are
pretty enough, if unspectacular, and it would take a hard-bitten cynic not to
be a little bit moved by the *Imagine* mosaic on the pathway.

here were the old **Penn Railroad Yards**, abandoned for nearly two
decades and now being replaced by a towering luxury apartment
development, spearheaded by none other than Donald Trump.
Riverside Drive starts here and winds north, flanked by palatial townhouses and multistory apartment buildings put up in the early part of
the twentieth century by those not quite rich enough to compete with
the folks on Fifth Avenue. A number of historic, landmarked districts
lie along it, particularly in the mid-70s, mid-80s, and low-100s.
Riverside Park also begins here, marked by a welcome recent addition to the neighborhood: the **Eleanor Roosevelt Monument** (corner
of 72nd St and Riverside Drive), dedicated in 1996 by First Lady
Hillary Rodham Clinton. The monument consists of a large, planted
base with a pensive statue of Eleanor Roosevelt standing in its center.
The stone statue, by Penelope Jencks, surrounded by well-kept
benches make it an inviting spot for contemplation.

The park itself is one of only eight designated scenic landmarks in
New York City. It was conceived as a way of attracting the middle
class to the (then) remote Upper West Side and covering the unappealing Hudson River Railway tracks that had been built along the
Hudson in 1846. Not as imposing or spacious as Central Park, it was
designed by the same team of architects; **Frederic Law Olmsted**
started the plans in 1873, but it took 25 years to complete, and other

architects, including his partner, **Calvert Vaux**, contributed designs.
Rock outcroppings and informally arranged trees, shrubs and flowers surround its tree-lined main boulevards. The park was widened in
the 1930s by **Robert Moses**, who typically added some of his own
concrete touches, including the rotunda at the 79th Street Boat
Basin. Between 72nd and 79th streets, the park is at its narrowest
and not as interesting (or scenic) as it becomes farther north.
However, along Riverside Drive there are lovely turn-of-the-century
townhouses, many with copper-trimmed mansard roofs and private
terraces or roof gardens. **West End Avenue**, a unique New York
avenue in that it is purely residential, lined with elegant prewar
apartment buildings and townhouses, and few, if any, modern high-
rises.

Verdi Square is a good place to take a breather and contemplate
the ornate balconies, round corner towers and cupolas of the
Ansonia Hotel (2109 Broadway between W 73rd and W 74th sts).
Completed in 1904, this dramatic Beaux Arts building is still the
artsy grande dame of the Upper West Side. Never a hotel but an
upscale apartment house, it has welcomed such luminaries as Enrico
Caruso, Arturo Toscanini, Lily Pons, Florenz Ziegfeld, Theodore
Dreiser, Igor Stravinsky and even Babe Ruth. **The Beacon Theater**
(2124 Broadway, between W 74th and 75th sts; ☎ 496-7070) is
nothing particularly special from the outside. But step into the lobby,
or better yet the 2700-seat auditorium (a designated landmark) to
get the full effect of its extravagant Greco-Deco-Empire interior. It is
also a great venue for rock shows.

Built in 1930 and taking up the entire block, the **San Remo** at
145–146 Central Park W between 74th and 75th streets, is one of the
most famous components of the Central Park skyline with its ornate
twin towers topped by columned, mock-Roman temples visible from
most points in the park. It is also very exclusive: some years ago
Madonna attempted to buy a multimillion dollar apartment here, but
was roundly refused approval by the building's co-op board.
Unaccountably, many other celebrities have been allowed to live
here, including Warren Beatty and Diane Keaton (when they were an
item), and Mary Tyler Moore. A block farther north is the **Central
Park Historic District**, from 75th to 77th streets on Central Park
West, and on 76th Street toward Columbus Avenue. Here you will
find a number of small turn-of-the-century rowhouses, and the
Kenilworth Apartments (151 Central Park W), which was built in
1908 and boasts an unusual mansard roof and a wildly carved limestone exterior.

Further north is the **New York Historical Society** (2 W 77th St at
Central Park West; ☎ 873-3400), which has a permanent collection
of books, prints, portraits, and the 432 original watercolors of
Audubon's *Birds of America*, as well as a research library (see
p.299). On the next block is the pride of the neighborhood, the

American Museum of Natural History (Central Park W between 77th and 81st sts; ☎769-5100). Said to be the largest museum of any kind in the world (its collection consists of over 34 million artifacts) this elegant giant fills four blocks with a strange architectural mélange of heavy Neoclassical and rustic Romanesque styles that was built in several stages, the first by Calvert Vaux and Jacob Wrey Mould in 1872. The Museum's vast front steps are a great reading-and-sunning place, with an appropriately haughty statue of President Theodore Roosevelt looking out with a resolute gaze from his perch atop a horse, flanked by a pair of Native Americans marching gamely beside him. For a full account of the museum and its exhibits, see p.285.

Take a moment to stroll west along 77th Street to admire all the beautiful townhouses and prewar apartment buildings with premium views of the Natural History Museum. If you are here on a Sunday, check out the extensive **flea market** that takes place year-round in the PS 44 school yard, on the corner of 77th Street and Columbus Avenue. It's a good place to pick up new and vintage jewelry, clothes and knickknacks, and even some fresh veggies from the green market located inside the 77th Street entrance.

Back on Broadway, the enormous limestone **Apthorp Apartments** (2211 Broadway) occupies an entire block from Broadway to West End and West 78th to West 79th streets. Built in 1908 by William Waldorf Astor, the ornate iron gates of the former carriage entrance lead into a central courtyard with a large fountain, visible from Broadway. Some of the best bagels in New York can be found nearby at **H&H Bagels** (2239 Broadway, at the corner of 80th St), where they are said to bake over 50,000 bagels a day. Another culinary attraction is **Zabar's** (2254 Broadway, between 80th and 81st sts), the Upper West Side's principal gourmet shop and area landmark. Here you can find more or less anything connected with food; the ground floor is given over to things edible, the upper floor contains cooking implements and kitchenware, a collection which, in the obscurity of some of its items, must be unrivaled anywhere. What kitchen, for example, could do without a duck press?

Another delightful place for a break is the **79th Street Boat Basin** in Riverside Park, with paths leading down to it located on either side of 79th Street at Riverside Drive (you'll hit a concrete rotunda first – keep going until you see water). There is a ramp entrance for the disabled, or people with bikes or baby carriages, on the north side of 79th Street. Often overlooked by tourists, this is a small harbor where a couple of hundred Manhattanites live on the water in houseboats, while others just moor their motor boats and sailboats there. It's one of the city's most peaceful locations, and while the views across the water to New Jersey aren't exactly awesome, they're a tonic after the congestion of Manhattan proper.

See p.368 for details on the Boat Basin Café.

On Riverside Drive between 80th and 81st streets there are a row
of historic **landmarked townhouses,** classics of the brownstone
genre, with bowed exteriors, bay windows, gabled roofs and lovely
detail. Nearby is the **Children's Museum of Manhattan** (212 W 83rd
St, between Broadway and Amsterdam; ☎721-1234), a delightful
five-story space that offers interactive exhibits that stimulate learning, in a really fun, relaxed environment for kids (and babies) of all
ages. The Dr. Seuss exhibit and the storytelling room (filled with
books kids can choose from) are particular winners. See Chapter 23,
"Kid's New York" for hours and admission information. The location
of the Children's Museum is appropriate, as Broadway in the 80s is
characterized more than anything else by parents with babies in
strollers or young children in hand, promenading along the boulevard, eating in the cafés and playing in the parks.

At 215 W 84th St, there's a plaque marking the one-time address
of **Edgar Allen Poe** (he lived in a farmhouse on the site in 1844,
while he finished *The Raven*), now sadly just a faceless condo; if
you're a real Poe fan, head over to Riverside Park and sit on the
rocky outcropping known as **Mount Tom** at 83rd Street, where Poe
was said to have written a few works, such as the poem "To Helene."

West 86th Street to 110th Street

The northern part of the Upper West Side has seen a lot of changes
in the last few years. Gentrification is slowly creeping northward,
sometimes for the better, sometimes not. The obligatory Starbucks
have proliferated around here, as have chain clothing stores and (on
the upside) nicer restaurants of all stripes. Check out one of the few
real old-timer spots left in the neighborhood, **Barney Greengrass
(the Sturgeon King),** opened its doors in 1908 and specializes in
smoked fish, located on Amsterdam Avenue, between 86th and 87th
streets.

The multistory **Claremont Riding Academy** (175 W 89th St
between Columbus and Amsterdam aves; ☎724-5100), home to the
steeds of New York's privileged Upper West Siders, is the oldest
functioning commercial stable in Manhattan. You can take a lesson
or ride in the bridle paths of Central Park a few blocks away (see
p.430). Although there are fewer elegant apartment buildings north
of 90th Street on Central Park West itself, some lovely old townhouses and prewar apartments remain, the most luxurious being the
Art Deco **Eldorado Apartments** (300 Central Park W between 90th
and 91st sts), built in 1931. The northernmost of Central Park West's
twin-towered apartment buildings, it peaks tantalizingly over the
Central Park skyline and helps to mark the transition from fabulous
residences below 96th Street to housing projects and a certain
amount of disrepair above.

If you are exploring West End Avenue or vicinity in the 90s and
low 100s, there are a few interesting monuments nearby in Riverside

Park. **The Soldiers' and Sailor's Monument** (1902), a marble
memorial to the Civil War dead, is located at Riverside Drive and
89th Street. The **Joan of Arc Monument** at West 93rd Street and
Riverside sits atop a 1.6-acre cobblestone and grass park named
Joan of Arc Island. Last, and most impressive, is the **Fireman's
Memorial** at West 100th Street, a stately commemorative frieze
designed in 1913 with the statues of *Courage* and *Duty* at its top.
There is also a large, beautifully planted **community garden** in
Riverside Park just south of 96th Street, lovingly cared for by local
volunteers.

As you weave your way through inevitably crowded sidewalks,
you will reach the **Symphony Space** (2537 Broadway between W
94th and 95th sts; ☎864-5400), one of New York's primary performing arts centers, known for its sophisticated, if slightly quirky,
programming. The Symphony Space regularly sponsors short story
readings (called Selected Shorts), as well as classical and world
music performances. But it is perhaps best known for its free,
twelve-hour performance marathons, like the annual Leonard
Bernstein Marathon and the uninterrupted reading of James Joyce's
Ulysses every Bloomsday (June 16). The theater is currently open,
but if you are interested in a performance call for an update on its
status. Another interesting sight is the **Metro Theater** (Broadway
and 99 St), one of the few old movie theaters left in New York that
still has part of its original facade, look above the glitzy marquee –
you'll see the Art Deco design with the Greek comedy/tragedy
masks at its center. Further north on Riverside Drive between 105th
and 106th streets is a lovely block of historic apartments. It begins
with **330 Riverside Drive**, now the Riverside Study Center, a glorious five-story Beaux-Arts house built in 1900 – note the copper
mansard roof, stone balconies and delicate iron scrollwork. **331
Riverside Drive** is the current headquarters of the New York
Buddhist Church but formerly the home of Marion Davies, a 1930s
actress most famous for her role as William Randolph Hearst's mistress. Hearst actually had this small mansion built for her in 1902,
and sometimes stayed here with her, while his family lived not too
far away Downtown.

The odd little building next door is also part of the **New York
Buddhist Church** showcasing a larger than life-size bronze statue of
Shinran Shonin (1173–1262), the Japanese founder of the Jodo-
Shinsu sect of Buddhism. It originally stood in Hiroshima, Japan and
somehow survived the atomic explosion of August 1945. It was
brought to New York in 1955 as a symbol of "lasting hope for world
peace" and has been in this spot ever since. Local lore had it that the
statue was still radioactive, so in the 1950s and 60s children were
told to hold their breath for protection as they went by. At **337
Riverside Drive**, the River Mansion, at the corner of 106th Street
was once home to Duke Ellington. In fact, this stretch of West 106th

Street has been renamed Duke Ellington Boulevard to honor the great composer and musician. At 107th Street, Broadway and West End Avenue meet at the recently remodelled **Strauss Park**, a small vest-pocket space centered on an **Augustus Lukeman statue** of a reclining woman gazing over a water basin. It was dedicated by Macy's founder Nathan Strauss to his brother/business partner Isidor and Isidor's wife Ida, both of whom lived nearby and went down with the *Titanic* in 1912 – legend has it that Ida refused to leave Isidor for the lifeboats.

The Cathedral Church of St John the Divine, Columbia University and Morningside Heights

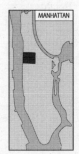

One area just north of the Upper West Side, has also undergone several waves of gentrification in the last decade. Happily, it has managed to retain its own slightly funky, college-town aura, resisting the urge (so far) to convert small stores to large impersonal chains or build luxury high-rise apartments. Filled with Columbia students and professors, middle class families who can't quite afford the rents farther Downtown, and a mix of whites, blacks, Latinos and Asians, it forms an eclectic, quintessentially New York neighborhood. There aren't a lot of sights in the area besides the Cathedral and Columbia, but it is worth a trip just for those.

The Cathedral Church of St John

The Cathedral Church of St John the Divine (Amsterdam Ave between 110th and 113th sts), rises out of the urban landscape with a sure, solid kind of majesty – far from finished, but still one of New York's most impressive sights, it is frequently visited by dignitaries and world leaders, including the Dalai Lama. If you happen to be here around Christmas, stop in for the Christmas Eve Candlelight Carol Service at 10pm, but, as with all things in New York, get here early – St John's is packed by the time the music begins, with standing room even hard to come by. Everyone is welcome, and if you want to leave after the caroling (and before the service), feel free; lots of people come from all over the city just for the music and the ambience.

Work on the Episcopal church began in 1892 to the specifications of a Romanesque design that, with a change of architect in 1911, became French Gothic. Work progressed quickly for a while but stopped with the outbreak of war in 1939 and only resumed again in the mid-1980s. The church declared bankruptcy in 1994, fraught with funding difficulties and hard questioning by people who think the money might be better spent on something of more obvious ben-

The
Cathedral
Church of
St John the
Divine,
Columbia
University
and
Morningside
Heights

efit to the local community, and has since launched a massive international fund-raising drive in the hope of resuming building work soon.

That said, St John's is very much a community church, housing a soup kitchen and shelter for the homeless, AIDS awareness and health outreach initiatives, and other social programs, as well as a gymnasium and plans for an amphitheatre for theater and music productions. And some of the building work itself is being undertaken by local African-Americans who are trained by English stonemasons in the church's own sculpture/stone workshops. The cathedral appears finished at first glance, but when you gaze up into its huge, uncompleted towers, you realize how much is left to do. Only two-thirds of the cathedral is finished, and completion isn't due until around 2050 – even assuming it goes on uninterrupted. Still, if finished, St John the Divine will be the largest cathedral structure in the world, its floor space – at 600 feet long and at the transepts 320 feet wide – big enough to swallow both the cathedrals of Notre Dame and Chartres whole, or, as tour guides are at pains to point out, two full-size football fields.

The Portal of Paradise at the Cathedral's main entrance, was recently completed, and is dazzlingly carved, with 32 biblical figures both male and female, despite the original men-only design, and such startling images as a mushroom cloud rising apocalyptically over Manhattan, all chiseled in limestone and painted with metallic oxide. But progress is long and slow; the portal alone took ten years to complete.

Walking the length of the **nave**, these figures seem much more than just another piece of bigger-is-better Americana – the size is truly awe-inspiring and adds to the spiritual power of the space. Here, too, you can see the welding of the two styles, particularly in the choir, which rises from a heavy arcade of Romanesque columns to a high, light-Gothic vaulting, the temporary dome of the crossing to someday be replaced by a tall, delicate Gothic spire. The open-minded, progressive nature of St Johns is readily visible throughout the cathedral itself: note the intricately carved wood **Altar for Peace**, the **Poets Corner**, with the names of American poets carved into its stone block floor, and an altar honoring AIDS victims. For some idea of how the completed cathedral will look, glance in on the gift shop, housed, for the moment, in the north transept, where there's a scale model of the projected design, as well as an interesting array of books and souvenirs.

Next to the cathedral on the south side are the **Bestiary Gates**, their grillework adorned with animal imagery (celebrating the annual blessing of the animals ceremony held here on the Feast of St Francis), and a **Children's Sculpture Garden** showcasing small bronze animal sculptures that were created by local schoolchildren. Afterwards, take a stroll through the cathedral yard and workshop, where if work has begun again, you can watch Harlem's apprentice masons tapping away at the stone blocks of the future cathedral.

Columbia University and Morningside Heights

The area to the east of the Cathedral is known as **Morningside Heights**, so called because of its large park of that name, acting as a buffer zone between East Harlem sprawling below and the academic, relatively affluent Columbia neighborhood up on the hill, bounded by Morningside Drive. **Morningside Park**, stretching from 110th to 123rd streets, was landscaped in 1887 by Frederick Law Olmsted; its foliage is lush and attractive, but after dark at least, it's to be treated with more than a bit of caution.

A block away, Broadway is characterized by a livelier bustle, with numerous inexpensive restaurants, bars and cafés, and a few bookstores. The **West End** (2911 Broadway, between 113th and 114th sts) was formerly the hangout of Jack Kerouac, Allen Ginsberg and the Beats in the 1950s; "one of those nondescript places," wrote Joyce Johnson, "before the era of white walls and potted ferns and imitation Tiffany lamps, that for some reason always made the best hangouts." It still serves the student crowd from the nearby university, though stand-up comedy and karaoke have replaced *Howl* as the performances of choice.

The **Columbia University** campus fills seven blocks between Broadway and Morningside Drive from 114th to 121st streets, with its main entrance at Broadway and 116th Street. It is one of the most prestigious academic institutions in the country, ranking with the other Ivy League colleges of the Northeast and boasting a campus laid out by McKim, Mead and White in grand Beaux Arts style. Of the buildings, the domed and colonnaded **Low Memorial Library** (built in 1902) stands center-stage at the top of a wide flight of stone steps, a focus for somewhat violent demonstrations during the Vietnam War. Tours leave regularly Monday to Friday during the school year from the **information office** on the corner of 116th Street and Broadway. Call ahead (☎ 854-4900) to schedule a tour or get additional information. For a culinary treat and great wraparound views of Manhattan (beware, it is very pricey), eat at *The Terrace* restaurant (400 W 119th St; reservations recommended ☎ 666-9490) on the top floor of **Butler Hall** (not to be confused with Butler Library).

Across Broadway is **Barnard College**. Part of Columbia University, it was the place where women had to study for their degrees until Columbia finally removed their "men-only" policy. Many women still choose to study here, and Barnard retains its status as one of America's elite "Seven Sisters" colleges. **Riverside Church**, located north of here on Riverside Drive between 120th and 121st streets (daily 9am–4.30pm, Sun service 10.45am), has a

The
Cathedral
Church of
St John the
Divine,
Columbia
University
and
Morningside
Heights

graceful French Gothic Revival tower, loosely modeled on Chartres and, like St John's, turned over to a mixture of community center and administrative activities for the surrounding parish. Take the elevator to the 20th floor and ascend the steps around the carillon (the largest in the world, with 74 bells) for some classic spreads of Manhattan's skyline, New Jersey and the hills beyond – and the rest of the city well into the Bronx and Queens. Take a look too at the church, whose open and restrained interior (apart from the apse, which is positively sticky with ornament) is in stark contrast to the darkened mystery of St John the Divine.

Up the block from the church is **Grant's Tomb** (Riverside Drive between 122nd and 131st sts; daily 9am–5pm; ☎666-1620), a Greek-style memorial and the nation's largest mausoleum in which, the old joke notwithstanding, conquering Civil War hero and blundering eighteenth US president Grant really is interred with his wife, in a black-marble Napoleonic sarcophogi. The tomb was refurbished in 1996, so current visitors will be spared the graffiti and trash that for some years festooned the resting place of a national hero.

The Upper East Side

The defining characteristic of Manhattan's **Upper East Side**, a two-square-mile grid scored with the great avenues of Madison, Park and Lexington, is wealth – and wealth does have its privileges. While other neighborhoods are affected by incursions of immigrant groups, artistic trends, and the like, this remains primarily an enclave of the well-off, with tony shops, clean and relatively safe streets, well-preserved buildings and landmarks, and some of the city's finest museums. East of Lexington Avenue was until recently a working-class district of modest houses, though not surprisingly, gentrification has quickly changed its character, although it still remains markedly more downbeat towards the river.

Fifth, Madison and Park avenues

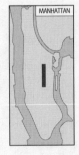

Fifth Avenue has been the haughty patrician face of Manhattan since the opening of Central Park in 1876 lured the Carnegies, Astors, Vanderbilts, Whitneys and other capitalists north from lower Fifth Avenue and Gramercy Park to build their fashionable residences on the strip alongside. Once unthinkable, upper Fifth Avenue addresses not only became acceptable but stylish. To this day the address remains so prestigious that buildings with no Fifth Avenue entrance to speak of call themselves by their would-be Fifth Avenue addresses instead of the more accurate side-street address, the latter being much too common. Gazing out over the park, these buildings went up when Neoclassicism was the rage, and hence the surviving originals are cluttered with columns and classical statues. A great deal of what you see, though, is third- or fourth-generation building: through the latter part of the nineteenth century, fanciful mansions were built at vast expense, to last only ten or fifteen years before being demolished for even wilder extravagances or, more commonly, grand apartment blocks. Rocketing land values made the chance of selling at vast profit irresistible.

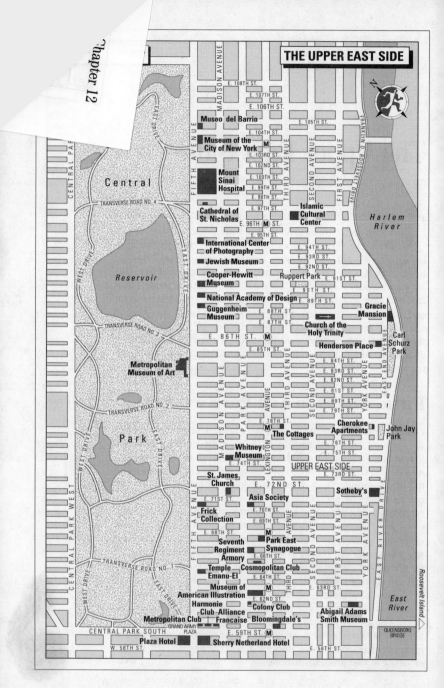

Chapter 12

THE UPPER EAST SIDE

E. 108TH ST.
E. 107TH ST.
E. 106TH ST.
E. 105TH ST.
Museo del Barrio
E. 104TH ST.
Museum of the
City of New York
E. 103RD ST.
E. 102ND ST.
E. 100TH ST.
Mount
Sinai
Hospital
E. 99TH ST.
E. 98TH ST.
E. 97TH ST.
Cathedral of
St. Nicholas
Islamic
Cultural
Center
E. 96TH ST.
E. 95TH ST.
International Center
of Photography
E. 94TH ST.
Jewish Museum
E. 93RD ST.
E. 92ND ST.
Cooper-Hewitt
Museum
Ruppert Park
E. 91ST ST.
E. 90TH ST.
National Academy of Design
E. 89TH ST.
Guggenheim
Museum
E. 88TH ST.
Gracie
Mansion
E. 87TH ST.
Church of the
Holy Trinity
E. 86TH ST.
E. 85TH ST.
Henderson Place
Carl
Schurz
Park
E. 84TH ST.
Metropolitan
Museum of Art
E. 83RD ST.
E. 82ND ST.
E. 81ST ST.
E. 80TH ST.
E. 79TH ST.
E. 78TH ST.
Cherokee
Apartments
John Jay
Park
The Cottages
E. 76TH ST.
Whitney
Museum
E. 75TH ST.
E. 74TH ST.
UPPER EAST SIDE
E. 73RD ST.
St. James
Church
E. 72ND ST.
Asia Society
Sotheby's
Frick
Collection
E. 70TH ST.
E. 69TH ST.
E. 68TH ST.
Seventh
Regiment
Armory
Park East
Synagogue
E. 66TH ST.
Temple
Emanu-El
Cosmopolitan Club
E. 64TH ST.
Museum of
American Illustration
E. 63RD ST.
Harmonie
Club
Colony Club
E. 62ND ST.
Alliance
Francaise
Bloomingdale's
Abigail Adams
Smith Museum
Metropolitan Club
GRAND ARMY
PLAZA
E. 59TH ST.
CENTRAL PARK SOUTH
QUEENSBORO
BRIDGE
Plaza Hotel
Sherry Netherland Hotel
E. 58TH ST.
W. 58TH ST.

Central
Park
Reservoir
TRANSVERSE ROAD NO. 4
TRANSVERSE ROAD NO. 3
TRANSVERSE ROAD NO. 2
TRANSVERSE ROAD NO. 1
EAST DRIVE
WEST DRIVE
CENTRAL PARK WEST

Harlem
River
East
River
Roosevelt Island

MADISON AVENUE
FIFTH AVENUE
PARK AVENUE
LEXINGTON AVENUE
THIRD AVENUE
SECOND AVENUE
FIRST AVENUE
YORK AVENUE
EAST END AVENUE
FRANKLIN D. ROOSEVELT DRIVE
EAST RIVER DRIVE

Southern Fifth Avenue

Grand Army Plaza is the southernmost point of introduction to all this, an oval at the junction of Central Park South and Fifth Avenue that marks the division between Fifth as a shopping district to the south and a residential boulevard to the north. This is one of the city's most dramatic public spaces, boasting a fountain and a recently replated gold statue of Civil War victor General William Tecumseh Sherman, and flanked by the extended copper-lined chateau of the **Plaza Hotel**, with the darkened, swooping television screen facade of the **Solow Building** behind. Across the plaza, the imposing marble-faced lines of the **General Motors Building** offer six stories of toys inside at **F.A.O. Schwarz**, the building's main commercial tenant. Two more hotels, the high-necked **Sherry Netherland** and **Pierre**, luxuriate nearby. Many of the rooms here have permanent guests; needless to say, they're not on welfare.

Fifth Avenue and its environs are dotted with the (traditionally men's) clubs which serviced, and still cater to, its mainly wealthy population. When **J.P. Morgan**, William and Cornelius Vanderbilt, and their pals arrived on the social scene in the 1890s, established society still looked askance at bankers and financiers, and its Downtown clubs were closed to Morgan and anyone else it considered less than up to snuff. Never to be slighted or outdone, Morgan commissioned Stanford White to design him his own club, bigger, better and grander than all the rest – and so the **Metropolitan Club** at 1 East 60th St was born, an exuberant confection with a marvelously outrageous gateway. Just the thing for arriving robber barons.

Another unwelcome group, affluent Jews, founded the elegant **Harmonie Club** in the 1850s and erected its home at 4 E 60th St around the same time. So many *parvenus* caused alarm, and in 1915 the **Knickerbocker Club**, a handsome brick Federal-style building on the corner of Fifth Avenue and 62nd Street, was erected in response to the "relaxed standards" of the **Union Club** (101 E 69th St), which had admitted several of Morgan's and Vanderbilt's friends. Before even the thought of admitting women to these hallowed bastions of old guard maleness occurred, there was the **Colony Club** on Park Avenue at 62nd Street, founded in 1903, and is the city's earliest social club organized by women for women. In 1933, Delano & Aldrich, the firm which had designed the Knickerbocker Club, constructed an elaborate Colonial building with extensive gymnasium and spa facilities as the **Cosmopolitan Club**, at 122 E 66th St. This was originally a place where rich women sent their governesses, but they eventually reclaimed the building for themselves. It's a strange apartment-block-like building, with white ironwork terraces reminiscent of New Orleans, and a private garden in the back.

On the corner of 65th Street and Fifth Avenue, America's largest reform synagogue, the **Temple Emanu-El**, strikes a more sober aspect, a brooding Romanesque–Byzantine cavern that manages to be bigger inside than it seems out. The interior melts away into mysterious darkness, making you feel very small indeed (Mon–Fri & Sun 10am–5pm, Sat noon–5pm; ☎744-1400 for special high holy day schedules). To get your fix of things Gallic go to the **Alliance Française** (22 E 60th St; ☎355-6100), the French cultural institute that hosts a number of noteworthy lectures as well as a Ciné Club series of classic and contemporary French films.

The rest of the East 60s are typical Upper East Side, a trim mix of small apartment houses and elegant town. One of the most beautiful private homes up here is the turn-of-the-century **Ernesto and Edith Fabbri House** at 11 E 62nd St, built for a Vanderbilt daughter in a Parisian Beaux Arts style with curving iron balconies. **The Sarah Delano Roosevelt Memorial House** at 47 E 65th was commissioned by Sarah Delano Roosevelt as a handy townhouse for her son Franklin, no. 142 belonged to Richard Nixon, and no. 115 is the US headquarters of the PLO. Quite a neighborhood.

Museum Mile and beyond

As Fifth Avenue progresses north, it becomes Museum Mile, New York's greatest concentration of art and exhibitions – several of them housed in a few remaining mansions. Henry Clay Frick's house at 70th Street is marginally less ostentatious than its neighbors and is now the deliciously intimate and tranquil home of the **Frick Collection**, one of the city's musts – even the lush gardens that surround it are a treat. Along the avenue (or just off it) are the **Whitney** (modern American art), the **National Academy of Design**, the **Metropolitan Museum** (the "Met"), the **Guggenheim Collection** (twentieth-century painting housed in Frank Lloyd Wright's helter-skelter mustard pot), the **Cooper-Hewitt Museum of Design**, the **International Center of Photography** and, pushing further north, the **Museum of the City of New York** and **El Museo del Barrio**. There's more than enough to keep you busy for a week at least; for listings see Chapter 15, "Museums and Galleries."

Take away Fifth Avenue's museums and a resplendent though fairly bloodless strip remains. Immediately east is **Madison Avenue**, a strip that was entirely residential until the 1920s. Today it is mainly an elegant shopping street, lined with top-notch designer clothes stores, some of whose doors are kept locked. At 699 Madison (63rd Street) is the tiny home of the **Margo Feiden Galleries**, which represent the work of the great New York caricaturist Al Hirschfeld, famous for his swirly portraits of Broadway stars. It's fun to admire the wedding dresses in **Vera Wang**'s bridal boutique at 991 Madison Avenue (between 77th and 78th sts). One notable exception to the demure commercialism here is the stately **St James' Church** at 865 Madison Ave, between 71st and 72nd streets, with its graceful Byzantine altar. A block away, **Park Avenue** is less extravagant, yet still as stolidly comfortable and often elegant. In the low 90s, the large black shapes of the **Louise Nevelson sculptures** stand out on the traffic islands, and just above 96th Street the neighborhood abruptly transforms into **Spanish Harlem** at the point where the subway line emerges from underground. One of the best features of this boulevard is the sweeping view, as Park Avenue coasts down to the **New York Central** and **Met Life** (originally Pan Am) buildings.

Architectural gems and homes of the rich and (in)famous nestle in the side streets. The **Wildenstein family**, premier art dealers now under attack for handling art stolen by the Nazis, and beneficiaries of bizarre plastic surgery, have both their gallery and private mansion on East 64th Street between Park and Madison. **Andy Warhol** spent the last 13 years of his life, from 1974 to 1987, in a surprisingly conservative and extremely private narrow brick house at **57 E 66th St**: no friends were allowed inside, and when Warhol died he left behind oddities like a massive collection of cookie jars. While you're here, have a look at **no. 64** across the street, an elegant sandstone house with a green copper bay window and stained glass. At Park and East 66th Street are several **stables**, built a few blocks east of Fifth for use by the mansions, and now transformed into expensive art galleries (**no. 126**, with its Romanesque facade, is especially handsome).

Dominating a square block is the **Seventh Regiment Armory** (Park Ave between 66th and 67th sts), built in the 1870s with pseudo-medieval crenellations and, inside, a grand double stairway and spidery wrought iron chandeliers – the only surviving building from the era before the New York Central's railroad tracks were roofed over and Park Avenue became an upscale residential neighborhood. There are two surviving Aesthetic Movement interiors inside, executed by the firm which included Louis Comfort Tiffany and Stanford White – the Veterans' Room and the Library; call ahead for a tour (☎ 744-8180; times vary). Frequent art and antique shows provide an opportunity to gawk at the enormous drill hall inside. Down the street from the armory's rear, on East 67th Street and Lexington Avenue, is a remarkable ensemble of fanciful **Victorian buildings** which narrowly escaped destruction and now resemble a movie set: the baby blue-trimmed local **Police Precinct**, the **Fire Station** with its bright red garage doors, and the whimsical ochre **Park East Synagogue**, with its Moorish arches, floral stained glass and campanile. Further north, **The Asia Society** (725 Park Ave between E 70th and 71st sts; ☎ 288-6400) has a permanent display of the Rockefeller Collection of Asian art and often hosts symposia, lectures, performances and film series and has a well-stocked bookstore on the ground floor.

At the northernmost part of this stretch, as the museums keep rolling by, is **Carnegie Hill**, an historic district bounded by 86th and 99th streets and Fifth and Lexington avenues. This well-tended and well-policed area retains the air of a gated community without the

Fifth, Madison and Park avenues

gates, and is largely inhabited by the more recently *riche*; you might catch a glimpse of celebrity tenants such as Bette Midler or Michael J. Fox, and their bodyguards, jogging down to Central Park. Aside from art and celebrity-sightings, the highlight here is the **Russian Orthodox Cathedral of St Nicholas** (15 E 97th St), most notable for its polychromatic Victorian body and five onion domes on top. Get too much past here, and the upscale living quickly fades.

Lexington Avenue and around

Lexington Avenue is Madison without the class; as the west became richer, property developers rushed to slick up real estate in the east. The signs of its 1960s heyday – hot bars like *Maxwell's Plum*, big stores like Alexander's – are gone, and this is now one of the cheaper areas for studio apartments. Much of the East 60s and 70s now houses young, unattached and upwardly mobile professionals – as the number of "happening" singles bars on Second and Third avenues will attest.

The southern stretches

On the southern perimeter of the Upper East Side, **Bloomingdale's** at 59th and Third is the celebrated American store for clothes and accessories, skillfully aiming its wares at the stylish and affluent (see p.453). Nearby, at 421 E 61st St between York and First Avenue, is the **Abigail Adams Smith Museum** (Mon–Fri noon–4pm, Sun 1–5pm; closed in August; adults $3, students and senior citizens $2, children under 12 free; ☎838-6878), another of those eighteenth-century buildings that managed to survive by the skin of its teeth. This wasn't the actual home of Abigail Adams, daughter of President John Quincy Adams, just its stables, restored with Federal-period propriety by the Colonial Dames of America. The furnishings, knickknacks and the serene little park out back are more engaging than the house itself, but there's an odd sort of pull if you're lucky enough to be guided around by a chattily urbane Colonial Dame.

The house is hemmed in by decidedly unhistoric buildings and overlooked by the **Queensboro Bridge**, which may stir memories as the **59th Street Bridge** of Simon and Garfunkel's *Feeling Groovy* or from the title credits of TV's *Taxi*. This intense profusion of clanging steelwork links Manhattan to Long Island City in Queens, but is utterly unlike the suspension bridges that elsewhere lace Manhattan to the boroughs. "My God, it's a blacksmith's shop!" was architect Henry Hornbostel's comment when he first saw the finished item in 1909.

There's not much just north of this way, save a few yuppie strip clubs, until you hit the New York auction gallery of London-based

Sotheby's, the oldest fine arts auctioneer in the world, at 1334 York Ave between East 71st and 72nd streets (☎606-7000). Admission to a few of the largest auctions is by ticket only, but all viewings are open to the public.

Yorkville

It's left to **Yorkville**, originally a German–Hungarian neighborhood that spills out from East 77th to 96th streets between Lexington and the East River, to try to supply the Upper East Side with a tangible ethnicity. Much of New York's German community arrived after the failed revolution of 1848–49, to be quickly assimilated into the area around Tompkins Square. The influx of Italian and Slavic immigrants to the Lower East Side, the tragic sinking of an excursion steamer carrying Tompkins Square residents, and the opening of the Elevated Railway all around the turn of the century hastened their move Uptown to Yorkville. Other groups followed not long after, and some splendid little townhouses were built for these newcomers, such as **The Cottages** on Third Avenue between East 77th and 78th streets, whose stylish English Regency facades and courtyard gardens remain intact.

Today, you have to search hard to detect a German flavor to the area, and the prospect of cheap rent with an Upper East Side address has lured many folks fresh-out-of-college who now blend amicably with the few elderly German-speaking residents who remain. There are some hints of the old neighborhood, such as the traditional German delicatessens **Schaller and Weber** (1654 2nd Ave between 84th and 85th sts) and **Bremen House** (218–220 E 86th St between Second and Third aves). But otherwise, the area has succumbed to its newer residents: video stores and fast-food restaurants now dominate these blocks.

South of here, beginning on East 76th Street and East End Drive is **John Jay Park**, a lovely patch of green centering around a beautiful pool and gym – which unfortunately only New Yorkers with Parks Department passes can use ($35 per year). Fronting the park on Cherokee Street between 77th and 78th streets are the **Cherokee Apartments**, originally the Shively Sanitarium Apartments, an understatedly elegant row with a splendid courtyard. Up the block at 81st Street is **John Finley Walk**, with its concrete promenade that runs north into the park named after **Carl Schurz**, a nineteenth-century German immigrant who rose to fame as Secretary of the Interior under President Rutherford B. Hayes and as editor of *Harper's Weekly* and the *New York Evening Post*. Winding pathways lead through this small, model park – a breathing space for elderly German speakers and East Siders escaping their postage-stamp apartments. The **FDR Drive** cuts beneath, and there are uninterrupted views across the river to Queens and the confluence of dangerous currents where the Harlem River, Long Island Sound and Harbor meet – not for nothing known as **Hell Gate**.

Gracie Mansion and Henderson Place

One of the reasons Schurz Park is so exceptionally well-manicured and maintained is the high-profile security that surrounds **Gracie Mansion** at 88th Street nearby. Built in 1799 on the site of a Revolutionary fort as a country manor house, it is one of the best-preserved colonial buildings in the city. Roughly contemporary with the Morris–Jumel Mansion (see p.211) and the Abigail Adams house, Gracie Mansion has been the official residence of the mayor of New York City since 1942, when Fiorello LaGuardia, "man of the people" that he was, reluctantly set up house – though "mansion" is a bit overblown for what was a rather cramped clapboard cottage. The mansion is open for tours, usually on Wednesday, though you need to book in advance. (Suggested admission $4, $3 for seniors; ☎570-4751.)

Across from the park and just below Gracie Mansion at East 86th Street and East End Avenue is **Henderson Place**, a set of old servants' quarters now transformed into an "historic district" of luxury cottages. Built in 1882 by John Henderson, a fur importer and real-estate developer, the small and sprightly Queen Anne-style wooden and brick dwellings were constructed to provide close and convenient housing for servants working in the palatial old East End Avenue mansions, most of which have now been torn down. Ironically, these servants' quarters now represent some of the most sought-after real estate in the city, offering the space, quiet and privacy that most of the city's housing lacks.

Around Yorkville's outskirts

Just west of here is **Ruppert Park**, a shaded and civilized bit of village green between East 90th and 91st streets and Second and Third avenues. The remainder of the area's attractions consists of two religious centers. The **Church of the Holy Trinity** (316 E 88th St between First and Second aves) is a picturesque and discreet Victorian church with an enchanting little garden. On Third Avenue at East 96th Street is the **Islamic Cultural Center**, New York's first major mosque, whose orientation toward Mecca was precisely pinpointed with a computer. It was here that the funeral of **Betty Shabazz**, widow of **Malcolm X,** was held in July 1997.

North of here, the mood begins to change rapidly as the bright turquoise facade of the diagonal housing projects on 97th Street and First Avenue signal the change as the streets become busier with the offshoots of El Barrio, the best-known part of New York's significant Latino community. Further west, the elevated tracks of the #4, #5 and #6 Bronx-bound trains surface at Park Avenue and 96th Street, signaling the end of Park Avenue's old-money dominance, while Madison and Fifth avenues retain their grandeur for only a few blocks more.

Roosevelt Island

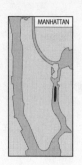

An **aerial tramway** near **Queensboro Bridge** connects mainland Manhattan with **Roosevelt Island** across the water. Though the island was connected by tunnel to the subway system a few years back, the tram is more fun (trams run every 15min, Mon–Thurs & Sun 6am–2am, Fri–Sat 6am–3.30am; every 7½ min during rush hours; $1.50 one way). Once on the island, you can jump on the bright-red minibus that will shuttle you off to the northern end of the island for 25¢. If you feel like exploring, Roosevelt Island rewards with some imaginative housing and unusual views.

Only two miles long and no more than 800 feet wide, Roosevelt Island was owned, inhabited and farmed by the **Blackwell** family from 1676 to 1826, and the brick paving and narrowness of **Main Street** preserve the small-town feel virtually unavailable in any other part of the city today. **Meditation Steps** and the **East River Walk**, a walking and rollerblading path on the western side of the island, permit uncluttered views of Manhattan's East Side and the rattling grates of Queensboro Bridge's metalwork overhead.

On paper this should long have been an ideal residential spot, but its history as "**Welfare Island**," a gloomy quarantine block of jail, poorhouse, lunatic asylum and smallpox hospital, for years put it out of bounds to Manhattanites. The stigma only started to disappear in the 1970s when Johnson and Burgee's master plan spawned the Eastview, Westwood, Island House and Rivercross housing areas. Today these and other residential complexes house deliberately racially and ethnically diverse residents of low-income and market-value housing. The narrow streets, bold signage and modular buildings are locally considered a triumph of urban planning; outsiders may find it reminiscent of the village in the TV series *The Prisoner*.

Grim reminders of Welfare Island remain. The **Octagon Tower**, now off-limits, at the island's north end was once an insane asylum (it briefly housed Mae West after an unpalatably lewd performance in 1927). At the northernmost point of the island the **Lighthouse** affords excellent views of the upper reaches of the East River and the surging waters of Hell Gate, and **Lighthouse Park** is a romantic retreat of grassy knolls and weeping willows.

To the south are the stabilized ruins of what was once the island's **Smallpox Hospital**, now a ghostly Gothic shell, and the **Strecker Laboratory**, the city's premier laboratory for bacteriological research when it opened in 1892. The ruins can be easily spotted from the Manhattan side of the East River but are all but impossible to see from the island itself, as the area surrounding the hospital is boarded up with rows of corrugated metal fencing.

Roosevelt Island seems far away from New York City, a sort of post-Manhattan purgatory before the borough of Queens. Crossing back over the bridge gives a spine-tingling panorama of the city, the one Nick Carraway described in F. Scott Fitzgerald's *The Great Gatsby*:

> *Over the great bridge, with the sunlight through the girders making*
> *a constant flicker upon the moving cars, with the city rising up across*
> *the river in white heaps and sugar lumps all built with a wish out of*
> *non-olfactory money. The city seen from the Queensboro Bridge is*
> *always the city seen for the first time, in its wild promise of all the*
> *mystery and the beauty in the world . . . "Anything can happen now*
> *that we've slid over this bridge" I thought; "anything at all ..."*

Chapter 13

Harlem, Hamilton Heights and the North

This chapter covers the most northerly stretches of Manhattan Island, which comprises a disparate group of localities. **Harlem** has long been synonymous with racial conflict and urban deprivation, though as a visit here will reveal, that's only part of a much bigger picture, one often simplified and jaundiced by media hostile to the black culture here. Though Harlem has its problems, it's a far less dangerous neighborhood than its reputation suggests, especially in light of solid city and neighborhood improvement efforts. Spanish Harlem – **El Barrio** – has an undeniably rougher edge to it, and reasons for visiting are far fewer than for Harlem proper. Further north, **Hamilton Heights** is richer and more residential, an old house and an excellent small museum its main draws. Continuing up, **Washington Heights** is a patchy neighborhood with little in the way of attractions, though you still may have reason to pass through. Because, oddly enough, the most visited site north of Central Park lies very near the top end of the island – the **Cloisters Museum**, a mock medieval monastery that holds the Metropolitan Museums superlative collection of medieval art.

Harlem

As goes Harlem, so goes Black America.

Langston Hughes

Harlem is a part of Manhattan that only some New Yorkers bother to see. This is a rather unfortunate by-product of an enduring legacy: it has languished under a reputation of racial tension and urban decay earned from years of outward neglect and internal strife throughout the 1940s, 1950s and 1960s. Yet Harlem is the most famous African-American community in America, and, arguably, the bedrock of black culture in this century. The Harlem Renaissance of the 1920s and 1930s, during which the talents of such icons as

0   900 yards

W. 164TH ST.
W. 163RD ST.
Riverside
Park
Morris-Jumel
Mansion
W. 160TH ST.
W. 159TH ST.
W. 158TH ST.
W. 157TH ST.
W. 155TH ST.
MACOMBS BRIDGE
Hispanic
Museum
W. 154TH ST.
W. 153RD ST.
W. 150TH ST.
W. 147TH ST.
W. 146TH ST.
146TH STREET
BRIDGE
W. 145TH ST.
W. 145TH ST.
W. 144TH ST.
W. 144TH ST.
W. 141ST ST.
Aunt Len's Doll
& Toy Museum
Hamilton Grange
W. 142ND ST.
W. 141 ST.
Strivers' Row
W. 140TH ST.
HAMILTON
HEIGHTS
Renaissance
Ballroom
Abyssinian
Baptist Church
Nicholas
Schomburg
Center
Small's
Park
Paradise
W. 134TH ST.
W. 133RD ST.
Well's
W. 132ND ST.
W. 131ST ST.
W. 130TH ST.
THIRD AVENUE BRIDGE
City
College
W. 129TH ST.
W. 129TH ST.
WALLIS AVENUE
HARLEM
W. 128TH ST.
W. 127TH ST.
Apollo
Theater
E. 126TH ST.
E. 125TH ST.
W. 125TH ST.
Sylvia's
TRIBOROUGH BRIDGE
Grant's
Tomb
Theresa
Towers
Studio Museum
of Harlem
Marcus
Garvey
Park
E. 120TH ST.
Riverside
Church
Morningside
Park
W. 121ST ST.
W. 120TH ST.
Columbia
University
Minton's
Playhouse
E. 116TH ST.
E. 115TH ST.
W. 116TH ST.
EL BARRIO
Cathedral
W. 112TH ST.
E. 112TH ST.
CENTRAL PARK NORTH
E. 110TH ST.
W. 109TH ST.
W. 109TH ST.
W. 107TH ST.
E. 109TH ST.
E. 108TH ST.
W. 106TH ST.
E. 106TH ST.
E. 105TH ST.
W. 105TH ST.
W. 104TH ST.
E. 104TH ST.
Central
Park
Museo del
Barrio

See 'Upper West Side' Map

Billie Holiday, Paul Robeson and James Weldon Johnson took root,
set the course for the generations of musicians, writers and performers that followed. Harlems history is rich and not a little turbu-
lent. Up until recently, because of its near-total lack of support from
federal and municipal funds, Harlem formed a self-reliant and
inward-looking community. For many downtown Manhattanites,
white and black, 125th Street was a physical and mental border not
willingly crossed.

Today, the fruits of a cooperative effort involving business, residents and City Hall funding are manifest in new housing, retail and community projects. But while brownstones triple in value and Harlems physical proximity to the Upper West Side is touted, poverty and unemployment are still evident in large patches of Harlem. To fully understand New York and its ethnic and economic contradictions, it is, however, necessary to understand and explore this part of the city.

Some hints and history

Practically speaking, Harlems sights are too spread out to amble between. You'll do best to make several trips, preferably beginning with a **guided tour** (see "Information, Maps and Tours" in Basics) to get acquainted with the area and to help you decide what to come back and see on your own. If youre a white visitor, it should be obvious to you that you *will* stand out in this almost exclusively black neighborhood. If you intend to tour Harlem on your own, it will serve you well to feel comfortable about where you're going beforehand, stick to the well-trodden streets and be relaxed once there. Thanks to their strong sense of community, Harlem residents are generally receptive to a friendly smile from passersby, and community businesses and organizations are actively seeking the tourist trade.

Harlems beginnings

As the name suggests, it was the **Dutch** who founded the settlement of **Nieuw Haarlem**, naming it after a town in Holland. Until the mid-nineteenth century this was farmland, but when the New York and Harlem railroad linked the area with Lower Manhattan it attracted the better-off immigrant families (mainly German Jews from the Lower East Side) to newly-built, elegant and fashionable brownstones in the steadily developing suburb. When work began on the IRT Lenox line later in the century, property speculators were quick to build good-quality homes in the expectation of seeing Harlem repeat the success of the Upper West Side. They were too quick and too ambitious, for by the time the IRT line opened most of the buildings were still empty, their would-be takers uneasy at moving so far north. Black real-estate agents saw their chance, bought the empty houses cheaply and rented them to blacks from the Midtown districts and from the South, lured north by industrial work during World War I.

The black community

Very quickly the Jewish, German and Italian populations of Harlem began moving farther north, spurred in part by the influx of blacks, and Harlem became predominantly black. The western areas along **Convent Avenue** and **Sugar Hill** (immortalized in Duke Ellington's *A Train*) were for years the home of the middle classes and preserve traces of a well-to-do past. In the east, the bulge between Park

Avenue and the East River became **Spanish Harlem**, now largely peopled by Puerto Ricans and more properly called **El Barrio** – the Neighborhood. In between live the descendants of West Indian, African, Cuban and Haitian immigrants, often crowded into poorly maintained housing.

This cramping together of dissimilar cultures has long caused tensions and problems not easily understood by the city's bureaucracy. Dotted around Harlem are buildings and projects that attest to an uneasy municipal conscience but have not in any real sense solved the problems of unemployment and urban decay. Sometimes, amid the boarded-up storefronts and vacant lots, it's hard to believe you're but a mile or two away from the cosily patrician Upper East Side.

The 1920s and 1930s: The Harlem Renaissance

There was a brief period when Harlem enjoyed a golden age. In the 1920s whites began to notice the explosion of black culture that had occurred here: jazz musicians like Duke Ellington, Count Basie and Cab Calloway played in nightspots like the *Cotton Club*, *Savoy Ballroom*, *Apollo Theater* and *Smalls Paradise*; the drink flowed as if Prohibition had never been heard of, and the sophisticated set drove up to Harlem's speakeasies after Downtown had gone to bed. Maybe because these revelers never stayed longer than the last drink, neither they, nor history, recall the poverty then rife in Harlem. One of the most evocative voices heard in the clubs those days was of Ethel Waters, who sang in the *Sugar Cane Club*:

> *Rent man waitin for his forty dollars,*
> *Aint got me but a dime and some bad news.*
> *Bartender give me a bracer, double beer chaser,*
> *Cause I got the low-down, mean, rent man blues.*

Equally symbolic, if not more so, of the Harlem Renaissance was the literature of the time – the rich writings of Langston Hughes, Jean Toomer and Zora Neale Hurston, among many others, which caught the fancy of blacks and whites alike. Still, music and literature were not enough to sustain a neighborhood where most were on the economic brink; even before the Depression, it was hard to scrape out a living, and decline drove middle-class blacks out of Harlem.

Harlem today

By the early 1970s, the genesis of redevelopment had begun. Disgraceful living conditions brought residents to a boiling point and fingers were pointed at the slumlords and absentee landlords who were allowing Harlem to fall apart. The city, which had become accustomed to letting Harlem implode for decades, was ultimately stirred into long-overdue action. A plethora of urban and community development grants were put into effect for commercial and retail development, housing and general urban renewal (unlike many so-called ghettos, the quality of the nineteenth-century housing here is excellent and ripe for modernization). Twenty-five years later, the investment is paying off: Harlem's historic areas are well maintained and everywhere you turn, construction seems to be in progress.

Currently, the federally-established Upper Manhattan Empowerment Zone, encompassing Harlem and part of the South Bronx, is pumping $550 million into various area projects. Community-led development organizations involving ninety local churches, spearheaded by the Abyssinian Baptist Church, have become the developers and owners of a number of business sites. But the spectacular recent opening of a Pathmark megastore supermarket on the corner of 125th Street and Lexington Avenue, the first chain supermarket (and the first high-quality one) to open in the neighborhood in three decades, and its coffee-chain neighbor

---

Harlem's music venues

There were once plenty of black-owned and frequented **nightspots** in Harlem, which catered to a black audience only, many of them housed somewhat unglamorously in private brownstones. Most have been converted to other uses. However, several of Harlem's larger jazz venues have survived, and although their current boarded-up state is sobering, these beautiful buildings are slated for restoration and reuse. The Abyssinian Development Corporation has acquired the **Renaissance Ballroom**, (Adam Clayton Powell Blvd between 137th and 138th sts), a tile-trimmed, square- and diamond-shaped Twenties dance club which hosted Duke Ellington, Cab Calloway and Chick Webb, among others. The Rennie, as it was known, was a haven for middle-class blacks and today its original light-up Chop Suey sign (once considered an exotic and fashionable dish) can be seen rusting away on the exterior. The 1925 **Smalls Paradise**, a finial-topped brick building down the boulevard at 135th Street, hosted a mixed black and white crowd. Once known as The Hottest Spot in Harlem, *Smalls* was briefly revived by basketball great Wilt Chamberlain in the Sixties, and is also now owned by Abyssinian (the Harlem Chamber of Commerce has discussed turning it into a tourism center). Malcolm X worked as a waiter at *Smalls* while staying at the *YMCA* at No. 180 on 135th Street. The ground floor of the *Cecil Hotel* at 206-210 W 118th St still displays the light-up sign advertising **Mintons Playhouse**, birthplace of bebop (the precursor to improvisational jazz) in the 1940s, when Thelonious Monk, Dizzy Gillespie, Charlie Parker and John Coltrane would gather here for late-night jam sessions after playing at Harlem's jazz clubs. The hotels current owner hopes to revive *Mintons*. For a look at a venue which has survived the decades check out the legendary **Apollo Theater** at 253 W 125th St, which has been a supporter of black entertainment since the 1930s (see p.398). Another survivor, memorable in part for its unusual pairing of jazz, fried chicken and waffles is **Wells** at 2249_7 Powell Blvd, with its striking mirrored bar and Monday Big Band jazz nights. *Wells* has been in business since 1938 and has played host to The Rat Pack (Sammy Davis Jr, Frank Sinatra, Dean Martin, Peter Lawford, Joey Bishop), Aretha Franklin, and Nat King Cole tied the knot here.

Starbucks at Lenox Avenue, have been met with a mixed reception. Activists (with good reason) point out that community businesses have not been receiving the loans offered to the white-owned mega-stores. And some have suggested that the revitalization effort is nothing more than a thinly-veiled land-grab aimed at gentrifying the neighborhood for the benefit of affluent whites. Fortunately, many affluent blacks are making a point of moving back to Harlem already. In fact, Harlem residents have taken to saying that a Second Harlem Renaissance is underway. Combined with recent figures that show a dramatic drop in crime in the neighborhood and a renewed community spirit, this may not be an overly optimistic view.

Exploring Harlem

125th Street between Broadway and Fifth Avenue is the working center of Harlem and serves as its main commercial and retail drag. The subway lets you out here, and the **Adam Clayton Powell, Jr. State Office Building** on the corner of Seventh Avenue provides a looming concrete landmark. Commissioned in 1972, it replaced a constellation of businesses which included Elder Louis Michauxs bookstore, one of Malcolm X's main rallying points. When construction began, the protests of squatters were so vehement that the city made several concessions: the bookstore was relocated one avenue eastward, and the building was named in the honor of Adam Clayton Powell Jr, Harlem's first black Congressman. 125th Street was Malcolm X's beat in the 1950s and 1960s – this is where he strolled and preached, and photos of him and his followers have passed into legend.

Walk a little west from here and you reach the legendary **Apollo Theater** at no. 253. Not much to look at from the outside, this venue was, from the 1930s to the 1970s, the center of black entertainment in New York City and northeastern America. Today, it continues to launch and host great performers. Almost all the great figures of jazz and blues played here along with singers, comedians and dancers. Past winners of its famous Amateur Night have included Ella Fitzgerald, Billie Holiday, Luther Vandross, The Jackson Five, Sarah Vaughan, Marvin Gaye and James Brown. Since its heyday it's served as a warehouse, movie theater and radio station, and in its latest incarnation is the venue for a weekly TV show, *Showtime at the Apollo*. Now an officially landmarked building, the *Apollo* offers daily 45-minute tours, Mon, Tues, Thurs & Fri 11am, 1pm and 3pm, Wed 11am only, Sat & Sun call to arrange a tour (☎531-5337). Across the way at 125th Street and Seventh Avenue, the tall, narrow Theresa Towers office building was until the 1960s the **Theresa Hotel**: its gleaming white terra cotta patterns with sunbursts at the top make it stand out from the shabbiness of the rest of the street. Desegregated only in 1940, it became known as the Waldorf of Harlem. Fidel Castro was a guest here in

1960 while on a visit to the United Nations, shunning Midtown luxury in a popular political gesture; the hotel's first black manager
was William Harmon Brown, whose son, Ron Brown, became
President Clinton's Secretary of Commerce until his untimely death
in a 1995 plane crash. At no. 230 W 125th St is another historic
location, **Blumsteins**, fronted by its dilapidated neon sign. Once
the largest department store in Harlem, founded by a German-
Jewish immigrant in 1898, Blumsteins refused to hire black workers except as menial laborers (like many white-owned local businesses), and was the focal point in 1934 of a community-wide boy-
cott led by Adam Clayton Powell, Jr – pointedly called Don't Buy
Where You Can't Work. The campaign worked here: the department store not only began hiring blacks, but became the first in the
area with à black Santa and black mannequins. Nearby is the
Studio Museum in Harlem, at no. 144, featuring various exhibitions of African-American art (see p.295).

The open-market feel of this stretch has dimmed somewhat to
make way for chain-store development, and the much-heralded
Harlem USA theme-mall at the corner of 125th Street and Frederick
Douglass Boulevard, under construction at press time, will house a
Disney Store, an HMV, a Gap and a Cineplex Odeon, among other
mega-commercial tenants. To get a sense of what local retailers do
(and do well), drop in to **Our Black Heritage** at 2295 Adam Clayton
Powell Blvd, a charming and friendly little store selling children's
books, greeting cards, historic newspaper clippings and videotapes
– all with a black cultural theme.

Mount Morris Park Historical District
Centered on Lenox Avenue between West 118th and 124th streets,
the area west of **Mount Morris Park**, now known as the **Mount
Morris Park Historic District**, was one of the first to attract residential development after the elevated railroads were constructed.
White Protestant Downtown commuters gave way to the second
largest neighborhood of Eastern European Jewish immigrants after
the Lower East Side, and finally to black households starting in the
late 1920s – complex demographics which explain the heavy concentration of religious structures here. The neighborhood is now on
the National Register of Historic Places, and the landmarked district
will most likely be extended towards Powell Boulevard.

At 201 Lenox Ave (at 120th St) stands the **Mount Olivet Church**,
an American version of a Greco-Roman temple which was a synagogue, and one of literally hundreds of religious buildings dotted
around Harlem. The somber, bulky, Gothic **St Martins**, at the southeast corner of Lenox Avenue and 122nd Street is among them, and
both have been fortunate in avoiding decay as church and community declined. Elsewhere the Mount Morris District comprises some
lovely **rowhouses** that went up in the speculative boom of the 1890s.

*Lenox Avenue
was officially
renamed
Malcolm X
Boulevard in
1987 – but it's
still known by
the old name.*

Harlem

Most outstanding of all are 133–143 W 122nd St, arguably the finest row of Queen Anne-style homes in the city, constructed by leading architect Francis H. Kimball in 1885–87 of gabled and dormered orange brick, with lovely stained glass. No. 131 is a Romanesque Revival house faced in Indiana limestone. Double back west and pause in front of **Hale House** at no. 154, established by Mother Clara Hale whose program for substance-addicted (and now HIV-infected) infants and mothers was one of the first in the country. A plaque in front is decorated with bronze faces of children and enfolds a statue of Mother Hale herself.

When you reach the edge of the park itself, **Mount Morris Park West**, you may find it hard to appreciate some of the noteworthy houses, overshadowed as they are by one of Harlem's great architectural tragedies. Smack dab in the middle of the ensemble is a block of rowhouses so neglected that the facades of several have literally been stripped away. Notoriously known as **The Ruins**, this ensemble was callously destroyed by New York State when under the right of eminent domain it began stripping several of the houses with plans to create a drug rehabilitation center in 1968. Once again, late-Sixties community opposition was fierce: this proposal and later plans were shelved, and the future of the ghostly, crumbling block is unknown (there is some talk of turning it into condos). Still, looking at Mount Morris Park West you can't help but feel that it too will go the way of Greenwich Village and the Lower East Side – the quality of building is so good, the pressures on Manhattan so great, it seems just a matter of time.

The former Mount Morris Park is now **Marcus Garvey Park**, taking its name from the black leader of the 1920s, it's an odd urban space with jutting outcrops contradicting the precise lines of the houses around. At the summit, an elegant octagonal fire tower of 1856 is a unique example of the early-warning devices once found throughout the city. Spiral your way to the top for a great view.

Continue down Lenox Avenue to 116th Street at no. 102 to find the green onion-dome of the **Masjid Malcolm Shabazz** mosque, named after Malcolm X who once preached here. Between Lenox and Fifth avenues you'll pass the new home of the bazaar-like **Malcolm Shabazz Harlem Market**, its entrance marked by colorful fake minarets. The markets offerings include cloth, T-shirts, jewelry, clothing and more with a distinctly African flavor. Ironically, the former street vendors, who used to run from police and clash with other local merchants, now pay taxes, accept credit cards, and take accounting courses at the mosque. Originally moved off the street by city authorities, the vendors were then moved down the block to make way for several massive development projects being supervised by the mosque (which functions much like the Abyssinian Development Corporation). One of them is **Malcolm Shabazz Gardens**, a series of income-capped houses modeled on the derelict brownstones they replaced, lining 117th Street. At 116th and Fifth, the barn-like **Baptist Temple Church** was originally a synagogue; at 116th and Powell Boulevard, the fanciful blue-and-white 1912 Moorish-style Regent Theater, one of America's earliest movie palaces, has become the **Corinthian Baptist Church**. Many of black Harlem's churches are buildings built by other congregations or with other original intents; to see one of the few churches actually built by a black architect, head up to 134th Street between Frederick Douglass and Powell boulevards, and have a look at **St Philips Church**, an elegant brick and granite building constructed by Vertner Tandy in 1910–11.

Powell Boulevard

Above 110th Street, Seventh Avenue becomes **Adam Clayton Powell Jr Boulevard**, a broad sweep pushing north between low-built houses that for once in Manhattan allow the sky to break through. Since its conception Powell Boulevard has been Harlem's main concourse, and it's not difficult to imagine the propriety the shops and side streets had in their late nineteenth-century heyday. As with the rest of Harlem, Powell Boulevard shows years of decline in its graffiti-splattered walls and storefronts punctuated by demolished lots. The recent injection of funds into this area should impact it for the better; in fact if the current investments don't make some difference, its hard to say what will.

To look back at past times rather than the uncertain future, it's worth checking out the angular brick **Schomburg Center for Research in Black Culture** at 515 Lenox Ave at 135th Street (Mon–Wed noon–8pm, Thurs–Sat 10am–6pm, library closed Sun; ☎491-2200) for its exhibitions and resources on the history of black culture in the US: see p.303. On your way up Lenox Avenue, at no. 328 (126th St), is the most renowned soul food restaurant in New York, *Sylvias*.

Abyssinian Baptist Church

A few streets north at 132 W 138th St (☎862-7474) is the **Abyssinian Baptist Church**, interesting primarily because of its long-time minister, the **Reverend Adam Clayton Powell Jr**. In the 1930s Powell was instrumental in forcing the mostly white-owned, white-workforce stores of Harlem to begin employing the blacks who ensured their economic survival, such as Blumensteins. Later he became the first black on the city council, then New York's first black representative in Congress – a career which came to an embittered end in 1967, when amid strong rumors of the misuse of public funds he was excluded from Congress by majority vote. This failed to diminish his standing in Harlem, where voters twice reelected him before his death in 1972. In the church there's a small collection of artifacts related to Powell's life, including copies of bills for which he was responsible – like the first minimum wage law in the country.

Sunday gospel

Lately it's the incredible **gospel music** that has attracted visitors up to Harlem. And for good reason: the music and the entire revival-style Baptist experience can be both amazing and invigorating. Gospel tours are becoming big business, and churches seem to be jockeying to get the most tourists. Many of the arranged tours (outlined in "Information, Maps and Tours" in Basics) are pricey, but they usually offer transportation Uptown and brunch afterwards. You can, however, easily go it on your own if you're looking for a more flavorful view. The choir at the Abyssinian Baptist Church is arguably the best in the city, but others of note include **Metropolitan Baptist Church** (151 W 128th St at Adam Clayton Powell Jr Blvd; ☎289-9488), **Mount Moriah** (2050 5th Ave at W 127th St; ☎722-9594) and **Mount Nebo** (1883 7th Ave at W 114th St; ☎866-7880). Keep in mind, if you do attend one of the services, that this isn't a tourist attraction but an actual church where worship is taken especially seriously. Dress accordingly: jackets for men and skirts or dresses for women.

The scandal is of course unmentioned, but a more fitting memorial is the boulevard that today bears his name. The collection may or may not be open when you visit: construction in the late 1990s forced it to be temporarily dismantled. Still it's worth a trip if you can see the gut-busting **choir** – call the number overleaf, or see "Information, Maps and Tours" in Basics for details.

Strivers Row

Near the Abyssinian Baptist Church at 138th Street between Powell and Eighth Avenue (aka Frederick Douglass Blvd) are what many consider the finest, most articulate blocks of rowhouses in Manhattan – **Strivers Row**. Commissioned during the 1890s housing boom, Strivers Row consists of 138th and 139th streets. Three sets of architects were commissioned: James Brown Lord, Bruce Price and Clarence Luce, and the best, McKim, Mead and White's north side of 139th: the results are uniquely harmonious, a dignified Renaissance-derived strip that's an amalgam of simplicity and elegance. Note the unusual rear service alleys of the houses, reached via iron-gated cross streets. Within the burgeoning black community of the turn of the century this came to be the desirable place for ambitious professionals to reside – hence its nickname.

El Barrio

From Park Avenue to the East River is Spanish Harlem or **El Barrio**, dipping down as far as East 96th Street to collide head on with the affluence of the Upper East Side. The center of a large Puerto Rican community, it is quite different from Harlem. El Barrio was originally a working-class Italian neighborhood (a small pocket of Italian families survives around 116th St and 1st Ave) and the quality of building here was nowhere as good as that immediately to the west. The result is a more intimidating atmosphere. It has been predominantly Puerto Rican since the early 1950s, when the American government offered Puerto Ricans incentives to emigrate to the US under a policy known as "Operation Bootstrap" (so named in the theory that the scheme would help pull Puerto Rico up "by the straps of its boots" by reducing its overpopulation problem). But the occupants have had little opportunity to evolve Latino culture in any meaningful or noticeable way; the main space where cultural roots are in evidence is **La Marqueta** on Park Avenue between 111th and 116th streets, a five-block **street market** of Spanish products. Originally a line of pushcart street vendors hawking their wares, it's more regulated now, selling everything from tropical fruit and vegetables, jewelry, figurines and clothing to dried herbs and snake oils. To get some background on the whole scene, **Museo del Barrio** at Fifth Avenue and 104th Street (see p.302) is a showcase of Latin American art and culture and also includes **La Casa de la Herencia Cultural Puertorriquena**, a Puerto Rican heritage library. To the northeast, El Barrio's **International Art Gallery** at 309 108th St (between 3rd and Lexington aves) is an alternative space for local artists of Latin, African-American and Asian origin.

Hamilton Heights

The further Uptown you venture, the less like New York it seems. Much of Harlem's western edge is taken up by the area known as **Hamilton Heights**, like Morningside Heights to the south, a mixed bag of campus, trash-strewn streets and slender parks on a bluff above Harlem. However, one stretch, the **Hamilton Heights Historic District** that runs down Convent Avenue to City College, pulls Hamilton Heights well up from the ranks of the untidily mediocre. Years ago the black professionals who made it up here and to Sugar Hill a little further north could glance down on lesser Harlemites with disdain: it's still a firmly bourgeois residential area – and one of the most attractive Uptown.

But even if this mood of shabbiness around a well-heeled neighborhood is to your liking, there's little in the way of specific sights. The 135th Street St Nicholas subway is as good a place to start as any, for up the hill and around the corner is Convent Avenue, containing the Heights' single historic lure – the 1798 house of Alexander Hamilton, **Hamilton Grange**, at 287 Convent Ave, at 142nd Street (Fri–Sun 9am–5pm; free; ☎666-1640). The Grange, which used to stand at 143rd Street, may soon be moved to a site in St Nicholas Park more similar to its original environment; alterations to its original porches and doors would also be reversed. For now, the city is mulling over the Parks Service's recommendation, and the

Federal-style mansion sits uncomfortably between the fiercely
Romanesque St Luke's Church – to which the transplanted house
was originally donated – and an apartment building.

Alexander Hamilton's life is as fascinating as it was flamboyant,
and several period rooms inside the house contain a few of his belongings, like a set of Louis XVI chairs. He was an early supporter of the
Revolution, and his enthusiasm quickly brought him to the attention of
George Washington. He became the general's aide-de-camp, later
founding the Bank of New York and becoming first Secretary to the
Treasury. Hamilton's headlong tackling of problems made him enemies as well as friends: alienating Republican populists led to a clash
with their leader Thomas Jefferson, and when Jefferson won the pres-
idency in 1801, Hamilton was left out in the political cold. Temporarily
abandoning politics, he moved away from the city to his grange here
(or rather near here – the house was moved in 1889) to tend his plan-
tation and conduct a memorably sustained and vicious feud with one
Aaron Burr, who had beaten Hamilton's father-in-law to a seat in the
Senate and then set up the Bank of Manhattan as a direct rival to the
Bank of New York. After a few years as vice president under Jefferson,
Burr ran for the governorship of New York; Hamilton strenuously
opposed his candidature and after an exchange of extraordinarily bitter letters, the two men fought a **duel** in Weehawken, New Jersey,
roughly where today's Lincoln Tunnel emerges. Hamilton's eldest son
had been killed in a duel on the same field a few years earlier, which
may explain why, when pistols were drawn, Hamilton honorably dis-
charged his into the air. Burr, evidently made of lesser stuff, aimed
carefully and fatally wounded Hamilton. So died "the most restless,
impatient, artful, indefatigable and unprincipled intriguer in the United
States," as President John Adams described him. He's only one of two
non-presidents to find his way on to US money (Benjamin Franklin's
the other): you'll find his portrait on the back of a $10 bill.

Convent Avenue and City College

If you've just wandered up from Harlem, **Convent Avenue** comes as
something of a surprise – and a quite welcome one at that. Its secluded, blossom-lined streets have a garden suburb prettiness that's
spangled with Gothic, French and Italian Renaissance hints in the
happily eclectic houses of the 1890s. Running south, the feathery
span of the **Shepard Archway** announces **City College**, a rustic-feel-
ing campus of Collegiate Gothic halls built from gray Manhattan
schist dug up during the excavations for the IRT subway line and
mantled with white terra cotta fripperies. Founded in 1905, City
College made no charge for tuition, so becoming the seat of higher
learning for many of New York's poor – and future illustrious.
Though free education came to an end in the 1970s, 75 percent of
the students still come from minority backgrounds to enjoy a campus
that's as warmly intimate as Columbia is grandiose.

Washington Heights

The change from Convent Avenue to Broadway is almost as abrupt as it is up from Harlem. Broadway here is a once-elegant, now raggy sweep that slowly rises to the northernmost part of Manhattan Island, **Washington Heights**. From Morningside Heights, the haul is a long one, though the best stopoffs are easily reached from the #1 train to 157th and Broadway or the A to 155th or 163rd; if you're in Hamilton Heights, just continue north for a largely uneventful walk. **Audubon Terrace** at 155th and Broadway is an Acropolis in a cul-de-sac, a weird, clumsy nineteenth-century attempt to deify 155th Street with museums dolled up as Beaux Arts temples. Officially the **Washington Heights Museum Group**, it was originally built in the vain anticipation of the movement north of New York's elite aristocratic society. Now the complex stands in mocking contrast to its still decrepit area. Included here is the **American Academy of Arts and Letters**, the **American Numismatic Society** and the **Hispanic Society of America**. As you might expect from something so far from the center of town, the complex is little known and little visited, though the Hispanic Museum alone is worth the trip. For a full account of these museums, see Chapter 15 "Museums and Galleries", 289 and 300 respectively. One avenue east, at 155th Street and Amsterdam, is the **Trinity Church Cemetery**, its large, placid grounds dotted with some fanciful mausolea; the remains of robber baron John Jacob Astor are said to be buried up here. At 166th and Broadway, now controversially incorporated into the Columbia-Presbyterian Hospital complex, is the **Audubon Ballroom**, scene of Malcolm X's assassination in 1967; a Malcolm X museum at this site is under consideration.

The Morris–Jumel Mansion

Within easy walking distance of Audubon Terrace and the cemetery, the **Morris–Jumel Mansion** (65 Jumel Terrace at 160th and Edgecombe Ave; ☎923-8008; Wed–Sun 10am–4pm; $3) is another Uptown surprise: cornered in its garden, the mansion somehow survived the destruction all around, and today is one of the more successful house museums, its proud Georgian outlines faced with a later Federal portico. Inside, the mansion's rooms reveal some of its engaging history: built as a rural retreat in 1765 by Colonel Roger Morris, it was briefly Washington's headquarters before falling into the hands of the British. A leaflet describes the rooms and their historical connections, but curiously omits much of the later history. Wealthy wine merchant Stephen Jumel bought the derelict mansion in 1801 and refurbished it for his wife Eliza, formerly a prostitute and his mistress. New York society didn't take to such a past, but when Jumel died in 1832, Eliza married ex-vice-president Aaron Burr (the nemesis of Alexander Hamilton) – she for his connections, he for her money. Burr was 78 when they married, twenty years older

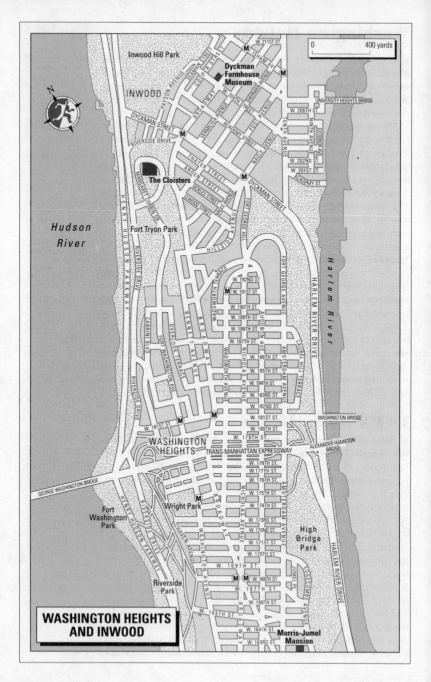

WASHINGTON HEIGHTS
AND INWOOD

than Eliza: the marriage lasted for six months before old Burr upped and left, to die on the day of their divorce. Eliza battled on to the age of 91, and on the top floor of the house you'll find her obituary, a magnificently fictionalized account of a "scandalous" life.

Just opposite the entrance to the mansion's grounds is the quaint block of **Sylvan Terrace**, a tiny cobblestone mews lined with yellow and green wooden houses – and seeming impossibly out of place just barely off the wide-open intersection of Amsterdam and St Nicholas avenues.

From most western stretches of Washington Heights you get a glimpse of the **George Washington Bridge**, linking Manhattan to New Jersey. It's arguable that the feeder road to the bridge splits two distinct areas: below is bleakly run-down, the biggest area of illegal drug activity in the city, mainly serving New Jersey residents making good use of the bridge; above, the streets relax in smaller, more diverse ethnic neighborhoods of old-time Jews, Greeks, Central Europeans and especially Irish, though a major Hispanic community has recently built up. A skillful, dazzling sketch high above the Hudson, the bridge skims across the channel in massive metalwork and graceful lines, a natural successor to the Brooklyn Bridge. "Here, finally, steel architecture seems to laugh," said Le Corbusier of the 1931 construction. To appreciate what he meant, grit your teeth and walk – midtown Manhattan hangs like a visible promise in the distance.

The Cloisters Museum and Inwood

What most visitors pass through Washington Heights to see, though, is **The Cloisters**, the Metropolitan Museum's collection of medieval art housed in a beautiful ersatz monastery in Fort Tryon Park. Unequivocally, this is a must (see p.282 for persuasion), and should you plump for riding up on the subway you'll find an additional reward in the park itself, cleverly landscaped by Frederick Law Olmsted, Jr – son of the famed Central Park and Prospect Park architect. The stone-walled promenade overlooking the Hudson and English-style garden make for a sweepingly romantic spot. Inside the museum, the central cloister, its pink marble arcades and fountain purchased from the impoverished French monastery of St-Michel-de-Cuixa at the turn of the century, will trick you into believing that you're really in southwestern France.

Inwood

Fort Tryon Park joins **Inwood Park** by the Hudson River and, despite the presence of the Henry Hudson Parkway running underneath, it is possible to walk across Dyckman Street and into Inwood Park. The path up the side of the river gives a beautiful view of New Jersey, sur-

**The
Cloisters
Museum
and Inwood**

prisingly hilly and wooded this far upstream. Keep walking and you will reach the very tip of Manhattan, an area known as *Spuyten Duyvil* ("the spitting devil" in Dutch), nowadays Columbia University's Athletic Stadium. Inwood Park itself is wild and rambling, often confusing and a little threatening if you get lost. It was once the stamping ground for Indian cave dwellers, but unfortunately the site of their original settlement is now buried under the Henry Hudson Parkway. Inwood's main tourist attraction is the **Dyckman Farmhouse Museum** (4881 Broadway at 204th St; ☎304-9422; Tues–Sun 11am–4pm; free), an eighteenth-century Dutch farmhouse restored with period pieces – pleasant enough but hardly worth the journey.

Chapter 14

The Outer Boroughs

anhattan is a hard act to follow, and the four Outer
Boroughs – Brooklyn, Queens, the Bronx and Staten Island
– inevitably pale in comparison. But while they lack the
glamour (and the mass money) of Manhattan, and life in them, essentially residential, is less obviously dynamic, they all offer uniquely
unexpected and refreshing perspectives on the city.

Most visitors never set foot off Manhattan Island, but if you have
more than a few days there's much out here to be recommended. The
most common places to start are a trip on the **Staten Island ferry** or
a walk over the Brooklyn Bridge to the **Brooklyn Heights
Promenade**. Other attractions abound: in Brooklyn, there's salubrious **Brooklyn Heights** and beautiful **Prospect Park**, along with the
evocatively run-down seaside resort of **Coney Island**. **Queens**,
scarcely visited by outsiders, has the bustling Greek community of
Astoria and **Flushing Meadows**, a vast park which played host to the
1939 and 1964 World's Fairs. As for **Staten Island**, the ferry is its
own justification. The **Bronx** has in recent years begun to supersede
its unfair reputation as a vast danger zone; the infamous **South
Bronx** has been largely rehabilitated, and the country's best zoo and
several historic private estates are outstanding highlights.

Perhaps the Outer Boroughs's most fascinating quality is their rich
assortment of ethnic neighborhoods: Orthodox Jews in
Williamsburg, Russians in **Brighton Beach**, and Poles in
Greenpoint (all in Brooklyn); Greeks in **Astoria**, Indians and South
Americans in **Jackson Heights** (all in Queens); Italians in **Belmont**
(the Bronx); and the list goes on. These towns have been first stops
for immigrants for more than two hundred years; as such, much of

---

Be warned that the Outer Boroughs are much larger than Manhattan, and
to get to some of the highlights you'll have to take various **subways and
buses** in succession. It can be a long haul, but you'll grow to appreciate
the MTA's ability to connect vastly separated areas. Make sure you're
familiarized with the transit system by studying "Getting around the city"
in Basics, plus the maps at the back of the book, before you start.

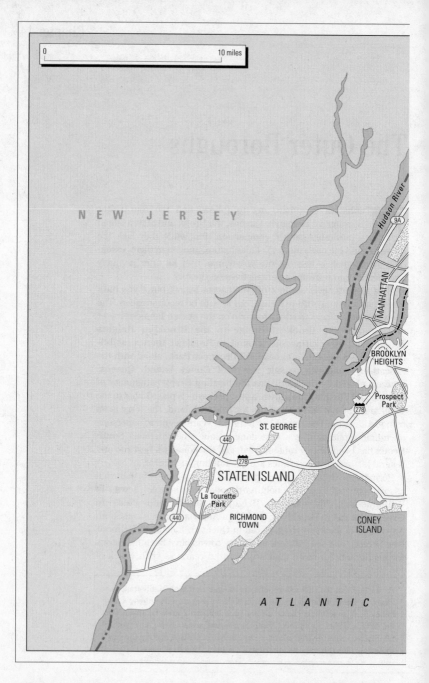

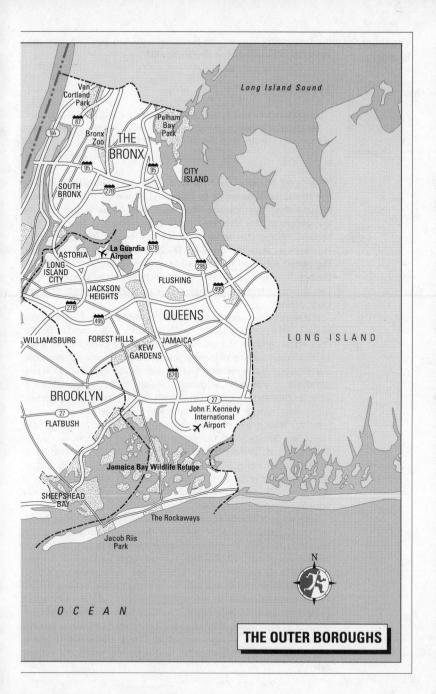

THE OUTER BOROUGHS

the best ethnic cuisine can be found here and you can walk long
stretches without hearing English spoken.

THE OUTER BOROUGHS

Brooklyn

*Maybe he's found out by now dat he'll neveh live long enough to know
the whole of Brooklyn. It'd take a guy a lifetime to know Brooklyn
t'roo an' t'roo. An' even den, you wouldn't know it at all.*

Thomas Wolfe, *Only the Dead Know Brooklyn*

"The Great Mistake." So New York writer Pete Hamill summed up
the **Brooklyn** annexation in 1898, and in a way, that's how most
longstanding Brooklynites feel even today, traditionally seeing
themselves as Brooklyn residents first, inhabitants of New York City
second. Maybe this sense of autonomy comes from the strong
Brooklyn legacy – the Brooklyn Dodgers, the unmistakable accent,
the famed sons and daughters like Woody Allen, Mel Brooks and
Barbra Streisand, all of which have become part of the urban folk-
lore that's a common heritage for Brooklynites of vastly different
backgrounds.

If it were still a separate city Brooklyn would be the fourth largest
in the United States, with its population of 2.3 million and its 93 distinct ethnic groups. But until as recently as the early 1800s, it was
no more than a group of loosely connected towns and villages existing relatively autonomously from already thriving Manhattan across
the water. It was with the arrival of Robert Fulton's steamship service, linking the two, that Brooklyn began to take on its present
form, starting with the establishment of a leafy retreat in Brooklyn
Heights. What really changed the borough, was the opening of the
Brooklyn Bridge, and thereafter development began to spread
deeper inland, as housing was needed for the increasingly large
workforce necessary to service a more commercialized Manhattan.
By the turn of the century, Brooklyn was fully established as part of
New York City, and its fate as Manhattan's perennial kid brother was
sealed.

You can go to almost any neighborhood and find something worthwhile; the most obvious – and justly the most visited district – is
Brooklyn Heights. Though many never get past this, the other areas
around downtown – **Cobble Hill**, **Carroll Gardens** and **Fort Greene**
– offer a lively enough mix. **Park Slope** has some of the city's best-
preserved brownstones and is home to many up-and-coming professionals and a large lesbian community; Olmsted and Vaux's **Prospect
Park** is for many an improvement on their more famous bit of landscaping in Manhattan. **Williamsburg**'s converted lofts are a favorite
for artists and East Village transplants; **Coney Island** and **Brighton
Beach** are nothing if not unique, and definitely worth the subway
ride.

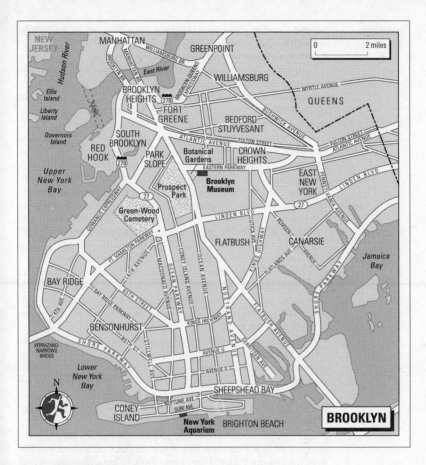

Downtown Brooklyn

This area is made up of **Brooklyn Heights**, **Atlantic Avenue** and **Fort Greene**, and stretches from the water to the Brooklyn Academy of Music, quickly moving from warehouses to brownstownes to the staid buildings found in most any civic center. Getting there, if you choose to walk, could turn out to be the most exciting part of your trip.

The Brooklyn Bridge and Fulton Ferry District

If you are going to Brooklyn, begin by walking over the **Brooklyn Bridge** – it's not too long (less than a mile across) and it may hold the best views of Manhattan that you will get. The walkway begins at City Hall Park next to the Municipal Building and ends in Brooklyn either at the corner of Adams and Tillary streets or at the more convenient Cadman Plaza East staircase. If you're not up to walking (though it really is the best way), the #2, #3, #4, #5, N, R, A, C and F subways all stop in downtown Brooklyn.

Arriving in Brooklyn from the bridge, walk down the stairs and bear right, following the path through the park at Cadman Plaza. If you cross on to Middagh Street, you'll soon find yourself in the heart of the Heights; follow Cadman Plaza West down the hill to Old Fulton Street, and you'll find yourself in the **Fulton Ferry District**.

Hard under the glowering shadow of the **Watchtower Building** (the world headquarters of the Jehovah's Witnesses) is where Robert Fulton's ferry used to put in: during the nineteenth century it grew into Brooklyn's first and most prosperous industrial neighborhood. With the coming of the bridge it fell into decline, but these days it's on the way up again: its aging buildings are being slowly tarted up as loft spaces (check out the imposing **Eagle Warehouse**, 28 Old Fulton St; its penthouse, with the huge glass clock-window is one of the city's most coveted apartments). Down on the ferry slip itself, a couple of barges-cum-restaurants – most notably the *River Café* – entice die-hard Manhattanites across the bridge by night, as well as Wall Street types for power lunching. Locals are more likely to follow their noses to the equally view-blessed *Pete's Downtown*, the delicious Italian eatery, or the brick-oven *Patsy's Pizza* for some of the best pizza in New York.

If it's open, the **Brooklyn Bridge Anchorage** across Old Fulton Street is well worth a visit. A cavernous space, cool and quiet under (inside, actually) the bridge, it's home to sporadic art and performance art happenings. There's no central number to call for information, but a call to events organization Creative Time ☎212/206-6674 in the summer months should get you a schedule of their events.

Just north of here, reachable by walking through the garden of the *River Café*, is a waterfront warehouse district ripe for renewal. For now, the **Empire Fulton Ferry State Park** offers a beautiful view of the river at river level – something increasingly rare – and occasional art and sculpture exhibits. Behind the park, the area beginning to be known as **DUMBO** (Down Under Manhattan Bridge Overpass) is rumored to be the next big thing. So far, it's not – but if you make it over that way by daylight, the warehouse buildings and cobblestone streets are quite interesting.

Brooklyn Heights

Brooklyn Heights is one of New York City's most beautiful and wealthy neighborhoods. From the early eighteenth century on, bankers and financiers from Wall Street could live among its tranquil exclusivity and imagine themselves far from the tumult of Manhattan, but close enough to keep an eye on the moneyed spires. Today the Heights are not far different.

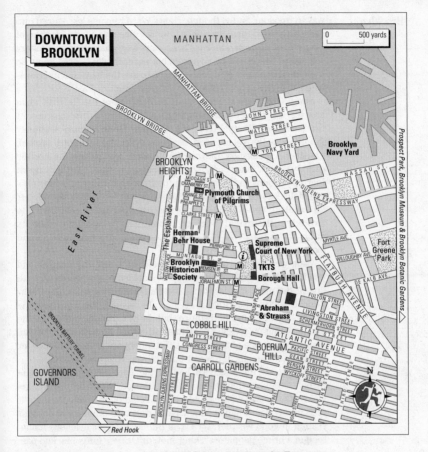

Walking up the hill from Old Fulton Street, you can take Everett or Henry streets into the oldest part of Brooklyn Heights proper. It's easy and enjoyable to wander these streets – so many houses have plaques on them that you can take yourself on a self-guided walking tour. One house that doesn't have a plaque is 24 Middagh St (at the corner of Willow); an unassuming but perfectly preserved Federal-style wooden house dating to 1824, it's the neighborhood's oldest house. Two streets down, on Orange between Hicks and Henry, you'll see the **Plymouth Church of the Pilgrims**, a simple church that went up in the mid-nineteenth century and became famous as the preaching base of **Henry Ward Beecher**, abolitionist and campaigner for women's rights. Horace Greeley, Mark Twain, even Abraham Lincoln all worshipped here on more than one occasion; drawn to Beecher's reputation as a great orator. The church was also used as a stop on the Underground Railroad, hiding slaves on their way to freedom. Sadly, though, Henry Ward remains less known outside New York than his sister, Harriet Beecher Stowe, author of *Uncle Tom's Cabin*, since his later years were marred by an adultery scandal of which he was acquitted but never finally cleared in public esteem. These days, your only chance to see the barn-like interior is when a service is on – otherwise no great loss.

South from here is **Pierrepont Street**; one of the Heights' main arteries, it's studded with delightful – and fantastic – brownstones. At the corner of Henry Street the **Herman Behr House**, a chunky Romanesque Revival mansion, has been, successively, a hotel, brothel, Franciscan monastery (it was the brothers who added the horrific canopy) and, currently, private apartments. Further down Pierrepont, look in if you can on the **Brooklyn Unitarian Church** – originally known as the Church of the Savior – which is notable for its exquisite neo-Gothic interior. Across the road at no. 128 is the **Brooklyn Historical Society**, which has temporarily shut its doors for at least two years, to undertake a major renovation and expansion.

Walk west on any of the streets between Clark and Remsen and you'll reach the **Promenade** (aka "the Esplanade"), a boardwalk with one of the most spectacular – and renowned – views in all of New York. It's hard to take your eyes off the skyline, the water and the Statue of Liberty in the distance, but do turn around and notice the creeper-hung palaces set back modestly from the walkway. Norman Mailer lives in one of these, and a few others are weekend homes for the rich and famous: it doesn't hurt to keep your eyes peeled.

Leading off the southern end of the Promenade is **Montague Street**, Brooklyn Heights' lively main thoroughfare, lined with bars and restaurants. The area looks like it could be in Manhattan, but it feels more relaxed and subdued. Numerous restaurants have outdoor seating in good weather: try *Caffè Buon Gusto* for delicious Italian food in a prime people-watching spot, or *Ozzie's* for coffee and pastries on their secluded back patio.

South of Montague, the brownstone streets continue, taking you toward Atlantic Avenue and Cobble Hill. Between Remsen and Joralemon, look for **Grace Court Alley** and **Hunts Lane**, two mews tucked away off Hicks and Henry respectively.

Downtown Brooklyn and Fulton Mall

The eastern end of Montague is known as "Bank Row" – downtown Brooklyn's **business center** – and leads on to what is in effect the borough's **Civic Center**, with the end of the residential Heights signaled by the tall Art Deco buildings of Court Street. Across the road the sober Greek-style **Borough Hall** is topped with a cupolaed belfry; further east are the massive State Supreme Court and Romanesque **post office**, next to which stands a bronze statue of Henry Ward Beecher. There's little to linger for, but your tired feet should know that this is where to find the large Borough Hall subway station.

Beyond the civic grandeur **Fulton Street** leads east, the principal shopping street for the borough as a whole. There are some good bargains to be found here, but all in all the streets – lined with fast-food franchises – can be a little depressing. What you will find here is *Gage & Tollner*, one of Brooklyn's most famous restaurants, which serves seafood and steaks in a setting determinedly left unchanged. However, the food doesn't come cheap. Another neighborhood landmark, and one more affordable, is *Junior's* on the corner of Flatbush and DeKalb avenues; the cheesecake is justly famous and their other dishes aren't far behind.

Just south of Fulton Mall, Adams Street turns into Boerum Place, and at the corner of Schermerhorn you'll see a subway entrance that actually leads to the **New York Transit Museum**, housed in an unused station that hasn't seen a train for over forty years: see p.299 for details.

Fort Greene and the Brooklyn Academy of Music

To the east of downtown Brooklyn and easily navigated by keeping an eye on the **Williamsburg Savings Bank** – Brooklyn's tallest building – sits **Fort Greene**, named after Nathaniel Greene, a prominent general in the American Revolution. Long established as a strong multiracial community, Fort Greene is now home to a growing African-American, professional contingent (film director Spike Lee is a native son), and a number of exciting venues for music and events have opened up: check out the Friday night poetry readings at the *Brooklyn Moon Café* (745 Fulton St at S Portland; ☎718/243-0424). Along with these are several good ethnic restaurants such as *Keur N'Deye* (737 Fulton St between S Elliott and S Portland sts), a delicious Senegalese restaurant with African decor. Most restaurants and cafés here are located along Fulton Street. Fort Greene also boasts America's oldest performing arts center, the **Brooklyn Academy of Music** (BAM to its fans, who come from all over the city) at 30 Lafayette Ave (☎718/636-4100). BAM is one of the borough's most hyped institutions, and has played host over the years to a glittering – and innovative – array of artists, albeit at considerably higher prices (and profile) than the newer spots opening up. BAM's new four-screen, state-of-the-art cinema features art films and the occasional new release.

Around Fulton Street, Fort Greene's newest draw is a cluster of African-inspired designer clothing **boutiques** whose customers include Ziggy Marley, Stevie Wonder and Erykah Badu; one standout is **4W Circle of Art and Enterprise** at 704 Fulton St ☎718/875-6500.

Atlantic Avenue

South of Brooklyn Heights is **Atlantic Avenue**, which runs from the East River all the way to Queens. This stretch – and spilling south into Cobble Hill – is the center of a vibrant Middle Eastern community. There are some fine and reasonably priced Yemeni and Lebanese restaurants here and a good sprinkling of Middle Eastern grocers and bakeries. Take a wander through the *Sahadi Importing Co.* at no. 187, known throughout the city for nuts, dried fruit, halva, and more than a dozen varieties of olives along with delicacies from other parts of the world. Next door at no. 185, *Peter's Ice Cream Parlor and Coffeehouse* is a neighborhood institution for both its fabulous homemade ice cream and its friendly atmosphere (☎718/852-3835).

South Brooklyn

Across Atlantic Avenue, **Cobble Hill**, **Boerum Hill** and **Carroll Gardens** – along with the old wharfing community of **Red Hook** – make up the area once known as **South Brooklyn**. Carroll Gardens and Boerum Hill have the unfortunate distinction of being traversed by the fetid Gowanus Canal, although attempts to clean it up are currently under way. **Court Street** holds the most interest here, with its restaurants, cafés and shops; the world's oldest **railroad tunnel**, built in 1844, is at Atlantic Avenue and Court Street (☎718/941-3160 for guided tours). **Atlantic Avenue** in Boerum Hill between Smith Street and Fourth Avenue is also known for its array of antiques dealers.

Cobble Hill

The main streets of **Cobble Hill** – Congress, Warren and Amity – are a mixture of solid brownstones and colorful redbrick rowhouses, most of which have long been a haven of the professional classes: rents here are beginning to approximate those of Brooklyn Heights, and signs of the young professional migration can be seen in the cafés springing up in the area. Among the best are *Bagel Point Café* (231 Court St), which has good brunch and a nice outdoor patio, and the charming *Roberto Cappuccino Café and Tea Room* (221 Court St). The who-was-who tour of Cobble Hill should take you to 197 Amity St, where **Jenny Jerome**, later Lady Randolph Churchill and mother of Winston, was born – the house is unfortunately disfigured by aluminum windows and a modern rustic facing. **Warren Place** is worth a look as well – easy to miss if you're not looking carefully, this tiny alley of late nineteenth-century workers' cottages is a shelter of quiet on the last block of Warren Street, just a stone's throw from the thunder of the Brooklyn–Queens Expressway. The Bergen stop on the F train will get you to and from this area, as well as neighboring Boerum Hill.

Boerum Hill

To the east of Cobble Hill, and south of Atlantic Avenue, **Boerum Hill** is scruffier and less architecturally impressive than its neighbors, though it has its share of sober Greek Revival and Italianate buildings – and gentrification is slowly but surely underway. One of the more solidly integrated neighborhoods in Brooklyn, it's home to Italian- and Irish-descended families, Arabs and a long-established Puerto Rican population which has since become part of a more diverse Latino community. They bring salsa music and dancing to the stoops of the neighborhood brownstones, and single-room storefront social clubs are a common sight on Smith Street, the commercial strip of this neighborhood.

Carroll Gardens

Going south along Court Street, Cobble Hill merges into **Carroll Gardens** around De Graw Street (also serviced by the F train; stop at Carroll St). Originally a middle- and upper-class community of many nationalities, this part of South Brooklyn was invaded by a massive influx of Italian dockworking immigrants who came in the early 1900s; the area was later named after Charles Carroll, the only Roman Catholic signee of the Declaration of Independence. Today, youthful professionals are a new sight coming out of the brownstones. But you'll still find plenty of pizza and pastry on Court Street, and a strong sense of community prevails, as the lower-middle-class, family-oriented, Italian population manages to coexist peacefully with the newcomers. If you are looking for a place to relax, stop by *Shakespeare's Sister* at 270 Court, a gift shop and café.

Carroll Gardens residents are also known for their fantastic, if not somewhat garish, holiday decorations. Although there are religious shrines and statues decorating many of the neighborhood gardens year round, Christmas and Easter bring out the festivities in full force, as neighbors vie to outdo each other with flashing lights, incandescent monuments, and even appropriate music to produce the most all-encompassing display.

Red Hook

After Carroll Gardens, the desolation of **Red Hook** is striking. The growing automatization of the docking industry (vividly portrayed in the film and the notorious novel *Last Exit to Brooklyn*) left Red Hook behind; the building of the Gowanus Expressway shortly thereafter isolated the area, and it's never been able to recover. Today a small Italian contingent remains and shares the now-cheap housing with African-Americans and Latinos, many of whom live in the infamous Red Hook housing projects. This is not a place for casual sightseeing.

There are, however, a few things that could point to better days ahead. In 1995, community volunteers presented their own ambitious urban renewal plan, though it has yet to be realized; meanwhile, two arts organizations are contributing to the revitalization of the waterfront area, where artists have taken over a number of Civil War-era warehouses. The **Hudson Waterfront Museum**, housed in a restored barge and run by a former professional clown, now makes its home at Pier 45 (Conover St at Beard St; ☎718/624-4719) and sometimes sponsors concerts – there's a shuttle bus available to fetch visitors from various Brooklyn neighborhoods. The **Brooklyn Waterfront Artists Coalition** holds its month-long Spring Show in May (call ☎718/596-2507 for specifics) on the piers as well. Still, change in this neighborhood is slow, and it remains not a highly recommended area to visit.

Prospect Park, Park Slope and Flatbush

Where Brooklyn really asserts itself – architecturally, at any rate – as a city in its own right is Flatbush Avenue leading up to **Grand Army Plaza**: pure classicism, with traffic being funneled around the central open space (best reached by the #2 or #3 train, Grand Army stop). It was laid out in the late nineteenth century by Olmsted and Vaux, who designed it as a dramatic approach to their newly completed Prospect Park just behind. The triumphal **Soldiers and Sailors' Memorial Arch**, which you can climb (spring and autumn weekends only), was added thirty years later and topped with a fiery sculpture of Victory, in tribute to the triumph of the north in the Civil War. On the far side of the square, the creamy-smooth **Brooklyn Public Library** continues the heroic theme, its facade smothered with stirring declarations to its function as fountain of knowledge, and with an entrance displaying the borough's home-grown poet, Walt Whitman. Behind, there's the **Brooklyn Museum of Art**, the **Brooklyn Children's Museum** (see p.289) and the **Brooklyn Botanic Garden** (April–Sept Tues–Fri 8am–6pm, Sat & Sun 10am–6pm; Oct–March Tues–Fri 8am–4.30pm, Sat & Sun 10am–4.30pm; ☎718/623-7200.

The Botanic Garden is one of the most enticing park spaces in the city, smaller and more immediately likeable than its more celebrated rival in the Bronx, and making for a relaxing place to unwind after a couple of hours in the museum. Sumptuous but not overplanted, it offers a Rose Garden, Japanese Garden, a Shakespeare Garden (laid out with plants mentioned in the Bard's plays), the Celebrity Path (a winding walk studded with leaf-shaped plaques which honor Brooklyn's famous), and some delightful lawns draped with weeping willows and beds of flowering shrubs. There's also a conservatory, housing among other things the country's largest collection of bonsai, and there's a gift shop that stocks a wide array of exotic plants, bulbs and seeds.

Prospect Park

The Botanic Garden is about as far away from Manhattan's bustle as it's possible to get, but if you can tear yourself away there's also **Prospect Park** itself. Energized by their success with Central Park,

Olmsted and Vaux landscaped this one in the early 1890s, completing it just as the finishing touches were being put to Grand Army Plaza outside. In a way it's better than Central Park, having more effectively managed to retain its pastoral quality. Although there have been encroachments over the years – tennis courts, a zoo – and plenty of people use the park for picnics, walks and soccer games, it remains for the most part remarkably bucolic in feel. Focal points include the **Lefferts Homestead**, an eighteenth-century colonial farmhouse shifted here some time ago and now open, free of charge, on weekends; the **Wildlife Center** (formerly the Zoo), open (for a small charge) every day, complete with a restored carousel and a lake in the southern half. Many of the various park attractions have been specially geared to children, so if you're traveling with kids, it's definitely worth a trip. And if you're worried about exhaustion – it's about 3.5 miles around the park on the main road – there's a free trolley bus (☎718/965-8967) that makes the rounds of the popular spots on weekends. The **boathouse** has maps and information on events in the park; dance, drama and music are performed in the bandshell during summer weekends; call for information ☎718/855-7882). You can also pick up all kinds of park information at ☎718/965-8999.

Park Slope

The western exits of Prospect Park leave you on the fringes of **Park Slope**. Walk down any of the quiet cross-streets (with some of New York's best-preserved brownstones) and you'll reach the trendy shopping street of Seventh Avenue (you can also get here by the F train, 7th Ave stop), where new restaurants and cafés share space with more longstanding businesses and some grandiose churches. This area has become a serious rival to Brooklyn Heights, with some of the city's fastest-soaring property prices. As young professionals and families flock to its amenities, even the more downmarket Fifth Avenue – until recently solidly Hispanic – is showing signs of taking some of Seventh's overflow, though it already had some of the most favored neighborhood eateries, especially *Aunt Suzie's* at no. 247 and *Cucina* at no. 256, two fine Italian joints.

The Slope is also home to a thriving lesbian and gay population, more famously the former. The action is split between Fifth and Seventh avenues: there's the specialty bookstore *Beyond Words* (186 5th Ave), and its next-door neighbor *Rising Café*; down Seventh Avenue is the prime gay lounge in the area, *Sanctuary* (444 7th Ave at 15th St).

Walk back down Fifth Avenue, across the Prospect Expressway, and you reach **Green-Wood Cemetery**: larger even than Prospect Park and very much the place to be buried in the last century if you could afford an appropriately flashy headstone or, better still, mausoleum. The main entrance, at fifth Avenue and 25th Street, is distinguished by its cathedral-like Gothic revival gates, constructed in the 1860s by R.M. Upjohn, son of Trinity Church architect Richard Upjohn (both of whom are buried here). Among the other permanent residents are Horace Greeley, politician and campaigning newspaper editor, resting relatively unpretentiously on a hill; William Marcy "Boss" Tweed, nineteenth-century Democratic chief and scoundrel, slumbering deep in the wilds; and the Steinway family, of piano fame, at peace in their very own 119-room mausoleum. Look out also for the tomb of one John Matthews, who made a fortune out of carbonated drinks and had himself a memorial carved with birds and animals, some fierce-looking gargoyles and (rather immodestly) scenes from his own life. You can stroll around the cemetery and find all this for yourself; or try to catch one of the **tours** given by the Brooklyn Center for the Urban Environment (see p.26).

Flatbush

Southeast of Prospect Park is **Flatbush**, a busy though largely uninteresting residential and shopping area inhabited mostly by West Indians – though that makes it a good place to get food or other wares from that part of the world. There are a couple of other notable highlights. An exclusive (and exhaustively planned) community of large single-family houses developed in 1899, **Prospect Park South** is a surprising haven centered on several quiet, secluded streets around Albemarle Road – just walk south from Church Avenue (reachable from the park or the D and Q trains), on either Buckingham Road or Coney Island Avenue. Back on Church, at the corner of Flatbush Avenue, stands the **Reformed Protestant Dutch Church of Flatbush**, which was founded in 1654 by Peter Stuyvesant. This isn't the original building, but it's still attractive: the small graveyard in the back is a jewel. Many of the headstones have sunk into the ground or are hard to read, but if you try to make out the names and inscriptions, you'll see that at least several are in Dutch. The large Gothic building across the street is **Erasmus Hall High School** (founded as a private academy by the church in 1786), meriting a mention as it's Barbra Streisand's alma mater.

Central Brooklyn

The areas loosely comprising **Central Brooklyn** are slightly rougher terrain. Known mostly these days as pockets of violence and decline, they are not without historical appeal.

Bedford-Stuyvesant

Immediately east of Fort Greene, though quite different in feel, is **Bedford-Stuyvesant**, once one of the most elegant neighborhoods in the city, and now, struggling to come out of a protracted period of neglect. Originally it was two separate areas, populated by both blacks and whites; the opening of the Brooklyn Bridge and later the construction of the A train brought a massive influx of African-Americans into the area. (Duke Ellington's *Take the A Train* commemorates that exodus from Harlem, which many hoped would give them a better life.) This led to increased hostility between the two groups, which in turn led to fighting, and in the 1940s the white population left, taking funding for many important community services with them. This was the start of the economic decline of "Bed-Stuy," as it has become colloquially known, and though the area has suffered the all-too-usual problems of inner-city neglect, today the African-American community here, which surpasses Harlem in size, is desperately trying to stop Bed-Stuy's rot and take advantage of an architectural legacy of some of the best Romanesque Revival brownstones in the city.

There is a historical legacy here which was largely forgotten until the 1960s and which remains unknown to many outside the area still. The nineteenth-century village of **Weeksville** – named after one of the first black landowners to move there – was a community of free blacks which evolved after slavery was abolished in New York State in 1827. Little remains of Weeksville today, but **The Society for the Preservation of Weeksville and Bedford-Stuyvesant History** operates a **museum** of African-American history in these houses and, while its efforts are directed primarily at local school groups, the Society welcomes visitors. It's best to call ahead (☎718/756-5250). To get to Weeksville take the A train to Utica Ave.

East of Bedford-Stuyvesant, there's not a lot to see. The neighborhood of Brownsville is notable for historic reasons: in the early part of this century, it was notorious as a hotbed for prominent anarchists, Bolsheviks and other political free thinkers. Emma Lazarus, author of the spirited inscription on the Statue of Liberty, lived here, and in 1916, with more than 150 prospective clients waiting outside its doors, the first birth control clinic in America opened here – only to be raided and closed nine days later by the vice squad, and its founder, Margaret Sander, imprisoned for thirty days as a "public nuisance."

Crown Heights

Fulton Street and Atlantic Avenue separate Bedford-Stuyvesant from **Crown Heights**, home to the largest West Indian neighborhood in New York, and to an active, established community of Hasidic Jews. Brooklyn in fact, has the largest Afro-Caribbean population outside the Caribbean itself, surpassing a million people, a great many of them Haitian. Coexistence between these two groups has often been strained, though things have largely settled down since the accidental death of a black child and the subsequent murder of a Hasidic man set off riots in 1991. Relations are getting better, however, the name "Crown Heights" remains synonymous with racial tension to many New Yorkers. Generally speaking, it's not dangerous to wander Crown Heights, and the lively atmosphere of Eastern Parkway (reachable by the #2 or #3 to Eastern Parkway/Brooklyn Museum or the #2, #3 or #4 to Franklin Ave) can be extremely enjoyable. If you're in town on Labor Day, too, this is the place to be, when the annual **Mardi Gras Carnival** (aka West Indian Day Parade) bursts into life (held in September rather than February because of the climate) with music, food, costumes and general revelry.

Coastal Brooklyn

It's possible, in theory, to walk, rollerblade or bike almost the entire **southern coast** of Brooklyn. On occasion, paths disappear, leaving you to share the service road off the highway with cars, but you'll never be on the actual highway itself. In short, it can be done. Even if you're of less sturdy stock it's worth making the trip to at least one of these areas to take in the often breathtaking views.

Bay Ridge

Way down south at the end of the R train is **Bay Ridge**, a traditionally Scandinavian community that's now more Irish and Italian (with a smattering of Russians and Arabs), although the annual Norwegian Independence Day Parade on May 17 still remains. It's a relaxed place, where newcomers and old-timers share space comfortably, as immortalized in the film *Saturday Night Fever*. Third Avenue is known for the huge proliferation of bars and restaurants; there's a lot to choose from, but for the sheer history of it, go to *Lento's* (7003 3rd Ave at the corner of Ovington St) and ask any of the waiters to explain some of the pictures that cover the wall.

From Bay Ridge Avenue (locals call it 69th Street) stop on the R train, walk west – passing the **Shore Belt Cycle Club** (29 Bay Ridge Ave ☎718/748-5077; basic bikes for $6 an hour, 25¢ extra for hand brakes) – and keep going until you get to the 69th Street pier, start of the **Shore Road Bike Path**. (Rollerblade enthusiasts should get off the subway at 95th St and detour to Panda Sport at 9213 5th Ave and 92nd St ☎718/238-4919, where rentals are $20 for the day. There's an entrance to the Bike Path at 95th St.) Looking north from the shoreline, lower Manhattan seems further away than expected; just to the south of the pier is the shimmering **Verrazano Narrows Bridge**, flashing its minimalist message across the entry to the bay. This slender, beautiful span was, until Britain's Humber Bridge opened, the world's longest at 4260 feet – so long, in fact, that the tops of the towers are visibly an inch or so out of parallel to allow for the curvature of the earth.

The Bike Path, part of a narrow strip of park that follows the coast south and then east, is a lovely stroll, marred only by the roar of the Belt Parkway it runs alongside. Follow it till you get to the larger expanse of **Dyker Beach Park** (named after the beach that still exists underneath the lawn; at low tide, you can see sand at the water's edge), where old and young from the surrounding neighborhood come for sunshine and expert kite-flying. After that, you can turn back, or follow the path to the end, turn left on Bay Parkway, and walk to the end of the B train. The truly determined can continue east to Coney Island.

Coney Island

Accessible to anyone for the price of a subway ride, the beachfront amusement spot of **Coney Island** has long given working-class New Yorkers the kind of holiday they just couldn't get otherwise. Look at old Buster Keaton movies and black-and-white photos from the earlier part of this century to get a sense of the fantasy land it was; then take the subway to Stillwell Avenue (last stop on the B, D, F or N) to see for yourself. These days, the music blares louder than it once did, the language of choice on the boardwalk is Spanish as often as English and the rides look a bit worse for the wear; but step out into the sunshine on a summer day and you'll feel the same excitement that's filled generations of kids about to ride the *Cyclone* for the very first time.

You do have to be in the right frame of mind. On weekdays, rainy days and off-season, the festive atmosphere can disappear, making for an experience that's bittersweet, if not downright depressing and even a bit creepy. The beach can be overwhelmingly crowded on hot days, and it's never the cleanest place in or out of the water. But show up for the annual **Mermaid Parade** on the first Saturday of summer (late June, but check the newspapers), and you'll get caught up in the fun of what's got to be one of the oddest – certainly glitziest – small-town festivals in the country, where paraders dress in King Neptune and mermaid attire.

On arrival, head for **Nathan's**, the fast-food spot on the corner of Surf Avenue when you get off the subway. This is the home of the "famous Coney Island hot dog" advertised in *Nathan's* branches elsewhere in the city, and while that delicacy is eminently skippable in Manhattan, only vegetarians have an excuse for missing it here. (*Nathan's* holds an annual "Hot Dog Eating Contest" on July 4th – so far the record is 24 1/2 hot dogs, with buns, in 12 minutes.) One block from *Nathan's* is the boardwalk, where a leisurely stroll gives you ample opportunity to people-watch as you look for clues to Coney Island's past in the fading paint on the sides of buildings.

Go west to see the vine-covered, sunken remains of Coney Island's other wooden **roller coaster** and the landmark parachute jump, now parachute-less and painted orange for no particular reason. Coney Island's real amusement area comprises several amusement parks, none of which are connected. What this means is that the **POP** (pay-one-price) **tickets** each park offers don't really make a lot of sense unless you have kids (nearly all the children's rides are in Deno's

Wonder Wheel Park) or plan on riding one ride more than four times. The **Wonder Wheel** ($3, plus a free children's ticket to the New York Aquarium, see below) is a must – after 75 years, it's still the tallest ferris wheel in the world, and the *only* one in the world on which two-thirds of the cars slide on serpentine tracks, shifting position as the wheel makes its slow circle twice around. The **Cyclone roller coaster** ($4; $3 for a repeat ride) is another landmark attraction, but if you're used to slick modern loop-coaster rides, be forewarned: this low-tech creaky wooden coaster is not for the faint of heart. Further down the boardwalk, halfway to Brighton Beach, is the seashell-shaped **New York Aquarium** (☎718/265-FISH; see p.444 for details) – well worth a visit if you have the time.

The **Coney Island Museum,** maintained by a nonprofit organization also known as Sideshows by the Seashore, is one indoor destination on the drab stretch of Surf Avenue which you won't want to miss. You may get to see such longstanding performers as the Human Blockhead, the Illustrated Man and the Snake Woman. Unofficial, somehow more authentic, sideshows (such as the Two-Headed Baby, the Headless Woman and the Giant Killer Rat) abound on the side streets, but don't expect much for your money.

Brighton Beach

East along the boardwalk from Coney Island, **Brighton Beach**, or "Little Odessa" (the film of the same name was set here), is home to the country's largest community of Russian émigrés, who arrived in the 1970s following a relaxation of emigration restrictions on Soviet citizens entering the US. There's also a long-established and now largely elderly Jewish population. You know when you're out of Coney Island – not only have the amusements disappeared, but there's a residential aspect to the place that gives Brighton Beach appeal.

The neighborhood's main drag, **Brighton Beach Avenue**, runs parallel to the boardwalk, underneath the elevated subway until the train swings north (the D and Q stop here). The street is a bustling mixture of **foodshops**, appetizing **restaurants**, and shops selling every type of Russian **souvenir** imaginable. Eating is half the reason to go to Brighton Beach: for a taste of tradition, try the long-established *Mrs Stahl's Knishes* on the corner of Brighton Beach and Coney Island Avenue, right where the train turns. Even more fun is to pick one of the many grocers/deli shops and try ordering yourself a picnic lunch – maybe some caviar or smoked fish as a topping to some heavy black bread. Be brave: the further away from the subway you get, the less English is spoken, and this community is not known for its outward friendliness. Sit-down food is also readily available throughout Brighton Beach, though you'd be better off waiting until evening as it's then the restaurants really heat up, becoming a near-parody of a rowdy Russian night out with loud live music, much glass-clinking and the frenzied knocking back of vodka. Guests are

Stop in at Harvey's Sporting Goods at 3179 Emmons Ave (☎718/743-0054), for information on diving in the area and to rent bikes and rollerblades or see p.464.

dressed to the nines, and the dancing girls will have you feeling like you've landed in a foreign Vegas. The most popular and accessible spots are *National*, *Ocean* and *Odessa*, all on Brighton Beach Avenue at 273, 1029 and 1113 respectively.

Sheepshead Bay

Next stop on the D or Q subway line heading back to Manhattan is **Sheepshead Bay**, which claims distinction as "New York's only working fishing village" (though City Island in the Bronx – see p.250 – might beg to differ). Much quieter than Coney Island or even Brighton Beach, Sheepshead Bay's **Emmons Avenue** maintains a definite charm, with locals strolling past the piers of fishing boats and relaxing at outdoor cafés whenever the weather is fine. One of America's most famous seafood restaurants, *Lundy's*, is here, housed in its recently-landmarked pink Moorish "palace" at 1901 Emmons Ave (☎718/743-0022). In the early evening, the adventurous can shop the boats themselves for what is undoubtedly the freshest **fish** in the city; all others can sample an earlier catch anywhere along the strip. Truly dedicated fish fanatics can go out on one of the many **boats** that take out visitors (for $25), all you have to do is show up at the piers before 7am and see who's around. Many of the fishing boats also do **sunset cruises** (for $15) to various points of interest in New York Harbor. You can either wander the piers after 5pm to see who's going out or check the ads in the *Daily News*.

Just across the wooden Ocean Avenue Bridge from Sheepshead Bay is the affluent (if occasionally tacky) neighborhood of **Manhattan Beach**, where the beach of the same name is popular with locals and largely unknown to most New Yorkers. It's a very pleasant spot to swim, especially on less-crowded weekday afternoons. Just northeast of Sheepshead Bay (although more easily accessible by bus from Flatbush) are the marshland of **Marine Park** and **Floyd Bennett Field** – an old airfield that serves as headquarters for the Gateway National Recreation Area in **Jamaica Bay**.

Northern Brooklyn

Head south from **Newtown Creek**, the separation between Long Island City in Queens and **Greenpoint** in Brooklyn. Between Polish north Greenpoint and Hasidic south **Williamsburg** there are worlds of difference.

Greenpoint

Greenpoint (reachable by the G to Greenpoint Ave or L to Bedford Ave) hasn't been green for a long time. The Industrial Revolution was good to the economy here, but the environment bears its legacy: the "Black Arts" – printing, pottery, gas, glass and iron – thrived, creating jobs for a growing community, although the pollution was considerable, and the industries that replaced them – primarily fuel and garbage – haven't really improved matters. That said, it's surprising to discover what a truly pleasant community Greenpoint is. And if you can manage to get a glimpse of the Manhattan skyline from between the buildings, so much the better.

To really understand what makes Greenpoint tick, take a look at the imposing **Russian Orthodox Church of the Transfiguration**, south of McCarren Park, at the corner of North 12th St and Driggs Avenue along Bedford Avenue and/or Berry Street. The dominant language around here is Polish, and it's a great place to try Polish food.

Williamsburg

South of here, the neighborhood turns Hispanic, and you're in **Williamsburg**, where, as in many other such enclaves throughout the city, a strong family atmosphere offsets the feeling of menace instilled by run-down commercial buildings. Williamsburg's emerging art scene and embryonic hipness have been getting a lot of press in the past several years: as in the formative days of SoHo and TriBeCa, many of the dilapidated buildings are being put to creative use, and the face of the neighborhood is quickly changing. Indeed, with easy access to Manhattan and waterfront views it's not hard to see why this area has exploded.

The best time to come to Williamsburg is over the weekend, when local art galleries are open to the public. The L train, one stop under the East River from 14th Street in Manhattan, will drop you off on **Bedford Avenue**, Williamsburg's main drag; the J, M or Z will drop you off farther south at the Marcy Avenue station, near the intersection of Bedford and Driggs avenues with Broadway.

If you get off at the L stop, you'll emerge on Bedford Avenue, at the upper end of a string of restaurants, bars, antique stores, bookstores and art galleries. *PlanEat Thailand*, at 184 Bedford Ave (☎718/599-5758) is already a neighborhood institution; the *Charleston Bar & Grill*, across the street at no. 174 (☎718/782-8717), is a comfy old-timer selling pizza and hosting local bands; and down the road, the established *Peter Luger's Steak House* at 178 Broadway and Driggs Avenue, still draws a conservative Wall Street crowd, in search of the best steak in the city. Another fun stop is a visit to the *Brooklyn Brewery* at 118 N 11th St; a century ago there were nearly fifty breweries in Brooklyn, but now the tradition has mostly died out. You can tour this one on Saturdays from noon to 4pm; it's relatively small and always a good time.

Williamsburg also boasts more than a dozen contemporary **art galleries** ranging in ambience from ultra-professional to makeshift, and run by an international coterie of artists; the most sophisticated is, Pierogi 2000, at 177 N 9th St; there's also Eyewash, in a tenement flat on the third floor of 143 N 7th St, and the tiny barn-like Holland Tunnel, at 61 S 3rd St. Farther south, in the shadow of the Williamsburg Bridge at 135 Broadway (corner of Bedford Ave; ☎718/486-7372; Sat–Sun noon–6pm), is the imposing **Victorian Kings Co. Savings Bank**, now home to the somewhat misleadingly named Williamsburg Art and Historical Center (or "WAH," which means "harmony" in Japanese). One of several landmarked nineteenth-century banks in Williamsburg, founded to service local industrialists, the building was renovated and opened as a multimedia arts center in 1996 by Japanese artist Yuko Nii, self-appointed grande dame of the Williamsburg art scene. Stop by for information on lectures and events.

For more details on Williamsburg galleries, see p.307.

The Williamsburg Bridge increasingly divides "hip" Williamsburg from "traditional" Williamsburg. A little farther south, **Division Avenue** marks the longstanding divide between the Hispanic community and the **Hasidic Jewish** part of Williamsburg, where the men wear black suits and long *payess* (curls) hang from under their hats, while women are conservatively dressed with scarves or wigs. The Jewish community has been prominent here since the **Williamsburg Bridge** linked the area to the Lower East Side, and many of the Jews from that neighborhood left for the better conditions across the East River (the bridge was unkindly nicknamed the "Jew Plank"). During World War II a further settlement of Hasidim, mainly from the ultraorthodox Satmar sect, established Williamsburg as a firmly Jewish area, and Puerto Ricans to the north and east began to arrive, since which time the two communities have coexisted in a state of strained tolerance.

The best place to start exploring Jewish Williamsburg is **Lee Avenue**, or Bedford Avenue which runs parallel (take the J, M or Z to Marcy Ave to get there). On both you'll see manifestations of the neighborhood's character: *Glatt Kosher* delicatessens line the streets; signs are written in both Yiddish and Hebrew. Don't take it personally if you're ignored – you may feel like you've dropped in from another planet, and the residents may feel like you have, too. Further south on Lee Avenue, you're far away from any subway – the B44 bus will get you back to the Williamsburg Bridge; the B61 will take you to downtown Brooklyn.

At the southern tip of the neighborhood is the vast **Brooklyn Navy Yard**, a crucial World War II construction ground for famous battleships such as the *Iowa*, *New Jersey*, *Arizona* and *Missouri*. Today, Robert DeNiro and Miramax Studio's Weinstein brothers are negotiating with city officials to construct a $150 million Hollywood-style soundstage complex on a fifteen-acre portion of the Navy Yard. Many New Yorkers have their fingers crossed, as the addition promises to employ hundreds of local residents.

Queens

Of New York City's four Outer Boroughs, **Queens**, named after the wife of Charles II, is probably the least visited by outsiders – not counting when they arrive at one of the two airports. In fact, that's as

THE OUTER BOROUGHS

far as most other New Yorkers get. It seems that the diversity of this, the largest borough geographically, works against it somehow: unlike Brooklyn, the Bronx or Staten Island, Queens has no focal point so compelling as to require attention. Queens was never its own city before incorporating into New York in 1898; it was a county of separate towns and villages, a legacy that is seen today in the individuality of its neighborhoods, not to mention their mailing addresses.

With some exceptions, you can see all the highlights by taking the elevated **#7 train**, which cuts through neighborhoods of ever-shifting ethnic diversity. If you're pressed for time, the train itself offers some view of the urban landscape and excellent people-watching. Go from Greek **Astoria** through Irish **Woodside** to Indian and South American **Jackson Heights** and finally Asian **Flushing**, which can feel as suburban as Long Island some days and as exotic as Hong Kong on others. South of the #7 train, reachable by taking the E or F from Manhattan or even the R from Jackson Heights, are the solidly Jewish neighborhoods of Rego Park, Forest Hills and Kew Gardens, where city and suburbia really do manage to combine in the same locale.

Long Island City and Astoria

Industrial **Long Island City** (which really was a city, and the largest community in Queens county, from 1870 until incorporation) is most people's first view of Queens: it's through here that the #7 and N subway trains cut above ground after crossing over from Manhattan. The area has been attracting artists to its affordable studio spaces for a number of years now, although it hasn't been the mass migration some predicted. In fact, there's not much to see here but if you're keen to visit, **Isamu Noguchi Garden Museum** (p.292), **Socrates Sculpture Park** (p.295), and **PS 1 Contemporary Art Center** (p.308) offer some interesting art displays. Otherwise, stay on the train, or if you've arrived by a more adventurous route (options include walking – though the Queensboro Bridge is not a very pleasant or peaceful stroll – and taking the new New York Waterway Ferry from Manhattan's 33rd St; ☎1-800/533-3779 for information), get on the train and take the N into the heart of Astoria.

Astoria is one of Queens' original communities and is famous for two things: filmmaking and the fact that it has the largest single concentration of Greeks outside Greece itself, or so it claims (whatever Melbourne says to the contrary). Until the **movie industry** moved out to the West Coast in the early 1930s, Astoria was the cinematic capital of the world, and Paramount had its studios here until the lure of Hollywood's reliable weather left Astoria empty and disused by all except the US Army. That's how it remained until recently, when Hollywood's stranglehold on the industry weakened and interest – in New York in general and Astoria in particular – was renewed. The

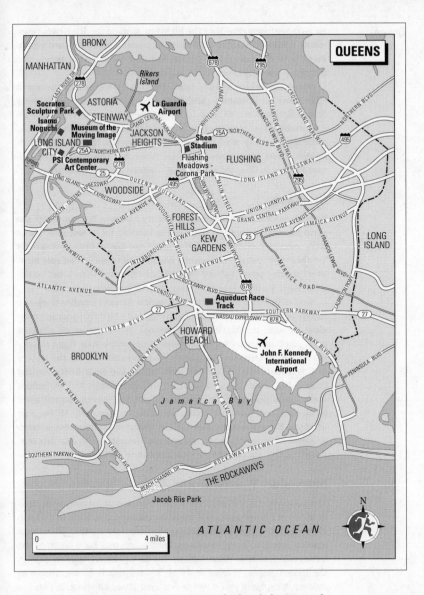

new studios here now rank as the country's fourth largest and, encouraged by the success of films done in New York, are set for a major expansion. They're not open to the public at present, but you can visit the **American Museum of the Moving Image** in the old Paramount complex at 34–31 35th St, close to Broadway (near the

Broadway stop on the N or the Steinway stop on the R). Newly renovated, it houses a stellar collection of posters, stills, sets and equipment both from Astoria's golden age and more recent times. See
p.288 for opening times and a full description.

Greek Astoria stretches from Ditmars Boulevard in the north
right down to Broadway, and from 31st Street across to Steinway
Street. Between 80,000 and 100,000 Greeks live here (together with
a substantial community of Italians) and the evidence is on display in
a sizeable quantity of **restaurants** and **patisseries** that require a closer look. There's not a great deal else to see, but check out the restaurant listings in Chapter 17, "Eating", before you write the area off.

Steinway

East of Astoria lies **Steinway**, a district that was bought up by the
great piano manufacturer and used as housing for its workers. These
were mainly Germans, and the area had for a time a distinctly
Teutonic feel, but the community has long since gone. You can, however, see the piano factory (☎718/721-2600 for visits), but otherwise, there's only a long shopping strip to grab your interest.

Next door the noise-trap of **La Guardia Airport** handles domestic
flights to and from the city. It's unlikely that you'll find yourself traveling through the **Marine Air Terminal**, but if you're an airplane
buff, you might want to leave a little time before your flight to take
one of the free **shuttle buses** over. A small exhibit details the history
of this stylish building, which was built in the early 1930s for the
huge flying boats that took off from the lake outside. Its best feature
is the mural depicting the history of flight, uncovered recently after
being declared "Socialist" and painted over in the early 1950s. Just
offshore, **Rikers Island** holds the city's largest and most overcrowded **prison**. It's very much in use and not for visiting casually. Not surprisingly, this isn't the city's most appealing corner.

Sunnyside, Woodside and Jackson Heights

From Astoria and Steinway, the R train bypasses the largely Irish communities of **Sunnyside** and **Woodside**, taking you straight to Jackson
Heights at the Roosevelt Avenue stop. Architecturally, you're not
missing much, although planning enthusiasts may have heard of the
Sunnyside Gardens development, the first planned "garden city" in
the United States. Started in 1924, it's not nearly as impressive to
modern eyes, but if you'd like to see what it was all about, get off the
#7 at the 46th Street stop and walk down 46th Street, on the opposite
side of Queens Boulevard from the Art Deco "Sunnyside" sign. Other
than that, the two neighborhoods are mainly noteworthy for being
home to Irish immigrants of several generations. On a Friday or
Saturday night, the area's active **bar scene** comes alive.

Jackson Heights

After Sunnyside the #7 train swings away from Queens Boulevard and up narrow Roosevelt Avenue, and the accent of the neighborhood changes. Get off at 74th Street and you'll find yourself in the heart of South American **Jackson Heights**, where at least 150,000 or so Colombians, half as many Ecuadorians, and a good number of Argentinians and other South American peoples make their home in a self-contained area where English is rarely the language of choice. The neighborhood first became Hispanic in the 1960s, when huge influxes of people came over – many illegally – to find work and escape from the poverty and uncertain politics of their own countries, and it's now the largest South American contingent in the States. Tighter immigration controls, however, have radically cut the intake, and the community here is now more or less static.

Roosevelt Avenue and, running parallel, 37th Avenue between 82nd Street and Junction Boulevard are the focuses for the district, and eating-wise, there's no better part of Queens for exotic, unknown and varied **cuisines**. Along both streets you'll find Argentinian steakhouses, Colombian restaurants, and pungent coffeehouses and bakeries stacked high with bread and pastries. But head back down 37th Avenue to 74th Street, and you'll see sudden contrast. With its proliferation of colorful sari, spice and video stores, **Little India** is the largest Indian community in New York, with numbers around 100,000; and the restaurants here far surpass the fare on well-known 6th Street in Manhattan. Try the fare at the popular *Jackson Diner* (74th St at 37th Ave), or see Chapter 17, "Eating" for restaurant listings. If you're into such things, the Menka Beauty Salon (74th St between Roosevelt and 37th aves) is a good place to indulge in the henna trend (hands, not hair).

Corona, Shea Stadium and Flushing Meadow Park

East of Jackson Heights you hit **Corona**, its subway yards ringed by menacing barbed wire and patrolled by dogs to deter graffiti artists – no visit required here. A few steps away is **Shea Stadium**, home of the New York Mets. The Beatles, too, played here in 1965 (little did their manager know that he had just originated the concept of the stadium rock concert) as did the Rolling Stones in 1989. Concerts out here are rare but appreciated; baseball games, on the other hand, are frequent and, attendance-wise, a bit lacking, though the Mets do have a solid fan base. For details on the Mets and when they play, see Chapter 21, *Sports and Outdoor Activities*.

Shea Stadium went up as part of the 1964 World's Fair, held in adjoining **Flushing Meadows-Corona Park**. This is now the **USTA National Tennis Center**, site of the US Open Tennis Championships at the end of each summer, and boasts around thirty courts and seating for well over 25,000 people (again see Chapter 21). Even if you can't get tickets to the Open, this is the best time of year to visit the park, since it's the only event for which air traffic is rerouted. At most other times, the roar of the jet engines can be deafening, marring what would otherwise be a truly lovely place to spend a day.

Flushing Meadows-Corona Park literally rose out of ashes – replacing a dumping ground known to locals as "Mount Corona" and described by F. Scott Fitzgerald in *The Great Gatsby* as "a fantastic farm where ashes grow like wheat into ridges and hills and grotesque gardens." Begun for the 1939 World's Fair, it took its present shape around the time of the later fair, and today it's a beautifully landscaped park with a couple of key attractions that may make the schlep out here well worthwhile.

From Shea, you'll easily find your way to the park; from the 111th Street stop on the #7 train, it's not as obvious, but if you walk *down* 111th Street itself, you'll come to it, starting with the **New York Hall of Science**, a concrete and stained-glass structure retained from the 1964 World's Fair (you'll see the best remaining structures deeper within the park). This is an interactive science museum kids will love, it's fun but can be exhausting for adults. The adjacent **Wildlife Center** (once the zoo) is interesting in that it features exclusively North American animals. But the main reason to come here is to see the **Queens Museum** and the **Unisphere**. Created for the 1964 World's Fair, the Unisphere is a 140-foot-high, stainless steel globe that weighs 380 tons – probably the main reason why it never left its place in the park. It was finally declared a landmark, to the delight of the borough, and it's now lit at night – you may have seen it when you came in from the airport. Robert Moses intended this park to be the "Versailles of America," and it's from this vantage point that you can see that plan in action: carefully designed pathways connect lawns, small pools and two lakes. On a summer day, the park is swarming with kids on bikes and rollerblades; you can rent a bicycle yourself, or even a boat.

See "Museums and Galleries," Chapter 15, for more on Queens' museums.

The park puts out a good map, which you can pick up free from inside the Queens museum, housed in a 1939 World's Fair building which served briefly as the first home of the United Nations. Here the must-see is the **Panorama of the City of New York**, which was built for the 1964 World's Fair. With one inch of model equal to one hundred feet of city, the Panorama (and its 895,000 individual structures) is the world's largest architectural model. It was recently updated, and new remodeling of the space allows you to walk all around (and occasionally over) the parameters of the five boroughs. For $1, you can rent binoculars, which for any kind of close scrutiny are essential. The rest of the museum is almost as fascinating: there are aerial photos, games, toys and other paraphernalia from the World's Fairs on view, plus a collection of glassworks by Louis Comfort Tiffany, who established his design studios in Corona in the 1890s.

While the Panorama is useful for understanding the geography of the city, the fun really comes when you know what you're looking at

– to that end, it's possible (though not easy) to make this your last stop in New York on the way to the airport. Assuming you can haul your luggage back to Roosevelt Avenue, the Q48 bus goes to La Guardia; alternatively, a cab (called from inside the museum) to either airport shouldn't cost more than $10.

Flushing

At the other end of the park (Main St, last stop on the #7 train) lies **Flushing**, most notable for its status as New York's second Chinatown. In actuality, Flushing is home to immigrants from many different Asian countries – too many cuisines to choose from if you're only going to be there for an hour or so. Chinese, Japanese, Korean, Malaysian and Vietnamese restaurants, along with pastry shops and ubiquitous fruit stalls selling a variety of surprises, line Roosevelt Avenue and Main Street – although you may not always be able to read the signs to figure out what's what.

The **historic** side of Flushing is also interesting. The Quaker **Bowne House** still stands; one of the oldest houses in the city (it dates from 1661), the slope-roofed structure is open to the public on Tuesday, Saturday and Sunday afternoons (2.30–4.30pm) and furnished with seventeenth-, eighteenth- and nineteenth-century artwork and furniture belonging to nine generations of the Bowne family. John Bowne helped Flushing aquire the tag "birthplace of religious freedom in America" by resisting official discrimination at a time when anyone who wasn't a Calvinist was persecuted by the Dutch. You'll run into Bowne Street walking east on Roosevelt; just make a left, and the house will be a few blocks up, between 37th and 38th avenues. More information about Queens history (and a map for a do-it-yourself walking tour of the historic sites) can be had at the **Queens Historical Society** (☎718/939-0647) at the Kingsland Homestead across the way – an historic house in its own right, shifted here from its original site about a mile away and reputedly the first house in Flushing to release its slaves. The houses are worth stopping by if you're out here for ethnic eats – *Kum Gang San*, a Korean restaurant on 138-28 Northern Blvd at Union Street is recommended – but it might not be worth a special trip.

Forest Hills and around

South of Flushing Meadows, the stretch of Queens Boulevard that comprises **Rego Park**, **Forest Hills** and **Kew Gardens** is a comfortable, residential area that's more than sixty percent Jewish, something that's manifest in the abundance of synagogues and Jewish centers, although the area is much more secular than the Orthodox enclaves of Williamsburg and Crown Heights in Brooklyn. The Rego Park stretch isn't much of a draw, and you may as well take the E or F straight to 71st Street – Continental Avenue in the heart of Forest

Hills. Incidentally, the name "Rego" comes from the "Real Good Construction Company" – the Queens construction company responsible for much of the original development here.

Forest Hills was for a long time one of the choicest Queens neighborhoods, home to the West Side Tennis Club, which used to host the US Open and still holds important matches. The priciest part of Forest Hills is still largely unchanged: **Forest Hills Gardens**, a mock Tudor village interesting not for what it is but for what it might have been, since it was built originally as housing for the urban poor until the rich grabbed it for themselves. Walk through to see for yourself and, if you do, wind your way to *Eddie's Sweet Shop* on the corner of Metropolitan and 72nd avenues – reckoned by many who've frequented it in its seventy-year history to have the best ice cream in the world.

Further down Queens Boulevard (at the Union Turnpike stop on the E or F) is another planned neighborhood, **Kew Gardens**, which extends south from Queens Boulevard and skirts the edge of Forest Park, a pleasant but unspectacular wilderness. At the turn of the century, Kew Gardens was a watering-hole popular with aging New Yorkers, complete with hotels, lakes and a whole tourist infrastructure. That's all gone now, but Kew Gardens remains, in a leafy and dignified kind of way, one of Queens' most visually enticing districts. The Q10 bus to JFK airport gives you a nice view if you don't actually wish to visit.

Jamaica Bay and the Rockaways

What you may have not noticed when you flew into New York for the first time is that JFK airport is situated on the edge of the wild, island-dotted marshlands of **Jamaica Bay**, named for the Jameco Indians whose territory this was. At the **Wildlife Refuge**, near Broad Channel on the largest of these islands (take the A train to Broad Channel and walk a half-mile; the Q53 bus from Rockaway or Jackson Heights also stops there), you can hike the trails and observe the diverse habitats of more than 300 varieties of migrating **birds**, including several endangered species. For more information, call the Refuge (☎718/318-4340), or, to find out more about the federally administered **Gateway National Recreation Area** of which it is a part, call ☎718/388-3799.

Partly enclosing the bay, the narrowing spit of the Rockaways is the largest **beach area** in the country, stretching for ten miles back toward Brooklyn – most of it strollable along the boardwalk. The action really centers around Beach 116th Street (a subway stop serviced by the A or the Rockaway Shuttle, depending on the time of day), where the boardwalk bustles and the surfers gather. This is the only place to surf in New York City proper, so it's popular with expat Californians. For more information on surfing and beaches, see Chapter 21.

At the far western end, **Jacob Riis Park** is also part of the Gateway area, but is a quieter beach, much less built-up, mostly because the subway doesn't go there (take the Q22 from Beach 116th or the Q35 from Flatbush in Brooklyn). Named for the crusading journalist who battled for better housing and recreation facilities, it features architecture reminiscent of less accessible beaches created by Robert Moses in later years, including a stately brick bathhouse and an outdoor clock, which have been New York City landmarks since the 1930s. The country's only all-women lifeguard tournament is held here every summer, a popular athletic event (call Gateway for dates, or ☎718/318-4300 for specific info). In the eastern corner of the beach, nude bathing is tolerated (if not officially allowed); it's also an area frequented by predominantly gay male naturists.

The Bronx

The city's northernmost borough, **The Bronx**, was for a long time believed to be its toughest and most notoriously crime-ridden district – and presented as such in films like *Fort Apache, The Bronx* and books like *Bonfire of the Vanities*, even after urban renewal was underway. Indeed, there was no other part of the city about which people were so ready to roll out their most gruesome horror stories. Nowadays its poorer reaches still suffer from severe urban deprivation, but almost all of the borough has undergone a successful recent transformation (parts were in any case always prime residential territory). Even in the notorious **South Bronx** – where landlords once burned their own buildings to collect insurance money – things are looking up. There were always plenty of attractions, beautiful parks and vistas in the Bronx, including a world-class botanical garden and zoo; and there are more improvements on the way, such as a plan for a network of promenades and paths designed for walkers and bikers. Much credit should go to community group efforts, as the **Bronx Tourism Council** (198 E 161 St; ☎718/590-3518) will no doubt be glad to tell you. Go there to pick up a visitor's pass, which will get you some discounts on your wanderings.

THE OUTER BOROUGHS

The Bronx is New York's only mainland borough, and as might be expected it has more in common, geographically, with Westchester County to the north than it does with the island regions of New York City: steep hills, deep valleys and rocky outcroppings to the west, and marshy flatlands along Long Island Sound to the east. Economically, the Bronx developed – and declined – more quickly than any other part of the city. First settled in the seventeenth century by a Swedish landowner named Jonas Bronck, like Brooklyn and Queens it only became part of the city proper at the turn of the last century – in two stages, with the area west of the Bronx River being annexed in 1874, and the area to its east in 1895. From 1900 onwards things moved fast, and the Bronx

The Bronx became one of the most sought-after parts of the city in which to live, its main thoroughfare, the **Grand Concourse**, becoming edged with increasingly luxurious Art Deco apartment buildings. This avenue runs the length of the borough, and many places of interest lie on it or reasonably close by.

Unlike Brooklyn or Queens, the Bronx doesn't lend itself to extensive wandering from neighborhood to neighborhood, perhaps because some of the main attractions (like the **Zoo** and the **Botanical Gardens**) take a long time to explore, while others (like **Wave Hill** or **Orchard Beach**) take a long time to get to. An excellent way to get around is by bus – the Bx12, in particular (which actually begins in Inwood, the northernmost part of Manhattan), winds a useful route past many of the places described on the following pages. Pick up a Bronx bus map (the driver may have one if you don't have time in

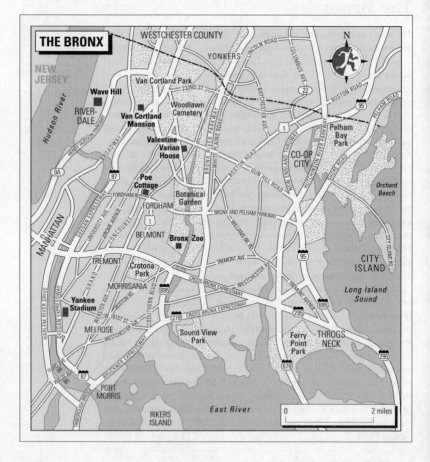

advance). MetroCards now facilitate the many subway-to-subway and subway-to-bus exchanges you'll need to make up here.

Yankee Stadium and the South Bronx

The first stop on the C and D subways after leaving Manhattan, and the third such stop on the #4, is **Yankee Stadium**, home to the New York Yankees baseball team with some of the best facilities for the sport in the country. You can tour the stadium – including the field, clubhouse and dugout – Monday–Friday 10am–4pm and Saturday 10am–1pm (last tour at noon); if there is a day game scheduled there will be no tours, and on night game days the last tour is at noon. (☎718/579-4531; $8, $4 kids and seniors). The Yankees played in north Harlem before moving here in 1923, a move that was in part due to their most famous player ever, **George Herman "Babe" Ruth**, who joined the team in the spring of 1920 and led them for the next fifteen years. It was the star quality of Babe Ruth, the original Bronx Bomber (who lent that nickname to the entire team), that helped pull in the cash to build the current stadium, still known as the "House that Ruth Built." Inside, Babe Ruth, Joe di Maggio and a host of other baseball heroes are enshrined by plaques and monuments, but unless you're coming here to see a game (or on occasion be blessed – the Pope said Mass in 1965 and 1979 to more than 50,000 New Yorkers), there's little reason to visit. (See p.426 for ticket information.)

A trip on the elevated #4 train down to Yankee Stadium affords a good general view of the South Bronx (see below) if you haven't got time to go neighborhood-seeing. The **Grand Concourse**, in its lower reaches, is appealing, and quite safe during the day. On the Concourse itself is the ever-busy **Bronx County Court House**, at 161st Street, where part of *The Bonfire of the Vanities* was filmed, and further along at 1040 Grand Concourse and East 165th Street, the greenhouse-like **Bronx Museum of the Arts** with temporary and permanent exhibits, oriented toward the Bronx and its urban art forms (including graffiti, which was more or less born here).

If you disembark at the first stop on the #4 train out of Manhattan, you'd be right near the neighborhood of **Port Morris**, an industrial part of town whose recently-emerged small outpost of antique shops is a good example of the South Bronx's resurgence. A number of local antique dealers, like the owner of Tigris & Euphrates at 79 Alexander St, hope that restaurants will not lag far behind; for now, the *Schlitz Inn* at no. 767 E 137th St and Willow Avenue is a 1950s-era best bet for German pub food and Schlitz beer (only open on weekdays). Poke around this industrial zone a bit if you have the chance: there are colorful sunken rowhouses (built before the street grade level was raised) on 137th and 136th streets, and the dark, satanic hulk of the **Philips Knitting Mills** is also on 136th Street.

The South Bronx is a term conceived in the Sixties to designate the rapidly declining areas south of Fordham Road. This was the first part of the borough to become properly urbanized, then scarred in the 1960s until fairly recently by huge squares of rubble, leveled apartments sprawling between gaunt-eyed tenements and groups of aimless teenagers. New York City Mayor, Ed Koch, and the Federal Government began to take an interest in rebuilding this part of the city and subsidizing middle-income and low-income housing in the late 1970s, while local heroes like Catholic Father Louis Gigante of Longwood and his South East Bronx Community Organization (SEBCO) had been trying to improve housing since the late 1960s. Indigenous art forms, meanwhile, developed with the times: graffiti, rap and break dancing's early explosions occurred in the South Bronx during the 1970s.

Once the most famous slum in the country, the infamous **Charlotte Street** (east of Crotona Park and north of Morrisania, now called Charlotte Gardens) is the symbolic ground zero of a revitalization now twenty years in the works. Presidents Carter and Reagan visited the desolate site of wholesale demolition in 1977 and 1980 respectively, and in 1978 Deputy Mayor Hermann Badillo, former Bronx Borough president, began actively seeking to redevelop the South Bronx. By the late 1990s the entire area had become known as the Bronx Miracle, and by the time President Clinton visited Charlotte Street in 1997, it had been transformed into the pleasantly, if eerily, suburban Charlotte Gardens. Elsewhere in the South Bronx, abandoned buildings have been renovated into co-operative apartments; backed by federal funds, private investments and a myriad of involved community groups, retailers long missing in this area – basic ones such as Rite-Aid, Pathmark, Caldor and other chains – have moved in. Aficionados of urban renewal and those fascinated by the unlikely survival of historic districts will love it up here – particularly since people innocuously washing their cars have roundly replaced crack addicts on the streets during daylight hours. That being said, you should still exercise caution in the somewhat downtrodden areas, which still exist.

Central Bronx

For simplicity's sake, Fordham Road, which runs west–east at the level of 189th Street, can be said to divide the South and North Bronx. Get off the B, D or #4 train at the junction of Fordham Road and the Grand Concourse, and you'll find yourself between two main **shopping districts**. East Fordham and West Fordham roads are the focus of Saturday afternoon shopping, with Fordham Road boasting every fast-food franchise imaginable, and hundreds of families and street vendors vying for space on the crowded sidewalk. If you take East Fordham Road downhill (or get on the Bx12 bus, which will do it for you) you'll arrive at the Fordham University Campus: continue east, and Arthur Avenue will branch off to your right. Beyond 180th

Street the Bronx improves radically. This is the main thoroughfare of Belmont, a strange mixture of tenements and clapboard houses that is home to one of the largest segments of New York's Italian community – and the most authentically provisioned. It's a small area, bordered to the east by the Zoo and the west by Third Avenue, with 187th Street as its axis. While there has been a small influx of other ethnic groups – most notably Haitians, Mexicans and Albanian Yugoslavs (who love Italian food) – the staunch Italian community is still the dominant force.

Few tourists come here, a shame, since where real Italian flavor is concerned, Belmont makes Little Italy look like Disneyland. There's no better part of the Bronx if you want to eat, particularly if you're on your way to the zoo. Choose restaurants with care: swanky *Mario's* (supposedly where Al Pacino shot the double-crossing policeman in *The Godfather*) is popular but pricey, whereas *Dominick's*, where the daily menu is in your waiter's head, is preferred by locals (see Chapter 17, "Eating", for more details).

The Bronx Zoo
Follow 187th to the end and you're on the edge of the **Bronx Zoo/Wildlife Conservation Park** (Apr–Oct Mon–Fri 10am–5pm, Sat & Sun 10am–5.30pm; Nov–Mar daily 10am–4.30pm; admission Apr–Oct $7.75, $4 for seniors and kids; Nov–Dec $6 and $3; Jan–Mar $4 and $2; free to all on Wed; parking is $6; rides and some exhibits are an additional charge; ☎718/367-1010), accessible either by its main gate on Fordham Road or by a second entrance on Bronx Park South. (This last is the entrance to use if you come directly here by subway – the East Tremont Ave stop on the #2 or #5.)

The Zoo is probably the only reason many New Yorkers from outside the borough ever visit the Bronx. Opened in 1899 and centered around a cluster of original buildings, this is arguably America's greatest zoo, its largest urban one, and one of the first to realize that animals both looked and felt better out in the open; something that's been artfully achieved through a variety of simulated natural habitats. Visit in summer to appreciate it at its best; in winter, a surprising number of the animals are kept in indoor enclosures without viewing areas. One of the most interesting parts is the Wild Asia exhibit, an almost forty-acre wilderness through which tigers, elephants and deer roam relatively freely, viewable either by walking or (for $2 extra, and only from May to October) from an elevated monorail train. Look in also on the World of Darkness (a re-creation of night, holding nocturnal species) and a simulation of a Himalayan mountain area, with endangered species like the red panda and snow leopard. There's a children's section where kids can climb spider webs and wriggle through prairie dog tunnels. As a park, the zoo functions particularly well, too, making for nice strolling. All in all, it's a great focus for a day-trip to the Bronx.

New York Botanical Gardens

Across the road from the zoo's main entrance is the back turnstile of the **New York Botanical Gardens** (Tues–Sun 10am–6pm; $3, $2 seniors and students, $1 kids, free to all on Wed; ☎718/817-8500), which in their southernmost reaches are as wild as anything you're likely to see upstate. Further north near the main entrance (the D train to Bedford Park Blvd, or more conveniently, the Metro-North train – from Grand Central or 125th St – ☎532-4900 for costs and package deals) are more cultivated stretches. The Enid A. Haupt Conservatory, a landmark, turn-of-the-century crystal palace, show-cases jungle and desert ecosystems, a palm court and a fern forest, among other seasonal displays ($3.50, $2.50 students and seniors, $2 kids). In addition, there are tram tours and plant sales, and the gardens themselves are enormous enough to wander around happily for hours.

The Poe Cottage and the Museum of Bronx History

Leave the gardens by their main entrance and walk west (or take the D or #4 train to Kingsbridge Road or the Bx9 up Fordham Rd) – and you'll come eventually to the Grand Concourse and Kingsbridge Road site of the **Poe Cottage**, in Poe Park. This tiny, white-clapboard anachronism in the midst of a now-working-class Hispanic neigh-borhood was Edgar Allan Poe's rural home for the last three years of his life, from 1846 to 1849, though it was only moved here recently when threatened with demolition. Never a particularly stable charac-ter and dogged by problems, Poe was rarely happy in the cottage, but he did manage to write the short, touching poem "Annabel Lee." The house is open to the public on weekends only (Sat 10am–4pm, Sun 1–5pm; $2; ☎718/881-8900); it has displays of memorabilia and manuscripts, as well as an audiovisual presentation on Poe's life and work in the Bronx. On Halloween there are readings of his works.

A bit north of here (at 3266 Bainbridge Ave and E 208th St; D to 205th St or #4 to Mosholu Parkway) is the Valentine-Varian House, an eighteenth-century Georgian stone farmhouse that now houses the **Museum of Bronx History**. Considering how much the Bronx has changed – there was still plenty of farm country left only fifty years ago – the old photographs and lithographs can be fascinating. Like the Poe Cottage, though, the museum is only open on weekends (Sat 10am–4pm, Sun 1–5pm; $2; ☎718/881-8900).

North Bronx

The **North Bronx** is the topmost fringe of New York City, and if any-one actually makes it up here it's to see the luminary-filled **Woodlawn Cemetery**. Accessible from Jerome Avenue at Bainbridge (last stop, Woodlawn, on the #4), this is a prime exam-ple of how New Yorkers in the 1850s took in the air: before the age of public parks, they went to visit the dead (and the idea of city parks grew out of such excursions' popularity). For many years, Woodlawn has been the top people's cemetery, and like Green-Wood in Brooklyn (see p.227) boasts a number of tombs and mausolea that are memorable mainly for their garishness. It's a huge place, but there are some monuments that stand out: one Oliver Hazard Belmont, financier and horse dealer, lies in a dripping Gothic fantasy near the entrance, modeled on the resting place of Leonardo da Vinci in Amboise, France; F.W. Woolworth has himself an Egyptian palace guarded by sphinxes; while Jay Gould, not most people's favorite businessman when he was alive, takes it easy in a Greek-style temple. Pick up a guide from the office at the entrance to locate the many larger-than-life individuals buried here: they include Herman Melville, Irving Berlin, George M. Cohan, Fiorello LaGuardia, Robert Moses, Miles Davis and Duke Ellington, among others.

Van Cortlandt Park

West of the cemetery lies **Van Cortlandt Park**, a forested and hilly all-purpose recreation space, used in fall and spring by high-school cross-country track teams. Apart from the sheer pleasure of hiking through its woods, the best thing here is the **Van Cortlandt Mansion**, nestled in its southwest corner not far from the subway station. This is the Bronx's oldest building, an authentically restored Georgian structure, very pretty, and with its rough-hewn gray stone really rather rustic. During the Revolution it changed hands a number of times, and was used as an operations headquarters by both the British and the Patriots. On the hills above, New York City's archives were buried for safekeeping during the Revolution, and it was in this house that George Washington slept before heading his victory march into Manhattan in 1783 (Tues–Fri 10am–3pm, Sat & Sun 11am–4pm, closed Mon; $2, $1.50 seniors and students, free to kids ☎718/543-3344).

Riverdale

Immediately west rise the moneyed heights of **Riverdale** – one of the most desirable neighborhoods in the city, and so far from the South Bronx in feel and income it might as well be on the moon. This part of the Bronx (and it is part of the Bronx, though some residents and real-estate agents would prefer to forget that) is extremely hard to get to without a car; Metro-North to Riverdale or the #1 or #9 to West 242nd Street are the closest rail options, and even the buses cover little of the residential streets. If you do make the trip, you'll be rewarded with suburban escape and – when you can get through the trees – spectacular views. Well worth a visit is **Wave Hill**, a small country estate overlooking the Hudson River and Palisade Cliffs which was donated to the city a couple of decades back; in previous years, it was briefly home to Mark Twain and, later, Teddy Roosevelt.

The delightful grounds boast gorgeous botanical gardens, and the nineteenth-century mansion is now a forum for temporary art installations, concerts and workshops (Tues–Sun 9am–5.30pm, Apr–Oct open Wed until dusk, free Tues all day and Sat until noon; $4, $2 students and seniors; ☎718/549-3200).

City Island

On the east side of the Bronx, jutting out into Long Island Sound, **City Island** is, historically, a fishing community and while much of the industry has gone, the atmosphere remains, despite the proximity of the urban Bronx (a short causeway takes the Bx29 bus – pick it up at the Pelham Bay Park subway stop on the #6 – to and from the mainland). With all the historic house-moving that goes on these days, it's easy to believe that City Island was imported from Maine or Massachusetts by some nautically minded philanthropist.

Most people come here for the **restaurants** – in fact, on a weekend night, it's nearly impossible for the bus to get down the traffic-clogged City Island Avenue, and the restaurants overflow with "off islanders." You're better off making the trip on a weekday; not only will the "clamdiggers" (as those born on the island call themselves) be more friendly, but you'll stand a better chance of getting something fresh when you order your dinner. You stand a good chance at either the *Lobster House* (691 Bridge St) or *JP Waterside Restaurant* (703 Minneford Ave) for seafood and outdoor seating.

Aside from the restaurants, City Island is interesting primarily for its New England-style houses and its small-town feel. You can easily walk the length of it, and though walking back and forth can be tiring, both the main drag and the back roads deserve a look. On **City Island Avenue**, small **shops** are the rule of the day – stop in at Mooncurser Antiques to see one of the largest collections of **vinyl records** assembled anywhere. In the last few years, an **arts community** has begun to thrive here too, led by CIAO Gallery and Arts Center (278 City Island Ave; ☎718/885-9316). While there, pick up a brochure listing the twelve other spaces on the island to view and buy arts and handicrafts; as well, there's an annual arts and crafts fair held here during the last weekend of May. Heading back toward the causeway, turn right on Fordham Street and then left on King Street. King and Minneford streets are where the bigger houses on City Island have remained; to make yourself really jealous, look back behind the houses at the private piers and beaches.

Before you head back to the mainland, stop in at the **North Wind Undersea Institute**, 610 City Island Ave (Mon–Fri 1–5pm, Sat & Sun noon–5pm; $3, $2 students and seniors; ☎718/885-0701), a quaint museum that, strangely, was co-founded by Woodstock legend Richie Havens. Housed in an old ship captain's retirement home, its exhibits center around an ecological theme, with particular attention to its own role in the rehabilitation and rescue of threatened and stranded marine life. Prowl around to see the collection of old diving gear, whaling artifacts and bones dating back to 1502 and a superb collection of scrimshaw (whalebone etched with intricate designs), which many consider to be the first true American folk art form.

Pelham Bay Park and Orchard Beach

From City Island, it's an easy walk to **Orchard Beach**, the eastern-most part of the expansive **Pelham Bay Park** – just make a right after the causeway, and take the scenic park path. These days, Orchard is known locally as the "Spanish Riviera," and beach and boardwalk pulse constantly with a salsa beat. **Free concerts** in summer are common, and even if nothing is going on, wander long enough and you're bound to hear music: beachgoers often bring their own instruments, and impromptu jam sessions (complete with dancing) spring up all over the place.

At the northernmost end of the boardwalk, a sign for the **Kazimiroff Nature Trail** takes you into a wildlife preserve that's also part of Pelham Bay Park. It's named after Theodore Kazimiroff, a noted naturalist, who helped stop these wetlands from being turned into a landfill. The trail winds through meadow, shrubland, forest and marsh, and is serene and peaceful – a stark contrast to much of the rest of the park, which is now crisscrossed by highways that take away from its original charm. Without a car, unfortunately, exploring the further reaches of Pelham Bay Park is difficult.

The **Bartow-Pell Mansion Museum and Gardens** (Wed, Sat & Sun noon–4pm; $2.50, $1.25 students and seniors, kids free; ☎718/885-1461) is a national landmark worth seeing for its beauti-fully furnished interior, and magnificent formal gardens that over-look Long Island Sound, but to get there you have to go back to the Pelham Bay Park subway #6 station and take bus Bx45 (no service Sunday).

Staten Island

Until just over thirty years ago **Staten Island**, the common name for what's officially Richmond County, was isolated – getting to it meant a ferry trip or long ride through New Jersey (to which it's physically closer), and daily commuting into town was almost an eccentricity. Staten Islanders enjoyed an insular, self-contained life in the state's least populous borough, and the stretch of water to Manhattan marked a cultural as much as physical divide. In 1964 the opening of the **Verrazano Narrows Bridge** changed things; land-hungry Brooklynites found cheap property on the island and swarmed over the bridge to buy their parcel of suburbia. Today Staten Island has swollen into tightly packed residential neighborhoods amid the ram-bling greenery, forming endless backwaters of tidy, look-don't-touch homes.

THE OUTER BOROUGHS

If New Yorkers from other boroughs know anything about Staten Island – and it's not guaranteed that they would – it's limited to two words: garbage and secession. Though recycling efforts have significantly reduced the amount of **garbage** the city produces, more than 75,000 tons a week are dumped in Staten Island's Fresh Kills landfill. This is the largest landfill in the world, holding 2400 million cubic feet of refuse (that's 25 times the size of the Great Pyramid at Giza), and it's a claim to fame over which residents feel strong resentment, particularly in the light of citywide political reforms that have left Staten Island vulnerable to decisions made by the votes in more populous boroughs. The landfill is, however, scheduled to close on December 31, 2001, with parkland promised in its wake.

Over the years there's been much talk of Staten Island **seceding** from the city, and a recent referendum showed overwhelming support for the idea; that vote, however, decided nothing more substantial than that the state legislature will look into the feasibility of the proposal.

With this stellar reputation, it's no wonder that nine out of ten tourists who take the Staten Island ferry to drool over the view turn back to Manhattan immediately on arrival. We won't berate them for that; travel by public transportation on Staten Island can be slow-going (bicycle may be the best way to get around), and there's nothing so unbeatable there that you should lose any sleep if you miss out on it. Should you decide to stay, however, your efforts will be rewarded – since each of the few, spread-out attractions here is a worthwhile excursion in itself.

The ferry, St George and the Snug Harbor Cultural Center

The **Staten Island ferry** sails from the tip of Manhattan Island (the Battery) around the clock, with departures every 15–20 minutes at rush hours, every 30 minutes mid-day and evenings, and every 60 minutes late at night – weekends less frequently. It is truly New York's best bargain: completely free (a 1997 innovation), with wide-angled views of the city and the Statue of Liberty becoming more spectacular as you retreat. By the time you arrive, Manhattan's skyline stands mirage-like, filtered through the haze as the romantic, heroic city of a thousand and one posters. The ferry terminal at the Staten Island end lacks the commuter grandeur of the one at the Battery, but is conveniently attached to the **bus station** – which you will need to use to get anywhere on the island (MetroCards will provide you with a free transfer if you've used the subway to get to the ferry, but have change, token or MetroCard with you as they are unavailable at the station). Arm yourself with a bus map, and – if you can find one – a *Staten Island Sites and Scenes* brochure (available free in the ferry terminals), and you're on your way. For an advance brochure, call ☎ 1-800/573-SINY.

The town of **St George** is adjacent to the ferry terminal, and it's a strange, underutilized place for a spot with such obvious potential. In an area that should be reaping the benefits of its closeness to Manhattan, empty storefronts abound, and crowds that should flock on nice days to hilly streets with fabulous views are nowhere to be found. There is a landmarked Historic District with a wonderful collection of residential buildings in shingle, Queen Anne, Greek Revival and Italianate styles.

In contrast, the **Snug Harbor Cultural Center**, 1000 Richmond Terrace ☎ 718/448-2500, in nearby New Brighton (take the S40 bus from the ferry terminal), thrives with signs of cultural growth. This arts center's 28 buildings are spread out over a campus that once served as a retirement home for sailors. With galleries and studios for up-and-coming artists, an annual outdoor Summer Sculpture Festival, and events and concerts year-round (including summer

performances of the Metropolitan Opera and New York Philharmonic
– good music in outdoor surroundings more intimate than anywhere
in Manhattan), it draws visitors from all over the borough and
beyond. There's also the lively Harmony Street Fair, held annually
the second Sunday in June. Also in the same park area are the **Staten
Island Children's Museum** and the **Botanical Gardens**. The Snug
Harbor grounds are open all the time and are free to the public;
tours, also free, are given on weekend afternoons.

The Alice Austen House

If you pack a picnic lunch for your trip to Staten Island (not a bad
idea, since there's little guarantee that your necessary bus stop will
be near anywhere to eat), enjoy it on the grounds of the **Alice
Austen House**, 2 Hylan Blvd (Thurs–Sun noon–5pm, ☎718/816-
4506; suggested donation $3). Easily reachable by the S51 bus to
Hylan Boulevard (walk down the hill), this Victorian cottage faces
the waters of the Narrows, and from the front lawn it's easy to
understand why Alice Austen's grandparents dubbed their house
"Clear Comfort" – today the spectacular view takes in the
Verrazano Bridge as well as the Brooklyn Shore. But the attraction
of this place is actually the story of Alice Austen herself, a pioneering photographer whose work comprises one of the finest records
of turn-of-the-century American life. At a time when photography
was both difficult and expensive, Alice Austen developed her talent
and passion for the art expertly. Her tragedy is that she never considered the possibility of going professional, even when the stock
market crash of 1929 lost her the family home and left her in the
poorhouse, and her work was only rediscovered shortly before her
death in 1952. The house exhibits a relatively small selection of her
photographs (the whole collection is owned by the Staten Island
Historical Society), but they're fascinating to look at, and as more
of the rooms are restored and refurnished, the museum can only
improve.

South Beach and the southeast shore

Stretching below the Verrazano Narrows, along the eastern part of
the island, are a series of public beaches, starting with **South Beach**,
a once-thriving resort for New York's wealthy, and stretching down
to **Great Kills Park**, a place surfed by locals. Few visitors come to
New York for its beaches, and those who do most likely head to the
Rockaways in Queens – for good reason – but these aren't bad if
you're looking for less crowded and more casual alternatives. At
South Beach, reachable by the S51 bus, there is a two-and-a-half-mile
boardwalk – the fourth largest in the world and a great place to jog
or rollerblade; otherwise, just hit its fairly quiet sands for sunning. If
you're in need of nourishment, great pizza can be had at *Good Fellas*

Brick Oven Pizza, on 1718 Hylan Blvd (☎718/987-2422) – a good mile and a half walk inland from the beach.

Staten
Island

Lighthouse Hill: The Jacques Marchais Museum of Tibetan Art

In the middle of Staten Island's residential heartland, the **Jacques Marchais Museum of Tibetan Art** at 338 Lighthouse Ave (April–Nov Wed–Sun 1–5pm, other times by appointment; $3, $2.50 seniors, $1 kids; ☎718/987-3500) is an unlikely find; the bus drivers don't know it's there, so ask to be let off at Lighthouse Avenue – it's a trek of about a mile up the steep hill until you hit it on your right. Jacques Marchais was the alias of Jacqueline Klauber, a New York art dealer who reckoned she'd get on better with a French name in the 1920s and 30s. She did, and used her own comfortable income and that of her husband to indulge her passion for Tibetan art. Eventually she assembled the largest collection in the Western world, reproducing a *gompah*, or Buddhist temple, on the hillside in which to house it in 1947. Even if you know nothing about such things the exhibition is small enough to be accessible, with magnificent bronze Bodhisattvas, fearsome deities in union with each other, musical instruments, costumes, and decorations from the mysterious world of Tibet. Give it time – after a while the air of the temple and its terraced gardens is heady. Best time to visit is on a Sunday, when lectures focus on different aspects of Asian culture around the world, and in the first or second week of October when the Tibetan festival takes place: Tibetan monks in maroon robes perform the traditional ceremonies, and Tibetan food and crafts are sold. Phone ahead for the exact date.

While you're up on the hill, there are two more items of note, neither of which is open to the public – but walking by won't hurt anyone. The **Staten Island Lighthouse** on Ediboro Road can be seen from Lighthouse Avenue, appropriately enough, and though it's a strange thing to see so far inland – ships used to line it up with other lighthouses on the water as a guide into New York harbor – it's been in pretty much constant use since it first started guiding ships into New York Harbor in 1912. Around the corner, at **48 Manor Court**, the private home known as "Crimson Beech" was designed by Frank Lloyd Wright and is significant as the only Wright residence within the New York City limits.

Historic Richmond Town

Back on the main Richmond Road, a short walk, or the S74 bus from the central terminal, brings you to **Historic Richmond Town** (July & August Wed–Fri 10am–5pm, Sat & Sun 1–5pm; Sept–June Wed–Sun 1–5pm; $4, $2.50 students, seniors and under-18s; ☎718/351-1611), home to the **Staten Island Historical Society**, and a charm-

ing "reinvention" of the seventeenth-to-nineteenth-century village of
Richmond comprised of about forty historic houses original to the
town, some transplanted from their original sites. Richmond was the
nexus of old Staten Island and the frontier outpost-like crossroads of
the route from Manhattan to New Jersey. Starting from the
Historical Museum, half-hourly tours negotiate such gems as the
1695 Dutch-style **Voorlezer's House**, oldest elementary school in
the country; a picture-book general store whose contents span the
nineteenth and twentieth centuries; and the atmospheric **Guyon-
Lake-Tysen House** of 1740. What brings this all to life are costumed
volunteer craftspeople using traditional techniques to make wooden
water buckets, bake bread and weld tin, all of them enthusiastic
experts on their activities and the houses and shops in which they
"work." It's all carried off to picturesque and ungimmicky effect, and
by the end of your visit you're likely to be so won over that you'll
want to work there yourself – or at least come back for one of their
special events. The rustic setting makes it difficult to believe you're
just twelve miles from downtown Manhattan.

Conference House

At the southern tip of the island is the **Conference House**, at 7455
Hylan Blvd, a stately seventeenth-century stone structure whose
claim to fame is acting as host to failed peace talks, led by Ben
Franklin and John Adams, during the American Revolution – and it
feels like it hasn't seen much action since, other than perhaps the
manicuring of its rolling lawns, from which there is a lovely beachfront view of Perth Amboy, New Jersey. Today, the house is open for
tours (call ☎718/984-6046); step inside for a peek at the period furnishings and its original kitchen, now restored to working order.

Chapter 15

Museums and Galleries

As a city, New York does not lack visual stimulation, and you may find there's enough on the streets to look at without walking inside a museum. But you should be aware of what you're missing. New York offers an extraordinary array of museums, large and small, dedicated to showcasing art and design, history, nature, film and television, ethnic themes and more. In the big two Manhattan museums alone – the **Metropolitan** and the **Museum of Modern Art** – there are few aspects of Western art left untapped. The Metropolitan, in particular, is exhaustive (mercilessly so, if you try to take in too much too quickly), with arguably the world's finest collection of European and American art as well as superlative displays of everything from ancient Egyptian to Chinese art. The Museum of Modern Art (MoMA) takes over where the Met leaves off, emphasizing exactly why (and how) New York became the art capital of the world.

Among the other **major museums**, there are exciting collections of contemporary art and invariably excellent temporary shows at the **Whitney** and **Guggenheim**; a wide array of seventeenth- and eighteenth-century paintings at the **Frick**; and – amid an unexpectedly pastoral setting – a glorious display of medieval art at **The Cloisters**. **The American Museum of Natural History** offers the largest exhibition in the world of items related to evolution, biology, and the natural world. All things, time permitting, are worth seeing. So also are many of the **smaller museums**, often quirkily devoted to otherwise obscure subjects and perfectly sized for a quick visit.

Opening hours and admission fees

Opening hours don't fall into any fixed patterns; many museums are closed on Mondays (and national holidays) and are open into the early evening one or two nights a week. Admission charges are high, with a slight discount for those with student ID cards; to offset the prices, some major museums are free or offer a much-reduced entrance charge one evening a week. Some museums also utilize the

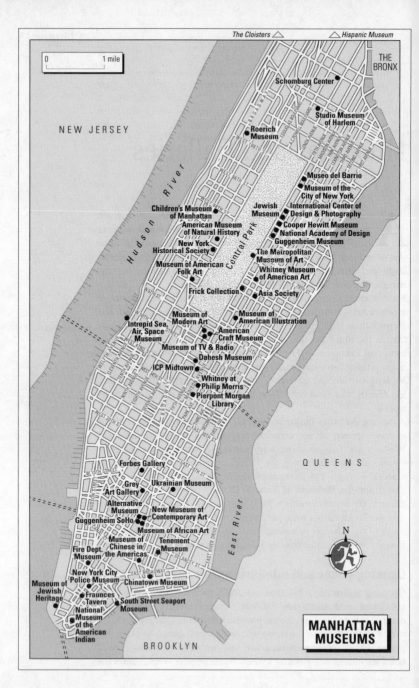

The Cloisters △   △ Hispanic Museum

0   1 mile

THE BRONX

NEW JERSEY

Schomburg Center

Studio Museum of Harlem

Roerich Museum

Museo del Barrio

Museum of the City of New York

Children's Museum of Manhattan

Jewish Museum

International Center of Design & Photography

American Museum of Natural History

Cooper Hewitt Museum

National Academy of Design

New York Historical Society

Guggenheim Museum

Museum of American Folk Art

The Metropolitan Museum of Art

Whitney Museum of American Art

Frick Collection

Asia Society

Central Park

Museum of American Illustration

Museum of Modern Art

Intrepid Sea, Air, Space Museum

American Craft Museum

Museum of TV & Radio

Dahesh Museum

ICP Midtown

Whitney at Philip Morris

Pierpont Morgan Library

QUEENS

Forbes Gallery

Ukrainian Museum

Grey Art Gallery

Alternative Museum

New Museum of Contemporary Art

Guggenheim SoHo

Museum of African Art

Museum of Chinese in the Americas

Tenement Museum

East River

Fire Dept. Museum

New York City Police Museum

Chinatown Museum

Museum of Jewish Heritage

Fraunces Tavern

South Street Seaport Museum

National Museum of the American Indian

N

BROOKLYN

MANHATTAN MUSEUMS

Free museums

The following museums are free at the stated times:

Tuesday Cooper-Hewitt (5–9pm), International Center of Photography Uptown and Midtown (5–8pm, pay what you wish), Jewish Museum (5–8pm).

Thursday Asia Society Gallery (6–8pm), Whitney (6–8pm, first Thurs of the month), New Museum of Contemporary Art (6–8pm).

Friday Guggenheim (6–8pm, pay what you wish), Museum of Modern Art (4.30–8.15pm, pay what you wish).

"suggested donation" system. In theory, this means you're allowed to give as little or as much as you'd like for an entry fee (hence enabling museums to keep their charitable status). A few (like the American Museum of Natural History) are quite amenable to taking an amount lower than the suggested one, others (like the Met) are less open-minded – so it really all depends on how brazen you are feeling.

The Metropolitan Museum of Art

5th Ave at 82nd St. Subway #4, #5 or #6 to 86th St–Lexington Ave. Tues–Thurs & Sun 9.30am–5.15pm, Fri & Sat 9.30am–8.45pm, closed Mon; suggested donation $10, students $5 (includes admission to The Cloisters on the same day, see p.282); recorded "acoustiguide" tours of the major collections $5; free conducted tours, "Highlights of the Met," daily; also highly detailed tours of specific galleries, call for details; several restaurants and excellent book and gift shops; ☎879-5500 or 535-7710 for recorded information.

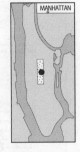

The Met, as it's usually called, is the foremost museum in America. Expanded piecemeal from its original Gothic Revival-style building designed by Calvert Vaux, most of its present Fifth Avenue facade is the work of McKim, Mead and White and was completed in 1926. The Met's collection takes in over two million works of art and spans the cultures of America, Europe, Africa, China, the Far East, and the classical and Islamic worlds. Any overview of the museum is out of the question: the Met demands many and specific visits or, at least, self-imposed limits.

Broadly, the museum breaks down into **seven major collections**: European Painting and Sculpture; Asian Art; American Painting and Decorative Arts; Egyptian Antiquities; Medieval Art; Ancient Greek and Roman Art; and the Art of Africa, the Pacific and the Americas. You'll find the highlights of these and the Twentieth Century Art collection detailed below. Keep in mind, however, that there is much, much more for which space forbids anything other than a passing mention. Among the **less famous Met collections** are Islamic Art

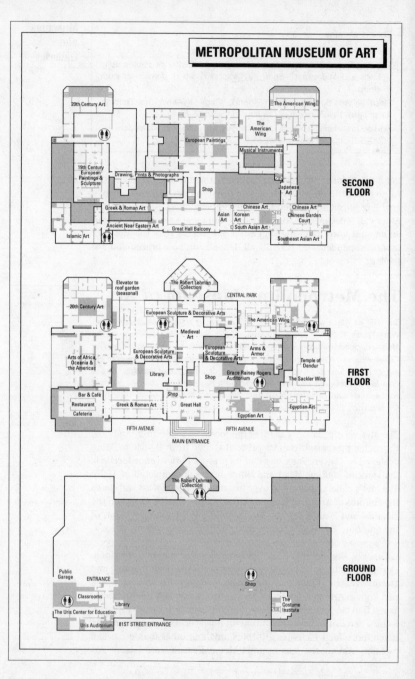

METROPOLITAN MUSEUM OF ART

SECOND FLOOR

20th Century Art

The American Wing

The American Wing

European Paintings

Musical Instruments

19th Century European Paintings & Sculpture

Drawing, Prints & Photographs

Shop

Japanese Art

Greek & Roman Art

Chinese Art

Ancient Near Eastern Art

Asian Art

Korean Art

Chinese Art

Chinese Garden Court

Islamic Art

Great Hall Balcony

South Asian Art

Southeast Asian Art

FIRST FLOOR

Elevator to roof garden (seasonal)

The Robert Lehman Collection

CENTRAL PARK

20th Century Art

European Sculpture & Decorative Arts

The American Wing

Medieval Art

Arts of Africa, Oceania & the Americas

European Sculpture & Decorative Arts

European Sculpture & Decorative Arts

Arms & Armor

Temple of Dendur

Library

Shop

Grace Rainey Rogers Auditorium

The Sackler Wing

Bar & Café

Shop

Restaurant

Great Hall

Cafeteria

Greek & Roman Art

Egyptian Art

Egyptian Art

FIFTH AVENUE

FIFTH AVENUE

MAIN ENTRANCE

GROUND FLOOR

The Robert Lehman Collection

Public Garage

ENTRANCE

Shop

Classrooms

The Uris Center for Education

Library

The Costume Institute

Uris Auditorium

81ST STREET ENTRANCE

Problems in visiting the Met

There are three main **difficulties** in visiting, other than the obvious frustrations of size and time:

Scheduling. Certain collections are open only on a rotating basis, so if you're intent on seeing anything less than obvious, phone ahead (☎879-5500). The rotating schedule affects galleries on Tuesdays, Wednesdays and Thursdays.

Layout. The Met has developed in a piecemeal way, for its nineteenth-century multimillionaire benefactors were often as intent on advertising their own tastes as setting America on the cultural high road. Therefore, their bequests often stipulated that their donations be housed in distinct galleries. If you're interested in one particular period or movement of art, you won't necessarily find all of its examples in the same place.

Reorganization. The museum is constantly reorganizing its galleries: rotating the works, creating space for special exhibits, loaning out pieces for retrospectives, and refurbishing rooms. This means that although the master works stay pretty much in the same locations, the order in which we've listed various standouts may not be that in which they appear and some might be away on loan.

(possibly the largest display anywhere in the world); European Decorative Arts; Arms and Armor Galleries (the largest and most important in the Western hemisphere); a Musical Instrument Collection (containing the world's oldest piano); and the spectacular Costume Institute.

Despite the museum's size, **initial orientation** is not too difficult. There is just one main entrance, and once you've passed through it you find yourself in the **Great Hall**, a deftly lit Neoclassical cavern where you can consult plans, check tours and pick up info on the Met's excellent lecture listings. Directly ahead is the Grand Staircase and what is, for many visitors, the single greatest attraction – the European Painting galleries.

European Art galleries

The Met's **European Art galleries**, located on the second floor at the top of the main staircase, are divided in two parts: the European Painting section – which traces several centuries worth of work – and the nineteenth-century European Paintings and Sculpture section.

The European Painting galleries begins with a scattering of portraits then branches off into **two paths**: the one to the right moves through the Italian Renaissance, chronicles the seventeenth-century Dutch masters, passes through a small but fine English collection and ends with a clutch of Spanish, French and Italian works painted in the Baroque style; the path to the left begins in the Gothic period, passes through the religious works of the Northern Renaissance, offers glances at Baroque and Italian Mannerism and finally culminates in Italian Baroque.

Make sure you pick up the detailed room-by-room gallery maps for the European Painting and Nineteenth-Century Painting collections, available at the main information desk in the Great Hall.

Spanish and Italian Painting

After looking through a preliminary section that contains works by
Tiepolo and Neoclassical/Romantic portraits by David and Greuve,
you'll pass through glass doors, **head to your right** and arrive at the
beginning of the Italian painting gallery. The **Italian Renaissance**
isn't spectacularly represented, but there's a worthy selection from
the various Italian schools, including an early *Madonna and Child
Enthroned with Saints* by **Raphael**, a late **Botticelli**, the crisply lin-
ear *Three Miracles of Saint Zenobius*, **Filippo Lippi**'s *Madonna
and Child Enthroned with Two Angels*, and **Michele de Verona**'s
handsome *Madonna and Child with the Infant John the Baptist*,
rendered in the fifteenth-century Italian tradition with a marmoreal
surface bathed in soft light. Also look out for the roaring dragon in
Crivelli's *St George* and **Mantegna**'s rigid and sculptural *Adoration
of the Shepherds*. At the end of the Italian section is a room filled
with luminous works by **Titian** and **Tintoretto**.

Dutch Painting

This collection, dominated by the major works of **Rembrandt,
Vermeer** and **Hals**, is the culmination of the main European galleries
– and arguably the finest single group of paintings in the museum.

Vermeer, genius of the domestic interior, is represented by some
of his best works. His *Young Woman with a Water Jug*, which
hints at themes of purity and temperance, is a perfect example of his
skill in composition and tonal gradation, combined with an uncannily naturalistic sense of lighting. *A Girl Asleep* is deeper in its composition, or at least appears to be, the rich fabric separating the
foreground from the rooms beyond. Vermeer often used this trick,
and you'll see it again in *Allegory of the Faith*, where the drawn
curtain presents the tableau and separates the viewer from the lesson presented. Most haunting of all is the great *Portrait of a Young
Woman*, displaying Vermeer at his most complex and the Met at its
most fortunate.

As Vermeer's pictures depict the domestic harmony of seventeenth-century Holland, **Hals**'s early paintings reveal its exuberance.
In *Merrymakers at Shrovetide*, the figures explode out from the
canvas in an abundance of gesture and richness. *Young Man and a
Woman at an Inn*, painted five years later, shows a more subdued
use of color (yet not at the expense of vitality).

The best of **Rembrandt**'s works here are also portraits. There is a
beautiful painting of his common-law wife, *Hendrike Stoffjels*, finished three years before her early death – a blow that marked a further decline in the artist's fortunes. In 1660, he went bankrupt, and
the superb *Self-Portrait* of that year shows the self-examination he
brought to later works. A comparison between the flamboyant 1632
Portrait of a Lady and the warmer, later *Lady with a Pink* reveals
his maturing genius.

In addition to these three famous artists, the Dutch rooms also display a good scattering of works by their contemporaries. Most memorable is **Pieter de Hooch**'s *Two Men and a Woman in a Courtyard of a House*, his acknowledged masterpiece, with its perfect arrangement of line, form and color. While de Hooch was painting peaceful courtyards and Vermeer lacemakers and lute players, **Adrian Brouwer** was turning his eye to the seamier side of Dutch life. When he wasn't drunk or in prison he came up with works like *The Smokers*, typical of his tavern scenes. *The Smokers* is a portrait of Brouwer and his drinking pals – he's the one in the foreground, in case you hadn't guessed.

English Painting

Though the Met's **English gallery** is essentially a prelude to the other major collections here, it's an unusually brilliant and elegant collection of paintings. At its heart are a group of portraits by **Sir Joshua Reynolds**, **William Gainsborough** and **Thomas Lawrence**, the trio of great eighteenth-century English portraitists. **Gainsborough's** *Mrs Grace Dalrymple Elliott* is typical of his portrait style – an almost feathery lightness softening the monumental pose. Lawrence is best represented by *The Calmady Children*, a much-engraved portrait that was the artist's favorite among his works, and by his likeable and virtuoso study of *Elizabeth Farren*, which he painted at the precocious age of 21. Upon seeing the picture, Sir Joshua Reynolds remarked, "This young man begins where I leave off," a rather modest comment considering the number of portraits by Reynolds that are included here.

Continue on, and as you loop back to the entrance to the painting galleries you'll pass through another smattering of works by **Spanish**, **French** and **Italian** painters, most notably **Goya** and **Velázquez**. The latter's piercing and somber *Portrait of Juan de Parej* shouldn't be missed; when it was first exhibited, a critic dramatically remarked, "All the rest are art, this alone is truth."

Early Flemish and Netherlandish Painting

Follow the **left-hand fork** from the preliminary rooms and you'll arrive at Early Flemish and Netherlandish Painting, precursors of both the Northern and Italian Renaissances. Inevitably, the first paintings are by **Jan van Eyck**, who is generally attributed with beginning the tradition of North European realism. *The Crucifixion* and *The Last Judgement* – painted early in his career and much like the miniatures he painted for the Turin-Milan Hours – are bright, realistic and full of expressive (and horrific) detail.

There's more allusion to things Gothic in **Rogier van der Weyden**'s *Christ Appearing to his Mother*, the apocryphal visit surrounded by tiny statuary depicting Christ's earlier and Mary's later life. It's one of the most beautiful of all van der Weyden's works, quite different in feel from Van Eyck, with a warmth of design and feeling replacing the former's hard draughtsman's clarity. Another great Northern Gothic painter, **Gerhard David**, also used local settings for his religious scenes; the background of his exquisite *Virgin and Child with Four Angels* is medieval Bruges and *The Rest on the Flight to Egypt* also features Low Country scenes. **Bruegel's** *Harvesters*, one of the Met's most reproduced pictures and part of the series of twelve paintings that included his (Christmas-card familiar) *Hunters in the Snow*, shows how these innovations were assimilated.

Cutting left at this point brings you to the **Italian Baroque** period, which culminates in a room dedicated to the formidable works of **El Greco**. His extraordinary *View of Toledo* – all brooding intensity as the skies seem about to swallow up the ghost-like town – is perhaps the best of his works anywhere in the world, and a satisfying conclusion to the gallery.

The nineteenth-century galleries

A suite of twenty rooms recently redesigned in Beaux Arts style (the decorative detail was adapted from designs made for the museum by architects McKim, Mead and White early this century) displays a startling array of **Impressionist and Post-Impressionist art** and **nineteenth-century European sculpture**. The main entrance is located on the second floor to the south (left) of the main staircase, through the Drawings, Prints and Photographs exhibit.

Impressionist Painting

Establishment artists and precursors of the Impressionists such as **Ingres** and **Delacroix**, as well as artists from the **Barbizon School**, are located to the far left of the gallery. Straight ahead are exhibits centering around **Édouard Manet**, the Impressionist movement's most influential precursor, whose early style of contrasting light and shadow with modulated shades of black can be firmly linked to the tradition of Hals, Velázquez and Goya. The *Spanish Dancer*, an accomplished example of this tradition, was well received on Manet's debut at the Paris Salon in 1861. Within a few years, though, he was shocking the same establishment with *Olympia*, *Déjeuner sur l'Herbe* and the striking *Woman with a Parrot* – the same woman, incidentally, modeled for all three paintings.

Gustave Courbet and **Edgar Degas**, too, are well represented – Courbet with examples of every phase and period of his career, including *Young Ladies from the Village*, a virtual manifesto of his idea of realism, and *Woman with a Parrot*, a superbly erotic and exotic work that gave Manet the idea for his work of the same name. As for Degas, there are studies in just about every medium, from pastels to sculpture. Many examine the theme he returned to again and again – dancers, a lovely example of which is *Dancers Practicing at* *the Bar*. In addition to showing the grace and beauty of the dancers, the painting is about structure, alluded to in the way the dancer on the right picks up the form of the watering can used to lay the dust in the studio. Also here is a casting of his *Little Dancer*, complete with real tutu, hair ribbon and slippers.

Claude Monet was one of the movement's most prolific painters. He returned again and again to a single subject to produce a series of images capturing different nuances of light and atmosphere. There are a number of his works here, including three superb examples – *Rouen Cathedral*, *The Houses of Parliament from the Thames* and *The Doge's Palace Seen from San Giorgio Maggiore* – which show the beginnings of his final phase of near-abstract Impressionism.

Paul Cézanne's technique was very different. He labored long to achieve a painstaking analysis of form and color, something clear in the *Landscape of Marseilles*. Of his few portraits, the jarring, almost Cubist angles and spaces of *Mme Cézanne in a Red Dress* seem years ahead of their time. Take a look, too, at *The Card Players*, whose dynamic triangular structure thrusts out, yet retains the quiet concentration of the moment. **Auguste Renoir** is perhaps the best represented among the remaining Impressionists, though his most important work here dates from 1878, when he began to move away from the mainstream techniques he'd learned while working with Monet. *Mme Charpentier and her Children* is a likeable enough piece, one whose affectionate if unsearching tone manages to sidestep the sugariness of Renoir's later work. Other rooms are devoted to works by **Corot** and **Sisley**, among others.

Post-Impressionist Painting

The Post-Impressionists, logically enough, follow Monet and Cézanne, with one of the highlights being **Paul Gauguin**'s masterly *La Orana Maria*. The title, the archangel Gabriel's first words to Mary at the Annunciation, is the key to the work. The scene was a staple of the Renaissance, transferred here to a different culture in an attempt to unfold the symbolic meaning, and perhaps voice the artist's feeling for the native South Sea islanders, whose cause he championed. *Two Tahitian Women* hangs adjacent, a portrait of his lover Pahura – skillful, studied simplicity.

Henri de Toulouse-Lautrec delighted in painting the world Gauguin went to Tahiti to escape. *The Sofa* is one of a series of sketches he made in Paris brothels. The artist's deformity distanced him from society, and he identified with the life of the prostitutes in his sketches. He also hated posed modeling, which made the bored women awaiting clients an ideal subject.

All of this scratches little more than the surface of the galleries. There are also major works by **Van Gogh** (including *Irises*, *Woman of Arles* and *Sunflowers*), **Rousseau**, **Bonnard**, **Pissarro** and **Seurat**.

Twentieth-century art

Housed over two floors in the Lila Acheson Wallace Wing, the Met's **twentieth-century collection** is a fascinating and relatively compact group of paintings. The first floor begins with the collection's most recent acquisitions and proceeds with a chronological installation of American and European art **from 1905 to 1940**. Such paintings as **Charles Demuth's** *The Figure Five in Gold* and **Picasso's** *Portrait of Gertrude Stein* are here, alongside works by **Klee**, **Modigliani**, **Braques** and **Klimt**. Other highlights include **Hopper's** *Views From Williamsburg Bridge*, a visually stunning if somewhat idealized take on brick tenements in Brooklyn, a wall of **Georgia O'Keefe's**, including the sumptuous, erotic *Black Iris*, and **Chaim Soutine's** *Houses at Cagnes*, a Cézanne townscape gone mad – off-kilter and vaguely sinister. In addition there is a small design collection, featuring changing pieces of furniture, ceramics and almost anything else from the museum's holdings. There are also temporary exhibits of relevant works here and on the mezzanine between the first and second floors of the wing.

The top floor contains European and American painting **from 1945 to the present**, opening with a room filled with the gigantic, emotional canvases of Abstract Expressionist **Clyfford Still**. Highlights on this floor include **Jackson Pollock's** masterly *Autumn Rhythm (Number 30)*, **R.B. Kitaj's** *John Ford on his Deathbed*, a dream-like painting of the director of western movies, an **Ellsworth Kelly** thirteen-panel color-block installation called *Spectrum V* (very reminiscent of a child's xylophone) and **Andy Warhol's** *Last Self-Portrait*. There are also works by **Max Beckmann**, **Roy Lichtenstein** (*Painting Since 1945*), **Mark Rothko** and **Willem de Kooning**.

From May through October, you can continue up to the **Cantor Roof Garden** (accessible by the elevator from the first floor) located on top of the Wallace Wing, which displays **contemporary sculpture** against the dramatic backdrop of the New York skyline. In October this also happens to be a great place to see colorful fall foliage in Central Park. Drinks and snacks are served, and while the drinks may be on the expensive side, the breathtaking views make up for it.

Asian Art

Recently redesigned and greatly expanded, the second floor's **Asian Art galleries** – while lacking in the prestige and the named artists of the Western holdings – gather an impressive and vast array of Chinese, Japanese, Indian and Southeast Asian sculpture, painting, ceramics and metalwork, as well as an indoor replica of a Chinese garden. Fourteen recently renovated and expanded galleries showcase Chinese painting, calligraphy, jade, lacquer and textiles, making this collection one of the largest in the world.

Approach from the Great Hall balcony: lining the corridor's back wall is an exhibit of fifth- to eighth-century Kuran pottery, which includes some fancifully glazed and decorated ceremonial pieces among the everyday jugs and bowls. First up is Chinese Sculpture, a collection of stone works arranged around two twenty-foot-high buddhas. The focal point, however, is not any one sculpture but an enormous (and exquisite) fourteenth-century mural, *The Paradise of Bhaishajyaguru*. This piece, masterfully reconstructed after being severely damaged in an earthquake, is a study in calm reflection.

Take the right fork from this gallery to arrive at **South Asian Art**. Note the ancient pair of golden earrings from India as you enter – actually quite rare, for it was custom there to melt down and recast jewelry after the owner died to avoid inheriting that person's karma. **Statues** of Hindu and Buddhist deities form the bulk of the works, alongside numerous pieces of **friezes**, many of which still possess exceptional detail despite years of exposure. *The Great Departure and the Temptation of the Buddha*, carved in the third century, is a particularly lively example: Siddhartha setting out on his spiritual journey being chased by a harem of dancing girls and grasping cherubs.

Past a set of stairs that leads to a small third-floor gallery (for temporary exhibits) is **Chinese Art.** There is so much here – painting, jewelry, jade carvings – that the works tend to run into one another, but don't miss *Lotus and Water Birds*, a pair of painted hanging scrolls from about 1300, or *Riverbank*, the earliest example of landscape painting, circa 962. The highlight in this area, however, is the **Chinese Garden Court,** a serene, minimalist retreat enclosed by the galleries. The naturally lit garden is a reconstruction of one found in Chinese homes, assembled by experts from the People's Republic: a pagoda, small waterfall and stocked goldfish pond landscaped by limestone rocks, trees and shrubs – all of which conjure a sense of peace and well-being.

After your meditation, forge right to the Sackler Wing, part of a cluster of rooms dedicated to **Japanese art**. Less structured than the other galleries, this section holds objects from the prehistoric era to the present, divided into thematic sections: "Gods and Ancestors," "Spirits and Teachers," "Characters in a Story" and "The Moral and Immoral." Complementing this core are rotating exhibits of textiles, paintings and prints. Earliest of Japanese **religious art** are the *dogu*, female figurines dating from 10,500 BC up to 400 BC, none of which remains a whole piece. Probably due to deliberate acts of superstition rather than general wear and tear, the figures are broken or missing a limb.

The coming of Buddhism in the sixth century changed the strategy of Japanese art, and the results – greatly exaggerated depictions of physical perfection – can be seen in the **Japanese Buddhist painting and sculpture** collection. All of which is a prelude to the exhibit's crown jewel – the several galleries of seventeenth- and eighteenth-century **hand-painted Kano screens**. The screens range from the

elegantly mundane (books on a shelf) to elaborate scenes of historical allusion and divine fervor, such as *Gods of Good Fortune and
Chinese Children*, a six-fold screen of delicate inkwork and vivid
colors by **Kano Chikanobu** that resides in a place of honor in the
shoin (study) room.

The American wing

The American wing comes nearest to being a museum in its own
right, and it's a thorough introduction to the development of fine and
decorative art in America.

Galleries lead off from the **Charles Engelhard Court**, a shrub-
filled sculpture garden enclosed at the far end by the *Facade of the
United States Bank*, lifted in its entirety straight from Wall Street.
Step through this facade and you'll be standing in the **Federal period rooms,** surrounded by the restrained Neoclassical elegance of the
late eighteenth century – the first of twenty-five **furnished historical
rooms** that lie adjacent to the American painting galleries on three
floors. If this is your first visit to this section of the Met, go up to the
third floor and work your way down from there; that way you'll see
the rooms in (roughly) chronological order. The **early Colonial period,** represented most evocatively in the Hart room of around 1674,
begins the tour; **Frank Lloyd Wright's** *Room from the Little House,
Minneapolis*, with its windowed walls demonstrating Wright's concept of minimizing interior–exterior division, ends it. On the second
floor balcony, don't miss the iridescent Favrile glass of **Louis
Comfort Tiffany**: an elegant Art Nouveau accompaniment to the
decor.

The American painting collection

The American paintings galleries begin in a maze of rooms on the
second floor with **eighteenth-century** portraits, but really get going
with the works of **Benjamin West**, an artist who worked in London
and taught or influenced many of the American painters of his day –
The Triumph of Love is typical of his Neoclassical, allegorical
works. More heroics come with **John Trumbull**, one of West's
pupils, in *Sortie Made by the Garrison of Gibraltar* and the fully
blown Romanticism of *Washington Crossing the Delaware* by
Emanuel Leutzes. This last enormous canvas shows Washington
escaping across the river in the winter of 1776; although historically
and geographically inaccurate – the American flag, shown dramatically flowing in the background, hadn't yet been created – the picture
is nonetheless a national icon.

Early in the nineteenth century, American painters embraced landscape painting and nature. **William Sidney Mount** depicted scenes
from his native Long Island, often with a sly political angle as with
Cider Makers and *The Bet*, and the painters of the **Hudson Valley
school** glorified the landscape in their vast lyrical canvases. **Thomas**

Cole, the school's doyen, is represented by *The Oxbow*, his pupil **Frederick Church** by an immense *Heart of the Andes* – combining the grand sweep of the mountains with minutely depicted flora. **Albert Bierstadt** and **S.R. Gifford** continued to concentrate on the American west – their respective works *The Rocky Mountains, Lander's Peak* and *Kauterskill Falls* have a near-visionary idealism, bound to a belief that the westward development of the country was a manifestation of divine will.

Winslow Homer is allowed most of a gallery to himself – fittingly for a painter who so greatly influenced the late nineteenth-century artistic scene in America. Homer began his career illustrating the day-to-day realities of the Civil War – there's a good selection here that shows the tedium and sadness of those years. His talent in recording detail carried over into his late, quasi-Impressionistic studies of seascapes; *Northeaster* is one of the finest of these.

The mezzanine below brings the Met's account of American art into the late nineteenth and early **twentieth century**. Some of the initial portraiture here tends to the sugary, but **J.W.** **Alexander's** *Repose* deftly hits the mark – a simple, striking use of line and light with a sumptuous feel and more than a hint of eroticism. By way of contrast, there's **Thomas Eakin's** subdued, almost ghostly *Max Schmitt in a Single Scull*, **Childe Hassom's** *Avenue of the Allies: Great Britain 1918*, patriotic art filled with light and color, and **William Merritt Chase's** *For the Little One*, an Impressionist study of his wife sewing. Chase studied in Europe and it was there that he painted his *Portrait of Whistler*. Whistler returned the compliment but destroyed the work on seeing Chase's (quite truthful) depiction of himself as a dandified fop, done in a teasing style that mimicked his own. Whatever **Whistler's** conceits, though, his portraits are adept: witness the *Arrangement in Flesh Color and Black: Portrait of Theodore Duret* nearby.

The reputation of **John Singer Sargent** has suffered its ups and downs over the years, but now he seems to be coming back into fashion. There is certainly a virtuosity in his large portraits, like that of *Mr and Mrs I.N. Phelps Stokes*, the couple purposefully elongated as if to emphasize their aristocratic characters. The *Portrait of Madam X* (Mme Pierre Gautreau, a notorious Parisian beauty) was one of the most famous pictures of its day: exhibited at the 1884 Paris salon, it was considered so improper that Sargent had to leave Paris for London. "I suppose it's the best thing I've done," he said wearily on selling it to the Met a few years later.

The Egyptian collection

"A chronological panorama of ancient Egypt's art, history and culture," boasts the blurb to the **Egyptian collection**, and it is no exaggeration, as nearly all of the 35,000 objects in the collection are on lavish display. Brightly efficient corridors steer you through the treasures of the museum's own digs during the 1920s and 1930s, as well as other art and artifacts from 3000 BC to the Byzantine period of Egyptian culture.

Enter from the Great Hall on the first floor and be prepared to be awed: the large **statuary** are the most immediately striking of the exhibits, such as those from Queen Hatshepsut's Temple, along with numerous **tombs** and **sarcophagi** in the first few rooms. But after a while it's the smaller **sculptural** pieces that hold the attention longest. Figures like *Merti and his Wife* were modeled as portraits, but often carvings were made in the belief that a person's *Ka*, or life force, would continue to exist in an idealized model after his or her death – there's a beautifully crafted example in the *Carving of Senebi* in gallery 8; what was probably **Senebi's tomb** is displayed nearby. Also in this room is the dazzling collection of **Princess Sithathorunet's jewelry**, a pinnacle in Egyptian decorative art from around 1830 BC; the models of *Mekutra's House* (around 1198 BC); and the radiant *Fragmentary Head of a Queen*, sensuously carved in polished yellow jasper.

The Temple of Dendur

At the end of the collection sits the **Temple of Dendur**, housed in a vast airy gallery with photographs and information about the temple's history and its original site on the banks of the Nile. Built by the Emperor Augustus in 15 BC for the Goddess Isis of Philae, the temple was moved here as a gift of the Egyptian people during the construction of the Aswan High Dam – otherwise it would have been drowned. Though you can't walk all the way inside, you can go in just enough to get a glimpse of the interior rooms, their walls filled with hieroglyphs. The temple itself is on a raised platform, surrounded by a narrow moat which in the front widens to become a rather pretty reflecting pool, no doubt designed to make us think of the Nile – it doesn't, but it's a nice touch anyway. The entire high-ceilinged gallery is glassed-in on one side, and looks out onto Central Park. Illuminated at night, the gallery seems to glow, lending the temple an air of mystery that is missing during the day.

Medieval art

Although in theory you could move straight to the **medieval galleries** from the American wing, you'd miss out on the museum's carefully planned approach. Instead, enter these galleries via the **corridor** from the back of the Great Hall, to the left of the main staircase; there you'll see displays of the sumptuous **Byzantine metalwork and jewelry** that J.P. Morgan donated to the museum in its early days. At the end of the corridor is the main **sculpture hall**, piled high with religious statuary and carvings (a tremendous *St Nicholas Saving Three Boys in the Brine Tub*) and divided by a massive *reja* (a decorative open-work, iron altar screen) from Valladolid

Cathedral. If you're here in December, you'll see a highlight of New York's Christmas season: a beautifully decorated, twenty-foot-high **Christmas tree** lit up in the center of the sculpture hall.

The **medieval treasury** to the right of the hall has an all-embracing – and magnificent – display of objects religious, liturgical and secular. And beyond are the **Jack and Belle Linski Galleries**: Flemish, Florentine and Venetian painting, porcelain and bronzes.

Scattered throughout the medieval galleries are later **period rooms**: paneled Tudor bedrooms and Robert Adam fineries from England, florid rococo boudoirs and salons from France, and an entire Renaissance patio from Velez Blanco in Spain. It's all fascinating, but a bit much, leaving you with the feeling that J.P. Morgan and his robber baron colleagues would probably have shipped over Versailles if they could have laid their hands on it.

The Lehman Pavilion

The **Lehman Pavilion** was tacked on to the rear of the Met in 1975 to house the collection of Robert Lehman, millionaire banker and art collector. This section breaks from the Met's usual sober arrangement of rectangular floor plans: Rooms are laid out beside a brilliantly lit atrium, with some rooms re-created from Lehman's own home.

Most important, Lehman's enthusiasms fill the gaps in the Met's account of **Italian Renaissance** painting. This period was his passion, and his personal collection is shown on the first floor of the pavilion, centering around **Botticelli's** *Annunciation*, a small but exquisite celebration of the Florentine discovery of perspective. From the Venetian school comes a sculptural *Madonna and Child* by **Giovanni Bellini** and, following **Bartolomeo Vivarini**'s exquisitely detailed altarpiece *Death of the Virgin*, a quartet of works by the Sienese **Giovanni di Paolo**; most notable are *The Creation of the World* and the *Expulsion from Paradise*, in which an angel gently ushers Adam and Eve from Eden, while a Byzantine God points to their place of banishment.

Continuing on, there is a small but strong group of sixteenth-century portraits by **El Greco**, **Ingres** (the luminescent *Princesse de Broglie*), **Ter Bosch** and **Velázquez**. One painting stands out from them all, though: **Rembrandt**'s *Portrait of Gerard de Lairesse*. Although de Lairesse was supposedly disliked for his luxurious tastes and unpleasant character, his most apparent flaw was his disfigured face – ravaged by congenital syphilis.

In the gallery to the left of this collection are works from the **Northern Renaissance**, highlighted by a trio of paintings by **Memling**, **Hans Holbein the Younger** and **Petrus Christus**, most notably Memling's *Annunciation*, in which cool colors and a gentle portrayal of Mary and her attendant angels illuminate the Flemish interior. Holbein's *Portrait of Erasmus of Rotterdam* was one of

three he painted in 1523 that established his reputation as a por-
traitist.

On the ground floor, there is also a small collection of **nineteenth-
and twentieth-century art**, mostly minor works by major artists –
Renoir, Van Gogh, Gauguin, Cézanne and Matisse – along with some
less well-known painters.

Greek and Roman galleries

This is one of the largest such collections in the world, its display of
classical Greek art second only to Athens. The collection is now exhibited in eight newly renovated and expanded galleries on the first floor,
re-created according to original McKim, Mead and White designs.
Enter from the museum's Great Hall, and you'll soon find yourself in
the **Belfer Court**, a sort of preamble to the exhibit in that it displays
prehistoric and early Greek art – characterized by simpler, more geometric shapes and patterns, such as a fanciful **Minoan vase** in the
shape of a bull's head from around 1400 BC and a charming sculpture
of a seated man playing the harp from around 3000 BC. The central
hall, which displays fourth- to sixth-century marble sculptures including several large sphinxes, is flanked by three rooms on either side,
each fully renovated, with exhibits arranged by theme, medium and
chronology. You'll find everything from large **funerary monuments** to
tiny **terra-cotta figures** to intricately carved **gold jewelry** in the same
room, with artfully arranged display cases that you can circle to get
views from all angles. Standing in the center of the first gallery to the
left of the central hall is a marble sculpture of a nude boy – known as
the **New York Kouros** – one the of earliest *kouros*, or funerary statue,
to have survived intact. Dating from 580 BC and originally from Attica,
it marked the grave of the son of a wealthy family, created according
to tradition as a memorial to ensure he would be remembered.

Art of Africa, the Pacific and the Americas
(The Michael C. Rockefeller Wing)

Son of Governor Nelson Rockefeller, Michael C. Rockefeller disappeared during a trip to West New Guinea in 1961. The Rockefeller
Wing, on the first floor past the Greek and Roman Art galleries,
stands as a memorial to him, and includes many of his finds of Asmat
objects from Irian Jaya, alongside the Met's comprehensive collection of art from these three regions. It's a superb set of galleries, the
muted, understated decor throwing the exhibits into sharp and often
dramatic focus. The **African exhibit** has recently been completely
renovated, expanded and reinstalled, offering an overview of the
major geographic regions and their cultures, though West Africa is
better represented than the rest of the continent. Particularly awe-
inspiring is the new display of art from the Court of Benin in present-
day Nigeria – tiny **carved ivory statues and vessels**, created with

astonishing detail. The **Pacific collection** covers the islands of Melanesia, Micronesia, Polynesia and Australia, and contains a wide array of objects such as wild, somewhat frightening, **wooden masks** with piercing all-too-realistic eyes. Sadly **Mexico, Central and South America** get somewhat short shrift here, though there is a nice collection of **pre-Columbian jade**, Mayan and Aztec pottery, and Mexican ceramic sculpture. But the best part by far is the entire room filled with **gold jewelry and ornaments**: particularly the exquisite hammered gold nose ornaments and earflares from Peru and the richly carved, jeweled ornaments from Colombia.

Other collections

The Met's other collections include **Islamic Art; European Decorative Arts; Arms and Armor; Musical Instruments;** and the spectacular **Costume Institute**, which shows rotating exhibitions on the ground floor drawn from its collection of more than 60,000 international costumes and accessories, dating from the fifteenth century to the present day. The expanding **Department of Photographs** has also been busily acquiring work, and now commands a collection to rival that of the Museum of Modern Art.

The Museum of Modern Art

11 W 53rd St (between 5th and 6th aves). Subway E or F to 5th Ave–53rd St. Sat–Tues & Thurs 10.30am–6pm, Fri 10.30am–8.30pm, closed Wed; $9.50, students $6.50, Fri 4.30–8.15pm pay what you wish; recorded audio tour $4. Free gallery talks held Mon, Tues, Thurs, Sat & Sun 1pm & 3pm; Fri 3pm, 6pm & 7pm; Call ☎708-9480 for exhibit information.

Founded in 1929 by three wealthy women, including Abby Aldrich Rockefeller, as the very first museum dedicated entirely to modern art, The Museum of Modern Art moved to its present home ten years later. Philip Johnson designed expansions in the Fifties and Sixties, and in the mid-1980s Cesar Pelli designed a steel pipe and glass renovation that doubled its gallery space. **MoMA**, as it is affectionately called, offers the finest and most complete account of late nineteenth- and twentieth-century art you're likely to find, with a permanent collection of over 100,000 paintings, sculptures, drawings, prints, photographs, architectural models and design objects, as well as a world-class film archive.

Yet another extension and renovation is in the works, slated to begin in early 2001 and be completed by some time in 2005. After a bitterly contested, multi-year design competition that involved many of the world's top architects, the design contract was awarded to Yoshio Taniguchi, architect of several prominent museum buildings in Japan, including a wing of the Tokyo National Museum. Plans call

The Museum of Modern Art

The museum's layout: MoMA 2000

The MoMA building is designed to guide you effortlessly and easily into the collections – and, with glass-enclosed landings and gliding escalators, it's an enjoyable place to explore. On the **first floor**, you'll find the usual pairing of restaurant and shop; outside, a **sculpture garden**, designed by Philip Johnson, offers the works of Rodin and Matisse alongside such artifacts as an Art Nouveau Paris metro sign (in the summer light snacks and drinks are available here, making it an even more relaxing spot). Downstairs on the **ground floor** there are several film theaters (pick up a leaflet for a list of current showings – MoMA is justly famous for its 14,000 plus **film archive**, often showing retrospectives and rare films you have little chance of seeing elsewhere).

The museum proper begins upstairs, with the second and third floors usually devoted to the **main painting and sculpture galleries**, the fourth to **architecture and design**. However, for the next five years at least, all that will change, as the museum launches its ambitious **MoMA 2000** exhibit, and soon afterwards begins its renovation and expansion. Beginning in October 1999 and continuing until March 2001, the entire museum, including its film programming, will be given over to a special integrated exhibit of all aspects of the permanent collection entitled MoMA 2000. The exhibit will be held in three successive chronological stages:

Cycle I: Modern Starts runs from October 1999 to March 2000 and focuses on the period 1880 to 1920; organized around the themes of people, places and things, it explores representations of figures, sites and landscapes, and objects in all mediums. Exhibits include figurative works by Matisse and Picasso, landscapes by Cézanne, modern cityscapes by Léger, and photographs by Steichen and Bellocq among others. In addition, furniture created by Frank Lloyd Wright and Marcel Duchamp, along with advertising posters and collages, will explore the increasing importance of both objects and design in everyday life.

Cycle II (as yet unnamed) runs from March 2000 to September 2000, and focuses on the period 1920 to 1960, with themes of war, social and political upheaval, and the advance of technology. It encompasses all of the various traditions of modern art, from the Dada and Surrealist schools to the development of abstract art by artists such as Mondrian, Malevich and others. A large photography installation includes a retrospective of the work of Walker Evans, revered, early twentieth-century photographer, as well as his contemporaries and those who he later influenced. An exhibit of furniture, architectural models and design objects embodying the domestic ideals that arose after each of the World Wars is also on display.

Cycle III: Open Ends runs from September 2000 through February 2001, and concentrates on 1960 to the present – the first time that most of MoMA's holdings of contemporary art have been displayed together, and – a prelude to an increased focus on contemporary art when the museum expansion is completed. Highlights include masterworks by Warhol, Rothko, Twombly and Jasper Johns, along with works by newer artists shown here for the first time, along with integrated exhibits in every medium from painting to photography to film.

for creating new galleries and updating existing space, with the expansion of the central sculpture garden, the restoration of the famous Bauhaus staircase in the main building, and the addition of a building connected to the Pelli Museum Tower, among other things. The expansion will allow MoMA to display more of its permanent collection, as well as mount even larger temporary exhibits.

Highlights of the Permanent Collection

As all the galleries of MoMA will be continuously reshuffled for the foreseeable future, it is impossible to predict what will be on display, much less where. So instead, here are some highlights of each of the three major sections of the collection (early-modern painting and sculpture, late-modern/contemporary painting and sculpture, and architecture and design), to give you an idea of what you may see.

Early-modern painting and sculpture

This collection boasts an impressive array of **Post-Impressionist** masterworks such as **Cézanne**'s *Bather* (1885) and paintings by **Gauguin**, **Seurat** and **Van Gogh**, including *Starry Night*, not to mention **Monet**'s *Water Lilies*: enormous, stirring attempts to abstract color and form, their swirling jades, pinks and purples creating the feeling of sitting in a giant aquarium. **Cubism** is represented by **Picasso, Derain** and **Braque**, among others. Most notable is Picasso's *Demoiselles d'Avignon* (1907), a jagged, sharp and, for its time, revolutionary clash of tones and planes which some hold to be the embodiment of Cubist principles. Picasso's later works include the *Charnel House*, which, like *Guernica*, is an angry protest against the horrors of war.

There are paintings by **Chagall** and **Mondrian**, including the latter's *Broadway Boogie Woogie*, painted in 1940 after he had moved to New York and reflecting his love of jazz music – its short, sharp stabs of color conveying an almost physical rhythm. MoMA's **Matisse** collection centers on the *Dancers* (1909), the *Red Studio*, a depiction of Matisse's studio in France in which all perspective is resolved in shades of rusty red, and *Le Bateau* – when this painting was first exhibited, MoMA had it hanging upside down for 47 days before noticing the mistake. Other highlights include swirling canvases by **Kandinsky**, the brooding skies of **de Chirico**, works by **Miró**, notably his hilarious *Dutch Interior*, and a handful of dreamlike paintings by **Dali** (*Persistence of Memory*) and **Magritte** (*The Menaced Assassin*).

Late-modern and contemporary painting and sculpture

The late-modern and contemporary painting collection continues chronologically, with an inevitably more American slant. It features paintings such as **Andrew Wyeth**'s *Christina's World*, one of the best known of all modern American paintings, and works by **Edward**

Hopper including *House by the Railroad* and *New York Movie*, potent and atmospheric pieces that give a bleak account of modern American life. There are also more abstract pieces: **Gorky**'s Miró-like doodles, and the anguished scream of **Bacon**'s *No. 7 from 8 Studies for a Portrait*.

Some of the biggest draws are the paintings from the **New York School** – large-scale canvases meant to be viewed from a distance, perfect for MoMA's large, airy rooms. The best examples are the paintings of **Pollack** and **de Kooning** – wild, and in Pollack's case, textured patterns with no clear beginning or end – and the more ordered **Color Field** works. In **Barnett Newman**'s words, their paintings are "drained of impediments of memory, association, nostalgia, legend, myth, and what have you," in other words pure color, as in the radiating, almost humming blocks of color by **Mark Rothko** and perhaps, most palpably, in the black canvases of **Ad Reinhardt**.

Lastly, there are famous examples of **Pop Art** including **Jasper Johns**'s *Flag*, a well-known piece in which a cloth Stars and Stripes is painted onto newsprint, transforming America's most potent symbol into little more than an arrangement of shapes and hues, and **Warhol**'s *Gold Marilyn Monroe* and the familiar *Campbell Soup* canvas.

Architecture and design

Architecture and design are, after painting and sculpture, MoMA's most important concern. Models and original drawings by the architects of key modern buildings include **Frank Lloyd Wright**'s *Falling Water*, and projects by **Le Corbusier** and **Mies van der Rohe**. Further aspects of modern design are traced through the overdone glasswork of **Tiffany**, and **furniture** designed by Mies van der Rohe, Charles Rennie Mackintosh, Alvar Alto and Henri van den Velde, to name a few, some of which represent more successful examples of applied design than others. There are usually a few oversized items as well, look for an E-type 1963 Jaguar roadster and a green Bell helicopter from 1945, generally hung above one of the escalators for effect.

Photography and film

In addition to the above, the museum also has an extraordinary collection of **photographs**, **prints** and **drawings**. The photographs, in particular, are marvellous – one of the finest, most eclectic collections around, and a vivid evocation of twentieth-century America, from the dramatic landscapes of Ansel Adams to Stieglitz's dynamic views of New York to the revealing portraits of Man Ray. MoMA's **film and video collection** is also justly famous, with 13,000 films and four million film stills. It includes silent works by D.W. Griffith, Sergei Eisenstein, Charlie Chaplin and Buster Keaton, as well as films by later directors including John Ford, Orson Welles, Akira Kurasawa and Ingmar Bergman, to name a few.

The Guggenheim Museum

1071 5th Ave (88th St). Subway #4, #5 or #6 to 86th St–Lexington Ave. Sun–Wed 9am–6pm, Fri & Sat 9am–8pm, closed Thurs; $12, seniors, students $7, children under 12 free, Fri 6–8pm pay what you wish. ☎423-3500 for exhibit information.

Multistory parking lot or upturned beehive? Whatever you think of the Guggenheim Museum, it's the building that steals the show. **Frank Lloyd Wright**'s structure, designed specifically for the museum and sixteen years in the making, caused a storm of controversy when it was unveiled in 1959, bearing little relation to the statuesque apartment buildings of this most genteel part of Fifth Avenue. Reactions, though Wright didn't live long enough to hear many (he died six months before construction was completed), ranged from disgusted disbelief to critical acclaim – "one of the greatest rooms erected in the twentieth century," wrote Philip Johnson, quite rightly. The years have given the building a certain respectability and made it a widely recognized landmark much loved by New Yorkers and visitors alike, so much so that any proposed changes can cause an uproar, as the debate over the museum's extension proved. From 1990 to summer 1992 the museum was closed, undergoing a $60 million facelift of the original Lloyd Wright building that opened the whole space to the public for the first time. Dull offices, storage rooms and bits of chicken wire were all removed to expose the uplifting interior spaces so that the public could experience the spiral of the central rotunda from top to bottom. At the same time a clever extension added the sort of tall, straight-walled, flat-floored galleries that the Guggenheim needed to offset its distinct shape. Though at the time the merits of the plans were hotly debated in the press and in art circles, the consensus is that the remodeled building is now a much better museum.

The Guggenheim SoHo branch has changing exhibits from the Guggenheim permanent collection; see p.291.

Some history

Solomon R. Guggenheim was one of America's richest men, his mines extracting silver and copper – and a healthy profit – all over the US. Like other nineteenth-century American capitalists, the only problem for Guggenheim was how to spend his vast wealth, so he started collecting Old Masters – a hobby he continued halfheartedly until the 1920s, when various sorties to Europe brought him into contact with the most avant-garde and influential of European art circles. Abstraction in art was then considered little more than a fad, but Guggenheim, always a man with an eye for a sound investment, started to collect modern paintings with fervor, buying wholesale the paintings of **Kandinsky**, adding works by **Chagall, Klee, Léger** and others, and exhibiting them to a bemused

American public in his suite of rooms in the *Plaza Hotel*. The Guggenheim Foundation was created in 1937 and after exhibiting the collection in various rented spaces, commissioned Wright to design a permanent home.

The collection

In addition to the works collected by Guggenheim himself, a number of acquisitions and donations have broadened the collection so that it spans the late 1800s through most of the twentieth century. In 1976, the collector Justin K. Thannhauser bequeathed masterworks by **Cézanne, Degas, Gauguin, Manet, Toulouse-Lautrec, Van Gogh and Picasso**, among others, greatly enhancing the museum's Impressionist and Post-Impressionist holdings. The Guggenheim's collection of American minimalist art from the 1960s is also particularly rich. The **Robert Mapplethorpe** Foundation recently gave 196 photographs that span the artist's entire career, now housed in a brand new Mapplethorpe gallery on the fourth floor. Other photographers are also well represented, though not in such quantity, including **Joseph Albers**, **Rineke Dijkstra** and **Max Becher**.

As a general rule of thumb, the permanent collection is housed on a rotating basis in the new tower and the small north rotunda, while **temporary exhibitions** based on aspects of the collection, picking up themes from the various styles and periods, are held in the main rotunda – between the two, a significant part of the museum's collection is always on display. Even so, it's the original space itself which dominates; it's hard not to be impressed (or sidetracked) by the tiers of cream concrete that open up above like the ever-widening ribs of some giant convector fan. Since the circular galleries increase upward at a not-so-gentle slope, it may be preferable to start at the top of the museum and work your way down; most of the temporary exhibits are planned that way.

Though the entire museum can easily be seen in an afternoon, two galleries offer a representative sample of the Guggenheim's **permanent collection**: The first, on **the second floor of the tower**, gives a quick but enjoyable look at the **Cubists**. The other, in the restored **small rotunda**, offers a collection of Impressionist, Post-Impressionist and early modern masterpieces.

The Frick Collection

1 E 70th St. Subway #6 to 68th St–Lexington Ave. Tues–Sat 10am–6pm, Sun 1–6pm, closed Mon; $7, students $5. Children under 10 are not admitted to the collection. A 22 min audiovisual presentation in the Music Room tells Henry Clay Frick's story and details the mansion and its collection, every hour on the half hour. Concerts of classical music are held each month; call ☎288-0700 for details.

Housed in the former mansion of **Henry Clay Frick**, the immensely enjoyable Frick Collection comprises the art treasures hoarded by Frick during his years as one of the most ruthless of New York's robber barons. Vicious, uncompromising and anti-union, Frick broke strikes with state troopers and was hated enough to only narrowly survive a number of assassination attempts. However, the legacy of his ill-gotten gains – he spent millions on the best of Europe's art treasures – is a superb collection of works, and as good a glimpse of the sumptuous life enjoyed by New York's early industrialists as you'll find.

First opened in the mid-1930s, the museum has been largely kept as it looked when the Fricks lived there. The decor is in dubious taste for the most part, much of the furniture heavy eighteenth-century French, but the nice thing about it – and many people rank the Frick as their favorite New York gallery because of this – is that it strives hard to be as unlike a museum as possible. Ropes are kept to a minimum, fresh flowers are on every table, and even in the most sumptuously decorated rooms there are plenty of chairs you can freely sink into. When weary, you can take refuge in the central enclosed courtyard, whose cool marble floors, fountains and greenery are simply and classically arranged, and whose serenity you'd be hard pressed to beat.

A **new gallery** on the ground level shows temporary exhibits from the permanent collection, as well as pieces on loan from other institutions. Though it is a limited space – just three small rooms – it is the first time the Frick has had any place for special exhibits. It is a more modern space, with pale, paneled walls and beige wall-to-wall carpeting, so, unlike the rest of the museum, it won't compete with whatever is on display. It is accessible only by a narrow, steep spiral staircase located just outside the entry hall – easy to miss unless you're looking for it.

The collection

The collection itself was acquired under the direction of Joseph Duveen, notorious – and not entirely trustworthy – adviser to the city's richest and most ignorant. For Frick, however, he seems to have picked out the cream of Europe's post-World War I private art collections, with a magnificent array of works by Rembrandt, Vermeer, Turner and Whistler, among other masters.

Keep an open mind as you enter through the **Boucher Room** – not to twentieth-century tastes, with its heavily flowered, painted walls, overdone furniture and Boucher's succulent, rococo representations of the arts and sciences in gilded frames. Next along, the **Dining Room** is more reserved, its Reynoldses and Hogarths overshadowed by the one non-portrait in the room, **Gainsborough**'s *St James's Park*: a subtly moving promenade under an arch of luxuriant trees; "Watteau far outdone," wrote a critic at the time. Outside in the hall there's more lusty French painting (Boucher again) and, in the next room, **Fragonard's** *Progress of Love* series, which was painted for Madame du Barry, mistress of Louis XV, in 1771 and rejected by her soon after in favor of another artist's work.

Better paintings follow in the Living Hall, not least of them **Bellini's** *St Francis*, which suggests his vision of Christ by means of pervading light, a bent tree and an enraptured stare. **Titian's** *Portrait of a Man with a Red Cap* hangs pensively along one wall and **El Greco's** *St Jerome*, above the fireplace, reproachfully surveys the riches all around. In the South Hall hangs one of Boucher's odder depictions of his wife, dressed shepherdess-style, with a prissy air about her, and an early **Vermeer**, *Officer and Laughing Girl*: suggestive and full of lewd allusions to forthcoming sex. The Library holds a number of British works, most notably one of **Constable's** *Salisbury Cathedral* series, **Turner's** idyllic *Fishing Boats Entering Calais Harbor* and a number of Gainsboroughs; and in the North Hall hangs Degas' *Rehearsal*, dancers rehearsing elegantly to a violinist's accompaniment, along with several soothingly washed out, scenic works by **Corot**.

The West and East galleries

The **West Gallery**, beyond here, is the Frick's major draw, holding some of its finest paintings in a magnificent setting – a long elegant room with a concave glass ceiling and ornately carved wood trim. Two **Turners**, views of Cologne and Dieppe, hang opposite each other, each a blaze of orange and creamy tones; **Van Dyck** pitches in with a couple of uncharacteristically informal portraits of Frans Snyders and his wife – two paintings only reunited when Frick purchased them; along with several portraits by **Frans Hals**, and *Vincenzo Anastagi* by El Greco, a stunning portrait of a Spanish soldier resplendent in green velvet and armor. **Rembrandt**, too, is represented by a set of piercing self-portraits and the enigmatic *Polish Rider* – more fantasy-piece than portrait.

At the far end of the West Gallery is a tiny room called the Enamel Room, so named because of the exquisite set of Limoges enamels on display, mainly sixteenth century, as well as a collection of small painted altarpieces by **Piero della Francesca**, and a *Virgin and Child* by **Jan van Eyck** – one of the artist's very last works, and among the rare few to have reached America. At the other end of the West Gallery, is the Oval Room with Houdon's sculpture of *Diana*, and a quartet of spare, elegant portraits by **Van Dyck** and **Gainsborough**, all the same size and painted against similar backdrops – unintended matched sets. Past here, the **East Gallery** hosts a slew of famous paintings including **Whistler's** portrait of fellow-artist *Rose Corder* posed to the point where she would have to faint before Whistler would stop painting. Other highlights of this final gallery include several massive **Turner** seascapes and a portrait of an expressive Spanish officer by **Goya**.

The Whitney Museum of American Art

945 Madison Ave (75th St). Subway #6 to 77th St–Lexington Ave. Tues, Wed & Fri–Sun 11am–6pm, Thurs 1–8pm, closed Mon; $12.50, seniors and students with ID $10.50; first Thurs of every month 6–8pm pay as you wish (free); excellent and free gallery talks take place Wed–Sun, call for times; ☎570-3600 for exhibit information.

Located in a heavy, gray, arsenal-like building designed by Marcel Breuer in 1966, the Whitney, from the outside, has an intimidating and suspiciously institutional air. Within, however, such impressions are quickly dispelled. This is some of the best gallery space in the city, and the perfect forum for one of the pre-eminent collections of twentieth-century American art. In addition to its permanent holdings, the Whitney is also known for its superb temporary exhibitions, and, like the Guggenheim, devotes much of its time and rooms to this end; the majority of these given over to retrospectives and debuts of lesser-known themes and artists. Jasper Johns, Cy Twombly and Cindy Sherman were all given their first retrospectives here.

Every other year, though, there is an exhibition of a wholly different nature – the **Whitney Biennial** – designed to give a provocative overview of what's happening in contemporary American art. It is often panned by critics (sometimes for good reason) but always packed with visitors. Catch it if you can between March and June in even-numbered years.

Some history

Gertrude Vanderbilt Whitney, a sculptor and champion of American art, established the Whitney Studio in 1914 to exhibit the work of living American artists who could not find support in established art circles. By 1929 she had collected over 500 works (including paintings by Hopper, Prendergast and Sloan) which she offered, with a generous endowment, to the Met. When her offer was refused, she set up her own museum in Greenwich Village in 1930, with her collection as its core exhibit. The first Biennial was held two years later. The small museum soon outgrew its Village home, and, after several interim moves, the Whitney relocated to its current spot in 1966.

The permanent collection

Currently, the museum owns over 11,000 paintings, sculptures, photographs and films by artists as diverse as Calder, Nevelson, O'Keefe, de Kooning, Rauschenberg, Le Witt and Nam June Paik. For an overview, see the **Highlights of the Permanent Collection** on the fifth floor, a somewhat arbitrary pick of the Whitney's best, arranged by both chronology and theme. The works form a superb introduc-

The Whitney Museum of American Art

tion to twentieth-century American art, best evaluated with the help of the gallery talks, designed to explain the paintings and sculptures, and their place within various movements.

The collection is particularly strong on **Edward Hopper** (2000 of his works were bequeathed to the museum in 1970), and several of his best paintings are here: *Early Sun Morning* is typical, a bleak urban landscape, uneasily tense in its lighting and rejection of topical detail. The street could be anywhere (in fact it's 7th Avenue); for Hopper, it becomes universal. Other major bequests include a significant number of works by **Milton Avery**, **Charles Demuth** and **Reginald Marsh**.

As if to balance the figurative works that formed the nucleus of the original collection, more recent purchases include an emphasis on abstract art. **Marsden Hartley**'s *Painting Number 5* is a strident, overwhelmed work, painted in the memory of a German officer friend killed in the early days of World War I. **Georgia O'Keefe** called it "a brass band in a closet," and certainly her own work is gentler, though with its own darkness: her *Abstraction* was suggested by the noises of cattle being driven to the local slaughterhouse. Have a look, too, at O'Keefe's flower paintings: verging on abstraction but hinting at deeper organic, erotic forms.

The **Abstract Expressionists** are featured strongly, with great works by masters **Pollock** and **de Kooning**. **Mark Rothko** and the **Color Field** painters are also well-represented – though you need a sharp eye to discern any color in **Ad Reinhardt**'s *Black Painting*. In a different direction, **Warhol**, **Johns** and **Oldenburg** each subvert the meaning of their images in different ways. Warhol's silk-screened *Coke Bottles* fade into motif; Jasper Johns's celebrated *Three Flags* erases the emblem of patriotism and replaces it with ambiguity; and Claes Oldenburg's light-hearted *Soft Sculptures*, with its squidgy toilets and melting motors, falls into line with his declaration, "I'm into art that doesn't sit on its ass in a museum."

The Cloisters

Fort Tryon Park. Subway A to 190th St–Washington Ave. Tues–Sun 9.30am–5.15pm (closes 4.45pm Nov–Feb), closed Mon; suggested donation $10, students $5 (includes admission to Metropolitan Museum on same day); call ☎923-3700 for exhibition information.

High above the Hudson in Fort Tryon Park in Upper Manhattan, The Cloisters stands like some misplaced Renaissance palazzo-cum-monastery, which was presumably the desired effect, for portions of five medieval cloisters are incorporated into the structure, the folly of collectors **George Grey Barnard** and **John D. Rockefeller, Jr**. A branch of the Metropolitan Museum of Art, it is well worth a visit – a tranquil spot perfect for picnics, with great views of the Hudson and a magnificent collection of medieval tapestries, metalwork, paintings and sculpture.

Some history

Barnard started a museum on this spot in 1914 to house his own medieval collection, mostly sculpture and architectural fragments acquired in France. Later, Rockefeller donated funds enabling the Metropolitan Museum to purchase the site and its collection, along with 66 acres of land around it – now Fort Tryon Park – and, with commendable foresight, he also purchased 700 acres of land across the way in New Jersey to ensure perpetual good views. Barnard and Rockefeller each shipped over the best of medieval Europe to be part of the museum: **Romanesque chapels** and **Gothic halls**, dismantled and transplanted brick by brick, along with tapestries, medieval paintings and sculpture. Despite the hodgepodge of styles, it is all undeniably well carried off, superb in its detail and with great atmosphere. The completed museum opened in 1938, and is still the only museum in the US specializing in medieval art. The best approach if you're coming from the 190th Street subway is directly across the park; the views are tremendous.

The collection

Starting from the entrance hall and working counterclockwise, the collection is laid out in roughly chronological order. First off is the simplicity of the **Romanesque Hall**, featuring French remnants such as an arched, limestone doorway dating to 1150 and a thirteenth-century portal from a monastery in Burgundy; and the frescoed Spanish **Fuentiduena Chapel**, dominated by a huge, domed twelfth-century apse from a tiny town near Madrid, that immediately induces a reverential hush. They corner on one of the prettiest of the five cloisters here, **St Guilhelm**, ringed by strong Corinthian-style columns topped by busily carved capitals with floral designs from thirteenth-century Southern France. The nearby **Langon Chapel**, attractive enough in itself, is enhanced by a twelfth-century **ciborium** that manages to be formal and graceful in just the right proportions, and an emotive wooden sculpture of the **Virgin and Child** beneath.

At the center of the museum is the **Cuxa cloister**, from the twelfth-century Benedictine monastery of Saint Michel de Cuxa near Prades in the French Pyrenées; its Romanesque capitals are brilliantly carved, many with weird, grotesque creatures with two bodies and a shared head. Central to the scene is the garden, planted with fragrant, almost overpowering, herbs and flowers and offering (bizarrely) piped-in plainsong.

The museum's smaller **sculpture** is equally impressive. In the **Early Gothic Hall** are a number of carved figures, including one memorably tender and refined **Virgin and Child**, carved in England in the fourteenth century, probably for veneration at a private altar. The stained glass here is also worth noting. The next room holds a collection of **tapestries**, including a rare surviving Gothic work showing the **Nine Heroes**. The heroes, popular figures of the ballads of the Middle Ages, comprise three pagans (Hector, Alexander, Julius Caesar), three Hebrews (David, Joshua, Judas Macabeas) and three Christians (Arthur, Charlemagne, Godfrey of Bouillon). Five of the nine are here, clothed in the garb of the day (around 1385) against a rich backdrop. The **Unicorn Tapestries** (*c.*1500) in the succeeding room are even more spectacular – brilliantly alive with color, observation and Christian symbolism, more so now than ever, as all seven were recently repaired, restored and rehung in a refurbished gallery with new lighting.

Most of the Met's medieval painting is to be found Downtown, but one important exception is **Campin**'s *Merode Altarpiece*, created for the private use of its owners. Housed in its own antechamber, this fifteenth-century triptych depicts the Annunciation scene in a typical bourgeois Flemish home of the day. On the left, the artist's patron and his wife gaze timidly on through an open door; to the right, St Joseph works in his carpenter's shop. St Joseph was mocked in the literature of the day, which might account for his rather ridiculous appearance – making a mousetrap, a symbol of the way the Devil traps souls. Through the windows behind, life goes on in a fifteenth-century market square, perhaps Campin's native Tournai. The **Late Gothic Hall** next door is filled with large sculptural **altarpieces** depicting biblical scenes and is noteworthy for the expressive detail of the stone carvings and figures.

On the ground floor there is a large Gothic chapel, boasting a high vaulted ceiling and fourteenth-century Austrian stained-glass windows, along with a number of funerary sculptures, such as the monumental **sarcophagus of Ermengol VII**, with its whole phalanx of family members and clerics carved in stone to send him off. Two further cloisters are here to explore, along with an amazing **Treasury**. This is crammed with items but two can easily be singled out: the *Belles Heures de Jean, Duc de Berry*, perhaps the greatest of all medieval Books of Hours, executed by the Limburg Brothers with dazzling miniatures of seasonal life; and the twelfth-century **altar cross** from Bury St Edmunds in England, a mass of tiny expressive characters from biblical stories. Finally, hunt out a minute **rosary** bead from sixteenth-century Flanders: with a representation of the Passion inside, it seems barely possible that it could have been carved by hand.

The American Museum of Natural History

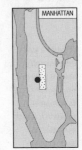

Central Park W at 79th St. Subway B or C to 81st St–Central Park West. Sun–Thurs 10am–5.45pm, Fri & Sat 10am–8.45pm; suggested donation $8, students $6, children $4.50; IMAX films, the Hayden Planetarium and certain special exhibits cost extra, call for details; several restaurants and gift shops; ☎ 769-5100 for exhibit information.

One of the best museums of its kind, an enormous complex of buildings full of fossils, gems, skeletons and other natural specimens, along with a wealth of man-made artifacts from indigenous cultures worldwide, the **American Museum of Natural History** is one of the oldest such museums in the world – founded in 1869. It is also one of the largest, and once you've paced the length of its four floors of exhibition halls and witnessed a fair number of the 32 million items on display, you'll feel it in your feet. There's a fantastic amount to see, but be selective; depending on your interests, anything from a highly discriminating couple of hours to half a day should be ample.

The collection

The main entrance up the marble steps on Central Park West is the one to make for, leaving you well placed for a loop of the more interesting halls on the **second** (entry-level) **floor**: principally the **Hall of Asian People** and **Hall of African People**, each filled with fascinating, often beautiful, art and artifacts, backed up with informal commentary and lent atmosphere with piped-in drums and ethnic music. The Hall of African People displays ceremonial costumes, musical instruments and masks from all over the continent. The Hall of Asian People, interestingly, begins with Russian and Central Asian artifacts, moves on to Tibet – with a gorgeous re-creation of an ornate, gilded Tibetan Buddhist shrine – and then on to China and Japan, with displays of some fantastic textiles, rugs, brass and jade ornaments. Another highlight of this floor, is the lower half of the **Hall of African Mammals**, a double-height room whose exhibits continue on to the third floor balcony. Don't miss (how can you?) the life-size family of elephants in the center of the room. Also worth seeing on the third floor are the **Reptiles and Amphibians Hall**, filled with samples of every such species one can think of, and the **Eastern Woodlands and Plains Indians** exhibit, a somewhat pedestrian display of artifacts, clothing and the like.

*If you're not
sure exactly
where you are
on a floor (and
it can easily
happen), check
the pillars
near each
staircase and
between exhib-
it halls – they
contain good
locator maps.*

The **fourth floor** is almost entirely taken up with the wildly popular **Dinosaur Exhibit**; renovated and expanded in 1996 into five spacious, well-lit and well-designed halls, it is the largest collection in the world, with more than 120 specimens on display. Here, you can watch two **robotic dinosaur jaws** chew; walk on a transparent bridge erected over a fifty-foot long Barosaurus spine; and **touch fossils**. The multilevel exhibits are also supplemented by interactive computer programs and claymation videos, which adds a nice hands-on appeal to the exhibit. "Profiles in Palaeontology" is another new display, which details the men who dug these treasures out of the dirt, and examines what their experiences were like. The **Astor Turret**, in the back left corner of the **Primitive Mammals** exhibit, offers a quiet, resting spot away from the crowds, with benches at each of the giant windows overlooking Central Park.

Downstairs on the **first floor** (the floor below where you entered) is the **Hall of Gems and Minerals**, well laid-out and including some strikingly beautiful crystals – not least the *Star of India*, the largest blue sapphire ever found; the enormous double-height gallery dedicated to **Ocean Life**, which includes a 94-foot-long (life-size) **Blue Whale** suspended from the high ceiling (disconcertingly hanging over a food court); and the exhibit of **North American Mammals** which hasn't changed in fifty years – dark halls, marble floors and illuminated diorama cases filled with stuffed specimens. The greatest draw on this floor, however, is the new **Hall of Biodiversity**. Opened in 1998, it focuses on both the ecological and evolutionary aspects of biodiversity, with multimedia displays on everything from the changes humans have wrought on the environment (with examples of solutions brought about by local activists and community groups in all parts of the world) to videos about endangered species. The centerpiece of the exhibit is a living re-creation of a **Central African Republic rainforest** that you can walk through, to the sounds of birdcalls and forest noises, accompanied by detailed texts about the ecology of the area and the need for conservation. The **Spectrum of Life**, a new addition to the rainforest, is a display of 1500 specimens of various life forms, from plants, mollusks and worms, to birds and animals, grouped according to related species, and revealing some surprising cousins. The **NatureMax Theater**, located on this floor, presents some interesting nature-oriented IMAX films; check to see what's playing (there is an additional charge for these).

The Rose Center for Earth and Space

Across from the Hall of Biodiversity lies the first installation of the Rose Center for Earth and Space – the spanking new **Hall of Planet Earth**, a multilevel and multimedia exploration of how the earth works, with displays on a wide variety of subjects such as the formation of planets, underwater rock formation, plate tectonics and carbon dating. Items on display include a 2.7 billion-year-old specimen of a banded iron formation and volcanic ash from Mount Vesuvius. The centerpiece of the room is the Dynamic Earth Globe, where visitors seated below the globe, are able to watch the earth via satellite go through its full rotation, getting as close as possible to the views astronauts see from outer space.

The Hall of Planet Earth links visitors to the rest of the Rose Center for Earth and Space, which is made up of the new Hall of the Universe and the Hayden Planetarium, both due to open in early spring 2000. Bearing no resemblance to the rather fusty old planetarium, which was torn down, the new center boasts an enormous sphere, 87-feet in diameter, which appears to be floating inside a huge metal and glass cube above the main arched entrance to the center. The sphere actually houses the planetarium itself, which includes two theaters and the Hall of the Universe, as well as research facilities and classrooms, and is illuminated rather eerily at night.

Inside, the state-of-the-art Sky Theater uses a Zeiss projector to create sky shows with sources like the Hubble telescope and NASA laboratories and can zoom in on any planet at will; the Big Bang Theater offers a multisensory re-creation of the "birth" of the universe. The Cosmic Pathway is a sloping spiral walkway that takes you through 13 billion years of cosmic evolution via an interactive computerized timeline (all of recorded history takes up less space than the width of a human hair). It leads to the Hall of the Universe, offering exhibits and interactive displays on the formation and evolution of the universe, the galaxy, stars and planets, including a mini-theater where visitors can journey inside a black hole through computerized effects. There is even a display here entitled "The Search For Life" which examines on which of the planetary systems life could exist – in case you hadn't questioned the meaning of existence enough by this point.

Other museums

While you could fill weeks wandering through New York's great museums listed earlier in this chapter, the city is awash with smaller museums, and the collections are so varied as to have something to interest everyone. On a highly selective basis, highlights include the Cooper-Hewitt National Design Museum, the International Center for Photography, The Pierpont Morgan Library, the National Museum of the American Indian, the Lower East Side Tenement Museum, a clutch of first-rate ethnic museums and, for all you TV and film buffs, the Museum of Television & Radio and the American Museum of the Moving Image.

Art, visuals and design

Alternative Museum

594 Broadway, Suite 402 (between Houston and Prince sts). Subway N or R to Prince St. Tues–Sat 11am–6pm, closed mid-Aug to mid-Sept; suggested donation $3. ☎966-4444 for exhibition information.

Temporary exhibitions of contemporary art, emphasizing international developments, and cultural and racial issues. Founded in 1975, it is well organized and adventurous, with 6–12 temporary exhibits a year supplemented by regular musical events and poetry readings.

American Craft Museum

40 W 53rd St. Subway E or F to 5th Ave–53rd St. Tues–Sun 10am–6pm, Thurs until 8pm, closed Mon; $5, students $2.50, free Thurs 6–8pm. ☎956-3535 for exhibition information.

Three floors of contemporary crafts presented by the American Craft Council. Changing exhibits cover every material (from paper to porcelain to metal to glass) and all styles, and are accompanied by lectures and workshops. Bright, brash and good fun.

American Museum of the Moving Image

35th Ave at 36th St, Astoria, Queens. Subway R or G to Steinway St. Tues–Fri noon–5pm, Sat & Sun 11am–6pm, closed Mon; $8.50, students/seniors $5.50, children 5–12 $4.50, children under 5 free; price includes all film and video programs. ☎718/784-0077 for exhibition information.

Housed in a part of Astoria Studios previously used by Woody Allen and the *Cosby Show*, among others, this museum chronicles the art, technology and cultural impact of film, TV and video. Its exhibit halls are filled with historic costumes, cameras and props, as well as the entire *Seinfeld* set. The second and third floors contain its core exhibition, "Behind the Screen," which has ten interactive displays and four hours' worth of audio and visual material. You can view demonstrations of non-linear editing and computerized special effects; select a song from a soundtrack jukebox and learn more about its composer; or read a scene from *Dressed to Kill* and see how it was actually shot on film. Other exhibits include a popular interactive one on computer games, where visitors can play their way through the history of video game technology.

The museum also offers special screenings designed to explain the technical development of an art form that, to millions around the world, defines America. You can listen to directors explaining sequences from famous movies; watch short films made up of well-known clips; even add your own sound effects to movies. Insider guided tours are given daily at 3pm and a wide array of film screenings are presented every weekend. A fascinating place, and well worth a visit. See also "Astoria", p.236.

American Numismatic Society

Broadway at 155th St (Audubon Terrace). Subway #1 to 157th St–Broadway, or B to 155th St–Amsterdam Ave. Tues–Sat 9am–4.30pm, Sun 1–4pm (exhibition hall only), closed Mon; free. ☎234-3130 for exhibition information.

For those who think that coin collecting is sheer dullsville, the Numismatic Society might change your mind: it's dedicated to the preservation and study of coins, medals and paper money, and offers changing exhibits on numismatic history, design and politics. The Society's library contains an enormous number of numismatic periodicals, books and illustrations – all there for the researcher or intrigued collector.

Asia Society Gallery

725 Park Ave (70th St). Subway #6 to 68th St–Lexington Ave. Tues–Sat 11am–6pm, Thurs until 8pm, Sun noon–5pm; $4, students/seniors $2; free Thurs 6–8pm. ☎517-ASIA for exhibit information.

A prominent educational resource on Asia founded by John D. Rockefeller 3rd, the society offers a modest exhibition space dedicated to both traditional and contemporary art from all over Asia. Worth the admission fee if the accompanying temporary exhibition looks promising. Also holds intriguing performances, political roundtables, lectures, films and free events.

Bronx Museum of the Arts

1040 Grand Concourse, corner of 165th St, the Bronx. Subway #4 to 161st St–Grand Concourse. Wed 3–9pm, Thurs & Fri 10am–5pm, Sat & Sun noon–6pm; suggested donation $3, students $2, children under 12 free. ☎718/681-6000 for exhibition information.

Small collection of twentieth century American art housed in a converted synagogue. Includes a few Romare Beardens, otherwise not much of any great note. Also changing exhibitions of Bronx-based artists.

The Brooklyn Museum of Art

200 Eastern Parkway, Brooklyn. Subway #2 or #3 to Eastern Parkway–Brooklyn Museum. Wed–Fri 10am–5pm, Sat & Sun 11am–6pm, first Sat of every month 11am–11pm, closed Mon & Tues; $4, students $2. ☎718/638-5000 for exhibition information. The museum's gift shop sells genuine ethnic items from around the world at reasonable prices.

When Judy Chicago's *Dinner Party* was exhibited here back in the early 1980s, the Brooklyn Museum had people lining up all the way around the block. Since then, however, the museum has reverted to its former status: good in its own right, but perpetually doomed to

Other Museums

stand in the shadow of the Met. Which is a pity, for it's a likeable place, and – together with a visit to the adjacent Botanical Garden – is a good reason for forsaking Manhattan for an afternoon.

A trip through the museum, one of the largest art museums in the US, with 1.5 million objects in its collection and five floors stacked with exhibits, does require considerable selectivity. The highlights include recently renovated and expanded exhibitions of art from **Africa, Oceania and the Americas** on the ground floor; **Greek classical and Middle Eastern art** on the second floor; a world-class collection of **Egyptian Antiquities** in a new chronological installation on the third floor; and 28 evocative **period rooms**, ranging from an early American farmhouse to a nineteenth-century Moorish castle.

Be sure to also look in on the **American and European Painting and Sculpture galleries** on the top story, which progress from eighteenth-century portraits – including one of George Washington by Gilbert Stuart – and bucolic paintings by members of the Hudson River school to works by Winslow Homer and John Singer Sargent to pieces by Charles Sheeler and Georgia O'Keefe. A handful of paintings by European artists – Degas, Cézanne, Toulouse-Lautrec, Monet and Dufy, among others – are also displayed, although nothing approaching their best work. You will also find a large collection of Rodin sculptures.

Cooper-Hewitt National Design Museum (Smithsonian Institute)

2 E 91st St. Subway #4, #5 or #6 to 86th St–Lexington Ave. Tues 10am–9pm, Wed–Sat 10am–5pm, Sun noon–5pm, closed Mon; $5, students & seniors $3, free Tues 5–9pm. ☎849-8400 for exhibition information. The Design Resource and Study Center is open weekdays by appointment only. The gift shop boasts an array of innovative and inexpensive items.

The permanent collection is on view by appointment only to design professionals and students (you must have a clear idea of what you want to see and meet with a curator beforehand).

When he decided to build at what was then the unfashionable end of Fifth Avenue, millionaire industrialist Andrew Carnegie asked for "the most modest, plainest and most roomy house in New York." What he got was a bit more than that; a beautiful, spacious mansion filled with wood-paneled walls, carved ceilings and parquet floors – too decorative to be plain, too large to be modest. These lovely rooms now constitute the gallery space for the Cooper-Hewitt National Design Museum run by the Smithsonian. Two floors of temporary exhibits focus on the history, nature and evolution of design and decorative arts – commercial, utilitarian and high art (it is the only museum that boasts a curator just of wall coverings). Very little of the large permanent collection is on view to the public, except when pieces are involved in a special exhibition. The skillful curating and insightful commentary make a trip to the Cooper-Hewitt highly entertaining, and the building itself is worth a look. Themes vary, so check what's on first.

Dahesh Museum

601 5th Ave (at 48th St). Subway B, D, F or Q to 47th–50th St (Rockefeller Center)–6th Ave. Tues–Sat 11am–6pm; free. ☎759-0606 for exhibition information.

A small museum featuring nineteenth- and early twentieth-century European artwork collected by Dr Dahesh, a Lebanese writer and philosopher passionate about European academic art. The permanent collection contains over 3000 works.

Forbes Galleries

62 5th Ave (at 12th St). Subway #4, #5 or #6 to 14th St–Union Square, or F to 14th St & 6th Ave. Tues, Wed, Fri & Sat 10am–4pm (Thurs group tours only), closed Sun & Mon; free. ☎206-5549 for exhibition information.

The world's largest private collection of Fabergé eggs, along with 500 model boats, 10,000 toy soldiers, and over 4000 historical documents, including some presidential papers of George Washington and Thomas Jefferson.

Grey Art Gallery & Study Center, New York University

100 Washington Square E. Subway A, B, C or D to W 4th St, or R to 8th St, or #6 to Astor Place. Tues, Thurs & Fri 11am–6pm, Wed 11am–8pm, Sat 11am–5pm, closed Sun & Mon, also closed Christmas Eve–New Year's Day for winter recess; suggested donation $2.50. ☎998-6780 for exhibition information.

This NYU-run gallery hosts traveling art exhibitions as well as its own temporary shows of a wide range of media–sculpture, painting, printmaking, photography, video and more. Due to limited space, their permanent collection is only shown when pieces are included in special exhibits, which is a shame as they are known for two outstanding collections: the **New York University Art Collection** – 6000 works, including a strong group of American paintings from the 1940s onwards and prints by Picasso, Miró and Matisse, and the **Abbey Weed Grey Collection of Contemporary Asian and Middle Eastern Art**.

Guggenheim Museum SoHo

575 Broadway at Prince St. Subway N or R to Prince Street–Broadway, or #6 to Spring St; Wed–Sun 11am–6pm, closed Mon–Tues; $8, students and seniors $5, children under 12 free. ☎423-3500 general information for both Guggenheim Museums.

By renting two floors of a loft building in the heart of SoHo in 1992, the Guggenheim was the first major museum to move downtown to where New York's contemporary art scene really happens. After a brief closing for self-examining, it reopened in mid-1999 with a show of Warhol's last works (the *Last Supper* series), signaling its new role as more of an outpost for the Guggenheim's permanent collection. It now aims to have longer exhibitions, with an emphasis on sin-

gle artist retrospectives and in-depth interpretations of the collection, particularly postwar art. It remains to be seen what direction
this branch will take and whether it will continue to provide an historical context for the area's new art. It's certainly worth calling or
dropping by to see what's on. Make sure to stop into the museum
shop – it's an excellent source for art books, colorful jewelry and creative household and design objects.

International Center of Photography – Midtown

*1133 Avenue of the Americas (at 43rd St). Subway B, D, F or Q to 42nd St.
Hours and admission prices same as ICP below; free Fri 5–8pm. ☎768-
4682 for exhibition information.*

This branch will be closed for renovations until Summer 2000, while
it doubles its gallery space and installs a state-of-the-art climate control system. Call to check on the reopening schedule.

International Center of Photography – Uptown

*1130 5th Ave at 94th St. Subway #6 to 96th St–Lexington Ave.
Tues–Thurs 10am–5pm, Fri 10am–8pm, Sat & Sun 10am–6pm, closed
Mon; $6, students $4, free Fri 5–8pm. ☎860-1777 for exhibition infor-
mation.*

Founded and directed by Cornell Capa, brother of Robert, the ICP
exhibits all aspects of photography. The Center's permanent
archived collection holds most of the greats – Cartier-Bresson,
Adams, Kertesz, Eugene Smith – and there are often three temporary
shows on at any given time. At least one of these is bound to be
worthwhile, often featuring the city's most exciting avant-garde and
experimental work from around the world. Overall, an excellent
adjunct to MoMA's collection.

Isamu Noguchi Garden Museum

*33rd Rd and Vernon Blvd, Long Island City, Queens. Subway N to
Broadway station, Queens, or Sat & Sun shuttle bus from in front of the
Asia Society (Park Ave and E 70th St) every hour on the half-hour
11.30am–3.30pm, with return trip every hour on the hour noon–5pm, $5
round trip. Museum open April–Oct only: Wed–Fri 10am–5pm, Sat & Sun
11am–6pm, guided tours at 2pm daily, closed Mon & Tues; suggested
donation $4, students $2. ☎718/204-7088 for more information. First
floor and garden are wheelchair accessible.*

Although it seems ironic that a garden museum is located in an abandoned industrial area of Queens, it's fitting in this instance. **Isamu
Noguchi** (1904–88), an abstract Japanese sculptor, strove to inte-
grate art with nature and the urban environment. More than three
hundred of his stone, metal, wood and paper works are on show in
this gutted warehouse and small garden; the pieces are elegant and
Zenlike in their simplicity.

Museum for African Art

593 Broadway between Houston and Prince. Subway N or R to Prince St. Tues–Fri 10.30am–5.30pm, Sat & Sun noon–6pm; $5, students $2.50. ☎966-1313 for exhibition information.

Two floors of changing exhibitions of the best of modern and traditional African art; paintings, sculpture, masks, sacred objects and more. The understated museum interior was designed in 1993 by Maya Lin, who designed the Vietnam War Memorial in Washington DC. Temporary exhibits focus on regional art, cultural/political themes and contemporary African painting and sculpture – an eye-opener compared to the token ethnic collections usually seen. Film screenings, lectures and weekend family workshops are held regularly, call ahead for schedules.

Museum of American Folk Art

2 Lincoln Square, Columbus Ave (between 65th and 66th sts). Subway #1 or #9 to 66th St. Tues–Sun 11.30am–7.30pm; suggested admission $3. ☎595-9533 for exhibition information.

Changing exhibitions of multicultural folk art from all over the US, with a permanent collection that includes over 3500 works from the seventeenth to twentieth centuries. The Folk Art Institute, a division of the museum, runs courses, lectures and workshops open to the public.

Museum of American Illustration

128 E 63rd St. Subway #4, #5 or #6 to 59th St–Lexington Ave. Tues 10am–8pm, Wed–Fri 10am–5pm, Sat noon–4pm, closed Sun and Mon; free. ☎838-2560 for exhibition information.

Rotating selections from the museum's permanent collection of over 2000 illustrations, from wartime propaganda to contemporary ads, with all manner of cartoons and drawings in between. Exhibitions center on a theme or illustrator – designed primarily for aficionados, but always accessible, well mounted and topical.

Museum of Television & Radio

25 W 52nd St (between 5th and 6th aves). Subway E or F to 5th Ave–53rd St. Tues, Wed & Fri–Sun noon–6pm, Thurs noon–8pm (theaters open until 9pm Friday). Suggested donation $6, students $4, children under 13 $3. ☎621-6600 for information on daily events.

Dedicated to preserving our television and radio heritage, this museum holds an archive of 60,000 mostly American TV and radio broadcasts. The museum's excellent computerized reference system allows you to research news, public affairs, documentaries, sports, comedies, advertisements and other aural and visual oddities. You can select up to four programs at a time, and watch them on any one of the eight dozen video consoles. Service is quick, and multiple copies exist of the more popular choices; perfect if you want to settle down to a day's worth of *I Love Lucy*.

To appease wary pop cult critics, the museum also conducts educational seminars and screenings in its four theaters; organizes thematic festivals; and broadcasts live from its in-house radio station. A warning, though: the museum becomes a noisy hothouse on weekends and holidays, so try to visit at other times.

National Academy of Design

1083 5th Ave (89th St). Subway #4, #5 or #6 to 86th St–Lexington Ave. Wed–Thurs & Sat–Sun noon–5pm, Fri 10am–6pm, closed Mon & Tues; $8, seniors $4.50, students $4.25, Fri 5–6pm free (pay as you wish). ☎369-4880 for exhibition information.

Samuel Morse founded the National Academy of Design along the lines of London's Royal Academy, and though 1083 Fifth Ave is not nearly as grand as Burlington House, similarities remain: a school of fine art, exclusive membership and regular exhibitions of art, in this case mostly American. There's a tradition that academicians and associates donate a work of art on their election here: associates a self-portrait, academicians a "mature work." One hundred and fifty years' worth of these pictures are now held by the Academy and form the mainstay of the Selection from the Permanent Collection – varied throughout the year but always with a strong slant toward portraiture. The icing on the cake is the building itself: an imposing Beaux Arts townhouse donated to the academy by the husband of sculptor Anna Hyatt Huntingdon; her *Diana* gets pride of place below the cheerful rotunda.

New Museum of Contemporary Art

583 Broadway (between Prince and Houston sts). Subway N or R to Prince St, or #6 to Spring St. Wed & Sun noon–6pm, Thurs–Sat noon–8pm, closed Mon & Tues; $5, students, seniors and artists $3, free Thurs 6–8pm. ☎219-1355 for exhibition information.

Regularly changing exhibitions by contemporary American and international artists. Offbeat and eclectic, the New Museum will mount risky works that other museums are unable – or unwilling – to show. Its new bookstore is devoted to contemporary art criticism and theory, along with artists' monographs and an array of gift items. Pick up the museum's calendar for details on current and forthcoming exhibits and lectures. A must.

The Pierpont Morgan Library

29 E 36th St (between Madison and Park aves). Subway #6 to 33rd St–Park Ave. Tues–Thurs 10.30am–5pm, Fri 10.30am–8pm, Sat 10.30am–6pm, Sun noon–6pm, closed Mon; $7, students, seniors $5, children 12 and under free; guided tours available Tues–Sat, call for schedule. ☎685-0610 for more information.

Built by McKim, Mead and White for financier J. Pierpont Morgan in 1906, this gracious Italian Renaissance-style mansion holds one of

New York's best small museums. Originating with Morgan's own impressive collection of manuscripts, the museum has grown to include nearly 10,000 drawings and prints (including works by da Vinci, Degas and Dürer), and an extraordinary array of historical, literary and musical manuscripts.

The focal point of the museum are the two **Historic Rooms** located off a corridor sometimes lined with a fine assortment of **Rembrandt prints**. The first room you come to, the **West Room**, served as Morgan's study and has been left much as it was when he worked here, with a carved sixteenth-century Italian ceiling, a couple of paintings by Memling and Perugino and, among the few items contemporary with the building, a desk custom-carved to a design by McKim. From here, through a domed and pillared hallway, lies the **East Room** or library, a sumptuous three-tiered cocoon of rare books, autographed musical manuscripts and various trinkets culled from Morgan's European travels. Many of the exhibits change so regularly that it's difficult to say precisely what you'll see – the only item from the permanent collection that is always on display is one of the museum's three copies of the Gutenberg Bible from 1455 (of eleven surviving). Also in the permanent collection but displayed only on a rotating basis are original manuscripts by Mahler (the museum holds the world's largest collection of his work), Beethoven, Schubert and Gilbert and Sullivan; the only complete copy of Thomas Malory's *Morte d'Arthur*; as well as letters from the likes of Vasari, Mozart and George Washington, and the literary manuscripts of Thoreau, Dickens and Jane Austen among others.

Roerich Museum

319 W 107th St (between Broadway and Riverside Drive). Subway #1 to 110th St–Broadway. Tues–Sun 2–5pm, closed Mon; free. ☎864-7752.

Nicolas Roerich was a Russian artist who lived in India, was influenced by Indian mysticism, and produced strikingly original paintings. This is a small, weird and virtually unknown collection of his work on three floors of the brownstone where he lived. Free concerts and other events – call for the schedule.

Socrates Sculpture Park

Broadway at Vernon Blvd, Long Island City, Queens. Subway N to Broadway. Daily 10am–sunset; free. ☎718/956-1819.

Disused park turned sculpture gallery, with exhibits changing every six months or so and sculptures on loan from international institutions. Not well-kept, but worth peeking into after visiting the nearby Isamu Noguchi Garden Museum (p.292).

Studio Museum in Harlem

144 W 125th St (between Lenox and 7th aves). Subway #2 or #3 to 125th St–Lenox Ave. Wed–Fri 10am–5pm, Sat & Sun 1–6pm, closed Mon & Tues;

$5, students and seniors $2, children under 12 $1, free admission on the first Sat of every month. ☎864-4500 for exhibition informatiom.

Founded in 1968, the museum has over 60,000 square feet of exhibition space dedicated to showcasing contemporary African-American painting, photography and sculpture. The permanent collection is displayed on a rotating basis and includes works by Harlem Renaissance-era photographer James Van Der Zee, and paintings and sculptures by postwar artists. At least a dozen temporary exhibits are mounted a year, and lectures, author readings and music performances are held regularly.

Historical museums

Edgar Allan Poe Cottage

Grand Concourse and E Kingsbridge Rd, the Bronx. Subway D or #4 to Kingsbridge Rd. Sat 10am–4pm, Sun 1–5pm, closed weekdays except for tour groups by appointment only; $2. ☎718/881-8900.

Built in 1812, this wood farmhouse was the final home of Edgar Allan Poe, who lived here from 1846 until his death in 1849 and wrote "Annabel Lee," "The Bells" and other works here. Owned by a number of people in the interim, the cottage was purchased by the City of New York in 1913, made into a museum in 1917 and is listed on the National Register of Historic Places. A film about Poe and a small gallery of 1840s artwork and photographs are also on view. See p.248 for more details.

Ellis Island Museum of Immigration

Ellis Island, access by the Circle Line Statue of Liberty Ferry from Battery Park. Daily 9.30am–5pm, admission is free; ☎363-3200. Ferries run on a seasonal schedule, call to confirm, generally run every half-hour from 9.30am–3.30pm (though you need to be on the 3pm ferry at the latest to see the museum), adults $7 round-trip, children 3–17 $3, call ☎269-5755 for ferry info; www and www (a searchable database of the names of the people who came through the immigration center).

Artifacts, photographs, maps and personal accounts tell the story of the immigrants who passed through Ellis Island on their way to a new life in America. Ellis Island became an immigration processing station in 1892, and in 1990 the main buildings were renovated and reopened as a museum. Features include a film about the island and its temporary occupants; "Ellis Island Stories," a half-hour dramatic re-enactment of the immigrant experience based on oral histories (April–Sept only, $3 for adults, $2.50 for children, call ahead for schedule); the Wall of Honor, with the names of many of those that came through Ellis Island; and Treasures From Home, a collection of family heirlooms, photos, and other artifacts donated by descendants of the immigrants. For extensive details, see P.66.

Fraunces Tavern

54 Pearl St (at Broad). Subway #4 or #5 to Bowling Green, or N or R to Whitehall St, or #1 or #9 to South Ferry, or #2 or #3 to Wall St. Mon–Fri 10am–4.45pm, Sat & Sun noon–4pm; $2.50, students $1. ☎*425-1778 for exhibition information.*

Revolutionary-era rooms and objects housed in a 1719 residence that was converted into a tavern in 1762. Special events and rotating exhibitions are offered as well – a great stop if you're in the area; see p.74 for more details.

Intrepid Sea-Air-Space Museum

W 46th St and 12th Ave at Pier 86. Summer hours: April 1–Sept 30 Mon–Sat 10am–5pm, Sun 10am–6pm; Winter hours: Oct 1–March 31 Wed–Sun 10am–5pm, closed Mon & Tues, closed January for repair and cleaning; last admission 1 hour prior to closing; adults $10, children 12–17 $7.50, children 6–11 $5, children 3–5 $1, 2 years and under free. ☎*245-0072.*

This old aircraft carrier has a distinguished history, including hauling Neil Armstrong and co. out of the ocean following the *Apollo 11* moonshot. Today it holds an array of modern and vintage air and sea craft including the A-12 Blackbird, the world's fastest spy plane, and the *USS Growler*, a guided missile submarine. It also has interactive CD-ROM exhibits and a restaurant onboard.

Morris–Jumel Mansion and Museum

65 Jumel Terrace at 160th St and Edgecombe. Subway A, B to 163rd St. Wed–Sun 10am–4pm, closed Mon & Tues; $3, students, seniors $2. ☎*923-8008.*

One of the few remaining pre-Revolutionary War buildings in New York City, this mansion was originally built in 1765 as a summer house for a British colonel; later George Washington used it as a headquarters during the war. The rooms have been preserved as a museum since 1903, and are quite interesting, as are the historical exhibitions on view – a worthwhile stop, especially if combined with sights at nearby Audubon Terrace, such as the Hispanic Society. See pp.211 & 300 for more information.

Museum of American Financial History

28 Broadway at Bowling Green Park. Subway #4, #5 or #6 to Bowling Green, #1 or #9 to Rector St. Tues–Sat 10am–4pm; $2. ☎*908-4110 or 1/877–98-FINANCE.*

Located in the former headquarters of John D. Rockefeller's Standard Oil Company, this is the largest public archive of financial documents and artifacts in the world, features finance-related objects such as the bond signed by George Washington bearing the first dollar sign ever used on a Federal document, and a stretch of ticker tape from the

opening moments of 1929's Great Crash. Also on view are early photographs of Wall Street and furnishings from *Delmonico's* restaurant
where the Robber Barons held court. Fortunately this isn't just a self-
congratulatory temple to big business: changing educational exhibits
concentrate on such themes as the colonies' emergence from debt in
the wake of the Revolutionary War to the process by which companies
raise capital. The museum also offers a "World of Finance" walking
tour ($15 adults, $10 students).

Museum of Bronx History

*3266 Bainbridge Ave, the Bronx. Subway D to 205th St–Bainbridge Ave,
or #4 to Kingsbridge Rd. Closed weekdays except for group tours by
appointment only, Sat 10am–4pm, Sun 1–5pm; $2. ☎718/881-8900 for
exhibit information.*

Housed in the landmarked Valentine-Varian House, a fieldstone
farmhouse built in 1758, this museum is more notable for its historic
building than for its exhibitions of Bronx-related artifacts from the
pre-Colonial era to the Depression.

Museum of the City of New York

*5th Ave (103rd St). Subway #6 to 103rd St–Lexington Ave. Wed–Sat
10am–5pm, Sun 1–5pm, Tues 10am–2pm for pre-registered tour groups
only, closed Mon; suggested donation $5, students $4, families $10.
☎534-1672 for exhibit information.*

Spaciously housed in a neo-Georgian mansion, the permanent collection of this museum provides a history of the city from Dutch
times to the present. Paintings, prints, photographs, costumes and
furniture are displayed on four floors, and a film about the city's history runs continuously. The museum runs lectures, workshops and
Sunday walking tours of New York neighborhoods. A worthwhile
and engaging stop.

New York City Police Museum

*25 Broadway, 2nd floor of Bowling Green Post Office, corner of Morris St
at Bowling Green. Subway #4, #5 or #6 to Bowling Green, #1 or #9 to
Rector St. Daily 10am–6pm; free. ☎301-4440.*

A collection of 250 years worth of memorabilia of the New York
Police Department, the largest and oldest in the country. Staffed
by cops from the force's Community Affairs department, it showcases the history and personal effects of New York's Finest: night
sticks, guns, uniforms, photos and the like – over 10,000 items in
all. There's a copper badge from 1845 that was worn by the
sergeants of the day, earning them the nickname of "coppers," and
a pristine-looking Tommy gun – in its original gangster-issue vio-
lin case – that was used to rub out Al Capone's gang leader,
Frankie Yale.

The New York Historical Society

2 W 77th St at Central Park W. Subway B or C to 81st St–Central Park W. Tues–Sun 11am–5pm; suggested donation $5, children, students and seniors $3. Library hours Tues–Sat 11am–5pm. ☎873-3400.

More a museum of American than New York history, this is a venue well worth keeping an eye on: its temporary exhibitions are more daring than you'd expect, mixing high and low culture with intelligence and flair. On the second floor, **James Audubon**, the Harlem artist and naturalist who specialized in lovingly detailed watercolors of birds, is the focus of one room; other galleries hold a broad sweep of **nineteenth-century American painting**, principally portraiture (the "missing" White House portrait of Jacqueline Kennedy Onassis, and the picture of Alexander Hamilton that found its way onto the $10 bill) and Hudson River school landscapes (among them Thomas Cole's famed and pompous *Course of Empire* series). A new permanent children's exhibit called **Kid City** has opened, with interactive exhibitions such as a child-size re-creation of a block on Broadway in 1901.

Don't miss the museum **library**, which holds 650,000 books, over 2 million manuscripts, letters and historical documents, and 30,000 maps and atlases in its collection; it boasts such diverse items as the original Louisiana Purchase document and the correspondence between Aaron Burr and Alexander Hamilton that led up to their duel (see p.210). An interesting museum too often overlooked.

New York Transit Museum

Old subway entrance at Schermerhorn St and Boerum Place, Brooklyn. Subway #2, #3, #4, #5 or F to Borough Hall. Tues–Fri 10am–4pm, Sat & Sun noon–5pm, closed Mon; adults $3, children $1.50; ☎718/243-3060. Also: The Transit Museum Gallery and Store at Grand Central Terminal, open Mon–Fri 8am–8pm, Sat 10am–4pm; free admission.

Housed in an abandoned 1930s subway station, this museum offers more than 100 years worth of transportation history and memorabilia, including more than twenty restored subway cars and buses dating back to the turn of the century (including, amazingly, a wooden train car from 1914). The New York Transit Museum Gallery and Store on the main floor of Grand Central Terminal has small changing exhibits and a gift shop selling transit-related items, including – a chocolate metrocard.

Both Transit Museum locations, as well as the Transit Museum kiosk at Times Square, sell the elusive (they're not sold in subway stations) MetroCard Fun Pass, which for only $4 offers one-day unlimited rides on public transportation.

Queens Museum of Art

New York City Building, Flushing Meadows-Corona Park, Queens. Subway #7 to Willets Point–Shea Stadium. Wed–Fri 10am–5pm, Sat & Sun noon–5pm, closed Mon, Tues open to group tours by appointment only; suggested donation $4, students $2, children under 5 free. ☎718/592-9700 for exhibit information.

Primarily worth the trip for its biggest permanent item: the Panorama of the City of New York – a 9300-square-foot model of the five boroughs of New York City, spectacularly lit, originally conceived for the 1964 World's Fair by Robert Moses, and updated in 1994. Great fun if you know the city, and useful orientation if you don't. The Wildlife Conservation Society zoo across the street has an aviary in one of Buckminster Fuller's geodesic domes, while the museum itself displays an interesting array of paraphernalia from the World's Fairs.

Skyscraper Museum

16 Wall St (at Nassau St). Subway #2, #3, #4, #5 to Wall St. Tues–Sat noon–6pm, closed Sun & Mon; suggested donation $2, children, students, seniors free. ☎968-1961.

This new museum is only temporarily housed in this spot, appropriately surrounded by Wall Street skyscrapers. If all goes according to plan, it will eventually be located on the ground floor of the new *Ritz Carlton Hotel* expected to open in 2001 near the Museum of Jewish Heritage (see p.302). This nonprofit institution offers a fascinating historical look at skyscrapers, from how they were built to why they became the defining New York structure.

South Street Seaport Center and Museum

207 Front St at the end of Fulton and the East River. Subway A, C to Broadway-Nassau, #2, #3, #4 or #5 to Fulton St. April–Sept daily 10am–6pm, Thurs until 8pm; Oct–March 10am–5pm, closed Tues; $6, students $4, children under 12 $3. ☎748-8600.

Eighteenth- and nineteenth-century buildings house three galleries, a children's center, a maritime craft center and a library, and the adjacent dock is home to a large fleet of historic ships. On exhibit are Fulton Fish Market artifacts, steamship memorabilia, maps, model ships, and photographs. New York Unearthed at 6 Pearl St is a site the museum has devoted to archeological work currently being done in the city. See p.74 for more information, and also Chapter 23, "Kid's New York" pp.442–443.

Community and ethnic museums

Hispanic Society of America

Audubon Terrace, 3753 Broadway (between 155th and 156th sts). Subway #1 to 157th St–Broadway. Tues–Sat 10am–4.30pm, Sun 1–4pm, closed Mon, Library closed Aug; free. ☎926-2234 for exhibit information.

One of the largest collections of Hispanic art outside Spain, with over 3000 paintings, including works by Spanish masters such as Goya, El Greco and Velázquez, and more than 6000 decorative works of art. The collection consists of everything from a 965 AD intricately carved ivory box to fifteenth-century textiles to the joyful mural series *Provinces of Spain* by Joaquin Sorolla y Bastida (commissioned specifically for the Society). Displays of permanent collection works rarely change so you can be fairly certain you'll see the highlights. The library of 200,000 books, including over 16,000 printed before the eighteenth century, is a major center for research on Spanish and Portuguese art, history and literature. Worth a trip, especially in conjunction with the nearby Morris–Jumel Mansion (see p.297) and other Audubon Terrace sights.

Jewish Museum

1109 5th Ave (92nd St). Subway #4, #5 or #6 to 92nd St–Lexington Ave. Sun–Thurs 11am–5.45pm, Tues until 8pm, closed Fri & Sat, closed on major legal and Jewish holidays; $8, students $5.50, children under 12 free, free Tues 5–8pm. ☎423-3200 for exhibit information.

The largest museum of Judaica outside Israel. Its centerpiece is a permanent exhibition on the Jewish experience – the basic ideas, values and culture developed over four thousand years. More vibrant and exciting, however, are the changing displays of works by major international artists, and theme exhibitions (for example, a recent major exhibit on Freud containing nearly 200 artifacts from his Vienna offices), as well as the children's "hands-on" area on the fourth floor.

Kurdish Library and Museum

144 Underhill Ave (corner of Park Place), Brooklyn. Subway D to 7th Ave, or #2 or #3 to Grand Army Plaza. Mon–Thurs 1–4pm, Sun 2–5pm, Library opened same hours or by appointment; free. ☎718/783-7930.

A collection of Kurdish photographs, traditional costumes and crafts that seek to place in context the fourth largest group of people in the Middle East. The museum, American-founded and sponsored, also publishes two journals about the Kurds; the library provides reference material of all kinds on their history, culture and politics.

Lower East Side Tenement Museum

90 Orchard St. Subway F to Delancey St–Essex St. Tues–Fri 1–5pm, Thursday until 8pm, Sat & Sun 11am–4.30pm; $8, students $6. Guided tours of the renovated tenement building are held every half-hour – last tour Tues–Fri is at 4pm (Thurs at 7pm), last one on weekends is at 3.30pm. In addition, walking tours of different ethnic neighborhoods are conducted April–Dec on Sat & Sun at 1.30pm and 2.30pm, call for price and details. ☎431-0233.

Housed in a former tenement building, the Tenement Museum aims to present a complete picture of lower Manhattan's immigrant history via a variety of temporary exhibitions. The two galleries show photographs and community-based displays, which concentrate on the multiple ethnic heritages in the area. If you elect to take the tenement tour (which is well worth your time), you'll be taken across the street to New York's first tenement building (*c.* 1863), which has been preserved more or less as it was when it was occupied by immigrant families earlier this century. In all, an earnest and sympathetic attempt to document the immigrant experience. Note: come early on weekends as the tours sometimes sell out.

Museo del Barrio

1230 5th Ave (104th St). Subway #6 to 103rd St–Lexington Ave. Wed–Sun 11am–5pm, May–Sept Thurs 11am–8pm; suggested donation $4, students $2. ☎831-7272 for exhibition information.

Literally translated as "the neighborhood museum," the Museo was founded in 1969 by a group of Puerto Rican parents, educators and artists from Spanish Harlem who wanted to teach their children about their roots. Now, although the emphasis remains largely Puerto Rican, the museum embraces the whole of Latin America and the Caribbean, with five major loan exhibits of painting, photographs and crafts each year, by both traditional and emerging artists. Make sure to see the *santos de palo* – an exquisite collection of carved votive figures. Educational programs, lectures and films.

Museum of Chinese in the Americas

70 Mulberry St, 2nd floor (corner of Bayard St). Subway N or R to Canal St, #6 to Canal St. Tues–Sat noon–5pm, closed Sun & Mon; suggested admission $3, students, seniors $1, children under 12 free. ☎619-4785.

Look for the community center with big red doors – hidden away on the second floor you'll find this tiny museum dedicated to documenting the experiences of Chinese immigrants in North and Latin America. Permanent exhibitions illustrate the Chinese-American experience through photographs, personal artifacts and oral histories.

Museum of Jewish Heritage

18 First Place, Battery Park City, Subway #1 or #9 to South Ferry, #4 or #5 to Bowling Green; N or R to Whitehall. April–Sept: Sun–Fri 9am–5pm, Thurs until 8pm; Oct–March Fri closes at 3pm, otherwise same hours; closed Sat and Jewish holidays; $7 ☎509-6130. Tickets may be purchased at the museum (call ☎945-0039) or through Ticketmaster (in New York call ☎307-4007).

Opened in late 1997, the Museum of Jewish Heritage was created as a living memorial to the Holocaust. Three floors of exhibits feature historical and cultural artifacts ranging from the practical accoutrements of everyday Eastern European Jewish life to the prison garb survivors wore in Nazi concentration camps, along with photographs, personal belongings and narratives. Recent acquisitions include Himmler's own annotated copy of *Mein Kampf* and a notebook filled by the inhabitants of the "barrack for prominent people" in the Terazin Ghetto.

Multimedia montages and archival films catalogue the Jewish experience this century: Europe's pre-World War II ghettos, the establishment of Israel, even the successes of entertainers and artists like Samuel Goldwyn and Allen Ginsberg. Steven Spielberg's moving Survivors of the Shoah Visual History Project (taped interviews with Holocaust survivors) is also on view here. The hexagonal granite structure itself is symbolically part of the exhibit, referencing the six million Jews who perished and the six points of the Star of David.

The National Museum of the American Indian (Smithsonian Institute)

Alexander Hamilton US Customs House, One Bowling Green. Subway #1 or #9 to South Ferry, or #4 or #5 to Bowling Green, or N or R to Whitehall St. Open daily, 10am–5pm, Thurs until 8pm; free. ☎*514-3700 for exhibition information;* www.si.edu/nmai.

An excellent and innovative collection of artifacts from almost every tribe native to the Americas, now part of the Smithsonian and relocated from Harlem to the landmarked Customs House in Lower Manhattan. Amazingly, many of the million-plus artifacts in the permanent collection were collected by one man, George Gustav Heye (1874–1957), who traveled throughout North and South America for over fifty years acquiring artwork and cultural artifacts, and who founded the museum in its original location in 1922. Only a small portion of the collection is on view here – more will be displayed in a new museum being built on the Mall in Washington DC (scheduled to be completed in 2002). In addition to several temporary shows a year, there are two large permanent exhibitions: "Creation's Journey: Masterworks of Native American Identity and Belief," consisting of 165 artifacts chosen by the museum's curators, and "All Roads are Good: Native Voices on Life and Culture," with over 300 artifacts chosen by different Native American groups to represent their world views and beliefs.

Interestingly, a large number of the staff here, including the director, are Native American, so, unlike other such museums, here you are really getting the inside perspective, so to speak. That may explain a rather extraordinary facet of the museum: its **repatriation policy**, adopted in 1991, which mandates that it give back to Indian tribes, upon request, human remains, funerary objects, and ceremonial and religious items it may have illegally acquired – if the major museums of the world followed suit, they would all be virtually empty (and we'd never have to hear about the Elgin Marbles again).

Schomburg Center for Research in Black Culture

515 Lenox Ave (135th St). Subway #2 or #3 to 125th St–Lenox Ave. Mon–Wed noon–8pm, Thurs–Sat 10am–6pm, Sun 1–5pm (exhibits only); free. ☎*491-2200 for exhibit information.*

Thought-provoking exhibitions of art, photographs and documents that detail the history of blacks in the US. The five million items in its

collection make the Center the world's pre-eminent research facility
for the study of black history and culture. Special exhibitions, lectures and events.

Ukrainian Museum

*203 2nd Ave. Subway #4, #5 or #6 to Astor Place. Wed–Sun 1–5pm; $3,
students $1.* ☎ *228-0110 for exhibition information.*

Situated in the heart of the Ukrainian East Village, this small collection offers little to entice outsiders. Crammed into two tiny floors,
the museum divides itself between recounting the history of
Ukrainian immigration to the US and showing (more interestingly)
some ethnic items and costumes from the country.

Commercial galleries

Art, and especially contemporary art, is big in New York: there are
roughly 500 art galleries in the city, the majority in SoHo and
Chelsea, and as many as 90,000 artists living in the area. Even if you
have no intention of buying, many of these galleries are well worth
seeing, as are some of the alternative spaces, run on a nonprofit
basis and less commercial than mainstream galleries.

Broadly, galleries fall into five main areas: along **Madison Avenue**
in the 60s and 70s for antiques and the occasional (minor) Old
Master; **57th Street** between Sixth and Park avenues for big, established modern and contemporary names; **SoHo** and **Chelsea** for
trendy and up-and-coming artists; and **TriBeCa** for more experimental displays. More and more respected galleries are moving to
Chelsea, pushed out of SoHo by ever-soaring rents and the chic boutiques and chain stores that now line its streets. The large old warehouse spaces in Chelsea offer better space for the money and are
perfectly suited for galleries. An emerging scene in **Williamsburg**,
Brooklyn, is also gathering momentum and a few worthwhile galleries are listed if you want to check out what's going on in the independent world of art in New York City.

A few of the more exclusive galleries are invitation only, but
most accept walk-ins (sometimes with a bit of attitude). One of the
best ways to see the top galleries is with Art Tours of Manhattan
(see p.25), which runs informed (if pricey) guided tours. Also, pick
up a copy of the **Gallery Guide** – available upon request in the larger galleries – for listings of current shows and each gallery's specialty. The weekly **Time Out New York** offers broad listings of the
major commercial galleries.

Listed below are some of the more interesting options in
Manhattan. **Opening times** are roughly Tuesday to Saturday
10am–6pm, but note that many galleries have truncated summer
hours and are closed during August. The best time to gallery-hop is

on weekday afternoons; the absolute worst time is on Saturday, when out-of-towners flood into the city's trendy areas. **Openings** – usually free and identifiable by crowds of people drinking wine from clear plastic cups – are excellent times to view work and eavesdrop on art gossip. A list of openings appear in the *Gallery Guide*.

SoHo and TriBeCa galleries

123 Watts, 123 Watts St ☎219-1482. Trendy gallery known for its photography, along with other forms of contemporary art; has shown work by Robert Mapplethorpe, Arturo Cuenca and Bruno Ulmer.

14 Sculptors Gallery, 168 Mercer St ☎966-5790. Just as the name implies, a gallery formed by fourteen sculptors to exhibit figurative and abstract contemporary art.

A.C.E. Gallery New York, 275 Hudson St ☎255-5599. Hosting several shows at a time, Ace is the place to see the work of young, emerging international and US artists. Also known for its shows of abstract Expressionist and Pop Art from the 1960s and 70s.

The Drawing Center, 35 Wooster St ☎219-2166. Offers shows of contemporary and historical works on paper, with an emphasis on emerging artists.

Edward Thorp, 103 Prince St ☎431-6880. Mainstream, contemporary American and European painting and sculpture.

Gemini GEL at Joni Weyl, 375 W Broadway, 2nd floor ☎219-1446. Contemporary graphics, with some vintage prints; has shown works by Roy Lichtenstein and Robert Rauschenberg.

Holly Solomon, 172 Mercer St (at Houston) ☎941-5777. A dramatic display space with an emphasis on installations and multimedia; artists have included Laurie Anderson, William Wegman and Nam June Paik.

John Gibson, 568 Broadway (at Prince), 2nd floor ☎925-1192. Avant-garde and old school American painting, sculpture and prints, with an emphasis on conceptual art and abstract works.

Leo Castelli, 420 W Broadway, 2nd floor ☎431-5160. One of the original dealer-collectors, Castelli was instrumental in aiding the careers of Rauschenberg and Warhol, and offers big contemporary names at big prices. Recent shows have included works by Jasper Johns and Frank Stella.

Louis Meisel, 141 Prince St (at W Broadway) ☎677-1340. Specializes in Photorealism – past shows have included Richard Estes and Chuck Close – as well as Abstract Illusionism (Meisel claims to have invented both terms).

O K Harris, 383 W Broadway ☎431-3600. Named after a mythical traveling gambler, O K is the gallery of Ivan Karp, a cigar-munching champion of Super-Realism. One of the first SoHo galleries and, although not as influential as it once was, worth a look. Also displays an interesting array of collectibles and Americana.

Sonnabend, 420 W Broadway, 3rd floor ☎966-6160. A top gallery featuring cross-the-board painting, photography and video from contemporary American and European artists, including Robert Morris and Gilbert and George.

Sperone Westwater, 142 Greene St, 2nd floor ☎431-3685. High quality European and American painting and works on paper. Artists have included Francesco Clemente, Frank Moore and Susan Rothenberg.

Chelsea galleries

Several large warehouse spaces in this neighborhood hold multiple galleries and are worth exploring as a group – in particular check out the four floors of galleries at **529 W 20th St**, in addition to some of the ones listed below which are also part of larger groups of galleries.

Annina Nosei Gallery, 530 W 22nd St, 2nd floor ☎741-8695. Global works, especially contemporary pieces by emerging Latin American and Middle Eastern artists.

Barbara Gladstone, 515 W 24th St ☎206-9300. Paintings, sculpture and photography by hot contemporary artists such as Matthew Barney and Rosemarie Trockel.

Greene/Naftali, 526 W 26th St, 8th floor ☎463-7770. A wide-open, airy space noted for its large group shows and conceptual installations.

John Weber, 529 W 20th St (between 10th and 11th aves), ☎691-5711. Shows conceptual, minimalist and highly unusual works, including those by Sol LeWitt and younger, similarly inspired, artists.

Matthew Marks Gallery, 522 W 22nd St (between 10th and 11th aves) ☎243-1650. A very hot gallery and the centerpiece of Chelsea's art scene, it shows the work of such well-known minimalist and abstract artists as Cy Twombly, Ellsworth Kelly and Lucien Freud. See also the branch at 523 W 24th St.

Pat Hearn, 530 W 22nd St ☎727-7366. This long-time gallery was an influential presence in its former SoHo location, and continues to specialize in abstract and conceptual artists, and risky exhibits.

Paula Cooper, 534 W 21st St ☎255-1105. An influential gallery that shows a wide range of contemporary painting, sculpture, drawings, prints and photographs, particularly minimalist and abstract works. Recently relocated from SoHo.

Thomas Healy, 530 W 22nd St ☎243-3753. No longer affiliated with Paul Morris, this gallery still specializes in contemporary installations, drawings and sculpture, with a stable of resident artists. Also recently relocated from SoHo.

Upper Eastside and Midtown galleries

Knoedler & Co., 19 E 70th St ☎ 794-0550. Highly renowned gallery specializing in abstract and Pop artists – showing some of the best-known names in twentieth-century art, including Stella, Rauschenberg and Fonseca.

Marlborough/Marlborough Graphics, 40 W 57th St ☎ 541-4900. Internationally renowned galleries show the cream of modern and contemporary artists and graphic designers. The broad sweep includes works by Red Grooms, Francis Bacon, R.B. Kitaj and others.

Mary Boone, 745 5th Avenue, 4th floor ☎ 752-2929. Leo Castelli's protégé who specializes in installations, paintings and works by up-and-coming European and American artists. A top gallery.

PaceWildenstein, 32 E 57th St ☎ 421-3292. This famous gallery has carried works by most of the great modern American and European artists; from Picasso to Calder to Rothko. Also has a good collection of prints and African art. A Downtown satellite located at 142 Greene St (☎ 431-9224) specializes in edgier works and large installations.

Robert Miller, 41 E 57th St (at Madison Ave) ☎ 980-5454. Exceptional shows of twentieth-century art, including paintings by David Hockney and Lee Krasner, and photographs by artists such as Diane Arbus and Robert Mapplethorpe.

Williamsburg galleries

Eyewash, 143 N 7th St, 3rd floor ☎ 718/387-2714. Housed in a tenement flat, this gallery showcases the works of local rising stars.

Holland Tunnel, 61 S 3rd St (between Berry St and Wythe Ave) ☎ 718/384-5738. Situated in the garden of Dutch artist Paulien Lethen, this tiny barn-like gallery is a gem. Best to call ahead before visiting.

Pierogi 2000, 177 N 9th St ☎ 718/599-2144. This stark-white former workshop, mounts installations of various kinds and is noted in the art world for its "flatfiles," a collection of gray folders containing the work of 400 or so artists and stored clinically and provocatively in metal, sliding cabinets. Peirogi also provides the names and addresses of other Williamsburg galleries.

Alternative spaces

The galleries listed above are part of a system designed to channel artists' work through the gallery spaces and, eventually, into the hands of the collector. While initial acceptance by a major gallery is an important rite of passage for an up-and-coming artist, it shouldn't be forgotten that the gallery system's philosophy is centered on making money for the owners, who normally receive fifty percent of the sale price. In these galleries, for an artist's work to be uncommercial is perhaps even more damming than to be socially or politically

Commercial galleries

unacceptable. The galleries below, often referred to as **alternative spaces**, provide a forum for the kind of risky and non-commercially viable art that many other galleries may not be able to afford to show. The recession of the 1990s has given the alternative space a new lease of life, and those mentioned here are at the cutting edge of new art in the city.

55 Mercer, 55 Mercer St, 2nd floor ☎226-8513. An artist-run co-operative that shows mostly abstract works by New York-area artists. High quality group and solo shows.

Art in General, 79 Walker St ☎219-0473. An experimental gallery with multimedia exhibits and performances, and an emphasis on multicultural themes.

Artists' Space, 38 Greene St, 3rd floor ☎226-3970. One of the most respected alternative spaces, with frequently changing theme-based exhibits, film screenings, videos and installations, as well as events. Their Artists' File is a computerized slide registry of more than 2500 New York State artists, and can be scanned free of charge.

Clocktower, 108 Leonard St ☎233-1096. Temporary exhibitions, and an annual studio program in which artists work in the studio space within the clock tower. When this is happening, you're allowed to wander around and talk to the artists about their work. Go just to see the incredible views of Downtown.

DIA Center for the Arts, 548 W 22nd St ☎989-5912. The pre-eminent Alternative Art Foundation's largest gallery space shows year-long exhibitions of work by artists such as Joseph Beuys, Dan Graham, Robert Ryman and Kids of Survival. The exhibition space on the roof has a café and chairs designed by artists. Other exhibit spaces include the New York Earth Room (see below), and "the Broken Kilometer" exhibit at 383 W Broadway (☎925-9397).

Exit Art, 548 Broadway ☎966-7745. A young, hip crowd frequents this huge alternative gallery that favors big installations, multimedia, and edgy cultural and political subjects. Make sure to have some espresso and ginger cookies from the café.

New York Earth Room, 141 Wooster St (between Prince and Houston sts) ☎431-3789. An incredible permanent exhibit by Walter de Maria, featuring a room filled, as the name suggests, with masses of dirt. Also changing exhibitions, installations and performances by contemporary artists.

PS 1 Contemporary Arts Center, 46-01 21st St in Long Island City, Queens ☎718/784-2084. $2 suggested donation. Part of the same organization (the Institute for Art and Urban Resources) as Clocktower, and based in an old schoolhouse, this is the place for avant-garde and experimental new art – so new that some Downtown galleries cull new talent from the exhibits here.

PS 122, 150 1st Ave ☎228-4249. Nonprofit gallery space open from September to June, which highlights emerging artists.

Storefront for Art and Architecture, 97 Kenmore St ☎431-5795. Innovative design shows exploring the use of urban space, be it in the form of architects' drawings, sculpture or painting. Housed in an incredible building that literally folds out to greet you.

Thread Waxing Space, 476 Broadway ☎966-9520. A trendy Downtown space that re-creates the 1960s "loft scene" – multimedia events, performance artists and even live bands play in this gallery decorated with avant-garde paintings, computer art and the like. Admission charges vary.

White Columns, 320 W 13th St ☎924-4212. Focuses on emerging artists, and is considered very influential. Check out the changing group shows.

Listings

Chapter 16

Accommodation

Accommodation in New York is a major cost. The majority of **hotels** in the city charge well over $100 a night, not to mention the **taxes** tacked on to that. Obviously the best way to cut this expense is to utilize contacts in the New York area – friends, or friends of friends – and perhaps sleep on a few floors along the way. However, there are a number of exceptions to the hotel rule – places that offer decent double rooms for as little as $65 a night – and some other less grand, but more practical, options for finding a bed for the night.

For the young and sociable there are plenty of **hostels** with dormitory accommodation offering a bed for as little as $20 a night. Other budget options include private rooms in a **YMCA/YWCA** (a *Y* as they're known), which run to around $50 for a double, or a **bed and breakfast**, which basically means staying in somebody's spare room, but with all the amenities of a private apartment. These rooms go for $65 and up for a double and can be booked through any of the agencies listed under "Bed and breakfast" (see p.16).

Whichever option you decide to go for, **booking ahead** is very strongly advised. At certain times of the year – Christmas and summer particularly – you're likely to find everything (and we mean this) chock full. You can book a room in a hotel or hostel yourself, by phoning direct to the hotel (☎001/212 before the listed number if you're dialing from Britain, or if there's an 800 number

listed you can use it to call toll-free from within the States, though this may only work outside the city), or by going through a specialist **travel agent** – which can sometimes work out cheaper (see "Getting there" in Basics for addresses). Bear in mind, too, the possibilities of all-in flight and hotel package vacations, again detailed under "Getting there." For hotels, there are also booking services – see box, p.319 – that reserve rooms at discount prices and usually for no extra charge.

Hostels and YMCAs

Hostels and **YMCAs** are just about the only option for cash-strapped backpackers in New York, with dorm beds for as little as $20 a night. Most hostels are fine as long as you don't mind sleeping in a bunk bed and sharing a room with strangers (if you're traveling in a group of four or six you could get a room to yourselves), though they do vary in quality. YMCAs are better if you want privacy because they have private single and double rooms, though they tend to have a more institutional feel than the more relaxed hostels. Note that hostels are especially busy and fairly rowdy in August and September when the legions of camp counselors descend on the city. For a comprehensive listing of hostels in New York and across North America you should obtain *The Hostel Handbook* for $4 by phoning ☎926-7030 or emailing *editor@hostelhandbook.com*. Or, you can

For the precise locations of most of the hotels and hostels we've listed, see the Accommodation map at the back of the book.

Accommodation

visit the *Internet Guide to Hosteling* at *www.hostelhandbook.com*.
The following is a small selection of the best hostels and *Y*s.

Hostels and Ys

Aladdin, 317 W 45th St, NY 10036 ☎246-8580, fax 246-6036. Don't be deceived by the dimly lit lobby or the black clad desk staff – accommodation here is basic and the single elevator takes forever. However, you don't have much choice in this part of town if you're on a tight budget. Dorm beds from $30 plus tax; private rooms from $89 plus tax.

Banana Bungalow, 250 W 77th St (at Broadway), NY 10024 ☎769-2441, fax 877-5733; *www.bananabungalow.com*. Popular dorm hostel at the corner of 77th St and Broadway, on the Upper West Side. Rates are $23–28 per person per night. Sun deck on the top floor, a shared tropical themed kitchen/lounge and free continental breakfast.

Blue Rabbit International House, 730 St Nicholas Ave, NY 10031 ☎1-800/6-HOS-TEL or 491-3892; *bluerabbit@hostelhandbook.com*. Recently opened by the owners of *International House – Sugar Hill*, four doors away, and charging the same price ($20) for dorms. With a limited number of double rooms, available only on a first-come, first-served basis, for $25 per person per night, which may be the cheapest doubles in the city. Check-in between 9am and 10pm. Has kitchens, and bed linen is included in the price.

Chelsea Center Hostel, 313 W 29th St near 8th Ave, NY 10001 ☎643-0214, fax 473-3945. Office hours: 8.30am to 11pm. No curfew. Small, clean, safe and friendly, Chelsea hostel has beds for $25 with breakfast and clean sheets and blankets included. The privately run hostel has no sign outside, which adds to its security, and it's well situated for Midtown, Chelsea and the West Village. It's good to book well in advance in high season. Two mixed dorms sleep a

total of twenty and facilities include a safe for valuables and summer barbecues in the garden courtyard. Cash only.

Chelsea International Hostel, 251 W 20th St, NY 10011 ☎647-0010, fax 727-7289; *www.chelseahostel.com*. Situated in the heart of Chelsea, between 7th and 8th aves, this is the closest hostel to Downtown and with a police precinct across the street, one would assume it's also pretty safe. Beds (130 in all) are $23 a night, including tax, and the rooms, which sleep four or six, are small with bathrooms in the hall (though there are larger rooms for six at the back of the hostel which have their own bathrooms). They also have private rooms for two at $55 a night. There are communal areas, free lockers, a laundry room, a backyard, and free pizza parties once a week. Accommodation is rudimentary, as befits the price, but it's the location that is the hostel's main attraction. 24-hour check-in, though it's worth calling ahead.

De Hirsch Residence at the 92nd St Y, 1395 Lexington Ave, NY 10128 ☎415-5650, fax 415-5578; *dehirsch@92ndsty.org*. For tourists there's a three-night minimum stay with singles at $75 a night and doubles at $48 per person per night. If you're a full-time student, working full-time or on an internship the *De Hirsch Residence* has single or shared bright, dormitory-style rooms for $835 (or $680 each if shared) per month with a 2-month minimum stay. Cooking and laundry facilities are available on each floor, along with shared bathroom facilities. Applications for residence must be made months in advance. An added bonus: the *92nd St Y* is renowned for its poetry and music events (to which residents get a discount), along with a host of other social activities.

> For details of **long-stay residences, particularly ones geared specifically to women**, see p.52

Gershwin Hotel, 7 E 27th St, NY 10016 ☎545-8000, fax 684-5546. A fun new hostel/hotel located in the Flatiron district, just off 5th Ave, and handy for just about any part of town. Beds in dorms (which sleep four to twelve) are $27 a night including tax, the only catch being they only accept a limited number of reservations – mostly it's a first-come, first-served basis. Imaginatively decorated with a Pop Art theme that spills out onto the sidewalk, and geared toward young travelers, there's an astroturfed rooftop terrace (where parties are held on summer weekends), a small bar, a well-priced restaurant and friendly staff. Don't expect anything but the barest necessities as far as sleeping arrangements are concerned, but there's so much going on here you'll probably want to be awake. See also p.322 for details of the *Gershwin's* private rooms.

Hosteling International – New York, 891 Amsterdam Ave at W 103rd St, NY 10025 ☎932-2300, fax 932-2574. High up on the Upper West Side, this historic building has 480 dormitory-style beds for $22–29 for IYHA members (on-the-spot membership is $25 for US citizens or $18 for those with a foreign address); $3 extra for nonmembers per night. Facilities include a library, kitchen, lounge, coffee bar and a large outdoor patio. Though large there's a good chance it'll be heavily booked, so reserve at least 24 hours in advance (at least a week in the summer). Open 24 hours.

International House of New York, 500 Riverside Drive at 122nd St, NY 10027 ☎316-8400. This graduate student residence hall up at Columbia University also functions as a hostel for travelers, though the cheapest rooms, with shared bathrooms, are only available to nonstudents during Christmas and summer, and cost $40 a night, or $35 if you stay fifteen days or more. Singles with private bathroom are available year-round for $95, doubles for $105 and triples for $120. Write or phone for reservations.

International House – Sugar Hill, 722 St Nicholas Ave at 145th St, NY 10031

☎926-7030; sugarhill@hostelhandbook. com. Friendly, well-run dorm hostel in a reputedly safe, middle-class neighborhood on the border of Harlem and Washington Heights. $20 per night, tax included, no curfew, no chores and no lockout during the day. Hostel sleeps about 25 with 6 people per dorm. Check-in between 9am and 10pm. You will need to book in advance for Aug and Sept. Also a limited number of double rooms, available only on a first-come, first-served basis, for $25 per person per night. Take the A or D train to 145th St – the hostel is just above the subway station.

Jazz on the Park, 36 W 106th St (at Central Park W), NY 10025 ☎932-1600, fax 932-1700; www.jazzhostel.com. Barely a year old, this groovy bunkhouse, just a stone's throw from the park, boasts a TV/games room, rooftop barbecues, the *Java Joint Café* plus activities galore. The rooms, sleeping between 2 and 14, are clean, bright and air-conditioned. Beds cost between $27 and $37 a night (including tax, linen and a light breakfast). Reservations essential June–October and over Christmas and New Year's.

McBurney YMCA, 24th St and 7th Ave, NY 10011 ☎741-9226, fax 741-8724. Situated in Chelsea, just behind 23rd St. Single rooms are $57 or $59, doubles $69, triples $89 and quads $100. Air conditioning costs $3 extra per night, there's a refundable $5 key deposit and a limit of 25 consecutive days on any stay. Showers and restrooms are shared. Out-of-town reservations require a $57 deposit or may be guaranteed with a major credit card at least two weeks in advance. Free use of gym, pool and sauna don't cover up the grim, institutional feel of the place, and it's only recommended if all else fails.

Uptown Hostel, 239 Lenox Ave at 122nd St, NY 10026 ☎666-0559. Small hostel just north of Central Park and well situated for the clubs, restaurants and shopping in Harlem. Clean bunk beds for 25–30 people a night at $14 per person.

Accommodation

Accommodation

Decent-size hall bathrooms, communal kitchen and pleasant common area. Summer lockout from 11am–4pm. Very helpful staff.

Vanderbilt YMCA, 224 E 47th St (between 2nd and 3rd aves), NY 10017 ☎756-9600. Smaller and quieter than most of the hostels mentioned above, and neatly placed in midtown Manhattan, just five minutes' walk from Grand Central Station. Inexpensive restaurant, swimming pool, gym and laundromat. Singles $68, doubles $81. All rooms are air-conditioned; handicapped access and non-smoking rooms available.

Webster Apartments, 419 W 34th St, NY 10001 ☎967-9000, outside city ☎1-800/242-7909, fax 268-8569. One of the nicer women-only residences, founded in 1923, the *Webster* has 390 rooms and is mainly for single women working short-term in the city, rather than for tourists. Though the rooms – all singles, with shared bathrooms on each floor – are small and rudimentary, the communal areas are the building's greatest asset. There are several lounges with piano or stereo, a large dining room and a library, and, best of all, the plant-filled rooftop terrace which has amazing views, and the lovely, leafy private garden, which is an invaluable haven in New York. The immediate location outside is unexciting, but it is well placed for access to all parts of the city. Contact the *Webster* on a weekday to set up a personal interview. The weekly rate is $162–199 depending on salary with special rates for students and those on an internship. This includes two meals a day and daily maid service; all prices before taxes. Visitors can stay for $60 a night including full breakfast.

Westside YMCA, 5 W 63rd St, NY 10023 ☎875-4173 or 875-4273, fax 875-1334. A wonderfully located *Y* right next to Central Park and Lincoln Center with single rooms for $68/$95 per night (with or without bath), doubles for $80/$110, and free use of two pools, saunas, gym and sports facilities. All rooms A/C. Early booking advisable.

Camping

You won't necessarily save a great deal on any of the above options by camping. Most of the campgrounds that could conceivably serve New York City are situated so far out as to make travel in and out a major cost and inconvenience. These are the most accessible:

Battle Row Campground, Claremont Rd, Old Bethpage, Long Island ☎516/572-8690. Situated a short way up Long Island and accessible via the Long Island Railroad. Site is open April to November; cost is $8.75 and up for a tent site, first-come, first-served.

Hecksher State Park Campground, East Islip, Long Island ☎516/581-2100. Beautiful situation and easier to reach than *Battle Row* – from Penn Station take the Long Island Railroad to Great River Station. Open mid-May to mid-September; prices around $14 for a tent and up to six people. In each party one of the campers must be over 21.

Liberty Harbor, Liberty Harbor Marina, 11 Marin Blvd, Jersey City, NJ 07302 ☎1-800/646-2066. Situated in New Jersey, right across the Hudson and 4 blocks north of the Grove St "PATH" Station (which will take you into Manhattan for just $1), this is probably your best bet. A tent site costs $25 while a motor home or trailer is $40. Call for directions. Reservations are strongly advised for the summer.

Bed and breakfast

Choosing a **bed and breakfast** can be a good way of staying bang in the center of Manhattan at a reasonably affordable price. But don't expect to socialize with your temporary landlord/lady – chances are you'll have a self-contained room and hardly see them – and don't go looking for B&Bs on the streets; all rooms – except for a few which we've found off the beaten track (listed below) – are let out via the following official agencies and they all recommend making your reservations as far in advance as possible – especially for the cheapest rooms.

B&B agencies

Bed and Breakfast in Manhattan, PO Box 533, NY 10150-0533 ☎472-2528, fax 988-9818. The ex-casting director head of this agency really knows her hosts and will match you up with the place and people where you'll be most comfortable. (She comes with many accolades from successful clients.) Rooms in a hosted apartment cost between $90 and $110 a night; unhosted places go for between $100 and $350 a night; an unusual option are the semi-hosted places (a private floor in a townhouse, for example) where you have plenty of space and privacy but there are hosts on hand for advice if you need it.

Bed and Breakfast Network of New York, Suite 602, 134 W 32nd St, NY 10001 ☎645-8134, Mon–Fri 8am–6pm. Growing network with hosted singles for $70–100, doubles $100–150; prices for unhosted accommodation run from $120 to luxury multibedded apartments for $450. Weekly and monthly rates also available. For an assured booking write at least a month in advance, though short-notice reservations should be made by phone.

City Lights Bed & Breakfast, PO Box 20355, Cherokee Station, NY 10021 ☎737-7049, fax 535-2755. More than 400 carefully screened B&Bs on its books, with many of the hosts involved in theater and the arts. Hosted singles run from $90–115, doubles $90–135. Unhosted accommodation costs $130 to $300 per night depending on whether it's a studio or four-bedroom apartment. Minimum stay two nights, with some exceptions. Reserve well in advance.

Colby International, 139 Round Hey, Liverpool L28 1RG, England ☎0151/220 5848, fax 0151/228-5453.

If you want guaranteed B&B accommodation, Colby International is without doubt your best bet – based in the UK, they are Europe's oldest and best established agency. Excellent-value rooms start at $75 single; $95 double. Self-catering apartments $120–300 per night. Book in advance, though they can take last minute reservations. Very knowledgeable staff.

Gamut Realty Group, 301 E 78th St, ground floor, NY 10021 ☎879-4229, outside city ☎1-800/437-8353, fax 517-5356; *Gamut@GamutNYC.com*; *www.GamutNYC.com*. Fully automated agency that can fax or email you sample listings of available rooms and apartments for nightly or longer-term stays. Hosted singles and doubles for $110–115; unhosted studio apartments for $120–145, and one-bedroom apartments for $145 and up. Has accommodation all over Manhattan, some in luxury buildings or artists' lofts.

New World Bed & Breakfast, Suite 711, 150 5th Ave, NY 10011 ☎675-5600, outside city ☎1-800/443-3800, fax 675-6366. Hosted singles and doubles $85–110; studios $90–165. Larger apartments are available from $130 up; call for a brochure.

Urban Ventures, PO Box 426, NY 10024. Personal visitors welcome at Suite 1412, 38 W 32nd St ☎594-5650; *www.nyurbanventures.com*. The first and largest registry in the city. Their budget double rooms go for $75 upwards, "comfort range" rooms (with private bath) from about $95. If you wish, you can rent a studio apartment minus hosts from $105 a night. Three nights minimum stay for hosted B&B, four nights for unhosted. You can book up until the last minute.

West Village Reservations, 425 W 13th St, NY 10014 ☎614-3034, fax 674-3393; *www.westvillagebb.com*. Small, personalized B&B/short-term apartment agency specializing in Downtown accommodation in both West and East villages. Singles $80–110; doubles

Accommodation

Accommodation

$95–135; self-catering apartments $110–175.

B&B properties

Bed & Breakfast on the Park ☎718/499-6115, fax 718/499-1385; *www.bbnyc.com.* In Brooklyn. A handsome 1892 limestone townhouse with views over Prospect Park, with seven double rooms ranging $125–275 a night.

Chelsea Brownstone ☎206-9237, fax 388-9985. Conveniently located on a safe, quiet street in Chelsea, this well-maintained, family-run brownstone contains a number of private, self-contained apartments costing between $120 and $150 per night (with discounts for stays of more than a week), each with their own TV, phone, bathroom and fully equipped kitchen. One has its own patio, and one has access to a back garden. Best to book well in advance by phone, though last-minute bookings are possible.

Foy House ☎718/636-1492. Beautiful 1894 brownstone in heart of Park Slope, with rooms for $95 (shared bath), $125 (private bath) and a garden suite for $150. Close to subways. Smoking not permitted.

Inn at Irving Place, 56 Irving Place, NY 10003 ☎1-800/685-1447 or 533-4600, fax 533-4611; *www.innatirvingplace.com.* It costs $295–450 a night for one of the 20 rooms – each named after a famous architect, designer or actor – in this handsome pair of 1834 brownstones, which must rank as one of the most exclusive guesthouses in the city. Frequented by celebrities, the *Inn* offers five-course "European Teas" along with free access to a local gym. A very special place for a very special occasion.

New York Bed and Breakfast, 134 W 119th St at Lenox Ave ☎666-0559, fax 663-5000. A lovely old brownstone in the heart of Harlem, just north of Central Park with nice double rooms for $45 a night for two people. The owner also runs the *Uptown Hostel* a few blocks up

the road with beds for $14 a night (see p.315).

Hotels

Most of New York's **hotels** tend to be in midtown Manhattan, which is fine if you want to be close to theaters and the main tourist sights, and fairly near the Park, but is hardly the loveliest part of the city. Unfortunately there aren't many other options, but if you're going to be spending a lot of time in the East or West Village or SoHo, you might want to try one of the handful of Downtown hotels. Or if museums, the Park and Lincoln Center are more your kind of thing, you should try the Upper West Side. The selections below cover the range from the cheapest to New York's most luxurious and/or hippest, the latter a small and select group of "special" places for which you may consider it worth paying over the odds. Finally, it's worth mentioning the latest fad in hotel design and marketing – the so-called "boutique" hotel. These are typically smaller, European in style, establishments, where what you sacrifice in room size is more than compensated for in terms of comfort, style and ambience.

Within each area group below, the hotels are listed alphabetically. For an overview of where to find a listed hotel, see the map at the back of the book.

Taxes and other hidden costs

The bad news is that there are **additional taxes** added to your hotel bill, and that hotels will nearly always quote you the price of a room *before* tax. The good news is that New York City and State hotel taxes have dropped quite considerably in the past few years. Taxes will add 13.25% to your bill (State taxes are 8.25%, city taxes 5%), and there is also an additional $2 per night "occupancy tax." This will add about $15 to a $100 room. The **price codes** at the end of each of the following listings represent the price of the hotel's cheapest double room inclusive of all taxes.

Hotel booking services

Accommodations Express
☎ 609/391-2100 or 1-800/444-7666, fax 609/525-0111; *www.accommodationsexpress.com.*

CRS ☎ 305/408-6100 or 1-800/950-0232, fax 305/408-6100; *www.reservation-services.com.*

Express Reservations (weekdays only) ☎ 1-800/356-1123 or 303/440-8481, fax 303/440-0166; *www.hotel-res.com.*

Hotel Reservations Network ☎ 1-800/964-6835; *www.hoteldiscount.com.*

Meegan's Services ☎ 1-800/441-1115 or 718/995-9292, fax 718/917-6278.

The Room Exchange 450 7th Ave, NY 10123 ☎ 1-800/846-7000 or 212/760-1000, fax 212/760-1013; *www.hotelrooms.com.*

Most hotels do not offer free **breakfast**, though continental breakfasts, for what they're worth, are becoming increasingly popular. If you have to pay for breakfast you can probably get better value at a nearby diner (we've listed some choices on p.342). At the more upmarket hotels, **tipping** will absorb at least some of your cash: unless you firmly refuse, a bell hop will grab your bags when you check in and expect $5 for carrying them to your room. It's appreciated if you tip the cleaning staff when you leave. Watch out for the luxuriously stocked **minibars**, with booze and chocolate goodies at astronomical prices, and hotel shops that sell basic necessities at three times the street price. Also, it's worth checking on the hotel's **phone charge** policy. Some hotels will charge you even if you call toll-free numbers or use your own calling card, so beware.

Discounts and special deals

With almost any hotel room it's possible to **cut costs** slightly if you can fill a double with three or even four people. This is normal practice in the US and managements rarely mind, providing an extra bed or two for an extra $20 or so. If you're staying long enough, you may also be able to pay a special **weekly rate**, maybe getting one night in seven for free. Some hotels also lay on special **weekend discounts** if you stay two nights or more, though these are often not available during the busiest season from September through December. Discounts may also be available in the form of off-season **summer rates**, **promotional specials** or **corporate rates**.

Accommodation

One good thing: almost all US hotels, even the most basic, have TVs in their rooms as a matter of course – so if you've spent all your money on a bed for the night you can always curl up in front of David Letterman. Also, in some of the pricier hotels, especially those recently renovated, you may find in-room CD players, VCRs (along with a CD/video library at the front desk), modem connections, a health club and business center. For full hotel listings and prices, consult the New York Convention and Visitors Bureau **leaflet**, *Hotels in New York City*, available from one of their offices.

Hotel price codes

The **code** in the following listings refers to the price of a hotel's cheapest double room and includes all taxes (State tax at 8.25%, city tax at 5% and occupancy tax of $2). Where there's a significant seasonal variation, the high season rate is usually given. Where prices are based on a per-person rate, however, they are given in dollars. Hotels in each geographical section are listed alphabetically.

① under $100
② $100–130
③ $130–160
④ $160–200
⑤ $200–250
⑥ $250–300
⑦ $300–350
⑧ over $350

Accommodation

Downtown: Below 14th Street

Cosmopolitan, 95 W Broadway, NY 10007 ☎1-888/895-9400 or 566-1900, fax 566-6909; *www.cosmohotel.com*. Great TriBeCa location, with smart, well-maintained rooms at an affordable price. Excellent value. ③.

Holiday Inn Downtown, 138 Lafayette St, NY 10013 at corner of Howard St ☎966-8898 or 1-800/HOLIDAY, fax 966-3933. Located just north of busy Canal St where Chinatown spills over into Little Italy, this idiosyncratic member of the well-known chain is also a stone's throw from SoHo and TriBeCa, where hotels are few and far between. Though the rooms themselves are small for the highish price, the rates fluctuate according to availability so booking early should get you a better deal. ④.

Larchmont, 27 W 11th St (between 5th and 6th), NY 10011 ☎989-9333, fax 989-9496. Fairly new budget hotel in the heart of Greenwich Village, on a beautiful tree-lined street, just off 5th Ave. Hotels are a rarity in this residential area, so this is a real find. Rooms are small but nicely decorated and clean, and all have TV, air conditioners, phones and wash-basins. Small kitchens and bathrooms with showers are on each corridor. Prices include continental breakfast. Very small singles as low as $70 a night plus tax, with doubles at ②.

Marriott Financial Center, 85 West St (between Carlisle and Albany sts), NY 10006 ☎385-4900. On summer weekends, doubles at ⑤ make this civilized business hotel with superb views of the World Trade Center, the Hudson and New York Harbor fairly affordable. Weekdays are a different story, but the high rates (⑧) are well worth it. Service is excellent.

The Mercer, 147 Mercer (at Prince St) ☎1-888/918-6060 or 966-6060, fax 965-3838. The last word in discreet "boutique" chic. Rooms are stylish with simple furnishings, high-ceilings, walk-in closets and over-sized bathrooms. Smart lobby with the staff dressed in Isaac Mizrahi designed uniforms. All this in the heart of SoHo. ⑧

Millennium Hilton, 55 Church St (between Fulton and Dey St), NY 10007 ☎693-2001 or 1-800/752-0014. The *Millennium* is designed for style-conscious businesspeople on expense accounts – but lower weekend rates with full breakfast and use of the hotel pool and fitness center make it well worth consideration. Relax in the sky-lit swimming pool overlooking St Paul's Chapel, enjoy your cocktail at the bar overlooking the World Trade Center Plaza, or eat in two, not overly expensive, restaurants, or the café. Rooms are fairly luxurious: ask for one with a view (unforgettable) of the Brooklyn Bridge. ⑦, but sometimes as low as ⑥ on weekends, and a slightly better choice than the nearby *Marriott*.

Off SoHo Suites, 11 Rivington St (between Christie and Bowery), NY 10002 ☎1-800/OFF-SOHO or 979-9808; fax 979-9801; *www.offsoho.com*. These small, apartment-style suites are well located for Little Italy, East Village, SoHo and Chinatown, but are in a rather depressed Lower East Side neighborhood. Very good value for two or four, the suites include fully equipped kitchen, TV, and use of laundry and fitness room. This part of town can be a little desolate after the sun sets – you may want to make use of the hotel's discount cab service at night. Suite for two with a shared bathroom ②; suites for four with private bath ⑤.

Soho Grand Hotel, 310 W Broadway at Grand St, NY 10013 ☎1-800/965-3000 or 965-3000, fax 965-3200; *www.sohogrand.com*. Great location at the edge of SoHo, and many guests exude the attitude that comes with the territory: rock stars, models, actors and the like. Still, the staff is surprisingly helpful, the rooms are stylishly appointed, if a bit small, with classic New York photographs from a local gallery and an optional goldfish (ask and you shall receive). The hotel also boasts a bar, restaurant and fitness center. ⑧.

Washington Square, 103 Waverly Place, NY 10011 ☎777-9515 or 1-800/222-0418, fax 979-8373. An ideal location: bang in the heart of Greenwich Village, just off Washington Square Park, and a stone's throw from the NYU campus. The rooms are more than adequate and some have views over the park. Continental breakfast and use of the exercise room are included in the price. Book two months in advance in the summer. ③

Chelsea and the West Side: 14th to 36th streets

Allerton Hotel, 302 W 22nd St (corner of 8th Ave), NY 10011 ☎243-6017; *www.allerton-hotel.com*. This family-run hotel on a quiet, tree-lined residential street has fair-sized, well-maintained rooms, some with kitchenette. Excellent value. ②.

Arlington Hotel, 18 W 25th St (between 6th Ave and Broadway), NY 10010 ☎645-3990, fax 633-8952. Chinese-run hotel with very good prices near Madison Square Park and equidistant from Downtown and Midtown. Clean rooms and free continental breakfast ②; with two-room suites for four at ③.

Best Western Manhattan, 17 W 32nd St (between 5th Ave and Broadway), NY 10001 ☎1-800/567-7720 or 736-1600, fax 563-4007. Recently refurbished hotel (previously called the *Aberdeen*) whose tranquil lobby offers a welcome respite from this rather hectic part of town. ④.

Chelsea, 222 W 23rd St (between 7th and 8th aves), NY 10011 ☎243-3700, fax 675-5531; *www.hotelchelsea.com*. One of New York's most noted landmarks, both for its ageing neo-Gothic building and, more importantly, its long list of alumni, from Dylan Thomas to Bob Dylan, including Sid Vicious and his girlfriend Nancy (see p.122 for the full cast). It's still something of a haunt of musicians and art-school types, though these days it's as much an apartment building as a hotel with its majority of guests being semi-permanent. If you check into the *Chelsea* you may find yourself staying in somebody's apartment, surrounded by their belongings. Ask instead for a renovated room with polished wood floors, log-burning fireplaces, and plenty of space to cram a few extra friends into. ③ for a studio room, ⑥ for a suite.

Accommodation

Chelsea Inn, 46 W 17th St, NY 10011 ☎645-8989, fax 645-1903. A long-term hostel as well as hotel in the heart of Chelsea, not too far from the Village. It's low on services and a bit rough around the edges, but with a choice of guestrooms (with or without bathroom), studios and suites, most equipped with kitchenettes, it can be a good deal. Studio with bathroom ④.

Chelsea Savoy Hotel, 204 W 23rd St, NY 10011 ☎929-9353, fax 741-6309. A few doors away from the *Chelsea Hotel*, the *Savoy* has none of its neighbor's funky charm but its rooms, though small, are clean and nicely decorated and the staff helpful. ③.

Comfort Inn Manhattan, 42 W 35th St, NY 10001 ☎947-0200. The best thing about the *Comfort Inn* is the deluxe continental breakfast and newspapers they give you in the elegant lobby each morning. It's a solid, good-value place to stay but the management can be unhelpful – you may not be able to see a room before you hand over your cash, for example. ⑤; summer weekends can drop to ④.

Herald Square, 19 W 31st St (between 5th Ave and Broadway), NY 10001 ☎1-800/727-1888 or 279-4017, fax 643-9208; *www.heraldsquarehotel.com*. Home of the original *Life* magazine, and with Philip Martiny's sculptured cherub known as *Winged Life* still presiding over the doorway of this Beaux Arts building. Inside it's meticulously clean and somewhat soulless. ①; triples and quads ④. Very small single rooms go for as low as $60 a night with shared bathroom.

Pennsylvania Hotel, 401 7th Ave, NY 10001 ☎1-800/223-8585 or 736-5000, fax 502-8712. Boasting the same

Accommodation

telephone number since 1917 (the "Pennsylvania six five thousand" of the Glenn Miller song), this is located across from Madison Square Garden, and offers every possible convenience, though you can't help thinking it looked better when it was a good old-fashioned hotel. ④, dropping to ③ in summer.

Southgate Tower, 371 7th Ave (at 31st St) NY 10001 ☎1-800/ME SUITE or 563-1800, fax 465-3697. A member of the excellent Manhattan East Suites chain, *Southgate Tower* is opposite Penn Station and Madison Square Garden. All double rooms are suites with kitchens. ⑥.

Stanford, 43 W 32nd St (between Broadway and 5th Ave), NY 10001 ☎1-800/365-1114 or 563-1500, fax 629-0043. Clean, inexpensive hotel on the block known as "Little Korea." As well as the basic hotel facilities the *Stanford* offers free continental breakfast and valet laundry, a cocktail lounge and good Korean cuisine in the very relaxing surroundings of the *Gam Mee Ok* restaurant. ④.

Wolcott, 4 W 31st St (between 5th Ave and Broadway), NY 10001 ☎268-2900. A surprisingly relaxing budget hotel, with a gilded, ornamented lobby and more than adequate rooms, all with bathrooms. A very good deal. ④ with occasional promotional offers at ③.

Midtown East: 14th to 45th streets

Carlton, 22 E 29th St (at Madison Ave), NY 10016 ☎1-800/542-1502 or 532-4100, fax 889-8683; *www.carltonhotelny.com.* A fairly well-priced, nicely modernized hotel in a Beaux Arts building. There are two pluses: you're in the safe residential area of Murray Hill, and you also get room and valet service, not often associated with hotels in this price bracket. Note that the *Carlton* is in the process of renovation – including moving its entrance onto Madison Ave – which should result in a rise in prices. ⑤ with summer rates at ④.

Carlton Arms, 160 E 25th St (between 3rd and Lexington aves), NY 10010 ☎679-0680. A strong contender for the city's latest bohemian hangout, with eclectic interior decor by would-be artists, very few comforts, and a clientele made up of Europeans, down-at-heel artists and longstay guests. People either love it or hate it – so check it out before you commit yourself to staying. Discount rates available for students and foreign travelers, with an extra 10 percent discount if you pay for seven nights in advance. Singles can be as low as $57 plus tax. Reserve well in advance for summer. ①.

Doral Park, 70 Park Ave (at 38th St), NY 10016 ☎1-800/223-6725 or 687-7050, fax 808-9029; *www.doralparkavenue. com.* A multimillion-dollar restoration has turned the *Doral Park* into one of the snazziest deluxe hotels, with re-creations of classical friezes and frescoes and original designs for lighting and furnishings. Service is excellent. ⑤.

Gershwin Hotel, 7 E 27th St, NY 10016 ☎545-8000, fax 684-5546. A young persons' hotel just off 5th Ave in the Flatiron district which also functions as a hostel (see p.315). There are 110 private double rooms with bathrooms which cost between $95 and $135 a night (plus tax); weekends are $12 extra. Imaginatively decorated with a Pop Art theme, the *Gershwin* has an astroturfed rooftop (where parties are held on the weekend), a small bar, a well-priced restaurant and a friendly staff. Try to book well in advance. ②.

Gramercy Park, 2 Lexington Ave (at 21st St), NY 10010 ☎1-800/221-4083 or 475-4320, fax 505-0535. Pleasant enough hotel perfectly situated in a delightful area next to the only private park in the city (residents get a key) and popular with Europeans. It also boasts one of the most unsuspecting bar scenes in New York; where a mix of hotel guests, locals and publishing types buzz over stiff drinks. Non-smoking rooms can be requested, though not guaranteed, and there's a mixture of fair-

ly recently renovated and tatty rooms. ④.
One bedroom family suites from ⑤. The
#6 train is one block away.

Grand Union, 34 E 32nd St (between
Madison and Park aves); ☎683-5890,
fax 689-7397. Comfortable budget
hotel, recently renovated. Well situated
and well priced, perfect for those who
won't mind its lackluster appearance.
②.

Jolly Madison Towers, Madison Ave at
38th St, NY 10016 ☎802-0600, fax 447-
0747. Italian chain hotel with restful,
clean, fairly spacious rooms and the
nautical themed *Whaler Bar*. ⑤; occasional promotional rates at ④.

Madison Hotel 21 E 27th St (between
Madison and 5th aves), NY 10017 ☎1-
800/9MADISON or 532-7373, fax 686-
0092; *www.madison-hotel.com*. Clean, if
basic, rooms, all with A/C and private
bathroom and a free continental breakfast. At ② for a double room this is a
good deal.

The Metro, 45 W 35th St, NY 10001
☎1-800/356-3870 or 947-2500, fax
279-1310; *www.hotelmetronyc.com*. A
very stylish hotel – recently renovated,
with a delightful rooftop terrace, spacious
communal areas, clean rooms and the
highly recommended *Metro Grill* restaurant on the ground floor. ⑤; summer
specials at ④.

Morgans, 237 Madison Ave (between
36th and 37th sts), NY 10016 ☎1-
800/334-3408 or 686-0300, fax 779-
8352. Created by the instigators of
Studio 54, this is self-consciously – and
quite successfully – one of the chicest
flophouses in town. Discreet furnishings
are by André Putnam, and a good-looking young staff clothed in Klein and
Armani are welcoming. Although the
black-white-gray decor is starting to look
too self-consciously 1980s and hence a
little passé, stars still frequent the place,
able as they are to slip in and out unno-
ticed. And you do get a jacuzzi, a great
stereo system and cable TV in your
room. Great bar downstairs. ⑦; promotional specials at ⑥.

Murray Hill Inn, 143 E 30th St (between
Lexington and 3rd aves), NY 10016 ☎1-
888/996-6376 or 683-6900, fax 545-
0103; *www.murrayhillinn.com*. It's easy
to see why young travelers and backpackers line the *Inn's* narrow halls.
Although the rooms are smallish and
basic, they are air-conditioned and all
have telephone, cable TV, and sink;
some also have private bathrooms. With
a friendly staff and a residential locale
that offers a breather from the bustle.
Rates per room are: singles for $75; dou-
bles are $95 (shared bath); $125 (private), additional costs if more than two
in a room. They also have weekly rates
for single rooms. ①.

Quality Hotel 5th Avenue, 3 E 40th St,
(between 5th and Madison), NY 10016
☎1-800/228-5151 or 447-1500. This is
a motel-style hotel, with helpful, friendly
staff, owned by a Canadian chain.
Rooms are bright and well-furnished,
and there's a very comfortable lounge
and restaurant on the premises. ⑥; with
weekend rates from ④.

Roger Williams, 131 Madison Ave (at
31st St), NY 10016 ☎877/847-4444 or
448-7000, fax 448-7007; *www.
rogerwilliamshotel.com*. At some point
during its $2 million "boutique" renova-
tion, this hotel made a right turn onto
Madison Ave and its prices shot up
exponentially. Still, Rafael Vinoly's mellow, Scandinavian/Japanese fusion
rooms and fluted zinc pillars in the
lobby, make it well worth the extra
bucks. ⑦, with occasional summer specials at ⑤.

Seventeen, 225 E 17th St (between 2nd
and 3rd), NY 10003 ☎475-2845, fax
677-8178. Budget accommodation as
you'd expect it to look: rudimentary bedrooms, and bathrooms on the corridors
that have seen better days. But
Seventeen is clean and friendly, and it
can't be beaten either for location – it's
on a pleasant, tree-lined street between
2nd and 3rd aves; and very handy if you
want to spend your time in the East
Village, only a few blocks away. Weekly
rates, including tax, come to $467 (single

Accommodation

room) or $580 (double); nightly, including tax is $75 (single) or $90 (double). ①.

Shelburne Murray Hill, 303 Lexington Ave (between 37th and 38th), NY 10016 ☎1-800/ME SUITE or 689-5200; *www.mesuite.com*. Luxurious Manhattan East Suite hotel, in the most elegant part of Murray Hill. All the rooms have kitchenettes and the *Secret Harbour Bistro* presents, each Wednesday and Thursday, a Maryland Crab Bash. ⑥; promotional rates drop to ④.

Thirty-One, 120 E 31st St (between Lexington and Park aves), NY 10016 ☎685-3060, fax 532-1232. A new hotel in Murray Hill brought to you by the folks who own *Seventeen*. The rooms are clean and the street is quiet and pleasant. ① (shared bathroom) or ③ (private bathroom).

UN Crowne Plaza, 304 E 42nd St (between 1st and 2nd aves), NY 10017 ☎986-8800, fax 986-1758. One of the more stylish hotels close to Grand Central Station, in the unique residential area built in the 1920s known as "Tudor City." Rooms are deluxe, with minibar, cable and in-room movies, hair dryer and opulent marble bathrooms. There's a fitness room and sauna too. Service is excellent. ⑧; promotional specials at ⑤.

Midtown West: 36th to 60th streets

Algonquin, 59 W 44th St (between 5th and 6th aves), NY 10036 ☎1-800/555-8000 or 840-6800. New York's classic literary hangout, as created by Dorothy Parker and her associates and perpetuated by Noel Coward, Bernard Shaw, Irving Berlin and most names subsequent. Decor remains little changed except in the bedrooms, which have all been refurbished to good effect. ⑦; summer rates at ⑤.

Ameritania Hotel 54, 230 W 54th St (at Broadway), NY 10019 ☎1-800/922-0330 or 247-5000; *www.ameritaniahotel.com*. One of the coolest looking hotels in the city. The well-furnished rooms come with marble bathroom, cable TV and CD play-

er; and there's a bar/restaurant off the high-tech, neo-classical lobby. $5 off their basic rates if you mention *Rough Guides*. ⑤, with July/August specials at ③.

Amsterdam Court Hotel, 226 W 50th St (between Broadway and 8th), NY 10019 ☎1-800/341-9889 or 459-1000, fax 265-5070. Well positioned and eminently affordable, this is currently undergoing a stylish renovation – and with it a rise in prices. Still worth a look. ②.

Best Western Ambassador, 132 W 45th St (between 6th Ave and Broadway), NY 10036 ☎1-800/242-8935 or 921-7600, fax 719-0171. Located on the edge of the theater district, this newly renovated hotel (previously the *Chatwal Inn* and the *Travelodge Midtown*) is an oasis of calm in a bustling part of town. Suites are very spacious and can easily accommodate four people; decor is in the English Georgian tradition. Continental breakfast is included in the price. ⑤, with rates dropping as low as ② in January and February.

Best Western President, 234 W 48th St (between 8th Ave and Broadway), NY 10036 ☎1-800/826-4667 or 246-8800, fax 974-3922. A solid, easy-going hotel with an Italian restaurant, and offers small, fairly recently renovated rooms. ③.

Best Western Woodward, 219 W 55th St (at Broadway), NY 10019 ☎1-800/336-4110 or 247-2000. Recently renovated Beaux Arts building and handy for the Museum of Modern Art. ③.

Broadway Inn, 264 W 46th St, NY 10036 ☎1-800/826-6300 or 997-9200, fax 768-2807; *www.broadwayinn.com*. Cozy, resonably priced bed-and-breakfast hotel in the heart of the theatre district on the corner of charmless 8th Ave, but a skip away from Times Square and Restaurant Row. All rooms are pleasantly decorated and have private bathrooms. Continental breakfast is included in the price and all guests get a 20 percent discount at the restaurant downstairs. ③.

Comfort Inn Midtown, 129 W 46th St (between 6th and 7th aves), NY 10036 ☎1-800/567-7720 or 221-2600, fax 764-7481. A clean, if somewhat bland, chain hotel (previously known as the *Remington*) in Times Square. ④; promotional specials can drop rates to ②.

Edison, 228 W 47th St (just west of Broadway), NY 10036 ☎1-800/637-7070 or 840-5000, fax 596-6850; *www.edisonhotelnyc.com*. The most striking thing about the distinctly funky 1000-room *Edison* is its beautifully restored Art Deco lobby, a re-creation of the original from 1931. All rooms have been recently renovated. ③.

Essex House, 160 Central Park S (between 6th and 7th aves), NY 10019 ☎1-800/WESTIN-1 or 247-0300, fax 315-1839. A beautiful hotel for a special occasion, *Essex House* has been restored by new Japanese owners to its original Art Deco splendor. The best rooms have spectacular Central Park views. Despite the excellent service the atmosphere is not at all formal or hushed. ⑦, dropping to ⑤ on summer weekends.

Gorham, 136 W 55th St (between 5th and 6th aves), NY 10019 ☎1-800/735-0710 or 245-1800, fax 582-8832. European-style Midtown hotel renovated in 1992. Handy for Central Park and the Museum of Modern Art. All rooms have self-service kitchens; suites have whirlpool baths. Doubles ⑥, with occasional promotional specials for ⑤.

Helmsley Windsor, 100 W 58th St (between 6th and 7th aves), NY 10019 ☎1-800/221-4982 or 265-2100, fax 315-0371. Enjoy coffee on the house each morning in the richly decorated, wood-paneled lobby. Like the other Helmsley hotels, the *Windsor* has a pleasantly old-fashioned air, with plenty of useful extras in the rooms. Central Park is a short walk away. ⑤; summer weekends at ④.

Howard Johnson Plaza, 8th Ave at 52nd St, NY 10019 ☎581-4100. Not the usual bland, chain hotel you might have expected. Here you'll find well-decorated rooms, space to spread out and a "Beefsteak Charlie's" restaurant. ④.

Iroquois, 49 W 44th St (between 5th and 6th aves), NY 10036 ☎840-3080, fax 398-1754. What was once a haven for down-at-heel rock bands and rebels without a cause is currently reinventing itself as a somewhat stuffy "boutique" hotel with health center, library and five-star restaurant. ⑥ with special summer rates at ⑤.

Mansfield, 12 W 44th St, NY 10036 ☎1-877/847-4444 or 944-6050, fax 764-4477; *www.mansfieldhotel.com*. A "boutique" make-over has transformed a rather mangy Midtown flophouse into one of the loveliest hotels in the city. Winner of the 1997 Interiors Magazine Best Hotel Design, the *Mansfield* manages, somehow, to be both grand and intimate. With its copper-domed salon, its clubby library, its nightly jazz and Tamara de Lempicka's "Polo Player" welcoming guests from behind the front desk, there's a charming, slightly quirky feel about the place – an echo, perhaps, of its turn-of-the-century role as a pad for New York's most eligible bachelors. ⑤.

Marriott Marquis, 1535 Broadway at 45th St, NY 10036 ☎398-1900. The enormous *Marquis* is perfect for conference and convention guests; it's worth dropping by to gawk at the split-level atrium and to ride the glass elevators to NY's only revolving bar and restaurant, but the rooms themselves are modest for the high price. ⑤.

Mayfair, 242 W 49th St (between Broadway and 8th Ave), NY 10019 ☎1-800/556-2932 or 586-0300, fax 307-5226; *www.mayfairnewyork.com*. This new, non-smoking, "boutique"-style hotel, across the street from the St Malachay Actor's Chapel, has beautifully decorated rooms, its own restaurant and a charming "old-world" feel, emphasized by the historic photographs on loan from the Museum of the City of New York that are everywhere on display. ⑤, with summer rates at ③.

Accommodation

Accommodation

Michelangelo, 152 W 51st St (between 6th and 7th aves), NY 10019 ☎1-800/237-0990 or 765-0505, fax 541-6604. An Italian chain took over recently and created a palazzo on Broadway, with acres of marble, and no expenses spared in the luxurious and super-large rooms. In terms of decor, the suites offer a choice of Art Deco, Empire or Country French styles. On weekends and some holidays prices drop from ⑦ to ⑥.

Milford Plaza, 270 W 45th St (8th Ave between 44th and 45th sts), NY 10036 ☎1-800/221-2690 or 869-3600, fax 944-8357. Rooms are tiny in this Ramada hotel and the atmosphere is impersonal, but hordes of theater-goers still flock here for the "Lullabuy [sic] of Broadway" deals. ④.

Millennium Broadway, 145 W 44th St (between Broadway and 6th), NY 10036 ☎1-800/622-5569 or 768-4400, fax 768-0847. Black marble and wall-to-ceiling art works dominate the *Millennium Broadway's* lobby; the sleek lines continue in the beautiful off-white bedrooms. A good place to come for an intimate after-theater supper, even if you decide against the (justifiably) high room rates. ⑦; weekends sometimes ⑥.

Novotel, 226 W 52nd St (on Broadway), NY 10019 ☎315-0100, fax 765-5369. Chain hotel large enough to offer a decent range of facilities, while small enough to avoid anonymity. The decor is sophisticated, the food good, as you would expect from a French-owned establishment, and the hotel offers special rooms for the disabled. ⑦, with summer rates dropping to ⑥.

Paramount, 235 W 46th St (between Broadway and 8th Ave), NY 10036 ☎764-5500. For the past few years now, this has been one of the hippest places in town to stay, popular with a pop and media crowd, who come to enjoy an interior designed by Philippe Starck and be waited on by sleek young things. The branch of *Dean and DeLuca* off the lobby, the *Whiskey Bar* and the newly opened *Coco Pazzo Teatro* restaurant are all busy and fun. ⑥, with summer rates at ⑤.

Park Savoy, 158 W 58th St (between 6th and 7th aves), NY 10019, ☎245-5755. With cozy rooms, all with private bath, and just a block from Central Park this hotel offers good value for the area. ④.

Plaza, 768 5th Ave (at Central Park S), NY 10019 ☎1-800/527-472 or 759-3000, fax 546-5234. The last word in New York luxury, at least by reputation, and worth the money for the fine old pseudo-French chateau building if nothing else. Doubles start at $365 and run to $15,000 (no kidding!) for a specialty suite, and that's before taxes. A place to stay if someone else is paying. ⑧.

Portland Square, 132 W 47th St (between 6th and 7th aves), NY 10036 ☎1-800/388-8988 or 382-0600, fax 382-0684; *www.portlandsquarehotel. com*. A theater hotel since 1904, and former home to Jimmy Cagney and other members of Broadway casts, the *Portland* has a few more comforts than its sister hotel *Herald Square*, but is still a budget operation, good for a few nights' sleep but not for hanging out in. The cheapest rooms go as low as $60 plus tax for a small single with a shared bathroom. Doubles ②; triples and quads ③.

Quality Midtown, 59 W 46th St (between 5th and 6th aves), NY 10036 ☎1-800/567-7720 or 719-2300, fax 790-2760. Near Diamond Row and a stone's throw from Rockefeller Center. All rooms in this comparatively inexpensive chain hotel come with private bath, cable TV and telephone. Free continental breakfast. ④.

Royalton, 44 W 44th St (between 5th and 6th aves), NY 10036 ☎1-800/635-9013 or 869-4400, fax 869-8965. Owned by the same management as the *Paramount*, the *Royalton* attempts to capture the market for the discerning style-person, with more interiors designed by Philippe Starck. It has tried to become the *Algonquin* of the 1990s, and is as much a power-lunch venue for NYC's media and publishing set as a place to stay. ⑦, with discounts sometimes available at ⑥.

St Moritz on the Park, 50 Central Park S (59th St between 5th and 6th aves), NY 10019 ☎1-800/444-4786 or 755-5800, fax 688-6619. If you'd like a view of Central Park but you don't want to pay the $300–400 a night room rates of the other hotels around here, then this is the place for you. The catch is that the rooms are tiny, so enjoy the views and then spend time in *Max's Bar*. ④.

Salisbury, 123 W 57th St, NY 10019 ☎246-1300. Good service, large rooms and proximity to Central Park are the main attraction of this recently renovated hotel. A good deal. ④.

Warwick, 65 W 54th St (at 6th Ave), NY 10019 ☎1-800/223-4099 or 247-2700. Stars of the 1950s and 1960s – including Cary Grant, Rock Hudson, the Beatles, Elvis Presley and JFK – stayed at the *Warwick* as a matter of course. Although the hotel's lost its showbusiness cachet now, it's a pleasant place to stay, from the elegant lobby to the *Ciao Europa* restaurant and *Randolph's* cocktail lounge. The staff are helpful and friendly. ⑦, with summer specials at ⑤.

Wellington, 7th Ave at 55th St, NY 10019 ☎1-800/652-1212 or 247-3900, fax 581-1719; *www.wellingtonhotel.com*. The *Wellington's* gleaming, mirror-clad lobby is the result of recent renovations, and similar attention has been paid to the rooms. Some have kitchenettes, and family rooms offer two bathrooms. Close to Carnegie Hall and handy for Lincoln Center, the hotel's a fair price for this stretch of town. ④.

Westpark, 308 W 58th St (between 7th and 8th aves), NY 10019 ☎1-800/248-6440 or 246-6440, fax 246-3131. The best rooms look out over Columbus Circle and the southwestern corner of Central Park. Although the staff are somewhat offhand, it's great value for the area, especially handy for Lincoln Center and the Park. ②.

Wyndham, 42 W 58th St (between 5th and 6th aves), NY 10019 ☎1-800/257-1111 or 753-3500, fax 754-5638. The *Wyndham's* large rooms and suites vary enormously in terms of decor and it's the kind of place where the hotel's devotees – many of whom are Broadway actors and actresses – request their favorite each time they stay. All the rooms are homely, though, and the place feels more like an apartment building than a hotel. ③. Summer specials ②.

Accommodation

The Mid and Upper East Side: East 45th to 92nd streets

Beekman Tower, 3 Mitchell Place (between 49th St and 1st Ave), NY 10017 ☎1-800/ME-SUITE or 320-8018, fax 465-3697. One of the more expensive of the Manhattan East Suite hotel chain and also one of the most stylish. All the rooms are suites and come with fully-equipped kitchens. The Art Deco top floor, *Top of the Towers*, restaurant offers superb East Side views. ⑦; in summer prices can drop to ④. Weekend and extended stay rates also available.

Box Tree, 250 E 49th St (between 2nd and 3rd aves), NY 10017 ☎758-8320, fax 308-3899. Thirteen elegant rooms and suites fill two adjoining eighteenth-century townhouses and make one of New York's more eccentric lodgings. The Egyptian-, Chinese- and Japanese-style rooms have fur throws on the beds, great lighting, and ornaments and decoration everywhere. A credit of up to $100 toward the hotel bill is offered to weekend diners in the excellent *Box Tree Restaurant*. Worth it for a splurge. ⑥; weekend rates are $100 more expensive.

Drake, 440 Park Ave at 56th St, NY 10022 ☎421-0900. A first-class hotel, and member of the Swissotel chain, with bustling cocktail bar and superb French restaurant, a spa and gym. This used to be an apartment building, so the rooms are large. ⑤.

Elysee, 60 E 54th St, NY 10022 ☎753-1066. The *Elysee* was until recently famed for its eccentric, theatrical style, but sadly enthusiastic new management have refurbished the whole place in the

Accommodation

best possible taste. A fine place to stay, if you can afford it though, with a great bar and close to 5th Ave. ⑤.

Fitzpatrick Manhattan, 687 Lexington Ave (between 56th and 57th sts), NY 10022 ☎355-0100, outside city ☎1-800/367-7701, fax 355-1371. Opened in 1991, this handsome Irish-owned and Irish-themed hotel is perfectly located for Midtown shopping, Upper East Side museums and Central Park. A hearty Irish breakfast is served all day long. Doubles and suites for ⑥, with weekend deals available.

Habitat, 130 E 57th St (between Lexington and Park), NY 10022 ☎1-800/255-0482 or 753-8841, fax 829-9605; www.stayinny.com. Centrally located in a very classy part of town, this hotel was once the women-only *Allerton House*. Its rooms are small, yet perfectly adequate. ④ (with private bathroom); ② (without). Note that the hotel is currently being remodeled and these rates may increase once that work is complete.

Lowell, 28 E 63rd St, NY 10021 ☎838-1400. Madonna loved to work out so much when she stayed here (so it's said) that the *Lowell* built a suite with its own fitness machines. Then Roseanne and Tom Arnold stayed in it and now you can too, for just $815, plus taxes. Along with the room you get great views of New York, a woodburning fireplace and tons of posh seclusion. ⑧.

Lyden House, 320 E 53rd St (between 1st and 2nd aves), NY 10022 ☎1-888-6070. One of the friendliest of the Manhattan East Suite chain, situated in exclusive Sutton Place, where even the smallest suites are apartment-sized by New York standards and could sleep four (second two adults at $20 plus tax per person per night). All suites have eat-in kitchens and have the luxury of a maid to do the dishes. ⑥; off-season rates can drop to ⑤ if available.

Mark, Madison Ave at E 77th St, NY 10021 ☎744-4300, fax 744-2749. One of a handful of NYC hotels which really does live up to its claims of sophistica-tion and elegance. A recent renovation has kitted the lobby out with Biedermeier furniture and sleek Italian lighting. In the guestrooms, restaurant and invitingly dark *Mark's Bar*, there's a similar emphasis on the best of every-thing. ⑦.

Pickwick Arms, 230 E 51st St, NY 10022 ☎355-0300. A thoroughly pleasant bud-get hotel, and for the price, one of the best deals you'll get on the East Side. All 400 rooms are air-conditioned, with cable TV, direct-dial phones and room service. The *Pickwick*'s open-air roof deck with stunning views and café are added attractions. A single room with a shared bathroom is $75. ①.

Pierre, 795 5th Ave at 61st St, NY 10021 ☎1-800/332-3442 (US), 1-800/268-6282 or 940-8101, fax 758-1615. The *Pierre* has consistently retained its repu-tation as one of New York's top hotels and is certainly luxurious. It was Salvador Dali's favorite place to stay in the city, but the only surreal aspects today are the prices. If these prohibit a stay, have afternoon tea in the gloriously frescoed *Rotunda*, or experience a power-break-fast in the *Café Pierre*. ⑦.

Roger Smith, 501 Lexington Ave at 47th St, NY 10017 ☎1-800/445-0277 or 755-1400, fax 319-9130. One of the best Midtown hotels with very helpful service, individually decorated rooms, a great restaurant, and art works and sculpture on display in the public areas. Breakfast is included in the price, along with a refrigerator and coffee-maker in all rooms and VCRs in most with 2000 videos available from the hotel's library. Popular with bands, and guests who like the arty ambience. ⑥; summer rates drop to ④.

Roosevelt, 45 E 45th St (at Madison Ave), NY 10017 ☎1-888/TEDDY NY or 661-9600, fax 885-6161. The *Roosevelt*'s heyday was in the Railway Age, when its proximity to Grand Central Station meant that thousands of travel-ers came to stay. It has recently under-gone extensive renovations, with new suites and the prices to match. Has nice, if traditional, bar and restaurant. ⑥; summer rates at ⑤.

San Carlos, 150 E 50th St (between Lexington and 3rd aves), NY 10022 ☎1-800/722-2012 or 755-1800, fax 688-9778; *www.sancarloshotel.com*. The *San Carlos* is well-located in the East 50s near plenty of bars and restaurants, and most of the large rooms have fully equipped kitchenettes. This is a useful standby when everything else is booked solid. ⑤; summer rates can drop to ④.

Sherry Netherland, 781 5th Ave, NY 10022 ☎355-2800. The place to rent a whole floor and live in permanently, if a large sum of money ever comes your way. Many of the *Sherry Netherland*'s guests already do this, and the service is geared to satisfying their every whim. Room service is by renowned restaurateur Harry Cipriani. ⑧.

Surrey, 20 E 76th St, NY 10021 ☎288-3700. A genteel Manhattan East Suite hotel, in the heart of the "Museum Mile." Recently renovated, with a new fitness center. ⑦.

W, 541 Lexington Ave (between 49th and 50th sts), NY 10022 ☎755-1200, fax 319-8344. If the crowd hanging out in the *Whiskey Blue* bar, dining at *Heartbeat* or just posing on the sidewalk are anything to go by, the *W*, which opened its doors in December 1998, might well be the hippest dosshouse in town. Clean, stylish rooms. ⑦ – though weekend specials can drop to ⑥.

Waldorf-Astoria, 301 Park Ave at E 50th St, NY 10022 ☎1-800/WALDORF or 355-3000, fax 872-7272. One of the great names among New York hotels, and restored to its 1930s glory, making it a wonderful place to stay if you can afford it or someone else is paying. ⑧; promotional rates can drop to ⑤.

Wales, 1295 Madison Ave at 92nd St, NY 10128 ☎1-877/847-4444 or 876-6000. Almost in Spanish Harlem, though very definitely Upper East Side in feel. Excellent prices for the high standard of accommodation: the original oak moldings and mantles have been lovingly restored, and tea, cookies and classical music are served up every afternoon in the parlor. ⑥ or summer rates, when available, at ⑤.

The Upper West Side: Above 60th Street

Amsterdam Inn, 340 Amsterdam Ave (at 76th St), NY 10023 ☎579-7500, fax 579-6127; *www.amsterdaminn.com*. From the owners of the lauded *Murray Hill Inn* this new addition is centrally located within walking distance of Central Park, Lincoln Center and the Museum of Natural History. Rooms are very basic (no closets) but clean. Twenty-four hour concierge and a friendly, helpful staff, plus rooms have TVs, phones and maid service. Singles with shared bath ①; doubles ①. Rooms with private bath ②.

Beacon, 2130 Broadway at 75th St, NY 10023 ☎1-800/572-4969 or 787-1100, fax 724-0839; *www.beaconhotel.com*. A pleasantly buzzing hotel with fair-sized rooms, deep closets, color cable TV and fully equipped kitchenettes. *Zabar's*, NYC's famous gourmet deli, is just a few blocks up Broadway. ③.

Lucerne, 201 W 79th St (at Amsterdam Ave), NY 10024 ☎1-800/492-8122 or 875-1000, fax 721-1179. This beautifully restored 1904 brownstone, with its extravagantly baroque entrance, charming rooms, and friendly, helpful staff is just a block away from the Natural History Museum and close to the liveliest stretch of the Columbus Ave scene. ⑤, with summer rates at ④.

Malibu Studios, 2688 Broadway (at W 103rd St), NY 10025 ☎222-2954, outside the city 1-800/647-2227, fax 678-6842. Excellent value budget accommodation. A fair step from the heart of things up at the Morningside Heights end of the Upper West Side, but adjacent to the 103rd St stop on the #1 and #9 subway lines, and within walking distance of plenty of restaurants and nightlife due to the nearby presence of Columbia University. Prices, all before

Accommodation

Accommodation

taxes, are $49 for a single room ($99 with private bathroom), $69 for a double ($109 with private bathroom). Also triples and quads. Mention the *Rough Guides* and pay for three nights or more upfront and get a 10 percent discount on any room. Friendly, helpful management too. Credit cards not accepted. ①.

Mayflower, 15 Central Park W at 61st St, NY 10023-7709; ☎1-800/223-4164 or 265-0060, fax 265-0227; *www. mayflowerhotel.com*. A slightly down-at-heel but very comfortable hotel a few steps from Central Park and Lincoln Center. It's so close to the latter, in fact, that performers and musicians are often to be seen in the hotel's very good . *Conservatory Café.* ⑤, with occasional promotional rates at ③.

Milburn, 242 W 76th St ☎362-1006 or 1-800/833-9622, fax 721-5476. Welcoming and well-situated suite hotel, great for families, which has recently been renovated in very gracious style. There are studios and one-room suites with fully equipped kitchenettes, bathrooms and TV.

Practical extras are in-room safes, laundry and maid service. ④.

Radisson Empire, 44 W 63rd St (at Broadway), NY 10023 ☎1-888/822-3555 or 265-7400, fax 315-0349. A lavishly renovated member of the Radisson chain, the *Empire* will suit music lovers – not only is it opposite the Metropolitan Opera House and Lincoln Center, but also each (box-sized) room comes equipped with excellent CD player and VCR. ⑦, but summer rates can drop to ⑥.

Riverside Tower, 80 Riverside Drive at W 80th St, NY 10024 ☎1-800/724-3136 or 877-5200, fax 873-1400. Although the rooms – all with small kitchenettes – are fairly basic, it's the location in this exclusive and safe neighborhood, flanked by one of the city's most beautiful parks and with stunning views of the Hudson River, which sets this budget hotel apart from the others. And it's worth noting that quads work out at around $35 per person, per night. Reservations a few weeks in advance are recommended. ①.

Chapter 17

Eating

There are plenty of reasons why New Yorkers like to **eat out** so much. Many of them work long hours and don't have time to cook dinner; still more live in very small apartments, and restaurants serve as their dining rooms. Of course, there are other reasons – New York is a rich port city that can get the best foodstuffs from anywhere in the world, and, as a major immigration gateway, it attracts chefs who know how to cook the world's cuisines properly, sometimes exceptionally. So not only can you get Senegalese, French provincial, or any other kind of food you can think of, you can also get outstanding versions of it. As you stroll through the heavenly odors that emanate from the city's delis, bagel shops, Chinese restaurants and upscale eateries, it's hard not to work up an appetite.

Budget food

In the early morning you'll see frazzled New Yorkers lining up in front of **street vendors** for a breakfast on the run of bagels, doughnuts and coffee. Summer's chilly treats include ice-cream bars, soft ice cream and *helados* – shaved ice with flavored syrup poured on top – while street staples like hot dogs, gyros, New York pretzels and honey-roasted nuts are available all year round. Street food makes for a cheap, greasy and sometimes sublimely satisfying meal, or for around $1.50 you can always get a slice of **pizza**. Of course, there are the

predictable *Burger King* and *McDonald's* **burger chains**, but with the abundance of good, cheap food available, you shouldn't have to resort to them.

For **quick snacks**, many delis also do ready-cooked hot meals. Though most are truly less than appetizing, delis are a sure-bet, and often all-night, place to get a salad, sandwich or quick pre-cooked meal in a pinch. **Diners** are a little more expensive, but you get the advantage of a table, seat, bathroom and possibly a quiet pay telephone. They serve filling breakfasts, burgers, sandwiches and basic American fare from a usually enormous menu, which often includes good-value lunchtime specials, either at formica-topped tables or at stools set around a counter. Prices are around $6 for a heavily garnished burger and fries, $8 or so for anything more elaborate, making diners a good value for a filling lunch or dinner on a budget, and they have a distinctly overdone style with an ambience all their own.

Breakfast

Although many hotels serve a breakfast of some kind, it is usually much cheaper (not to mention more interesting) to go out to a coffee shop for the first meal of the day. Most diners offer **breakfast specials** until 11am, allowing you to eat and drink until you're full for under $7. Figuring prominently on **breakfast menus** are sausages and bacon (streaky, cut very thin and fried to a crisp), along with eggs, toast, waffles and pancakes – the latter

Eating

thick and heavy, and usually served with a smothering of maple syrup. Be prepared to be interrogated as to how you want your eggs, and be ready to snap back with an answer – breakfast may be taken seriously, but it is never taken slowly. Basically, "sunny side up" means eggs fried unturned and "over easy" turned for a few seconds only. A typical breakfast special usually includes some combination of eggs (fried or scrambled), home fries (chunky potatoes fried with onions) or French fries, toast, juice and coffee (with free refills) for a fixed price.

Lunch

Most restaurants in New York open at lunchtime. In addition to diners, one of the best **lunchtime deals** can be had in **Chinatown**, where you can get a massive plate of meat with noodles or rice for around $5, or, if you're feeling a little more adventurous, feast at a dim sum restaurant for $7–8. Dim sum (literally "your heart's delight") consists of small dishes that you choose from a moving trolley and pay for at the end, according to the empty dishes in front of you.

Another option for lunch – and one that's not just limited to Manhattan – is to get a **sandwich "to go"** from a **deli**. Once again, be prepared for a quick-fire question-and-answer session with the counter person, who will not only ask which kind of bread you want – white, whole wheat, rye or French – but also whether you want mayonnaise, lettuce or anything else. Deli sandwiches are custom-built and constrained only by your imagination, so bear in mind the size of the thing you're creating; if you hear them say "full house" it means you've ordered everything. You can expect to pay around $4–6 for a sandwich, and it is easily a meal in itself.

Brunch

Brunch can also be a good-value deal, and is something of a New York institution, usually served on weekends between 11am and 4pm. Lox and cream cheese on a bagel, omelettes, French toast, eggs Benedict and pancakes are favorite brunch items. Many restaurants compete for customers by laying on a special well-priced brunch menu – sometimes including a free cocktail – basically, because the place specializes in dinner fare and wants to fill some seats in the afternoon. There's a list of recommended brunch venues on p.362.

Bar food and bargains

Bars are often the cheapest places to eat in New York, but they're by no means the only budget option. In the ritzier bars there are almost invariably hot **hors d'oeuvres**, laid out during happy hour between 5pm and 7pm Monday to Friday; one of the city's best scams if you're on a tight budget. For the price of a single drink (it won't be cheap) you can stuff yourself silly on pasta, seafood, chili or whatever. Remember, though, that the more you look like an office-person (it's for them, after all, that the hors d'oeuvres are put out) the easier you'll blend in with the freeloading crowds.

Most **bars** serve food of one kind or another, and you'll find a substantial – and inevitable – crossover between our "Eating" and "Drinking" chapters. Even in the lowliest bar there's a good chance they'll cook you at least a burger or a plate of potato skins, and many places offer a full menu, particularly the more upscale Irish and American hangouts. Though bars stay open late, their kitchens are usually closed by midnight. Bars that serve serious food are detailed along with restaurant listings later in this chapter.

For **further cheap eating options**, be sure to look also at the places detailed in the following "Restaurants" section. Although Chinese and Eastern European food, and of course pizza, are perhaps the only cuisines that are reliably cheap pretty much everywhere, there are bargains to be had in every category.

Coffee, tea and soft drinks

Served black or "regular" (with cream or milk, though in other parts of the States

Eating

Service, tipping . . . and home deliveries

Whatever you eat, **service** is likely to be decent, since not only is the notion of customer service deeply ingrained into the American psyche, but the system of tipping, whereby (in New York) you double the figure on the bill for tax (8.25 percent) to work out the minimum tip, can make the staff almost irritatingly attentive. There's no way round this: if you either refuse or forget to tip there's little point in going back to that restaurant. As far as actual **payment** is concerned, most – although by no means all – restaurants take credit/charge cards

(if you use one you'll find a space left for you to write in the appropriate tip); travelers' checks are also widely accepted (see Basics, "Money and Banks"). If you're not in the mood to get dressed up or fight the crowds, you might consider having food **delivered** to your hotel or host's home. These days almost every kind of New York neighborhood restaurant offers this service for free if the order exceeds a given minimum (generally $10–15) and you're within a reasonable distance – though you should, of course, tip the bearer.

"regular" coffee is black coffee), **coffee** is usually freshly brewed (high-maintenance New Yorkers consume coffee in large quantities), though it frequently tastes stale. You can get coffee "to go" in most delis, and many restaurants serve a "bottomless cup," i.e. you can keep asking for refills at no extra charge. More and more restaurants (and even some delis) provide brewed decaffeinated coffee (if you see two glass-globe pots of coffee behind the counter, the one with an orange or green band around the neck is the brewed decaf). Coffee is now big business in New York; in addition to the omnipresent (and generally good) Starbucks and Timothy's chains, coffeehouses of all sorts have popped up in the city in the last few years, offering a wide array of coffee concoctions and baked treats. **Tea** is also becoming more popular and will normally be served straight or with lemon; if you want milk request it, and specify if you want it hot or it will come ice cold. **Soft drinks** (sodas) come in caffeine-free versions as well. These are drunk in three sizes: small (large), regular (bigger) and large (practically a bucket); stick to cans and bottles so you'll know what you're in for.

New York has a number of **cafés** and **tea rooms**, which don't always serve alcohol but concentrate instead on pro-

viding fresh coffee and tea, fruit juices, and pastries and light snacks, and sometimes full meals. Many of the more long-established cafés are Downtown, congenial places with a European emphasis; indeed they're often determinedly Left Bank in feel (like the grouping at the junction of Bleecker and MacDougal sts) and perfect for lingering or just resting up between sights. The more upscale Midtown **hotels** are good places to stop for tea too, if you can afford the prices they charge for the English country-house atmosphere they often try to contrive.

American food and ethnic cuisines

American cooking, as served by New York restaurants, tends to be served in huge portions. Salads are frequently eaten with meals, not as a main course but as an appetizer, and ordering one entails fielding more rapid questions as to the kind of dressing you want. Main dishes include steaks and burgers, fried chicken, and often a choice of fish and seafood. Side dishes will almost certainly include a choice of French fries and baked potato, and a vegetable. Ordering a burger may be more complicated than you're used to: they're treated like regular steaks and you'll be asked how you want them cooked – rare, medium or

Eating

well-done. (Only have them rare if you're sure of the quality of the meat.) You'll also find many American restaurants offering a rich array of regional specialties such as **Southern, Cajun, Southwestern** and **Tex-Mex**, everything from jambalaya to grits to barbecue spare ribs. **Continental** cuisine, is generally a hybrid of American, Italian and French influences, featuring pastas, meat and poultry in light sauces, fish, seafood and an array of nightly specials.

Be prepared to be confronted with a startling variety of **ethnic cuisines**. In New York, none has had so dominant an effect as Jewish food, to the extent that many **Jewish** specialties – bagels, pastrami, lox and cream cheese – are now considered archetypal New York. Others retain more specific identities. **Chinese** food, available not just in Chinatown but all over Manhattan, includes the familiar Cantonese, as well as spicier Szechuan and Hunan dishes – most restaurants specialize in one or the other. Chinese prices are usually among the city's lowest, especially in the numerous takeout places (which are not very good). **Japanese** food is generally expensive – but very good. New Yorker's insist upon fresh, high-quality sushi and there is plenty of it throughout Manhattan. Other Asian cuisines include **Indian**, increasingly popular though still not as ubiquitous – or as good – as their British counterparts (with a few exceptions), and a broad and increasing sprinkling of **Thai, Korean, Vietnamese** and **Indonesian** restaurants, all of which tend to be pricier than Chinese but not prohibitively so.

Irish food dominates the city's pubs, with corned beef (more like salt beef than the tinned British bully), various forms of potatoes, and shepherd's pie. **Italian** cooking is also widespread and not terribly expensive, especially if you stick to pizza or pasta; **Spanish** food, though not as common, can be a good deal if you order the huge seafood paella dishes – an economical night out for those in a group (and don't forget the large pitchers of sangria). **French** restaurants tend to be pricier, although there are an increasing number of bistros and brasseries turning out authentic and reliable French nosh for attractive prices. The newest trend is **Belgian** food; a surprising number of Belgian brasseries and steak frites joints have opened in the last year, making it the hot new cuisine and the subject of numerous articles in New York papers.

There is also a whole range of **Eastern European** restaurants – Russian, Ukrainian, Polish and Hungarian – located mainly on the lower and upper East Side, that serve well-priced, filling fare (emphasis on the filling). **Caribbean, Central** and **South American** restaurants are on the rise in New York, and often offer a good deal and a large, satisfying meal. Other sundry places include **Cuban-Chinese** and **Kosher-Chinese** hybrids, and any number of **vegetarian** and **wholefood** eateries to cater to any taste or fad. The key is to keep your eyes peeled and not be afraid to be adventurous. Eating is one of the great joys of being in New York, and it would be a shame to waste it on the familiar.

Restaurant prices

New York's ethnic make-up is at its most obvious and accessible in the city's restaurants. Don't, however, make the mistake of assuming all ethnic food is necessarily inexpensive. Often it's not. You pay Manhattan's highest **prices** for the better Italian, French and Japanese eateries; Greek and Spanish food, too, often work out to be expensive, and really only Chinese, Jewish, Mexican and Eastern European are dependably low-budget. One other thing to bear in mind is that these days many of New York's most interesting and affordable ethnic restaurants are in the Outer Boroughs.

The **selections** offered here run from the best, more expensive New York restaurants to the bare-bones basic, but the emphasis throughout is on getting the best **value for your money** – most selections shouldn't break the bank, and you'll often find special deals or set menus that make them even better. The listings that follow are by neighborhood and then country of origin or ethnic group, with closing sections on seafood and vegetarian options.

Where you'll find ethnic food

African

Budget **African** restaurants are becoming increasingly common, their pulse-based meals almost always including vegetarian options. The most common are **Ethiopian**, often designed with great atmosphere and furnished with low-to-the-ground wicker seats and tables (not recommended for people with bad backs). The food is eaten with your hands, with the aid of a delicious flat bread to sop up the sauce.

American and continental

In addition to the forementioned coffee shops and bars serving generic **American** food such as burgers and fried chicken, there are numerous regional American restaurants serving specialties from the **South**, such as grits, smothered pork chops and black-eyed peas; **Southwestern** food, including variations on Mexican dishes such as fajitas, as well as ribs, and cilantro-based sauces; **Cajun Creole**: jambalaya (a rich, spicy seafood and sausage stew) and crawfish. **Tex-Mex** cuisine is a common hybrid all over America (though not at its best in New York City) and despite varying quality, ensures a filling meal. In the past few years there has been an eruption of restaurants serving up **continental** cuisine: traditional American fare with a light and creative twist.

Asian

Chinese cuisine provides one of the city's best bargains, particularly if you pick up dim sum and other lunchtime specials. As far as areas go, Chinatown, not surprisingly, has the highest restaurant concentration, but there's another good contingent on the Upper West Side. More expensively (though still usually quite affordable), **Thai** food has become prevalent of late and you'll find Thai restaurants springing up all over Manhattan, as well as an increasing number of **Vietnamese** restaurants – many of which are, like Chinese spots, quite inexpensive and tasty. The high demand for **Japanese** specialties resulted in an explosion of sushi bars and such in the mid-1980s and it's still one of the city's most popular cuisines. Sushi is almost invariably expensive, but if you know where to go, it's possible to experiment without breaking the bank.

Caribbean, Central and South American

There has been an influx of **Cuban**, **Puerto Rican**, **Dominican** and **Jamaican** restaurants in New York, ranging from hole-in-the-wall rice and beans joints to wildly decorated restaurants serving jerk chicken, fricasseed goat and black bean soup. Fewer Central and South American restaurants exist here, though there are a few standouts. Both Caribbean and Latin American restaurants tend to be clustered in the same areas in Manhattan: the Lower East Side, Ninth Avenue in the forties, the Upper West Side, and, especially, Washington Heights, with a smattering elsewhere in the city.

Fish and seafood

Budget **fish restaurants** are a rarity in the city, especially since the area around the Downtown fish market was dolled up into the South Street Seaport. However, fish and particularly seafood remain something New York does extremely well, and a couple of the places listed here are among its most unbeatable culinary treats – though they rarely come cheap.

French and Belgian

French restaurants tend to trade on their names in New York: those that are good know it and make you pay accordingly, although a handful have slipped through with value-for-money intact. Beware the

Eating

Eating

wine list: prices for French vintages can be considerably more than Californian wines of comparable quality. As always, the least expensive route is to ask for the house wine – though even that can carry a hefty price at the better restaurants. **Belgian** restaurants have seen a surge in popularity in the last year, with a slew of new ones popping up all over the city. Their specialties are mussels, steak frites and *waterzooi* – a creamy chicken or fish stew.

Greek and Middle Eastern

While **Greek** restaurants are plentiful, few make it on to anyone's list of top ten places to eat: vegetarians in particular may be faced with few options, and for the best Greek cooking you should head for Astoria in Queens, home turf of most of the city's Greek population. Greek food tends to be pricey for what you get, as are the city's **Turkish** restaurants. Other than a handful of places serving pita-related snacks, **Middle Eastern** food was rather thin on the ground in Manhattan till recently; some splendid restaurants have now begun to crop up.

Indian

Indian restaurants are numerous, and like most other cuisines vary considerably in quality. The best deals (and generally the best meals) can be found on East 6th Street between First and Second avenues in the village, where there are a dozen or so Indian restaurants to choose from in the space of less than two blocks – local lore has it that they are really all serviced by one enormous kitchen underneath the street (not true). Another good place to look for Indian food is in mid-town Manhattan, along Lexington Avenue between 28th and 30th streets, called Little India because of the large number of Indian restaurants and food shops in the area (a great place to buy good curry ingredients).

Italian

Little Italy is the most obvious location for **Italian** food, though much of the area

is geared toward tourists these days and consequently can be pricey: pick with care. There are literally hundreds of Italian restaurants throughout the city, so again choose carefully – some are quite overpriced unless you stick to veggie pasta dishes. Or content yourself with pizza, you can rarely go wrong in this town, though most New Yorkers have strong opinions on where you can find the best slice of pizza around.

Jewish and Eastern European

The city's large **Jewish** community, most of which originated in Eastern Europe, means that kosher restaurants (serving dairy and non-dairy menus) are found all over town, with Manhattan's highest concentration in the East Village and Lower East Side. They cover all price ranges, but usually represent good, and very filling, value – as do the various and consistently delicious **Polish, Hungarian** and **Ukrainian** restaurants. Eastern European cuisine is famous for its dumplings, roast duck and stews, so be prepared for a heavy, fat- and choles-terol-saturated (albeit satisfying) meal.

Spanish

Downtown, in Greenwich Village especially, there are a number of enjoyable **Spanish** restaurants, mostly not too pricey, and certainly nowhere near as expensive as their French counterparts. Paellas, often intended to be eaten by two, will cut costs, and house wines are affordable, as are the usually excellent pitchers of sangria.

Vegetarian

Surprisingly, exclusively **vegetarian** restaurants are fairly rare in New York, although most places serve fish and poultry along with meatless dishes, and unless you're in a real carnivore's haven it's unusual to find a menu that doesn't have something completely meat-free. Italian, Chinese and Japanese restaurants are your best bets, if there's no vegetarian restaurant in sight.

Financial District and Civic Center

The culinary focal point of lower Manhattan is the Fulton Fish Market, so not surprisingly many of the restaurants in the **Financial District** and **Civic Center** serve seafood. Unfortunately, with few exceptions, most overcharge the power-broker lunch regulars for relatively unimpressive fare. And remember, the place revolves around trading hours, so many restaurants close early, and are closed or have reduced hours on weekends.

American and continental

Bridge Café, 279 Water St (at Dover St) ☎227-3344. They say there's been a bar here since 1794, but this place looks very up-to-the-minute. The good crab cakes come from the local fish market, and there are plenty of upscale beers with which to wash them down. The rare eighteenth-century frame house, painted red with black trim, is well worth a look. Entrees are priced at around $15.

Fraunces Tavern, 54 Pearl St (at Broad St) ☎269-0144. Where George Washington ate back when; they try to keep it as much like that as modern hygiene allows. The typical pub food's so-so, but atmosphere is the reason to come, as well as the museum.

Harry's at Hanover Square, 1 Hanover Square (between Pearl and Stone sts) ☎425-3412. Clubby bar that gets into its stride when the floor traders come in after work. Great burgers, but only open during the work-week.

Paris Café, 119 South St ☎240-9797. Established in 1873, this old-fashioned bar and restaurant serves plentiful servings of traditional American fare – including very fresh fish and seafood, entrees are about $18–25.

Caribbean, Central and South American

Radio Mexico, 259 Front St (at Dover St) ☎791-5416. Good Tex-Mex food in enjoyable, if often crowded surroundings.

Specialty eating

We've highlighted **particular types and styles of restaurant**, and places to eat that can't easily be listed elsewhere, and listed them in boxes on the following pages.

Bagels p.353

Breakfast: coffee shops and diners p.342

Brunch p.362

Coffee and tea p.352

Expense-account restaurants p.374

Restaurants with outdoor seating p.373

Restaurants with views p.368

Smoker-friendly restaurants p.348

24-hour food p.379

Eating

About the only such choice in the neighborhood, it's fun, reliable and has good margaritas.

Fish and seafood

Jeremy's Alehouse, 254 Front St (at Dover St) ☎964-3537. Once a waterside sleaze bar in the shadow of the Brooklyn Bridge, *Jeremy's* fortunes changed with the aggrandizement of the nearby South Street Seaport. However, it still serves well-priced pint mugs of beer and excellent fish fresh from the adjacent Fulton Fish Market, as well as burgers. Expect to spend $10–15 per person.

Johnny's Fish Grill, 4 World Financial Center ☎385-0333. Cozy New England-style seafood house featuring very fresh clams on the half-shell and superior grilled swordfish at moderate prices. Open Mon–Fri, serving dinner until 10pm.

Sloppy Louie's, 92 South St (at Fulton St) ☎509-9694. If you take in the South Street Seaport, you'll have a lot of fresh fish options. You could do worse than this clean, well-lit joint dating back to the 1930s, where you can get large combination platters of just about anything that comes out of the water.

Eating

Italian

Carmine's Bar and Grill, 140 Beekman St (at Front St) ☎962-8606. In business since 1903, this place specializes in Northern Italian-style seafood and exudes a comfortable, Financial-District ambience. Try a glass of the house wine and a bowl of linguini in clam sauce for lunch.

Chinatown, Little Italy and the Lower East Side

Three of New York's most prominent cuisines huddle together in these crowded adjoining neighborhoods. If authentic Chinese, Thai and Vietnamese food is what you're after, best head for the busy streets of **Chinatown**, where you'll find *the* best budget eats in the city. Little Italy and the Lower East Side are less of a bargain but as much of an institution. Mulberry Street is **Little Italy**'s main drag, and though often crowded with Bridge and Tunnel weekend tourists, the Southern Italian food and carnival atmosphere make dinner and coffee a worthwhile excursion. A turn down one street may leave you standing in front of an overpriced and quintessentially touristy restaurant; a turn down a nearby side street and you arrive at the **Lower East Side**, which at times seems like a throwback to early immigrant sweatshop days and others an overpriced and tourist experience. Either way, it's still the best place to get a pickle.

Bakeries and cafés

Café Gitane, 242 Mott St (between Prince and Houston sts) ☎334-9552. Sunny little café serving coffee and creative light lunch fare.

Caffè Biondo, 141 Mulberry St (between Grand and Hester sts) ☎226-9285. A little brick-walled cappuccino shop with excellent Italian desserts.

Caffè Roma, 385 Broome St (between Mulberry and Mott sts) ☎226-8413. Old Little Italy pasticceria, ideal for a drawn-out coffee and pastry. Try the homemade Italian cookies, exceptionally good cannoli (plain or dipped), or gelato at the counter in back.

Ceci-Cela, 55 Spring St (at Mulberry St) ☎274-9179. Tiny French patisserie with a stand-up counter and bench out front for immediate consumption of coffee and delectable baked goods. Croissants and palmiers are divine. Recommended.

Ferrara's, 195 Grand St (between Mott and Mulberry sts) ☎226-6150. The best-known and most traditional of the Little Italy coffeehouses, this neighborhood landmark has been around since 1892. Try the cheesecake, cannoli or granite (Italian ices) in summer. Outside seating. See also the newer Midtown locations at 1700 Broadway (at 53rd St) and 201 W 42nd St (at 7th Ave).

American and continental

Baby Jupiter, 170 Orchard St (at Stanton St) ☎982-2229. The front room serves a melange of tasty Asian-influenced Cajun barbecue dishes, all reasonably priced, while the back room serves as live music venue, no cover required. Can get pretty loud and rowdy later in the evenings, especially on weekends, so if you're coming for the food, come early. Otherwise, be prepared to party.

Asian

Bo Ky, 80 Bayard St (between Mott and Mulberry sts) ☎406-2292. Cramped Chinese-Vietnamese serving very inexpensive noodle soups and seafood dishes. The house specialty is a big bowl of rice noodles with shrimp, fish or duck.

Canton, 45 Division St at the Manhattan Bridge (between Bowery and Market sts) ☎226-4441. Fairly upscale compared to other Chinatown restaurants in terms of decor, style and service, but only marginally more expensive. Seafood is the specialty here; bring your own booze. Closed Mon and Tues.

Chinatown Ice Cream Factory, 65 Bayard St (between Mott and Elizabeth sts) ☎608-4170. A must after you've stuffed yourself in one of the restaurants nearby, but the wondrously unusual flavors make it good anytime. Specialties include green tea, ginger, almond cookie and lychee.

Excellent Dumpling House, 111 Lafayette St (between Canal and Walker sts) ☎219-0212. The thing to order is obviously the most excellent dumplings, any way you like them. Their scallion pancakes are also delicious.

Joe's Shanghai, 9 Pell St (between Bowery and Mott sts) ☎233-8888. New Chinatown entry of famed Queen's restaurant, this place is most always packed, with good reason. Start with the soup dumplings and work through some seafood dishes for the main course.

New York Noodle Town, 28 Bowery St (at Bayard St) ☎349-0923. Despite the name, noodles aren't the real draw at this down-to-earth eatery – the soft shell crabs are, spicy, crisp and delicious. Good roast meats and soups too.

Nice Restaurant, 35 E Broadway (between Catherine and Market sts) ☎406-9510. Vast Cantonese restaurant especially good for dim sum (and barbecued duck). Usually crowded and noisy, particularly on Sundays.

Nom Wah, 13 Doyers St (between Bowery and Pell sts) ☎962-6047. A fairly mellow, even downbeat place to enjoy tea and Chinese snacks.

Oriental Pearl, 103 Mott St (between Hester and Canal sts) ☎219-8388. Great dim sum served in a huge and hectic Chinatown restaurant.

Pho Pasteur, 85 Baxter St (between Canal and Bayard sts) ☎608-3656. Quick, hot and filling Vietnamese noodles. Very cheap.

Say Eng Look, 5 E Broadway (at Chatham Square) ☎732-0796. Good-value Shanghai restaurant that'll tailor your meal to fit your budget. Just tell them how much you can afford and they'll do the rest. They rarely miss.

Silver Palace, 50 Bowery (between Bayard and Canal sts) ☎964-1204. A predominantly dim sum restaurant. Take the escalator up to the enormous dining room with dragon pillars and peacock murals. Not recommended for vegetarians.

69 Mott Street Restaurant, 69 Mott St (near Bayard St) ☎233-5877. Small, clean spot serving amazingly cheap Cantonese food, including barbecued meats, squid and other treats. If you're really feeling adventurous you can try the pig bowel.

Thailand Restaurant, 106 Bayard St (at Baxter St) ☎349-3132. Well-priced Thai food, eaten at long communal tables. The deep sea bass, crispy and spicy, is a standout.

20 Mott, 20 Mott St (at Canal St) ☎964-0380. The place for shark's-fin soup and other Hong Kong-style seafood delicacies, as well as superb dim sum. Very popular, so expect to wait.

Wo Hop, 17 Mott St (between Canal St and Park Row) ☎267-2536. Heaping plates of food, many for less than $6. Anything with duck and noodles is recommended. Best of all, *Wo Hop* is open all night.

Wong Kee, 113 Mott St (between Canal and Hester sts) ☎226-9018 or 966-1160. Good, cheap, reliable Cantonese.

Caribbean, Central and South American

El Cibao, corner of Clinton and Rivington sts, no phone. The best of a slew of Dominican and Puerto Rican restaurants in the Lower East Side. Hearty and inexpensive fare, with great sandwiches, particularly the *pernil* (pork), toasted crisp in a sandwich press.

El Sombrero, corner of Stanton and Ludlow sts, no phone. Known to the local demimonde as "The Hat," this unprepossessing Mexican restaurant serves generous portions of wholesome food and wonderful frozen margaritas.

Fish and seafood

Vincent's Clam Bar, 119 Mott St (at Hester St) ☎226-8133. Little Italy restau-

Eating

Eating

rant serving fresh, cheap and spicy seafood dishes – clams, mussels and squid.

Italian

Benito I, 174 Mulberry St (at Broome St) ☎226-9171; **Benito II**, 163 Mulberry St (between Grand and Broome sts) ☎226-9012. The smell of garlic lures you in to these two homey little Italian spots that serve simple Sicilian fare. Closed Sun.

Grotta Azzurra, 387 Broome St (at Mulberry St) ☎925-8775. Bustling Little Italy institution that serves garlicky home-cooked Sicilian food. Closed Mon.

Il Fornaio, 132a Mulberry St (between Hester and Grand sts) ☎226-8306. Stylish, bright, tiled Italian restaurant with good lunch deals – fine calzone and pizza for $4. Affordable and tasty Southern Italian cooking: pastas, Italian stews and the like. Recommended.

La Luna, 112 Mulberry St (between Canal and Hester sts) ☎226-8657. One of Little Italy's longest established and best value choices. The attitude of the waiters is gruff, and the food middling to good – but the atmosphere is fun and it's a popular joint, packing in a crowd.

La Mela, 167 Mulberry St (between Grand and Broome sts) ☎431-9493. Established Little Italy restaurant serving food in huge family-style portions, with an equally huge selection of pastas. Best for groups.

Pellegrino, 138 Mulberry St (between Hester and Grand sts) ☎226-3177. Laid-back Little Italy restaurant serving good homemade pastas and other dishes for good prices.

Puglia, 189 Hester St (between Mulberry and Mott sts) ☎226-8912. One of Little Italy's more affordable (and tacky) restaurants, where they cut costs and sharpen the atmosphere by sitting everyone at communal trestle tables. Consistently good Southern Italian food, consumed loudly and raucously. Closed Mon.

Jewish and Eastern European

Katz's Deli, 205 E Houston St (between Essex and Ludlow sts) ☎254-2246. Cafeteria-style or sit down and be served. The overstuffed pastrami or corned beef sandwiches, doused with mustard and with a side pile of pickles, should keep you going for about a week. If you've seen the movie *When Harry Met Sally*, you may recognize this as the site of the famous "orgasm" scene. Also famous for their egg creams; open 7 days a week.

Ratner's, 138 Delancey St (between Norfolk and Suffolk sts) ☎677-5588. Massive kosher dairy restaurant, crowded at all times of the day. High on atmosphere, though on the pricey side. Some of the best prune Danishes in the city. Closed Sat.

Sammy's Roumanian Restaurant, 157 Chrystie St (between Delancey and Rivington sts) ☎673-0330. The food, at around $25 or so for a full meal, is undeniably good, but most people come for the raucous live music. *Zagat's* calls its huge platters of heavy, greasy food "a heart attack on a plate."

Yonah Schimmel's, 137 E Houston St (between Forsyth and Eldridge sts) ☎477-2858. Knishes, baked fresh on the premises, and wonderful bagels. Unpretentious and patronized by a mixture of wrinkled old men wisecracking in Yiddish and – on Sundays especially – young uptowners slumming it while they wade through the Sunday papers.

SoHo and TriBeCa

Still New York's two trendiest neighborhoods, in **SoHo** and **TriBeCa** you often pay for the vista rather than the victuals. Even so, there are appropriately divine meals, and on occasion even deals, to be had. And the people-watching's not bad either.

Bakeries and cafés

Bouley Bakery, 120 W Broadway (between Duane and Reade sts) ☎964-2525. *Wunderkind* David Bouley's latest, a tiny bakery-restaurant with truly great breads and baked goods, as well as light food, all at the star-chef prices you might expect.

Once Upon a Tart, 135 Sullivan St (between Houston and Prince sts) ☎387-8869. Tiny café serving good coffee and homemade muffins and scones.

Yaffa Tea Room, 19 Harrison St (at Greenwich St) ☎966-0577. Hidden in an unassuming corner of TriBeCa next to the *Yaffa Bar*, this restaurant serves Mediterranean-style dinners, good brunch and a cozy high tea (reservations required). Eclectic decor composed of flea market bric-a-brac finds.

African

Abyssinia, 35 Grand St (between 6th Ave and W Broadway) ☎226-5959. A comfy Ethiopian restaurant popular with a youthful crowd. A good array of vegetarian dishes.

Ghenet, 284 Mulberry St (between Houston and Prince sts) ☎343-1888. New, atmospheric Ethiopian restaurant serving a changing menu of unusual spicy dishes that you can eat with your hands and sop up with some good bread. Very inexpensive.

American and continental

Bodega, 136 W Broadway (between Thomas and Duane sts) ☎285-1155. Across the street from its pricier sister, *Odeon* (see below), this family-style restaurant serves great burritos, burgers and home-cooked specials all for under $12 per entree.

Bubby's, 120 Hudson St (between Franklin and N Moore sts) ☎219-0666. A relaxed TriBeCa restaurant serving homey health-aware American food. Great scones, mashed potatoes, rosemary chicken and soups. A good, moderately priced brunch spot too.

Cody's Bar and Grill, 282 Hudson (at Dominick St) ☎924-5853. A newish restaurant-bar with tasty pub food at reasonable prices, and a relaxed, homey atmosphere. A good option for this area, which lacks in choices.

Cupping Room Café, 359 W Broadway (between Broome and Grand sts) ☎925-2898. Absurdly quaint American restaurant that serves good wholesome food to live jazz on Friday and Saturday nights. An eclectic and creative mix of food styles, from basic American (good steaks) to Cajun to French, mostly well pulled off, with entrees running the gamut from $10 to $18. Brunches are excellent, with huge portions of freshly baked breads and muffins, though you'll probably need to wait. Recommended.

Jerry's Restaurant, 101 Prince St (between Greene and Mercer sts) ☎966-9464. Casual American-continental restaurant with a funky, upscale diner atmosphere. Good lox for brunch. Moderate prices. Closed Sun night.

La Cigalle, 231 Mott St (between Spring and Prince sts) ☎334-4331. A comfortable, quiet, garden-equipped eatery where you can have plain (pork chops, steak) or fancy (ceviche, farfalle), all good, relatively inexpensive, and served with a refreshing lack of pretension.

Moondance Diner, 80 6th Ave (between Grand and Canal sts) ☎226-1191. This authentic old diner car turns out cheap and filling meals of great burgers, onion rings, omelettes and apple pancakes. Open 24 hours on weekends.

Odeon, 145 W Broadway (at Thomas St) ☎233-0507. Very long-established restaurant featuring American/Continental/Mediterranean food served to a still largely chic clientele. Immortalized as the 1980s place to be in Jay McInerney's *Bright Lights Big City* (in fact a picture of it is on the cover of the book), it has shown surprising staying power, perhaps because the eclectic food choices are actually pretty good and the people-watching still can't be beat. Entrees go for around $15–20 and, on the whole, are worth it. Steak frites and crab fritters are recommended.

Prince Street Bar, 125 Prince St (at Wooster St) ☎228-8130. SoHo bar and

Eating

Eating

Breakfast: coffee shops and diners

You rarely have to walk more than a block or two in Manhattan to find somewhere that serves **breakfast**. Coffee shops and diners all over town serve up much the same array of discounted specials before 11am. But when you're desperate for a shot of early morning coffee, the following checklist should help you avoid traipsing too far from wherever you happen to be staying. You'll find full reviews elsewhere in this chapter; otherwise just expect standard American burgers, sandwiches and breakfasts.

DOWNTOWN MANHATTAN

Around the Clock, 8 Stuyvesant St (between 2nd and 3rd aves) ☎598-0402

Bendix Diner, 219 8th Ave (at W 21st St) ☎366-0560

Jones Diner, 371 Lafayette (at Great Jones St) ☎673-3577

Kiev, 117 2nd Ave (at E 7th St) ☎674-4040

KK Restaurant, 192–194 1st Ave (between E 11th and 12th sts) ☎777-4430

Odessa, 117–119 Ave A (between E 7th St and St Mark's Place) ☎473-8916

Triumph Restaurant, 148 Bleecker St (between LaGuardia and Thompson sts) ☎228-3070

Veselka, 144 2nd Ave (between E 9th St and St Mark's Place) ☎228-9682

Waverly Restaurant, 385 6th Ave (between W 8th St and Waverly Place) ☎675-3181

MIDTOWN MANHATTAN

Broadway Diner, 590 Lexington Ave (at E 52nd St) ☎486-8838; 1726 Broadway (at W 55th St) ☎765-0909

Chez Laurence, 245 Madison Ave (between E 37th and 38th sts) ☎683-0284

Ellen's Stardust Diner, 1377 6th Ave (at W 56th St) ☎307-7575; 1650 Broadway (at W 51st St) ☎956-5151

Jerry's Metro Delicatessen, 790 8th Ave (at W 48th St) ☎581-9100

Market Diner, 572 11th Ave (at W 43rd St) ☎695-0415

Olympic Restaurant, 809 8th Ave (between W 48th and 49th sts) ☎956-3230

Westway Diner, 614 9th Ave (between 43rd and 44th sts) ☎582-7661

UPTOWN MANHATTAN

EJ's Luncheonette, 433 Amsterdam Ave (between W 81st and 82nd sts) ☎873-3444

Googie's Diner, 1491 2nd Ave (at E 78th St) ☎717-1122

Gracie Mews Diner, 1550 1st Ave (at E 81st St) ☎861-2290

Tom's Restaurant, 2880 Broadway (at W 112th St) ☎864-6137

Tramway Coffee Shop, 1143 2nd Ave (at E 60th St) ☎758-7017

Viand, 673 Madison Ave (between E 61st and 62nd sts) ☎751-6622

---

restaurant used by the local art-house clique. Broad array of different dishes, and, for the area, not terribly expensive.

Rialto, 265 Elizabeth St (between Houston and Prince sts) ☎334-7900. Serious home-style American cooking in unlikely surroundings – a chic room with curved red leather banquettes, filled with beautiful, chic people, and a refreshing

garden in back. Not as expensive as the clientele looks either; entrees are around $15.

Silver Spurs, 490 LaGuardia (at W Houston St) ☎228-2333. Brighter and better sister to the lower Broadway original. Burgers are the specialty, cooked on an open grill under metal pots to lock in the juices. Inexpensive.

Tennessee Mountain, 143 Spring St (at Wooster St) ☎431-3993. Though situated in the heart of SoHo, this is a very un-SoHo-like restaurant, serving huge portions of barbecued meat and fish. Good value if you're hungry.

TriBeCa Grill, 375 Greenwich St (at Franklin St) ☎941-3900. Part-owned by Robert De Niro, so some people come for a glimpse of the actor when they should really be concentrating on the food – fine American cooking with Asian and Italian accents at around $30 a main course. The setting is nice too; an airy, brick-walled eating area around a central Tiffany bar (rescued from the legendary Upper East Side singles' hangout, *Maxwell's Plum*). Worth the money as a treat, despite the trendy scene and gawking tourists.

Zoë, 90 Prince St (between Broadway and Mercer St) ☎966-6722. One of SoHo's trendier places to eat, with a California-style setting and menu packed full of intriguing and often delicious New American cuisine combinations. Not cheap; entrees are around $16–25, but chic and highly popular.

Asian

Blue Ribbon Sushi, 119 Sullivan St (between Prince and Spring sts) ☎343-0404. Widely considered one of the best sushi restaurants in New York, the lines for a table can be long and it doesn't allow reservations. Our advice: have a cup of sake and relax.

Kelley and Ping, 127 Greene St (between Prince and W Houston sts) ☎228-1212. Sleek pan-Asian tea room and restaurant that serves a tasty bowl of noodle soup. Dark wooden cases filled with Thai herbs and cooking ingredients add to the casually elegant (and unusual) setting. Recommended.

Nobu, 105 Hudson St (at Franklin St) ☎219-0500. Robert De Niro's best-known New York restaurant, headed up by celebrated chef Nobu Matsuhisa. A lavish woodland decor complements really superlative Japanese cuisine, especially sushi, at the high prices you would expect.

Omen, 113 Thompson St (between Prince and Spring sts) ☎925-8923. Zen-inspired SoHo spot featuring authentic Kyoto flavors and flair, including good sushi. Expensive.

Penang, 109 Spring St (between Greene and Mercer sts) ☎274-8883; 1596 2nd Avenue (at E 83rd St) ☎585-3838; 240 Columbus Ave (at 71st St) ☎769-3988. Superlative Malaysian food served in a wildly overdone jungle setting with bamboo interior walls and tropical plants. The seafood is particularly fresh – try the whole spiced sea bass in banana leaves. Reservations are recommended as it can be crowded (especially at the SoHo branch).

Rice, 227 Mott St (between Prince and Spring sts) ☎226-5775. Small, inexpensive pan-Asian spot, where you mix-and-match various rices (black, sticky, etc) with interesting meat choices (lemongrass chicken, beef salad and the like).

Thai House Café, 151 Hudson St (at Hubert St) ☎334-1085. Small, friendly TriBeCa Thai restaurant, popular for its inexpensive authentic food. The Pad Thai and red curries are excellent. Closed Sun.

Caribbean, Central and South American

Brisa del Caribe, 489 Broadway (at Broome St) ☎226-9768. Very good and very cheap rice and beans in an unlikely SoHo no-frills eatery.

El Teddy's, 219 W Broadway (between Franklin and White sts) ☎941-7070. Eccentrically decorated restaurant that serves creative Mexican food, like goat cheese quesadillas, and the best margaritas in town. Try the fried tortillas wrapped around spicy chicken for starters. Entrees, around $15–19, are a little pricey.

Fish and seafood

Aguagrill, 210 Spring St (at 6th Ave) ☎274-0505. Fresh seafood expertly cooked to your taste and a first-rate raw

Eating

Eating

bar. They serve over a dozen varieties of oyster, and the wait staff actually knows the difference between all of them. Excellent wine list and service. Prices to match, with entrees from $18. Reservations recommended.

Le Pescadou, 18 King St (off 6th Ave, south of W Houston St) ☎924-3434. A chic seafood bistro in a charming French setting. Moderate prices.

French and Belgian

Alison on Dominick, 38 Dominick St (between Hudson and Varick sts) ☎727-1188. Alison is Alison Price, the owner and chef of this famed French country restaurant. About as tucked away and romantic as you can get in the middle of a huge city, with great Southwestern French food that is served with a creative, light touch. Very expensive, but worth it for a special occasion with the one you love.

Balthazar, 80 Spring St (between Crosby St and Broadway) ☎965-1414. After two years this is still one of the hottest reservations in town and the raves keep pouring in. The tastefully ornate Parisian decor and non-stop beautiful people keep your eyes busy until the food arrives; then all you can do is savor the fresh oysters and mussels, the exquisite pastries and everything in between. It's worth the money and the attitude.

Capsouto Frères, 451 Washington St (at Watts St) ☎966-4900. Tucked away in a discreet corner of TriBeCa is this wonderful, if pricey, French bistro with a lofty feel. Dinner entrees are about $14–24. Try the duck with ginger and cassis, and don't miss the dessert soufflés the *Frères* is best known for.

Chanterelle, 2 Harrison St (at Hudson St), ☎966-6960. Some say while in New York you should live on stale bread all week and spend all your money on one of Chef David Waltuck's meals here. Haute French cuisine of the finest order, with wines so rare you are advised to reserve your bottle ahead of time so they can properly decant it, all served

impeccably in a small, stately room. Very pricey.

Country Café, 69 Thompson St (between) ☎966-5417. Small, utterly charming restaurant with French doors opening out into the street, lovely country decor (understated not cutesy), Edith Piaf on the stereo and a terrific menu. The food is French with a Moroccan twist; rich tagines and a curried pork tenderloin accompany the more traditional fare, including truly superb mussels in a white wine, shallot and basil sauce. Entrees run between $14 and $22. Note: smoking is permitted, as it seats fewer than 35 people. Highly recommended.

L'Ecole, French Culinary Institute, 462 Broadway (at Grand St) ☎219-3300. Students of the French Culinary Institute serve up affordable French delights – and they rarely fail. The three-course prix fixe dinner costs $25.95 per person, one of the best deals in town, but book well in advance. Closed Sun.

Le Jardin Bistro, 25 Cleveland Place (between Kenmare and Spring sts) ☎343-9599. Unpretentious French bistro with a garden in the back and reliably good food, including very fresh seafood. Romantic and moderately priced for what you get, with entrees around $16–20. Recommended.

Manhattan Bistro, 129 Spring St (between Greene and Wooster sts) ☎966-3459. Your basic bistro – familiar French dishes, plus pastas and focaccia sandwiches – that has lasted in a fad-obsessed neighborhood because the food is well-prepared and not overpriced, and the room is classy and quiet.

Provence, 38 MacDougal St (between Prince and Houston sts) ☎475-7500. Very popular SoHo bistro that serves excellent food but at around $15–19 for a main course. A nice place for a special occasion, though, with a lovely, airy, eating area and a garden for the summer.

Raoul's, 180 Prince St (between Sullivan and Thompson sts) ☎966-3518. French bistro seemingly lifted from Paris. The food, especially the *steak au poivre*, and service are wonderful, as you'd expect at the high prices you'll find here. Reservations recommended. Closed Aug.

Vandam, 150 Varick St (at Vandam St) ☎352-9090. A brand new restaurant from the people who brought you *Balthazar*, and it's already causing a stir with its sumptuous decor and French food with a new twist – a Latin American twist, that is. Want some yucca with your foie gras? Now you can have it.

Greek and Middle Eastern

Delphi, 109 W Broadway (at Reade St) ☎227-6322. Accommodating Greek restaurant with good menu, great portions and unbeatable prices. The antipasti and fish are excellent value at $8–10.75 or there's kebabs and the like from $7–10 and sandwiches as low as $4. Best Manhattan choice for bargain Greek eating.

Layla, 211 W Broadway (at Franklin St) ☎431-0700. Middle Eastern theme restaurant from Drew Nieporent and the *TriBeCa Grill* boys, where you can get a very nice $24 kebab, as well as calamari stuffed with *merguez* sausage. Wild, rich Persian-style decor and belly-dancers add a great deal to the experience. Expensive.

Italian

Cucina della Nonna, 104 Grand St (at Mercer St) ☎925-5488. Unpretentious, home-style Italian, with very reasonable prices (especially considering the neighborhood) and friendly service. In all, it's a good deal.

Mezzogiorno, 195 Spring St (at Sullivan) ☎334-2112. Bright SoHo restaurant that's as much a place to people-watch as eat. A little overpriced, but a good and inventive menu, including excellent wood-burning-oven pizzas, great salads and carpaccio – thinly sliced raw beef served in various ways.

Oro Blu, 333 Hudson St ☎645-8004. Great Italian food in a modern airy setting – a mixture of savory classics and

more innovative fare. It is a good option in a fairly sparse part of town.

Jewish and Eastern European

Triplet's Roumanian, 11–17 Grand St (at 6th Ave) ☎925-9303. Noisy neighborhood restaurant that is like crashing a loud Jewish wedding. Egg creams made at your table are a real highlight. A guaranteed blast. Closed Mon and Tues.

Vegetarian

Spring Street Natural Restaurant, 62 Spring St (at Lafayette St) ☎966-0290. Not wholly vegetarian, but very good, freshly prepared health food served in a large airy space. Moderately priced, with entrees from $9. Very popular with locals, but crowds add to sometimes already slow service.

Greenwich Village

The bohemian edge that once characterized **Grenwich Village** became the most seductive of marketing ploys, attracting visitors from near and far. Now many restaurants are overcrowded and overpriced, particularly in and around the New York University area and along Seventh Avenue. Move a little west towards Hudson Street or north around the meat packing district and you'll find some cozier, more affordable nooks. In spite of tourist traffic, the hub of Italian cafés around Bleecker and MacDougal remains a good place to recuperate with a healthy infusion of sugar and caffeine.

Bakeries and cafés

Anglers & Writers, 420 Hudson St (at St Luke's Place) ☎675-0810. Village café serving high tea from 4pm to 7pm, as well as decent continental fare – soups and desserts are a specialty. A good place to just have a coffee, a snack or a full meal.

Café Le Figaro, 184 Bleecker St (at MacDougal St) ☎677-1100. Former Beat hangout during the 1950s now ersatz Left Bank, serving cappuccino and

Eating

Eating

pastries. If you want to watch weekend tourists flooding West Village streets, this is a good place to do it.

Caffè Dante, 79 MacDougal St (between Bleecker and Houston sts) ☎982-5275. A morning stop-off for many locals since 1915. Good cappuccino, double espresso and caffè alfredo with ice cream. Often jammed with NYU students and teachers.

Caffè Reggio, 119 MacDougal St (between Bleecker and W 3rd sts) ☎475-9557. One of the first Village coffeehouses, dating back to the 1920s, always crowded and with tables outside for people- or tourist-watching in warm weather.

Caffè Vivaldi, 32 Jones St (between Bleecker and W 4th sts) ☎929-9384. An old-fashioned Viennese-style coffeehouse with fireside coziness.

Tea and Sympathy, 108 Greenwich Ave (between W 12th and 13th sts) ☎807-8329. Self-consciously British tearoom, serving an afternoon high tea full of traditional British staples like jam roly-poly and treacle pud, along with shepherd's pie and scones. Perfect for British tourists feeling homesick.

Thé Adoré, 17 E 13th St (between 5th Ave and University Place) ☎243-8742. Charming little tea room with excellent pastries, scones, croissants and coffee. Sit upstairs and have a sandwich and a tasty bowl of soup. Daytime hours only; closed Sundays; generally closed Saturdays in August, but it varies so call ahead.

Xando, 504 Avenue of the Americas (corner of 13th St) ☎462-4188. An inviting, airy, coffeehouse, offering an extraordinary array of coffee concoctions, as well as light snacks, ice cream and the *very* American treat – s'mores – a combination of marshmallow, graham crackers and chocolate, melted together. They bring it to your table with a flame so you can roast them yourself. Go ahead, relive your youth (or pretend you're American for a bit) at $7.50 for two giant helpings.

American and continental

Aggie's, 146 W Houston St (at MacDougal St) ☎673-8994. Funky upscale diner serving fresh and generous, if a bit overpriced, salads and sandwiches, and good brunch items. *Aggie's* friendly cats roam their turf while you eat.

Bagel Buffet, 406 6th Ave (between W 8th and 9th sts) ☎477-0448. Wide selection of fillings and good-value bagel and salad platters for around $5. Open 24 hours.

Brother's Bar-B-Q, 255 Varick St (corner of Clarkson) ☎727-2775. A huge airy room with firehouse decor, kitschy Dixieana displays, big booths, and piped-in country/blues music, serving some of the best barbecue north of the Mason-Dixon line. The ribs, mashed potatoes and collard greens are not to be missed. Cheap too – two people can eat handsomely for around $25. Also really good $3 margaritas during happy hour, Mon–Fri 4–7pm.

Caliente Cab Co, 61 7th Ave (at Bleecker St) ☎243-8517. Average Tex-Mex food but with some good bargains: Mon–Fri happy hour (4–8pm) has free bar food; weekend brunch buffet (Sat & Sun noon–3pm) comes with as many margaritas, mimosas or screwdrivers as you can drink.

Corner Bistro, 331 W 4th St (at Jane St) ☎242-9502. Down-home pub with cavernous cubicles, paper plates and healthy servings of tasty burgers, BLT's, fries, beer and desserts for reasonable prices. Longstanding haunt of West Village literary and arty types, a mix of locals and die-hard fans line up nightly, but don't be discouraged, the line moves faster than it looks. Great bar and jazz jukebox too.

Cowgirl Hall of Fame, 519 Hudson St (at W 10th St) ☎633-1133. Down-home Texan-style barbecue amidst cowboy kitsch and memorabilia. Huge selection of tequilas served in a glass cowboy boot. Try the meaty ribs or fried chicken.

Elephant and Castle, 68 Greenwich Ave (between 6th and 7th aves) ☎243-1400. Old Village favorite serving up well-priced food and drink. Known for its burgers, excellent omelettes, and Caesar salad, it's especially good for breakfast and lunch.

Home, 20 Cornelia St (between Bleecker and W 4th sts) ☎243-9579. There's no place like it, as the saying goes. *Home* is one of those rare restaurants that manages to pull off quaint and cozy with flair. The creative American food is always fresh and wonderful, perhaps a better deal at lunch than dinner. Try the cheese fondue or cumin-crusted pork chops.

Indigo, 142 W 10th St (between Greenwich and Waverly) ☎691-7757. Home-style American food with a creative Mediterranean (and once in a while Asian) twist. Delicious roast chicken served with polenta and artichokes, thick tasty soups and unusual salads. Entrees cost about $16 and are worth it.

The Pink Teacup, 42 Grove St (between Bleecker and Bedford sts) ☎807-6755. Longstanding Southern soul-food institution in the heart of the Village. Relatively inexpensive (entrees around $12) and filling. Brunch too, but no credit cards.

Shopsin's General Store, 63 Bedford St (at Morton St) ☎924-5160. Leave your attitude at the door when you come to *Shopsin's*. This tiny, family-run restaurant serves a Bible-length menu of home-made soups and sandwiches. Closed weekends just because they feel like it. No credit cards.

Tavern on Jane, 31 8th Ave (at Jane St) ☎675-2526. Formerly *Jane Street Seafood Café*, this is now a pleasant bar/restaurant that serves a wide range of beers and good basic American pub food, including excellent mashed potatoes.

Asian

Japonica, 100 University Place (at 12th St) ☎243-7752. Spacious, elegant restaurant serving a large Japanese menu, including some of the freshest sushi in the city, at some of the most reasonable prices. Sat and Sun brunch deals are excellent – big plates of sushi or sashimi (teriyaki too), with salad and beer or plum wine for around $12 a head. For dinner, the teriyaki and tempura entrees run $11–16, the sushi bar averages about $25 for a whole dinner. Be prepared to wait in line after 7pm.

Lemongrass Grill, 80 University Place (at 11th St) ☎604-9870. Popular Thai restaurant with quick service and inexpensive food. One of several branches, it offers a limited menu featuring the usual noodle dishes and stir-fried meat and veggie fare – fine if you're in a hurry.

Toons, 417 Bleecker St (at Bank St) ☎924-6420. Relatively high prices, but a low-lit, homey place with an intimate atmosphere and tasty authentic food. A Thai community favorite.

Caribbean, Central and South American

Benny's Burritos, 113 Greenwich Ave (at Jane St) ☎727-0595; 93 Avenue A (at E 6th St) ☎254-2054. Huge, inauthentic burritos with all kinds of fillings and speedy service. Cheap too. First-rate margaritas.

Caribe, 117 Perry St (between Hudson and Greenwich sts) ☎255-9191. A funky Caribbean restaurant filled with leafy jungle decor and blasted with reggae music. Jerk chicken, washed down with wild tropical cocktails, makes it the place for a fun night out. Entrees in the range of $7–10.

Day-O, 103 Greenwich Ave (at W 12th St) ☎924-3161. A young crowd enjoys the food and lively atmosphere at this Downtown Caribbean/Southern joint. Highlights include fried catfish, jerk chicken, coconut shrimp and a choice of two veggie dishes. Deadly tropical drinks too.

Flying Fish, 395 West St (between Christopher and W 10th sts) ☎924-5050. Crowded Caribbean place offering cheap Jamaican food.

Lupe's East LA Diner, 110 6th Ave (at Watts St) ☎966-1326. Very laid-back,

Eating

Eating

hole-in-the-wall restaurant serving excellent burritos and enchiladas. Good fun, and cheap.

Mi Cucina, 57 Jane St (at Hudson St) ☎627-8273. Authentic Mexican food in a simple setting. Good prices – entrees in the range of $9–14. Often crowded, so be prepared to wait.

Panchito's, 105 McDougal (between W 3rd and Bleecker sts) ☎473-5239. No, it's not "authentic," but so what? A big, lively and attractive room, with cheap and filling food (beans, rice, burritos). And the bar is excellent, with some very rare brandies.

Tortilla Flats, 767 Washington St (at W 12th St) ☎243-1053. Cheap West Village Mexican dive with great margaritas, a loud jukebox and plenty of kitsch.

French and Belgian

Au Troquet, 328 W 12th St (entrance on Greenwich St) ☎924-3413. Romantic Village haunt that has an authentic Parisian feel. Decent food, moderately priced.

Café de Bruxelles, 118 Greenwich Ave (at W 13th St) ☎206-1830. Very authentic – and popular – Belgian restaurant in

---

Smoker-friendly restaurants

At 12:01am on April 10, 1995 a hitherto inconceivable thing happened in New York: restaurants, or at least the majority of them, went **smokeless**. A complicated new law prohibits smoking in the dining area of all New York restaurants with a capacity of more than 35 people. In these restaurants, smoking is restricted to the bar area or designated enclosed lounges. Smoking is still permitted in bars and restaurants that seat fewer than 35 persons. When in doubt, call ahead, or ask before you light up. What follows is a listing of some restaurants that, at the time of writing, continue to permit smoking in at least part of their space.

DOWNTOWN MANHATTAN

Admiral's Gallery, 160 South (at Dover St) ☎608-6455

Au Troquet, 328 W 12th St (at Greenwich St) ☎924-3413

Bayamo, 704 Broadway (between E 4th St and Washington Place) ☎475-5151

Bell Caffè, 310 Spring St (between Greenwich and Hudson sts) ☎334-2355

Benito I, 174 Mulberry St (between Grand and Broome sts) ☎226-9171

Café Tabac, 232 E 9th St (between 2nd and 3rd aves) ☎674-7072

Corner Bistro, 331 W 4th St (between W 12th and Jane sts) ☎242-9502

Country Café, 69 Thompson St ☎966-5417

Cucina Della Fontana, 368 Bleecker St (at Charles St) ☎242-0636

Ear Inn, 326 Spring St (between Washington and Greenwich sts) ☎226-9060

El Teddy's, 219 W Broadway (between Franklin and White sts) ☎941-7070

Fanelli, 94 Prince St (at Mercer St) ☎226-9412

Florent, 69 Gansevoort St (between Washington and Greenwich aves) ☎989-5779

Gotham Bar & Grill, 12 E 12th St (between 5th Ave and University Place) ☎620-4020

Home, 20 Cornelia St (between Bleecker and W 4th sts) ☎243-9579

John's of 12th Street, 302 E 12th St (between 1st and 2nd aves) ☎475-9531

La Cigalle, 231 Mott St (between Spring and Prince sts) ☎334-4331

Greenwich Village. Moderately priced, interesting food – try the *waterzooi*, a rich and creamy chicken stew. Also excellent frites and mussels.

Chez Brigitte, 77 Greenwich Ave (between Bank St and 7th Ave) ☎929-6736. Only a dozen people fit in this tiny restaurant that serves homey soups, stews, all-day roast meat dinners for under $10, and other bargains from a simple menu.

Chez Ma Tante, 189 W 10th St (between W 4th and Bleecker sts) ☎620-0223. A tiny French bistro that's most fun in summer, when the doors open out onto the street. NYC rustic, with

a charming feel and good food, also known for their brunches.

Chez Michallet, 90 Bedford St (at Grove St) ☎242-8309. A cozy Village version of a French country inn. Moderate to expensive but, at $19.95 for a three-course meal, the nightly prix fixe menu is great value.

Florent, 69 Gansevoort St (between Washington and Greenwich sts) ☎989-5779. Ultra-fashionable bistro on the edge of the meat-packing district that serves good French food, either à la carte or from a prix fixe menu ($18.50, or $16.50 before 7.30pm). Coffee shop decor, always busy. The mussels are so

Eating

Le Pescadou, 18 King St (off 6th Ave, south of W Houston St) ☎924-3434

Lucky Strike, 59 Grand St (between W Broadway and Wooster St) ☎941-0479

Raoul's, 180 Prince St (between Sullivan and Thompson sts) ☎966-3518

Rio Mar, 7 9th Ave (at W 12th St) ☎243-9015

TriBeCa Grill, 375 Greenwich St (at Franklin St) ☎941-3900

MIDTOWN MANHATTAN

Aquavit, 13 W 54th St (between 5th and 6th aves) ☎307-7311

Blue Moon Café, 150 8th Ave (between W 17th and 18th sts) ☎463-0560

P.J. Clarke's, 915 3rd Ave (between E 55th and 56th sts) ☎759-1650

The Coffee Shop, 29 Union Square W (between E 16th and 17th sts) ☎243-7969

Dawat, 210 E 58th St (between 2nd and 3rd aves) ☎355-7555

El Rio Grande, 160 E 38th St (between Lexington and 3rd aves) ☎867-0922

La Bonne Soupe, 48 W 55th St (between 5th and 6th aves) ☎586-7650

Landmark Tavern, 626 11th Ave (between W 45th and 46th sts) ☎757-8595

Mickey Mantle's, 42 Central Park S (W 59th St between 5th and 6th aves) ☎688-7777

Mike's American Bar & Grill, 650 10th Ave (between W 45th and 46th sts) ☎246-4155

Orson's, 175 2nd Ave (between 11th and 12th sts) ☎475-1530

Oyster Bar, Lower level, Grand Central Terminal (at 42nd St and Park Ave) ☎490-6650

Trattoria dell'Arte, 900 7th Ave (between W 56th and 57th sts) ☎245-9800

Zarela, 953 2nd Ave (between E 50th and 51st sts) ☎644-6740

UPTOWN MANHATTAN

Asia, 1155 3rd Ave (between E 67th and 68th sts) ☎879-5846

Bangkok House, 1485 1st Ave (between E 77th and 78th sts) ☎249-5700

Bella Donna, 307 E 77th St (between 1st and 2nd aves) ☎535-2866

Le Monde, 2885 Broadway (at 112th St) ☎531-3939

Madame Romaine de Lyon, 29 E 69th St (between Park and Madison aves) ☎759-5200

Rathbones, 1702 2nd Ave (between E 88th and 89th sts) ☎369-7361

Eating

good it almost doesn't matter how obnoxious the waiters are. Open 24 hours, it's a favorite late-night hangout for clubbers and low-level celebrities and also serves weekend brunch.

La Bohème, 24 Minetta Lane (between W 3rd and Bleecker sts) ☎473-6447. Bright and amiable, if cramped, restaurant in the heart of the Village with pasta, brick-oven pizza, and provençal-style meat and fish dishes for $12–15. Good food, and nice in the summer when they open the French doors to the street. Closed Sun and Mon during Aug.

La Metairie, 189 W 10th St (at W 4th St) ☎989-0343. Tiny, charming West Village bistro serving excellent French country fare. Entrees in the range of $14–24.

Paris Commune, 411 Bleecker St (between W 11th and Bank sts) ☎929-0509. Romantic West Village bistro with reliable French home cooking and a fireplace. Memorable French toast and wild mushroom ravioli at moderate prices. Long lines for brunch.

Waterloo, 145 Charles St (at Washington St) ☎352-1119. A tranquil spot in the West Village, serving good Belgian fare at modest prices for what you get (entrees run around $15). Most traditional dishes – mussels and frites for example – are particularly good here. Be prepared to wait for a table.

Italian

Arturo's Pizza, 106 W Houston St (at Thompson St) ☎475-9828. Moderately priced entrees and coal-oven pizzas big enough to share for even less. While-you-eat entertainment includes live music. Convivial, if not the cheapest or most attractive feed in town.

Baboo, 110 Waverly Place (between 6th Ave and MacDougal St) ☎777-0303. New, inviting restaurant with creative Italian dishes and attentive service. The combination of good food (by chef Mario Batali from *Po* – see below), surprisingly moderate prices (entrees around $18) and relaxed decor make this very popular, so reserve in advance.

Cent' Anni, 50 Carmine St (between Bleecker and Bedford sts) ☎989-9494. Small, low-key, old time Village restaurant serving consistently delicious, and sometimes pricey Florentine dishes.

Cucina Della Fontana, 368 Bleecker St (at Charles St) ☎242-0636. From the outside this place looks like a normal bar, but out in the back there's a plant-filled atrium where you can eat fine Italian food. Mussels, fish, pasta all very good.

Cucina Stagionale, 275 Bleecker St (between 6th and 7th aves) ☎924-2707. Enormously popular restaurant in the West Village, with most dishes at around $8. Expect to wait in line, and bring your own wine – there's no license. Try the calamari or *pasta puttanesca*.

Ennio and Michael, 539 LaGuardia Place (between Bleecker and W 3rd sts) ☎677-8577. Old-fashioned Italian bistro favorite, intimate and cozy. Outdoor seating in warm weather.

John's Pizzeria, 278 Bleecker St (between 6th and 7th aves) ☎243-1680. No slices, no takeaways. A full service restaurant that serves some of the city's best and most popular pizza, with a crust that is thin and coal-charred. Be prepared to wait in line. Uptown branches at 408 E 64th St (between 1st and York aves) ☎935-2895; and 48 W 65th St (between Columbus Ave and Central Park W) ☎721-7001.

Minetta Tavern, 113 MacDougal St (at Minetta Lane) ☎75-3850. One of the oldest bars in New York, decorated with murals showing Greenwich Village as it was in the 1930s. A casual restaurant out back turns out dependable Italian food.

Po, 31 Cornelia St (between Bleecker and W 4th sts) ☎645-2189. Chef Mario Batali's small signature restaurant, serving delicious and creative Italian food, made with fresh, interesting ingredients – his pastas are amazing. Reserve well in advance, as it's still one of the hotspots in the Village. Entrees run about $25.

Stromboli Pizzeria, 112 University Place (between E 12th and 13th sts) ☎255-0812. Excellent thin-crust pizzas – a good place for a quick slice.

Two Boots-to-go West, 75 Greenwich Ave (between 7th Ave and 11th St) ☎633-9096. Great thin-crust pizzas with a Cajun flavor – crawfish and jalapeño peppers are common toppings. Excellent value.

Middle Eastern

Moustache, 90 Bedford St (between Grove and Barrow sts) ☎229-2220. There are scores of falafel joints in the West Village, but *Moustache* is a real step up: clean, delicious and clever as well. The gimmick is "pitza," fresh pitas with pizza-like toppings; better still is the lamb sandwich with cumin and mayo dressing. The food takes a while though, so sit back and relax.

Spanish

Café Español, 63 Carmine St (at 7th Ave S) ☎675-3312; 172 Bleecker St (between MacDougal and Sullivan sts) ☎505-0657. Hole-in-the-wall restaurants serving garlicky Spanish fare for $10–15 a plate. Try the paella or *mariscada* – a filling seafood dish that can easily feed two. Also good sangria.

El Faro, 823 Greenwich St (at Horatio St) ☎929-8210. A dark, lively restaurant, where garlic smells from the kitchen and the look of the food at the next table (it's a tight fit) are guaranteed to stir any appetite. You can't go wrong with the paella or seafood in green sauce. Moderate prices too, and you can share most main dishes. Crowded, especially on weekends.

Rio Mar, 7 9th Ave (at W 12th St) ☎243-9015. A welcoming Spanish restaurant that serves low-priced and authentic food, albeit in a fairly down-beat setting. Recommended.

Sevilla, 62 Charles St (at W 4th St) ☎929-3189. Wonderful Village old-timer that is still a favorite neighborhood haunt. Dark, fragrant (from garlic) restaurant with good, moderately priced food. Terrific paella and large pitchers of strong sangria.

Spain, 113 W 13th St (between 7th and 8th aves) ☎929-9580. Modest prices (entrees are $11–16) and large portions are the prime attractions of this cozy Spanish restaurant. Casual atmosphere and tacky decor in the larger back dining room – this neighborhood place has been here forever. Order the paella and split it with a friend.

Vegetarian

Eva's, 11 W 8th St (between 5th and 6th aves) ☎677-3496. Healthy food in a coffee-shop setting. Nice grub, speedily served, and very cheap. Try the vegetarian falafel combo.

Souen, 210 6th Ave (at Prince St) ☎807-7421; 28 E 13th St (between 5th Ave and University Place) ☎627-7150. Politically correct vegetarian, macrobiotic. Serves organic vegetables, fish, shrimp and grains.

Vegetarians' Paradise, 144 W 4th St (between MacDougal St and 6th Ave) ☎260-7130; 33–35 Mott St (at Pell) ☎406-6988; 48 Bowery ☎571-1535. Village vegetarian Chinese – pricier than ordinary Downtown Chinese restaurants but still pretty reasonable.

Eating

East Village

Grittier than its western counterpart, the **East Village** is a mixed bag of radicals, students, immigrants (mostly Puerto Ricans and older Eastern Europeans), and an increasingly large number of young professionals and trendy trans-plants. It seems a new upscale Italian restaurant, sushi bar, or chic café opens every day on Avenue A. By con-trast the homey and cheap restaurants of **Little India**, E 6th St between 1st and 2nd aves, and **Little Ukraine**, around E 7th to E 9th St between 1st and 3rd aves, remain consistently good and satisfying.

Bakeries and cafés

Caffè Della Pace, 48 E 7th St (at 2nd Ave) ☎529-8024. Dark and cozy East Village café with decent food and a

Eating

Coffee and tea

Lately, New York has been invaded by cookie-cutter **coffee chains**, large and small, each professing to offer the final word in the java experience. Chains like *Starbuck's*, *New World Coffee*, *Dalton's*, *Timothy's*, *Seattle Coffee Roasters* are consistently good and serve just about any caffeinated concoction you can dream up. But when you're looking to get your caffeine high, you might just want a little more ambience. For that kind of mood, we suggest the following:

DOWNTOWN MANHATTAN

@ Cafe, 12 St Mark's Place (between 2nd and 3rd aves) ☎979-5439

alt.coffee, 137 Ave A (between 9th and 10th sts) ☎529-2233

Anglers & Writers, 420 Hudson St (at St Luke's Place) ☎675-0810

Café Gitane, 242 Mott St (between Prince and Houston sts) ☎334-9552

Caffè Della Pace, 48 E 7th St (between 1st and 2nd aves) ☎529-8024

Caffè Vivaldi, 32 Jones St (between Bleecker and W 4th sts) ☎929-9384

City Bakery, 22 E 17th St (between Broadway and 5th Ave) ☎366-1414

Cyber Cafe, 273 Lafayette (at Prince St) ☎334-5140

Danal, 90 E 10th St (between 3rd and 4th aves) ☎982-6930

De Robertis, 176 1st Ave (between E 10th and 11th sts) ☎674-7137

Dean and DeLuca Café, 121 Prince St (between Wooster and Greene sts) ☎254-8776; 75 University Place (at E 11th St) ☎473-1908

Kaffeehaus, 131 8th Ave (between W 16th and 17th sts) ☎229-9702

Limbo, 47 Ave A (between E 3rd and 4th sts) ☎477-5271

Sticky Fingers, 121 1st Ave (between E 7th St and St Mark's Place) ☎529-2554

T, 142 Mercer St (at Prince St) ☎925-3700

Tea and Sympathy, 108 Greenwich Ave (between W 12th and 13th sts) ☎807-8329

Thé Adoré, 17 E 13th St (between 5th Ave and University Place) ☎243-8742

Veniero's, 342 E 11th St (between 1st and 2nd aves) ☎674-4415

Xando, 504 Avenue of the Americas (at 13th St) ☎462-4188

Yaffa Tea Room, 353 Greenwich St (at Harrison St) ☎274-9403

MIDTOWN MANHATTAN

Algonquin Oak Room, 59 W 44th St (between 5th and 6th aves) ☎840-6800

Big Cup, 228 8th Ave (between W 21st and 22nd sts) ☎206-0059

News Bar, 2 W 19th St (between 5th and 6th aves) ☎255-3996; 366 W Broadway (at Broome St) ☎343-0053

UPTOWN MANHATTAN

The Bread Shop, 3139 Broadway (at W 123rd St) ☎666-4343

Café Mozart, 154 W 70th St (between Central Park W and Columbus Ave) ☎595-9797

Caffè la Fortuna, 69 W 71st St (between Central Park W and Columbus Ave) ☎724-5846

Food Attitude, 127 E 60th St (between Lexington and Park aves) ☎980-1818

Les Friandises, 922 Lexington Ave (between E 70th and 71st sts) ☎988-1616

great selection of coffees and desserts, especially the tiramisu.

Cloister Café, 238 E 9th St (between 2nd and 3rd aves) ☎777-9128. Don't come

here for the food, which hovers somewhere between mediocre and really bad. Come for the spacious garden dining area and a big mug of coffee. Popular late-night spot.

Limbo, 47 Ave A (between E 3rd and 4th sts) ☎477-5271. Sweets are decent (the blackout cake is more than that) and the coffee is good. You end up sharing tables with would-be screenwriters and novelists. A good selection of magazines to read. Avoid the infrequent poetry readings.

Moishe's, 115 2nd Ave (between E 7th St and St Mark's Place) ☎505-8555. Good prune Danishes, excellent humentashen, seeded rye and other kosher treats.

Sticky Fingers, 121 1st Ave (between 7th St and St Mark's Place) ☎529-2554. Friendly East Village refuge with kids' artwork on the wall. Good coffee and great pastries and breads.

Taylor's, 175 2nd Ave (between E 11th and 12th sts) ☎378-2892; 523 Hudson St (between W 10th and Charles sts) ☎378-2890; 228 W 18th St (between 7th and 8th aves) ☎378-2895. They have soups and salads, but come for the oversized muffins and astonishing pas-

tries. Try the monkey bread, a kind of sugary baked doughnut, zebra brownies, flourless chocolate soufflé cake or blueberry muffins.

Veniero's, 342 E 11th St (between 1st and 2nd aves) ☎674-4415. East Village bakery and over a century-old institution that sells wonderful pastries and has a recently expanded seating area in the back. Desserts and decor are fabulously over-the-top. Try the ricotta cheesecake and homemade gelati in the summer.

American and continental

Around the Clock, 8 Stuyvesant St (between 2nd and 3rd aves) ☎598-0402. Centrally situated East Village restaurant serving crepes, omelettes, burgers and pasta at reasonable prices. Open 24 hours.

Bowery Bar & Grill, 358 Bowery (at E 4th St) ☎475-2220. A former gas station turned restaurant serving overpriced and rather ordinary fare, but still the place to be for the terminally hip.

Eating

Bagels

Theories abound as to the origin of the modern **bagel**. Most likely, it is a derivative of the pretzel, with the word *bagel* coming from the German *beigen*, "to bend." Modern-day bagels are probably softer and have a smaller hole than their ancestors – the famous hole made them easy to carry on a long stick to hawk on street corners. Whatever their birthplace, it is certain that bagels have become a **New York institution**. Since they are boiled before being baked, bagels have a characteristically chewy texture. They are most traditionally (and famously) served with cream cheese and lox (smoked salmon), though of course they can be topped with anything you like.

Until the 1950s bagels were still hand-crafted by Eastern European Jewish immigrants in two- or three-man cellars scattered around New York's Lower East Side. Today they can be found **almost everywhere**, but many New Yorkers would say only a few places serve the real thing. Here is a list of some of the better bagelsmiths.

Bagel Buffet, 406 6th Ave (between W 8th and 9th sts) ☎477-0448

Bagelry, 1324 Lexington Ave (between E 88th and 89th sts) ☎996-0567

Bagels on the Square, 7 Carmine St (between Bleecker St and 6th Ave) ☎691-3041

Columbia Hot Bagels, 2836 Broadway (between W 110th and 111th sts) ☎222-3200

Ess-A-Bagel, 359 1st Ave (at E 21st St) ☎260-2252

H & H Bagels, 2239 Broadway (at W 80th St) ☎595-8000

Yonah Schimmel's, 137 E Houston St (between Forsyth and Eldridge sts) ☎477-2858

Eating

First, 87 1st Ave (between E 5th and 6th sts) ☎674-3823. Sophisticated East Village newcomer serving innovative combinations of New American fare, like tuna *steak au poivre* and double-thick pork chops. Moderately priced – entrees average about $14, but noisy.

Life Café, 343 E 10th St (between Ave A and B) ☎477-8791. Peaceful and long-established East Village haunt right on Tompkins Square that hosts sporadic classical and other music concerts. Food is sandwiches, California/Mexican, and vegetarian – plates all around $8–10.

Marion's Continental Restaurant and Lounge, 354 Bowery (between Great Jones and E 4th sts) ☎475-7621. Superb *steak au poivre* and martinis in a casually elegant atmosphere. Turf is consistently better than surf. Service is slow – all the better for taking in the kitsch decor.

Miracle Grill, 112 1st Ave (between E 6th and 7th sts) ☎254-2353. Moderately priced Southwestern specialties with interesting taste combinations and an attractive garden out back. Save room for the vanilla bean flan. A new branch recently opened at 415 Bleecker.

Old Devil Moon, 511 E 12th St (between Ave A and B) ☎475-4375. Filled with thrift store *tchotchkes*, this East Village dive hangout serves enormous brunch portions, most notably the Road Side breakfast (sloppy, greasy and perhaps better described as "road kill"). Try the catfish sandwich or corn meal pancakes with fresh fruit of the day.

Pierrot, 28 Avenue B at 2nd St ☎228-8194. This bistro/bar keeps everyone happy with its eclectic menu of appetizers, salads, sandwiches and more complex entrees, plus a wine list featuring many good Californian choices. While you wait to be seated, have a drink at the attractive and well-stocked bar.

Radio Perfecto, 190 Avenue B (between 11th and 12th sts) ☎477-3366. Cozy in the winter and airy in the summer this place has it all covered. Antique radios (for sale) line the walls and airplane pro-

pellers, recycled as ceiling fans, whirl above the tables. It also boasts a friendly wait staff, excellent menu – featuring continental fare with a definite French twist and a solid wine list. Check out the backyard garden in the summer.

Stingy Lulu's, 129 St Mark's Place (between 1st Ave and Ave A) ☎674-3545. This retro diner serves decent, simple American fare and is a good place to people-watch.

Time Café, 380 Lafayette St (between Great Jones and E 4th sts) ☎533-7000. Happening restaurant with a reasonably priced eclectic California-Southwestern menu and a large outdoor seating area perfectly positioned for people-watching. Downstairs the *Fez* lounge offers poetry readings, regular live jazz (usually on Wednesdays) and periodic campy 1970s music revues called The Loser's Lounge – along with strong drinks and tasty appetizers. There is also a West Village location at 87 7th Ave at Barrow St ☎220-9100 – featuring the above menu plus a great rooftop garden.

Asian

Dok Suni, 119 1st Ave (between E 7th St and St Mark's Place) ☎447-9506. This dimly lit, somewhat cramped East Village restaurant has fast become a favorite for Korean home cooking. Try the spicy squid and black bean rice.

Elephant, 58 E 1st St (between 1st and 2nd sts) ☎505-7739. The menu is a delicious fusion of Thai and French delicacies and features innovative fish specials and superb noodle dishes. The bright blue-and-yellow awning makes sure you can spot this tiny, eclectic, East Village favorite.

Indochine, 430 Lafayette St (between E 4th St and Astor Place) ☎505-5111. Not the kind of place you go to save money; more to lap up the elegant surroundings and excellent French-Vietnamese food. Good people-watching, too. Recommended.

Lucky Cheng's, 24 1st Ave (between 1st and 2nd sts) ☎473-0516. An over-the-top spot with creative combinations of California and Asian cuisines, served by outrageous waiters in drag; $6–16 for entrees. Go for the show more than the food.

Mee Noodle Shop, 219 1st Ave (between E 13th and 14th sts) ☎995-0333; 922 2nd Ave (at E 49th St) ☎888-0027; 795 9th Ave (at 53rd St) ☎765-2929. You can create endless combinations of noodles, broths and toppings at *Mee*. The food is so inexpensive that you won't notice the lack of decor. Try Mee Fun Soup with chicken or Dan Dan noodles, served with black mushrooms in a spicy meat sauce.

Sapporo Village Japanese Restaurant, 245 E 10th St (at 1st Ave) ☎260-1330. Good noodle dishes and better than average sushi, along with a tasty seaweed salad. The remarkably low prices keep this restaurant crowded and lively.

Shabu Tatsu, 216 E 10th St (between 1st and 2nd aves) ☎477-2972. This place offers great Japanese barbecue. Choose a combination of foods, and have them cooked right at your table. Moderate pricing.

Takahachi, 85 Ave A (between E 5th and 6th sts) ☎505-6524. Superior sushi, the best in the neighborhood, at affordable prices. For dinner you'll probably have to wait – they don't take reservations.

Caribbean, Central and South American

Bayamo, 704 Broadway (between E 4th St and Washington Place) ☎475-5151. Chinese-Cuban food, served in vast portions at moderate prices – around $10 to $16 for entrees. Try the stir-fried duck with rice and Cuban chicken cutlets. Live Latin music Tues, Thurs and Fri evenings – no cover. Also a fun, though crowded, brunch spot.

Boca Chica, 13 1st Ave (at 1st St) ☎473-0108. This is real Brazilian stuff, piled high and washed down with black beer and fancy, fruity drinks. It gets crowded, especially late and on weekends, and the music is loud, so come in a party mood and bring your dancing shoes. Inexpensive.

Pedro Paramo, 430 E 14th St (between 1st Ave and Ave A) ☎475-4851. Authentic Mexican food in a quiet, homey restaurant. Have a mole and an excellent margarita. Entrees are about $8–12.

French and Belgian

Belgo, 4152 Lafayette St (below Astor Place) ☎253-2828. Neoindustrial mussels and Belgian beer hall, constantly crowded and perhaps a better bet for its $8 lunch deal.

Casimir 103 Ave B (between 6th and 7th sts) ☎358-9683. Dark, spacious French bistro, specializing in straightforward pleasures. Try the filet mignon, an excellent – and, surprisingly, well-priced – cut of meat.

Chez Es Saada, 42 E 1st St (between 1st and 2nd sts) ☎777-5617. The decor evokes visions of Tangiers in the early 1950s while rose petals line the stairs. The menu is a mix of French and Moroccan fare, and is pretty expensive. Meanwhile, the bar scene is hopping and nightly DJs pull in the black-clad crew – it's worth it to get a drink and an appetizer and take it all in.

Danal, 90 E 10th St (between 3rd and 4th aves) ☎982-6930. Charming and cozy French café in what used to be an antiques store. French toast made with croissants and topped with cinnamon apples. Great for dinner, brunch and high tea on weekends from 4–6pm.

Jules, 65 St Mark's Place (between 1st and 2nd aves) ☎477-5560. Comfortable and authentic French restaurant, a rarity in the East Village, serving up moderately priced bistro fare and a good-value brunch on weekends.

Opaline, 85 Ave A (between E 5th and 6th sts) ☎475-5050. It's hip, it's loud, it has roast ostrich – but you can also get crepes and confit, and you don't have to dress up (but bring a full wallet).

Eating

Eating

Greek and Middle Eastern

Khyber Pass, 34 St Mark's Place (between 2nd and 3rd aves) ☎473-0989. Afghan food, which, if you're unfamiliar, is filling and has plenty to offer vegetarians (pulses, rice, eggplants are frequent ingredients). Also tasty lamb dishes. Excellent value for around $10.

Indian

Gandhi, 345 E 6th St (between 1st and 2nd aves) ☎614-9718. One of the best and least expensive of the E 6th St Indian restaurants – also one of the more spacious, with two open dining areas. Try the lamb Muglai and the light, fluffy poori bread.

Mingala Burmese, 21 E 7th St (between 2nd and 3rd aves) ☎529-3656. Indian, Thai and Chinese cuisines combine in Burmese food – here made well and relatively inexpensively. Try the Thousand Layer Pancakes and the crispy lentil fritters. Delicious.

Mitali East, 334 E 6th St (between 1st and 2nd aves) ☎533-2508. Though more expensive than the other 6th St Indians, this one is well worth it, and still at half the price of spots further Uptown. There's another branch across town, *Mitali West*, at 296 Bleecker St (at 7th Ave) ☎989-1367.

Passage to India, 308 E 6th St (between 1st and 2nd aves) ☎529-5770. North Indian tandoori dishes and breads at very cheap prices.

Rose of India, 308 E 6th St (between 1st and 2nd aves) ☎533-5011. Good workmanlike curries, and if you tell them it's your birthday they'll turn on the "disco lights" and bring you a free dessert.

Italian

Cucina di Pesce, 87 E 4th St (between 2nd and 3rd aves) ☎260-6800. There are better Italian restaurants around, but not at these prices. The room is attractive and underlit, and the help is friendly. Squid-ink linguini and various seafood specials are the standouts. There's a big local crowd at dinnertime; get a drink at the bar and nibble on the free stewed mussels while you wait.

Frank, 88 2nd Ave (between 5th and 6th sts) ☎420-0202. Tiny, neighborhood favorite serving basic, traditional Italian dishes at a reasonable price. It's packed every night with hungry locals looking for the closest thing to a home cooked meal.

John's of 12th Street, 302 E 12th St (between 1st and 2nd aves) ☎475-9531. Heaping portions of Southern Italian food in a dark, candlelit room, with red-checked tablecloths and an informal feel. Good pastas.

La Foccaceria, 128 1st Ave (between 7th and 8th sts) ☎254-4946. Cheap, filling Sicilian meals in a tiny, down-home setting, with wine served in water glasses.

Lanza Restaurant, 168 1st Ave (between E 10th and 11th sts) ☎674-7014. A prix-fixe lunch for $8.50 or a late-night prix-fixe at 9–11pm for $13.95 makes this basic Italian-fare, like linguini with white clam sauce, seem extra-special.

Orologio, 162 Ave A (between E 10th and 11th sts) ☎228-6900. Clocks are the theme (on the walls, on tables, in cases...) in this rustic Italian eatery that offers reasonably priced food in a happening, and usually very crowded, environment. Outdoor seating in the summer.

Two Boots, 37 Ave A (between E 2nd and 3rd sts) ☎505-2276. Unique East Village restaurant serving great thin-crust pizzas with a Cajun flavor – crawfish and jalapeño peppers are common toppings. A full restaurant, it serves main dishes too, including mostly spicy pasta and seafood options. Excellent value, and fun.

Two Boots To Go, 42 Ave A (at 3rd St) ☎505-5450; 74 Bleecker St (at Broadway) ☎777-1033; Park Slope, Brooklyn ☎718/499-3253. Takeout pizzerias offering an even cheaper way to sample the thin-crust Cajun-Italian pizza combinations available at the restaurant (see above). There's also *Two Boots-to-go West*, at 75 Greenwich Ave (between 7th Ave and 11th St) ☎633-9096.

Jewish and Eastern European

B & H Dairy, 127 2nd Ave (between E 7th St and St Mark's Place) ☎505-8065. Tiny luncheonette serving homemade soup, challah and latkes. You can also create your own juice combination to stay or go. Good veggie choice.

Christine's, 208 1st Ave (between E 12th and 13th sts) ☎254-2474. Longstanding Polish coffee shop, one of several such places in the area – great soups, blintzes and *pierogies*.

Kiev, 117 2nd Ave (at E 7th St) ☎674-4040. Eastern European dishes and burgers. Great and affordable food at any time of the day or night. Open 24 hours.

KK Restaurant, 192–194 1st Ave (between E 11th and 12th sts) ☎777-4430. Polish home cooking with cheap breakfast specials. Try to sit in the tranquil garden out back.

Odessa, 117–119 Ave A (between E 7th St and St Mark's Place) ☎473-8916. The scramble for a seat may put you off, but the food here – a filling array of dishes from the Caucasus – and prices (around $8 for a meal) are impressive. There are actually two places right next to each other. One has coffee-shop decor, loud, plastic and brightly lit. Go to the one with the bar – it's dimly-lit, has more atmosphere and is a popular late-night slumming spot (with food).

Second Avenue Deli, 156 2nd Ave (between E 9th and 10th sts) ☎677-0606. An East Village institution, recently renovated, serving up marvellous burgers, hearty pastrami sandwiches, and other deli goodies in ebullient, snap-happy style. The star plaques in the sidewalk out front commemorate this area's Yiddish theatre days. They're famous for their matzoh ball soup.

Veselka, 144 2nd Ave (corner of E 9th St) ☎228-9682. East Village institution, recently spruced up, that offers fine homemade hot borscht (and cold in summer), latkes, *pierogies*, and great burgers and fries. Open 24 hours.

Spanish

Helena's, 432 Lafayette St (between Astor Place and E 4th St) ☎677-5151. Tapas is the focus here, and though there are other dishes on the menu, the tapas choices are so varied and delicious that you don't need anything else. The place itself is lively with brightly painted red and yellow walls, huge flower arrangements and an airy two-tier main dining area. There is also a tented garden space out back, in case you get tired of the main room. Moderate prices. Recommended.

Xunta, 174 1st Ave (between 10th and 11th St) ☎614-0620. Below 1st Ave this electric East Village gem buzzes with hordes of young faces perched on rum barrels downing pitchers of sangria and choosing from the dizzying tapas menu – try the mussels in fresh tomato sauce, shrimp with garlic, and the mushrooms in brandy. You can eat (and drink) very well for around $20.

Vegetarian

Anjelica Kitchen, 300 E 12th St (between 1st and 2nd aves) ☎228-2909. Vegetarian macrobiotic restaurant with various daily specials for a decent price. Patronized by a colorful Downtown crowd.

Dojo, 24–26 St Mark's Place (between 2nd and 3rd aves) ☎674-9821; also at 14 W 4th St (between Broadway and Mercer St) ☎505-8934. Popular East Village hangout, with reasonably priced vegetarian and Japanese food in a brash, fun environment. One of the best-value restaurants in the city (breakfasts run as low as $2, and veggie sandwiches are $2.50–3.95), and certainly one of the cheapest Japanese menus you'll find.

Chelsea

Retro diners, Cuban-Chinese greasy spoons along 8th Ave, increasingly

Eating

Eating

trendy restaurants, and cute brunch spots characterize **Chelsea** – a neighborhood of mixed and multiple charms. Perhaps the best and most reasonably priced offerings are to be had in the area's Central American establishments, though there is also a mosaic of international cuisines – Thai, Austrian, Mexican, Italian and traditional American – to choose from.

Bakeries and cafés

Big Cup, 228 8th Ave (between 21st and 22nd sts) ☎206-0059. Popular coffee shop with fresh muffins and (big) hot cups of joe. Comfortable couches and chairs make it the perfect place to read the papers and relax into your day.

News Bar, 2 W 19th St (between 5th and 6th aves) ☎255-3996. Tiny minimalist café with equally great selections of pastries and periodicals. Draws photographer and model types as well as regular people, making it good for people-watching.

American and continental

Eighteenth and Eighth, 159 8th Ave (between W 17th and 18th sts) ☎242-5000. Ever so tiny, upscale Chelsea coffee shop popular with a hip, gay crowd. Great for homey brunch fare, especially the brioche French toast.

Empire Diner, 210 10th Ave (between W 22nd and 23rd sts) ☎243-2736. With its gleaming chrome-ribbed Art Deco interior, this is one of Manhattan's original diners, still open 24 hours and still serving up plates of simple American food such as burgers and grilled cheese sandwiches. The food is average, but the place is a beauty – a real New York institution. Free postcards, too.

Food Bar, 149 8th Ave (between W 17th and 18th sts) ☎243-2020. The food at this Chelsea restaurant, part of the Chelsea gay scene, is not quite as good as the view. Even so, well-priced salads and sandwiches.

Moran's, 146 10th Ave (at 19th St) ☎627-3030. Listed in the phone book

as "Moran's Chelsea Sea Food," but while you can get good swordfish, lobster and sole here, it's the steaks and chops that impress – as well as the plush stained-wood decor. Try and get the cozy back room, especially in winter, when the fireplace is roaring.

The Old Homestead, 56 9th Ave (between 14th and 15th sts) ☎242-9040. Steak. Period. But really gorgeous steak, served in an almost comically old-fashioned walnut dining room by waiters in black vests. Huge portions, but expensive.

O'Reilly's, 56 W 31st St (between Broadway and 6th Ave) ☎684-4244. Posh Irish pub/restaurant with standard American dishes at $6–12. Good value.

Asian

Bendix Diner, 219 8th Ave (at W 21st St) ☎366-0560. For breakfast, your all-American greasy-spoon diner, but with an unusually large lunch and dinner menu that includes a lot of Thai-inspired dishes.

Meri Ken, 189 7th Ave (at W 21st St) ☎620-9684. Stylish Art Deco sushi place, with reliably fresh fish and a faithful crowd.

Pad Thai, 114 8th Ave (at 16th St) ☎691-6226. Good noodle dishes, stews and other classics, all at very low prices. Also a wide array of vegetarian choices.

Royal Siam, 240 8th Ave (between 22nd and 23rd sts) ☎741-1732. Reasonably priced Thai restaurant, with surprisingly flavorful renditions of the old standards.

Caribbean, Central and South American

Blue Moon Café, 150 8th Ave (between W 17th and 18th sts) ☎463-0560; 1444 1st Ave (at 75th St) ☎288-9811. Standard Mexican food at moderate prices. Hockey fans may be interested to know the restaurant was once owned by the NY Rangers. Try their large Blue Moon margaritas – yes, they're blue; they're also quite potent.

Kitchen, 218 8th Ave (between W 21st and 22nd sts) ☎243-4433. Mexican cuisine to go with a slew of daily burrito specials to choose from.

La Taza de Oro, 96 8th Ave (between 14th and 15th sts) ☎243-9946. Changing daily specials, each served with a heaping of rice and beans makes this a cheap place to get a tasty, filling meal with a Puerto Rican twist.

Negril, 362 W 23rd St (off 9th Ave) ☎807-6411. An enormous aquarium and colorful decor add to the pleasure of eating at this Jamaican restaurant. Spicy jerk chicken or goat, stews and other dishes keep 'em coming, as do the reasonable prices (especially the lunch specials). At dinner expect to pay around $10–12 for an entree – well worth it.

Sam Chinita, 176 8th Ave (between W 18th and 19th sts) ☎741-0240. Old-fashioned boxcar diner serving cheap Cuban-Chinese combos (the Cuban side of the menu is better).

French and Belgian

Markt, 401 W 14th St (at 9th Ave) ☎727-3314. A new Belgian brasserie, with a spacious wood-paneled dining room and lots of tasty standards, including mussels, seafood stews and a great selection of Belgian beers. Crowded and lively.

Greek and Middle Eastern

Periyali, 35 W 20th St (between 5th and 6th aves) ☎463-7890. Gourmet Greek food that's a cut above the rest, both in quality and price, in a cheerful Mediterranean setting. Closed Sun.

Italian

Caffè Bondí, 7 W 20th St (between 5th and 6th aves) ☎691-8136. This Flatiron district restaurant serves up Sicilian specialties and divine desserts. Try to sit in the garden, and go for dinner, as it's often packed at lunchtime.

Chelsea Trattoria, 108 8th Ave (between W 15th and 16th sts) ☎924-7786. A brick-walled Northern Italian restaurant

that's cozy and enjoyable as much for the ambience as the moderately priced food.

Frank's, 85 10th Ave (at W 15th St) ☎243-1349. Long-established Italian-American steakhouse, with pasta and other Italian dishes from $10 up. The casual atmosphere provides a real taste of old New York.

Le Madri, 168 W 18th St (at 7th Ave) ☎727-8022. Named after the Italian "mothers" who work in the kitchen, this elegant Tuscan eatery's marvellous food and wine are only slightly marred by the snooty service and clientele. On the pricey side, but worth it. Try and get a table in the patio out.

Spanish

El Quijote, 226 W 23rd St (between 7th and 8th aves) ☎929-1855. Has changed very little over the years; it was not too long ago used as the setting for a dinner scene in *I Shot Andy Warhol* (which takes place in 1968) with minimal makeover. Still serves lovely *mariscos* and fried meats amidst the deep burgundy lighting and dark-stained wood setting.

Union Square, Gramercy Park, Murray Hill

Due at least in part to the success of the Union Square Greenmarket, the area around **Union Square** and **Gramercy Park** has become the site of many a culinary adventure of late. Save some of the more expensive restaurants for lunch, but by all means come to sample the fresh and largely Californian cuisine-influenced restaurants the Flatiron district has to offer. Like Little India in the East Village, the area **around Lexington Ave in the upper 20s** is a good place to sample cheap and filling Indian fare.

Bakeries and cafés

Chez Laurence, 245 Madison Ave (corner of 38th St) ☎683-0284. Well-placed, friendly little patisserie that makes cheap breakfasts and decent, inexpensive

Eating

Eating

lunches – and good coffee at any time of the day. Closed Sun.

City Bakery, 22 E 17th St (between Broadway and 5th Ave) ☎366-1414. Minimalist bakery that uses fresh Greenmarket ingredients from around the corner. Serves reasonable soups and light lunch fare, but above all masterfully delicate tartlets, creamy hot chocolate, and crème brûlée. Closed Sun.

La Boulangère, 49 E 21st St (between Broadway and Park Ave S) ☎475-8772; 66 Mercer (between Broome and Spring sts) ☎475-8582. French bakery-café featuring breads, pastries, soups and salads; good for a midday pick-me-up.

American and continental

Alva, 36 E 22nd St (between Broadway and Park Ave S) ☎228-4399. Mirrors and photos of Thomas Alva Edison cover the walls in this eclectic continental restaurant. Specialties include grilled duck, double garlic roast chicken and soft-shell crabs. It's expensive, but the weekday pre-theater prix-fixe dinner (served 5.30–7pm; 3 courses and a glass of wine for about $30) is good value. If you have the cash, it's certainly an excellent place to explore American cooking. Beware heavy smoking (cigars as well as cigarettes) at the bar.

Café Beulah, 39 E 19th St (between Broadway and Park Ave S) ☎777-9700. A little pricey but still the best southern food in the area. Try the free-range duck in a tangy barbecue wine sauce.

Chat 'n' Chew, 10 E 16th St (between 5th Ave and Union Square W) ☎243-1616. Riding the "trailerpark chic" wave, this trendy spot offers up some of the best macaroni and cheese, meatloaf, grilled cheese and turkey dinners in the city. The kitsch decor adds to the Americana theme and brings a pleasant, relaxed feeling to this part of town. Recommended.

El Rio Grande, 160 E 38th St (between Lexington and 3rd aves) ☎867-0922. Long-established Murray Hill Tex-Mex place with a gimmick: you can eat Mexican, or if you prefer, Texan, by simply crossing the "border" and walking through the kitchen. Personable and fun – and the margaritas are earth-shattering.

Friend of a Farmer, 77 Irving Place (between E 18th and 19th sts) ☎477-2188. Rustic Gramercy café known for its old-fashioned chicken pot pie and homey "comfort meals." Also a popular brunch spot.

Mayrose, 920 Broadway (at E 21st St) ☎533-3663. High-ceilinged upscale diner serving solid American food in the Flatiron district. Crowded at lunch.

Mesa Grill, 102 5th Ave (between W 15th and 16th sts) ☎807-7400. One of lower Manhattan's more fashionable eateries, serving eclectic Southwestern grill fare at relatively high prices. During the week it's full of publishing and advertising types doing lunch – at dinner things liven up a bit.

Reuben's, 244 Madison Ave (at E 38th St) ☎867-7800. A busy Midtown diner that makes a fine and filling haven in between the sights and shops of lower 5th Ave.

Scotty's Diner, 336 Lexington Ave (at E 39th St) ☎986-1520. Conveniently placed Midtown diner, close to Grand Central and the Empire State Building. Solid diner food, good breakfasts until 11am and a friendly Spanish owner. Open 24 hours.

Union Square Café, 21 E 16th St (between 5th Ave and Union Square W) ☎243-4020. Choice California-style dining with a classy but comfortable Downtown atmosphere. No one does salmon like they do. Not at all cheap – prices average $100 for two – but the creative menu (and great people-watching) is a real treat. Don't miss it if you have the bucks.

Verbena, 54 Irving Place (between E 17th and 18th sts) ☎260-5454. This simple and elegant restaurant serves a seasonal menu of creative (and pricey) New American food. Don't miss the crème brûlée with lemon verbena, the herb for which the restaurant was named. Try to get seated in the garden, and reserve in advance.

Asian

Asia de Cuba, 237 Madison Ave (between 37th and 38th sts) ☎726-7755. If you feel like treating yourself, this Asian/Latin American hot spot is where to go. Celebrity sightings have launched this place to fame of its own, while the streamlined white decor, enormous communal dining table and flavorful menu has kept the buzz alive. The bar upstairs is also a great place to enjoy neon cocktails and strong martinis – while perusing the very well-heeled crowd.

Choshi, 77 Irving Place (at E 19th St) ☎420-1419. Modestly priced Gramercy Japanese serving first-rate fresh sushi. The $22 prix-fixe menu is a good deal, including drinks, soup, appetizer, main dish (even sushi) and dessert.

Jaiya Thai, 396 3rd Ave (between E 28th and 29th sts) ☎889-1330. Spicy, delicious and affordable. Pad Thai for $8.

Republic, 37 Union Square W (between 16th and 17th sts) ☎627-7172. Pleasant decor, fast service, low prices and serviceable noodle dishes make this a popular Pan-Asian spot. The tasty appetizers are the best part.

Tina, 118 3rd Ave (between 13th and 14th sts) ☎477-1761. Good Chinese in an area not usually known for its Chinese restaurants.

Fish and seafood

City Crab, 235 Park Ave S (at E 19th St) ☎529-3800. A large and very popular joint that prides itself on a large selection of fresh East Coast oysters and clams, which can be had in mixed sampler plates. Overall, a hearty place to consume lots of bivalves and wash 'em down with pints of ale. Sometimes with

jazz at weekend brunch. Roughly $20–30 per person for a full dinner.

French and Belgian

Les Halles, 411 Park Ave S (between E 28th and 29th sts) ☎679-4111. Noisy, bustling bistro with carcasses dangling in a butcher's shop in the front. Very pseudo *rive gauche*, serving rabbit, steak frites and other staples. Pricey; dinners in the range of $25–35 a person. Not recommended for veggies.

L'Express, 249 Park Ave S (at 20th St) ☎254-5858. A good, airy bistro with the usual food (galatine, smoked salmon a la Lyonnaise) at somewhat reasonable prices, but with two important points of distinction: the waiters are actually friendly, and it's open 24 hours – by far the classiest all-night place in the neighborhood.

Park Bistro, 414 Park Ave S (between E 28th and 29th sts) ☎689-1360. Sister to *Les Halles* (see above) and similar in prices and style, though a little less hectic. Friendly bistro à la Paris in the 1950s.

Pitchoune, 226 3rd Ave (at 19th St) ☎614-8641. Provençal French bistro fare served by a friendly wait staff in a comfortable, relaxed setting. The sidewalk tables, when whether permits, add to the pleasant ambience. Entrees are $15–20 and well worth it.

Steak Frites, 9 E 16th St (between Union Square W and 5th Ave) ☎463-7101. Classic European feel, with an upscale ambience and good service. As the name suggests, great steak and frites, for about $19. Other main courses $12–20.

German

Rolf's, 281 3rd Ave (at 22nd St) ☎473-8718. A nice, dark, chintz-decorated Old World feeling dominates this East Side institution. Schnitzel and sauerbraten are always good but somehow taste better at the generous bar buffet, commencing around 5pm all through the week.

Eating

Eating

Indian

Annapurna, 108 Lexington Ave (between E 27th and 28th sts) ☎679-1284. Good value Indian restaurant.

Curry in a Hurry, 119 Lexington Ave (between E 27th and 28th sts) ☎683-0900. A quick, inexpensive and delicious spot where you can eat for around $8.

Madras Mahal, 104 Lexington Ave (between E 27th and 28th sts) ☎684-4010. A kosher vegetarian's dream . . . and really good for everyone else, too. Entrees are round $10.

Jewish and Eastern European

Eisenberg's Sandwich Shop, 174 5th Ave (between W 22nd and 23rd sts) ☎675-5096. This narrow little restaurant is a Flatiron institution. A tuna sandwich and some matzoh ball soup will cure what ails you.

Vegetarian

Hangawi, 12 E 32nd St (between 5th and Madison aves) ☎213-0077. A strictly vegetarian Korean restaurant. Pumpkin porridge, shredded mountain root and bamboo rice are among the standouts. A little pricey, but quite good.

Zen Palate, 34 Union Square E (at E 16th St) ☎614-9291; 663 9th Ave (at W 46th St) ☎582-1669; 2170 Broadway (between 76th and 77th sts) ☎501-7768. Stylish and modern, with what it calls a "Zen atmosphere," these reliable restaurants serve up health-conscious vegetarian Asian food prepared to look, and sometimes even taste, like meat. Sit at the counter and pick an appetizer from the extensive list of "Tasty Morsels" for quick snacks alone.

Brunch

Weekend **brunch** is a competitive business in New York, and the number of restaurants offering it is constantly expanding. Selections below (most of which are covered in more detail elsewhere in the listings) all offer a good weekend menu, sometimes for an all-inclusive price that includes a free cocktail or two – though offers of freebies are to be treated with suspicion by those more interested in the food than getting blitzed. Above all, don't regard this as a definitive list. You'll find other possibilities all over Manhattan.

DOWNTOWN MANHATTAN

Aggie's, 146 W Houston St (at MacDougal St) ☎673-8994

Anglers & Writers, 420 Hudson St (at St Luke's Place) ☎675-0810

Caliente Cab Co, 61 7th Ave (at Bleecker St) ☎243-8517

Cupping Room Café, 359 W Broadway (between Broome and Grand sts) ☎925-2898

Danal, 90 E 10th St (between 3rd and 4th aves) ☎982-6930

Elephant and Castle, 68 Greenwich Ave (between 6th and 7th aves) ☎243-1400

Home, 20 Cornelia St (between Bleecker and W 4th sts) ☎243-9579

Japonica, 100 University Place (at E 12th St) ☎243-7752

Jerry's Restaurant, 101 Prince St (between Greene and Mercer sts) ☎966-9464

Jules, 65 St Mark's Place (between 1st and 2nd aves, ☎477-5560

Old Devil Moon, 511 E 12th St (between aves A and B) ☎475-4375

Paris Commune, 411 Bleecker St (between W 11th and Bank sts) ☎929-0509

7A, 109 Ave A (between E 6th and 7th sts) ☎673-6853

Yaffa Tea Room, 353 Greenwich St (at Harrison St); 19 Harrison St (at Greenwich St) ☎274-9403

Midtown west

Manifold good meals await you on the **western side of Midtown**, a neighborhood whose restaurants encompass Greek, South American, Japanese, African, French and everything in between. **Restaurant Row**, W 46th St between 8th and 9th aves, is a frequent stopover for theater-goers seeking a late-night meal, though **9th Ave** offers cheaper alternatives. Further east is the infamous galaxy of **Planets** – Hollywood, Harley Davidson and Hard Rock– that are not worth a visit as much as a laugh. Be aware that most restaurants in the **Times Square** area (now that it's a tourist hot spot) are overpriced and not great quality, with a few exceptions to that rule noted below.

Bakeries and cafés

Algonquin Hotel, 59 W 44th St, lobby (between 5th and 6th aves) ☎840-6800. The archetypal American interpretation of the English drawing room, located in the airy, attractive lobby of the hotel (home of the notorious Round Table). Good for afternoon teas (not high tea, though), or a drink.

Brasserie Centrale, 1700 Broadway (at W 53rd St) ☎757-2233. A rare Midtown place where you can linger over coffee, freshly baked treats or a full meal. The menu offers a range of burgers, soups, salads, pastas and average French-tinged brasserie standards (stick with the simpler items on the menu). Large outdoor seating area. Open 24 hours.

Cupcake Café, 522 9th Ave (at W 39th St) ☎465-1530. A delightful little joint, offering decent soup and sandwiches at bargain prices, and great cakes, cupcakes and pies. Anything with fruit is a must.

Eating

MIDTOWN MANHATTAN

Eighteenth and Eighth, 159 8th Ave (between W 17th and 18th sts) ☎242-5000

Food Bar, 149 8th Ave (between W 17th and 18th sts) ☎243-2020

Friend of a Farmer, 77 Irving Place (between E 18th and 19th sts) ☎477-2188

Royal Canadian Pancake Restaurant, 1004 2nd Ave (between E 53rd and 54th sts) ☎980-4131; also 2286 Broadway (between W 82nd and 83rd sts) ☎873-6052; 180 3rd Ave (between E 16th and 17th sts) ☎777-9288

UPTOWN MANHATTAN

Barking Dog Luncheonette, 1678 3rd Ave (at E 94th St) ☎831-1800

Copeland's, 547 W 145th St (between Broadway and Amsterdam Ave) ☎234-2357

E.A.T., 1064 Madison Ave (between E 80th and 81st sts) ☎772-0022

EJ's Luncheonette, 433 Amsterdam Ave (between W 81st and 82nd sts) ☎873-3444

Good Enough to Eat, 483 Amsterdam Ave (between W 83rd and 84th sts) ☎496-0163

Popover Café, 551 Amsterdam Ave (between W 86th and 87th sts) ☎595-8555

Sarabeth's Kitchen, 423 Amsterdam Ave (between W 80th and 81st St) ☎496-6280; 1295 Madison Ave (between E 92nd and 93rd sts) ☎410-7335

Shark Bar, 307 Amsterdam Ave (between W 74th and 75th sts) ☎874-8500

Sylvia's Restaurant, 328 Lenox Ave (between 126th and 127th sts) ☎996-0660

OUTER BOROUGHS

Montague Street Saloon, 122 Montague St (between Henry and Hicks sts), Brooklyn Heights ☎718/522-6770.

Oznot's Dish, 79 Berry (at N 9th St) ☎718/599-6596.

Eating

Poseidon Bakery, 629 9th Ave (between W 44th and 45th sts) ☎757-6173. Decadent baklava and other sweet Greek pastries, strudels and cookies, as well as spinach and meat pies. Known most of all for the hand-rolled phyllo dough that it makes on the premises and supplies to many restaurants in the city. Closed Sun and Mon.

American and continental

Arriba Arriba, 762 9th Ave (at W 51st St) ☎489-0810. Boozy Tex-Mex place, popular with the after-work crowd for the great margaritas as much as the inexpensive meals.

Bryant Park Grill, 25 W 40th St (between 5th and 6th aves) ☎840-6500. The food is standard-upscale (Caesar salad, grilled chicken, rack of lamb, hake), but the real reason to come is atmosphere, provided by the Park, whether viewed from within the spacious dining room or enjoyed al fresco on the terrace. The $15 prix-fixe weekend brunch is a good deal, otherwise it can be pricey, with dinner entrees in the $15–25 range. Also: *The Café at Bryant Park* next door on the terrace (May–Sept), serves less expensive, lighter options such as salads and a few main dishes ($5–15). But beware; it's a huge singles scene, and cigars rule.

Ellen's Stardust Diner, 1650 Broadway (at W 51st St) ☎307-7575. Another 1950s-style diner serving traditional American food and built around the "missed my subway home" theme.

Hamburger Harry's, 145 W 45th St (between Broadway and 6th Ave) ☎840-0566. Handy diner just off Times Square; some claim its burgers are the best in town.

Hard Rock Café, 221 W 57th St (between Broadway and 7th Ave) ☎489-6565. Burger restaurant that for some reason continues to pull in celebrity New York, or at least the odd rock star. Full to bursting with tourists most nights, especially on weekends. The food isn't bad, but only really worth it if you've a teenager in tow.

Jerry's Metro Delicatessen, 790 8th Ave (at W 48th St) ☎581-9100. Large deli restaurant with a huge choice of sandwiches, omelettes and burgers, etc. Good breakfasts, too.

Joe Allen's, 326 W 46th St (between 8th and 9th aves) ☎581-6464. Tried and true formula of checkered tablecloths, old-fashioned barroom feel, and reliable American food at moderate prices. The calf's liver with spinach and potatoes has been on the menu for 20 years. Popular pre-theater spot, so reserve well in advance unless you can arrive after 8pm. Either way, have a Bloody Mary.

Landmark Tavern, 626 11th Ave (at 46th St) ☎757-8595. A long-established Irish tavern popular with a yuppie crowd. Tasty menu with large proportions, and the Irish soda bread is baked fresh every day.

Market Diner, 572 11th Ave (at W 43rd St) ☎695-0415. The ultimate 24-hour diner, chrome-furnished and usually full of weary clubbers filling up on breakfast. A good place to refuel early evening, too.

Mike's American Bar & Grill, 650 10th Ave (between W 45th and 46th sts) ☎246-4155. Funky "downtown" bar in Midtown west (aka "Hell's Kitchen"). The decor changes each season, but the menu stays basic: burgers, nachos and the like.

Planet Hollywood, 140 W 57th St (between 6th and 7th aves) ☎333-7827. A tourist trap in the *Hard Rock Café* vein, but with movie rather than music memorabilia. Co-owned by Bruce Willis, Sylvester Stallone and Arnold Schwarzenegger.

Rock Center Cafe, 20 W 50th St (at Rockefeller Plaza) ☎332-7620. Gazing at the Rockefeller Center ice skating rink and plaza, is what this place has going for it. Slated to open in the winter of 2000, it is replacing the *American Festival Café* – call ahead to make sure it's open.

Stage Deli, 834 7th Ave (between W 53rd and 54th sts) ☎245-7850. Another reliable all-night standby, and longtime rival to the *Carnegie Deli*, p.367. More genuine New York attitude and big over-stuffed sandwiches but it's not at all cheap.

The Supper Club, 240 W 47th St (between Broadway and 8th Ave) ☎921-1940. Enormous restaurant/swing club, with an eclectic menu derived from the menus of famous old nightclubs of the 1940s and 1950s, great period decor, and a talented Big Band orchestra. If you enjoy the style, you'll love this grand palace (formerly a Broadway theater). Call ahead for the schedule and to book a table – it's still a hot spot, and as you might expect, not at all cheap.

Virgil's Real BBQ, 152 W 44th St (between Broadway and 6th Ave) ☎921-9494. Hardcore ribs and biscuits for barbecue enthusiasts, though the ambience leaves something to be desired. A bit pricey, so order light – chances are you'll still end up with too much. Very popular with tourists, especially pre-theater, so despite its huge size waits can be long. Also very noisy.

West Bank Café, 407 W 42nd St (at 9th Ave) ☎695-6909. Some French, some American, all delicious and not as expensive as you'd think – entrees are $9–16. Very popular with theater people before and especially after a performance. Recommended.

Zuni, 598 9th Ave (at W 43rd St) ☎765-7626. Pricey haute Mexican cuisine in an informal setting. They make the guacamole fresh at your table.

Asian

Dish of Salt, 133 W 47th St (between 6th and 7th aves) ☎921-4242. Tired of the linoleum-table Cantonese fare in Chinatown? For approximately five times as much money, you can dig into roast plum duckling and spinach with crabmeat, served impeccably at huge polished-wood tables at this Midtown institution.

Ollie's Noodle Shop, 190 W 44th St (between Broadway and 8th Ave) ☎921-5988; also 2315 Broadway (at W 84th St) ☎362-3111; 2957 Broadway (at W 116th St) ☎932-3300. Good Chinese restaurant that serves marvellous noodles, barbecued meats and spare ribs. Not, however, a place to linger. Very cheap, very crowded and very noisy. Also very popular pre-theater place, so don't be alarmed if there are long lines – but due to the rushed service, they move fast.

Pongsri Thai Restaurant, 244 W 48th St (between Broadway and 8th Ave) ☎582-3392; 106 Bayard St (at Baxter St) ☎349-3132; 311 2nd Ave (at E 18th St) ☎477-4100. Restaurant popular at lunchtime with local businesspeople for its extensive and good-value lunch menu – rice and noodle combos a specialty. A massive menu in the evenings.

Sukhothai, 411 W 42nd St (between 9th and 10th aves) ☎947-1930. Sumptuous, over-the-top decor, with sunken seating in the main dining area and beautiful multicolored kites hanging from the ceiling. The Thai food is better than one might expect, served in traditional brass pots and ranging from noodle dishes to spicy meat and seafood (even frogs legs), in curry and chili paste sauces. Entrees range from $7.95–14.95. A good choice for pre-theater.

Caribbean, Central and South American

Cabana Carioca, 123 W 45th St (between 6th Ave and Broadway) ☎581-8088. Animated restaurant decorated with colorful murals. A great place to try out Brazilian-Portuguese specialties, like *feijoada* (black bean and pork stew), washed down with fiery *caipirinhas*. Portions large enough for two make it reasonably inexpensive.

Via Brasil, 34 W 46th St (between 5th and 6th aves) ☎997-1158. Excellent place to taste *feijoada*, Brazil's national dish – a meaty black bean stew. A bit pricey, though, entrees are in the range of $13–22. Live music Wed–Sat nights.

Victor's Café 52, 236 W 52nd St (between Broadway and 8th Ave)

Eating

Eating

586-7714. A well-established hangout, serving real Cuban food at moderate prices. Great black bean soup and sangria.

French and Belgian

Café Un, Deux, Trois, 123 W 44th St (between Broadway and 6th Ave) ☎354-4148. Crowded French brasserie-style restaurant close to Times Square serving fair-to-middling food. Crayons for table-top doodling while you wait for your order. $12–25 for a main course.

Chantal Café, 257 W 55th St (between Broadway and 8th Ave) ☎246-7076. Quiet little bistro serving a savory chicken with rosemary and other continental specialties.

Chez Napoleon, 365 W 50th St (between 8th and 9th aves) ☎265-6980. Due to this neighborhood's proximity to the docks, it became a hangout for French soldiers during World War II, leading to the creation of several highly authentic Gallic eateries here in the 1940s and 1950s. This is one of them, and it lives up to its reputation. A friendly, family-run bistro; bring a wad to enjoy the tradition, though.

Hourglass Tavern, 373 W 46th St (between 8th and 9th aves) ☎265-2060. Tiny Midtown French restaurant – around eight tables in all – which serves an excellent-value, two-course prix-fixe menu for just $12.75. Choose between two appetizers and half a dozen or so main courses – a small range that guarantees good cooking. The gimmick is the hourglass above each table, the emptying of which means you're supposed to leave and make way for someone else. In reality they seem to last more than an hour, and they only enforce it if there's a line. Cash only.

La Bonne Soupe, 48 W 55th St (between 5th and 6th aves) ☎586-7650. Traditional French food at reasonable prices. Steaks, omelettes, snails and fondues from $14.

La Cité, 120 W 51st St (between 6th and 7th aves) ☎956-7100. A handsome Midtown French steakhouse. Expensive – entrees are $20–30.

Le Madeleine, 403 W 43rd St (between 9th and 10th aves) ☎246-2993. Pretty Midtown French bistro with good service, good food (including some knockout desserts) and moderate to expensive prices. Get a seat in the outdoor garden if you can. Usually crowded pre-theater.

René Pujol, 321 W 51st (between 8th and 9th aves) ☎246-3023. See *Chez Napoleon* above. This room is a little brighter and the food less traditional, *tant pis*. Expensive.

German

Hallo Berlin, 402 W 51st St (between 9th and 10th aves) ☎541-6248. On the West Side, the best for wursts. The owner used to sell this stuff from a pushcart, and made enough to open a restaurant. Pleasant bench-and-table beer-garden setting.

Greek and Middle Eastern

Afghanistan Kebab House, 1345 2nd Ave (between E 70th and 71st sts) ☎517-2776; 155 W 46th St (between 6th and 7th aves) ☎768-3875. Inexpensive lamb, chicken and seafood kebabs, served with a variety of side dishes. Complete dinners for under $15.

Ariana Afghan Kebab, 787 9th Ave (between W 52nd and 53rd sts) ☎262-2323. A casual neighborhood restaurant serving inexpensive kebab (chicken, lamb and beef) and vegetarian meals.

Lotfi's Couscous, 358 W 46th St (between 8th and 9th aves) ☎582-5850. Moderately priced Moroccan hidden away on the second floor. Lots of spicy dishes, vegetarian options and inexpensive salads. Closed in Aug.

Uncle Nick's, 747 9th Ave (between W 50th and 51st sts) ☎315-1726. A clean, sunny little restaurant with unimpassioned but filling Greek standards.

Italian

Becco, 355 W 46th St (between 8th and 9th aves) ☎397-7597. A welcome addition to "Restaurant Row" – and as such is busy with the pre-theater crowd –

where you get generous amounts of antipasto and pasta for around $20.

Carmine's, 200 W 44th St (between Broadway and 8th Ave) ☎221-3800; also 2450 Broadway (between W 90th and 91st sts) ☎362-2200. This restaurant made a name for itself with its combination of decent (and decently priced) Southern Italian food in mountainous portions meant to be shared and for the noisy, convivial atmosphere in which it's served. Prices can seem high until you see the portions; for example, the fried calamari ($16) or the osso bucco ($38), either of which could easily feed 3 to 4 people. Reservations for groups of 6 or more; otherwise be prepared to wait in line.

Julian's, 802 9th Ave (between 53rd and 54th sts) ☎262-4800. Light and inventive Mediterranean fare in a bright, pleasing room and clever dining garden tucked in an alley. Whether you want sandwiches or scalloppine, a safe bet in Hell's Kitchen.

Supreme Macaroni Co., 511 9th Ave (between W 38th and 39th sts) ☎564-8074. A macaroni shop with a small, divy but lovable restaurant attached.

Trattoria dell'Arte, 900 7th Ave (between W 56th and 57th sts) ☎245-9800. Unusually nice restaurant for this rather tame stretch of Midtown, with a lovely airy interior, excellent service and good food. Great, wafer-thin crispy pizzas, decent and imaginative pasta dishes for around $15 and a mouth-watering antipasto bar – all eagerly patronized by an elegant out-to-be-seen crowd. Best to reserve.

Jewish and Eastern European

Carnegie Deli, 854 7th Ave (between W 54th and 55th sts) ☎757-2245. This place is known for the size of its sandwiches – by popular consent the most generously stuffed in the city, and a full meal in themselves. The chicken noodle soup is good, too. Not cheap, however, and the waiters are among New York's rudest.

Firebird, 365 W 46th St (between 8th and 9th aves) ☎586-0244. A marble foyer leads to a lush dining room covered in rich reds and golds in this stand-out Russian eatery. It is an expensive but worthwhile dining experience – entrees are about $25 a plate but their pre-the-ater prix-fixe menu is a steal.

Uncle Vanya Café, 315 W 54th St (between 8th and 9th aves) ☎262-0542. White Russian delicacies, including more than just the obligatory borscht and caviar. Moderately priced. Sundays open only 2–11pm.

Vegetarian

Great American Health Bar, 35 W 57th St (between 5th and 6th aves) ☎355-5177. This Manhattan chain comes well praised, but in reality the food can be rather bland and uninviting. Committed veggies only.

Midtown east

Catering mostly to lunchtime office-going crowds that swarm the sidewalks on weekdays, the **eastern side of Midtown** overflows with restaurants, most of them on the pricey side. You probably won't want to make it the focal point of too many culinary excursions but, that said, there are a few time-worn favorites in the neighborhood.

American and continental

Broadway Diner, 590 Lexington Ave (at E 52nd St) ☎486-8838; 1726 Broadway (at W 55th St) ☎765-0909. An upscale coffee shop with 1950s-style ambience.

Comfort Diner, 214 E 45th St (between 2nd and 3rd aves) ☎867-4555; 142 E 86th St at Lexington Ave ☎369-8628. One of the friendliest spots in town, this retro diner serves up hearty staples like meatloaf, fried chicken, and macaroni and cheese. It's a great place to fill up and rest the weary toes.

Lipstick Café, 885 3rd Ave (at E 54th St) ☎486-8664. Unlike most restaurants in the neighborhood, this one serves up

Eating

Eating

delectable lunchtime food at affordable prices. Tasty homemade soups, salads and delicious baked goods. Closed weekends.

Rosen's Delicatessen, 23 E 51st St (between 5th and Madison aves) ☎541-8320. Enormous Art Deco restaurant, renowned for its pastrami and corned beef, and handily situated for those suffering from Midtown shopping fatigue. Good breakfasts too.

Royal Canadian Pancake Restaurant, 2286 Broadway (between W 82nd and 83rd sts) ☎873-6052; 180 3rd Ave (between E 16th and 17th sts) ☎777-9288. This chain serves up numerous kinds of vast – and delicious – pancakes, with fillings ranging from white chocolate and almonds to berries and bananas. Come hungry, and try sharing.

Smith and Wollensky, 797 3rd Ave (at 49th St) ☎753-1530. Clubby atmosphere in a grand setting, where waiters – many of whom have worked here for twenty years or more – serve you the primest cuts of beef imaginable. Quite pricey – you'll pay at least $30 a steak – but worth the splurge. Go basic with the sides and wines.

Asian

Hatsuhana, 17 E 48th St (between 5th and Madison aves) ☎355-3345; 237 Park Ave (at E 46th St) ☎661-3400. Every sushi lover's favorite sushi restaurant, now with two branches. Not at all cheap, so try to get there for the prix-fixe lunch.

Vong, 200 E 54th St (between 2nd and 3rd aves) ☎486-9592. This is the eccentrically, exotically decorated restaurant everyone was talking about last month – or was it last year? In any case it's still hot enough to make your wallet smoke. The chefs take a French colonial approach to Thai cooking, doing things like putting mango in foie gras, and sesame and tamarind on Moscovy Duck. Somehow it works. You can get a "tasting menu" of samples for the bargain price of $65 per person.

Caribbean, Central and South American

Zarela, 953 2nd Ave (between E 50th and 51st sts) ☎644-6740. If you've ever wondered what regional home-cooked Mexican food really tastes like, this festive restaurant is the place to go. It's noticeably more expensive than most Mexican places, but worth every bit.

Restaurants with views

This is a brief checklist of – mainly Manhattan – restaurants that draw many people just for their **views** or **location**. Some of the restaurants are covered in more detail in other sections (including "Expense-account restaurants," pp.374–375); where they're not, it's worth bearing in mind that the quality of the views will almost invariably be reflected in the size of your bill.

Boat Basin Cafe, W 79th St (at the Hudson River) ☎496-5542

Boathouse Café, Central Park Lake (east side, near 72nd St entrance) ☎517-2233

Hudson River Club, 4 World Financial Center, Upper Level (between Liberty and Vesey sts) ☎786-1500

River Café, 1 Water St (at the East River), Brooklyn ☎718/522-5200

Tavern on the Green, W 67th St (at Central Park W) ☎873-3200

The Terrace, 400 W 119th St (between Amsterdam Ave and Morningside Drive) ☎666-9490

The Water Club, 500 E 30th St (at the East River; access from 34th St) ☎683-3333

Windows on the World, World Trade Center, 107th floor (at West St) ☎938-1111

Fish and seafood

Goldwater's, 988 2nd Ave (between E 52nd and 53rd sts) ☎888-2122. Fish dishes in huge portions for $10–15 a head. Primarily a seafood restaurant, though some steaks and pastas are served. Recently renovated, the new slick look serves it well – occasional live music as well.

Oyster Bar, Lower level, Grand Central Terminal (at 42nd St and Park Ave) ☎490-6650. Atmospheric turn-of-the-century place located down in the vaulted dungeons of Grand Central, where Midtown execs and others break for lunch. Fish, seafood, and of course oysters, though none of it exactly budget-rated – reckon on a minimum of $25 and upwards per dish, for lunch. If you're hard up, eat at the bar and taste the clam chowder with bread – delicious, quite ample and around $8 – or great creamy bowls of pan-roast oysters or clams for around $15.

French

Lutece, see the box entitled "Expense-account restaurants" on page 375.

Rive Gauche, 560 3rd Ave (at 37th St) ☎ 949-5400. Pleasant, if unremarkable neighborhood French bistro, serving soups, salads and classic entrees at a reasonable price (for French food), around $15–20 an entree.

Spanish

Solera, 216 E 53rd St (between 2nd and 3rd aves) ☎644-1166. Tapas and other Spanish specialties in a stylish town-house setting. As you'd expect from the surroundings and the ambience, it can be expensive.

Upper West Side and Morningside Heights

Restaurants on the **Upper West Side** have been steadily improving in recent years, with a wide array of ethnic and price choices (particularly if you avoid the overpriced **Lincoln Center** area). There

are lots of generous burger joints, Chinese restaurants, friendly coffee shops, and delectable, if a bit pricey, brunch spots, so you'll never be at a loss for good meals.

Bakeries and cafés

The Bread Shop, 3139 Broadway (at W 123rd St) ☎666-4343. Rich homemade breads and buttermilk biscuits in the bakery section, and soup and pizza in the cozy little restaurant section. A good place to rest up if you're in the neighborhood.

Café Mozart, 154 W 70th St (between Central Park W and Columbus Ave) ☎595-9797. Faded old Viennese coffeehouse that serves rich tortes and apple strudel.

Caffè la Fortuna, 69 W 71st St (between Central Park W and Columbus Ave) ☎724-5846. The walls are covered with records and black-and-white photos of opera personalities. The atmosphere is dark, comfy and inviting. You can sip a coffee all day long in the shade of their peaceful garden, and their Italian pastries are heavenly. Recommended.

Edgar's Café, 255 W 84th St (between West End Ave and Broadway) ☎496-6126. A pleasant coffeehouse with good desserts and light snacks, great hot cider in the winter, and well-brewed coffees and teas all the time. Named for Edgar Allen Poe, who at one time lived a block or so farther east on 84th St.

Hungarian Pastry Shop, 1030 Amsterdam Ave (between 110th and 111th sts) ☎866-4230. This simple, no-frills coffeehouse is a favorite with Columbia University students and faculty alike. You sip your espresso and read all day if you like; the only problem is choosing amongst the pastries, cookies and cakes, all made on the premises.

African

The Nile, 103 W 77th St (between Amsterdam and Columbus aves) ☎580-3232. Ethiopian restaurant, where the

Eating

Eating

food is served on low tables, with even lower stools. Eat with your fingers using soft, flat *injera* bread. The food consists of rich meat stews and lentil and vegetable concoctions washed down with sharp African beer. Very tasty. Main dishes priced around $10.

American and continental

All State Café, 250 W 72nd St (between Broadway and West End Ave) ☎874-1883. Hamburgers, steaks and American food from $10–14 make this a popular Upper West Side hangout. Seating is limited, and it closes at 11.30pm; get here early to be sure of a place.

Amsterdam's, 428 Amsterdam Ave (between W 80th and 81st sts) ☎874-1377. Bar-restaurant serving burgers, great fries, chicken, pasta and the like for $12–15 per entree.

Big Nick's, 2175 Broadway (between 76th and 77th sts) ☎362-9238. If you want a hamburger or pizza on the Upper West Side, this is a fun, New York kind of place. In his crowded, chaotic little wooden-table restaurant, Big Nick has been serving them up all night long to locals for 20-plus years. Wash the stuff down with 12-ounce draft beers at $1 a pop.

Boat Basin Café, 79th St at the Hudson River (access through Riverside Park) ☎496-5542. An outdoor restaurant, open May through Sept, with informal tables covered in red-and-white checked cloths, some under a sheltering overhang. The food is standard, but inexpensive considering the prime location – burgers with fries ($7.50), hot dogs, sandwiches (also around $7) and some more serious entrees like grilled salmon ($13.50). On weekend afternoons a violin trio adds to the ambiance.

Boathouse Café, Central Park Lake (72nd St entrance) ☎517-2233. Peaceful retreat from a hard day's trudging around the 5th Ave museums. You get great views of the famous Central Park skyline and decent American/continental cuisine, but at very steep prices. Closed from Oct to March.

Dallas BBQ, 27 W 72nd St (between Columbus Ave and Central Park W) ☎873-2004; 1265 3rd Ave (at E 73rd St) ☎772-9393; 21 University Place (at E 8th St) ☎674-4450; 132 2nd Ave (at St Mark's Place) ☎777-5574. A real-value budget option for this part of town, just off Central Park. Barbecue chicken and burgers for $5–8, chili, and great racks of tangy ribs, not to mention their obscenely large onion loaf. Whichever branch you try it'll be crowded, and be prepared for fast, but less than gracious service. Great early bird specials (between 5pm and 7pm).

Diane's Uptown, 249 Columbus Ave (between W 71st and 72nd sts) ☎799-6750. Fast, quick hearty burgers, and handy for Ben & Jerry's ice cream next door. Inexpensive and fun.

EJ's Luncheonette, 447 Amsterdam Ave (between W 81st and 82nd sts) ☎873-3444. Diner that does its best to look retro, with mirrors, booths upholstered in turquoise vinyl, and walls adorned with 1950s photographs. Unpretentious, affordable American food that includes pancakes in many guises and banana splits to die for. Also great French-fried sweet potatoes. Expect long lines for brunch on Sun.

Good Enough to Eat, 483 Amsterdam Ave (between W 83rd and 84th sts) ☎496-0163. Cutesy Upper West Side restaurant known for its cinnamon-swirl French toast, award-winning meatloaf, and excellent brunch value.

Gray's Papaya, 2090 Broadway (at W 72nd St) ☎799-0243. Order two all-beef franks and a papaya juice for a true New York experience. No ambiance, no seats, just good cheap grub.

Hi-Life Bar and Grill, 477 Amsterdam Ave (at W 83rd St) ☎787-7199; also 1340 1st Ave (at E 72nd St) ☎249-3600. A hip spot offering basic American fare and good people-watching. The uneven food and service seem to make no difference to the crowds.

Josephina, 1900 Broadway (between W 63rd and 64th sts, across from Lincoln

Center) ☎799-1000. Large airy restaurant painted with colonial murals (albeit cut in half by their new banquette seating). Good salads, soups and the like; moderate prices.

Positively 104th St, 2725 Broadway (between W 104th and 105th sts) ☎316-0372. Basic American food, with good steaks and a friendly atmosphere, make this a good choice for this part of town. Reasonably priced too.

Santa Fe, 72 W 69th St (between Columbus Ave and Central Park W) ☎724-0822. Upscale Southwestern cuisine in lovely surroundings – muted earth tones, large arrangements of fresh flowers and a cozy fireplace. The food is first-rate and the prices steep; be prepared to spend about $30 per person.

Sarabeth's Kitchen, 423 Amsterdam Ave (between W 80th and 81st St) ☎496-6280; 1295 Madison Ave (between E 92nd and 93rd sts) ☎410-7335. Best for brunch, this country-style restaurant serves delectable baked goods and impressive omelettes. Dinner is very pricey, so you're better off at brunch. But expect to wait in line.

Tom's Restaurant, 2880 Broadway (at W 112th St) ☎864-6137. Cheap, greasy-spoon fare. This is the *Tom's* of *Seinfeld* and Suzanne Vega fame, usually filled with students from Columbia. Great breakfast deals – a large meal for under $5.

Vince & Eddie's, 70 W 68th St (between Columbus Ave and Central Park W) ☎721-0068. Slightly pseudo-country-style restaurant serving American food like American grannies supposedly used to make – hearty, wholesome and delicious. Moderately priced.

Asian

Fujiyama Mama, 467 Columbus Ave (between W 82nd and 83rd sts) ☎769-1144. The West Side's best – and most boisterous – sushi bar, with high-tech decor and loud music.

Hunan Balcony, 2596 Broadway (at W 98th St) ☎865-0400; 1417 2nd Ave (at E 74th St) ☎517-2088. Cheap and reliable Hunan-style food from $6–11. Soft-shell crab for $12.95.

Hunan Park, 235 Columbus Ave (between 70th and 71st sts) ☎724-4411. Some of the best Chinese on the Upper West Side, in a large, crowded room, with typically quick service and moderate prices. Try the spicy noodles in sesame sauce and the dumplings. A good, less expensive option within a few blocks of Lincoln Center.

Lemongrass Grill, 2534 Broadway (between W 94th and 95th sts) ☎666-0888. Very reasonable Upper West Side Thai restaurant serving delicious chicken soup with lime juice and red pepper, spicy curries, basil chicken and Pad Thai from $8–15.

Lenge, 200 Columbus Ave (at W 69th St) ☎799-9188; 1465 3rd Ave (between E 82nd and 83rd sts). Decent Japanese restaurant, with lots of sushi choices, average prices.

Monsoon, 435 Amsterdam Ave (at W 81st St) ☎580-8686. It's best to come here for lunch when the crowds are smaller and the food is apt to be more dependable. Otherwise be prepared to wait. Try the grilled chicken on skewers or coconut curry shrimp noodle soup.

Ollie's Noodle Shop, 2315 Broadway (at W 84th St) ☎362-3111; 2957 Broadway (at W 116th St) ☎932-3300; 190 W 44th St (between Broadway and 8th Ave) ☎921-5988. Good Chinese restaurant that serves marvellous noodles, barbecued meats and spare ribs. Not, however, a place to linger. Very cheap, very crowded and very noisy.

Rikyu, 210 Columbus Ave (between W 69th and 70th sts) ☎799-7847. A wide selection of Japanese food, including sushi made to order. Inexpensive lunches and early-bird specials make this place a relative bargain.

Ruby Foo's, 2182 Broadway (at 77th St) ☎724-6700. Pan-Asian cuisine in an enjoyable setting, with new twists on dim sum, dumplings and sushi.

Eating

Eating

Caribbean, Central and South American

Flor de Mayo, 2651 Broadway (at W 101st St) ☎663-5520. Very cheap, very popular Cuban-Chinese restaurant with coffee-shop decor and lots of food, though not much for vegetarians – spicy chicken, Cuban-style steaks, etc. You can eat well for around $12.

Gabriela's, 685 Amsterdam Ave (at 93rd St) ☎961-0574. Terrific, inexpensive, authentic Mexican – not just your usual enchiladas and burritos, but also a wide array of regional chicken and seafood dishes. Large crowded room, noisy, lively and thoroughly enjoyable, but be prepared to wait unless you get there early. Recommended.

La Caridad, 2199 Broadway (at W 78th St) ☎874-2780. Recently doubled in size, and redecorated (sort of), this is something of an Upper West Side institution, a tacky, no-frills eatery that doles out plentiful and cheap Cuban-Chinese food to hungry diners (the Cuban is better than the Chinese). Bring your own beer, and expect to wait in line.

Pampa, 768 Amsterdam Ave (between 87th and 98th sts) ☎865-2929. Argentine meats are the thing here, though there are other things on the menu. Huge steaks, grilled meats (*churrasco*) and cold beer to wash it down. Charming little neighborhood spot, with moderate prices (entrees are $10–14).

Fish and seafood

Dock's Oyster Bar, 2427 Broadway (between W 89th and 90th sts) ☎724-5588; also 633 3rd Ave (at E 40th St) ☎986-8080. Some of the best seafood in town at this popular Uptown restaurant, with a raw bar, great mussels and a wide variety of high-quality fresh fish. The Upper West Side is the original and tends to have the homier atmosphere – though both can be noisy and service can be slow. Reservations are recommended on weekends.

Fish, 2799 Broadway (at 108th St) ☎864-5000. A nice compromise

between *nouvelle* and old-fashioned; the dishes here aren't fussy, just incredibly tasty. Fried calamari with anchovy butter is a good example; prawns roasted with bacon, cognac and scallions is another. Or just content yourself with impeccably fresh raw oysters.

Fishin' Eddie, 73 W 71st St (between Central Park W and Columbus Ave) ☎874-3474. Fresh fish in a homey New England-style setting.

French and Belgian

Café Luxembourg, 200 W 70th St (between Amsterdam and West End aves) ☎873-7411. Trendy Lincoln Center area bistro that packs in (literally) a self-consciously hip crowd to enjoy its first-rate contemporary French food. Not too pricey – two people can eat for $60 or so.

La Boite en Bois, 75 W 68th St (between Central Park W and Columbus Ave) ☎874-2705. Rustic, moderately priced Lincoln Center bistro that has good country French food.

Le Monde, 2885 Broadway (at 112th St) ☎531-3939. An inviting and moderately priced newcomer serving the Columbia University area. The decor is in classic French bistro style, with food that is so far uneven, so stick with the simpler items on the menu, such as roast chicken with garlic, steak frites, or the various salads and soups.

Les Routiers, 568 Amsterdam Ave (between 87th and 88th sts) ☎874-2742. Excellent French country/Provençal cuisine, in an intimate and unpretentious setting. Lamb shanks in lentils, mussels in white wine and other hearty dishes are all prepared very well. Mostly a regular, neighborhood crowd, making it relaxed and casual – sit in the front room if you can, it has more charm. Entrees run from $14–22. Recommended.

Greek and Middle Eastern

Symposium, 544 W 113rd St (between Broadway and Amsterdam Ave) ☎865-1011. Neighborhood restaurant near

Columbia University, serving favorite Greek dishes in a relaxed, student atmosphere.

Indian

Indian Café, 2791 Broadway (between 107th and 108th sts) ☎749-9200. This light, airy restaurant serves good Indian food at moderate prices. A pleasant spot for lunch or dinner (weekday lunch specials run from $5 to $7).

Mughlai, 320 Columbus Ave (at W 75th St) ☎724-6363. Uptown, upscale Indian with prices about the going rate for this

strip: $10–15 an entree. The food, though, is surprisingly good.

Italian

Ernie's, 2150 Broadway (at W 75th St) ☎496-1588. Casual, extra-large Upper West Side Italian, serving staple, decent food at slightly inflated prices.

Gennaro, 665 Amsterdam Ave (between 92nd and 93rd sts) ☎665-5348. A tiny outpost of really great Italian food, with room only for about 25 people (and thus perpetual lines to get in). Standouts include a warm potato,

Eating

Restaurants with outdoor seating

The following is just a brief checklist of restaurants that regularly have **outdoor seating in summer**. Many Manhattan restaurants, especially in the Village and on the Upper East and West sides, put at least a few tables out on the sidewalk when the weather gets warm.

DOWNTOWN MANHATTAN

Caffè Reggio, 119 MacDougal St (between Bleecker and W 3rd sts) ☎475-9557

Cloister Cafe, 238 E 9th St (between 2nd and 3rd aves) ☎777-9128

The Coffee Shop, 29 Union Square W (between E 16th and 17th sts) ☎243-7969

KK Restaurant, 192–194 1st Ave (between E 11th and 12th sts) ☎777-4430

Miracle Grill, 112 1st Ave (between E 6th and 7th sts) ☎254-2353

Pisces, 95 Ave A (between E 6th and 7th sts) ☎260-6660

Provence, 38 MacDougal St (between Prince and Houston sts) ☎475-7500

Radio Perfecto, 190 Avenue B (between 11th and 12th sts) ☎477-3366

Spring Street Natural Restaurant, 62 Spring St (at Lafayette St) ☎966-0290

St Dymphnas, 118 St Mark's Place (between Ave A and 1st Ave) ☎254-6636

Time Café, 380 Lafayette St (at Great Jones St) ☎533-7000; 87 7th Ave (at Barrow) ☎220-9100

White Horse Tavern, 567 Hudson St (at W 11th St) ☎243-9260

MIDTOWN MANHATTAN

Brasserie Centrale, 1700 Broadway (at W 53rd St) ☎757-2233

Bryant Park Grill, 25 W 40th St (between 5th and 6th aves) ☎840-6500

Caffe Bondí, 7 W 20th St (between 5th and 6th aves) ☎691-8136

Empire Diner, 210 10th Ave (between W 22nd and 23rd sts) ☎243-2736

Le Madeleine, 403 W 43rd St (between 9th and 10th aves) ☎246-2993

Pete's Tavern, 129 E 18th St (at Irving Place) ☎473-7676

UPTOWN MANHATTAN

Boat Basin Cafe, W 79th St (at the Hudson River) ☎496-5542

Boathouse Café, Central Park Boating Lake (72nd St entrance) ☎517-2233

Caffe la Fortuna, 69 W 71st St (between Central Park W and Columbus Ave) ☎724-5846

The Saloon, 1920 Broadway (at W 64th St) ☎874-1500

Eating

mushroom and goat cheese tart (incredible) and braised lamb shank in red wine. The desserts are also worth the wait. Moderate prices – open for dinner only. Recommended.

Sambuco, 20 W 72nd St (between Columbus Ave and Central Park W) ☎787-5656. Serves up huge portions of good food at very reasonable prices.

Expense-account restaurants

Should you win the lottery or have rich relatives, New York has some superb restaurants to choose from, most of them serving French or French-tinged American food, or in some cases variations on California-style cuisine. Go expecting to pay upwards of $100 a head, dress up, and phone first for reservations. If, however, you want to try one of these more expensive eateries but have neither the will nor the way to pay for it, go for lunch instead. You'll get a much better deal, often for a fixed price.

Ambassador Grill, *Regal UN Plaza Hotel*, 1 UN Plaza (E 44th St just off 1st Ave) ☎702-5014. In the *UN Plaza Hotel*, so you know what kind of clientele it serves: one that appreciates quiet and demands excellent food and service. Food tends toward the old-fashioned coq au vin and medallions of whatever, but you aren't going to see it done much better elsewhere, and the sleek dining room is truly ambassadorial.

Aquavit, 13 W 54th St (between 5th and 6th aves) ☎307-7311. Superb Scandinavian food – pickled herrings, salmon, even reindeer – in a lovely atrium restaurant. A real treat.

Aureole, 34 E 61st St (between Madison and Park aves) ☎319-1660. Magical French-accented American food in a gorgeous old brownstone setting. The prix-fixe options should bring the cost down to $70 per head. Actually though, the late lunch special (after 2pm) is truly affordable (and a steal) at $19.98.

Bouley, 165 Duane St (between Greenwich and Hudson sts) ☎608-3852. One of New York's best French restaurants, serving modern French food made from the freshest ingredients under the eye of chef David Bouley. Popular with city celebrities, but costs for the magnificent meals can be soft-ened by opting for the prix-fixe lunch and dinner options.

Elaine's, 1703 2nd Ave (between E 88th and 89th sts) ☎534-8103. Remember the opening shots of Woody Allen's *Manhattan*? That was *Elaine's*, and today her restaurant is still something of a favorite with New York celebrities – though it's hard to see why. If you want to star-gaze there's no better place to come; if you're hungry for good food or watching the pennies, best go somewhere else.

Four Seasons, 99 E 52nd St (between Park and Lexington aves) ☎754-9494. Housed in Mies van der Rohe's Seagram Building, this is one of the city's most noted restaurants, not least for the decor, which includes murals by Picasso, sculptures by Richard Lippold and interior design by Philip Johnson. The food isn't at all bad either, and there's a relatively inexpensive pre-theater menu – around $40 – if you want to try it. Somewhat stuffier than the other top restaurants.

Gotham Bar & Grill, 12 E 12th St (between 5th Ave and University Place) ☎620-4020. This restaurant serves marvellous American fare in an airy, trendy setting. Generally reckoned to be one of the city's truly best restaurants; and it's at least worth a drink in the bar to see the city's beautiful people drift in.

Sfuzzi, 58 W 65th St (between Central Park W and Broadway) ☎385-8080. Swinging bar scene and lots of Italian hors d'oeuvres – easily enough to make yourself a mini dinner. Try the frozen *sfuzzi* drink – fresh peach nectar, champagne and peach schnapps.

V&T Pizzeria, 1024 Amsterdam Ave (between W 110th and 111th sts) ☎663-1708. Checked tablecloths and a

Hudson River Club, 4 World Financial Center, 250 Vesey St, Upper Level (at West St) ☎786-1500. Worth the $70 or so per head for the view over the harbor to the Statue of Liberty. The food is American, with special emphasis on cooking from New York State's Hudson River Valley. Try the pumpkin-apple soup or the roast free-range chicken with beet risotto, but save room for one of the scrumptious chocolate desserts.

Le Bernadin, 155 W 51st St (between 6th and 7th aves) ☎489-1515. Renowned as perhaps the best place in New York to eat fish, for which the chef has received rave reviews. However, to enjoy both that and the clubby teak decor of this place you have to book weeks in advance. And it's one of the city's most expensive restaurants, of any kind. Not for the faint of heart.

Le Cirque 2000, *New York Palace Hotel*, 455 Madison Ave (between 50th and 51st sts) ☎794-9292. Recently relocated, it is still widely considered to be one of the city's best restaurants, though not quite as good as it used to be. Very orchestrated, very expensive, and frequented over the years by the likes of Liza Minnelli, Richard Nixon and Ronald Reagan.

Lutece, 249 E 50th St (between 2nd and 3rd aves) ☎752-2225. Still rated one of the best restaurants in the country, and a favorite of many well-to-do New Yorkers. The classic French food is top-notch, the service elegant and understated. What's surprising is how low key and completely unpretentious it is, though you do need big bucks and reservations in advance. Worth every penny.

River Café, 1 Water St (at the Brooklyn Bridge), Brooklyn ☎718/522-5200. You probably won't be able to afford the food, but for the price of a drink you can enjoy the best view of the Lower Manhattan skyline there is. Try brunch – it's the best bargain.

Russian Tea Room, 150 W 57th St (between 6th and 7th aves) ☎265-0947. Recently renovated and, at the time of writing, predicting to be open by the year 2000 it is one of New York's favorite places to hobnob with the literati. Rates are perhaps not as high as in the city's top French dining spots, and it's easier to get a table (though unless you're a celeb you may get relegated to the 2nd floor dining room). The wonderfully garish interior makes eating here a real occasion, too, though choose carefully on the rather overrated menu, and stick to the old favorites – the blinis are among the city's best, as is the borscht and the chicken Kiev.

21 Club, 21 W 52nd St (between 5th and 6th aves) ☎582-7200. Though the days when the likes of Dorothy Parker regularly dined here are over, this remains a stylish, power-broking restaurant, enormously popular despite its deliriously high prices. (You can, however, get a prix-fixe luncheon for $24.)

Windows on the World, One World Trade Center, 107th floor (at West St) ☎524-7000. Recent renovations have cleaned it up a bit; the views remain unchanged and are the main attraction. But if you've money to burn the food's good too, and the wine cellar is said to be among the best in New York. A nice (pricey) venue for Sunday brunch; weekday lunch, previously only served to lunch club members, is now open to anyone with the money.

Eating

low-key, down-home feel describes this pizzeria near Columbia that draws a predictably college-aged crowd. Good though, and very inexpensive.

Vinnie's Pizza, 285 Amsterdam Ave (between W 73rd and 74th sts) ☎874-4332. Some say the best, cheesiest pizzas on the Upper West Side. Cheap too.

Jewish and Eastern European

Barney Greengrass (The Sturgeon King), 541 Amsterdam Ave (between W 86th and 87th sts) ☎724-4707. A West Side deli and restaurant that's been around since time began. The smoked salmon section is a particular treat.

Fine & Schapiro, 138 W 72nd St (between Broadway and Columbus Ave) ☎877-2721. Longstanding Jewish deli that's open for lunch and dinner and serves delicious old-fashioned kosher fare – an experience that's getting harder to find in New York. Great chicken soup. See p.466.

Upper East Side

Upper East Side restaurants cater mostly to a discriminating and well-heeled clientele; many of our French and Italian "Expense-account restaurants" (see box overleaf) call this neighborhood home. Otherwise, the cuisine here is much like that of the Upper West Side: a mixture of Asian, standard American and more reasonable Italian cafés. For a change of pace, try a wurst and some strudel at one of **Yorkville**'s old-world German luncheonettes.

Bakeries and cafés

Food Attitude, 127 E 60th St (between Lexington and Park aves) ☎980-1818. Sweet fruit tarts and chocolate truffle cakes make this tiny café a good place to rest up between sights. A display of crusty bread creatures graces the front window. Closed Sun.

Les Friandises, 922 Lexington Ave (between E 70th and 71st sts) ☎988-1616. A paradise of French pastries on the Upper East side. Wonderful croissants and brioches and a sublime *tarte tatin.*

Patisserie & Bistro, 1032 Lexington Ave (between 72nd and 73rd sts) ☎717-5252. This is real Parisian pastry – buttery, creamy and over the top. Cookies, cakes, and crème brûlée made to the exacting standards of the kitchen staffs of local millionaires.

American and continental

Barking Dog Luncheonette, 1678 3rd Ave (at E 94th St) ☎831-1800. Puppy motif at this Uptown diner with extra-special mashed potatoes and grilled cheese sandwiches. Expect lines for brunch.

Canyon Road, 1470 1st Ave (between E 76th and 77th sts) ☎734-1600. Yuppie Upper East Side place effecting a Santa Fe atmosphere. Moderate prices.

E.A.T., 1064 Madison Ave (between E 80th and 81st sts) ☎772-0022. Expensive and crowded but excellent food (Eli Zabar is the owner, so that's no surprise) – especially the soups and breads, and the *ficelles* and Parmesan toast. Unlike most in the city, the mozzarella, basil and tomato sandwiches are fresh and heavenly.

Googie's Diner, 1491 2nd Ave (at E 78th St) ☎717-1122. Arty diner with funky decor and Italian-influenced American food.

Madhatter, 1485 2nd Ave (between E 77th and 78th sts) ☎628-4917. Casual pub serving decent burgers and other simple food in a lively, sometimes loud setting.

Rathbones, 1702 2nd Ave (between E 88th and 89th sts) ☎369-7361. Opposite *Elaine's* (see "Expense-account restaurants", p.374) and an excellent alternative for ordinary humans. Take a window seat, watch the stars arrive, and eat for a fraction of the price. Burgers, steak, fish for under $15 – and a wide choice of beers.

Serendipity 3, 225 E 60th St (between 2nd and 3rd aves) ☎838-3531. Long-established eatery and ice-cream parlor adorned with Tiffany lamps. Has been a favorite spot for Sweet Sixteen parties and after-the-movie first dates for years. The frozen hot chocolate, a trademarked and copyrighted recipe, is out of this world, and the wealth of ice cream offerings are a real treat too.

Viand, 673 Madison Ave (between E 61st and 62nd sts) ☎751-6622. A bit pricier than most diner fare but worth it for the enormous turkey sandwiches, remarkable burgers, and tasty vanilla Cokes.

Asian

Asia, 1155 3rd Ave (between E 67th and 68th sts) ☎879-5846. Pan-Asian cuisine in a handsome wood-paneled setting.

Bangkok House, 1485 1st Ave (between E 77th and 78th sts) ☎249-5700. Terrific Thai food, fairly priced. Try the deep-fried fish with chili sauce, Pad Thai for $8.75, or masaman curry with shrimp, chicken or beef for $10.75-11.50.

Pig Heaven, 1540 2nd Ave (between E 80th and 81st sts) ☎744-4333. Good-value Chinese restaurant decorated with images of pigs, serving lean and meaty spare ribs, among other things. In case you hadn't guessed, the accent is on pork.

Sala Thai, 1718 2nd Ave (between E 89th and 90th sts) ☎410-5557. Restaurant serving creative combinations of hot and spicy Thai food for under $15 a head. Pleasant decor, good service and the best Thai food in the neighborhood.

Wu Liang Ye, 215 E 86th St (between 2nd and 3rd aves) ☎534-8899. Excellent, authentic Szechuan food. The menu here features dishes you've never seen before, and if you like spicy food, you will not be disappointed. Perhaps one of the best Chinese restaurants in the whole city.

Caribbean, Central and South American

Bolivar, 206 E 60th St (between 2nd and 3rd aves) ☎838-0440. New South

American venue serving mostly Peruvian dishes and large Argentine steaks and grilled meats. Entrees run about $16-20. The next-door café section is cheaper and more casual, serving essentially the same food in smaller portions.

El Pollo, 1746 1st Ave (between E 90th and 91st sts) ☎996-7810. Fast-food Peruvian-style restaurant, serving rotisserie chicken, flavored with a variety of spices to eat in or take out. Delicious – and very cheap.

Fish and seafood

Katch, 339 E 75th St (between 1st and 2nd aves) ☎396-4434. Not only is the fish fresh and well prepared, it's available till 3am all week long. And most of the entrees are under $12.

French and Belgian

Bistro du Nord, 1312 Madison Ave (at E 93rd St) ☎289-0997. A cozy bistro with excellent Parisian fare. Very stylish atmosphere with moderate to expensive prices – entrees run from $18-24. Try the duck confit.

Le Refuge, 166 E 82nd St (between Lexington and 3rd aves) ☎861-4505. Quiet, intimate and deliberately romantic old-style French restaurant situated in an old city brownstone. Bouillabaisse and other seafood dishes are delectable. Expensive but worth it; save for special occasions. Closed Sun during the summer.

Mme Romaine de Lyon, 29 E 61st St (between Madison and Park aves) ☎758-2422. The best place for omelettes: they've got 550 on the lunch menu, and dinner features an expanded non-omelette menu (though honestly, why bother? Eggs are the thing here).

Greek and Middle Eastern

Uskudar, 1405 2nd Ave (between E 73rd and 74th sts) ☎988-2641. Authentic Turkish cuisine at a rather spartan Upper East Side venue. Great prices – plan on $25 or so for two.

Eating

Eating

Indian

Dawat, 210 E 58th St (between 2nd and 3rd aves) ☎355-7555. The best elegant gourmet Indian dining in the city. Try the Cornish game hen with green chili or the leg of lamb. A bit pricey – entrees average about $16. For an extra charge, Beverly will give you a tarot card reading.

Italian

Caffè Buon Gusto, 243 E 77th St (between 2nd and 3rd aves) ☎535-6884. This stretch of the Upper East Side has plenty of cool, Italian joints: what *Buon Gusto* lacks in style it makes up for in taste and low prices.

Carino, 1710 2nd Ave (between E 88th and 89th sts) ☎860-0566. Family-run Upper East Side Italian, with low prices, friendly service and good food. Two can eat for under $25.

Contrapunto, 200–206 E 60th St (at 3rd Ave) ☎751-8616. More than twenty fresh pastas daily at this friendly, neighborhood Italian restaurant. Reasonably priced as well.

Ecco-Là, 1660 3rd Ave (between E 92nd and 93rd sts) ☎860-5609. Unique pasta combinations at very moderate prices make this place one of the Upper East Side's most popular Italians. A real find if you don't mind waiting.

Il Vagabondo, 351 E 62nd St (between 1st and 2nd aves) ☎832-9221. Hearty family-style Southern Italian food in a casual setting that includes the restaurant's own bocci court.

Jewish and Eastern European

Heidelburg, 1648 2nd Ave (between E 85th and 86th sts) ☎628-2332. The atmosphere here is *mittel*-European kitsch, with gingerbread trim and waitresses in Alpine goatherd costumes. But the food is the real deal, featuring excellent liver dumpling soup, Bauernfruestuck omelettes, and pancakes (both sweet and potato). And they serve Weissbeer the right way, too – in giant, boot-shaped glasses.

Ideal Restaurant, 238 E 86th St (between 2nd and 3rd aves)

☎535-0950. Before renovations a few years back, this was the place. Now, we're not so sure. But you can still get wursts and sauerkraut in huge portions for paltry prices.

Mocca Hungarian, 1588 2nd Ave (between E 82nd and 83rd sts) ☎734-6470. Yorkville restaurant serving hearty portions of Hungarian comfort food – schnitzel, cherry soup, goulash and chicken paprikash, among others. Moderately priced, but be sure to come hungry.

Spanish

Malaga, 406 E 73rd St (between 1st and York aves) ☎737-7659. Intimate Spanish restaurant frequented by locals. Good, wholesome food at decent prices.

Harlem, Washington Heights, Inwood

Cheap Cuban, African, Caribbean and the best soul-food restaurants in the city abound in and around Harlem; even institutions like *Sylvia's*, touristy and crowded as it may be, remain reasonably priced. Too many visitors to New York forgo excursions, culinary and otherwise, to Harlem, but it's well worth the trip.

Bakeries and cafés

Wilson's Bakery and Restaurant, 1980 Amsterdam Ave (at W 158th St) ☎923-9821. Luscious Southern specialties, like sweet potato pie and peach cobbler, but much more than desserts – try the chicken and waffle combination.

African

Koryoe Restaurant and Café, 3143 Broadway (between Tiemann Place and LaSalle St) ☎316-2950. Huge portions of West African specialties served with your choice of meat and sauce. Try the *wacheay*, rice with black-eyed peas, plantains and your choice of meat for $10. Also vegetarian selections.

Zula, 1260 Amsterdam Ave (at W 122nd St) ☎663-1670. High-quality and inexpensive ($7 up) Ethiopian food that's popular with the folk from Columbia University. Spicy chicken, beef and lamb dishes mainly, though a few veggie plates too.

American and continental

Copeland's, 547 W 145th St (between Broadway and Amsterdam Ave) ☎234-

2357. Soul food at good prices for dinner or Sunday Gospel brunch, with a more reasonably priced cafeteria next door. Try the Louisiana gumbo. Live jazz on Fri and Sat nights.

Emily's, 1325 5th Ave (at E 111th St) ☎996-1212. Barbecued chicken and some of the best ribs in New York in a convivial atmosphere.

Eating

24-hour food

This is simply a checklist for **late-night** – and mainly budget-constrained – hunger. For details, either check the individual listings, or assume they serve a straight coffee-shop menu. If you're nowhere near any of the addresses below, don't despair. There are numerous additional all-night delis (for takeout food), and in most neighborhoods of the city you'll also find at least one 24-hour Korean greengrocer – good for most food supplies.

DOWNTOWN MANHATTAN

Around the Clock, 8 Stuyvesant St (between 2nd and 3rd aves) ☎598-0402

Bagel Buffet, 406 6th Ave (between W 8th and 9th sts) ☎477-0448

Dave's Pot Belly, 94 Christopher St (at Bleecker St) ☎242-8036

Florent, 69 Gansevoort St (between Washington and Greenwich sts) ☎989-5779

French Roast Café, 456 6th Ave (at W 11th St) ☎533-2233

Greenwich Cafe, 75 Greenwich Ave (between 7th Ave S and Bank St) ☎255-5450

L'Express, 249 Park Ave S (at 20th St) ☎254-5858

Triumph Restaurant, 148 Bleecker St (between LaGuardia and Thompson sts) ☎228-3070

Veselka, 144 2nd Ave (between E 9th St and St Mark's Place) ☎228-9682

Waverly Restaurant, 385 6th Ave (between W 8th St and Waverly Place) ☎675-3181

Yaffa Café, 97 St Mark's Place (between Ave A and 1st Ave) ☎677-9001

MIDTOWN MANHATTAN

Brasserie Centrale, 1700 Broadway (at W 53rd St) ☎757-2233

Empire Diner, 210 10th Ave (between W 22nd and 23rd sts) ☎243-2736

Gemini Diner, 641 2nd Ave (at E 35th St) ☎532-2143

Lox Around the Clock, 676 6th Ave (at W 21st St) ☎691-3535

Market Diner, 572 11th Ave (at W 43rd St) ☎695-0415

Sarge's, 548 3rd Ave (between E 36th and 37th sts) ☎679-0442

Stage Deli, 834 7th Ave (between W 53rd and 54th sts) ☎245-7850

West Side Diner, 360 9th Ave (at W 31st St) ☎560-8407

UPTOWN MANHATTAN

Big Nick's, 2175 Broadway (between 76th and 77th sts) ☎362-9238

Gray's Papaya, 2090 Broadway (at W 72nd St) ☎799-0243

Green Kitchen, 1477 1st Ave (at E 77th St) ☎988-4163

H & H Bagels, 2239 Broadway (at W 80th St) ☎595-8000

Tramway Coffee Shop, 1143 2nd Ave (at E 60th St) ☎758-7017

Eating

Londel's, 2620 8th Ave (between 139th and 140th sts) ☎234-6114. A little soul food, a little Cajun, a little Southern-fried chicken. This is an attractive down-home place where you can eat upscale items like steak Diane or more common treats such as fried chicken; either way, follow it up with some sweet potato pie.

Sylvia's Restaurant, 328 Lenox Ave (between 126th and 127th sts) ☎996-0660. A legendary Southern soul-food restaurant in Harlem with exceptional greens and Southern fried chicken. Go early on a Wednesday night and get free tickets for amateur night at the *Apollo*. Also famous for the Sunday Gospel brunch – a New York must.

Wells, 2247 7th Ave (between 132nd and 133rd sts) ☎234-0700. Famous soul-food joint which has been a venue for the likes of Aretha Franklin, Sammy Davis Jr and other jazz legends. The crowd is a mix of regulars and visitors while the food is cheapish and tasty – they are best known for their odd mix of waffles and fried chicken.

Caribbean, Central and South American

Caridad Restaurant, 4311 Broadway (at W 184th St) ☎781-0431. Not to be confused with the Upper West Side restaurant of (almost) the same name, this place serves mountains of Dominican food at cheap prices. Try the *mariscos* or seafood, the specialty of the house to be eaten with lots of *pan y ajo*, thick slices of French bread, grilled with olive oil and plenty of garlic. Be sure to go feeling hungry.

The Outer Boroughs

If you decide to explore the **Outer Boroughs**, food could be as good a motivation as any. The ethnic communities here have for the most part retained their closed character – and their restaurants are similarly authentic, generally run by and for the locals. All of New York's ethnic groups are well represented, and you can eat more or less any-

thing: **Brooklyn** has some of New York's best West Indian and Italian food, not to mention its most authentic Russian restaurants; **Queens** holds the city's biggest Greek and South American communities; while Belmont in the **Bronx** is one of the best places in the city to eat authentic Italian cuisine.

Brooklyn Heights and Atlantic Avenue

Charleston Bar and Grill, 174 Bedford Ave, Williamsburg ☎718/782-8717. This local hangout is more bar than grill – go there primarily for the good cheap pizza and to listen to the assortment of bands playing there nightly.

Gage & Tollner, 372 Fulton St (between Jay and Boerum sts), downtown Brooklyn ☎718/875-5181. Old-fashioned seafood restaurant with an extensive menu that's long been part of the downtown Brooklyn eating scene. One of the oldest restaurants in New York (c. 1879), it's not as expensive as it looks. Serves great crab cakes, Charleston she-crab soup and clam bellies.

Henry's End, 44 Henry St (at Cranberry St), Brooklyn Heights ☎718/834-1776. Neighborhood bistro with a wide selection of seasonal dishes, appetizers and desserts. Normally crowded, and don't expect it to be all that cheap. Known for its wild-game festival in fall and winter.

Montague Street Saloon, 122 Montague St (between Henry and Hicks sts), Brooklyn Heights ☎718/522-6770. Burgers and salads for under $10; good fried calamari and Cajun catfish.

Moroccan Star, 205 Atlantic Ave (between Court and Clinton sts), Brooklyn Heights ☎718/643-0800. Perhaps New York's best Moroccan restaurant, with wonderful *tajines* and couscous with lamb. The chef once worked at the *Four Seasons*, and the quality of his cooking remains undiminished.

Moustache Pitza, 405 Atlantic Ave (at Bond St, Brooklyn Heights) ☎718/852-5555. Original and best branch of small

Middle-Eastern chain that has since migrated to Manhattan (see p.351).

Oznot's Dish, 79 Berry St (at N 9th St), Williamsburg ☎718/599-6596. Technically Middle Eastern, but in decor and spirit more Middle-East-Village. Plop down on one of the antique chairs and try grilled shrimp with jalapeño vinaigrette served on a grilled mango, or lamb chunks over basmati rice with melted leeks and tomatillos.

Patsy Grimaldi's Pizza, 19 Old Fulton St (between Water and Front sts) Brooklyn Heights ☎718/858-4300. Delicious, thin and crispy pies that bring even Manhattanites across the water – cheap and crowded.

Peter Luger's Steak House, 178 Broadway (at Driggs Ave), Williamsburg ☎718/387-7400. Pricey (around $50 a head), but reckoned by aficionados to have the best steaks in the city – which is quite a claim. Good service and pleasant ambiance make it a great place to eat a charred porterhouse steak (the only cut they serve) and drink a few brews. Cash only.

Petite Crevette, 127 Atlantic Ave (between Henry and Clinton sts) Brooklyn Heights ☎718/858-6660. Reasonably priced, comfortable French bistro with many simple fish dishes.

PlanEat Thailand, 184 Bedford Ave (between N 6th and 7th sts), Williamsburg ☎718/599-5758. A welcome addition to Bedford Ave that serves reasonably priced spicy Thai food. Worth a trip on the L train if you're in Manhattan.

Stacy's, 85 Broadway (at Berry St), Williamsburg ☎718/486-8004. Cheap neighborhood restaurant serving an eclectic mix of Moroccan, Middle Eastern and American fare. Works by local artists, a majority of the clientele, are displayed on the walls.

Teresa's, 80 Montague St (between Hicks St and Montague Terrace) ☎718/797-3996. Large portions of Polish home-cooking – blintzes, *pierogies* and the like – make this a good lunch time stop-off for those on tours of Brooklyn Heights.

Tripoli, 156 Atlantic Ave (at Clinton St), Brooklyn Heights ☎718/596-5800. Lebanese restaurant serving fish, lamb and vegetarian dishes for a low $8 or so. Miniature lamb pies in yogurt sauce are a standout.

Waterfront Ale House, 155 Atlantic Ave, Brooklyn Heights ☎718/522-3794. Old-style pub serving good spicy chicken wings, ribs and killer key lime pie (made locally and only available in Brooklyn). Also a terrific selection of Belgian and other beers. Inexpensive and good fun.

Eating

Central Brooklyn

Aunt Suzie's, 247 5th Ave (between Garfield Place and Carroll St), Park Slope ☎718/788-3377. Neighborhood Italian serving decent food for as little as $10 a person. Not a restaurant to drive from Manhattan for, but if you happen to be in the area, it's one of the best-value places around.

Cucina, 256 5th Ave (between Garfield Place and Carroll St), Park Slope ☎718/230-0711. Warm and inviting Italian restaurant serving exemplary food for affordable prices.

Fatoosh Babecue, 311 Henry St (at Atlantic Ave) ☎718/596-0030. Call it "hippie Middle Eastern," fresh, hearty falafel and babaganoush in a funky boîte on a shady Cobble Hill street.

Ferdinando's, 151 Union St (between Hicks and Columbia sts) ☎718/855-1545. Authentic Italian, cooked and served by the family that owns this tiny dining room. Nothing fancy, just your basic sauces, meats, and pastas made the same way they've been making them out here for decades.

Leaf 'n' Bean, 83 7th Ave (between Union and Berkeley sts), Park Slope ☎718/638-5791. Exotic coffees and teas plus excellent homemade soups and gourmet truffle candies. Brunch for about $10 on weekends. Outdoor seating when it's fine.

Once Upon a Sundae, 7702 3rd Ave (at 77th St), Bay Ridge ☎718/748-

Eating

3412. Turn-of-the-century ice-cream parlor.

Patois, 255 Smith St (between Douglass and Degraw sts) ☎718/855-1535. The newest restaurant from chef Alan Harding – a ten-table bistro with great food, a garden and reasonable prices. Arrive early, as this is one of the hottest spots around.

Sam's, 238 Court St (between Baltic and Kenneth sts), Cobble Hill ☎718/596-3458. Long-established restaurant serving standard Italian fare at reasonable prices.

Coney Island and Brighton Beach

Carolina, 1409 Mermaid Ave (at W 15th St), Coney Island ☎718/714-1294. Inexpensive, family-run Italian restaurant that's been around forever. Great food, great prices.

Gargiulo's, 2911 W 15th St (between Surf and Mermaid aves), Coney Island ☎718/266-4891. A gigantic, noisy family-run Coney Island restaurant famed for its large portions of cheap and hearty Neapolitan food.

Mrs Stahl's, 1001 Brighton Beach Ave (at Coney Island Ave), Brighton Beach ☎718/648-0210. Longstanding knish purveyor with over 20 different varieties.

Nathan's Famous, Surf and Stillwell aves, Coney Island ☎718/266-3161. New York's most famous hot dogs and crinkle-cut French fries. Not the ultimate in gastronomy but a legend nonetheless.

Odessa, 1113 Brighton Beach Ave (between 13th and 14th sts), Brighton Beach ☎718/332-3223. Excellent and varied Russian menu at unbeatable prices. Dancing and music nightly.

Primorski, 282 Brighton Beach Ave (between 2nd and 3rd sts), Brighton Beach ☎718/891-3111. Perhaps the best of Brighton Beach's Russian hangouts, serving up a huge menu of authentic Russian dishes, including blintzes and stuffed cabbage, at absurdly cheap prices. Live music in the evening.

The Bronx

Dominick's, 2335 Arthur Ave (at 187th St), Fordham ☎718/733-2807. All you could hope for in a Belmont neighborhood Italian: great, rowdy atmosphere, communal family-style seating, wonderful food and low(ish) prices.

Mario's, 2342 Arthur Ave (between 184th and 186th sts), Fordham ☎718/584-1188. Pricey but impressive Italian cooking, from pizzas to pastas and beyond, enticing even die-hard Manhattanites to the Bronx.

Astoria

Omonia Café, 32–20 Broadway (at 33rd St), Astoria ☎718/274-6650. Affordable Greek neighborhood restaurant.

Uncle George's, 33–19 Broadway (at 34th St), Astoria ☎718/626-0593. This 24-hour joint serves excellent and ultra-cheap authentic Greek food.

Jackson Heights

Inti-Raymi, 86–14 37th Ave (between 86th and 87th sts), Jackson Heights ☎718/424-1938. Unpretentious restaurant serving substantial low-priced Peruvian food in a jovial atmosphere. Try the *ceviche de mariscos* (raw fish in lime juice) or the Peruvian version of *lo mein*. The restaurant has very limited hours however: it is open for dinner only on Thurs and Fri, lunch and dinner on Sat and Sun, and closed the rest of the week.

Jackson Diner, 37–47 74th St (between 37th and Roosevelt Ave), Jackson Heights ☎718/672-1232. Come here hungry and stuff yourself silly with amazingly light and cheap Indian fare. Samosas and mango *lassis* are not to be missed.

La Pequeña Colombia, 83–27 Roosevelt Ave (at 84th St), Jackson Heights ☎718/478-6528. Literally "Little Colombia," this place doles out heaped portions of seafood casserole, pork and tortillas. Try the fruit drinks too, *maracuay* (passion fruit) or *guanabana* (sour soup).

Tabaq 74, 73-21 37th Ave (between

74th and 75th sts) ☎718/898-2837. Pakistani barbecue of the highest order. If you don't like beef brains (the house specialty), you can have chicken, lamb, or quail, generously spiced and prepared with skill and care.

Forest Hills, Jamaica, Bayside, Kew Gardens

Mardi Gras, 70-20 Austin St (between 70th Rd and 69th Ave) ☎718/261-8555. Tiny Cajun eatery, serving crawfish, muffalleta sandwiches and other tasty treats at moderate prices.

Pastrami King, 124-24 Queens Blvd (at 82nd Ave), Kew Gardens

☎718/263-1717. The home-smoked pastrami and corned beef are better than any you'll find in Manhattan. Closed Sat.

Staten Island

Aesop's Tables, 1233 Bay St (at Hylan Blvd), Rosebank ☎718/720-2005. Cozy and rustic restaurant serving interesting American regional variations. Try the catfish over greens or jerk chicken.

Goodfella's Pizza, 17–18 Hylan Blvd ☎718/987-2422. Not worth a special trip, but if you've ferried across, you'll find the pizza here more than up to the snuff.

Eating

Chapter 18

Drinking

Despite the image many Europeans have of puritanical, abstemious Americans living on bottled water, New York is a drinking town. You can't walk a block along most Manhattan avenues (and many of the side streets) without passing one or two **bars**. You can swig $2 drafts at your local dive or sip martinis in the city's most plush hotel bars. Specific **savings** on drinking can often be made in the larger bars by ordering quart or half-gallon pitchers of beer, which represent a considerable discount on the price per glass. Look out, too, for "happy hour" bargains (see box below) and two-for-the-price-of-one deals. Also, avoid bars or clubs that offer "free drinks for ladies" – they tend to be cattle markets or worse. Remember too that many serve some form of food, from basic chicken wings and ribs to full-blown meals.

Bars generally **open** from mid-morning (around 10am) to the early hours – 4am at the latest, when they have to close by law. As for prices, in a basic bar you'll be paying around $4 for a bottle or a glass of beer "on tap" (i.e. draft), although in a swankier and/or more fashionable environment, or in a singles joint, this may go up considerably. Detailed listings and recommendations begin on p.387.

What to drink

When you've made your choice of bar, the problem is deciding **what to drink**.

Beer

Beer is enjoying something of a renaissance these days – it's not unusual to see ten taps of draft and a half-dozen

---

Happy hours and free food

At the turn of the last century, Bowery barkeeps offered a "free lunch" of pickles and boiled eggs to attract workingmen during their mid-day break. This has evolved into **happy hour**, now designed to pull in the after-work crowds. It's generally a two-hour period, often 5–7pm, Monday to Friday only. Discounts are offered, either in two-for-one deals, or sometimes with special prices on specific drinks. Bars often put out thirst-inducing **snacks** like popcorn or pretzels during happy hour, but some

offer free hors d'oeuvres, particularly the swell Midtown joints. Since the idea in these cases is to draw in well-heeled clientele, you'll do well to **dress** appropriately, though most of these places will accommodate you as long as you perform with confidence and don't too obviously clear the tables. The **cost** of a regular drink or cocktail should work out around $3. For happy hour devotees, there are possibilities in addition to those listed: just check out the more upscale Midtown bars and hotels.

---

bottled beer options behind the bar – with a choosy clientele knowing just what they want. Microbrews are particularly popular: Sam Adams, Pete's Wicked and Anchor Steam are drunk as frequently as Budweiser, Miller or Rolling Rock – something you wouldn't have seen ten years ago. In addition, Belgian beers have stormed the market, edging out their European brethren vying for space. You'll find most bars have Stella Artois or Hoegarden on tap alongside German brands like Spaten and Paulaner – not to mention the usual assortment of Heineken, Guinness, Newcastle and Bass. Beer usually costs around $5 a pint, bottles are usually cheaper at $4 a pop. If price is a problem, then bear in mind you can walk into any supermarket or corner store and buy beer at around $1 a can.

Wines

Buying American **wine**, is one of the best deals around. Not only is the wine generally very good, but the price is quite fair at around $8–10 a bottle in a liquor store. If you're keen to sample something decent, try the varieties from the Napa or Sonoma valleys, just north of San Francisco, which between them produce some of the best-quality wines in the country. New York State also produces wine, though of a lesser quality than California. French and Italian wines come more expensive, but they're still by no means costly. In all cases, however, wine does demand a better-filled wallet when in a restaurant or bar: expect 100 percent mark-up on the bottle.

Spirits and liquor

As for the **hard stuff**, there are a number of points of potential confusion for overseas visitors. First bear in mind that whether you ask for a drink "on the rocks" or not, you'll most likely get it poured into a glass full to the brim with ice; if you don't want it like this ask for it "straight up." Don't forget either that if you ask for whiskey you will get one of the American kinds, most likely rye, of

Drinking

which the most common brand is Seagram's 7. If you want bourbon, Scotch or Irish whiskey you should ask for them by name. Pick a brand if you want something better than "speed rack" liquor (the cheap stuff a bartender serves if a brand choice is not indicated); it will cost more, but it will also be infinitely more drinkable. Jim Beam, Wild Turkey, and Maker's Mark are among the better readily available bourbons. For Irish, Paddy, Jameson and Murphy's are the safe bets, and unless you want to get into the thicket of single-malts available in the better bars, Johnny Walker (Black or Red) is the most popular Scotch. And neither should you ask for Martini if you want the herby drink drunk by beautiful people. To Americans, a martini is a mixture of gin and vermouth, usually with an olive or two, served in an elegant stemmed glass (and still drunk by beautiful people) – vermouth (pronounced "vermooth") to an American being what the British would call Martini.

Cocktails

Cocktails are popular all over the States, especially during happy hours and weekend brunch. The standards are list-

Drinking

ed opposite, but really varieties are innumerable, sometimes specific to a single bar. With any names you come across, experiment – that's half the fun. For novice drinkers, a word of advice: go slow with any drink containing more than three ingredients.

Non-alcoholic drinks

By law, all NYC bars must serve selections of **non-alcoholic drinks**. Even if you plump for (say) the dubious delights of the alcohol-free beers that have become popular in recent years, quaffing a Kaliber in an Irish bar is a bit like having a bath with your raincoat on. See "Coffee and tea" box on p.352 for details of places specializing in genteel refreshment – and those that will provide you with a serious caffeine hit.

Buying your own booze

When buying your own alcohol, you'll need to find a **liquor store** – supermarkets only have beer, just one of New York State's complex **licensing laws**. Other regulations worth keeping in mind are that you have to be over 21 to buy or consume alcohol in a bar or restaurant (and you'll be asked to provide evidence if there's any dispute); that it's against the law to drink alcohol on the street (which is why you see so many people furtively swigging from brown paper bags, though this still doesn't make it legal); and that you can't buy your own booze, other than beer, anywhere on a Sunday.

Where to drink

It's in Manhattan – and more specifically below 23rd Street – that you're likely to spend most time **drinking** (as well as eating). Many of the city's better bars are situated in this part of town, as well as the majority of the cheaper (and ethnic) restaurants. For drinking only, you'll find some of the bars listed here (music and gay-oriented places, most obviously) cross over into the "Nightlife" chapter that follows, both in terms of feel and often escalating prices.

The bar scene

The **bar scene** in New York City is a varied one, with a broader range of places to drink than in most American cities, and prices to suit most pockets. At the bottom end of the scale, the cheapest watering holes you'll find, all over the city, are roughish places – convivial enough, though difficult ground for women on their own, and sometimes for men. In addition to these, there are more mixed hangouts, varying from some of the long-established haunts in Greenwich Village to newer, louder and more deliberately stylish places that spring up – and die out – all the time in the Downtown neighborhoods.

Selections that follow are personal favorites. The potential choice, obviously, is a lot wider – below 14th Street it's hard to walk more than a block without finding a bar – and takes in the whole range of taste, budget and purpose. (Bear in mind that many places double as bar and restaurant, and you may therefore find them listed not here but in the previous chapter, "Eating".) The best hunting grounds are in the East Village, SoHo, and TriBeCa; there's a good choice of Midtown bars – though here bars tend to be geared to an after-hours office crowd and (with a few notable exceptions) can consequently be pricey and rather dull; Uptown, the Upper West Side, between 60th and 85th streets along Amsterdam and Columbus, has a good array of bars though these tend to cater to more of a clean-cut and dully collegiate crowd.

Hours of opening are generally mid-morning through to 2am; some stay open later but by law all must close by 4am. Bar kitchens usually stop operating around midnight or a little before. Wherever you go, even if you just have a drink you'll be expected to **tip**: the going rate is roughly ten percent of the bill or 50¢ for a single drink.

Groupings follow, approximately, the chapter divisions outlined in the *Guide*. For ease of reference, however, all specifically gay and lesbian bars are gathered together in a single section starting on p.394.

Cocktails

Bacardi	White rum, lime and grenadine – not the brand-name drink	*Manhattan*	Vermouth, whiskey, lemon juice and soda
Black Russian	Vodka with coffee liqueur, brown cacao and Coke	*Margarita*	Tequila, triple sec and lime (or strawberry) juice
Bloody Mary	Vodka, tomato juice, tabasco, worcester sauce, salt and pepper	*Mimosa*	Champagne and orange juice
Cosmopolitan	Pink New York martini made with vodka, cranberry juice and lime juice	*Mint Julep*	Bourbon, mint and sugar
		Pina Colada	Dark rum, light rum, coconut, cream and pineapple juice
Daiquiri	Dark rum, light rum and lime, often with fruit such as banana or strawberry	*Screwdriver*	Vodka and orange juice
		Tequila Sunrise	Tequila, orange juice and grenadine
Harvey Wallbanger	Vodka, galliano, orange juice	*Tom Collins*	Gin, lemon juice, soda and sugar
Highball	Any spirit plus a soda, water or ginger ale	*Vodka Collins*	Vodka, lemon juice, soda and sugar
Kir Royale	Champagne, cassis	*Whisky Sour*	Bourbon, lemon juice and sugar
Long Island Iced Tea	Gin, vodka, white rum, tequila, lemon juice and Coke	*White Russian*	Vodka, white cacao and cream

Drinking

Financial District and Civic Center

Greatest Bar on Earth, 1 World Trade Center, 107th Floor, Liberty St ☎524-7000. Posh, expensive bar with obviously excellent views; Wed night is Mondo 107, a popular lounge party featuring local DJs.

Jeremy's Alehouse, 254 Front St (at Dover St) ☎964-3537. Earthy bar near the South Street Seaport. Reputedly serves the city's best calamari and clams.

North Star Pub, 93 South St (at Fulton) ☎509-6757. "British" ale-house where you can wash down your bangers & mash with a pint of Newcastle Brown – or choose from some 80 single malt Scotch whiskies. Fairly small and very popular with Wall St locals and visiting Limeys.

SoHo and TriBeCa

Broome Street Bar, 363 W Broadway (at Broome St) ☎925-2086. A popular and long-established local haunt, these days more restaurant than bar, serving reasonably priced burgers and salads in a dimly lit setting. A nice place just to nurse a beer too, especially when footsore from SoHo's shops and galleries.

Café Noir, 32 Grand St (at Thompson St) ☎431-7910. Faux-Moroccan decor (think Sidney Greenstreet's place in *Casablanca*, without the flies) and lush cocktails. A place to be seen.

Ear Inn, 326 Spring St (between Washington and Greenwich sts) ☎226-9060. "Ear" as in "Bar" with half the neon "B" chipped off. Be that as it may,

Drinking

this cozy pub, a stone's throw from the Hudson River, has a good mix of beers on tap, serves basic, reasonably priced, American food and claims to be the second oldest bar in the city. It may also be one of the best.

Fanelli, 94 Prince St (at Mercer St) ☎226-9412. Established in 1872, *Fanelli* is one of SoHo's oldest bars, relaxed and informal. Food is simple American fare: burgers, salads and such.

Knitting Factory, 74 Leonard St (between Church St and Broadway) ☎219-3055. Street level bar and cozy downstairs taproom with 18 draft microbrews, $1 drafts from 5pm to 6pm weekdays and free live music from 11pm.

Liquor Store Bar, 225 W Broadway (at White St) ☎226-7121. Cozy little pub with sidewalk seating that feels like it's been around since colonial times. A welcome respite from the trendy local scene.

Lucky Strike, 59 Grand St (between W Broadway and Wooster St) ☎941-0479. Convivial bar/bistro patronized by a mixed bunch of young and middle-aged SoHo-ites. Food served out back (nothing special and not cheap), and DJs on Fri, Sat and Sun nights, when the scene can be buzzing.

Ñ, 33 Crosby St (between Broome and Grand sts) ☎219-8856. Laid-back in summer and packed on frosty winter nights, this long and narrow bar serves tasty tapas and $15 pitchers of not-too-sweet sangria. A favorite on the SoHo scene.

No Moore, 234 W Broadway (at White St) ☎925-2901. Sprawling, friendly lounge with live music at weekends (some weeknights too). No food, but, oddly, you can order in or byo dinner.

Puffy's Tavern, 81 Hudson St (at Harrison St) ☎766-9159. Small, funky TriBeCa bar with lunchtime food and bar pizza, cheap booze and a great jukebox.

Sporting Club, 99 Hudson St (between Leonard and Franklin sts) ☎219-0900.

Sports bar with a large electronic screen to keep up with the action. Up to nine different events can be screened at once, with college and pro scores posted on an electronic scoreboard. Closed on weekends during the summer.

Spring Lounge, 48 Spring St (at Mulberry St) ☎965-1774. Agreeable, downbeat hole-in-the-wall.

Sweet and Viscious, 5 Spring St (between Bowery and Elizabeth St) ☎334-7915. Although this gem of a bar is said to be named after the owners' cats, it could just as easily refer to the peachy-pink lighting and the two decrepit pistols (found while excavating the site) that hang next to the door. It also has as stylish a back yard as you'll find in the city.

Toad Hall, 57 Grand St (between W Broadway and Wooster St) ☎431-8145. Less hip, more of a local hangout than *Lucky Strike* next door. Still, a stylish alehouse with a pool table, good service and excellent bar snacks.

Greenwich Village

Art Bar, 52 8th Ave (between Horatio and Jane St) ☎727-0244. Forget the bland exterior, this hugely popular lounge has a cozy, dimly-lit interior with a good menu.

Barrow St Alehouse, 155 Barrow St (between Bleecker and 7th Ave S) ☎206-7302. Basic, no-nonsense tavern with cheap beer, pizzas and an affable young crowd.

Blind Tiger, 518 Hudson St (at W 10th St) ☎675-3848. The name is fitting as you could easily leave here with things looking a bit foggy after you choose from the 24 beers on tap and eclectic bottled selection.

Cedar Tavern, 82 University Place (between E 11th and 12th sts) ☎929-9089. Legendary Beat and artists' meeting point in the 1950s and now a cozy bar with food and well-priced drinks. All year round you can eat under the stars in their covered roof garden.

Hotel bars

There's no better place to go for a martini in New York when you're feeling fabulous. Hotel bars are posh watering holes for the well bred and well maintained and, lest you forget, their sole purpose is comfort. Sure the drinks are expensive, but you're paying for atmosphere, too. Sink back into a comfy banquette, sip your precious booze slowly and with dignity, and watch the parade of foreign dignitaries, royalty, well-groomed businesspeople, media celebs, chic socialites and mysterious strangers conducting important affairs.

Bemelman's, The Carlyle, 35 E 76th St (at Madison Ave) ☎744-1600.

The Blue Bar, The Algonquin Hotel, 59 W 44th St (between 5th and 6th aves) ☎840-6800.

Cibar, The Inn at Irving Place, 54 Irving Place (between E 17th and 18th sts) ☎460-5656.

5757, The Four Seasons, 57 E 57th St (between Madison and Park aves) ☎758-5700.

44, The Royalton, 44 W 44th St (between 5th and 6th aves) ☎944-8844.

Grand Bar, Soho Grand Hotel, 310 W Broadway (between Grand and Canal sts) ☎965-3000.

King Cole Bar, St Regis Hotel, 2 E 55th St (between 5th and Madison aves) ☎339-6721.

Mercer Kitchen, Mercer Hotel, 147 Mercer St (at Prince) ☎966-6060.

Monkey Bar, Elysee Hotel, 60 E 54th St (between Park and Madison aves) ☎838-2600.

The Oak Bar, The Plaza Hotel, 768 5th Ave (at 59th St) ☎546-5320.

The Pierre Hotel Bar, 2 E 61st St (at 5th Ave) ☎838-8000.

The View, The Marriott Marquis, 1535 Broadway (at W 45th St) ☎398-1900.

Whiskey Bar & Library Bar, Paramount Hotel, 235 W 46th St (between 8th Ave and Broadway) ☎819-0404 or 827-4183.

Whiskey Blue, The W, 541 Lexington Ave (between 49th and 50th sts) ☎755-1200.

Chumley's, 86 Bedford St (between Grove and Barrow sts) ☎675-4449. It's not easy to find but it's worth the effort – offering up a good choice of beers and food, both reasonably priced. Best arrive before 8pm if you want to eat at one of the battered tables – at which, supposedly, James Joyce put the finishing touches to *Ulysses*.

Fifty Five, 55 Christopher St (between 6th and 7th aves) ☎929-9883. Near the site of the late, lamented *Lion's Head*, this bar has a great jazz jukebox and live music 7 nights a week.

Hogs & Heifers, 859 Washington St (at W 13th St) ☎229-0930. Hogs as in the burly motorcycles parked outside; heifers as in, well, ladies. Though there's no more bar dancing (Julia Roberts was

famously photographed doing so here), those bold enough to venture into this rough-and-tumble meat-packing district joint can still drink to excess.

Jekyll and Hyde, 91 7th Ave S (between Barrow and Grove sts) ☎989-7701; 1409 6th Ave (between W 57th and 58th sts). Novelty pub with a haunted house theme that appeals to an under-25 crowd, mainly from out-of-town.

Kava Lounge, 605 Hudson St (at W 12th St) ☎989-7504. Maori-style murals grace the walls of this charming, intimate and truly original Village bar.

Kettle of Fish, W 3rd St (at 6th Ave) ☎533-4790. A refreshing dive, which

Drinking

houses the locals and old-timers in the area looking for a cheap drink in a laid-back atmosphere – that is until the rowdy NYU students move in. $3 bottled beer and $1.75 for a mug of ale.

Peculier Pub, 145 Bleecker St (between La Guardia and Thompson sts) ☎353-1327. Popular local bar whose main claim to fame is the number of beers it sells – more than 300 in all and examples from any country you care to mention.

Reservoir, 70 University Place (between 10th and 11th sts) ☎475-0770. The regular size TVs (6 of them) disqualify this affable NYU hangout from being listed as a fully-fledged sports-bar (which may be to its credit!). Still, it's a good place to enjoy a beer and watch a game – and that's not too easy to find in this part of town.

Time Café West, 87 7th Ave (at Barrow St) ☎220-9100. Great rooftop garden with good views of the city streets below and the people who occupy them. *Time Café*'s East Village location is listed on p.354.

Village Idiot, 355 W 14th St (at 9th Ave) ☎989-7334. Rowdy bar with cheap beer and, for some, a certain redneck charm. Tommy, the owner, eats beer cans and (when he's feeling really perky) shot glasses. You can feed four goldfish to the bar's snapping turtle for a buck or just enjoy the thirtysomething stripper on TV. Reported to be the best spot for a daytime buzz.

White Horse Tavern, 567 Hudson St (at W 11th St) ☎243-9260. Old-time village bar where Dylan Thomas supped his last before being carted off to hospital with alcoholic poisoning. Beer and food are cheap and palatable. Outside seating in the summer.

Lower East Side

bOb, 235 Eldridge St (between Stanton and Houston sts) ☎777-0588. A hip lounge with occasional DJs who do little to disturb the languid atmosphere.

Dharma, 174 Orchard St (between Stanton and Houston sts) ☎780-0313.

Live music wafts down from a balcony seven nights a week in this long, narrow and infinitely cool cocktail lounge.

Kush, 183 Orchard St (between Stanton and Houston sts) ☎677-7328. Beguiling Moroccan bar with live music Sunday nights and belly dancing on Tuesdays. If you're looking for something different, this is the place to be.

Lansky Lounge, 38 Delancey St (between Norfolk and Suffolk sts) ☎677-5588. The venerable dairy restaurant *Ratner's* has spun its back room into a retro cocktail lounge, to which jaded urban sophisticates flock.

Local 138, 138 Ludlow St (between Stanton and Rivington sts) ☎477-0280. A nice escape from the sometimes overwhelming hipster scene of Ludlow St. Simply, a relaxed bar with good beers on tap and a comfortable, friendly crowd.

Luna Lounge, 171 Ludlow St (between Houston and Stanton sts) ☎260-2323. Friendly spot without any attitude. Long, comfy bar serves up pints in the front, noisy rock bands or stand-up comedians perform in the back.

Sapphire Lounge, 249 Eldridge St (between Houston and Stanton sts) ☎777-5153. Very small, very dark and very popular with the cocktail-dress and martini-glass tribe.

Swim, 146 Orchard St (between Rivington and Stanton sts) no phone. A new addition to Orchard St's ever growing bar scene, this sleek newcomer packs in a well-heeled late night crowd in search of pulsing DJ beats, strong drinks and maybe a bite of sushi or two (it's also a sushi bar).

East Village

Ace, 531 E 5th St (between aves A and B) ☎979-8476. Behind the architectural glass brick is a noisy and strangely cavernous bar, with pool table, darts and a good jukebox. NYU students fill this place up on Thursdays.

Barmacy 538 E 14th St (between aves A and B) ☎228-2240. Cross a dive-bar and a pharmacy circa 1950 and this is what you get. Plus cheap beer, good DJs and a devoted regular crowd.

Beauty Bar, 231 E 14th St (between 2nd and 3rd aves) ☎539-1389. From the owner of *Barmacy*, this popular theme bar doubles as a semi-functioning beauty salon. It's hipper than you might expect.

Blue and Gold, 74 E 7th St (between 1st and 2nd aves) ☎473-8918. Popular dive with cheap beer and a great Eighties pop jukebox.

d.b.a., 41 1st Ave (between E 2nd and 3rd sts) ☎475-5097. A beer lover's paradise, *d.b.a.* has at least 60 bottled beers, 14 beers on tap and an authentic hand pump. Garden seating in the summer.

Decibel, 240 E 9th (between 2nd and 3rd sts) ☎979-2733. Downstairs sake bar in Little Tokyo, that feels uncannily like the real thing.

Detour, 349 E 13th St (between 1st and 2nd aves) ☎533-6212. Comfortable jazz bar with live music seven nights a week and no cover.

Doc Holliday's, 141 Ave A (at 9th St) ☎979-0312. A very rowdy bar with a cowboy theme. Now incorporating "Big Mama's world famous BBQ Buffet and Boutique". Beware.

Drinkland, 339 E 10th St (between aves A and B) ☎228-2435. Dizzying psychedelic decor fused with DJs spinning big-beat and trip-hop make this place a favorite among Downtown hipsters. Strong mixed drinks too.

Grassroots Tavern, 20 St Mark's Place (between 2nd and 3rd aves) ☎475-9443. Likeably scuzzy basement bar. Inexpensive, with a good oldies jukebox and two dartboards.

Holiday Cocktail Lounge, 75 St Mark's Place (between 2nd and 3rd aves) ☎777-9637. Unabashed dive with a mixed bag of customers, from old-world grandfathers to the younger set, and a bona-fide character tending bar (more or less). Good place for an afternoon beer, unless you find the *Lost Weekend* vibe a trifle too mellow. Closes early.

International Bar, 120 1/2 1st Ave (between E 7th St and St Mark's Place) ☎777-9214. Christmas lights year-round make this neighborhood bar a cozy choice for the East Village. Bring crisp bills to feed the moody jukebox.

KGB, 85 E 4th St (between 2nd Ave and Bowery) ☎505-3360. Soviet motif bar on the second floor. Popular with off-off Broadway theater crowds.

Lakeside Lounge, 162 Ave B (between 10th and 11th sts) ☎529-8463. Opened by a local DJ and a record producer who have stocked the jukebox with old rock, country and R&B. A down-home hangout, with live music four nights a week.

McSorley's, 15 E 7th St (between 2nd and 3rd aves) ☎473-9148. New York City's longest-established watering hole, so it claims, and a male-only bar until a 1969 lawsuit. These days it retains a saloon look, with mostly an out-of-town-er crowd. There's no trouble deciding what to drink – you can have beer, and you can have it dark or light.

The Opium Den, 29 E 3rd St (between Bowery and 2nd Ave) ☎505-7344. Fairly small, quite trendy and very red, this lounge offers an intoxicating mix of the exotic and the baroque.

7Bs (*Vazac's*), 108 Ave B (at 7th St) ☎473-8840. Known as "7Bs" for its location on the corner of Tompkins Square, this is a popular East Village hangout, with an extremely mixed crowd, that's often used as a sleazy set in films and commercials – perhaps most famously in the film *Crocodile Dundee*.

St Dymphna's, 118 St Mark's Place (between 1st Ave and Ave A) ☎254-6636. With a pleasant back garden, a tempting menu and some of the city's best Guinness, this snug Irish watering hole is, understandably, a favorite among young East Villagers.

Sophie's, 507 E 5th St (between aves A and B) ☎228-5680. $2 draft beer and oh-so-cheap mixed drinks make this bar

Drinking

Drinking

the consummate East Village hangout.
Pool table and jukebox.

Swift, 34 E 4th St (between Bowery and
Lafayette). Classy, Irish watering-hole
with a great beer selection, live music
each Tuesday and occasional poetry
readings in the Fall.

Temple Bar, 332 Lafayette St (between
Bleecker and Houston sts) ☎925-4242.
Elegant bar serving champagne and,
some claim, Manhattan's best martinis.

2A, 27 Ave A (at 2nd St) no phone. A
long, thin and wildly popular bar catering
to longtime East Village residents. Bar
sometimes manned by "Handsome Dick"
Manitoba of the legendary punk rock
group The Dictators.

WCOU Radio Bar/Tile Bar, 115 1st Ave
(at 7th St) ☎254-4317. This small, well-
lit bar with a good jukebox is a great
place to sit and chat with friends.

Union Square, Gramercy Park, Murray Hill and Midtown East

Belmont Lounge, 117 E 15th St
(between Park Ave S and Irving Place)
☎533-0009. Oversized couches, dark
cavernous rooms and an outdoor garden
reel in a continuous stream of twenty-
somethings. Strong drinks and a very
attractive staff helps things too.

British Open, 320 E 59th St ☎355-
8467. Shamelessly Anglophile pub/sports
bar with 5 TVs and a fetish for the royal
and ancient game.

The Coffee Shop, 29 Union Square W
(at E 16th St) ☎243-7969. A former
coffee shop turned trendy bar and
restaurant that is still a place to be
seen. With its original curvy counter and
bar stools from the old coffee shop, the
bar is a nice place to hang out at any
time. The noisy adjacent restaurant,
complete with booths, serves vaguely
Brazilian-style food – a little overpriced
but very tasty.

Divine Bar, 244 E 51st St (between 2nd
and 3rd aves) ☎319-9463. Although it's
often packed with corporate types com-
muning with their cellphones, this
swanky tapas lounge has a great selec-

tion of wines and imported beers, not to
mention the tasty appetizers.

Failte, 531 2nd Ave (between 29th and
30th sts) ☎725-9440. Perhaps the best
of the many Irish bars to be found in
this otherwise unappealing part of town.
Live music on Sunday nights, good
restaurant and cordial atmosphere make
it well worth a visit.

Heartland Brewery, 35 Union Square W
(between 16th and 17th sts) ☎645-3400.
Even with seating sprawled out onto the
sidewalk, this vast space still gets packed
out some nights. Good selection of beers
brewed on the premises.

19th Hole, 322 2nd Ave (between 18th
and 19th sts) ☎777-9176. Cozy golf-
themed bar, stuck in the middle of
nowhere, with more than a whiff of your
favorite putter.

No Idea, 30 E 20th St (between
Broadway and Park Ave S) ☎777-0100.
Stylish, yet quirky, it's only drawback is
that it serves No Food. Highly recommended, nonetheless.

Old Town Bar and Restaurant, 45 E
18th St (between Broadway and Park
Ave S) ☎473-8874. One of the oldest
and still one of the very best – and least
pretentious – bars in the city, although it
can get packed, especially when the
suits from the Flatiron district get off
work. High on authentic old-world
atmosphere, and with an excellent, if
standard, menu of chili, burgers and the
like. It was regularly featured on the old
NBC *David Letterman Show*.

Paddy Reilly's 519 2nd Ave (between
29th and 30th sts) ☎686-1210. A good
place to enjoy a few Guinness drafts, listen to live music and pretend you're
Irish. $5 cover some nights.

Pete's Tavern, 129 E 18th St (at Irving
Place) ☎473-7676. Former speakeasy
that claims to be the oldest bar in New
York – opened in 1864 – though these
days it inevitably trades on its history.
The food in the restaurant is neither
cheap nor particularly good.

P.J. Clarke's, 915 3rd Ave (between E
55th and 56th sts) ☎759-1650. One of

the city's most famous watering holes, this is a spit-and-sawdust alehouse with a not-so-cheap restaurant out the back. You may recognize it as the location of the film *The Lost Weekend*.

Revival, 129 E 15th St (between Irving Place and 3rd Ave) ☎974-9169. Walk down the stairs and into this friendly narrow bar with great outdoor seating and an excellent jukebox. Popular with fans waiting for a rock show at Irving Plaza around the block.

Thady Con's, 915 2nd Ave (between 48th and 49th sts) ☎688-9700. Although the *faux* Irish decor may be a tad over the top, this friendly bar/restaurant is chock-full of genuine charm, hosts a good mix of customers and serves great food.

Chelsea, Garment District and Midtown West

Candy Bar and Grill, 131 8th Ave ☎229-9702. Stylish hangout for a well-dressed crowd. Amazing martini's and mixed drinks plus an excellent menu of munchies and meals.

Chelsea Commons, 242 10th Ave (at W 24th St) ☎929-9424. Not only a personable bar but a great place to eat. Popular local hangout with a summer garden and winter fireplace.

Citron 47, 401 W 47th St (between 9th and 10th aves) ☎397-4747. Charming hybrid of a French bistro, hip Downtown bar and New England farmhouse situated in gentrified Hell's Kitchen. Great place to take a few back.

The Collins Bar, 735 8th Ave (between W 46th and 47th sts) ☎541-4206. Rising from the ashes of the *Full Moon Salon*, this sleek, stylish bar has choice sports photos along one side, original art works along the other – not to mention perhaps the most eclectic juke in the city.

Flight 151, 151 8th Ave (between 16th and 17th sts) ☎229-1868. This jolly neighborhood dive, with an aviation theme, cheap drinks and decent food, has been dubbed "The Cheers of Chelsea."

Jimmy's Corner, 140 W 44th St (between Broadway and 6th Ave) ☎221-9510.

The walls of this long, narrow corridor of a bar, owned by ex-fighter/trainer Jimmy Glenn, are a virtual Boxing Hall of Fame. You'd be hard pressed to find a more characterful dive anywhere in the city – or a better jazz/R&B jukebox.

Rudy's Bar and Grill, 627 9th Ave (between W 44th and 45th sts) ☎974-9169. One of New York's cheapest, friendliest and liveliest dive bars, a favorite with local actors and musicians. Great jukebox, free hot dogs and a back-yard in the summer.

Russian Vodka Room, 265 W 52nd St (between Broadway and 7th Ave) ☎307-5835. They have several different kinds of vodka, as you might expect, and a lot of Russian and Eastern European expatriates.

Siberia, 250 W 50th St (in the IRT subway station) ☎333-4141. One of New York's oddest exemplars of the "location, location, location" school: this small bar is in the 1/9 subway station at 50th St. It looks and feels like your parents' rec room; a good place for a shot of vodka or a late-night beer.

Ye Olde Tripple Inn, 263 W 54th St (between Broadway and 8th Ave) ☎245-9849. Basic Irish bar that serves inexpensive food at lunchtime and early evening. A useful place to know about if you're after affordable food in this part of town.

Upper West Side and Morningside Heights

Blondie's, 212 W 79th St (between Broadway and Amsterdam Ave) ☎877-1010. Comparatively civilized sports bar with a copy of the *USA Today* sports section at each table.

Cannon's Pub, W 108th St (at Broadway), no phone. Longtime favorite haunt of Columbia students. Four TVs, usually playing sporting events; $5 Rolling Rock pitchers, darts and draft Guinness.

Donohue's, 174 W 72nd St (at Broadway) ☎874-9304. It's much a local place – fairly atmospheric and good for an early drink or two.

Dublin House, 225 W 79th St (between Broadway and Amsterdam Ave)

Drinking

Drinking

☎ 874-9528. Brash Irish bar with a young crowd, good jukebox and inexpensive drinks. Recommended if you're up this way.

O' Neals', 49 W 64th St (between Central Park W and Broadway) **☎** 595-9545. This bar is the best place for a drink after a Lincoln Center show – or just about anytime, for that matter. And the restaurant at the back is upscale, yet reasonably priced.

Raccoon Lodge, 480 Amsterdam Ave (at W 83rd St) **☎** 874-9984. Simple bar with cheap drinks, jukebox, pinball and pool table. Also on the East Side at 1439 York Ave **☎** 650-1775 and Downtown at Warren St **☎** 766-9656.

Shark Bar, 307 Amsterdam Ave (between W 74th and 75th sts) **☎** 874-8500. Ultra-elegant African-American lounge with great soul food and a beat to go with it.

Smoke, 2751 Broadway (at W 105th St) **☎** 864-6662. Seductively mellow jazz lounge. Live music most nights. $8 cover at the weekend.

The West End, 2909-2911 Broadway (between 113th and 114th sts) **☎** 662-8830. Large bar/café across the street from Columbia University with a good mix of students, faculty and locals.

Upper East Side

Australia, 1733 1st Ave (at 90th St) **☎** 876-0203. Under new management, the "reigning Aussie-theme bar" aims to distance itself from the frat crowd that frequent most other watering holes around these parts (see *Bear Bar* below) while retaining an ambiance that feels, for better or worse, convincingly "Strine."

Bear Bar, 1770 2nd Ave (between 92nd and 93rd sts) **☎** 987-7580. Raucous, spit 'n' sawdust sports bar with too many cheap beer 'n' wings deals to list here.

Hunter's American Bar and Grill, 1387 3rd Ave (between 78th and 79th sts) **☎** 734-6008. On weekday afternoons, this amiable bar's "mature" clientele consists of residents from nearby retirement homes. The rest of the time you'll find a marginally funkier crowd. The restaurant at back serves tasty American basics, reasonably priced.

Kinsdale Tavern, 1672 3rd Ave (at 93rd St) **☎** 348-4370. Very Irish semi-sports bar/restaurant with a great beer selection, too many TVs to count and a good, eclectic jukebox.

Metropolitan Museum of Art, 1000 5th Ave (at 82nd St) **☎** 535-7710. Hard to imagine a more romantic spot to sip a glass of wine, whether it's up on the Cantor Roof Garden (open only in warm weather), enjoying one of the very best views in the city or on the Great Hall Balcony listening to live chamber music (Fri and Sat from 5–8pm).

Phoenix Park, 206 E 67th (between 2nd and 3rd aves) **☎** 717-8181. Nothing special about this Irish pub, except it's sociable, has a jukebox, TVs and a pool table – and there's very little else happening in this part of town.

Subway Inn, 143 E 60th St (at Lexington Ave) **☎** 223-8929. Downscale neighborhood dive bar across the street from Bloomingdale's. Definitely ungentrified, and great for a late afternoon beer.

Gay and lesbian bars

New York's **gay men's bars** cover the spectrum: from relaxed, mainstream cafés to some hard-hitting clubs full of glamour and attitude. Most of the more established places are in Greenwich Village and Chelsea, with the East Village and Murray Hill–Gramercy Park areas (the east 20s and 30s) up-and-coming. Things tend to get raunchier further west as you reach the bars and cruisers of the wild West Side Highway and meat-packing districts, both of which are hard-line and occasionally dangerous. **Lesbian bars** are fast growing in popularity, especially in the East Village. Perhaps even more popular are the roving "nights" that operate certain days of the week in bars throughout Downtown, like the "**Clit Club**" (**☎** 529-3300, see *Mother*, p.404). See "Nightlife", Chapter 19, for full listings. Check local weeklies, like the *Village Voice* and

MetroSource, and clubland's free 'zines like *H/X* for up-to-the minute listings.

Mainly for men

The Bar, 68 2nd Ave (at E 4th St) ☎674-9714. A longstanding neighborhood hideaway with a pool table in the East Village. Fairly relaxed on week nights, cruisier at the weekend.

Barracuda, 275 W 22nd St (between 7th and 8th aves) ☎645-8613. A favorite spot in New York's gay scene, featuring cheap drinks, a groovy vibe and, it's said, the best drag acts in the city.

The Boiler Room, 86 E 4th St (between 1st and 2nd aves) ☎254-7536. NYU/ local dive.

Brandy's Piano Bar, 235 E 84th St (between 2nd and 3rd aves) ☎650-1944. Handsome Uptown cabaret/piano bar. Definitely worth a visit. No cover, but a 2 drink minimum after 9.30pm.

The Break, 232 8th Ave (between 21st and 22nd sts) ☎627-0072. Hard-core Chelsea pick-up dive with cheap drinks, a pool table and free summer barbeques each Saturday in the back yard.

Dick's, 192 2nd Ave (at 12th St) ☎475-2071. Local dive with a pool table, an interesting jukebox and a good age mix.

The Dugout, 185 Christopher St (at Weehacken) ☎242-6113. Right by the river, this friendly West Village hangout with TV, pool table and video games might be the closest you'll find to a gay sports bar.

The Duplex, 61 Christopher St (at 7th Ave S) ☎255-5438. Big, welcoming two-level piano bar with regular cabaret and outdoor seating.

G, 223 W 19th St (between 7th and 8th aves) ☎929-1085. Nearly as stylish as its "guppie" clientele, this large and deservedly very popular lounge also features a regular DJ and juice bar.

Hell, 59 Gansevoort St (between Greenwich and Washington sts), ☎727-1666. An upscale lounge in the very hip meat-packing district.

Marie's Crisis, 59 Grove St ☎243-9323. Well-known cabaret/piano bar popular with tourists and locals alike. Features old-time singing sessions on Fri and Sat nights. Often packed, always fun.

The Monster, 80 Grove St (at Waverly Place) ☎924-3558. Large, campy bar with drag cabaret, piano and downstairs dance floor. Very popular, with a strong "neighborhood" feel.

Oscar Wilde, 221 E 58th St (between 2nd and 3rd aves). As you might guess from the name, not particularly rambunctious, but pleasant nonetheless.

Rawhide, 212 8th Ave (at 21st St) ☎242-9332. Hell-bent for leather, Chelsea's Rough Rider Room opens at 8am for those who are not yet ready for breakfast (and closes fairly late too).

Spike, 120 11th Ave (at W 20th St) ☎243-9688. Chelsea institution with a mostly middle-aged jeans and leather crowd, conveniently situated on the West Side Highway.

Stonewall, 53 Christopher St (between Waverly Place and 7th Ave S) ☎463-0950. Yes, *that* Stonewall, mostly refurbished and flying the pride flag like they own it – which, one supposes, they do.

Two Potato, 143 Christopher St (at Greenwich St) ☎255-0286. Cheap drinks, outrageous drag acts and a largely African-American crowd.

Wonder Bar, 505 E 6th St (between aves A and B) ☎777-9105. Cramped, festive and lesbian-friendly, though still boy-dominated.

The Works, 428 Columbus Ave (at W 81st St) ☎799-7365. Tropical theme bar with a fairly mixed crowd and friendly, laid-back atmosphere. One of the few options for this part of town. $1 margaritas on Thurs.

Mainly for women

Bar 4 (formerly Sanctuary), 444 7th Ave (at 15th St), Brooklyn ☎718/832-9800. Park Slope has the biggest Outer

Drinking

Drinking

Borough lesbian scene, and *Sanctuary* was its prime women's bar. Under the new name, *Bar 4* has gone fully democratic, welcoming everyone no matter what their inclination.

Crazy Nanny's, 21 7th Ave S (at Leroy St) ☎366-6312. Call for nightly events and activities.

Cubby Hole, 281 W 12th St (at W 4th St) ☎243-9041. Not exclusively gay, but this neighborhood hangout welcomes everyone.

Henrietta Hudson, 438 Hudson St (between Morton and Barrow St) ☎924-3347. Laid-back in the afternoon but brimming by night, especially on weekends. Guys are welcome too.

Julie's, 204 E 58th St (between 2nd and 3rd aves) ☎688-1294. Fairly sedate Sun–Tues: pretty wild the rest of the week. Wed and Sat are Latin Nights. One of your few choices around Midtown or Uptown, too.

Meow Mix, 269 E Houston St (at Suffolk St) ☎254-0688. Still one of the city's hottest girl clubs, way east Downtown. Bands or performances most nights, for which men are welcome if they behave themselves.

Chapter 19

Nightlife

New York's **music scene** reflects the city's diversity. Traditional and contemporary **jazz** are still in abundance, with the annual JVC and *Knitting Factory*'s "What Is Jazz?" festivals bringing top international talent to the city every year. The Downtown **avant-garde** scene – best personified by John Zorn, Arto Lindsay and Laurie Anderson – has petered out since the 1980s but still exists; its attendant art noise bands – the most famous being Sonic Youth – continue to influence the area's musicians both directly (the band runs the Sonic Youth Recordings label, and Thurston Moore does informal talent scouting) and indirectly (Kim Gordon's X-Girl fashion line). **Spoken word performers**, along with the current crop of singer/songwriters, are reviving the Beats' poetry scene. And, if you travel to the Outer Boroughs, you'll find pockets of **Brazilian music, West Indian music,** reggae and hip-hop. But if you stay within Manhattan (and chances are that you will), **indie rock** will fill your ears. The city's guitar bands have gotten sexier recently, with the punk revival giving way to acts that incorporate every type of gadget, pedal and sample into their tunes.

Despite what the designers on any avenue would like you to believe, New York is not uptight about appearance. In the trendiest **clubs**, however, appearances do matter: acolytes must adhere to the current look, with bouncers guarding the doors against the gauche. But if you just want to dance, there are plenty

of more casual places, especially the city's **gay clubs**, which often offer more creative music and less hassle.

The sections that follow provide accounts of the cream of current venues. Remember, though, that the music – and especially the club scenes – change continually. To ensure that techno night isn't now a drag-queen party, consult weekly **listings** publications. Excellent freebies include *The Village Voice, New York Press* and *Homo Xtra*, which contain detailed club, theater and venue listings for the straight and gay scenes; you can find them in corner self-serve newspaper boxes and music stores. It may seem a ridiculous and puritanical requirement, but you will most likely be "carded" at the door in New York, so it's imperative to bring your **ID** (driver's license or passport) with you when you go out. Venues and bars do enforce the legal drinking age of 21 and you must be 18 to enter some music venues.

Rock music

New York's **rock music** scene is still built on white-boy guitar bands, with three-chord rock the default setting. That said, many foreign acts – especially British bands – travel to New York's shores first when trying to break into America. Frequently you'll have the opportunity to see these groups play in small venues at low admission prices.

Rising rents have forced many musicians out of Manhattan and into the

Nightlife

Outer Boroughs and New Jersey; although the scene is still in Manhattan, the center has become more diffuse. There is a thriving off-Manhattan hub in Hoboken, New Jersey, centering on *Maxwell's* (see opposite); and in Brooklyn and Queens, large Latin, South American, Indian and reggae contingents exist – although the venues themselves are way off the average tourist circuit.

In Manhattan, most of the energy is provided by bars and venues located in the East Village and TriBeCa. The listings below will point you to the primary spots where you should find something for your ears, no matter what you're looking for.

The big performance venues

Madison Square Garden, 7th and 8th aves, W 31st–33rd sts ☎465-6741. New York's principal large stage, the Garden hosts not only hockey and basketball but also a good proportion of the stadium rock acts that visit the city. Seating 20,000-plus, the arena is not the most soulful place to see a band, but it may be the only chance that you get.

Meadowlands Stadium, East Rutherford, New Jersey ☎201/935-3900. The city's other really large venue, again with room for 20,000 of your closest friends.

Radio City Music Hall, 6th Ave and 50th St ☎247-4777. Not the prime venue it once was; most of the acts that play here now are firmly in the mainstream. The building itself has as great a sense of occasion, though, and Rockette dolls are still sold in the gift shop.

Smaller venues

Apollo Theater, 253 W 125th St (between 8th Ave and Powell Blvd) ☎749-5838 (show info) ☎531-5305 (tkts) ☎531 5337 (tours). Stars are born and legends are still made at the Apollo, which features a cast of black music acts, as well as weekly amateur nights (Wed). $13–35.

Arlene Grocery, 95 Stanton St (between Ludlow and Orchard sts) ☎473-9831.

An intimate, erstwhile *bodega* that hosts nightly free gigs by local, reliably good indie bands – and there's no cover charge. Frequented by musicians, some talent scouts and open-minded rock fans.

Baby Jupiter, 170 Orchard St (at Stanton St) ☎982-2229. Restaurant in front, performance space in back. Hosts a spectrum of rock (indie to avant-garde) bands and experimental performances. $2–5.

Beacon Theater, 2124 Broadway (74th St) ☎496-7070. Once the quirky Upper West Side host of off-the-mainstream names, now featuring divas such as Whitney, Cher and Tina. $20–40.

The Bitter End, 147 Bleecker St ☎673-7030. Young MOR bands in an intimate club setting. The famous people who've played the club are listed by the door: don't expect to see them there nowadays. Cover $5–10, with a two-drink at table, one at bar minimum.

The Bottom Line, 15 W 4th St (corner of Mercer St) ☎228-7880. Not New York's most adventurous venue but one of the better known – where you're most likely to see singer-songwriters. Cabaret setup, with tables crowding out any suggestion of a dance floor. Entrance $15–20, with shows at 7.30pm & 10.30pm. Cash only.

Bowery Ballroom, 6 Delancey St (corner of Bowery) ☎533-2111. A minimum of attitude among staff and clientele, great sound, and even better views has earned this site praise from fans and bands alike. Great bar and solid lineup – it's where British imports usually play in NYC. Many claim this place has set the standard for venues in New York. Shows $10–20.

Brownies, 169 Ave A (between 10th and 11th sts) ☎420-8392. The place to see major-label one-offs, bands on the cusp of making it big and impressive local talent. Around $6–8.

CBGB (and OMFUG), 315 Bowery (at Bleecker St) ☎982-4052. After 20+ years the black, sticker-covered interior may be the last of its kind in New York, but this legendary punk bastion (launch-pad for The Ramones, Blondie, Patti Smith and Talking Heads) is hardly as cutting-edge as it was. Noisy rock bands are the order now, often five or six a night. Weekday shows begin at 7 or 8pm, weekend shows at 9.30pm; occasional Sun matinees at 3pm. Prices about $3–9.

CB's 313 Gallery, 313 Bowery (at Bleecker St) ☎677-0445. Seven nights a week, *CBGB's* clean, spacious counterpart features folk, acoustic, and experimental music. $5.

Continental, 25 3rd Ave (between St Mark's Place and E 9th St) ☎529-6924. Loud alternative rock, with $2 shots at all times. Free entrance during the week, $5 on weekends.

The Cooler, 416 W 14th St (between 9th and 10th aves) ☎645-5189. Maybe it's the indigo lighting that lends a *Blue Velvet* feel to this underground bunker – or perhaps it's because the club is a former meat refrigerator. Adventurous indie rock and avant-garde attract a youthful, hip crowd. Mon–Thurs shows begin at 9pm; Fri & Sat shows start at 10pm. Free on Mon, otherwise $5–10.

Fez (Under Time Café), 380 Lafayette St (Great Jones St) ☎533-2680. The mirrored bar and sparkling gold stage curtain suggest a disco fantasy; poetry readings and acoustic performances are high caliber. Around $10.

Irving Plaza, 17 Irving Place (between E 15th and E 16th sts) ☎777-6800. Once home to an off-Broadway musical (hence the dangling chandeliers and blood-red interior), now host to an impressive array of rock, electronic and techno acts. The room has wildly divergent acoustics; stand toward the back on the ground floor for truest mix of sound. $10–25.

Koyote Kate's, 307 W 47th St (8th Ave) ☎956-1091. A baying coyote decorates the outside, while blues, jazz and rock music are performed live inside. No cover; bands daily except for Sun and Mon, with sets beginning at 9.30pm.

The Living Room, 84 Stanton St ☎533-7235. Comfortable couches and a friendly bar make for a relaxed setting in which to hear up-and-coming folk and rock. No cover, one drink minimum.

Manhattan-Center Hammerstein Ballroom, 311 W 34th St (between 8th and 9th aves) ☎564-4882. Refurbished ballroom that hosts a few shows a month, mostly indie rock and electronic music, in a 3600-seat venue. Uptight bouncers limit movement between seating levels and prohibit smoking on the balconies. $16–40.

Manny's Car Wash, 1558 3rd Ave (87th St) ☎369-BLUES. Smoky, Chicago-style blues bar, with a small dance floor, reasonable prices and Upper East Side clientele. Shows from 9.15pm. No cover Sun for blues jams; Mon women are admitted free and enjoy gratis tap beer and house wine. Otherwise, $4–15.

Maxwell's, Washington and 11th sts, Hoboken, New Jersey ☎201/798-0406. Neighborhood rock club hosting up to a dozen bands a week: some big names and one of the best places to check out the tri-state scene. Admission $6–10.

Mercury Lounge, 217 E Houston St (Essex St) ☎260-7400. Dark, medium-sized, innocuous space which hosts a mix of local, national and international pop and rock acts. It's owned by the same crew as Bowery Ballroom – who lately get the better bands. Around $7–12.

Roseland, 239 W 52nd St (between Broadway and 8th Ave) ☎249-0200. A historic ballroom that opened in 1919 and was once frequented by Adele and Fred Astaire, among others. Now a ballroom dancing school that, six times a month, turns into a concert venue, hosting big names and various pop and electronic acts. Take a gander at the shoes and photographs displayed in the entry hall. $10–50.

SOB's (Sounds of Brazil), 204 Varick St (corner of Houston St) ☎243-4940.

Nightlife

Nightlife

Premier place to hear Brazilian, West Indian, Caribbean and world music acts within the confines of Manhattan. Vibrant, with a high quality of music. Two shows nightly, times vary. Admission $12–20.

The Supper Club, 240 W 47th St (between Broadway and 8th Ave) ☎921-1940. White linen tablecloths, a large dance floor and upscale lounge jazz/hip-hop groups. Fri and Sat at 8pm, Eric Comstock and the *Supper Club's* house big-band swing with a vengeance. Around $20.

Surf Reality, 172 Allen St ☎673-4182. Welded metal parts make up the doorway to this velvet-draped offbeat venue, featuring contemporary vaudeville and open-mike performances, some of them truly bizarre. $6–8.

Terra Blues, 149 Bleecker St (between Thompson and LaGuardia sts) ☎777-7776. Great venue hosting jazz, blues and funk. No cover Sun–Wed. $5–15 other days.

Under Acme, 9 Great Jones St (Lafayette St) ☎420-1934. Seamy but laid-back basement club specializing in up-and-coming indie bands. Restaurant upstairs. Around $7.

Wetlands Preserve, 161 Hudson St (Laight St) ☎966-4225. A self-proclaimed "ecosaloon" that books reggae, hip-hop, world music and psychedelic blues bands. Admission $7–15, some free performances.

Jazz

The late 1980s and early 1990s were tough times for New York **jazz**. The city's clubs went through a rough patch, from which many a joint – including the landmark *Village Tavern* – did not recover. A clutch of new clubs has revived the scene, however, and there still are more than forty locations in Manhattan that present jazz regularly. Look mostly to **Greenwich Village** or **Harlem** for a good place; Midtown jazz clubs tend to be slick dinner-dance joints – expensive and overrun by businesspeople looking for culture.

To find out who's playing, check the usual sources, notably the *Voice*, *New York Magazine* and *Hothouse*, a free monthly magazine sometimes available at the venues; or the jazz monthly *downbeat*. The city's jazz-oriented **radio stations** are also sources of information: two of the best are **WBGO** (88.5 FM), a 24hr jazz station, and **WKCR** (98.7 FM), Columbia University's radio station. As a final resort, the **Jazz Line** (☎479-7888) provides recorded information about the week's events.

Price policies vary from club to club, but at most there's a hefty cover ($10–15) and always a minimum charge for food and drinks. An evening out at a major club will cost at least $15 per person, and more along the lines of $25–30 per person if you'd like to eat. Piano bars – smaller and often more atmospheric – come cheaper; some have neither an admission fee nor a minimum, but expect to pay inflated drink prices.

Jazz venues

Arthur's Tavern, 57 Grove St ☎675-6879. Small, amiable piano bar with some inspired performers and no cover or minimum. Drinks are pricey.

Birdland, 315 W 44th St (8th and 9th aves) ☎581-3080. Not the original place where Charlie Parker played, but an established supper club that's recently moved to Midtown. Hosts some big names. Sets nightly at 9pm and 11pm. Music charge of $10–20 at the bar, $15–30 at the tables, with a one-drink minimum at bar.

The Blue Note, 131 W 3rd St (6th Ave) ☎475-8592. Famous names with the attendant high prices. Cover charges vary wildly, from $7 to $65, plus a $5 minimum per person at the tables or a one-drink minimum at the bar. Sets are at 9pm & 11.30pm. On Fri & Sat, the jam sessions after 1am are free if you've seen the previous set, $5 if you haven't. Also offers a decent Sunday brunch for $18.50 that includes live music.

Detour, 349 E 13th St (1st Ave) ☎533-6212. Coffee and cocktail bar that fancies itself a bit of Paris in the East Village. Modern jazz and avant-garde experimentation nightly, no cover.

Dharma, 174 Orchard St (between Orchard and Stanton sts) ☎780-0313. A cozy setting for funky bop or experimentalism. Sets at 7 and 10pm. No cover.

Fifty Five, 55 Christopher St (between 6th and 7th aves) ☎929-9883. See p.389.

Iridium Room, 44 W 63rd St (Columbus Ave) ☎582-2121. Contemporary jazz performed 7 nights a week in a surrealist decor described as "Dolly meets Disney." Cover $20–35, $10 food and drink minimum.

Izzy Bar, 166 1st Ave (at 10th St) ☎228-0444. Popular with a European crowd, this cavernous hangout is more lounge than bar – but hosts jazz sessions and a variety of other music acts nightly. Admission is $5–10.

The Jazz Standard, 116 E 27th St ☎576-2232. A spacious room with great sound and even better performers has earned this club high praise and a loyal clientele. Sets Wed–Thurs at 8pm and 10pm, Fri and Sat 8pm, 10.30pm and midnight, Sun at 7pm and 9pm. $15–25.

Joe's Pub, 425 Lafayette St ☎539-8777. Stylishly classic bar in Joe Papp's Public Theater attracts the entertainment crowd. Performances six days a week, ranging from Broadway songbooks to readings from the New Yorker's fiction issues, with the likes of salsa, Indian music and jazz thrown in. Open daily 5pm–4am. $10–25.

Knickerbocker's, 33 University Place (at 9th St) ☎228-8490. A piano bar/restaurant decorated with Hirschfelds and featuring high-caliber bass/piano duos. Cover ($3–5) and minimum one-entree ($12–25) at the tables; cover ($3–5) and one-drink/$5 minimum at the lounge; and no cover but one-drink/$5 minimum at the bar (which offers the best view of the performers). Music

begins at 9.45pm and continues until 1–2am.

Knitting Factory, 74 Leonard St (between Broadway and Church St ☎219-3006. When it moved from its grubby East Village digs to a chichi space in TriBeCa, the *Knit* lost its street cred but gained an affluent clientele. The refurbished club – two performance spaces, two bars and a microbrewery with eighteen beers on draft – may be a baby boomer's dream, but for the rest of us, it's a place to see avant-garde jazz, experimental acts and big-name rock bands in an intimate setting. $15–20, with shows beginning from 8–10pm.

Roulette, 228 W Broadway (between Franklin and Broadway) ☎219-8242; *www.roulette.org*. Focusing on fringe music this TriBeCa living room hosts (very) experimental musicians performing jazz, rock and "new music." All shows begin at 9pm. $10.

Savoy Lounge, 355 W 41st St ☎947-5255. Just behind the Port Authority Bus Terminal, this Midtown joint has live jazz and blues nightly, and an increasingly rare Hammond organ. Sets Sun–Wed at 9pm, 10.30pm and midnight, no cover; jam session Thurs 11.30pm–4am, $5; sets Fri–Sat at 10pm, 11.30pm, 1am. $7.

Smalls, 183 W 10th St (7th Ave S) ☎929-7565. Tiny West Village club has the best jazz bargain in NY: ten hours of music for $10. The program comprises two sets and a late-night jam, by well-knowns and unknowns. Free juice and non-alcoholic beverages, or BYOB. Daily performances run 10pm–8am. Highly recommended.

Sweet Basil, 88 7th Ave (between Grove and Bleecker sts) ☎242-1785. One of New York's major – and most crowded – jazz spots, particularly at weekends, when there's brunch noon–5pm and free jazz 2–6pm. The walls are covered with photographs of past performers – just mere mortals like Dizzy Gillespie. Weekday evenings are the best times to go, and shows usually start at 9pm and

Nightlife

Nightlife

11pm (Fri and Sat offer an additional set at 12.30am). $17.50 cover during the week, $10 minimum per set at the tables, Fri and Sat $20–25 cover and a $10 minimum; $18 cover and one-drink minimum at the bar, with one free drink from the house.

Tonic, 107 Norfolk St ☎358-7503. Hip Lower East Side avant-jazzerie with Klezmer Sundays and a Monday-evening film series on the side. Cover varies.

Village Vanguard, 178 7th Ave (W 11th St) ☎255-4037. A NYC jazz landmark that celebrated its fiftieth anniversary a few years back, the *Vanguard* supplies a regular diet of big names. Mon–Thurs and Sun admission is $15, with a $10 minimum; Sat–Sun entry is $20, with a $10 minimum. Sets are at 9.30pm and 11.30pm, with a 1am set Sat and Sun.

Well's, 2247-9 Adam Clayton Powell Blvd (7th Ave between 132nd and 133rd sts) ☎234-0700. Harlem's "famous home of chicken and waffles," where Nat King Cole got married and the Rat Pack and Aretha Franklin used to hang out, has good jazz, a big mirrored bar – and a warm, authentic atmosphere. There's a trio on Fri and Sat nights (after 9.30pm), a five-piece band to accompany Sunday brunch (noon–4pm), and Mon is Big Band night with a 16-piece orchestra and dancing (after 9pm; $20 food and drink minimum).

Zinc Bar, 90 W Houston (at LaGuardia) ☎477-8337. Great jazz venue with strong drinks and a loyal bunch of regulars. The blackboard above the entrance announces the evening's featured band. Cover is $5 with a one-drink minimum. Hosts new talent and established greats such as Max Roach, Grant Green and Astrud Gilberto.

Folk, country and spoken word venues

Maybe it's the legacy of New York's Beatnik writers, so verbal and prolific in the 1950s and 1960s, or maybe it's a backlash against punk and grunge trends. Whatever the reason, there's been a resurgence of interest in poetry in New York's music scene. **Singer-songwriters** have returned, as have **readings**. Spoken word acts have evolved too: words are no longer just read off scraps of paper in a shaky voice – now they're also shouted and accompanied by music.

Centerfold Coffee House, Church of St Paul and St Andrew, 263 W 86th St (at Broadway) ☎362-3328. A 75-seat space with incredible acoustics that hosts occasional folk, jazz and bluegrass performances as well as small theater productions. Around $12.

Nuyorican Poets Café, 236 E 3rd St (between aves B and C) ☎505-8183. Beat poetry for the 1990s, performed both a cappella and accompanied by jazz and hip-hop. Café opens at 5pm; two shows nightly Tues–Sun. $5–10.

O'Lunney's, 204 W 43rd St ☎840-6688. Restaurant serving steaks, hamburgers and the like to traditional folk sounds.

People's Voice Cafe, 133 W 4th St (at Sullivan St) ☎787-3903. Tucked into the parlor of the Washington Square United Methodist Church, this space draws those in search of original music and cultural acts. $7 cover; seats about eighty.

Rodeo Bar, 375 3rd Ave (27th St) ☎683-6500. Dust off your spurs, grab your partner and head down to the *Rodeo* for live country tunes seven days a week.

Nightclubs

New York's – especially Manhattan's – **club life** is a rapidly evolving creature. While many of the name DJs remain the same, venues shift around, opening and closing according to finances and fashion. Musically, techno and house hold sway at the moment, with the emphasis on the deep, vocal style that's always been popular in the city; but reggae, hip-hop, funk, ambient and drum'n'bass all retain interest.

Recently, though, the club scene has endured tough times, with Mayor Rudolph Giuliani introducing a conservative strain into the city's nightlife. Under the guise of "quality of life" improvements, Giuliani has enacted laws requiring each nightspot to have a cabaret license in addition to an alcohol license if it intends to allow dancing. So while many bars might have a DJ playing in the corner, only the ones with the costly extra paperwork will permit their patrons to shake their hips.

Another problem that has dampened the scene came from within. Peter Gatien, the owner of New York's three largest nightclubs – *Limelight, Tunnel* and the *Palladium* – was indicted in May 1996 on drug distribution and conspiracy charges, and his biggest party promoter, Michael Alig, is currently in jail, charged with the murder of club kid Angel Melendez. *Limelight* was closed after the debacle but has now reopened, while the *Palladium* was not so lucky, and has closed its doors permanently. Though drugs are regarded by many as a natural accompaniment to clubbing, a word of warning: if you feel you must indulge, be very discreet.

Despite all this, **clubs** in New York can offer a good night out. The scene constantly changes, so to ensure that the party is still there, check such listings mags as *Time Out New York, Paper Magazine* or *Homo Xtra* – or freebies *The Village Voice* and *New York Press*.

Clubbing can be costly. In order to get the most for the least amount of money, here are some guidelines:

• The best time to go is during the week. Crowds are smaller, prices are cheaper, service is better, and clubbers are more savvy than during the weekend, which is when out-of-towners flood the floor.

• The fliers placed in record and clothing stores in the East Village and SoHo are the best way to find out about the latest clubs and one-off nights. Many fliers also offer substantial discounts.

• Style can be important, so make an effort and you'll probably get beyond the velvet rope (if there even is one).

• Nothing much gets going before midnight, so many places offer reduced admission before then.

• Expect to be thoroughly frisked by security before entering the larger dance clubs. Drugs, weapons and hip flasks will be confiscated; any sharp objects that could be used as weapons (Swiss Army knives, metal combs) will be held at the door, as will pepper sprays and bottles of water. Basically, if you'd like to keep it, don't take it to the club.

• When you eventually stagger out into the morning light, keep your wits about you. If you're taking a cab, specify the most direct route home, or you might find yourself taking a tour of the city.

Baktun, 418 W 14th St ☎206-1590. If you're in the mood to make the trek this far west the rewards are vast in one of the city's most unpretentious nightclubs. "Direct Drive" Saturdays feature drum'n'bass with DJ's Lion, Seoul, Cassien, Reid Speed and Chris Thomas. Great time guaranteed.

Bar d'O, 29 Bedford St (at Downing St) ☎627-1580. Drag-queen-about-town Joey Arias belts out show tunes that would bring a tear to any Streisand fan's eye. Mon and Wed at 10pm, Thurs at 7pm. $3–5.

bOb, 255 Eldridge St (at E Houston St) ☎777-0558. A friendly, 20-something art-school crowd lounges on the sofas while DJs spin hip-hop and soul grooves. Nightly, free.

Body and Soul, held Sun 3–10pm at *Vinyl*, 6 Hubert St (between Hudson and Greenwich sts, *see* p.405) ☎343-1379. DJ François K dishes up heavy house at this afternoon party. Popular with a mid-20s crowd that prefers dancing to body piercing and said to be the best club vibe in New York.

Cafe Con Leche, held Sun at 11pm at Speeed, 20 W 39th St (between 5th and

Nightlife

Nightlife

6th aves) ☎719-9867. Continually rated one of the best nights out in New York. DJ Junior O spins house, latin, hip-hop, salsa, merengue, reggae. Mainly gay crowd. $10.

Delia's, 197 E 3rd St (between aves A and B) ☎254-9184. A supper club whose sleazy location appeals to Upper East Siders. *Delia's* is anything but squalid, however: inside, the formidable mistress presides over a plush environment that caters to the needs of diners and dancers alike. Open Fri and Sat with prix-fixe dinner/dancing $39; dancing alone $10. Reservations encouraged.

Don Hill's, 511 Greenwich St (corner of Spring St) ☎219-2850. Drag queens, creative types, and slumming stars congregate at this dive on the outskirts of SoHo. Less trendy than it used to be, but still the place where your rubber gear won't get a second glance. Fri is Squeezebox, a cauldron of glam, punk and disco ($10); on Sat, Tiswas, featuring cutting-edge Britpop, is $7. Live bands both nights; other parties during the week.

Flamingo East, 219 2nd Ave (between 13th and 14th sts) ☎533-2860. Cozy seating, area rugs and the balcony overlooking 2nd Ave make the upstairs party space feel like a rich acquaintance's apartment. Kiki and Herb do musically diverse rock cabaret on Thurs at 9.30pm. Salon Wed, 10pm, for the chic gay crowd; the first Wed of the month is "Salonette," for the ladies. $7–15.

Giant Step, venues vary, call ☎414-8001 for time and place. After singlehandedly flooding NY with acid jazz, *Giant Step* has mercifully reinvented itself as a proponent of drum'n'bass and trip-hop. Hosts low-key shows that aren't well publicized, offering the chance to see name acts for cheap prices in small venues. $10–15.

Life, 158 Bleecker St (at Thompson St) ☎420-1999. Mirrored pillars, a huge dance floor, and "hidden" seating behind the bar make this trendy nightspot antiseptic and anachronistic, executed without a trace of humor. Leo DiCaprio, Mariah Carey and everyone else with an agent shows up to be seen. Wed night's "Lust for Life" pack in the crowds as do Thursday's "Get a Life," a favorite of the fashion crowd, Friday nights are owned by none other than Grandmaster Flash spinning hip-hop for "Flash Fridays." Tues–Sun, $20.

Limelight, 660 6th Ave (at 20th St) ☎807-7850. Back in business, and its drug-bustee owner, Peter Gatien, is even on the door some nights. The building is splendid: a church designed by Trinity Church-builder Richard Upjohn. Looking to the 1980s for inspiration, Gatien and his new partner, Irv Johnson, have added an art gallery/lounge behind the main dance floor, but moveable video screens still rule the day. Suffers from weekender syndrome. $25.

Meow Mix, 269 E Houston St (Suffolk St) ☎254-0688. Lipstick lesbians, leather ladies and all types in between drink and dance at this temple devoted to *la femme*. DJs play tunes that range from 1980s hits to sinewy soul. Free–$5.

Mother, 432 W 14th St (Washington St) ☎366-5680. Located among the warehouses and loading docks of the meatpacking district, this funhouse is so happening that it was immortalized in an Absolut vodka ad. Probably one of the few NY clubs left where anything goes. Fri is the "Clit Club", a techno, tribal extravaganza for gay women and friends; Sat is "Click + Drag", where leather and pleather fetishes reach cyberspace; Tues is the long-running "Jackie 60", a dress-to-excess party that sets no bounds. Tues–Fri, admission $10 (Sat $15).

Nell's, 246 W 14th St (between 7th and 8th aves) ☎675-1567. First of the so-called "supper clubs," still a plush venue with late supper and live music upstairs, and DJ dancing down, every night. Open-mike night on Tues with the occasional celebrity walk-on. Some nights the bridge-and-tunnel crowd (non-

Manhattanites) is in full force; but in general, it's a multiracial, well-dressed crowd. $10–15.

Ohm, 16 W 22nd St (between 5th and 6th aves) ☎229-2000. Formerly *Les Poulets*, glam supper club with three-level lounge area and upstairs dance space, mellower black-lacquered dance floor downstairs. Big names in Latin music and sensuously performed salsa – the only place in central Manhattan where the twain do meet. Frequented by a serious dance clientele, and extremely crowded on weekends. Prix-fixe breakfast served starting at 2am. Open for dinner and dancing Thurs–Sat; admission $20.

Sapphire Lounge, 249 Eldridge St (at Houston St) ☎777-5153. Cheesy'n'sleazy, with a black-lit interior and "arty" films in the back room. Frequented by hip Lower East Siders. Lots of house, garage and techno; "Infinity" on Saturdays a bit more diverse, with latin and reggae mixed in. Open every night, free–$5.

Shine, 285 W Broadway (at Canal St) ☎941-0900. Looking every bit what a nightclub should: velvet ropes and angry bouncers outside, high ceilings, plush red curtains and dim lights inside. Once important for up-and-coming rock bands it's still the place for music industry parties; DJ oriented theme nights line up a crowd on Fri for "Groove On." $10–20.

Sound Factory, 618 W 46th St (between 11th and 12th aves) ☎489-0001. Relocated yet again, the *Sound Factory* has been reborn as a mainstream house and techno club with security so tight they'll frisk your socks. The crowd lacks the flavor of the *Factory's* old days, and the spirit, though willing, is weak. Open Fri–Sun; $20-25.

Sway, 305 Spring St (between Hudson and Greenwich sts) ☎1620-5220. A late night incognito club with only a sign for *McGovern's* bar (the previous tenants) over the door. New York's beautiful people, celebrities and other venturesome night owls slink around till dawn. The ambiance is set with trance music, low lighting and big booths. 10pm–4am.

Tunnel, 220 12th Ave (W 27th St) ☎695-4682. A premier techno and house hall occupying a never-completed subway station, a tad the worse for wear. Check out the Kenny Scharf room with cartoonish decor by the artist and the unisex bathroom with full bar and lounge. The hip-hop lounge downstairs offers sanctuary but watch out for giant crowds of out-of-towners on the weekends. Open Fri–Sun; $15–20.

Twilo, 530 W 27th St (between 10th and 11th aves) ☎462-9422. Megadisco in the former home of the *Sound Factory*. Features name European DJs each Fri, DJ Junior Vasquez spinning house and trance on Sat nights. Fri mainly straight, Sat largely gay. Open Fri–Sat; $17–25.

2i's, 248 W 14th St (between 7th and 8th aves) ☎807-1775. Funky, posh dance club and lounge, rumored to surpass its passé neighbor, *Nell's*. $10–15.

Vanity, 28 E 23rd St ☎989-1038 ext 219. Fri nights are "GBH" (Great British House) while Sat's rock with "Sticky," a big-beat night featuring drum'n'bass mega-stars like David Holmes and Deejay Punk Roc. Mon–Thurs the club is a bit sleepy, Thurs–Sat you're destined to groove. $20–25.

Vinyl, 6 Hubert St (between Hudson and Greenwich sts) ☎343-1379. Considered one of New York's hottest venues, this big, dark, low-ceilinged warehouse is a techno sweatshop: packed full of rave kids and other slaves to the beat. Li'l Louis Vega spins here each Sat; expect to wait in line for a long time. Fri–Sun. $12–20.

Webster Hall, 125 E 11th St (between 3rd and 4th aves) ☎353-1600. A microcosmic venue with myriad private rooms, four floors of techno, acid jazz, jungle and the like, nooks and crannies – even a coffee shop. Expect to meet frat boys, homeboys, queens, Goths and the Wall Street crowd. Fantastical decor behind a stately turn-of-the-century facade. $10–20.

Nightlife

Chapter 20

The Performing Arts and Film

From Broadway glitter to NoHo grunge, from the high-culture polish of Lincoln Center to the rawest experimentalism of the Lower East Side, the range and variety of the performing arts in New York is exactly what you might expect. And prices, of course, vary accordingly, from $100 nights at the opera to free bring-your-own chair performances of Shakespeare in Downtown parking lots. Broadway, and even Off-Broadway theater is notoriously expensive, but if you know where to look, there are a variety of ways to get tickets cheaper, and on the Off-Off-Broadway fringe you can see a play for little more than the price of a movie ticket. Dance, music and opera are superbly catered for: again the big mainstream events are extremely expensive; but smaller ones are often equally as interesting as well as far cheaper. As for cinema, New York gets the first run of most American films and many foreign ones long before they reach Europe, and has a very healthy art-house and revival scene.

"What's on" listings for the arts can be found in a number of places. The most useful sources are the clear and comprehensive listings in *Time Out New York*, the free *Village Voice* (especially the pull-out "Voice Choices" section), or the *New York Press*, all especially useful for things Downtown and vaguely "alter-

native." For tonier events try the "Cue" section in the weekly *New York Magazine*, the "Goings On About Town" section of *The New Yorker*, or Friday's "Weekend" or Sunday's "Arts and Leisure" sections of *The New York Times*. Specific Broadway listings can be found in the free *Official Broadway Theater Guide*, available from theater and hotel lobbies or the New York Convention and Visitors' Bureau (see "Information, Maps and Tours" in Basics). Even more useful, if you want to plan your itinerary before you leave, are Web sites such as *newyork.citysearch.com* and *NewYork.sidewalk.com which* have up-to-the-minute information on arts and events in New York, as well as the Web site *NYTheatre.com*, a useful source of information about local theater.

Theater

Theater venues in the city are referred to as Broadway, Off-Broadway, or Off-Off-Broadway, groupings that represent a descending order of ticket price, production polish, elegance and comfort (but don't necessarily have much to do with the address) and an ascending order of innovation, experimentation and theater for the sake of art rather than cash. Broadway, for years dominated by grandiose tourist-magnet musicals, has, over the past couple of years, been getting its act together and getting serious. The record-breaking 1998–99 season was notable for acclaimed revivals of plays by those titans of American theater Eugene O'Neill, Tennessee Williams and Arthur Miller, as well as a slew of hot British imports like *Closer, Electra, The Weir, The Blue Room* (notable itself for a much ballyhooed naked Nicole Kidman), and at least a couple of plays by David Hare. On top of that, lively, imaginative musicals like *The Lion King, Rent, Fosse, Chicago* and *Cabaret* continue to draw crowds and acclaim. Off-Broadway, while less glitzy, is the best place to discover new talent and adventurous new American drama like recent sensations *Wit* or *How I Learned to Drive*. It's Off-Broadway where you'll find social and political drama, satire, ethnic plays and repertory: in short, anything that Broadway wouldn't consider a surefire money-spinner. Lower operating costs also mean that Off-Broadway often serves as a forum to try out what sometimes ends up as a big Broadway production. Off-Off-Broadway is New York's fringe. Unlike Off-Broadway, Off-Off doesn't have to use professional actors, and shows range from shoestring productions of the classics to outrageous and experimental performance art. Prices for Off-Off range from cheap to free, and quality can vary from execrable to electrifying. Use weekly reviews as your guide; the listings here should give you an idea of which venues and companies are worth a look.

For the record, it's the size of the theater that technically determines the category it falls into: under 100 seats and a theater is Off-Off; 100 to 500 and it's Off. Most Broadway theaters are located in the blocks just east or west of Broadway between 41st and 53rd streets; Off- and Off-Off-Broadway theaters are sprinkled throughout Manhattan, with a concentration in the East and West Villages, Chelsea, and several in the 40s and 50s west of the Broadway theater district.

Tickets

Tickets for Broadway shows can cost as much as $75 for orchestra seats (some-

times even $100 for the hottest show in town) and as little as $15 for day-of-performance rush tickets for some of the longer-running shows. Off-Broadway's best seats are cheaper than those on Broadway, averaging between $25–55. Off-Off Broadway, however, tickets should rarely set you back more than $15 at most. There are also a few methods for obtaining cheap seats on and Off-Broadway.

• Line up at one of two Manhattan **TKTS booths** run by the Theater Development Fund (☎768-1818), where you can obtain cut-rate tickets on the day of performance (up to half-off plus a $2.50 service charge) for many Broadway and Off-Broadway shows (though not always for the more recently opened popular shows). The booth in Times Square, at Broadway and 47th St, has the longest lines and opens Mon–Sat 3–8pm, 10am–2pm for Wed and Sat matinees, and 11am–7pm for all Sun performances. There's a less busy Downtown TKTS booth on the mezzanine of 2 World Trade Center (preferable if it's raining) open Mon–Fri 11am–5.30pm, Sat 11am–3.30pm (closed Sun), and on Fri and Sat tickets are sold for the *following day's* matinee shows. Both booths take cash or travelers' checks only; best days for availability and short lines are Tues, Wed and Thurs.

• Look for **twofer discount coupons** in the New York Convention and Visitors' Bureau and many shops, banks, restaurants and hotel lobbies. These entitle two people to a hefty discount (though the days when they really offered two-for-the-price-of-one are long gone) and unlike TKTS it's possible to book ahead, though don't expect to find coupons for the latest shows. The Hit Show Club (630 9th Ave at 44th St ☎581-4211) also provides discount vouchers up to fifty percent off which you present at the box office.

• If you're prepared to pay full price you can, of course, go directly to the theater, or call one of the following ticket sales agencies. **Tele-Charge** (☎239-6200, or

The Performing Arts and Film

The Performing Arts and Film

1-800/432-7250 outside NY), **Ticketmaster** (☎307-4100 or 1-800/755-4000 outside NY), and **Ticketron** (☎1-800/SOLD-OUT, Mon to Fri) sell tickets over the phone to Broadway shows, while **Tickets Central** (☎279-4200) sells tickets to many Off- and Off-Off-Broadway theaters 1–8pm daily. All these services charge a service fee of a couple of dollars or more. You can also buy theater tickets over the Internet at Ticketmaster's Web site (www.ticketmaster.com) or through Playbill-On-Line (www.playbill.com).

• Same-day standing-room tickets are also available for some sold-out shows for $10–20. Check listings magazines for availability.

Though you will want to check out the aforementioned journals to see what's playing the following theaters are worth attention for their specialized repertoire or for their long-running shows.

On and Off-Broadway

Actor's Playhouse, 100 7th Ave S ☎463-0060. West Village venue specializing in gay-themed theater.

American Jewish Theater, 307 W 26th St ☎633-9797. Produces four classical and contemporary plays a year on Jewish themes.

Astor Place Theater, 434 Lafayette St ☎254-4370. Showcase for much exciting work since the 1960s, when Sam Shepard's The Unseen Hand and Forensic and the Navigators had the playwright on drums in the lobby. Since 1992, however, the theater has been the home of the absurdist but tourist-friendly comic performance artists The Blue Man Group (www.blueman.com).

Brooklyn Academy of Music, 30 Lafayette Ave, Brooklyn ☎718/636-4100. Despite its name, BAM regularly stages theater on its three stages. They have imported a number of stunning productions directed by Ingmar Bergman in recent years, and every autumn the annual Next Wave festival is the city's most exciting showcase for large-scale performance art by the likes of Robert

Wilson, Robert LePage, Laurie Anderson and Pina Bausch. Not so much Off-Broadway as Off-Manhattan, but well worth the trip.

Daryl Roth Theatre, 20 Union Square E (at 15th St) ☎239-6200. Site of the rambunctious, airborne frat-party of a show that is De La Guarda. Wear old clothes and be prepared to be hoisted in the air by swooping performance artistes.

Irish Repertory Theater, 132 W 22nd St ☎727-2737. Specializes in Irish or Irish-themed theater.

Jane Street Theatre at the Hotel Riverview Ballroom, 113 Jane St at West Side Hwy ☎239-6200. Way out west in the meat-packing district, this little upstairs venue has spawned the strangest, hottest ticket in town: the transsexual German rock opera Hedwig and the Angry Inch.

The Joseph Papp Public Theater, 425 Lafayette St ☎239-6200. This major Downtown Off-Broadway venue produces serious and challenging theater from new, mostly American playwrights all year round, as well as being the major producer of Shakespeare productions in the city. In the summer the Public runs the free Shakespeare Festival at the open-air Delacorte Theater in Central Park (☎539-8750). Tickets are available on the day both at the Public Downtown and the Delacorte Uptown, but be prepared for long lines.

Manhattan Theater Club, 131 W 55th St ☎581-1212. Major Midtown venue for serious new theater, many of whose productions eventually transfer to Broadway. See them here first.

New Amsterdam Theater, 214 W 42nd St ☎307-4100. Disney's recently renovated Times Square palace is home to Julie Taymor's Tony award-winning extravaganza The Lion King.

Orpheum Theater, 126 2nd Ave (at St Mark's Place) ☎477-2477. One of the biggest theaters in the East Village, known for showing David Mamet and other new American theater, and home for the last few years to the British percussion performance troupe Stomp.

St Luke's Church, 308 W 46th St ☎239-6200. After a decade in the West Village, the audience participation comedy *Tony'n'Tina's Wedding* has moved nearer to Times Square. The audience attends a boisterously staged Italian-American wedding and then joins the party for dinner at Vinnie Black's Vegas Room in the *Hotel Edison*. (Price of dinner is included in the $65–75 ticket).

Studio 54, 524 W 54th St ☎239-6200. The legendary disco mecca has been recently transformed into the perfect setting for the Tony award-winning revival of *Cabaret*.

Sullivan St Playhouse, 181 Sullivan St ☎674-3838. Greenwich Village theater which has been home to *The Fantasticks*, the longest running show in American history, since 1960.

Vivian Beaumont Theater and Mitzi E. Newhouse Theater, Broadway at 65th St at Lincoln Center ☎239-6200. Technically Broadway theaters, though far enough away from Times Square in distance and, usually, quality, to qualify as Off. The place to see new work by Stoppard, Guare and the like.

Westside Theater, 407 W 43rd St ☎239-6200. Small basement theater known for productions of Shaw, Wilde, Pirandello and the like.

Off-Off-Broadway and performance art spaces

Bouwerie Lane Theater, 330 Bowery (at Bond St) ☎677-0060. Home of the Jean Cocteau Repertory which produces plays by Genet, Sophocles, Shaw, Strindberg, Sartre, Wilde, Williams, etc.

Dixon Place, 258 Bowery (between Prince and Houston sts) ☎219-3088. Very popular small venue upstairs in a Bowery loft dedicated to experimental theater. Once a month Dixon Place has an "Open Performance Night," where the first ten people to sign up can perform.

Expanded Arts, 85 Ludlow St (below Delancey) ☎253-1813. Lower East Side

performance venue that also produces the summer-long "Shakespeare in the Park(ing Lot)" series of free performances at the Municipal Parking Lot at Broome and Ludlow.

Franklin Furnace, 112 Franklin St ☎925-4671. An archive dedicated to installation work and performance art, the Franklin Furnace has launched the careers of performers as celebrated and notorious as Karen Finley and Eric Borgosian. Performances do not take place at the TriBeCa Furnace but at related venues Downtown.

Here, 145 6th Ave (at Spring St) ☎647-0202. Relatively new performance space on the western edge of SoHo.

Hudson Guild Theater, 441 W 26th St (between 9th and 10th aves) ☎760-9800. Introduces new American and European playwrights.

The Kitchen, 512 W 19th St (between 10th and 11th aves) ☎255-5793; *www.panix.com/~kitchen*. Well-established Chelsea venue for avant-garde performance art, theater, music and dance.

Knitting Factory, 74 Leonard St (between Broadway and Church St) ☎219-3006; *www.knittingfactory.com*. In its new, improved TriBeCa space this much-loved alternative music venue now hosts theater and performance art in its Alterknit Theater.

La Mama E.T.C. (Experimental Theater Club), 74A E 4th St (between the Bowery and 2nd Ave) ☎475-7710. The mother of all Off-Off-theaters and venue for some of the most exciting theater, performance and dance seen in the city in the past 30 years.

Nuyorican Poets Cafe, 236 E 3rd St (between aves B and C) ☎505-8183. For a number of years now the *Nuyorican* in Alphabet City has been one of the most talked-about performance spaces in town. Its "poetry slams" made it famous, but they also host theater and film script readings, occasionally with well-known Downtown stars.

The
Performing
Arts and
Film

The Performing Arts and Film

Ontological-Hysteric Theater at St. Mark's Church, 131 E 10th St (at 2nd Ave) ☎533-4650. Produces some of the best radical theater in the city; especially famous for the work of Downtown theater legend Richard Foreman.

Performing Garage, 33 Wooster St ☎966-3651. The well-respected experimental Wooster Group (whose most famous alumnus is Willem Dafoe) perform regularly in this SoHo space.

P.S. 122, 150 1st Ave (at 9th St) ☎477-5288. A converted school house in the East Village that is a perennially popular venue for a jam-packed schedule of radical performance art, dance and one-person shows.

Samuel Beckett Theater, 410 W 42nd St ☎332-0894. A repertory program of classic and new plays.

Surf Reality, 172 Allen St (between Stanton and Rivington sts) ☎673-4182. Eclectic performance art and comedy space on the Lower East Side.

Theater for the New City, 155 1st Ave (at 10th St) ☎254-1109. Known for following the development of new playwrights and integrating dance, music and poetry with drama. TNC also performs outdoors for free at a variety of venues throughout the summer and hosts the Lower East Side Festival of the Arts at the end of May.

Thread Waxing Space, 476 Broadway ☎966-9774. Beautifully named performance space in SoHo, inside an old factory, mostly used for music, but often hosts performance-based art too.

WPA Theater, 519 W 23rd St ☎206-0523. The Workshop of the Players Art performs neglected American classics and American Realist plays, many from the South, acted in a style described as "derived from Stanislavski."

Dance

With the astounding success of recent Broadway shows like *Fosse, Tap Dogs, Riverdance* and anything starring Savion Glover, **dance** is experiencing a surge in popularity in New York. And, as with theater, the range of dance on offer in the city is vast. New York has five major ballet companies, dozens of modern troupes and untold thousands of soloists and you would have to be very particular indeed in your tastes not to find something of interest. Events are listed in broadly the same places as for music and theater – though you might also want to pick up *Dance Magazine*. The official dance season runs from September to January and April to June. The following is a list of some of the major dance venues in the city though a lot of the smaller, more esoteric companies and solo performers also perform at many of the spaces like the Kitchen and P.S.122, which are listed above under "Off-Off Broadway and performance art spaces." Dance fans should also note that the annual **Dance on Camera Festival** (☎727-0764) of dance films takes place at the Walter Reade Theater at Lincoln Center in December.

Brooklyn Academy of Music, 30 Lafayette St (between Flatbush Ave and Fulton St), Brooklyn ☎718/636-4100. Universally known as BAM, this is America's oldest performing arts academy and one of the busiest and most daring producers in New York. In the autumn, BAM's Next Wave Festival showcases the hottest international attractions in avant-garde dance and music; in winter visiting artists appear, and each spring BAM hosts the annual DanceAfrica Festival, America's largest showcase for African and African-American dance and culture, now in its twentieth year. A great venue and one definitely worth crossing the river for.

City Center, 131 W 55th St (between 6th and 7th aves) ☎581-1212 or 581-7907. This large, Midtown venue hosts some of the most important troupes in modern dance, such as the Merce Cunningham Dance Company, the Paul Taylor Dance Company, the Alvin Ailey American Dance Theater, the Joffrey Ballet and the Dance Theater of Harlem.

Cunningham Studio, 55 Bethune St (at Washington St) ☎726-3432. The newish home of the Merce Cunningham Dance Company stages performances once a week by emerging modern choreographers.

Dance Theater Workshop's Bessie Schönberg Theater, 219 W 19th St (between 7th and 8th aves) ☎924-0077; *www.dtw.org*. Founded in 1965 as a choreographers' collective for the support of emerging artists in alternative dance, DTW boasts more than 175 performances from nearly 70 artists and companies each season. Located on the second floor of a former warehouse, the theater has an unintimidating, relaxed atmosphere and ticket prices are very reasonable.

Danspace Project, St Mark's-Church-in-the-Bowery, 131 E 10th St (at 2nd Ave) ☎674-8194. Experimental contemporary dance, with a season running from September to June in one of the more beautiful performance spaces.

The Joyce Theater, 175 8th Ave (at 19th St) ☎242-0800. Situated in Chelsea, the Joyce is perhaps the best-known Downtown dance venue. Hosts short seasons by a wide variety of acclaimed dance troupes such as Pilobolus, the Parsons Dance Company and Donald Byrd/The Group. The Joyce also recently opened a new space in SoHo at 155 Mercer St between Prince and Houston sts ☎431-9233.

The Judson Church, 55 Washington Square S (at Thompson St) ☎477-6854. Greenwich Village's historic venue for experimental dance.

Julliard Dance Workshop, Julliard Theater, 155 W 65th St (at Broadway) ☎799-5000. The dance division of the Julliard School often gives free workshop performances.

Lincoln Center's Fountain Plaza, 65th St at Columbus Ave ☎875-5766. Open-air summer venue for the enormously popular offering, Midsummer Night Swing, where you can learn a different dance en masse each night (everything from

polka to rockabilly) and watch a performance all for $11.

Metropolitan Opera House, 65th St at Columbus Ave, Lincoln Center ☎362-6000. Home of the renowned American Ballet Theater, which performs at the Opera House from early May into July. Prices for ballet at the Met range from more than $100 for the best seats to $15 for standing-room tickets, which go on sale the morning of the performance.

New York State Theater, 65th St (at Columbus Ave), Lincoln Center ☎870-5570. Lincoln Center's other major ballet venue is home to the revered New York City Ballet, which performs for a nine-week season each spring.

Pace Downtown Theater, Spruce St (between Park Row and Gold St) ☎346-1715. Venue for the Yangtze Repertory Theatre Company which stages work by Asian choreographers.

92nd Street Y, 1395 Lexington Ave (at 92nd St) ☎415-5552. Hosts performances and discussions, often for free, at the Y's Harkness Dance Center.

Classical music and opera

New Yorkers take **serious music** seriously. Long lines form for anything popular, many concerts sell out, and summer evenings can see a quarter of a million people turning up in Central Park for free performances by the New York Philharmonic. The range of what's on offer is wide, but it's big names at big venues that pull the crowds, leaving you with a good number of easily attended selections.

Opera venues

Amato Opera Theater, 319 Bowery (at 2nd St) ☎228-8200. This Downtown venue presents an ambitious and varied repertory of classics performed by up-and-coming young singers and conductors. Performances at weekends only, closed in the summer.

Julliard School, 60 Lincoln Center Plaza (at Broadway and 65th St) ☎769-7406.

The
Performing
Arts and
Film

The Performing Arts and Film

Right next door to the Met, Julliard students often perform under the control of a famous conductor, usually for low ticket prices.

Metropolitan Opera House, Columbus Ave (at 64th St), Lincoln Center ☎362-6000. Known as the Met, New York's premiere opera venue is home to the Metropolitan Opera Company from Sept to late April. Tickets are expensive and can be quite difficult to get hold of, though 175 standing-room tickets for $11–15 go on sale every Sat morning at 10am (though the line has been known to form at 5am).

The New York State Theater also in Lincoln Center (☎870-5570) is where Beverley Sills' New York City Opera plays David to the Met's Goliath. Its wide and adventurous program varies wildly in quality – sometimes startlingly innovative, occasionally mediocre, but seats go for less than half the Met's prices.

Concert halls

The Avery Fisher Hall, in Lincoln Center ☎875-5030; *www. newyorkphilharmonic.org*. Permanent home of the New York Philharmonic, and temporary one to visiting orchestras and soloists. Ticket prices for the Philharmonic are in the range of $12–50. An often fascinating bargain are the NYP open rehearsals at 9.45am on concert days. Tickets for these, non-reservable, cost just $6. Avery Fisher also hosts the very popular annual Mostly Mozart Festival (☎875-5103) in Aug.

The Alice Tully Hall ☎875-5050, also in Lincoln Center, is a smaller venue for chamber orchestras, string quartets and instrumentalists. Prices similar to those in Avery Fisher.

Bargemusic, Fulton Ferry Landing, Brooklyn ☎718/624-4061. Chamber music in a wonderful river setting below the Brooklyn Bridge on Thurs and Fri at 7.30pm, and Sun at 4pm. Tickets are

$23, $20 for senior citizens, $15 for students.

Brooklyn Academy of Music, 30 Lafayette Ave (near Flatbush Ave), Brooklyn ☎718/636-4100. See "Dance, p.410"

Cathedral of St. John the Divine, 1047 Amsterdam Ave (at 112th St) ☎662-2133. Magnificent Uptown setting which hosts both classical and New Age performances. Prices range from free to $60; call for details.

Carnegie Hall, 154 W 57th St (at 7th Ave) ☎247-7800. The greatest names from all schools of music performed here in the past, from Tchaikovsky and Toscanini to Gershwin and Billie Holiday. Recently called "one of the finest orchestral showplaces on the planet" by Alex Ross in *The New Yorker*.

Kaufman Concert Hall, in the *92nd St Y* at 1395 Lexington Ave ☎996-1100.

Lehman Center for the Performing Arts, Bedford Park Blvd, Bronx ☎718/960-8232. First-class concert hall drawing the world's top performers.

Merkin Concert Hall, 129 W 67th St (between Broadway and Amsterdam Ave) ☎501-3330.

Symphony Space, 2536 Broadway (at 95th St) ☎864-5400.

Town Hall, 123 W 43rd St (between 6th and 7th aves) ☎840-2824.

Cabaret and comedy

Comedy clubs and **cabaret spots** are rife in New York, with shows varying from stand-up and improvised comedy (amazing if you've never seen it before – quick-fire wit being part of the city psyche) to singing waiters and waitresses, many of whom are professional performers waiting for their big break. Most clubs have shows every night, with two at weekends, and charge a cover and usually a two-drink minimum. The list below represents the best-known venues in town, but there are performances to be found at a multitude of bars, clubs and art spaces all over the city. Check *Time Out New York* and *New York Magazine* for the fullest and most up-to-date listings.

Asti, 13 E 12th St ☎741-9105. Celebrating 70 years in business, *Asti* is an East Village restaurant with daily live entertainment from professional opera stars and singing waiters. A rowdy, fun night out. No cover. Closed in the summer from early August.

Boston Comedy Club, 82 W 3rd St (between Thompson and Sullivan sts) ☎477-1000. This long-running club in the heart of the Village has what *New York Magazine* calls "an *Animal House* ambience" so be warned. You might even be accosted on the street by house MC Lewis Schaffer hustling up an audience. $8 cover Sun–Thurs, $12 Fri–Sat. Two-drink minimum.

Brandy's Piano Bar, 235 E 84th St (between 2nd and 3rd aves) ☎650-1944. Small, Upper East Side piano bar featuring bar staff and waitresses who sing popular Broadway show hits and old TV theme tunes. Performances begin at 9.30pm when there's a two-drink minimum charge at the tables but no cover.

Caroline's on Broadway, 1626 Broadway (at 49th St) ☎757-4100. Moved to Times Square from its old location at the Seaport, *Caroline's* still books some of the best stand-up acts in town. $12–15 cover Sun–Thurs, $17–21.50 Fri and Sat. Two-drink minimum. Also has a restaurant, *Comedy Nation*, upstairs.

Chicago City Limits Theater, 1105 1st Ave (at 61st St) ☎888-5233. Improvisation theater playing one show nightly, two on weekends. Closed Tues. Admission is $20, $10 on Mon. New York's oldest improv club.

Comedy Cellar, 117 MacDougal St (between W 3rd and Bleecker sts) ☎254-3480. Popular Greenwich Village comedy club now in its 19th year of existence. A good late-night hangout. $5 cover Sun–Thurs, $12 Fri–Sat. Two-drink minimum.

Comic Strip Live, 1568 2nd Ave (between 81st and 82nd sts) ☎861-

The Performing Arts and Film

The Performing Arts and Film

9386. Famed showcase for stand-up comics and young singers going for the big time. Cover $8 Sun–Thurs, $12 Fri and Sat. Two-drink minimum.

Dangerfield's, 1118 1st Ave (between 61st and 62nd sts) ☎593-1650. Vegas-style new talent showcase founded 20 years ago by Rodney Dangerfield. Cover $12.50–15, with, unusually, no minimum drink charge.

Don't Tell Mama, 343 W 46th St (between 8th and 9th aves) ☎757-0788. Lively and convivial west Midtown piano bar and cabaret featuring rising stars and singing waitresses. Shows at 8pm and 10pm. Cover varies, two-drink minimum.

Duplex, 61 Christopher St (at 7th Ave) ☎255-5438. West Village cabaret popular with a boisterous gay and tourist crowd; it was here that Joan Rivers was discovered. Has a rowdy piano bar downstairs and a cabaret room upstairs. Hosts a "Star Search" show on Fri nights. Open 4pm–4am. Cover $3–12, two-drink minimum.

Gladys' Comedy Room, in the back room at *Hamburger Harry's*, 145 W 45th St (between Broadway and 6th Ave) ☎832-1762 or 840-0566. Small comedy club in its tenth year has shows Thurs, Fri & Sat, and an "Open mike" night on Wed at 7pm. Mention *Rough Guides* at the door and get in for $7 ($5 Wed) with a table minimum of $5 per person.

Gotham Comedy Club, 34 W 22nd St (between 5th and 6th aves) ☎367-9000. A swanky and spacious comedy venue in the Flatiron district. Cover $8 Sun–Thurs, $12 Fri and Sat. Two-drink minimum.

The Original Improv, at *Danny's Skylight Room*, 346 W 46th St (between 8th and 9th aves) ☎475-6147. New comic and singing talent – most, as the name suggests, improvised. Cover $12. $10 drink minimum. Shows at 10.45pm on Fri and Sat; 2pm on Sun.

Stand Up New York, 236 W 78th St (at Broadway) ☎595-0850. Upper West Side forum for established comics, many

of whom have appeared on Leno, Letterman and the like. Nightly shows, three on weekends. Weekdays $7 cover, Fri & Sat $12. Two-drink minimum.

Film

New York is rapidly becoming a **movie-lovers mecca**. New state-of-the-art movie theatres are popping up all over the city, with more than a hundred new screens due to be added over the next couple of years. Most of these will be in multiscreen complexes with all the charm of large airports but with the advantages of superb sound, luxurious seating and perfect stadium-seating sightlines, as in the recent megaplexes erected in Union Square and Kips Bay. Times Square, whose cinemas, with the exception of the enormous **Astor Plaza** (44th St and Broadway ☎869-8340), and the newish four-screen **State Theater** within the Virgin Megastore (1540 Broadway ☎391-2900), have tended to be small, noisy and worth avoiding, is getting an overhaul in keeping with its controversial ongoing gentrification. For a movie-going experience with more character, the venerable **Ziegfeld** (54th St at 6th Ave ☎765-7600) is an old-style Midtown movie palace that makes almost any film seen in it look good. Also worth a trip, if only to sit in an old-time movie balcony, is the **Paris Fine Arts** (58th St and 5th Ave ☎980-5656). For new foreign and independent films visit the six-screen **Lincoln Plaza** (Broadway at 62nd St ☎757-2280), on the Upper West Side; the ever popular, but increasingly less adventurous six-screen **Angelika Film Center** (corner of Houston and Mercer sts ☎995-2000), whose spacious café lobby is a great place to meet; the smaller four-screen **Quad** (13th St at 6th Ave ☎255-8800); the three-screen **Cinema Village** (22 E 12th St ☎924-3363); the TriBeCa **Screening Room** (54 Varick St at Canal St ☎334-2100) which has its own cocktail bar and restaurant; or the Brooklyn Academy of Music, which recently opened the four-screen arthouse **Rose Theater** (*www.bam.org*). The **Film Forum** (see overleaf) also screens a popular selection of new low-budget films and documentaries. For Imax films (both 3-D and 2-D) visit the **Sony Lincoln Square** (Broadway at 68th St ☎336-5000), near Lincoln Center. **For listings** your best bets are the weekly *Village Voice* or the *New York Press* (both free), *Time Out New York*, or the daily papers on a Friday when reviews come out. The weekly magazines (*New York*, *The New Yorker*) publish listings but without showtimes. Beware that listings in papers are not *always* entirely accurate, but you can phone ☎777-FILM or visit the Web site *www.moviefone.com* for accurate showtimes and computerized film selections. Ticket prices have recently risen to as high as $9.50, and there are no reduced matinee prices in Manhattan, nor cheap evenings, but if you're strapped for cash the six-screen **Worldwide** (50th St between 8th and 9th aves ☎504-0960) is a godsend, showing new films only just past their prime for $3.50. Note that theaters are very busy on Friday and Saturday nights,

and tickets for hot new releases can sell out early in the day on opening weekends.

Revivals

Outside of Paris, New York may well be the best city in the world to see a wide selection of old movies, but the cinema landscape has changed considerably in the past decade. The old repertory houses showing a regular turnover of scratchy prints of old chestnuts and recent favorites have all gone (the last five closed in the 1990s, including the much-loved **Theater 80 St Mark's**). But what remains, or has sprung up in its place, is an impressive selection of museums and revival houses showing an imaginatively programmed series of films – whether retrospectives of particular directors or actors, series from particular countries, or programs of particular genres. The theaters showing these films range from the dryly academic to the purely pleasurable, but what most of them have in common is an emphasis on good-quality prints (there are exceptions of course) and comprehensiveness. Of course, as a visi-

The Performing Arts and Film

Festivals

There always seems to be some **film festival** or other running in New York. The granddaddy of them all, **The New York Film Festival**, starts at the end of September, runs for two weeks at the Alice Tully Hall at Lincoln Center, and is well worth catching if you're in town. Unfortunately, tickets sell out quickly in mid-September for the most popular films, but it's often possible to purchase tickets on the night from people selling unwanted tickets at face value outside the theater (especially if the film has been panned that morning in *The New York Times*). Other New York film festivals include the **New York Jewish Film Festival** in January; **New Directors/New Films Festival** – which speaks for itself – at the Museum of Modern Art, and the rival Downtown **Underground Film**

Festival, both in March; the **GenArt Film Festival** of American independents, the **Women's Film Festival**, and the **Avignon/New York Festival** of French and American films in April; **Docfest** (the International Documentary Festival), the **Human Rights Watch Film Festival**, the **Lesbian and Gay Film Festival**, and the **Sierra Club Film & Video Festival** of environmental activist films in June; the **Asian American International Film Festival** and the **New York Video Festival** in July; the **Harlem Week Black Film Festival** in August; the **Hong Kong Film Series** at the Cinema Village in August and September; and the **Margaret Meade Festival** of anthropological films at the Museum of Natural History in October.

The Performing Arts and Film

tor, what you get to see is a matter of chance. If you're lucky your trip may coincide with retrospectives of your favorite director, your movie heartthrob, and that series of Lithuanian silents you'd been waiting all your life to see.

Schedules can be found in the publications listed overleaf, and all the following revival houses and museums publish calendars that can be picked up at the box office.

The American Museum of the Moving Image, 35th Ave (at 36th St), Astoria, Queens ☎718/784-0077. Showing films only on weekends during the day, AMMI is well worth a trip out to Queens (it's not as far as it sounds – call ☎718/784-4777 for directions) either for the films – serious director retrospectives, silent films, and a good emphasis on cinematographers – or for the cinema museum itself.

Anthology Film Archives, 32 2nd Ave (at 2nd St) ☎505-5110; *www.arthouseinc.com/anthology*. The bastion of experimental filmmaking where programs of mind-bending abstraction, East Village grunge-flicks, auteur retrospectives and the year-round Essential Cinema series rub shoulders. Around the corner, on E 4th St (between 2nd Ave and the Bowery), **Millennium** (☎673-0090) keeps the experimental candle burning with occasional screenings of new abstract and avant-garde work in film and classes in low-budget filmmaking.

Film Forum, 209 W Houston (between 6th and 7th aves) ☎727-8110; *www.filmforum.com*. The cozy three-screen Film Forum has an eccentric but famously popular program of new independent movies, documentaries and foreign films on two of its screens, and a repertory program in Film Forum 2 specializing in silent comedy, camp classics and cult directors. With its cappuccinos and popcorn and lively crowds, Film Forum is always worth a visit.

The Museum of Modern Art, 11 W 53rd St ☎708-9480; *www.moma.org*. Famous among local cinephiles for its vast collection of films, its exquisite pro-gramming and its regular audience of cantankerous senior citizens. Films range from Hollywood screwball comedies to hand-painted Super 8, and entry to either of MoMA's large movie theaters is free with museum admission.

Walter Reade Theater, 65th St (between Broadway and Amsterdam Ave) ☎875-5600; *www.filmlinc.com*. Programmed by the Film Society of Lincoln Center, the Walter Reade is simply the best place in town to see great films. Opened in 1991, this beautiful modern theater with perfect sightlines, a huge screen and impeccable sound elevates the art of cinema to the position it deserves within Lincoln Center. The emphasis is on foreign cinema and the great auteurs.

Also of note. . .

As if it were late-1950s Paris, a number of cine-clubs have sprung up in the last year or so in the more happening parts of town like Williamsburg in Brooklyn, or the Lower East Side. These clubs, like **Cinema Classics** (☎675-6692), the **Cine-Noir Film Society** (☎253-1922) and **Ocularis** (☎718-388-8713), screen an eclectic array of films once a week in the back rooms of bars and bookshops. If you'd rather watch your movies *en plein air*, **Bryant Park** (6th Ave and 42nd St ☎512-5700) hosts free, outdoor screenings of old Hollywood favorites on Monday nights at sunset throughout the summer, while **River Flicks** at the new Chelsea Piers (Pier 62 at W 23rd St) has free summer screenings of water-themed crowd-pleasers (like *Jaws* and *The Poseidon Adventure*) on Wednesday nights. Though primarily music venues, **Symphony Space** (2537 Broadway at 95th St ☎864-5400) hosts a repertory program of old favorites one night a week, and the **Knitting Factory** (74 Leonard St ☎219-3055) occasionally shows silent films with live modern accompaniment. There are also regular screenings, often of experimental cinema, at the **Whitney Museum** (see Chapter 15, *Museums and Galleries*) in conjunction with its exhibitions. German, Asian,

Japanese and French cinema can often be found at, respectively, the **Goethe Institute** (1014 5th Ave ☎439-8700), the **Asia Society** (725 Park Ave at 70th St ☎517-2742), the **Japan Society** (333 E 47th St ☎832-1155) and the **French Institute** (55 E 59th St ☎355-6160). And for night owls, there are special midnight screenings on Friday and Saturday nights at the **Angelika Film Center** and the **Screening Room** (see p.414); not to forget that New York institution, *The Rocky Horror Picture Show*, which has returned to the city with midnight weekend shows at the **Village East** (189 2nd Ave at 12th St ☎529-6799).

The Performing Arts and Film

Chapter 21

Sports and Outdoor Activities

Since New York is the media capital of the world, it's no surprise, given the ever intensifying synergy between the media and **sports**, that New York is, at the very least, the no. 1 "sports city" in America. The city's newspapers devote a great many pages to the subject, as do the TV stations, which cover most of the regular season games and all of the post-season games in the big four American team sports – **baseball, football, basketball** and **ice hockey**. If you want to watch a game, bear in mind that some tickets can be hard to find, some impossible, and most don't come that cheap. Remember, also, that bars – and specifically **sports bars** – are a good alternative to actually being there, especially those with king-sized screens (see box on p.425 for listings).

Many **participation sports** are affordable or free in the city. You can **swim** either at the local pools or the borough beaches, usually for a small fee; **jog**, still one of the city's main obsessions; or if you're into **soccer** there are generally many pick-up games on the Great Lawn in Central Park on summer Sundays. However, it is hard to find facilities for some sports, such as tennis, if you are not either a club member or a city resident. Many New Yorkers spend around $100 a month to be members of private health clubs. For anyone interested,

these places fill sizeable sections of the city's Yellow Pages.

Spectator sports

In this section we've included details of each of the main **spectator sports** and the teams which represent New York. Also included, are a run-through of the rules, where necessary – followed by a section detailing the venues.

Baseball

In the early 1840's, the New York Knickerbocker Club played "base ball" in the northeast part of Madison Square, in Manhattan, before moving to Elysian Fields, across the Hudson River in Hoboken, New Jersey. There, on June 26, 1846, they laid down the basic rules (the Knickerbocker Rules) of the game of **Baseball**, as it is played to this day.

For half a century, New York was home to three Major League baseball teams: the New York Giants and Brooklyn Dodgers representing the National League and the **New York Yankees** representing the American League. In addition, in the years before integration, the Negro League had several notable teams that were based in the Metropolitan area – the New York Lincoln Giants, the Royal Brooklyn Giants, the New York Black Yankees and the Newark Eagles.

By all accounts, the Golden Age of New York baseball was the decade following the end of World War II. Between 1947 and 1956, the Yankees faced the Dodgers six times and the Giants once in the World Series. The city still bears the scars from the Giants' and Dodgers' bolt to California after the 1957 season. New York was bereft of a National League franchise until the **Mets** arrived at the Polo Grounds in 1962, from where they would move, in 1964, to Shea Stadium, in Flushing, Queens.

There are two Major **Leagues**, the **National** and the **American**, which play with slightly different rules. Most significantly, National League pitchers are allowed to bat, whereas in the American League a Designated Hitter (known as the DH) hits in his place. 162 games are played from April through September (not for nothing is it called The Long Season) before two rounds of October playoffs set the stage for the World Series – a best-of-seven series between the champions of the two leagues.

NEW YORK YANKEES

Reciting the **Yankees**' (also lovingly called the Bronx Bombers) achievements over the decades can get tedious after a while. They are a team with the most World Series wins, the most players in the Hall of Fame, the most Most Valuable

Player awards, and the statistics just keep going. Suffice it to say that the 1998 Yankees, with their record-breaking 125 wins, including a 4-game World Series sweep of the San Diego Padres, played as a consummate team (all egos held firmly in check); and that their young shortstop Derek Jeter, is well on his way to becoming the most exciting and gifted all-round player in the game today. Ticket prices: $8–50.

NEW YORK METS

When the 1998 Yankees were making their bid to be "the greatest team of all time," the wildly dysfunctional **Mets** – bickering and backstabbing in the dugout while underachieving on the field – provided welcome comic relief. The Mets have been on a roller-coaster ride ever since the lovably inept Mets team of 1962 matured into the 1969 World Series Champions, and then taking a nose dive from their second World Series win in 1986 to the "worst team money can buy" of the early 1990s. Currently, they field the best hitting catcher in the history of the game (Mike Piazza), the National League's most dazzling defensive player (shortstop Rey Ordoñez) and of course, Mr Met, professional sport's cutest mascot.
Ticket prices: $10–30.

Yankee Stadium

Yankee Stadium, in the Bronx, is home to the New York Yankees and has witnessed more than a few awe-inspiring moments since it was consecrated with a home run by Babe Ruth, on Opening Day, in 1923. Here, "the greatest game ever played" took place between the New York Giants and the Baltimore Colts in December 1958 – a televised football Championship that went into a dramatic final overtime and helped legitimize and popularize (American) football from that day forth. The undisputed "Fight of the Century" took place on June 22, 1938, when black heavy-

weight champion Joe Louis knocked out Hitler's National Socialist hero Max Schmeling. In baseball alone, certain images from the stadium, recycled over and over, take root in the memories of sports fans nationwide: Babe Ruth tiptoeing daintily around the bases after yet another majestic clout, Joe di Maggio's phenomenal 56 game hitting streak and his effortless grace in centerfield, Mickey Mantle's awesome power and the dying Lou Gehrig's July 4, 1939 farewell to the game, in which he declared himself "the luckiest man on the face of the earth."

Sports and Outdoor Activities

STATEN ISLAND YANKEES

The 1999 season saw the birth of the first new local baseball franchise in several decades: the Minor League, **Staten Island Yankees**, who are part of the New York Penn League. Until their ballpark at the Ferry Terminal is ready for the year 2001, they play their home games at The College of Staten Island, Victory Blvd, Staten Island. The season runs from mid-June to early September. It's fun to check out if you're in the area. Call ☎718/982-3569 for game schedule. Ticket prices: $6–10.

Football

The **NFL (National Football League) season** stretches from September to the end of December, when the six division winners, plus the next three teams in each conference with the best records, meet in the playoffs to decide who goes to the Super Bowl – played on the third Sunday of January. New York's teams are the **NY Jets** and the **NY Giants**; both teams play at **Giants Stadium**, part of the Meadowlands Sports Complex in New Jersey. Although tickets are sold out for both teams well in advance, if you're willing to pay the price, you can often buy tickets outside the stadium before the game (from scalpers or just extra-ticket holders). Otherwise, at least two games are shown on TV every Sunday afternoon, with another on Monday night during the regular season.

NEW YORK GIANTS

With a 20+ year waiting list for season tickets, the franchise that lost the first ever NFL Championship game (to the

---

The rules of baseball and football: a primer for foreign visitors

Baseball

The basic set-up looks like the English game of rounders, with four **bases** set at the corners of a 90-foot-square **diamond**; at the bottom corner, the base is called **home plate** and serves much the same purpose as do the stumps in cricket. Play begins when the **pitcher**, standing on a low pitcher's mound in the middle of the diamond, throws a **ball** at upwards of 100mph, making it curve and bend as it travels toward the **catcher**, who crouches behind home plate; seven other defensive players take up **positions**, one at each base and the others spread out around the field of play. A **batter** from the opposing team stands beside home plate and tries to hit the ball with a tapered, cylindrical wooden **bat**. If the batter swings and misses, or if the ball is pitched in the **strike-zone**, it counts as a **strike**; if he doesn't swing and the ball passes outside of this strike zone, it counts as a **ball**. If the batter gets **three strikes** against him he's out; if the pitcher throws **four balls** or hits the batter with a pitch, then the batter gets a free **walk** and takes his place as a runner on first base.

If the batter succeeds in hitting the pitched ball into **fair territory**, which is the wedge between the first and third base, the batter runs toward first base; if the opposing players catch the ball before it hits the ground, the batter is out. Otherwise they field the ball and attempt to relay it to first base before the batter gets there; if they do he is **out**, if they don't the batter is **safe** – and stays there being moved along by subsequent batters until he makes a complete circuit of the diamond and scores a **run**. The most crowd-pleasing offensive play is the **home run**, when a batter hits the ball over the outfield fences, a boundary about 400 feet away from home plate; he and any runners on base when he hits the ball each scores a run. If there are runners on all three bases it's a **grand slam** and earns four runs.

Games tend to take around three hours to play and each side – made up of nine players – bats through nine

---

Chicago Bears) as well as the "greatest football game of all time" must be doing something right. Since they were founded in 1925, the **Giants** have won four NFL and two Super Bowl Championships, but they still hold the record for the most championship losses ever and are the only team to twice fail to make the playoffs in the season immediately following a Super Bowl victory. No one can ever claim they're boring.

Ticket prices: $45 and $50.

NEW YORK JETS

Too easily dismissed as the worst franchise in professional sports, the **Jets'** perennial underdog status makes them easier to root for than the more respectable Giants. Founded in 1960 as part of an upstart American Football League, the team originally known as the Titans, have yet to find a home of their own. The team shared Shea Stadium in Flushing, Queens with the Mets for a while (close proximity to La Guardia airport inspiring the nickname "Jets") before relocating, in 1984, to the Jersey suburbs as tenants of the New York Giants. The Jets 16–7 Super Bowl III victory in 1968 was particularly significant in that it earned respect for the fledgling AFL (which had suffered ugly losses to the NFL in Super Bowls I and II) and set the stage for the creation of the National Football League as it is today. After a dismal 1–15 record in 1996 and with the Jets facing the prospect of closing out the century as the only team since the 1970 AFL/NFL merger without a division title, Bill Parcells (architect of the Giants' two Super Bowl wins) was lured back to

Sports and Outdoor Activities

---

innings; each side gets **three outs** per **inning**. Games are normally held at night. There are no tied games; the teams play **extra innings** until either side pulls ahead and wins.

Football

Basically, the home-grown game Americans refer to as football is more like rugby than its International namesake (known here as soccer). The aim is to reach the **end zone** with the ball and score a **touchdown** earning the team six points (though players don't actually have to place the ball on the ground). The action is organized into a series of **plays** and each time the player with the ball is **tackled** to the ground or the ball goes off the pitch, that play is concluded. On each play the quarterback will either **hand-off** to a runner or fire off a **pass** to a teammate. Meanwhile, blockers try to prevent the defensive team from tackling the player with the ball.

The measurement of advancement is a **down**; with every **ten yards** counting as a **first down**. The offensive team has four attempts to move forward the ten yards. (Thus the enigmatic phrases uttered by commentators – Third (down) and 6 (yards are needed). If it seems unlikely that the offensive team will make their first down, a **kicker** may attempt a **field goal** (worth three points) by sending the ball through the goalposts. If the ball is too far to attempt a field goal and they have not achieved the first down, the ball is turned over to the opposition by having a **punter** drop-kick it as far downfield as possible. If a team makes a touchdown, they usually attempt to kick the ball between the goalposts for an **extra point**; although they may try to garner two points by running a player back into the end zone. Once either of these has been attempted, the ball is then kicked off a tee to the opposing team.

The game lasts for one hour of play, divided into four **quarters** with a halftime break after the second quarter. However, the clock only runs when the game is in progress, which means that it can run for three hours or more – more than enough time to master the complexities if you're prepared to sit back and listen, since on TV every play is subjected to pretty exhaustive analysis.

Sports and Outdoor Activities

the Garden State where it took him just two seasons to turn the sad-sack franchise, once again, into legitimate contenders.
Ticket prices: $40 and $50.

Professional basketball

Basketball is perhaps the most popular American game to be played outside the US. Played over 48 minutes (at the pro level), the game is conducted at a blistering pace. Since the clock only runs when the ball is in play, a game generally lasts about two hours.

The **National Basketball Association's** regular season begins in November and runs through the end of April, after which its playoffs begin with the eight best teams in each conference qualifying, and culminating in a best-of-seven finals between the Eastern and Western Conference Champions, around the middle of June. The two professional teams in the New York area are the **NY Knicks** (Knickerbockers), who play at Madison Square Garden, and the **New Jersey Nets**, whose venue is the Continental Airlines Arena at the Meadowlands Sports Complex in New Jersey.

NEW YORK KNICKS

It's not easy being a **Knicks** fan: Madison Square Garden must be one of the ugliest structures in North America (and to build it, one of the city's architectural treasures, Penn Station, was razed to the ground); the current team play with a strutting, chest-thumping arrogance, quite unjustifed by the franchise's actual accomplishments (the last Championship was way back in 1973); and after all that – tickets are expensive and impossible to come by. In fact, the vast majority of fiercely loyal and racially diverse fans can only dream of attending a game in person. Still, maybe because they are so flawed, so essentially New York, it's even harder *not* to be a Knicks fan.
Ticket prices constantly vary – it's best to call and see if you can even get a ticket.

NEW JERSEY NETS

The **Nets** began life, in 1967, as the New Jersey Americans, a founding franchise of the rogue American Basketball Association. At one point in their early history, they decked themselves out in patriotic red, white and blue, to match the ABA's funky, psychedelic ball. Led by the legendary Julius Irving (Dr J), they won two championships (1974 and 1976) before joining the NBA for the 1976 season (their last year as the New York Nets). Since then they've been rather less successful and, of late, appear to be in perpetual rebuilding mode. In 1999, however, Nets management, pulled off a major coup by acquiring Brooklyn playground legend Stephon Marbury. The Nets may be on the rise again.
Ticket Prices: $30–75.

NEW YORK LIBERTY

The **Women's National Basketball Association** season opens when the NBA season ends and runs through the summer to its playoffs in September. The league kicked off in 1997, with New York team, NY Liberty, finishing off as runners-up for the title their first year. Games are played at Madison Square Garden, and prices are a bargain compared to the Knicks. Also, while many games have near sell-out crowds, you can usually get a ticket.
Ticket Prices: $8–24.

College basketball

College basketball is a highly profitable business enterprise, earning millions for its Division one athletics programs as well as its star coaches. The metropolitan area has at least three Division One schools – **Long Island University, Seton Hall** and **St John's** – the last of whom are currently the most successful of the three. The season begins in November and ends with "March Madness," a series of conference tournaments culminating in a 64-team playoff – with the top four teams participating in the "Final Four" weekend around the end of

March/beginning of April. This time of year may well be the most exciting, eagerly anticipated sporting event in the US. Madison Square Garden hosts pre-season tournaments and the Big East Tournament, which is part of "March Madness." Call ☎465-6741.

ST JOHN'S RED STORM

St John's is part of the Big East Conference and with the leadership of their new coach, Mike Jarvis, there is a positive buzz about their future successes. They have a large and loyal fan base, they are always fun to watch in person or at a bar. Call ☎718/990-6211 for game schedule and ticket prices.

Street basketball

Free of the obsession with image building, maintenance and marketing that makes the NBA so seductive and so superficial, or the greedy economics that rule in the NCAA, street basketball presents the game in its purest and, arguably, most attractive form. New York City is the capital of playground hoops with a host of asphalt legends, past and present: Lew Alcindor (Kareem Abdul-Jabbar), Wilt Chamberlain, Julius Erving and Stephon Marbury are a few who made it to the pros. If you want to play yourself, *Hoops Nation* by Chris Ballard is an invaluable guide to basketball courts in the five boroughs (and across the nation) and a useful primer in the etiquette of pickup ball. Otherwise, the best place to check out the scene is W 4th St at 6th Ave in Manhattan. Scout the next NBA superstar – or look out for current ones dropping by for an off-season tune-up.

Ice hockey

To someone who isn't familiar with the game, ice hockey or **hockey**, as it's called in the US, might seem a very odd excuse for getting a bunch of guys to beat the hell out of each other for the benefit of the paying public. It is a violent sport, certainly, and some players are without doubt chosen mainly for their punching ability. But there's a huge amount of skill involved, too. It takes some watching to work out where the puck is – the speed the action takes place at is, without question, phenomenal. The two New York teams are the **Rangers**, who play at Madison Square Garden, and the New York **Islanders**, whose venue is the Nassau Coliseum on Long Island. There's also a local New Jersey side, the **Devils**, who play at Meadowlands. There are two conferences in the NHL (Eastern and Western) and six divisions with five to seven teams in each division – all three metro area teams are in the same division (the Atlantic division) and competition is fierce between them. Regular season lasts throughout the winter and into early spring, when the playoffs take place – a battle consisting of the top three teams in each division, whittling down to two teams in the Stanley Cup Finals.

NEW YORK RANGERS

One of the original six NHL teams, the **Rangers** were founded back in 1926, led the American division their first season and won three Stanley Cups over the next fifteen years. According to Hockey lore, giddy from their 1940 victory over the Toronto Maple Leafs, the Madison Square Garden owners paid off their $3 million mortgage and celebrated by burning the deed in Lord Stanley's cup – an act of desecration that provoked a curse upon the franchise and its fans, depriving them of another Championship for over half a century. When the Rangers finally put an end to the 54-year drought in 1994, the Stanley Cup accompanied the team on a celebratory tour of the city which included the Howard Stern Show, several bars and at least one strip joint. The team's mediocre performance since then suggests the Hockey Gods may be working on another almighty maledicton. Ticket prices: $22–55.

NEW YORK ISLANDERS

An expansion team, founded in 1972, the Islanders were fortunate enough to

Sports and Outdoor Activities

**Sports and
Outdoor
Activities**

string together their 4 Stanley Cups in consecutive years (1980–1983) and thus qualify as a bona-fide hockey dynasty. Since then, however, it's been mostly downhill, with the franchise failing to make the play-offs the last 5 years. Ticket prices: $15–70.

NEW JERSEY DEVILS

Since the team was founded in 1974, the **Devils** spent two seasons as the Kansas City Scouts and five as the Colorado Rockies before moving to New Jersey in 1982. Their succession of mediocre seasons was interrupted when they beat the heavily favored Detroit Red Wings in four straight games to win the 1995 Stanley Cup.
Ticket prices: $20–74.

Soccer

Although the game itself continues to grow in popularity, particularly in the city's Latin communities, the **US soccer** team's disappointing performance in the 1998 World Cup was further evidence, if any were needed, that the general standard of professional soccer in the US leaves much to be desired.

However, with the women's national team winning the 1999 Women's World Cup in a final estimated to be the most watched soccer match in network television history and achieving cult status virtually overnight, there is talk of a professional **Women's Soccer League** starting up as early as 2001. Whether the powers that be conclude that this is economically feasible remains to be seen.

In addition, European soccer turns up fairly regularly on cable TV (though usually delayed by at least a few hours due to the time difference) and some bars show British league games live via satellite (see box opposite).

METROSTARS

The New York/New Jersey **Metrostars** are the metropolitan area's Major League Soccer representatives – and so far it has been pretty dismal. The Metrostars have been among the bottom half of the

Eastern conference since the Major League's inception in 1996. But this may all change with Germany's national team captain, Lothar Matthäus, star defensive stopper for Bayern Munich and all-time world leader in World Cup appearances (25), coming to the rescue of both the team and its fans – when he joins the team in 2000.
Ticket prices: $15–30.

Horse racing

There are four **race tracks** in the New York area: the **Aqueduct Race Track**, the **Belmont Race Track**, the **Meadowlands Race Track** and **Yonkers Raceway**. Both the Aqueduct and Belmont have thoroughbred racing. Meadowlands, has both thoroughbred and standardbred racing and Yonkers has only standardbred.

The **Aqueduct** in Rockaway, Queens has racing from October through May. To get there take the A train, on the New York Subway line, to the Aqueduct station. The **Belmont Race Track** is in Elmont, Long Island, and is home to the Belmont Stakes, which, along with the Kentucky Derby and Preakness, is one of the big three American races of the year (the "Triple Crown"). The racing takes place May–July and September–October, with the Belmont Stakes held in June. You have two options to get there by public transit: take the E or F train to 169th St and then the #16 bus will get you to the track, or take the Long Island Railroad to the Belmont Race Track stop which is directly across from the track. For both Belmont and the Aqueduct, call ☎718/641-4700. Admission at both tracks ranges from $1 to $4 depending on where you park and sit. Valet parking costs $5 at the Aqueduct and $6 at Belmont. The **Meadowlands Race Track**, in the Meadowlands Sports Complex in New Jersey, holds harness racing eight months of the year (December–August) and thoroughbred racing September–December (☎201/935-8500). From Manhattan, the easiest way to get there is on NJ Transit, bus #164 from Port Authority. Parking is free, admission is

$1, and entry to the Clubhouse is $3. **Yonkers Raceway** holds harness racing only, but operates all year round every night except Sundays (☎914/968-4200). Take Subway #4 to Woodlawn and transfer to the #20 bus. If you drive, parking is $2; admission is $3.25.

To **place a bet** anywhere other than the racetrack itself you'll need to find an **OTB** – Off Track Betting – office. There are plenty around the city; call ☎221-5200 for locations (opening hours are Mon–Sat 11.30am–7pm, Sunday 11.30am–6.30pm). You need an established account to place a phone bet: to set one up, call ☎800/OTB-8118. To watch a race or two in comfort, try The Inside Track (run by OTB) at 991 2nd Ave at 53rd St (☎752-1940). They are open from 11.30am until the last race ends and offer food, drink and wagering on the premises.

Tennis

The **US Open Championships**, held in Queens each September at the National Tennis Center, Flushing Meadows, Corona Park, Queens is the top tennis event of the year. In 1997, the Flushing complex opened a new center court, the Arthur Ashe Stadium. When David Dinkins, an avowed sports fan, was mayor, he ordered the nearby La Guardia Airport planes to be rerouted during the championships, which greatly improves the volume level. For tickets, the Tennis Center's box office (☎718/760-6200) is open Mon–Fri 9am–5pm and Sat 10am–4pm for over-the-counter sales only. To book by phone call: Telecharge (☎888/673-6849). Promenade level at the stadium costs $21–82, while the better seats can cost several hundred dollars. If they are sold out, keep trying up to the day of the event because

Sports and Outdoor Activities

Sports bars

Boomer's Sports Club, 349 Amsterdam Ave (between 76th and 77th sts) ☎362-5400. Named after quarterback Boomer Esiason, the club is filled with memorabilia. Currently undergoing a makeover; it may change its name to *Time Out*.

British Open, 320 E 59th St (between 1st and 2nd aves) ☎355-8467. See p.392.

Entourage Bar, formerly *The Polo Grounds Bar & Grill*, 147 3rd Ave (at 83rd St) ☎570-5590. This bar tries (successfully) to be a bit classier than the average sports bar.

Jimmy's Corner, 140 W 44th St (between Broadway and 6th Ave) ☎221-9510. See p.393.

Kinsdale Tavern, 1672 3rd Ave (at 93rd St) ☎348-4370. See p.394.

Mickey Mantle's, 42 Central Park S (between 5th and 6th aves) ☎688-7777. Perhaps the city's most famous sports bar – jam packed with memorabilia, it's hard to tell which is more bland – the food or the decor.

Official All-Star Cafe, 1540 Broadway (at W 45th St) ☎840-8326. You really think Tiger or Junior are going to stop by your table to see how you're doing? They just might.

Sporting Club, 99 Hudson St (between Franklin and Leonard sts) ☎219-0900. Rated the no. 1 sports bar in Manhattan by *New York* magazine and has seven giant screens, a dozen smaller TVs, plus a pool table and other games.

Sushi Generation, 1572 2nd Ave (between 81st and 82nd sts) ☎249-2222. A combination Sushi/Sports bar. No Kidding.

The following bars show regular **European soccer games**. All with a cover charge.

British Open, 320 E 59th St (between 1st and 2nd aves) ☎355-8467. See p.392.

McCormack's, 365 3rd Ave (at 27th St) ☎683-0911. Irish neighborhood bar.

Nevada Smith's, 74 3rd Ave (between 11th and 12th sts) ☎982-2591. Jolly East Village dive.

Sports and Outdoor Activities

often corporate tickets are returned. Tickets for the big matches are incredibly difficult to get – you can either take a chance with scalpers or try your luck at the Will Call window for people who don't show up. Madison Square Garden also hosts the WTA Tour Chase Championships, held each year in the middle of November (☎465-6741). Tickets $10–60.

Track and field

The **Chase Bank Melrose Games**, played at Madison Square Garden in February each year, feature world-class athletes. The games include almost every **track and field** event such as the one-mile race, sprints, pole-vault, the high jump, the long jump and much more. The event is well attended, but tickets are easier to come by than other city sporting events. Call Madison Square Garden (☎465-6741) for more information.

Wrestling

Wrestling, held regularly at Madison Square Garden, is perhaps the least "sporting" of all the sports you can watch in New York, more of a theatrical event really, with a patriotically charged, almost salivating crowd cheering on all-American superheroes against evil and distinctly un-American foes. Bouts start with a rendition of *The Star-Spangled Banner*, after which the action – a stagey affair between wrestlers with names like Hulk Hogan and the Red Devil – takes place to a background of jingoistic roars, the true-blue US spirit invariably winning the day. Recently, some of the more flamboyant professional athletes from other sports – basketball's Dennis Rodman, football's Kevin Greene – have even tried their hands in the ring. For details of bouts, call Madison Square Garden direct (☎465-6741).

Tickets and venues

Tickets for most events can be booked ahead with a credit card through Ticketmaster ☎307-7171 and collected at the gate, though it's cheaper – and of course riskier for popular events – to pick up tickets on the night. You can also call or go to the stadium's box office and buy advance tickets. When the box office has sold out, you can call a **ticketing agency** such as **1-800 SOLD OUT** (☎1-800/765-3688), which buys quantities of tickets for resale. Expect to pay a little bit more to substantially more depending on the importance of the game and the seats – look in the Yellow Pages under tickets for others. **Scalping** (buying a ticket from an individual, usually the day of the event outside the arena at an inflated price) is illegal. If all else fails, simply catch the action on the big screen in a **sports bar**.

Madison Square Garden Center, 7th Ave (between W 31st and W 33rd sts) ☎465-6741. Subway #1, #2, #3, #9, A, C and E to 34th St Penn Station. Call box office for hours, which change by season and depend on the calendar of events.

Meadowlands Sports Complex, containing both Giants Stadium and the Continental Airlines Arena, off routes 3, 17, and Turnpike exit 16W, East Rutherford, New Jersey ☎201/935-3900. Regular buses from Port Authority Bus Terminal on 42nd St and 8th Ave. Box office open for all arenas Mon–Fri 9am–6pm, Sat 10am–6pm, Sun noon–5pm.

Nassau Coliseum, 1255 Hempstead Turnpike, Uniondale, New York ☎516/794-9300. Long Island Railroad to Hempstead, then bus N70, N71 or N72 from Hempstead bus terminal, one block away. Another option, which may be safer late at night, is to take the LIRR to Westbury, and take a cab (a 5–10 minute ride) to the stadium. Box office daily 10.45am–5.45pm.

Shea Stadium, 126th St (at Roosevelt Ave), Queens ☎718/507-8499. Subway #7, direct to Willets Point/Shea Stadium Station. Box office Mon–Fri 9am–6pm, Sat, Sun & holidays 9am–5pm. You can also buy tickets from the Mets Clubhouse Store in Manhattan, 575 5th Ave (at 47th St), Mon–Fri 10am–7pm, Sat

10am–6pm, Sun 1–5pm; their Web site is *www.mets.com*. Dress warmly in autumn and winter as Shea is a windy icebox.

Yankee Stadium, 161st St and River Ave, the Bronx ☎718/293-6000. Subway C, D or #4 direct to 161st St Station. Box office Mon–Sat 9am–5pm, Sun 10am–5pm and until one hour after completion of evening games. You can also buy tickets from these Yankees Clubhouse Stores in Manhattan: 110 E 59th St (between Lexington and Park aves) ☎758-7844; 393 5th Ave (between 36th and 37th sts) ☎685-4693; 8 Fulton St (South St Seaport) ☎514-7182; or on the Internet: *www.yankees.com*. Get to the game early and visit Monument Park where all the Yankee greats are memorialized.

Participatory sports

Central Park is the focus for almost all sports: from croquet to chess, soccer to hacky-sack, sunning to swimming. Joggers, in-line skaters, walkers and cyclists have the roads to themselves on weekdays 10am–3pm & 7–10pm and all day on weekends. The park is closed each night from 1–6am. To find out what is going on where and when, go to the *Arsenal*, at 830 5th Ave at the end of 64th St and pick up the following, or call and ask for them to be mailed to you:

• **Green Pages**, which tell you about every activity, from archery to wild-food walks ☎360-8111 ext 310.

• **Special Events Calendar**, a day-by-day listing of events in the parks in all the boroughs. There are races, dances, track meets as well as a lot of concerts and events for children ☎360-1492.

Chelsea Piers Sports and Entertainment Complex

Chelsea Piers is located at W 23rd St and the Hudson River (between 17th and 23rd sts) ☎336-6666 for general info. To get there, take the A, C, E, #1 or #9 trains to 23rd St and walk west, the M23 bus, which will drop you off at the front door, or the M14 which terminates

at 14th St and the West Side Highway which is close to the Piers' south entrance. The complex is the complete renovation of four piers, jutting out into the Hudson River, originally designed in 1912 by Warren & Wetmore, the architects of Grand Central Station. The **Golf Club** at Pier 59 features Manhattan's only outdoor driving range. The hours are 5am–11pm to midnight. You buy tee time at $15 for 94 balls. ☎336-6400.

The **Field House** connects the four piers. This facility houses the largest gymnastics facility in the state, and is where soccer and lacrosse leagues play. You can also rock climb or play basketball without being in a league. ☎336-6500.

Sports Center at Pier 60 features a quarter-mile running track, the largest rock-climbing wall in the northeast, three basketball/volleyball courts, a boxing ring, a 24-yard swimming pool and whirlpool, indoor sand volleyball courts, exercise studios scheduling over 100 classes weekly, cardiovascular weight-training room, a sundeck right on the Hudson River, and spa services.

You must be 16 or older to use the Sports Center. Day passes are available for $36 on weekdays and $50 on weekends. Mon–Fri 6am–11pm, Sat & Sun 8am–9pm. ☎336-6000.

The **Roller Rinks** are on Pier 62. They are outdoors and open all year round, weather permitting. Daily session starts at noon, exact times vary. $5; $4 for children under 12. Rentals available. ☎336-6200.

The **Sky Rink** is on Pier 61. Ice-skate year-round on this indoor rink. Daily sessions start at noon, exact times vary. $10.50; $8 children under 12; $7.50 seniors. Rentals are $5. ☎336-6100.

Golf

If you need any inducement to take out those clubs, then know that **golf** is the preferred leisure activity of New York's professional athletes. There are no public golf courses in Manhattan. Recommended among those in the outer boroughs are:

Sports and Outdoor Activities

Sports and Outdoor Activities

Dyker Beach Golf Course, 86th St and 11th Ave, Dyker Heights, Brooklyn, ☎718/836-9722. Easily accessible via the R train. Fees around $20.

Split Rock Golf Course & Pelham Golf Course, 870 North Shore Rd, Pelham ☎718/855-1258. *New York* magazine voted Split Rock the most challenging course in the city. Pelham, right next door, is somewhat easier. Located in the northwest Bronx. Fees $25.

Van Courtland Park Golf Course, Van Courtland Park S and Bailey Ave, The Bronx ☎718/543-4595 The oldest 18-hole public golf course in the country. Green fees range from $10 to $27.

Jogging

Jogging is still very much the number one fitness pursuit in the city: the number of yearly coronaries in Central Park, the most popular venue, probably runs well into double figures. A favorite circuit in the park is 1.58 miles around the Receiving Reservoir; just make sure you jog in the right direction – counterclockwise. The East River Promenade and almost any other stretch of open space long enough to get up speed are also well jogged. One of the more beautiful and longer routes is through the Bronx's Botanical Garden (☎718/817-8705): it's a two-mile loop with eight miles of adjoining trails. For company, contact the **New York Road Runners Club** and find out their schedule: 9 E 89th St ☎860-2280. They do several races/runs such as the Frostbite 10 Miler and the Valentine Run each year.

If, rather than bust your own guts, you'd prefer to see thousands of others do so, the **New York Marathon** takes place on the first Sunday of November. Two million people turn out each year to watch the 16,000 runners complete the 26.2-mile course, which starts in Staten Island, crosses the Verrazano Bridge and passes through all the other boroughs before ending up at the *Tavern on the Green* in Central Park. To take part you need to apply for an entry form from the New York Road Runners Club (see above).

Roller- and ice-skating . . . and tobogganing

In winter, the freezing weather makes for good **ice-skating**, while in summer **roller-skating** is a popular activity, on the paths in Central Park and specifically the northwest corner of the Sheep Meadow; also at Riverside Park and even the smaller open spaces. **Tobogganing** is another popular winter activity, up on the slopes of Van Cortlandt Park in the Bronx; phone ☎718/549-6494 to see if the snow's deep enough.

Lasker Rink, 110th St, Central Park ☎534-7639. The lesser-known ice rink in Central Park, situated at the north end of the park. Much cheaper than the Wollman Rink, though less accessible, and the neighborhood isn't great at night. Call for hours and prices.

Rockefeller Center Ice Rink, between 49th and 50th sts, off 5th Ave ☎332-7654. Without doubt the slickest place to skate, though you may have to wait in line and it's pricier than anywhere else. Call for hours and prices.

Wollman Rink, 62nd St, Central Park ☎396-1010. Lovely rink, where you can skate to the marvelous, inspiring backdrop of the lower Central Park skyline – incredibly impressive at night. Call for hours and prices.

In-line skating

You'll see commuters to freestylists on in-line skates – also known as **rollerblades** – in New York. For the best place to watch freestylists, go to the skate circle near Naumberg Bandshell in Central Park at 72nd St. World-class bladers maneuver between cones with all kinds of fancy footwork just inside Central Park's *Tavern on the Green* entrance, by 68th St. Other than Central Park, the best places to skate are Battery Park, and Flushing Meadow Park in Corona, Queens, which is forty minutes from Midtown on the #7 train.

Wollman Rink, 62nd St, Central Park, ☎396-1010. See above description. Open for in-line skating during the summer. Admission $4 ($3 for children under 12 and seniors) plus $6 for in-line skate rental.

Blades. Their many locations make it a convenient shop to rent in-line skates:
128 Chambers St (between W Broadway and Church St) ☎964-1944.
120 W 72nd St (between Columbus and Broadway) ☎787-3911.
160 E 86th St (between Lexington and 3rd aves) ☎996-1644.
1414 2nd Ave (at 73rd St) ☎249-3178. $16 for two hours and $27 a day on weekends; $16 all day weekdays. No overnight rentals on Fri or Sat.

Bicycling

There are 100 miles of **cyclepaths** in New York; other than Central Park, Riverside Park and the East River Promenade are some of the nicest. If you want to go further, the deal of the century is a MetroNorth Railroads lifetime bike pass for $5, available at the ticket windows of Grand Central Station. These trains will bring you to the scenic small towns of lower Hudson Valley and coastal Connecticut. When riding on the street, remember that by law you must wear a helmet. It's not enforced, but it's the safe thing to do. Most bike stores rent bicycles by the day or hour. What follows is a list of clubs and other good cycling info:

Bicycle Habitat, 244 Lafayette St ☎431-3315. Known for an excellent repair service and prices, as well as rentals $25 a day, plus a deposit equal to the value of the bike, and $7.50 an hour with a two-hour minimum. You can also have a tune-up (priced at $60 and up) if you think you'll be riding a lot. The very knowledgeable staff here will be able to help you no matter what level of cyclist you are. They also offer group rides.

Five Borough Bike Club. This club organizes rides throughout the year, including the Montauk Century a hundred-mile ride from New York to Montauk, Long Island. Call ☎932-2300 ext 115 for membership details.

New York Cycle Club ☎828-5711. A large club that offers many rides. Call for registration information.

Times Up ☎802-8222. They do a variety of rides such as Riverside Rides, Moonlight Rides, Cyclone Rides (to Coney Island) along with environment and ecology rides. Call for a schedule.

Transportation Alternatives, 115 W 30th St ☎629-8080. They have many interesting programs and many knowledgeable staffers. Stop by or call to find out more information.

Pool and snooker

Along with bars and nightclubs, a good option for an evening in Manhattan is to play **pool**, not in dingy halls but in gleaming bars where well-heeled yuppies mix with the regulars. A number of sports bars and dive bars have pool tables as well, though these are often much smaller than regulation size. **Snooker** fans will also find a few tables throughout the city.

Amsterdam Billiards, 344 Amsterdam Ave at 77th St ☎496-8180. Very popular Uptown billiards club with 31 tables. They now serve liquor along with beer and bar food.

The Billiard Club, 220 W 19th St (between 7th and 8th aves) ☎206-7665. A pool club with a nice, vaguely European atmosphere and a small bar serving beer, liquor and soft drinks.

Chelsea Billiards, 54 W 21st St (between 5th and 6th aves) ☎989-0096. A casual place with both snooker and pool tables. Bar serves beer and soft drinks.

Le Q Billiards, 36 E 12th St (between Broadway and University Place) ☎995-8512. Downtown hangout serving soft drinks and snacks only.

Hiking

For **hikes**, **nature walks** and other special activities around the city, you can try either of the following organizations:

Shorewalkers ☎330-7686.

Urban Park Rangers ☎360-2774 or ☎1-800/201-PARK.

Sports and Outdoor Activities

Sports and Outdoor Activities

Appalachian Mountain Club

To go off the beaten track and mix with locals, participate in the New York/New Jersey chapter of the worldwide **Appalachian Mountain Club.**

With friendly people of all ages, you can learn yoga on Fire Island, tour the historic neighborhoods of the five boroughs or hike the scenic Shawangunks.

Four-month Guest membership is available. Send $15, with your name and mailing address, to: AMC, 5 Tudor City Place, NY, NY 10017 ☎986-1430.

Horse riding

Claremont Riding Academy, 175 W 89th St ☎724-5100. For riding in Central Park, this place hires out ponies by the hour for $33. Saddles are English-style; lessons $38 per half-hour. You must be an experienced rider.

Jamaica Bay Riding Academy, 7000 Shore Parkway, Brooklyn ☎718/531-8949. Trail riding, with western-style saddles, around the eerie landscape of Jamaica Bay. $20 for a 45min ride; lessons $50 an hour.

Riverdale Equestrian Center in Bronx's Van Cortlandt Park (at W 254th and Broadway) ☎718/548-4848. Lessons only: $35 for 30min, $65 for full hour. Brand-new, beautiful country trails.

Bowling

Bowlmor Lanes, 110 University Place (between 12th and 13th sts) ☎255-8188. Long-established and large bowling alley with a bar and shop. Open Mon & Fri 10am–4am, Tues & Wed 10am–1am, Thurs 10am–2am, Sat 11am–4am, Sun 11am–1am. $4.25 per game per person before 5pm, $5.45 after 5pm. $3 shoe-hire.

Leisure Time Bowling, on 2nd floor of Port Authority, 625 8th Ave, near 40th St ☎268-6909. The nicest place in the city to bowl. $4.75 per game per person, plus $3 shoe-hire.

Tennis

Court space is at a premium in Manhattan so finding a court and being able to afford it can be tough, but you can call the following:

New York City Courts ☎360-8133 for information on all city courts. Ask about their $50 Permit, which runs from April to November, and gives you access to all municipal tennis courts in the five boroughs.

Sutton East Tennis Club (mid-Oct–April) 488 E 60th St ☎751-3452.

Health and fitness: pools, gyms and baths

There are several newly renovated city **recreation centers** that you can become a member of for $25 per year (ages 18–54) or $10 (kids 13–17 and seniors). All have gym facilities and most have an indoor and/or outdoor pool. Call ☎447-2020 or look in the Manhattan Blue Pages (within White Pages) under NY City Parks; there is a listing of centers under "Recreation" and under "Swimming Pools".

East 54th St Pool, 348 E 54th St ☎397-3154. Good-sized indoor pool; annual membership just $25. Bring check or money order, no cash. Exercise classes too. Open Mon–Fri 7am–9.30pm, Sat 9am–3pm, closed Sun.

John Jay Pool, 77th and Cherokee Place ☎794-6566. Above the FDR Drive, this six-lane, fifty-yard pool is surrounded by playgrounds and park benches. While it opened in 1940, it is in remarkably great condition. Free to anyone; bring a padlock.

Riverbank State Park, W 145th St and Riverside Drive ☎694-3600. Beautiful new facility built on top of a waste refinery in Harlem. Sounds strange, and it is, but there are great tennis courts, an outdoor track, an ice-skating rink and indoor facilities. Admission is free.

Sutton Gymnastics and Fitness Center, 20 Cooper Square ☎533-9390. One of the few gyms in New York where you don't have to be a member to use the facilities. Classes for around $20. Call for hours and schedule of classes.

Tenth Street Turkish Baths, 268 E 10th St ☎473-8806. An ancient place, something of a neighborhood landmark and still going, with steam baths, sauna and an ice-cold pool, as well as massage and a restaurant. Admission $20, extra for massage, etc. Open daily 9am–10pm; men only Sun & Thurs; women only Wed; co-ed Mon, Tues, Fri & Sat.

West 59th St Pool, 533 W 59th St (between 10th and 11th aves) ☎397-3159. Two pools, one indoor and another outdoor, gym and climbing wall. $25 annual membership (climbing wall extra) paid by money order. The gym is open Mon–Fri 11am–10.15pm, Sat 9am–5.30pm. Closed Sun. Call for pool hours.

Boating

Downtown Boathouse, Hudson River, Pier 26 ☎966-1852. Free kayaking on the weekends.

Loeb Boathouse, Central Park ☎517-2233. Rowing boats for hire between April and Oct, daily 9am–6pm. Rates are $10 an hour plus $30 deposit. Also gondola rides for $30 a half-hour, 5–10pm; reservations required.

Beaches

Few visitors come to New York for the **beaches**, and those New Yorkers with money tend to turn their noses up at the city strands, preferring to move further afield to Long Island, just a couple of hours away and much better. But the city's beaches, though often crowded, are a cool summer escape from Manhattan and most are also just a subway token away.

BROOKLYN

Brighton Beach, D train to Brighton Beach. Technically the same stretch as Coney, but less crowded and given color by the local

Russian community (pick up ethnic snacks from the boardwalk vendors).

Coney Island Beach, at the end of half a dozen subway lines: fastest is the D train to Stillwell Ave. After Rockaway (see below), NYC's most popular bathing spot, jam-packed on summer weekends. The Atlantic here is only moderately dirty and there's a good, reliable onshore breeze.

Manhattan Beach, D train to Sheepshead Bay Rd, walk to Ocean Ave and cross the bridge. Small beach much used by locals.

QUEENS

Jacob Riis Park, IRT #2 train to Flatbush Ave, then Q35 bus. Good sandy stretches, the western ones used almost exclusively by a gay male crowd.

Rockaway Beach, A and C trains to any stop along the beach. Forget California: this seven-mile strip is where New Yorkers – up to three-quarters of a million daily in summer – come to get the best surf around. So good that the Ramones wrote a song about it. Best beaches are at 9th St, 23rd St and 80–118th sts.

THE BRONX

Orchard Beach, subway train #6 local to Pelham Bay Park, then Bx12 bus. Lovingly known as "Horseshit Beach" – and in any case less easy to get to than the rest.

STATEN ISLAND

Great Kills Park, bus #103 from Staten Island Ferry Terminal. Quiet and used by locals.

South Beach, bus S52. New ballfields, rollerblading areas and low-key beaches.

Wolfe's Pond Park, bus #103 to Main St Tottenville, at Hylan and Cornelia. Regularly packs in the crowds from New Jersey.

Sports and Outdoor Activities

Chapter 22

Parades and Festivals

The other big daytime activities in New York, and often worth timing your visit around, are its **parades and street festivals**. The city takes these, especially the **parades**, very seriously. Almost every large ethnic group in the city holds an annual get-together, often using 5th Ave as the main drag; the events are often political or religious in origin, though now are just as much an excuse for music, food and dance. Chances are your stay will coincide with at least one: the list that follows is roughly chronological.

Also prominent in New York are summer-long **arts festivals**, or performance series, often held outdoors – Central Park, Prospect Park and South Street Seaport are all prime locations – and usually free. For more details and exact dates of parades, festivals and the like, phone ☎1-800/NYC-VISIT, or visit *www.nycvisit.com*. Also, look at listings in *New York* magazine's "CUE" section, *The New Yorker* magazine's "Goings on About Town" section, the Friday *New York Times'* "Weekend" section, and the *Village Voice's* "Cheap Thrills" section.

January

Chinese New Year (first day of the lunar year): a noisy, colorful occasion celebrated from noon to sunset around Mott St. Dragons dance in the street, firecrackers chase away evil spirits and the chances of getting a meal anywhere in Chinatown are slim; phone ☎431-9740

or 941-0923 for further details including the precise date, which varies each year.

Julliard's Focus, from the Julliard School of Music, is an annual festival with six contemporary music concerts held at the Julliard Theater (call for dates) ☎769-7406.

February

Empire State Building Run Up Foot Race (mid-month): where contenders race up 1575 steps ☎736-3100.

Manhattan Antiques and Collectibles (usually last two weekends of the month): Triple Pier Expo at the Passenger

---

Street fairs

Look out, too, for neighborhood **street fairs**. These are like urban village fetes, and more than 5000 crop up annually, most frequently in midsummer. They're advertised locally, on notice boards and in newspapers, and depending on the neighborhood it can be well worth going. More significantly, block fairs are a good way of getting a taste of real, neighborhood New York, beyond the sirens and skyscrapers. For a free, comprehensive list of street events, go to The Mayor's Office, Community Assistance Unit, 51 Chambers St, room 608 ☎788-7439; Mon–Fri 10am–4pm. Updated monthly. They will not mail or fax.

Ship Terminal (Piers 88, 90 and 92)
☎255-0020; www.stellashows.com.

Presidents Day Parade (2nd/3rd Mon): for Abe and George. Check newspapers and local TV news for parade route.

March

New York Underground Film Festival (mid-March): a bit out of the mainstream – but very usually showing very interesting films. Locations vary – call or check out their Web site ☎925-3440; www.nyuff.com.

St Patrick's Day Parade (March 17): Celebrating an impromptu march through the streets by Irish militiamen on St Patrick's Day 1762, it has become a draw for every Irish band and organization in the US and Ireland. Check newspapers and local TV News for parade route.

Greek Independence Day Parade (late March): not as long or as boozy as St Pat's, more a patriotic nod to the old country from floats of pseudo-classically dressed Hellenes. When Independence Day falls in the Orthodox Lent, the parade is shifted to April or May. It usually kicks off from 62nd St and 5th Ave at 1.30pm ☎718/204-6500.

Easter Parade (Easter Sun): from Central Park down to Rockefeller Center on 50th St, an opportunity for New Yorkers to dress up in outrageous Easter bonnets. 10am–5pm. There's also an **Eggstravaganza**, a children's festival including an egg-rolling contest in Central Park on the Great Lawn.

The Circus Animal Walk (call for exact date): where animals from Ringling Brothers' Barnum & Bailey Circus march from their point of arrival to Madison Square Garden. Call the Garden for details at ☎465-6741.

April

Bang on a Can Festival (late March-early May): a major "new music" festival featuring musicians from all over the world. Locations citywide ☎777-8442; www.bangonacan.org.

First Run Film Festival (beginning of the month): NYU's annual showcase of student shorts at Cantor Film Center, 36 E 8th St ☎998-4100. (Selected films are also shown at Lincoln Center.)

New Directors, New Films (Late March/early April): Lincoln Center and MoMA have presented this popular two-week film festival for more than 25 years ☎875-5638; www.filmlinc.com.

International African Dance/Drum Conference and Festival (first week): five days of African dance and drum lectures and classes. Benefit performance held at Symphony Space ☎718/455-7136; www.angelfire.com/ny/africandance.

Vintage Poster Fair (first weekend): a tradition for more than 15 years at the Metropolitan Pavilion at 110 W 19th St ☎206-0499; www.posterfair.com.

Annual Antiquarian Book Fair at the Park Ave Armory, Park Ave and 67th St, ☎777-5218. Admission (mid-April) $12.

Earth Day (April 22): in the weeks surrounding it, there are dozens of activities at parks and schools around the five boroughs, ranging from compost demonstrations to music festivals. Call ☎922-0048; or check out www.home.dti.net/earthday for a schedule.

Macy's Flower Show (late April/early May): fragrant flowers, plants and trees, lush landscapes and global gardens fill up Macy's main floor for one to two weeks a year ☎494-4495.

May

Sakura Matsuri (Cherry Blossom Festival) (first weekend): music, art, dance and food celebrating Japanese culture and the blossoming of the garden's 200 cherry trees. Free with garden admission. Brooklyn Botanic Garden ☎718/623-7200.

Rockefeller Center Flower and Garden Show (Spring/Summer; typically mid-May, sometimes as late as July; call for dates): landscaped gardens, etc ☎632-3975.

Ukrainian Festival (mid-May): this fills a weekend on E 7th St between 2nd and

Parades and Festivals

Parades and Festivals

3rd aves with marvelous Ukrainian costume, folk music and dance plus authentic foods. At the Ukrainian Museum (12th St and 2nd Ave) there's a special exhibition of *pysanky* – traditional hand-painted eggs ☎674-1615 for festival details.

Martin Luther King Jr Parade (mid-May): celebrating Dr King's contribution to civil rights; the parade travels along 5th Ave from 66th to 86th sts. The parade also pays tribute to the African-Americans who have served in the US military ☎374-5176.

Ninth Ave International Food Festival (weekend in mid-May): it closes down the avenue between 37th and 57th sts for the weekend and offers tantalizing food, delicious scents, colorful crafts and great deals ☎581-7217.

Lower East Side's Loisada Street Fair (traditionally held on the last weekend in May). Check newspapers for times and street address.

Crafts on Columbus (first 3 weekends in May): Columbus Ave between 77th and 81st sts ☎866-2239.

Salute to Israel Parade (call for date): on 5th Ave, between 52nd and 79th sts then east to 3rd Ave ☎245-8200 ext 106 or 255.

Fleet Week (end of May): the annual welcome of sailors from the US, Canada, Mexico, and the UK to New York, held at the Intrepid Sea-Air-Space Museum. Plus activities and events ☎245-0072.

Irish American Festival (last weekend): at Gateway National Recreation Area in Brooklyn ☎718/338-3687.

Washington Square Outdoor Art Exhibit (weekends; end May/mid-June): It's free, held for over 65 years and features over 200 artists ☎982-6255.

Memorial Day (last Mon in May): check out newspapers and local TV news for parade route and times.

June

Museum Mile Festival (first Tues evening in June): on 5th Ave from 82nd St to 105th St. Several museums are open free 6–9pm.

Philippine Independence Day Parade (early June; call for exact date and route) ☎683-2990.

Puerto Rican Day Parade (call for exact date): the largest of several Puerto Rican celebrations in the city, three hours of bands and baton-twirling from 44th to 86th sts on 5th Ave, then across to 3rd ☎718/665-4009.

Lower East Side Jewish Spring Festival (check *Jewish Weekly* for date and location): kosher foods, Yiddish and Hebrew folk singing and guided tours of the Jewish Lower East Side.

The Festival of St Anthony (begins the first Thurs of the month): a ten-day long, fun Italian celebration on Sullivan St from Spring to West Houston sts, culminating in a procession of Italian bands, led by a life-size statue of the saint carried on the shoulders of four men ☎777-2755.

Welcome Back to Brooklyn Homecoming Festival (second week of June): one of Brooklyn's largest festivals, held at Grand Army Plaza in Prospect Park ☎718/855-7882.

Mermaid Parade (first Sat after June 21): hilarious event where the participants are dressed up like mermaids and King Neptunes, and saunter down the boardwalk of Brooklyn's Coney Island, after which everyone throws fruit into the sea. If you're around – don't miss it ☎718/392-1267; *www.coneyislandusa.com*.

Gay Pride Week (last week in June): kicks off with a rally and ends with a march and a dance ☎807-7433; *www.nycpride.org.*

Brooklyn Arts Council International Film and Video Festival (June–July). Call for dates and locations ☎718/625-0080.

July

African Arts Festival (first week in July): held at 1700 Fulton St, in Brooklyn, and includes a parade, talent contest, children and family programs and all sorts of fun for families of all ages. From 10am to midnight.

Independence Day (July 4th): Macy's fireworks display – visible all over downtown Manhattan but best seen from Battery Park from around 9pm.

The Great July 4th Festival: at Battery Park ☎809-4900, a fantastic fair and more fireworks. For oratory, go to City Hall.

Bastille Day (Sun closest to July 14th): celebrate with the Alliance Francaise on 60th St between Lexington and 5th Ave ☎355-6100.

American Crafts Festival (two weekends around the end of June): at Lincoln Center. More than crafts, you'll also see demonstrations, puppets, clowns and singing ☎875-5593.

Japanese Obon Festival (Sat nearest July 15th): held in Bryant Park behind the New York Public Library, there's slow and simple dancing in the lantern-hung park and a service the following Sun ☎678-0305. Also on the same weekend are the **NYC Unfolds Street Fair** (mid-July), on W 3rd St from Broadway to LaGuardia, and the **Magic on Madison Ave Fair**, from 37th to 57th sts, ☎809-4900.

August

Harlem Month (culminates with Harlem Day on the 3rd Sun): a month-long celebration of African, Caribbean and Latin culture including a children's festival, a step show, a fashion parade, talent contest and other festivities, call ☎862-7200 for info.

Dance Theater of Harlem Street Festival (usually the second week of the month): a variety of dance performances plus events for children. The festival is more than a quarter-century old and takes place on 152nd St between Amsterdam Ave and Convent St, call ☎690-2800.

Macy's Tap A Mania (mid-Aug): It starts at noon, and there is a rain date. There have often been more than 3500

dancers, and Guinness lists this as the "record for the largest line of dancers ever to tap in unison." 34th St and 7th Ave, near Broadway ☎494-5247.

September

Tugboat Challenge (Sun before Labor Day): Labor Day Weekend also hosts this kid-pleasing annual – a race between NY's working tugboats. The finish line is Pier 86. It is the culmination of **Seafest**, when ships visit and pier events are held at the Intrepid Sea-Air-Space Museum ☎245-0072.

West Indian-American Day Parade Held in Brooklyn on Labor Day. Call for more details ☎718/774-8807.

Labor Day Parade and Street Fair (Labor Day). Check newspapers and local TV news for parade route and related events.

West Indian Day Parade and Carnival (Labor Day Weekend): in Crown Heights (see description in *Brooklyn* section).

Broadway on Broadway (Sun after Labor Day): Free performances feature songs performed by casts of virtually every Broadway musical, culminating in a shower of confetti; held at Times Square ☎768-1560.

American Crafts Festival (two weekends around the middle of Sept): at Lincoln Center. More than crafts, you'll also see demonstrations, puppets, clowns and singing ☎875-5593.

Festival of the Feast of San Gennaro (ten days in mid-Sept): celebrating the patron saint of Naples, held along Mulberry St in Little Italy. This feast has been held here for over 70 years: wonderful food, great people-watching and fun things to buy. A high spot is a procession of the saint's statue through the streets, with donations of dollar bills pinned to his cloak.

New York is Book Country (usually third Sunday): 11am–5pm on 5th Ave between 48th and 57th sts, and from Madison to 6th Ave on 52nd and 53rd sts. Every bookstore and publisher in the

Parades and
Festivals

Parades and Festivals

metropolitan area has stands, carts or stalls ☎207-7242.

African American Day Parade (call for exact date): runs from 111th St and Adam Clayton Powell Blvd to 142nd St then right to 5th Ave, Harlem ☎862-7200.

Korean American Parade (call for exact date): from 42nd St and Broadway to 23rd St ☎255-6969.

Steuben Day Parade (third weekend): the biggest German-American event. Baron von Steuben was a Prussian general who fought with Washington at the battle of Valley Forge, which is as good an excuse as any for a costumed parade in his honor from 63rd to 86th sts and 5th Ave ☎516/239-0741.

Washington Square Outdoors Art Exhibit (call for dates): along the sidewalks of the village centered around Waverly Place from 6th Ave to Broadway ☎982-6255.

Gracie Square Art Show (call for date): 11am–dusk, at Carl Shultz Park, on East End Ave from 84th to 87th sts ☎535-9132.

New York Film Festival (2 weeks late Sept–mid-Oct; held at Lincoln Center) ☎875-5610.

October

Promenade Art Show (call for dates): on Brooklyn Promenade, the historic walkway overlooking downtown Manhattan ☎718/625-0080.

Lexington Ave Octoberfest (usually the first weekend): on Lexington from 42nd to 57th sts ☎808-4900.

Pulaski Day Parade (call for exact date): on 5th Ave for the city's Polish immigrants ☎374-5176.

Hispanic Day Parade (on or around Oct 8): running on 5th Ave between 44th and 72nd sts ☎242-2360.

Columbus Day Parade (on or around Oct 12): one of the city's largest binges, commemorating the day America was put on the map. Runs on 5th Ave from 44th to 79th sts, ☎249-2360.

Children's Halloween Carnival is held around Halloween (usually a few days before Oct 31) at Chelsea Piers ☎336-6666.

Village Halloween Parade (Oct 31): a procession on 6th Ave from Spring to 23rd sts. 7pm. You'll see spectacular costumes, wigs and make-up. The music is great, the spirit is wild and be sure to get there early so you can get a good viewing spot – it gets packed every year. For more info call ☎914/758-5519. There's also a tamer, children's parade earlier that day, in Washington Square Park.

Antique and craft fairs include **Crafts on Columbus**, which runs the first three weekends behind the Museum of Natural History (☎866-2239) and **St Ignatius Loyola Antiques Show** at Park Ave and 84th St, a small and intimate show in a unique setting with quality antiques at affordable prices (call for dates ☎288-3588).

November

New York City Marathon (call for date): runners from all over the world assemble for this 26.2-mile run on city pavement through the five boroughs. One of the best places to watch is Central Park S, almost at the finish line ☎860-4455.

Veteran's Day Parade (Nov 11): The United War Veterans sponsor this annual event, which runs down 5th Ave from 39th St to 23rd sts ☎693-1475.

Triple Pier Expo (two weekends, mid-month): The largest metropolitan antiques fair, on piers 88, 90 and 92, ☎255-0020.

Macy's Thanksgiving Parade (last Thurs in Nov): New York's most televised parade, with floats, dozens of marching bands from around the country, the Rockettes, and Santa Claus's first appearance of the season. More than two million spectators watch it from 77th St down Central Park W to Columbus Circle, afterwards down Broadway to Herald Square, 9am–noon ☎494-4495.

Macy's Thanksgiving Day Parade

See Mickey Mouse and the other balloons being inflated the night before the parade. It's not as crowded, and you can experience something not televised to every home in America. They're blown up on W 77th and W 81st sts between Central Park W and Columbus Ave at the Museum of Natural History. Wander around these huge objects and watch their shapes appear. It starts at dusk and can go past midnight.

Thanksgiving Weekend Annual Uptown/Downtown Thanksgiving Crafts Fair: (Fri–Sun after Thanksgiving) For a more sedate scene, start your holiday shopping here. At Wallace Hall at 84th St and Park Ave ☎866-2239.

December

Out of the Darkness (Dec 1): public candle-lit march to City Hall in observance of World AIDS day. Coincides with the 24-hour reading of the Names Vigil ☎580-7668.

Miracle on Madison Avenue' Festival (first Sun): covers 15 blocks, between 57th and 72nd sts, with a variety of things to do and buy. Proceeds go to benefit needy children ☎988-4001.

Rockefeller Center (beginning of month): the lighting of the Christmas tree, begins the festivities ☎632-3975.

Chanukah Celebrations: for the eight nights of this holiday, a menorah lighting ceremony takes place at 59th St and 5th Ave.

Holiday Windows: the windows on 5th Ave are fun to look at, although you might have to wait in line especially for Lord & Taylor and Saks.

Kwanzaa Fest (call for dates): the world's largest celebration of African-American Arts and Culture. Live entertainment, a children's pavilion and much more. Held at the Jacob K Javits Convention Center ☎216-2000.

New Year's Eve (Dec 31): traditionally marked by 200,000 people gathering on Times Square where the last seconds of the year signal drunken but good-natured revelry in the snow ☎768-1560. There are also fireworks at South Street Seaport, and Brooklyn's Prospect Park. A more family-oriented, alcohol-free festival has started, called **First Night**, with dancing, music and food throughout the city ☎818-1777.

Summer arts' festivals

There are a number of performance series or ongoing arts festivals, mostly music-oriented, that take place throughout the summer in New York; best of all, most of these are free.

Anchorage Music and performance art inside the Brooklyn Bridge. Call for info ☎206-6674.

Bryant Park Summer Film Festival Mon nights at sunset (Tues rain date), mid-June to Labor Day, behind the 42nd St NY Public Library, between 5th and 6th aves. Much better sound than you'd expect. Bring a blanket and a picnic. Call ☎512-5700 for film schedule and details of other events. Free.

Celebrate Brooklyn Mid-June through mid-Aug. Concerts, plays and readings free at the Bandshell in Prospect Park. Call ☎718/855-7882 ext 52. See Brooklyn section of Outer Boroughs.

Center Stage Live performances at World Trade Center Plaza Tues–Fri, lunchtime and after work ☎435-4170.

JVC Jazz Festival Citywide during June, hear mythic names and new groups, indoors and out, in clubs and halls; some are even free. Call Jazz Line at ☎479-7888 for info or JVC Jazz at ☎501-1390.

Lincoln Center Out-of-Doors Aug evening, in and around Lincoln Center. Annual highlights include Roots of American Music, which celebrates the best in blues, gospel and folk plus special events for families and kids. Call ☎875-5108 for info. Free.

Parades and Festivals

Parades and Festivals

Midsummer Night Swing at Lincoln Center's Fountain Plaza, 65th St at Columbus Ave. Every Wed through Sat from mid-June to mid-July, 8.15–11pm, you can learn a different dance en masse each night to the rhythm of live swing, mambo, merengue, samba, country and other styles. Call ☎875-5766 for more info. $11, but you can dance and listen to the music from the areas surrounding for free.

Mostly Mozart July/Aug, at Lincoln Center's Avery Fisher Hall and Alice Tully Hall, at 8pm. Distinguished guests join the orchestra. Call ☎875-5103 for info.

Music at Castle Clinton Free waterside music performances in July and Aug by top named performers in Battery Park. Call ☎835-2789 for details.

Opera in the Parks June/July the Metropolitan Opera performs opera for free in New York parks. ☎362-6000; *www.metopera.org/news.*

New York Philharmonic Free concerts in all five boroughs with fireworks. Call ☎875-5709 for schedule.

River Flicks Summer Film Series at the Piers. Free films. Call ☎533-PARK for locations and schedules.

Shakespeare in the Park Delacorte Theater in Central Park, Tues–Sun,

July–Aug. ☎260-2400 for info. Free tickets given out at 1pm for 8pm performances, but line forms early in the morning.

Sounds at Sunset at the Battery Park Esplanade, June, July and Aug, at 6.30pm. Call ☎416-5300 for info. Free.

Summergarden Concerts Museum of Modern Art concerts in the sculpture garden, 54th St between 5th and 6th aves. Fri and Sat, July–Aug at 8.30pm. First-come, first-served, but it will be canceled if raining. Free. ☎708-9491; *www.moma.org.*

Summerstage at Central Park June–Aug at Rumsey Playfield in Central Park, mid-park at 72nd St. Concerts, performances and readings, plus the New York Grand Opera. Call ☎360-CPSS; *www.summerstage.org.* Free.

Washington Square Music Festival (Tues in July & Aug): 8pm at Washington Square Park. A village tradition since 1953: five free open-air concerts – 4 classical and 1 jazz.

The World Financial Center Arts & Events June–Aug. Dance on the waterfront to various types of music from Hungarian to swing. Call ☎945-0505 for info. Free.

Chapter 23

Kids' New York

Despite what you may have heard, New York can be a wonderful city to visit with **children** of all ages. There are the obvious attractions such as museums, skyscrapers and ferry rides, and the simple pleasures of just walking the streets, seeing the buskers and taking in the shopping scene. There are lots of free events year-round, but especially in the summer, ranging from puppet shows and nature programs in the city's parks to storytelling hours at local libraries and bookstores. In addition, many of the city's museums and theaters have specific children's programs. Following are details on some of the attractions that are especially appealing to kids. Always be sure to phone ahead for specific times, programs and availability to avoid any disappointment.

General Advice

For a further **listing** of what is available when you're in town, see the pages of Friday's *Daily News* or *New York Times*, and "Activities for Children" in the weekly *New York* magazine, as well as *Time Out* and *The Village Voice*. An excellent automated directory of family-oriented current events all around the city is available through the New York Convention and Visitors Bureau, 810 7th Ave (between 52nd and 53rd sts) NY 10019 ☎484-1222 Mon–Fri 8.30am–6pm, Sat & Sun 9am–5pm; *www.nycvisit.com*. They also have a free seasonal booklet, *The Big Apple Visitor's*

Guide, with a good map, directions and coupons. You can also check the family activity listings on the New York CitySearch Web site: *www.citysearch-nyc.com*

Your main problem won't be finding stuff to do with your kids, but perhaps how to transport the younger ones around: though many natives navigate the streets and subways with a stroller (note: it can be a hassle to get up onto buses and down into subways if you're alone), some prefer to keep infants and even toddlers conveniently contained in a **backpack** or **front carrier**. Indeed, most of the attractions listed here do not allow strollers, though most will store yours for you while you visit – call ahead for details. The majority of sights, restaurants and stores, however, are quite tolerant of children, if not actually child-friendly.

Public transit in the city got easier (and cheaper) with the introduction in 1998 of free transfers between buses and subways with the use of a **MetroCard** (see Basics for more information). Subways are the fastest way of getting around the city and are perfectly safe – there is no reason to feel worried about taking your kids on them, in fact they will probably get quite a kick out of them, crowds, noise and all. Buses are slower but give an antsy or bored kid the option of staring through the large windows and watching the hustle and bustle outside.

Don't hesitate to ask a stranger for help getting a stroller up (or down) steps

Remember that children under 44 inches (112cm) tall ride free on the subway and buses when accompanied by an adult.

**Kids'
New York**

to the subway, or directions to a sight or the nearest bathroom (large hotels and chain bookstores are great for this). Contrary to their reputation, most New Yorkers like kids and are quite willing to help.

Lastly, as the Scandinavian woman who left her sleeping baby outside a café while she ate quickly found out, such behavior is frowned upon – if you can't bring your child inside, don't go in at all. The woman in question was actually arrested and accused of child abuse after someone called the police and reported an abandoned baby. Though the charges were later dropped, the whole episode caused quite a sensation. Cultural differences notwithstanding, please don't leave your child unattended.

Museums

One could spend an entire holiday just checking out the city's many **museums**, which almost always contain something of interest for the kids; the following is a brief overview of the ones that should evoke more than just the usual enthusiasm. See Chapter 15, "Museums and Galleries," for more details of these and other museums.

American Museum of Natural History

Central Park W (at 79th St) ☎769-5100; *www.amnh.org.* Sun–Thurs 10am–5.45pm, Fri & Sat 10am–8.45pm; Hayden Planetarium closed until some time in the year 2000 due to massive new renovations; IMAX shows 10.30am–4.30pm, every hour on the half-hour. Suggested donation $8, children $4.50, students/seniors $6. Special exhibits and IMAX additional charge, combination packages available.

One of the best museums of its kind, an enormous complex of buildings full of fossils, gems, meteorites and other natural artifacts (34 million in all). The recently renovated Dinosaur Halls offer enormous, creative displays and interactive computer stations that are sure to please all ages and are a good first stop. Extensive diora-

mas of animals from around the world allow children an up-close look at wildlife, and the new Hall of Biodiversity offers video presentations about the world's environment and a multimedia re-creation of a Central African rainforest. Several interactive children's programs are held the last weekend of each month, Oct–May, call for the schedule.

American Museum of the Moving Image

35th Ave at 36th St, Astoria, Queens ☎718/784-0077. Tues–Fri noon–5pm, Sat & Sun 11am–6pm, closed Mon; $8.50 adults, students/seniors $5.50, children 5–12 $4.50, under five free (museum admission includes film screenings).

Located in an old movie lot, this museum is dedicated to all aspects of film, video and TV. Its exhibit halls are filled with historic costumes, cameras and props, as well as the entire *Seinfeld* set. Interactive displays, movie special effects demonstrations, and an exhibit of classic video games (that you can actually play) are just some of the things kids will love. Free film screenings are held in a lovely old movie palace on the premises. Definitely worth a visit, especially for kids 6 and older.

Brooklyn Children's Museum

145 Brooklyn Ave (on the corner of St Mark's Ave) ☎718/735-4400. Wed–Fri 2–5pm, Sat & Sun 10am–5pm; suggested contribution $3.

Founded in 1899, this is the world's first museum for children. A participatory, hands-on museum stacked full of authentic ethnological, natural history and technological artifacts with which to play. Fun for children of all ages as well as adults.

Children's Museum of the Arts

182 Lafayette St (between Broome and Grand) ☎274-0986. Wed noon–7pm, Thurs–Sun noon–5pm, closed Mon & Tues; children and adults $5, 12 months old and under free.

Art gallery of works by and/or for children. Children are encouraged to look at different types of art and then create their own, with paints, clay, plaster of Paris and any other simple medium. There are even projects for small toddlers.

Children's Museum of Manhattan

212 W 83rd St (between Broadway and Amsterdam in the Tisch building) ☎721-1234; www.cmom.org. Tues–Sun 10am–5pm, closed Mon; children and adults $5, under age 1 free.

A terrific participatory museum founded in 1973 to "inspire learning through interactive exhibits and educational programs." The exhibit space covers five floors, with imaginative displays; not to be missed is Seuss! a whimsical area with decor inspired by Dr. Seuss books, where kids can (literally) cook up some green eggs and ham. As if that's not enough, there is also a Media Center where children can produce their own television shows. For ages 1–12 years, and highly recommended.

Ellis Island Immigration Museum

Ellis Island, access by the Circle Line Statue of Liberty Ferry from Battery Park ☎363-3200; www.ellisisland.org or www.wallofhonor.com (a searchable database of the names of the people who came through the immigration center). Daily 9.30am–5pm, free. Ferries run every hour from 9.30am–3.30pm (though you need to be on the 3pm ferry at the latest to see the museum), adults $7 round-trip, children 3–17 $3. This is not only one of the least expensive ways to spend a day in New York, but also one of the best, as you can combine a fun trip on a ferry with visits to this and the Statue of Liberty. Ellis Island became an immigration processing station in 1894, and in 1990 the main buildings were renovated and reopened as the Immigration Museum. Special features include the "Ellis Island Stories," a dramatic re-enactment of the immigrant experience based on oral histories (April–Sept only, $3 for adults, $2.50 for children, call ahead for schedule); and "Treasures From Home," a collection of family heirlooms, photos, and other artifacts donated by descendants of the immigrants. When you're ready for a break, there is a lovely restaurant with a terrace and great views.

Fire Museum

278 Spring St (between Hudson and Varick) ☎691-1303. Tues–Sun 10am–4pm, closed Mon; adults $4, students $2, children 12 and under $1.

A sure hit with the pre-school crowd, it's an unspectacular but pleasing homage to New York City's firefighters, and indeed firepeople everywhere. On display are fire engines from the last century (hand-drawn, horse-drawn and steam-powered), helmets, dog-eared photos and a host of motley objects on three floors of a disused fire station. A neat and endearing display.

Intrepid Sea-Air-Space Museum

W 46th St and 12th Ave at Pier 86 ☎245-0072. Summer hours: April 1–Sept 30 Mon–Sat 10am–5pm, Sun 10am–6pm; winter hours: Oct 1–March 31 Wed–Sun 10am–5pm, closed Mon & Tues, closed January for repair and cleaning; last admission 1 hour prior to closing; adults $10, children 12–17 $7.50, children 6–11 $5, children 3–5 $1, 2 years and under free.

This old aircraft carrier has a distinguished history, including hauling Neil Armstrong and co out of the ocean following the Apollo 11 moonshot. Today it holds the world's fastest spy plane, a guided missile submarine, and other modern and vintage air and sea craft, as well as interactive CD-ROM exhibits and a restaurant. Not especially recommended for kids under 5 years.

Lefferts Homestead

Prospect Park, Willink Entrance, at Flatbush Ave and Empire Blvd. Subway D to Prospect Park. March–July, Sept–Dec, Sat & Sun noon–4pm; closed Aug, Jan & Feb, closed Mon–Fri; free. ☎718/965-6505.

Kids'
New York

See Chapter 2, "The Harbor Islands" for much more detail on Ellis Island and the Statue of Liberty.

Kids' New York

One of the few remaining Dutch farm-houses in New York, built around 1780 by Peter Lefferts, who was one of the richest men in the county at the time and a delegate to the state convention when New York ratified the constitution in 1788. The Dutch colonial-style house is now the Children's Historic House Museum, with refurbished rooms filled with period furniture, including a four-poster bed and other pieces owned by Lefferts. There are children's exhibits on life during the 1820s and the freeing of slaves in the New York area, along with craft workshops and other kid-friendly activities.

National Museum of the American Indian (Smithsonian Institution)

1 Bowling Green ☎514-3700; www.si.edu/nmai. Daily 10am–5pm, Thurs until 8pm; free.

A beautiful museum housing the largest collection in the world devoted to North, Central and South American Indian cultures. Though much of the exhibit is behind glass, the layout makes it very accessible and the background sound and music set the mood. Kids will enjoy looking at the ancient dolls, moccasins and the replicas of a reservation home and schoolroom. They often have programs that include theater troupes, performance artists, dancers and films.

New York Hall of Science

47–01 111th St (at 46th Ave), Flushing Meadows, Corona, Queens ☎718/699-0005; Mon–Wed 9.30am–2pm, Thurs–Sun 9.30am–5pm; in July & Aug Tues & Wed also 9.30am–5pm; $6, children $4.

Built for the 1964–65 World's Fair, this museum (ranked one of the top ten science museums in the country) continues to add the latest in scientific and techno-logical displays, with hands-on exhibits that make it really fun for kids. A highlight is the outdoor Science Playground (open May–Oct), for ages 6 and older. Not worth a special trip in itself, but it certainly merits a visit on the way out to nearby Shea Stadium, the Queens Zoo, Queens

Art Museum or the World's Fair grounds in Flushing Meadow Park.

New York Transit Museum

Old subway entrance (at Schermerhorn St and Boerum Place), Brooklyn ☎718/243-3060; www.mta.nyc.ny.us. Tues–Fri 10am–4pm, Sat & Sun noon–5pm, closed Mon; adults $3, children $1.50. Also: **Transit Museum Gallery and Store** at Grand Central Station, open daily, free admission.

Housed in an abandoned 1930s sub-way station, this museum offers more than 100 years worth of transportation history and memorabilia, including old subway cars and buses dating back to the turn of the century (including, amaz-ingly, a wooden train car from 1914). Frequent activities for children, including underground tours, workshops and an annual bus festival – all best for younger school kids. The NY Transit Museum Gallery and Store opened in Spring 1999 and has changing exhibits about public transit and a gift shop selling transit-related items.

Queens County Farm Museum

73-50 Little Neck Parkway, Queens. Subway E, F to Kew Gardens-Union Turnpike, transfer to Q46 bus to Littleneck Parkway. Museum open April–Dec, Sat & Sun 10am–5pm; farm grounds open year-round Mon–Fri, 9am–5pm, April–Dec also Sat & Sun 10am–5pm. ☎718/347-3276. Yes, there really is a working farm right in the middle of Queens, with cows, sheep, geese, ducks and other farm ani-mals, and a large orchard. Built in ☎772, this 47-acre farm was continuously worked for over 200 years, and has a lovely farmhouse with wooden-beamed ceilings and Dutch detail. Special events include apple festivals in the fall, craft shows, weekend hayrides and other reg-ular activities for kids.

South Street Seaport Center and Museum

207 Front St (at the end of Fulton St at the East River) ☎748-8600; www.

southstseaport.org. April–Sept daily
10am–6pm, Thurs until 8pm; Oct–March
10am–5pm, closed Tues; $6, students
$4, children $3.

Eighteenth- and nineteenth-century
buildings house three galleries, a children's center, a maritime craft center and
a library, and the adjacent dock is home
to a large fleet of historic ships. **New York
Unearthed** is a site the museum has
devoted to archeological work currently
being done in the city. Children can watch
archeologists work, see how artifacts discovered tell the story of New York's history, and ride an elevator into a simulated
"dig" site. During July and August there are
also free concerts on Saturday evenings.
Kids of all ages will enjoy the **street performers** who regularly perform around the
Seaport in warm weather.

Staten Island Children's Museum

Snug Harbor Cultural Center, 1000
Richmond Terrace, Staten Island
☎718/273-2060. Tues–Sun noon–5pm,
closed Mon; $4, children under 2 free.

This is a good way to round off a trip
on the Staten Island ferry; it's reachable
on a trolleybus from the ferry terminal.
There are many hands-on exhibits covering subjects like the environment and
technology, puppets and toys. In the
summer months the downstairs gallery
hosts many special exhibits and events
which are free with admission, but the
space is often full. Call for reservations.

Sights and entertainment

Again, this is just a small selection of the
top attractions children of all ages will
enjoy:

Bronx Zoo (formally known as the International Wildlife Conservation Park)

Bronx River Parkway at Fordham Rd,
☎718/367-1010; *www.wcs.org.*
Mar–Oct Mon–Fri 10am–5pm, Sat & Sun
10am–5.30pm; Nov–Feb daily
10am–4.30pm; adults $6.75, kids $3,
free to all on Weds, rides and some
exhibits are an additional charge.

The largest urban zoo in America, it is
truly spectacular, with over 4000 species
of animals, reptiles and birds on display,
many in huge simulated natural habitats
such as Wild Asia, where tigers, elephants and other large animals roam
(almost) free. A children's section allows
kids to climb around on large exhibits,
including a giant spider web, and pet
some of the tamer animals. Highly recommended for an all-day excursion.

Central Park

Year-round, Central Park is equipped to
provide sure-fire entertainment for children of all ages. In the summer it
becomes one giant playground, with
activities ranging from storytelling to
rollerblading to rowboating. The following are merely a few of the highlights –

Kids'
New York

*For more on
the Bronx Zoo,
see p.247. For
more on the
Central Park
Zoo see p.166.*

For more on the Bronx Zoo, see p.247. For more on the Central Park Zoo see p.166.

Babysitting

The Babysitters' Guild, 60 E 42nd St
☎682-0227, offers babysitting services
with approved sitters, and 16 foreign
languages spoken. Fees are $14 an
hour, depending on the age and how
many children there are, plus a flat fee
of $4.50 to cover transportation – after
midnight the fee for transportation is
$7. Most sitters have teaching and nurs-
ing backgrounds, and are fully licensed
and bonded. As always, call for the full
picture. Be sure to book as far in

advance as you can – at the latest the
day before you need the sitter, if possible.

Also, **The Avalon Nurse Registry
and Child Service**, 162 W 56th St
☎245-0250. Avalon arranges full- or
part-time nannies and babysitters at a
reasonable $10 per hour plus trans-
portation costs, and $2 extra for each
additional child, with a 4-hour minimum. English and Spanish languages
spoken.

**Kids'
New York**

for much more detailed information on these and other sights, see Chapter 10, "Central Park".

The Carousel, 64th St mid-park. For just $1, children can take a spin on the country's largest hand-carved horses. **Central Park Wildlife Conservation Center (Zoo)**, 5th Ave at 64th St. A small but enjoyable zoo, with sea lions, polar bears, monkeys and the new Tisch Children's Zoo. **Hans Christian Andersen statue**, 72nd St on the East Side (next to the **Boat Pond**), a forty-or-so-year tradition of storytelling sessions; Sat 11am–noon, June to Sept. **Loeb Boathouse**, 72nd St mid-park. Rent a rowboat on the Central Park lake and enjoy the views or take a gondola ride in the evening. Bike rentals available too. **Wollman Rink**, 62nd St mid-park ☎396-1010. Roller/in-line skating during the summer and ice-skating during the winter. Skate rental and instruction available.

Chelsea Piers Sports & Entertainment Complex

Piers 59–62 at W 23rd St and the Hudson River ☎336-6666 (general info) or ☎336-6500 (field house, soccer, basketball, etc.); each activity priced separately. This is a huge, wildly popular sports center, with 2 indoor ice-skating rinks, an outdoor rollerblading rink, basketball courts, a rock climbing wall for kids, 2 indoor astroturf soccer fields, batting cages, gymnastics facilities, and much more.

New York Aquarium

W 8th St and Surf Ave, Coney Island, Brooklyn ☎718/265-3474. Daily 10am–6pm; $8.75, children 2–12 $4.50, under 2 free.

First opened in 1896, the aquarium is a division of the Wildlife Conservation Society. Mostly it's a series of darkened halls containing creatures from the deep, but open-air shows of whales and dolphins are held several times daily, as are

---

Times Square

Just north of 42nd St, where Broadway and 7th Ave converge in midtown Manhattan, is the new **Times Square**, which has been transformed from an infamous den of iniquity into a family-oriented entertainment zone. Much of this has to do with Disney's new and very obvious presence in the area. For more on the neighborhood, see p.157. Below are some of the more kid-oriented options in the district.

The Disney Store, 210 W 42nd St at Broadway ☎221-0430. This retail outlet is found in many American malls, though this one is considerably larger than the standard. There is a giant movie screen running advertisements for DisneyWorld in Orlando, Florida, and of course segments of the many Disney movies.

New Victory Theater, 209 W 42nd St ☎382-4000. The city's first year-round theater for families. There is always a rich mix of theater, music, dance, storytelling, film and puppetry, in addition to pre-performance workshops and post-performance participation. The interior has been beautifully restored, the seats are plush but small. Everything about

this theater is child-oriented from the affordable cost (most shows $10–20) to the duration of performances (60–90 minutes).

XS Virtual Game Arena, 1457 Broadway between 41st and 42nd sts ☎1-888/972-7529; *www.xsnewyork.com*. Sun–Thurs 10am–midnight, Fri & Sat 10am–2am. This is a must-stop for the age 10 and over crowd. Upon entering this very dark and very loud futuristic world all senses go into overdrive, which is exactly the idea. There are tons of virtual reality games to try, from hang-gliding to a Western shoot-out, plus an underground lasertag arena and a number of computers with Internet access.

the shark, sea otter and walrus feedings. This is also the site of the famous **Coney Island boardwalk** and **amusement park** – older children and teens will find it a good spot to people-watch.

New York Botanical Garden

200th St and Southern Blvd (Kazimiroff Blvd), Bronx (across from the Bronx Zoo) ☎718/817-8777; www.nybg.org. Tues–Sun 10am–6pm, closed Mon; grounds only $3, students, children 2–12 $1, free admission on Wed.

One of America's foremost public gardens, with 250 acres of flowers, trees and park. The Enid A. Haupt Conservatory (known as the crystal palace) has been magnificently restored and is currently housing a rainforest containing several thousand medicinal herbs. The Everett Adventure Garden is a 12-acre kid's discovery center, with over 40 hands-on activities, as well as storytelling, music, puppet shows and other special events (summer: Tues–Fri 1–6pm, Sat & Sun 10am–6pm; adults $3, children 2–12 $1; call for events info). Otherwise, a beautiful, tranquil spot, perfect if you've got a baby or toddler in need of a nap (especially good for the adults).

Skyride

350 5th Ave (at 34th St) in the Empire State Building ☎279-9777. Daily 10am–10pm; $11.50, children 5–11 $9.50. Combination ticket to skyride and observatory $14 and $9.

Located in the Empire State Building, the Skyride is a big-screen thrill ride through the most well-known sights in the city, complete with tilting seats and surround sound. Bring a strong stomach; it may be too much for small children. Don't miss the observatory at the top of the Empire State Building, offering spectacular day and nighttime views 1050 feet above Manhattan.

Sony Imax Theater

1998 Broadway and 68th St ☎336-5000; www.sony.com. Adults $9.50, 12 and under $6.

See the city past and present in 3-D. Also housed in the Lincoln Square Entertainment Complex is a Sony twelve-screen movie theater and the *Real Java Café*. Show times vary daily.

Sony Wonder Technology Lab

550 Madison Ave (at 56th St) ☎833-8100. Tues–Sat 10am–6pm, Thurs until 8pm, Sun noon–6pm, closed Mon; free.

Offers amazing hands-on experience with communication technology, including everything from editing rock videos to editing or producing TV programs. You can even participate in directing an action movie while sitting in its audience. Very futuristic; every person receives a card-key that imprints your photo image, name and a voice sample, and a completion certificate is issued at the end. This is a hugely popular attraction, so get here early.

Shops: toys, books and clothes

Bank Street Bookstore, 610 W 112th St (between Broadway and Riverside Drive) ☎678-1654. Affiliated with Bank Street College of Education, the first floor is filled with children's books and games, while the second floor is devoted to educational material for parents and teachers. Their knowledgeable and helpful staff will recommend the perfect book for your child. Frequent special events.

Big City Kites, 1210 Lexington Ave (at 82nd St) ☎472-2623. Manhattan's largest and best kite store, with a huge range to choose from.

Books of Wonder, 16 W 18th St (between 5th and 6th aves) ☎989-3270. Excellent kids' bookstore, with a great story-hour on Sun at 11.45am, and author appearances Sat in the spring and fall.

Cozy's Cuts for Kids, 1125 Madison Ave (at 84th St) ☎744-1716; also 448 Amsterdam Ave (between 81st and 82nd sts) ☎579-2600. For the first haircut through 12 years old, kids can get their hair cut while sitting in a play jeep and

Kids' New York

watching videos. Little ones receive an honorary diploma for their first haircut.

Enchanted Forest, 85 Mercer St (between Spring and Broome sts) ☎925-6677. A marvellous shop that hides its unique merchandise – stuffed animals, puppets, masks and the like – partly in the branches of its mock forest.

F.A.O. Schwarz, 767 5th Ave (at 58th St) ☎644-9400. Showpiece of a nationwide chain sporting three huge floors of everything a child could want. Fans of Barbie will want to check out the Barbie store, in the back of F.A.O. Schwarz, with its own Madison Ave entrance. Not to be missed.

Gymboree, 2015 Broadway (at 69th St) ☎595-7662; also 1049 3rd Ave, at 62nd St ☎688-4044, and other locations in the city. Welcoming stores offering brightly colored kids clothes for new-borns through seven years old. Very reasonable prices and great sales.

Little Eric, 1331 3rd Ave (between 76th and 77th sts) ☎288-8987; also 1118 Madison (between 83rd and 84th sts) ☎717-1513. Large selection of shoes, mostly imported from Italy (and expensive), for children of all ages. Kids won't mind shopping here since they play videos and cartoons all day.

Monkeys and Bears, 506 Amsterdam Ave (between 84th and 85th sts) ☎873-2673. Charming small shop, filled with unique, often handmade clothes for kids. Can be pricey but usually a good value.

Noodle Kidoodle, 112 E 86th St (between Lexington and Park aves) ☎427-6611; also Broadway and 88th St ☎917/441-2066. Well-stocked educational toy shop.

New York for teens

Manhattan itself should be enough to excite and enrapture **teenagers**, but if you're searching for additional entertainment, there are a number of options. For high-tech thrills, check the **Sony Wonder Technology Lab** (overleaf) or **XS Virtual Game Arena** (p.444). Or you could hit one of the city's many music stores. **Manny's Music**, 156 W 48th St, has walls covered with hundreds of autographed photographs of music's biggest stars, past and present, in addition to musical instruments and recording gear. The **Virgin Megastore**, 1540 Broadway, at 46th St, is true to its name and has every kind of merchandise for the music enthusiast.

For a backstage look at real television production, take the **NBC Studio Tour** (30 Rockefeller Plaza–50th St, between 5th and 6th Aves ☎664-4000; Mon–Sat 9.30am–4.30pm, approximately every 15min; $10 per person; children under 6 not admitted). The tour is about one hour long and takes in the studios of *NFL Today*, *Dateline* and *Saturday Night Live*, as well as general production facilities. It also includes a mock radio show with audience participation. The **Kramer Reality Tour** (P.O. Box 391, NY 10036 ☎268-5525 or 1-800/KRAMERS; Sat & Sun tours at noon, $37.50) is a tour of New York spots highlighted in the popular *Seinfeld* sitcom, led by the person who inspired the character of Cosmo Kramer.

For the sports enthusiast the **Madison Square Garden Tour** (7th Ave between 33rd and 31st ☎465-5800) offers a 1-hour behind-the-scenes look at the arena, theater, and the Knick and Ranger locker rooms; and **Chelsea Piers** for participatory sports ☎336-6000, see p. 444. For a rockin' eating experience, there are the established favorites: **Hard Rock Café** (221 W 57th St ☎489-6565); **Planet Hollywood** (140 W 57th St ☎333-7827); **Harley Davidson Café** (1370 6th Ave ☎245-6000), which also has a cool retail shop; and **Motown Café**, 104 W 57th St ☎489-0097, serving up Motown music and southern-style food. For that **clothes-shopping** spree, head to the East Village and SoHo for all the funky stores and "in" fashions – see Chapter 24, "Shops and Markets."

Penny Whistle Toys, 1283 Madison Ave (at 91st St) ☎369-3868; also 448 Columbus Ave (at 81st St) ☎873-9090. Wonderful shop selling a fun, imaginative range of toys that deliberately eschews guns and war accessories, including replicas of old-fashioned toys rarely seen these days. Highly recommended.

Red Caboose, 23 W 45th St (between 5th and 6th aves); lower level – follow the flashing railroad sign in back of lobby ☎575-0155. A unique shop specializing in models, particularly trains and train sets.

Second Childhood, 283 Bleecker St (between 6th and 7th aves) ☎989-6140. Toys dating back to 1850, with a wide assortment of miniatures, soldiers and lead animals.

Space Kiddets, 46 E 21st St (between Park Ave and Broadway) ☎420-9878. Eclectic mix of unusual, funky clothes from newborn to size twelve. They also have shoes and toys.

Tannen's Magic Studio, 24 W 25th St (between Broadway and 6th Ave) ☎929-4500. Your kids will never forget a visit to the largest magic shop in the world, with nearly 8000 props, tricks and magic sets. The staff is made up of magicians who perform free magic shows throughout the day.

Warner Brothers Studios Store, 1 E 57th St (at 5th Ave) ☎754-0300. A dizzying array of merchandise featuring the Warner Bros cartoon characters. As if the merchandise isn't enough for children, video screens show cartoons around the clock.

Theater, puppet shows, circuses and others

The following is a highly selective round-up of other activities, particularly cultural ones, that might be of interest to young children. Bear in mind that you can – as always – find out more by checking the listings in local newspapers and magazines. Note too that stores like Macy's and F.A.O. Schwarz often have events for children – puppet shows, story-hours and the like – as do the children's bookstores (see above).

Barnum & Bailey Circus, Madison Square Garden ☎465-6741. This large touring circus is usually in New York between the end of March and the beginning of May.

Big Apple Circus, Lincoln Center ☎546-2656. Small circus that performs in a tent in Damrosch Park next to the Met, from late Oct to early Jan. Tickets $10–45.

Miss Majesty's Lollipop Playhouse, Children's theater company with performances at the Grove St Playhouse, 39 Grove St ☎741-6436, Sat & Sun at 1.30pm & 3.30pm, closed in the summer; and at the Gene Frankel Theater, 24 Bond St off Lafayette ☎375-8485, Sat & Sun at 1pm and 3pm, open year-round; tickets at both locations are $8 adults and children. Mostly comedies based on fairy tales, with audience participation, for kids 2–10. Well-done and quite popular – reserve your seats in advance.

New Victory Theater, see p.158 for details.

Puppet Playhouse, 555 E 90th St (at York Ave, within Asphalt Green) ☎369-8890. Puppet theater that puts on shows on weekends. Adults $6, kids $5; performances at 10.30am and noon. Seasons run Sept to May – call for a schedule; reservations only.

Thirteenth Street Repertory Company, 50 W 13th St (between 5th and 6th aves) ☎675-6677. Sat & Sun 1pm and 3pm, year-round; $7 adults and children. 45-minute original musicals, such as "Rumplewho?," specifically created for "little humans." Reservations needed, as these are very popular shows.

Kids'
New York

> ### Baby-changing facilities
>
> All the above establishments have restrooms, many with **baby-changing facilities**. Fast-food restaurants, too, will usually allow you to use their facilities without purchase; there are also facilities in hotel lobbies and larger department stores.

Chapter 24

Shops and Markets

New York is the consumer capital of the world. Its **shops** cater to every possible taste, preference, creed and perversity, in any combination and in many cases at any time of day or night. As such, they're as good a reason as any for visiting the city – particularly since exchange rates make merchandise here *cheap* by the standards of most of other Western countries. Unfortunately, though many of the best, the biggest, the oddest and the oldest stores still exist, the face of New York shopping is changing. With the invasion of America-wide superstores and chains, Barnes & Noble, Filene's Basement, T.J. Maxx, Bradley's and even the world's largest K-Mart have become ubiquitous in Manhattan. And there seems to be a Gap on every corner. But while the vast inventory and lower prices of the chains are appealing, nothing beats discovering a quirky, independent store that may only specialize in vintage cufflinks or rubber stamps.

When to shop, how to pay

Most parts of the city are at their least oppressive for shopping early weekday mornings, and at their worst around lunchtimes and on Saturday. There are few days of the year when most everything closes (really only Thanksgiving, Christmas and New Year's Day) and many shops, including the big Midtown department stores, are open on Sunday. Remember, however, that certain (usually ethnic) communities close their shops in accordance with religious and other holi-

days: don't bother to shop on the Lower East Side on Friday afternoon or on Saturday, for example, though places there are open on Sunday. By contrast, Chinatown is open all day every day, while the stores of the Financial District follow the area's nine-to-five routine and for the most part are shut all weekend.

Opening hours in midtown Manhattan are roughly Monday–Saturday 9am–6pm, with late closing on – usually – Thursday; Downtown shops tend to stay open later, at least until 8pm and sometimes until about midnight; bookstores especially are often open late.

As far as **payment** goes, credit and charge cards are as widely accepted as you'd expect: even the smallest of shops will take Visa, American Express, MasterCard (Access) and Diners Club; many department stores also run their own credit schemes. Travelers' checks are a valid currency too, though they must be in US dollars and you may have to provide ID. Remember that an 8.25 percent **city sales tax** will be added to your bill; this is bypassed sometimes when paying cash in a market or discount store. Finally, wherever you're shopping, be careful. Manhattan's crowded, frenzied stores are ripe territory for pickpockets and bag-snatchers.

Shopping neighborhoods of Manhattan

As in most large cities, New York stores are concentrated in specific **neighborhoods**, so if you want something partic-

Shops and Markets

ular you invariably know exactly where to head.

SOUTH STREET SEAPORT/FINANCIAL DISTRICT

This area is mostly composed of three malls – one at **South Street Seaport** and the other two in the **World Trade Center** and the **World Financial Center**. All contain stores that you can pretty much find elsewhere. South Street Seaport especially is very touristy but very historic and very pleasant, with a great view of the Brooklyn Bridge. There aren't too many other places to shop

Downtown, with the notable exception of two discount department stores: Century 21 (22 Cortlandt St) and Syms (42 Trinity Place).

LOWER EAST SIDE

Bordered by Canal St on the south and Houston St on the north, Orchard St is the main artery of the Jewish **Lower East Side**. It's worth a trip for its cheap clothes stores, especially on Sunday when its 200 shops are open only to pedestrians. With merchandise out on the street, it is something of an open-air bazaar. Some merchants, like Ben

Shops and Markets

Freedman (137 Orchard), have been there since its pushcart heyday around the turn of the century.

CHINATOWN

Bustling with energy and activity all the time, a trip to **Chinatown** is worthwhile just for the sights. While the two main streets are Canal and Mott, which bisect each other, Chinatown continues to grow. It has now completely encircled Little Italy, making it a sort of island in a Chinese sea. If you're interested in shopping, the food down here is beautiful, fresh and remarkably cheap. You can also get prepared food (noodles, fried rice, etc) for a few dollars from carts on the south side of Canal St. There is a wonderful grocery store, Kam-Man (200 Canal off Mulberry), that sells all sorts of paraphernalia downstairs, including dishware; Pearl River (277 Canal St) is a popular Chinese department store, while Pearl Paint across the street is one of the world's best art supply stores (see p.90).

SOHO

The area **So**uth of **Ho**uston, north of Broome and between Lafayette and 6th Ave, is one of the most lively and fashionable in the city. Along Broadway, from Canal St up to Astor Place, shoes, jeans and sneaker stores fill the blocks – most notably Canal Jeans Co (504 Broadway), where the assortment of clothes, old and new, is almost overwhelming. There are chains too, such as The Gap and Pottery Barn, and it is west of here, down Prince and Spring sts, that you encounter high fashion, trendy shoes, beautiful antiques and home furnishings along with all of the accompanying attitude – this is the place to go for up-to-the-minute fashion.

Just east of SoHo and north of Little Italy is a fairly new shopping neighborhood currently and cleverly known as **NoLIta** (centered in the area east from Lafayette to the Bowery, and between Prince and Houston). Many local artists, jewelry-makers and designers have set up shop here, such as at Push Jewelry (240 Mulberry St) and Kelly Christy (235 Elizabeth St). If you want to check out what's hip in New York don't skip over this section of town. It's also a good place to get away from central SoHo's more madding crowds.

GREENWICH VILLAGE

The **Village** plays host to a wide variety of more offbeat stores: small boutiques, secondhand bookshops and almost pedantically specialized stores, selling nothing but candles or a hundred different types of caviar. On Christopher St to the west of 7th Ave are several stores catering specifically to gays, with all sorts of merchandise options; 8th St is traditionally shoe central (erring on the hip side). Most shops are small and charming and can be found on the streets that fit the same description; the atmosphere itself makes this a fun shopping neighborhood.

THE EAST VILLAGE

For some shopping on the funkier side of life, hit the **East Village** – at its best along 9th St and also down Ave A. This neighborhood is crammed with one-of-a-kind shops and boutiques like Gabbriel Ichak Design Studio (430 E 9th St between 1st Ave and Ave A), where they specialize in accessories made of recycled materials, the self-explanatory Kimono House (93 E 7th St at 1st Ave), and Body Worship, nearby at 102 E 7th, with its stylish fetish wear. There are many other hip stores, mostly featuring local designers and elegant home furnishings, on 9th St between 2nd Ave and Ave A. If you're on the prowl for vintage clothes, head to the area to the south and west of Tompkins Square Park, mostly along side streets such as 7th St. The most famous consumer strip in the neighborhood, **St Mark's Place**, is now somewhat of a charmless sidewalk sale, but good for cheap CDs, T-shirts or jewelry.

CHELSEA

6th Ave in **Chelsea** is lined with places to shop, mostly giant superstores;

there's Barnes & Noble and Bed, Bath & Beyond, and cheap clothiers like Filene's Basement, Old Navy and Today's Man. However, as you move west toward 7th and 8th aves you encounter some smaller, more unusual shops like Eclectic Home (224 8th Ave at 21st St) and Roger & Dave (123 7th Ave between 17th and 18th sts), the latter good for kitschy T-shirts. Chelsea is also the home of the city's largest lesbian and gay bookstore (A Different Light at 151 W 19th St between 6th and 7th aves) as well as several other gay-friendly stores. For odds and ends, there's the Chelsea Antiques Fair and Flea Market at 26th St and 6th Ave on weekends. The **Flower District** is nearby on 6th Ave between 26th and 30th sts and has the city's largest concentration of plants and flowers. If you can't find what you want here, be it houseplant, tree, dried, cut or artificial flower, then it's a fair bet it's not available anywhere else in New York. Finally, as Manhattan's wholesale **garment district**, Chelsea is a best bet for warehouse sales of clothes and shoes (you're likely to get handed flyers on the street), and lingerie wholesalers are concentrated around and east of Broadway and W 28th St. The blocks between 6th and 7th aves in the 30s – can be a good place for picking up designer clothes, fabric and trimmings (beads, buttons and ribbon) at a discount. There's an office here for every women's garment retailer and manufacturer in the country, and though some are wary of selling to non-wholesale customers, you can pick up some enviable bargains at sample sales. Dave's A & N Jeans (779 6th Ave) is Manhattan's best spot for discount jeans; for a wonderful array of tassels and buttons, start at M & J Trimming (1008 6th Ave at 38th St).

LOWER FIFTH AVENUE/FLATIRON

Between the Flatiron Building at 23rd St and Union Square at 14th St, **5th Ave and Broadway**, and their side streets, have become a great shopping neigh-

borhood. You'll find street fashion standards like Banana Republic (17th St and 5th) and J. Crew (5th at 17th St) as well as new and established designers such as Eileen Fisher (5th between 17th and 18th sts) and Matsuda (5th and 20th St). Home furnishings are reigned over by ABC Carpet and Home (19th St and Broadway) and Domain (Broadway at 22nd St); and off-beat merchandise such as vintage gravy boats can be procured at Fish's Eddy (19th St and Broadway).

HERALD SQUARE

The small triangular park where 6th Ave and Broadway intersect, at 34th St, is named **Herald Square**, an unlikely center of New York's busiest shopping district. Locals and tourists alike come here for clothes, shoes and accessories; during holidays, the crowds are almost unfathomable. The main reason, of course, is Macy's department store, where 35,000 shoppers visit daily. Located one block east on 34th St are Limited Express, Lerner, Manhattan's flagship Gap, an HMV music store, and The Athlete's Foot. On the bargain end, there are several Conways for inexpensive clothes and housewares. There's also Daffy's, Toys R Us and Manhattan Mall along 6th Ave.

FIFTH AVENUE

Just south of Central Park, **5th Ave** in the 50s is a neighborhood filled with the best-known international designer stores: department stores like Henri Bendel (at 56th St), Saks (at 50th St, across the street from Rockefeller Center) and Takashimaya (between 54th and 55th sts); jewelry stores such as Bulgari (at 57th St) and Cartier (at 52nd St); and designer boutiques including Christian Dior (at 55th St) and Gucci (at 54th St). A lot of the little shops have been replaced by theme stores, like the Warner Brothers Studio Store (at 57th St) and the Coca-Cola Store (one of the earliest, at 55th St). As you travel Downtown toward 34th St, the prices and merchandise get more downscale. West of 5th Ave in the 40s is the **Diamond District**, where you

Shops and Markets

Shops and Markets

can browse the jewelry marts and select your own gems and settings. South of 42nd St is Lord & Taylor (at 39th St), many electronics and camera stores and inexpensive "going-out-of-business" stores selling fakes.

57TH STREET

This is one of the most exclusive shopping streets in the world, bound by Lexington on the east and capped by 7th Ave and Carnegie Hill on the west. Almost all top designers have a boutique on 57th St, only found elsewhere in Paris, Milan and LA, its classiness anchored by Bergdorf Goodman, Tiffany, Chanel, Escada and Tourneau. However, this junction with 5th Ave isn't only steeped in luxury, as evidenced by chains like Pottery Barn, Victoria's Secret, Limited Express, Bolton's and a Borders superstore. On Lexington, the glitter returns at fast and fun Bloomingdale's department store, which is surrounded by Banana Republic, Urban Outfitters and the Levi's 501 store.

UPPER WEST SIDE

Most of the shopping done between 66th and 86th sts, west of Central Park and north of Lincoln Center, happens on Broadway, Columbus Ave and Amsterdam Ave. The **Upper West Side** has perhaps the city's greatest concentration of intellectuals, especially if judged by the number of bookstores and cafés. Two giant Barnes & Noble bookstores (Broadway at 66th St and 82nd St) host readings almost every night, and Tower Records and HMV battle with one another for preeminence between 66th and 72nd sts. There's an array of off-the-wall stores, antique shops, secondhand clothing, craft and design shops to challenge any funky area in the city, including Allan & Suzi (416 Amsterdam at 80th St), which claims to have restarted the platform shoe craze and features chain-mail bikinis in its ever-changing window. On upper Broadway and Columbus Ave you'll find shopping staples of the

1990s: Laura Ashley, Ann Taylor, Gap, Body Shop, Banana Republic, Limited Express, Pottery Barn and Talbots, as well as unusual clothes and home shops like Handblock (487 Columbus Ave) and uppercrust thrift shops like Housing Works (306 Columbus Ave). The **Green Flea Market**, in the I.S. 44 schoolyard at 77th and Columbus, has become a neighborhood institution, with clothing, jewelry, collectibles, vintage clothes, lingerie and a farmer's market, and is nicely complemented in the spring and summer by the white canvas booths of art and fine jewelry vendors ranged alongside the American Museum of Natural History across the street.

UPPER EAST SIDE

Madison Ave in the 60s, 70s and 80s – the core of the **Upper East Side** shopping neighborhood – is filled with exclusive clothiers and antique and art dealers. Bloomingdale's department store marks the southern end of this neighborhood, at 59th St and Lexington Ave. Between 62nd and 72nd sts there are no fewer than twenty designer shoe stores, as well as dozens of European fashion boutiques including Armani, Gianni Versace, Krizia, Valentino and Prada. Ralph Lauren (at 71st St) is one of the few American designers here; also unusual is the designer discount store Bis (24 E 81st). Because this is also a residential neighborhood, there's a smattering of children's stores, coffee shops, restaurants and bars. The waning German community influence is most visible at the intersection of 82nd St and 2nd Ave, with Kramer's Pastries and Schaller & Weber butchers. Most of the museums on Museum Mile have elegant shops (museums unto themselves) – most notably the Metropolitan Museum, with its exquisite jewelry reproductions from all eras of history.

HARLEM

The main shopping district of **Harlem**, New York's most famous African-American community, is 125th St. The shopping district extends from Park Ave, where the MetroNorth commuter trains stop, to Frederick Douglass Blvd, where the new Harlem USA theme-mall, under construction at press time, will house a Disney Store, an HMV, a Gap and a Cineplex Odeon. The stores are mostly mundane and the goods mainly cheap. Though many vendors have been moved from the street due to political wrangling, Mart 123 (125th St between Frederick Douglas and Adam Clayton Powell blvds) holds nearly forty, selling everything from fresh produce and T-shirts to incense and kitchen appliances. Don't miss the Malcolm Shabazz Harlem Market, in its new minaret-framed home between Lenox and Fifth, for beautiful African imports, and the museum store at The Studio Museum in Harlem (144 W 125th St). The best shop in the city for African crafts is African Paradise (27 W 125th St), with its herbal medicines, black soaps, baskets, musical instruments and much more; Our Black Heritage at 2295 Adam Clayton Powell Blvd sells tapes of great speeches by black leaders and greetings cards and books with a black theme.

Department stores and malls

Saks Fifth Avenue, Lord & Taylor, Bloomingdale's and Macy's are among the world's greatest (and most beautiful) **department stores**. However, the last fifteen years or so have seen a number of the better established ones close down. Others have gone upmarket, making them less places to stock up on essentials and more outlets for designer clothes and chichi accessories, full of concessions on the top-line names. Most department stores offer restaurants and complimentary personal shopping, alterations and concierge service: they'll make your dinner reservations, secure tickets to the theater, call a taxi and more. Ask for details at each store's information desk.

Manhattan also has a number of **shopping malls**. Housed in purpose-built locations or in conversions of older premises, several of them are a lot of fun to shop in – and a far cry from the megamalls of the American suburbs. The larger and more important ones are listed below.

Department stores

Barney's, 600 Madison Ave (between 60th and 61st sts) ☎826-8900. Mon–Fri 10am–8pm, Sat 10am–7pm, Sun noon–6pm. Though a proper department store, Barney's actually concentrates on clothes, particularly men's, with the emphasis on high-flying, up-to-the-minute designer garments, alongside a relatively new women's wear department. If you've got the money, there's no better place in the city to look for clothes. There's a smaller branch at 225 Liberty St in the World Financial Center mall ☎945-1600.

Bergdorf Goodman, 754 5th Ave (at 58th St) ☎753-7300. Mon–Wed, Fri & Sat 10am–7pm, Thurs 10am–8pm. Come if only to ogle the windows, which approach high art with their rhinestone-encrusted diaphanous dress displays. Everything about Bergdorf's speaks of its attempt to be New York City's most elegant and wealth-oriented department store. Lucky that most of the folk who shop here have purses stacked with charge cards – the rustle of money would utterly ruin the feel. The men's store is across 5th Ave.

Bloomingdale's, 1000 3rd Ave (at 59th St) ☎355-5900. Mon–Fri 10am-8.30pm, Sat 10am–7pm, Sun 11am–7pm. New Yorkers are proud of Bloomingdale's: somehow it's an affirmation of their status, their sense of style, and, perhaps most importantly, their ability to inject a little whimsy into a major department store. Bloomies – as the store is popularly known – has the atmosphere of a large, bustling bazaar, packed full of concessions to perfumiers and designer clothes. Whatever you want, they're likely to stock it.

Henri Bendel, 712 5th Ave (between 55th and 56th sts) ☎247-1100.

Shops and Markets

Mon–Wed, Fri & Sat 10am–7pm, Thurs 10am–8pm, Sun noon–6pm. This store, is and always has been deliberately more gentle in its approach than the biggies, with a name for exclusivity and top-line modern designers. One of Manhattan's most refined shopping experiences, thanks in part to its classy reuse of the old Coty perfume building, with windows by Rene Lalique. Stylists on hand to escort the serious from boutique to boutique.

Lord & Taylor, 424 5th Ave (at 39th St) ☎391-3344. Mon, Tues & Sat 10am–7pm, Wed–Fri 10am–8.30pm, Sun 11am–6pm. Most venerable of the New York specialty stores, in business since 1826 and to some extent the most pleasant, with a more traditional feel than Macy's or Bloomingdale's. Though no longer at the forefront of New York fashion, it's still good for classic designer fashions, petites, winter coats, household goods and accessories, and the more basic items.

Macy's, 151 W 34th St (on Broadway at Herald Square) ☎695-4400. Mon–Sat 10am–8.30pm, Sun 11am–7pm. Quite simply, the largest department store in the world with two buildings, two million square feet of floor space, ten floors (four for women's garments alone). Unfortunately not the hotbed of top fashion it ought to be: most of the merchandise is of mediocre quality (particularly the jewelry), although real fashion is steadily returning. But The Cellar, the downstairs housewares department, is arguably the best in the city.

Saks Fifth Avenue, 611 5th Ave (at 50th St) ☎753-4000. Mon–Wed, Fri & Sat 10am–6.30pm, Thurs 10am–8pm, Sun noon–6pm. The name is virtually synonymous with style, and, although Saks has retained its name for quality, it has also updated itself to carry the merchandise of all the big designers. Shopping here is more like a stroll, along Saks' unique winding pathways. In any case, with the glittering array of celebrities that use the place regularly, Saks can't fail. The ground floor is lovely when decorated with sparkling white branches at Christmas time.

Sterns, 899 6th Ave (at 33rd St) ☎244-6060. Mon, Thurs, Fri 10am–8pm, Tues, Wed, Sat 10am–7pm, Sun 11am–6pm. The focus of the Manhattan Mall, this store is similar in look and merchandise to ones found in suburbs across the nation. Go to shop, not to soak in atmosphere.

Takashimaya, 693 5th Ave (between 54th and 55th sts) ☎350-0100. Mon–Wed, Fri & Sat 10am–6pm, Thurs 10am–8pm. A relative newcomer to New York, with other locations in Tokyo and Paris. Beautiful Japanese department store with a scaled-down assortment of expensive merchandise, simply displayed, and exquisitely wrapped purchases. Stop by the café, *The Tea Box*, on the lower level, where there is also an assortment of teapots and loose tea.

Shopping malls

Manhattan Mall, 100 W 33rd St (at 6th Ave) ☎465-0500. Perhaps because of its location a block away from Macy's, this large, mirror-fronted and rather glitzy multilevel shopping center has never really been a success, a humdrum string of mainstream stores in what resembles nothing so much as a suburban shopping mall.

Pier 17, South Street Seaport. Again, not quite the shopping experience it's cracked up to be, what with the preponderance of mall-style vendors, but the barn-like building and its historic surroundings of ships, docks and old warehouses are fascinating and fun, the river views from the deck are lovely, and The Sharper Image stocks some terrifying and ingenious toys for adults.

Trump Tower, 725 5th Ave (between 56th and 57th sts) ☎832-2000. Donald Trump's retail triumph was constructed in his own image. Gaudy caterer to the wealthy, with a range of exclusive boutiques set around a deep, marbled atrium with a several-story goldtone waterfall that marks it out as a tourist attraction in itself.

World Financial Center, Battery Park City. Centered around the huge, greenhouse-like Winter Garden, this is worth a visit just for a look at the development as a whole, and it has a handful of intriguing stores. On the other hand, it's rather out of the way just for a spot of shopping.

Clothes and fashion

Dressing right is important to many in Manhattan, and fashion is a key reference point, though you may find that **clothes** are more about status here than setting trailblazing trends. Although New York may be streets in front of the rest of the country fashion-wise, compared to the cutting-edge in Europe it can sometimes seem slightly behind, unless you are in an international designer's boutique. If you are prepared to search the city with sufficient dedication you can find just about anything, but it's **designer clothes** and the snob values that go with them that predominate. **Secondhand clothes**, of the "vintage" or "antique" variety, have caught on of late, and upscale designer vintage stores abound. Unfortunately this popularity has driven the prices up, but it is still possible to find bargains here and there.

Chain stores

Ann Taylor, 575 5th Ave (at 47th St; flagship store) ☎922-3621. Medium-priced business and elegant casual clothing for women. More than ten branches throughout the city; check the phone book for exact locations.

Banana Republic, 655 5th Ave (at 52nd St; flagship store) ☎644-6678. Owned by the same company that owns Gap, these stores originally stocked expensive wear for the chic traveler: boots, bags, designer safari suits, etc. Now they offer an upscale, minimalist version of Gap clothing. More than ten branches throughout the city; check the phone book for exact locations.

Benetton, 597 5th Ave at 48th St ☎593-0290. Italian chain offering youthful, contemporary, casual, bright-colored clothing for women, men and children.

The flagship store is located in the landmark Scribners building, an insult to many serious book buyers.

Brooks Brothers, 346 Madison Ave ☎682-8800; also 666 5th Ave. Something of an institution in New York. Classic conservative style selling the tweeds, gabardines and quietly striped shirts and ties it did fifty years ago. Women's line is catching up with its male counterpart.

Burberry's, 9 E 57th St (between 5th and Madison aves) ☎371-5010. Classic plaids and tweeds, with a distinctly British feel to the conservative designs.

Club Monaco, 160 5th Ave ☎352-0936; also 121 Prince St, 520 Broadway, 111 3rd Ave, 2376 Broadway. Understated simplicity is the theme at this newish chain of stylish and well-priced clothing for men and women. It's like New York's own version of the Gap.

Diesel, 770 Lexington (at 60th St) ☎308-0055. One of five stores in the States that sell this Italian-designed label. Funky, some vintage-inspired club wear, lots of denim. Two floors including a café.

Eileen Fisher, 103 5th Ave between 17th and 18th sts ☎924-4777. This is the largest of their four NY shops full of loose and elegantly casual clothes for women. Their outlet is on 9th St between 1st and 2nd aves ☎529-5715.

Gap, 60 W 34th St and Herald Square (flagship store) ☎643-8960. Dressing most of the United States (and, soon perhaps, most of Europe). You can get the essentials here – lots of denim and the latest casual cotton trends, including bathing suits and underwear. Gap Kids and Baby Gap now complement their parents. Branches on every other corner of the city (around 25 in Manhattan); check the phone book for exact locations. Circular sale racks in the back of many stores offer terrific reductions, as style turnover is high.

J. Crew, 99 Prince St (at Mercer; flagship store) ☎966-2739. Better known as a mail-order company, but its retail stores

Shops and Markets

Shops and Markets

are popping up all across the country. Serving both men and women, the casual clothing is a safe bet although they do offer some dressier pieces. Others at 91 5th Ave and 16th St, 770 Broadway, and 203 Front St (South Street Seaport area).

Laura Ashley, 398 Columbus Ave (at 79th St) ☎496-5110. Expanded beyond the floral prints this store is known for. Contemporary cotton, linen and silk clothing for women and children as well as country-style home furnishings.

The Limited, 691 Madison Ave (at 62nd St) ☎838-8787; another branch at 4 World Trade Center. Moderately priced casual clothing for women.

Limited Express, 7 W 34th St (between 5th and 6th aves) ☎629-6838; other branches include Pier 17 at the South Street Seaport and 46th St at 3rd Ave. An offshoot of The Limited stores, they carry similar, albeit trendier, versions of the same type of clothing.

Urban Outfitters, 628 Broadway (between Houston and Bleecker sts) ☎475-0009; at 360 6th Ave and Waverly Place, 162 2nd Ave and 127 E 59th St at Lexington Ave. Stylish and oh-so-trendy chain with prices which have raised dramatically but designs that are still irresistible.

Designer stores

As you might expect, New York has an unrivaled selection of **designer clothing stores**, and if you have any interest in clothes at all these should not be missed, even if only for an afternoon of people-watching. Internationally known **design houses** are concentrated Uptown on 5th Ave in the 50s and on Madison Ave in the 60s and 70s. Downtown the newer, younger designers are found in SoHo, the East and West Villages and TriBeCa. In any of these neighborhoods they are close enough to enjoy walking from one to another. Dress well, and you'll be welcomed whether browsing or buying. Most are open Mon to Sat 10am–6pm, but call to check.

UPTOWN DESIGNERS

April Cornell, 487 Columbus Ave (at 83rd St) ☎779-4342. Pastoral designs reminiscent of *Little House on the Prairie*, delicate dresses, lingerie, jewelry and colorful housewares as well.

Calvin Klein, 654 Madison Ave ☎292-9000.

Chanel, 15 E 57th St (at 5th Ave) ☎355-5050.

Charivari, 18 W 57th St ☎333-4040. Once a chain, now consolidated into one location, Charivari remains the solid bastion of ready-to-wear New York street fashion.

Christian Dior, 712 5th Ave (at 55th St) ☎582-0500.

Emanuel Ungaro, 792 Madison Ave (at 67th St) ☎249-4090.

Gianni Versace, 647 5th Ave ☎317-0224 or 755-4826.

Giorgio Armani, 760 Madison Ave (at 68th St) ☎988-9191.

Gucci, 685 5th Ave (at 54th St) ☎826-2600.

Hermes, 11 E 57th St ☎751-3181.

Krizia, 769 Madison Ave (between 65th and 66th sts) ☎879-1211.

Paul Stuart, Madison Ave at 45th St ☎682-0320. Classic men's garb, not unlike Brooks Brothers but more stylish.

Polo Ralph Lauren, 867 Madison Ave ☎606-2100; and **Polo Sport Ralph Lauren**, 888 Madison Ave ☎434-8000.

Prada, Madison Ave and E 70th St ☎327-0488.

Valentino Boutique, 747 Madison Ave (at 63rd St) ☎772-6969.

Yves Saint Laurent Boutique, 855 Madison Ave (between 70th and 71st sts) ☎988-3821.

DOWNTOWN DESIGNERS

agnès b, women's 116–118 Prince St (between Greene and Wooster sts) ☎925-4649; men's 79 Greene St ☎431-4339; 13 E 16th St ☎741-2585; 1063 Madison Ave (between 80th and 81st sts) ☎570-9333.

Clothing and shoe sizes

Women's dresses and skirts

American	4	6	8	10	12	14	16	18
British	6	8	10	12	14	16	18	20
Continental	38	40	42	44	46	48	50	52

Women's blouses and sweaters

American	6	8	10	12	14	16	18
British	30	32	34	36	38	40	42
Continental	40	42	44	46	48	50	52

Women's shoes

American	5	6	7	8	9	10	11
British	3	4	5	6	7	8	9
Continental	36	37	38	39	40	41	42

Men's suits

American	34	36	38	40	42	44	46	48
British	34	36	38	40	42	44	46	48
Continental	44	46	48	50	52	54	56	58

Men's shirts

American	14	15	$15\frac{1}{2}$	16	$16\frac{1}{2}$	17	$17\frac{1}{2}$	18
British	14	15	$15\frac{1}{2}$	16	$16\frac{1}{2}$	17	$17\frac{1}{2}$	18
Continental	36	38	39	41	42	43	44	45

Men's shoes

American	7	$7\frac{1}{2}$	8	$8\frac{1}{2}$	$9\frac{1}{2}$	10	$10\frac{1}{2}$	11	$11\frac{1}{2}$
British	6	7	$7\frac{1}{2}$	8	9	$9\frac{1}{2}$	10	11	12
Continental	39	40	41	42	43	44	44	45	46

Shops and Markets

Anna Sui, 113 Greene St (between Prince and Spring sts) ☎941-8406.

Bagutta, 402 W Broadway ☎925-5216. A confluence of top designers including Helmut Lang, Prada, Gaultier, Plein Sud, Dolce & Gabbana.

Beau Brummel, 421 W Broadway (between Prince and Spring sts) ☎219-2666.

Betsey Johnson, 130 Thompson St (between Prince and Houston sts) ☎420-0169; 248 Columbus (at 72nd St) ☎362-3364; 251 E 60th St (at 2nd Ave) ☎319-7699; 1060 Madison Ave (at 80th St) ☎734-1257.

Comme des Garçons, 116 Wooster St (between Prince and Spring sts) ☎219-0660.

Cynthia Rowley, 108 Wooster St (between Prince and Spring sts) ☎334-1144.

Daryl K, 208 E 6th St (between 2nd and 3rd sts) ☎475-1255; 21 Bond St at Broadway ☎777-0713. This Irish designer has taken NYC fashion by storm.

Emporio Armani, 110 5th Ave at (18th St) or 601 Madison Ave. Here you'll find the lower-priced, more mass-produced Armani line; and for his most relaxed, inexpensive look, head for **Armani Exchange**, 568 Broadway (at Prince St).

Helmut Lang, 80 Greene St ☎925-7214.

Meaghan Kinney Studio, 312 E 9th St (between 1st and 2nd aves) ☎260-6329. By designing clothes with classic lines complimenting the female form, Ms Kinney has made herself a stand out on 9th St.

Miu Miu, 100 Prince St ☎334-5156. Gorgeous fashion for women.

Shops and Markets

Paul Smith, 108 5th Ave (at 16th St) ☎627-9770. Excellent sophisticated menswear.

Tracey Feith, 280 Mulberry St ☎925-6544. Great new designer of women's clothing.

Vivienne Tam, 99 Greene St (between Prince and Spring sts) ☎966-2398.

Yohji Yamamoto, 103 Grand St (at Mercer St) ☎966-9066.

Funky, Trendy, Hip

Whatever you want to call it, you know what you're looking for. Check out 7th St and 9th St between 3rd Ave and Ave A for a prodigious number of stores carrying the above-mentioned desirables. And definitely search through Ludlow, Mott and Elizabeth sts south of Houston.

Big Drop, 174 Spring St (between Thompson and W Broadway) ☎966-4299. Clothes for forward-thinking women.

Calypso St Barth's, 280 Mott St ☎965-0990. Forget black, color is the game here. Vibrant fashions such as string bikinis for $70.

Canal Jean Co, 504 Broadway (between Spring and Broome sts) ☎226-1130. Enormous warehousey store sporting a prodigious array of jeans, jackets, T-shirts, dresses, hats and more, new and secondhand. Young, fun and reasonably cheap.

Center for the Dull, 216 Lafayette (between Spring and Broome sts) ☎925-9699. Psychedelic store with lots of funky "dead stock" (never-sold) from the 1960s, 1970s and 1980s, including go-go boots, halter tops, tube tops and slinky mylar shirts. Price range $10–100, most items around $20–40. For men and women.

Liquid Sky, 241 Lafayette (between Spring and Prince sts) ☎343-0532. Lots of club clothes and transferred T-shirts. Great designs. For men and women. Intriguing trance/techno music store downstairs.

Mode, 109 St Mark's Place ☎529-9208. Inspiring collection of clothes by new designers. Ask German designer and store employee Daniel L. to help uncover the hidden, stylish you.

Patricia Field, 10 E 8th St (between 5th Ave and University Place) ☎254-1699. Touted as Manhattan's most inventive clothes store, Pat Field was one of the first NYC vendors of "punk chic" and has since blossomed into one of the few Downtown emporia that yuppie Uptowners will actually visit.

Pierre Garroudi, 139 Thompson St (between Houston and Prince sts) ☎475-2333. A limited design line with unusual fabrics, colors and styles. Bias cut dresses, wedding gowns and tailored suits. All of the clothes are made on the premises and they can make any item for you overnight. Reasonable prices.

TG-170, 170 Ludlow St (between Houston and Stanton sts) ☎995-8660. Small, unique store featuring emerging local designers. A favorite with the East Village crowd.

Trash 'n' Vaudeville, 4 St Mark's Place (between 2nd and 3rd aves) ☎982-3590. Famous to the extent that it advertises its wares in British magazines like *ID*. Great clothes, new and "antique," in the true East Village spirit, including classic lace-up muscle shirts.

Utility Canvas, 146 Sullivan (just south of Houston St) ☎673-2203. Stylish and comfortable clothing line for men and women. Not so funky but definitely hip.

X-Large, 267 Lafayette ☎334-4480. Check out the Mini line for women, X-Large for men. Cutting edge streetwear, trendy club kid T-Shirts. Mike D of the Beastie Boys is a part-owner.

Vintage/secondhand

The East Village is the neighborhood for this kind of shopping. Wander up and down the side streets east of 3rd Ave and west of Ave B, where the stores are too numerous to mention. But there are many good options throughout the city.

a tempo couture, 290 Columbus Ave (between 73rd and 74th sts) ☎769-0368. Exquisite vintage dresses and evening gowns.

Alice Underground, 481 Broadway (between Broome and Grand sts) ☎431-9067. A large assortment contained in bins you have to dig through. A good selection of vintage linens, dresses, lingerie and shoes.

Allan & Suzi, 416 Amsterdam Ave (at 80th St) ☎724-7445. Beautiful far-out fashion from the last several decades. Claims to have single-handedly restarted the platform shoe craze.

Antique Boutique, 712–714 Broadway (at Washington Place); 227 E 59th St (between 2nd and 3rd aves) ☎460-8830. Wedding dresses from the 40s, used Levis, suede jackets and Diesel, Betsey Johnson and Pat Field meet up at this vintage institution.

Darrow, 7 W 19th St (between 5th and 6th aves) ☎255-1550. Designer and never-worn vintage, with a friendly and helpful staff. Popular with top models.

The Fan Club, 22 W 19th St (between 5th and 6th aves) ☎929-3349. An amazing selection of vintage clothes, many from movies, TV and theater, with a good supply of Marilyn Monroe frocks usually on display in the front window. The store benefits three AIDS charities.

Honeymoon Antiques, 105 Ave B ☎477-8768. A mix of old T-shirts and vintage fashion in the heart of Alphabet City. You won't leave empty-handed.

Housing Works Thrift Shop, 143 W 17th St (between 6th and 7th aves) ☎366-0820; 306 Columbus Ave ☎579-7566; 202 E 77th St ☎772-8461. Upscale thrift shops where you can find secondhand designer wear in very good condition. All proceeds benefit Housing Works, an AIDS social service organization.

Love Saves the Day, 119 2nd Ave (at 7th St) ☎228-3802. Fairly cheap vintage as well as classic lunchboxes and other kitschy nostalgia items, including valuable Kiss and Star Wars dolls.

Michael's: The Consignment Shop, 1041 Madison (between 79th and 80th sts) ☎737-7273. For bridal wear as well as slightly used designer women's clothing from names like Ungaro, Armani and Chanel.

Out of the Closet, 220 E 81st St ☎472-3573. One of the Upper East Side's most charming thrift shops, with an antique feel and a greenhouse. Established to help AIDS sufferers.

Out of Our Closet Consignment, 15 W 17th St (between 5th and 6th aves) ☎633-6965. Specializing in top-end designers like Gucci, Prada and Helmut Lang. You can also find new clothes direct from the showroom.

Reminiscence, 50 W 23rd St ☎243-2292. Remember the everything-with-palm-trees craze of the 1980s? Relive it here (the store's logo is a palm tree). They also carry funky secondhand and new clothes for men and women. Staples include Hawaiian shirts, tie-string overalls and tube tops.

Resurrection, 123 E 7th St (between 1st Ave and Ave A) ☎228-0063; and 217 Mott St ☎625-1374. Specializing in designer vintage (Pucci, Christian Dior) in excellent condition at reasonable prices. Attracts designers and models.

The Ritz Thrift Shop, 107 W 57th St (between 6th and 7th aves) ☎265-4559. New York's venerable and best source for used furs, known as "The Miracle on 57th Street." Imagine, get a $15,000 mink for only $2000!

Screaming Mimi's, 382 Lafayette St (between 4th St and Great Jones) ☎677-6464. One of the most established vintage stores in Manhattan. Vintage clothes (including lingerie), bags, shoes and housewares at reasonable prices.

Stella Dallas, 218 Thompson St (between Bleecker and 3rd sts) ☎674-0447. A relatively small selection, but very nice quality vintage clothing with a beautiful selection of scarves (most $1–3). Also hand-embroidered vintage linens.

Tokio 7, 64 E 7th St (between 1st and 2nd aves) ☎353-8443. Attractive sec-

Shops and Markets

Shops and Markets

ondhand and vintage consignment items.

Valentino Mastroianni, 218 W 29th St (between 7th and 8th aves) ☎947-9347. More like a museum than a vintage store, with the look of an old-moneyed attic. Arranged beneath the crystal chandelier are beaded bags, floppy hats, gowns and other fragile antiques, many reasonably priced.

The Village Scandal, 19 E 7th St (between 2nd and 3rd aves) ☎253-2002. Small and friendly shop, with fashionable clothing at decent prices.

What Comes Around Goes Around, 351 W Broadway (between Broome and Grand sts) ☎343-9303. Established and well-loved Downtown vintage store.

Discount clothing

Aaron's, 627 5th Ave (between 17th and 18th sts), Brooklyn ☎718/768-5400. This 10,000-square-foot store carries discounted designer fashions ranging from Jones

New York to Adrienne Vittadini at the beginning of each season, not the end. Prices are marked down about 25 percent. It's 30 minutes from Manhattan – take the R train to Brooklyn, get off at the Prospect Ave Station/4th Ave and 17th St in Brooklyn. Walk one block east to 5th Ave.

Century 21, 12 Cortlandt St ☎227-9092. A department store with designer brands for half the cost, a favorite among budget yet label-conscious New Yorkers. Only snag – no dressing rooms. If you can make the trip – there are better prices and more selection in the Brooklyn store at 472 86th St ☎718/748-3266 (take the R train to 86th St and 4th Ave).

Daffy's. Four locations in Manhattan; the biggest one is at Herald Square, 6th Ave and 34th St ☎736-4477. Name-brand clothes at discount prices for men, women and children. Specializes in Italian designers such as Les Copian.

Dave's Army & Navy Store, 581 6th Ave (between 16th and 17th sts) ☎989-

---

Sample sales

At the beginning of each season, designers and manufacturers' showrooms are full of **leftover merchandise** that is removed via these informal sales. You'll always save at least fifty percent off the retail price, though you may not be able to try on the clothes and you can never return them. As well, while some take credit cards, be prepared with cash. The best times for sample sales are spring and fall. Short of waiting for advertisement fliers to be stuffed into your hands while walking through the garment district, the following sources (particularly the up-to-the-minute Web sites) are helpful.

Nice Price, 493 Columbus Ave (at 84th St) ☎362-1020. The owners of this terrific designer outlet store run regular sample sales. Pick up a printed card at the store or call their sample sale hotline ☎947-8748.

S&B Report. Find out about designer showroom sales, as well as the best retail sales, and consignment and thrift shops in *Sales and Bargains* magazine. It is published monthly by NYC's other bargain expert, Elysa Lazar, who *Redbook* magazine called "the world's smartest shopper." Send

$9.95 for the month's issue that coincides with your trip to NY, or you can subscribe for $59 a year. The *Black Belt Bulletin*, which lists latebreaking sales, is $3 an issue; $124 is the yearly rate for both. Address: Lazar Media Group, Inc. 56 1/2 Queen St, Charleston, SC 29401 ☎toll free 877/579-0222; *www.lazarshopping. com*.

www.styleshop.com This Web site is a goldmine of detailed information about current designer sample sales, including collections, locations and dates.

6444. Comes recommended as the best place to buy jeans in Manhattan. Helpful assistants, no blaring music, and brands other than just Levi's.

Filene's Basement, a newcomer to NY's discount shopping, a favorite in the suburbs. 620 6th Ave (at 18th St) is the bigger one ☎620-3100: there is also one at Broadway and 79th St.

Labels for Less, biggest branch is at 1345 6th Ave (at 54th St) ☎956-2450. The name says it all – a national chain with 13 stores in Manhattan selling discount designer labels for women.

Loehmann's, biggest branch is at 101 7th Ave (between 16th and 17th sts), ☎352-0856. New York's best-known department store for designer clothes at knockdown prices. No refunds and no exchanges, but there are individual dressing rooms. Other locations are 2103 Emmons Ave, Brooklyn ☎718/368-1256; 60-06 99th St, Rego Park, Queens ☎718/271-4000; and the original store at 5740 Broadway, Riverdale, the Bronx ☎718/543-6420.

Nice Price, 493 Columbus Ave (at 84th St), ☎362-1020. An unprepossessing boutique chock-full of overruns and factory seconds from major designers like Max Studio, whose prices drop to unbelievable lows during clearance blitzes. Nice Price also runs sample sales (see box opposite).

Syms, 42 Trinity Place ☎797-1199; and 54th St and Park Ave ☎317-8200. "Where the educated consumer is our best customer." Combine the Downtown Syms and Century 21 in the same trip.

T.J. Maxx, 620 6th Ave (at 18th St) ☎229-0875. Another suburban discount chain, a lot like Filene's, and in the same shopping center.

Shoes

Most department stores carry two or more **shoe** salons – one for less expensive brands and one for finer shoes. Both Bloomingdale's and Lord & Taylor are known for their shoe departments, and

Loehmann's has a vast selection of designer shoes at discount prices. You'll find shoe stores in all clothes-shopping areas, such as 34th St, Columbus Ave, Broadway from Astor Place to Spring St, and Bleecker going south to 6th Ave. The greatest concentration of bargain shoe shops in hip fashions is on W 8th St between University Place and 6th Ave in the Village and on Broadway below W 8th St. **Shoes on Sale** is the largest shoe sale open to the public, with more than 50,000 pairs of shoes. It is held each year around the second week in October, in a tent in Central Park at 5th Ave and 60th St. Check the newspaper for details.

Charles Jourdan, 777 Madison Ave ☎585-2238. Outstanding French designer of fine shoes, who strikes a delicate balance between traditional and contemporary looks.

John Fluevog, 104 Prince St ☎431-4484. Innovative designs for a walk about town. Mostly casual, always hip shoes.

Juno, 550 Broadway (between Prince and Spring) ☎925-6415. High-quality imitations of designer shoes.

Kenneth Cole, 353 Columbus Ave (at 77th St) ☎873-2061; call for more locations. Classic and contemporary shoes, beautiful bags, excellent full-grain leather.

Lady Continental, 932 Madison Ave (at 73rd St) ☎744-2626. If you have $300 to spend, you can't go wrong with these stylish Italian shoes that last 10 years and more.

Manolo Blahnik, 31 W 54th St (between 5th and 6th aves) ☎582-3007. World-famous strappy stilettos – good for height (of fashion), hell for feet.

Manuela di Firenze (Maraolo), 131 W 72nd St ☎787-6550; 782 Lexington Ave ☎832-8182. Attractive, inexpensive Italian shoes in various styles. Seems to be holding a permanent clearance sale.

Otto Tootsi Plohound, 137 5th Ave ☎460-8650; 413 W Broadway ☎925-8931. If you want to run with a trendy crowd these shoes will help. Very current designs.

Shops and Markets

Shops and Markets

The Diamond District

The strip of 47th St between 5th and 6th aves is known as the **Diamond District** of New York. Crammed into this one block are more than 100 shops: combined they sell more jewelry than any other block in the world. The industry has traditionally been run by Hasidic Jews, and you'll run into plenty of black-garbed men with *payess* (side-locks) in this area.

At the street level are dozens of retail shops and over twenty "exchanges" – marts containing booths where many different dealers sell very specific merchandise. For example, 55 W 47th St is home to 115 independent jewelers and repair specialists. Lesser known is the Swiss Center at 608 5th Ave at 49th St, specializing in antique and estate jewelry and housed in an historic Art Deco building.

There are different dealers for different gems, for gold and silver – even dealers who will string your beads for you, and "findings" stores where you can pick up the basic silver makings of do-it-yourself jewelry, like chains and earring posts. Some jewelers trade only among themselves; some sell retail; and others do business by appointment only. Most shops are open Monday through Saturday 10am–5.30pm, though a few close on Friday afternoon and Saturday for religious reasons, and the standard vacation time is from the end of June to the second week in July.

It is very important that you go to the exchanges **educated**. Research what you are looking for and be as specific as possible. It's always better to go to someone who has been recommended to you if possible. Some good starting points are Andrew Cohen, Inc (579 5th Ave, 15th floor), for diamonds; Myron Toback (25 W 47th St), a trusted dealer of silver findings; and Bracie Company Inc (608 5th Ave, suite 806), a friendly business specializing in antique and estate jewelry. Once you buy, there's AA Pearls & Gems (10 W 47th St), the industry's choice for pearl and gem stringing; and, if you want to get your gems graded, the Gemological Institute of America (580 5th Ave, 2nd floor).

Patrick Cox, 702 Madison Ave (between 62nd and 63rd sts) ☎759-3910. Patrick Cox runs the gamut from fun sneakers to elegant evening shoes. Innovative styles and textures.

Salvatore Ferragamo, 663 5th Ave (at 52nd St) ☎759-3822 (women's) and 725 5th Ave (at 56th St), in Trump Tower ☎759-7990 (men's). Wonderful Italian shoes, as well as accessories and clothing.

Sigerson Morrison, 242 Mott St (at Prince St) ☎219-3893. Kari Sigerson and Miranda Morrison make rather timeless, simple and elegant shoes for women.

Steve Madden, 150 E 86th St (at Lexington) ☎426-0538; 540 Broadway (near Prince St) ☎343-1800; 2315 Broadway (near 84th St) ☎799-4221. Very popular copies of up-to-the-minute styles. Well-loved for their ability to take on New York's "shoe killing" streets.

Unisa, 701 Madison Ave ☎753-7474. The only retail shop for these comfortable affordable shoes imported from Spain and Brazil.

Finishing touches: bags, glasses, hair, make-up

As a rule of thumb you will find these **accessories** in major department stores and in areas where there is a high concentration of shopping such as SoHo and the Upper East Side. You can spend very little or a fortune – whatever suits you. What follows is a sampling of the best.

BAGS

Kate Spade, 454 Broome St (at Prince St) ☎274-1991. All the rage for several years running, these boxy fabric bags with the little logo-label are a generic assertion of "Manhattan chic."

Manhattan Portage, 242 W 30th St ☎594-7068; 333 E 9th St ☎995-5490. The now-classic canvas messenger bag with the red skyline-printed label appeared in 1980, but it's only in recent years that these practical, rugged New York carryalls have skyrocketed to chic-dom.

GLASSES

Alain Mikli, 880 Madison Ave (between 71st and 72nd sts) ☎472-6085. A wide selection of European and vintage frames for men and women.

Cohen's Optical, 117 Orchard St ☎674-5887. Nicaragua's Daniel Ortega supposedly spent $3000 here on a pair of bullet-proof glasses. You can probably get away with something less.

Lens Crafters, Manhattan Mall (at 34th St and 6th Ave) ☎967-4166; call for more locations. Chain store for glasses in an hour or a repair.

Morgenthal-Frederics, 944 Madison Ave (near 75th St) ☎744-9444; 685 Madison Ave ☎838-3090. Nice custom-made spectacles.

Oliver Peoples, 366 W Broadway ☎925-5400. This LA cult eyewear designer's New York outpost offers understated frames for $175–335.

Robert Marc, 575 Madison Ave ☎319-2000 and four other locations. Exclusive New York distributor of designer frames like Lunor and Kirei Titan; also sells Retrospecs, restored antique eyewear from the 1890s to the 1940s. Very expensive and very hot.

HAIR

Astor Place Hair Stylists, 2 Astor Place ☎475-9854. People line up six deep here. They'll do any kind of unusual style, and, most important, don't cost the earth – $11 and up for a straight cut.

Barrett Salon, 19 E 7th St (between 2nd and 3rd aves) ☎477-3236. Garrulous free spirit Adriana Barrett specializes in her own brand of multicolored extensions and caters to the stars. Haircuts around $50. Highly recommended.

Chelsea Barbers, 465 W 23rd St ☎741-2254. Bertilda "Betty" Garcia is drawing some of the glitterati away from their $300 haircuts; hers are closer to $15.

Jean Louis David, 1385 Broadway (at 37th St) ☎869-6921; call for more locations. They're everywhere if you need an inexpensive, respectable cut. You don't need an appointment but it helps.

The Spot, 521 Madison Ave (between 53rd and 54th sts) ☎688-4450. Get a great cut by some of the best apprentices in the city at a reduced rate. Starts at $50.

MAKE-UP

If you're looking for make-up lines such as Clinique, Elizabeth Arden, Bobbi Brown and the like, start by going to any of the department stores, since they all have large **cosmetics** departments. If you are looking for something a little different check out the following:

Aveda, 233 Spring (between 6th Ave and Varick St – 7th Ave) ☎807-1492. Call for more locations.

Face Stockholm, 110 Prince St ☎334-3900; and 224 Columbus Ave (between 70th and 71st sts) ☎769-1420.

MAC, 14 Christopher St (between 6th and 7th aves) ☎243-4150; and 113 Spring St ☎334-4641.

Make-up Forever, 409 W Broadway (between Prince and Spring sts) ☎941-9337. High quality make-up.

Sephora, 555 Broadway ☎625-1309. Breathtaking "warehouse" of perfumes, make-up and body care products. You have to see it to believe it.

Sporting goods

The **sporting goods** scene is dominated by chains such as Foot Locker, The Athlete's Foot, Sports Authority and Modell's, though there are a few other options: "theme park" sports clothes

Shops and Markets

Shops and Markets

stores, as well as stores tightly focused on one sport. Use them for merchandise as well as a wealth of information about that sport in NY.

Superstores

Niketown, 6 E 57th St (between 5th and Madison) ☎891-6453. You can enter this temple through Trump Tower, literally hearing crowds cheer as you pass through the door. Every 30 minutes, a screen descends the full five stories of the store and shows Nike commercials. There's tons of memorabilia, most notably relating to Michael Jordan. Oh, and you can also purchase Nike clothing and accessories.

Reebok Store, 160 Columbus Ave ☎595-1480. This is the flagship Reebok store; although there is an outlet at Chelsea Piers. The Reebok Store is not as dazzling as Niketown, but it does show ads on two big screens, houses the Reebok Sports Club and features European Reebok lines not found anywhere else in the States.

Specialty stores

Bicycle Habitat, 244 Lafayette ☎431-3315. This unassuming store is frequented by bike messengers. Buy a bike here, and they'll service your brakes forever.

Bicycle Renaissance, 430 Columbus Ave (at 81st St) ☎724-2350. A classy place with competitive prices; custom bike building and usually same-day service. Trek and Cannondale bikes and Campagnolo and Shimano frames in stock.

Blades, Board & Skate, 120 W 72nd St (between Broadway and Columbus Ave) ☎787-3911. Rent or buy rollerblades, snowboards and the like.

Eastern Mountain Sports (EMS), 20 W 61st St (between Broadway and Columbus) ☎397-4860; 611 Broadway (at Houston St) ☎505-9860. Top-quality merchandise covering almost all outdoor sports, including skiing and kayaking.

Harvey's Ski/Sport Shop, 3179 Emmons Ave, Sheepshead Bay, Brooklyn

☎718/743-0054. Friendly shop, selling ski gear, diving equipment and other sporting goods; also rents rollerblades and bikes.

Mason's Tennis Mart, 911 7th Ave (between 57th and 58th sts) ☎757-5374. New York's last remaining tennis specialty store, which lets you try out all racquets.

Paragon Sporting Goods, 871 Broadway (at 18th St) ☎255-8036. Family-owned, with three levels of general merchandise.

Soccer Sport Supply Company, 1745 1st Ave (between 90th and 91st sts) ☎427-6050. Half-century-old international soccer and rugby supply company with a professional staff.

Super Runners Shop, 1337 Lexington Ave (at 89th St) ☎369-6010; 360 Amsterdam Ave (at 77th St) ☎787-7665; 416 3rd Ave (at 29th St) ☎213-4560. Experienced runners work at all four locations; co-owner Gary Muhrcke won the first New York City Marathon in 1970.

Tents & Trails, 21 Park Place ☎227-1760. Bizarrely located in the Wall Street neighborhood, this small shop is a hiker's dream.

The World of Golf, 147 E 47th St (between Lexington and 3rd aves) ☎755-9398. Known for their large selection and discount policy.

Food and drink

Food – the buying as much as consuming of it – is a New York obsession. Nowhere do people take eating more seriously than Manhattan, and there's no better place in the world to shop for food. Where to buy the best bagels, who stocks the widest – and weirdest – range of cheeses, are questions that occupy New Yorkers a disproportionate amount of time. The proliferation of delis boasting diverse fresh salad bars packed to overflowing (and selling beautiful flowers on the side) will confirm for you that America is indeed the Land of Plenty. More sophisticated places, gourmet or specialty shops for example, will be enough to make you swoon – and as the bull market bullies ahead, new ones are opening every day in affluent neighborhoods to help absorb all of that excess wealth.

The listings below, while comprehensive, are by no means exhaustive. Wander the streets and you'll no doubt uncover plenty more besides. If you're after **drink**, remember that you can only buy liquor – i.e. wines, spirits or anything else stronger than beer – at a liquor store, and that you need to be 21 or over to do so.

Supermarkets, delis and greengrocers

For the most **general food requirements**, there are a number of **supermarket** chains that pop up all over the city. Big Apple, Sloan's and Food Emporium you'll find pretty much everywhere; D'Agostino and Gristedes tend to appear in the fancier neighborhoods. In addition, many of the department stores listed on pp.453–454 – principally Macy's and Bloomingdale's – have food halls. At night, Food Emporium's 15 locations are open 24hrs on weekdays – on Saturday and Sunday they close at midnight (see the phone book for locations).

On a smaller scale, there are **delis and greengrocers** that sell basic food and drink items, as well as sandwiches and coffee to take away, and sometimes hot ready meals and the chance to dip into a copiously provided salad bar. You should never have to walk more than a couple of blocks to find one, and most are open late or all night.

Gourmet markets

In the late Seventies there were three: Balducci's in the Village, Dean and Deluca in SoHo, and Zabar's on the Upper West Side. But in recent years a frenzy of new **gourmet markets** have glutted the scene. Essentially a step up from delis, they are gloriously stocked places, selling all manner of choice edible items in a super-abundant environment that will make your taste buds jump. In general – though not exclusive-

ly – they supply the more gentrified neighborhoods with their most obscure (and more mainstream) objects of desire.

Agata & Valentina 1505 1st Ave (at 79th St) ☎452-0690. A spinoff of Balducci's (see below); very classy, with an authentic Sicilian atmosphere.

Balducci's, 424 6th Ave (between 9th and 10th sts) ☎673-2600. The long-term Downtown rival of Zabar's (see overleaf), a family-run store that's no less appetizing – though some say it's slightly pricier.

Chelsea Market, 75 9th Ave (between 15th and 16th sts) ☎243-6005. A complex of eighteen former industrial buildings, among them the late 19th-century Nabisco Cookie Factory. A true smorgasbord of stores, including Amy's Bread, Bowery Kitchen Supplies, the Chelsea Wholesale Flower Market, the Chelsea Wine Vault, Hale & Hearty Soups, the Lobster Place and the Manhattan Fruit Exchange.

Citarella, 2135 Broadway (at 75th St) and 1313 3rd Ave (at 75th St); both ☎874-0383. Famous fish store gone full-service gourmet market (see also p.468).

Dean and Deluca, 560 Broadway (between Prince and Spring sts) ☎226-6800. One of the original big neighborhood food emporia. Very chic, very SoHo and not at all cheap. There's also a café on Prince St.

EAT Gourmet Foods, 1064 Madison Ave (at 80th St) ☎772-0022. A brother to Zabar's (and run by the owner of Zabar's brother, Eli; see below), primarily based in the East Side and packed with gourmet delights. Try the wonderful Eli's bread. Like Dean and Deluca, it has its own "Gourmet Café" next door.

Eli's Manhattan, 1411 3rd Ave (at 80th St) ☎717-8100. A slick, expensive counterpoint to Zabar's, run by Eli Zabar, owner of EAT.

Faicco's, 260 Bleecker St (between 6th and 7th aves) ☎243-1974. Very authentic Italian deli.

Fairway, 2127 Broadway (between 74th and 75th sts) ☎595-1888. Long-

Shops and Markets

Shops and Markets

established Upper West Side grocery store that for many locals is the better-value alternative to Zabar's. They have their own farm on Long Island, so the produce is always fresh, and their range in some items is enormous.

Fine & Schapiro, 138 W 72nd St (between Broadway and Columbus Ave) ☎877-2874. Excellent, principally kosher, meals to go and renowned sandwiches and cold meats. Also a restaurant – see p.376.

FoodWorks, 8 W 19th St (between 5th and 6th aves) ☎352-9333. Full-service gourmet market with eat-in café. Good selection of cheeses and better prices than most gourmet shops.

Gourmet Garage, 453 Broome St (at Mercer) ☎941-5850; Gourmet Garage East, 301 E 64th St ☎535-5880; Gourmet Garage West, 2567 Broadway ☎663-0656. Excellent value on cheeses, olives, produce and ready-made sandwiches. Purveyors to *Le Cirque 2000* and *The Four Seasons*.

Grace's Marketplace, 1237 3rd Ave (at 71st St) ☎737-0600. Gourmet deli offspring of Balducci's that is a welcome addition to the Upper East Side food scene. An excellent selection of just about everything.

Russ & Daughters, 179 E Houston St (between Allen and Orchard sts) ☎475-4880. Technically, this store is known as an "appetizing" – the original Manhattan gourmet shop, set up at the turn of the century to sate the appetites of homesick immigrant Jews, selling smoked fish, caviar, pickled vegetables, cheese and bagels. This is one of the oldest.

Schaller & Weber, 1654 2nd Ave (between 85th and 86th sts) ☎879-3047. Culinary heart of the Upper East Side's now sadly diminished German-Hungarian district of Yorkville, this shop is a riot of cold cuts, salami and smoked meats. Not for vegetarians.

Todaro Brothers, 555 2nd Ave (between 30th and 31st sts) ☎532-0633. An excellent selection of imported and domestic gourmet foods, plus a bakery.

Zabar's, 2245 Broadway (at 80th St) ☎787-2000. The apotheosis of New York food-fever, Zabar's is still the city's most eminent foodstore (run by Saul Zabar, brother of Eli). Choose from an astonishing variety of cheeses, cooked meats and salads, fresh baked bread and croissants, excellent bagels, and cooked dishes to go. Upstairs stocks miscellaneous shiny kitchen and household implements to help you put it all together at home; there are often good bargains on electric items like fans and European coffee-makers. Not to be missed.

Bakeries and patisseries

Cupcake Café, 522 9th Ave (at 39th St) ☎465-1530. Special-occasion cakes and cupcakes, all with buttercream frosting. Also serves light meals. Cozy place to sit.

Damascus Bakery, 56 Gold St, Brooklyn ☎718/855-1456. Syrian bakery, long established, with the city's best supply of different pita breads, as well as a dazzling array of pastries.

Ferrara, 195 Grand St (between Mulberry and Mott sts) ☎226-6150; 108 Mulberry St ☎966-7867. Legendary Little Italy café-patisserie. Specializes in gelati, cakes and coffees. Sit-down café.

Fung Wong, 30 Mott St ☎267-4037. Chinese pastries.

H&H Bagels, 639 W 46th (at 12th Ave) ☎595-8000; and 2239 Broadway at 80 St. Open 24hrs, seven days a week, this is the home of New York's finest bagel.

Hungarian Pastry Shop, 1030 Amsterdam Ave (between 110th and 111th sts) ☎866-4230. Rigojanci, bittersweet chocolate mousse cake, linzer tarts and other authentic Hungarian desserts as well as a bottomless cup of coffee. Popular with Columbia students.

Kossar's, 367 Grand St (at Essex St) ☎473-4810. Jewish baker whose bialys may be the best in New York.

Let Them Eat Cake, 287 Hudson St (at Spring St) ☎989-4970. Delicious carrot, chocolate, bourbon and pecan cakes, plus soups and sandwiches on the side.

Little Pie Company, 424 W 43rd St (between 9th and 10th aves) ☎736-4780. Specializes in traditional American pies and cakes.

Magnolia Bakery, 401 Bleecker St (at 11th St) ☎462-2572. Luscious cookies, pies and cakes baked to perfection. A neighborhood favorite.

Moishe's, 181 E Houston St (between Allen and Orchard sts) ☎475-9624; 115 2nd Ave (between E 6th and E 7th aves) ☎505-8555. New York's most authentic Jewish bakery – legendary cornbread, pumpernickel and challah.

Patisserie Claude, 187 W 4th St ☎255-5911. Delicious authentic French bakery.

Payard Patisserie, 1032 Lexington Ave ☎717-5252. Sophisticated pastries for those with a complex sweet tooth, but still delicious for those without.

Sticky Fingers, 121 1st Ave (at 7th St and St Mark's Place) ☎529-2554. Fresh breads daily, and homemade desserts. Sweeter than sweet sticky buns, cookies and cakes.

Taylor's, 156 Chambers St ☎962-0519. Baked goods, entrees and desserts to go, all baked on premises. Also at 523 Hudson, 228 W 18th St and 175 2nd Ave.

Veniero's, 342 E 11th St (between 1st and 2nd aves) ☎674-7264. Century-old Italian-style patisserie.

Vesuvio, 160 Prince St between Thompson St and W Broadway ☎925-8248. SoHo's most famous Italian bakery.

Yonah Schimmel's, 137 E Houston St between 1st and 2nd aves ☎477-2858. Forget the junk street vendors sell. Yonah Schimmel started selling his homemade knishes out of a pushcart in the early 1900s; now they are the stuff of New York legend. A variety of fillings (kasha, potato, spinach, cheese, etc) with a bona fide thin, flaky crust.

Zaro's Bread Basket, Grand Central Station; Penn Station; and several other locations in Manhattan; check the phone book for addresses. Croissants, bagels and all good things. A good place to stop off for a breakfast on your feet.

Zito's, 259 Bleecker St (between 6th and 7th aves) ☎929-6139. Long-established Downtown Italian baker, renowned for its fine round *pane di casa*.

Cheese and dairy

Alleva Latticini, 188 Grand St (at Mulberry St) ☎226-7990. Oldest Italian cheesery in America; also a grocer. Makes own smoked mozzarella and ricotta.

Cheese Unlimited, 240 9th Ave (between 24th and 25th sts) ☎691-1512. The name says it all . . . more than 40 varieties of cheese.

Di Paolo, 206 Grand St (at Mott St) ☎226-1033. A wide array of different cheeses, including fresh Italian dairy varieties made on the premises.

Ideal Cheese Shop, 1205 2nd Ave (between 63rd and 64th sts) ☎688-7579. A fine cheese emporium.

Joe's Dairy, 156 Sullivan St (between Houston and Prince sts) ☎677-8780. Family store considered New York's best bet for fresh mozzarella in several varieties.

Murray's Cheese Shop, 257 Bleecker St (between 6th and 7th aves) ☎243-3289. A variety of more than 300 fresh cheeses.

Third Avenue Cheese Shop, 141 3rd Ave (between 9th and 10th sts) ☎477-1221. Very inexpensive, with a nice selection; good breads, to boot.

Fish and seafood

Barney Greengrass, 541 Amsterdam Ave (between 86th and 87th sts) ☎724-4707. "The Sturgeon King." An Upper West Side smoked-fish brunch institution since 1908 which also sells brunch-makings to go.

Caviarteria, 502 Park Ave; enter on 59th St between Park and Madison aves ☎759-7410. Mainly caviar – more than a dozen varieties – and a stock of smoked fish and patés.

Shops and Markets

Shops and Markets

Central Fish Company, 527 9th Ave (between 39th and 40th sts) ☎279-2317. Friendly, knowledgeable staff, stocks thirty-five species, including fresh Portuguese sardines and live carp, at any given time – and at very reasonable prices.

Citarella, 2135 Broadway (at 75th St) ☎874-0383; 1313 3rd Ave (at 75th St). The largest and most varied fish and seafood source in the city, now with gourmet baked goods, cheese, coffee, meat, prepared food. Still, the specialty is seafood; there's a wonderful bar serving prepared oysters, clams and the like to take away. Famous for its artistic window displays, which make graceful use of squid.

Fulton Fish Market. For New York's freshest fish if you're up early enough (5am – see p.77). The market itself is a lively affair to visit.

Murray's Sturgeon Shop, 2429 Broadway (between 89th and 90th sts) ☎724-2650. Another popular Upper West Side haunt, this place specializes in smoked fish and caviar.

Petrossian, 182 W 58th St (at 7th Ave) ☎245-2214. This well-known shop imports only the finest Russian caviar, alongside a range of other gourmet products – smoked salmon and other fish mainly – as well as pricey implements to eat it all with. Quite the most exclusive place to shop for food in town, and with a restaurant attached to complete the experience.

Health food, vegetarian and spice shops

Angelica's Traditional Herbs & Foods, 147 1st Ave (at 9th St) ☎529-4335. An excellent selection of herbs, tinctures, spices and books.

Aphrodisia, 264 Bleecker St (between 6th and 7th aves) ☎989-6440. For herbs spices and seasoning oils only, this place is hard to beat.

Commodities Natural Foods, 117 Hudson St (between N Moore and Franklin sts) ☎334-8330. Huge health food store and café.

General Nutrition Center (GNC). The city's largest health food chain (check the phone book for addresses), and resembling nothing so much as a muscle-builders' supermarket, but prices are reasonable.

Good Earth Foods, 1334 1st Ave between (71st and 72nd sts) ☎472-9055; 167 Amsterdam Ave at (68th St) ☎496-1616. Not cheap but one of the best-equipped health food outlets in the city. Has a worthy juice and food café.

Good Food Co-op, 58 E 4th St. Cooperatively run but open to the public. Full market with a good amount of organic food.

Gramercy Natural Food Center, 427 2nd Ave (between 24th and 25th sts) ☎725-1651. Best known for its fish, poultry and organic dairy products.

The Health Nuts, 2141 Broadway (at 75th St) ☎724-1972; and other Manhattan locations. Good general health food and macrobiotic chain.

Kalustyan's, 123 Lexington Ave (between 28th and 29th sts) ☎685-3451. The best of the groceries that make up the tiny Little India district of Manhattan. Good spice selection.

Nature Food Center, 682 Broadway (at third street) ☎777-2330; and locations across Manhattan. The "department store" of natural foods – an excellent selection.

Prana, 125 1st Ave (between St Mark's and 7th St) ☎982-7306. Wholefood shop where you can make your own peanut butter.

Whole Foods in SoHo, 117 Prince St (between Greene and Wooster) ☎982-1000; 2421 Broadway and 89th St ☎874-4000. Health food supermarket, open daily with a very wide selection.

Ice cream and frozen yogurt

Two national chains have largely carved up the city's appetite for ice cream and frozen yogurt between them: Baskin-Robbins (traditionally famous for its thirty-one flavors), which has about half a dozen outlets spread between Wall St and Harlem, and the considerably better Häagen-Dazs, which trades from about fifteen locations across Manhattan; again, the phone book has details. Oddly, national frozen yogurt mega-chain TCBY ("The Country's Best Yogurt") has only two Manhattan locations, at 400 E 14th St and 237 Park Ave.

There are a few smaller operators which die-hard New York ice-cream freaks swear by, though in the ultra-competitive marketplace that is Manhattan a number have melted away. Ben & Jerry's (222 E 86th St; 680 8th Ave at 43rd St; 41 3rd Ave between 9th and 10th sts; World Trade Center) is still the jolly place it set out to be, if decidedly more commercial − and their esoteric ice cream and frozen yogurt flavors can't be beat. Chelsea Baking and Ice Company at 259−263 W 19th St (between 7th and 8th aves) offers 100 flavors of ice cream, 20 of gelati and 80 sorbets. The Chinatown Ice Cream Factory (65 Bayard St, south of Canal between Mott and Elizabeth sts) gets the most bemused reactions, since it's the only place that serves up mango, green tea and lychee flavors.

Sweets, nuts and chocolate

Bazzini, 339 Greenwich St (at Jay St) ☎334-1280. Nice selection of expensive gourmet nuts and sweets in all shapes and sizes, but a far cry from the unpretentious wholesaler it used to be.

Be-speckled Trout, 422 Hudson St ☎255-1421. Wonderful old-fashioned candy shop with jars of colorful sweets and rows of homemade lollypops.

Economy Candy, 108 Rivington St (between Essex and Ludlow sts) ☎254-1531. A candy junk shop on the Lower East Side, selling tubs of sweets, nuts and dried fruit at low prices

Elk Candy Co, 1628 2nd Ave ☎650-1177. A Yorkville candy store selling Yorkville-style candies − rich and marzipaned.

Godiva, 701 5th Ave (between 54th and 55th sts) ☎593-2845. This renowned

Belgian chocolatier has branches all over Manhattan − unbeatable for satisfying anyone's chocolate craving.

Leonidas, 485 Madison Ave (between 51st and 52nd sts) ☎980-2608. The only US franchise of the famous Belgian confectioner.

Li-Lac, 120 Christopher St (between Hudson and Bleecker sts) ☎242-7374. Delicious chocolates that have been hand-made on the premises since 1923, including fresh fudge. One of the city's best treats for those with a sweet tooth.

Teuscher, 620 5th Ave (between 49th and 50th sts) ☎246-4416; 25 E 61st St ☎751-8482. Upper East Side Swiss chocolate importer renowned for its truffles.

Treat Boutique, 200 E 86th St (at 3rd Ave) ☎737-6619. Six different kinds of homemade fudge and a broad selection of dried fruit and nuts.

Tea and coffee

McNulty's, 109 Christopher St (between Bleecker and Hudson sts) ☎242-5351. Expensive personalized coffee blends, and a wide selection of teas, since 1895.

Oren's, 31 Waverly Place (Greenwich Village) ☎420-5958; call for other locations along the East Side. Among the best beans in the city.

Porto Rico, 201 Bleecker St (between 6th Ave and McDougal St) ☎477-5421; also 40 1/2 St Mark's (off 2nd Ave) and 107 Thompson St (between Prince and Spring). Best for coffee, and with a bar for tasting. Rumor has it that the inexpensive house blends are as good as many of the more expensive coffees.

Sensuous Bean of Columbus Avenue, 66 W 70th St (just off Columbus Ave) ☎724-7725. Mostly coffee, with some tea.

Liquor stores

Prices for all kinds of **liquor** are controlled in New York State and vary little from one shop to another. There are, however, a

Shops and Markets

Shops and Markets

number of places that either have a particularly good selection or where things tend to be a touch less expensive. It's those that are listed here. Bear in mind there's a state law forbidding the sale of strong drink on Sundays, a day on which all liquor stores are closed; also, supermarkets are authorized to sell beer, but not wine or spirits (go figure). Many places will take orders over the phone if you would like your drink to come to you.

Acker, Merrall & Condit, 160 W 72nd St (between Broadway and Columbus Ave) ☎787-1700. Oldest wine store in America, founded in 1820. Has a very wide selection of wine from the US, especially California.

Astor Wines and Spirits, 12 Astor Place (at Lafayette St) ☎674-7500. Manhattan's best selection and most competitive prices.

Beekman Liquors, 500 Lexington Ave (between 47th and 48th sts) ☎759-5857. Good, well-priced Midtown alternative to Astor.

Best Cellars, 1291 Lexington Ave (between 86th and 87th sts) ☎426-4200. Wine store with 100 carefully chosen selections, each for under $10, and a very knowledgeable staff. Recommended.

Columbus Circle Liquor Store, 1780 Broadway (at 57th St) ☎247-0764. Uptown alternative to Astor.

Cork & Bottle, 1158 1st Ave (between 63rd and 64th sts) ☎838-5300. Excellent selection; deliveries too.

Garnet Wines & Liquors, 929 Lexington Ave (at 68th St) ☎772-3211. Possibly the city's most inexpensive source for specialty wines.

Maxwell Wines & Spirits, 1657 1st Ave (between 86th and 87th sts) ☎289-9595. Upper East Side liquor store, open until midnight every day except Sun (closed).

Morrell & Co, 535 Madison Ave (between 54th and 55th sts) ☎688-9370. One of the best selections of good-value wine in town.

Schapiro's, 126 Rivington St (between Essex and Norfolk sts) ☎674-4404. Kosher wines made on the premises. Free tours of the cellars, with wine tasting, Sun 11am–4pm on the hour.

Schumer's Wine & Liquors, 59 E 54th St (between Park and Madison aves) ☎355-0940. Stays open until midnight Fri & Sat, and will also deliver.

Sherry-Lehman, 679 Madison Ave ☎838-7500. New York's foremost wine merchant.

Spring Street Wine Shop, 187 Spring St (between Thompson and Sullivan sts) ☎219-0521. Well-stocked SoHo liquor store.

Warehouse Wines and Spirits, 735 Broadway (between 8th and Waverly) ☎982-7770. The top place to get a buzz for your buck, with a wide selection.

Books

Book lovers bemoan the steady disappearance of New York's independent bookstores, and directly attribute their loss to the phenomenon of Barnes & Noble superstores, where you can settle in comfortably at the table-filled café and use the place as your personal library-cum-newsstand. But there's still a fantastic selection of **books** in New York. Stores servicing a niche, such as mystery, are flourishing as a place to purchase books as well as meet like-minded people. More than 90 percent of the nation's publishers are located here, with their wares sold in more than 200 bookstores. New or secondhand, US or foreign, there's little that isn't available somewhere.

Superstores and chains

Barnes & Nobles are book department stores with temptingly comfortable chairs and nice views. Some people find them atmosphereless, some fun. But there's no question that their enormous stock makes it likely you'll find what you're looking for, and since Barnes & Noble made its reputation as a discount bookstore, bargains are common. Author readings take place about five evenings a week, and hours are 9am to midnight, every day. The store at 105 5th Ave (at E 18th St ☎807-0099) claims to be "The World's Largest Bookstore" and concentrates on **college text books**. There are nine **superstores** in Manhattan:

4 Astor Place (at Broadway and Lafayette) ☎420-1322; 675 6th Ave (at W 22nd St) ☎727-1227;. 600 5th Ave (at W 48th St) ☎765-0590; Citicorp Building at E 54th St and 3rd Ave ☎750-8033; 2289 Broadway (at W 82nd St) ☎362-8835; 240 E 86th St (at 2nd Ave) ☎794-1962; 1280 Lexington (at E 86th St) ☎423-9900; 1972 Broadway (across from Lincoln Center) ☎595-6859; Union Square (at 33 E 17th St) ☎253-0810.

Borders Books and Music, 5 World Trade Center (at Church and Vesey sts) ☎839-8049; 461 Park Ave (at 57th St) ☎980-6785; 550 2nd Ave (at 32nd St) ☎685-3938. This Ann Arbor-based chain rivals Barnes & Noble.

B. Dalton, 396 6th Ave (at 8th St) ☎674-8780. A nationwide chain, owned by Barnes and Noble, but this is the only branch left in Manhattan.

Tower Books, 383 Lafayette St (at 4th St) ☎228-5100. The literary arm of Tower Records, next door, focusing on pop culture, music, travel and film. Magazines too.

General interest and new books

Bookberries, 983 Lexington Ave (at 71st St) ☎794-9400. Classic Uptown New York bookstore with a fine selection of literature.

Coliseum Books, 1775 Broadway (at 57th St) ☎757-8381. Very large store, good on paperbacks and academic books.

Corner Bookstore, 1313 Madison Ave (at 92nd St) ☎831-3554. Upscale bookstore with an excellent literature selection in a lovely atmosphere.

Gotham Book Mart, 41 W 47th St ☎719-4448. Located in the heart of the Diamond District, for more than 75 years

this jewel has focused on the creative arts, stocking both new publications and out-of-print books – as well as smuggling in banned titles like *Tropic of Cancer*. The art department and gallery are on the second floor. Huge film and theater section, and excellent for the more obscure literary stuff. A notice board downstairs advertises readings and literary functions, and a gallery has sporadic exhibitions.

Papyrus, 2915 Broadway (at 114th St) ☎222-3350. New and used titles, especially good on literature. Many of their film, literature and political philosophy titles have a left-wing slant.

Posman Books, 1 University Place ☎533-2665. General college bookstore. New location to open soon at 9 Grand Central Terminal at 42nd St.

St Mark's Bookshop, 31 3rd Ave (between 8th and 9th sts) ☎260-7853. Nice selection of new titles from mainstream to way alternative; see p.474, under "Radical," for more.

Shakespeare & Co, 939 Lexington (at 68th and 69th sts) ☎570-0201; 716 Broadway and Washington Place ☎529-1330; 137 E 23rd St ☎220-5199; 1 Whitehall St ☎742-7025. New and used books, paper and hardcover. Great for fiction and psychology.

Three Lives & Co, 154 W 10th St and Waverly Place ☎741-2069. Excellent literary bookstore that has an especially good selection of books by and for women, as well as general titles.

Secondhand books

A neighborhood to browse through for book bargains is centered around 5th Ave and 18th St. There you'll find used bookstores Academy Books, Skyline Books and Books of Wonder (for children). The Strand is four blocks away at 12th St and Broadway. The Metropolitan Book Auction sells fine and rare used books – they're on the 4th floor of 123 W 18th St; call ☎929-4488 for schedule.

Academy Book Store, 10 W 18th St (between 5th and 6th aves) ☎242-4848.

Shops and Markets

Shops and Markets

Small shop carries used, rare and out-of-print books.

Argosy Bookstore, 116 E 59th St (between Lexington and Park aves) ☎753-4455. Unbeatable for rare books, and also sells clearance books and titles of all kinds, though the shop's reputation means you may well find mainstream works cheaper elsewhere.

Gryphon Bookshop, 2246 Broadway (between 80th and 81st sts) ☎362-0706. Used and out-of-print books, records, CDs and laser discs. Art books, illustrated books and antique children's books. Watch out for overpriced titles, of which there are a good few. There's also the Gryphon Record Shop next door to HMV at 251 W 72nd St, 2nd floor ☎874-1588 (see p.476).

Housing Works Used Books Cafe, 126 Crosby St (between Houston and Prince sts) ☎334-3324. Very cheap books, comfy and spacious. Proceeds benefit AIDS charity.

Ninth Street Books, 436 E 9th St (between 1st Ave and Ave A) ☎254-4603. General used books.

Pageant Book & Print Shop, 114 W Houston (between Thompson and Sullivan sts) ☎674-5296. Once located in the heart of New York's rare- and old-book district, this fine antiquarian bookshop carries a large selection of valuable secondhand books, prints, engravings and maps.

Ruby's Book Sale, 119 Chambers St ☎732-8676. Civic Center's used bookstore, dealing especially in paperbacks and ancient dog-eared magazines. Excellent value.

Skyline Books, 13 W 18th St (between 5th and 6th aves) ☎675-4773 or 759-5463. Concentration of beat literature, first editions and uncommon art and photography books. Cheerfully does book searches.

Strand Bookstore, 828 Broadway (at 12th St) ☎473-1452; annex at 95 Fulton St ☎732-6070. With around eight miles of books and a stock of over two and a half million, this is the largest

book operation in the city – and one of the few survivors in an area once rife with secondhand book stores. There are recent review copies and new books for half price; older books go for anything from 50¢ up. Also imports British remainders.

Special interest bookstores

New York has a good number of stores specializing in books on a particular area, from travel and art to more arcane subjects. The following is a selective list.

TRAVEL

The Civilized Traveler, 2003 Broadway (between 68th and 69th sts) ☎875-0306; 864 Lexington (at 65th St) ☎288-9190; 1 E 59th St ☎702-9502. Small selection of guidebooks, plus luggage, magazines and other travel accessories.

The Complete Traveler, 199 Madison Ave (at 35th St) ☎685-9007. Manhattan's premier travel bookshop, excellently stocked, secondhand and new – including a huge collection of Baedekers.

Rand McNally Map and Travel Store, 150 E 52nd St (between Lexington and 3rd aves) ☎758-7488; 555 7th Ave ☎944-4477. As much a map shop as a place for guidebooks, run by the major map and atlas publisher, with maps of all the world and specialist ones of New York State and city – along with luggage and other travel gear.

Travelers Choice Bookstore, 111 Greene (between Prince and Spring sts) ☎941-1535. This is a large, well-stocked store, affiliated with a travel agency.

ART AND ARCHITECTURE

Hacker Art Books, 45 W 57th St (between 5th and Madison aves) ☎688-7600. On the 5th floor.

Printed Matter, 77 Wooster St (between Spring and Broome sts) ☎925-0325. Retail arm of historic Municipal Art Society. Great space, exhibitions.

Urban Center Books, 457 Madison Ave (between 50th and 51st sts) ☎935-3592.

Architectural book specialists with a very helpful staff.

PHOTOGRAPHY, CINEMA AND THEATER

Applause Theater Books, 211 W 71st St (at Broadway) ☎496-7511. Theater, film, television, screenplays of films – some books unavailable elsewhere. New and used.

Drama Bookshop, 723 7th Ave (between 48th and 49th sts), on second floor ☎944-0595. Theater books, scripts and publications on all manner of drama-related subjects.

Photographer's Place, 133 Mercer St (just below Prince St) ☎431-9358. Lovingly run bookstore specializing in all aspects of photography and out-of-print titles.

Richard Stoddard Performing Arts Books, 18 E 16th St, room 605 ☎645-9576. Purchase a playbill from Broadway's yesteryear hits, plus good out-of-print theater book selection.

Theater Circle, 268 W 44th St ☎391-7075 or 944-1573. Theater books, posters, sheet music and souvenirs – in the heart of the theater district.

CRIME

Black Orchid, 303 E 81st St ☎734-5980. Secondhand and new novels.

Murder Ink, 2486 Broadway (between 92nd and 93rd sts) ☎362-8905. The first bookstore to specialize in mystery and detective fiction in the city, it's still the best, billed as stocking every murder, mystery or suspense title in print, and plenty out.

Mysterious Bookshop, 129 W 56th St (between 6th and 7th aves) ☎765-0900. The founder of this store started Mysterious Press (now owned by Warner Books). Signed first editions of new and used titles.

Partners in Crime, 44 Greenwich Ave ☎243-0440. Crime novels. Also home to the Cranston and Spade Theater Co. who perform classic radio scripts from the 1940s on Saturday nights. Call ☎462-3027 for info.

SCI-FI AND COMICS

Forbidden Planet, 840 Broadway (at 13th St) ☎473-1576. Science fiction, fantasy and horror fiction, graphic novels and comics. T-shirts and the latest toys, and collectibles including Star Wars and Star Trek paraphernalia.

St Mark's Comics, 11 St Mark's Place (between 2nd and 3rd aves) ☎598-9439. Tons of comic books, including underground comics; well known for their large stock. Action figures, trading cards, and a whole room of back issues.

Science Fiction Mysteries and More, 140 Chambers St ☎385-8798. Basic sci-fi bookstore.

Science Fiction Shop, 214 Sullivan St, #2D ☎473-3010. New and used science fiction records and books.

Village Comics, 215 Sullivan St (between Bleecker and W 3rd) ☎777-2770; 118 E 59th St, 2nd floor (between Park and Lexington aves) ☎759-6255. Old and new books, limited editions, trading cards, action figures and occasional celebrity appearances. Highly recommended.

LANGUAGE AND FOREIGN

Irish Book Shop, 580 Broadway, room 1103 ☎274-1923. Irish books and gifts.

Kinokuniya Bookstore, 10 W 49th St (at 5th Ave) ☎765-7766. The largest Japanese bookstore in NY, with English books on Japan, too.

Lectorum, 137 W 14th St ☎741-0220. Spanish books: fiction, reference, children's and business.

Liberation Bookstore, 421 Lenox Ave (at 131st St) ☎281-4615. Works from Africa and the Caribbean.

Librairie de France/Libreria Hispanica/The Dictionary Store, 610 5th Ave (in the Rockefeller Center Promenade) ☎581-8810. Small space housing a wealth of French and Spanish books, a dictionary store with over 8000 dictionaries of more than 100 languages, and a department of teach-yourself language books, records and tapes.

Shops and Markets

Shops and Markets

Rizzoli, 31 W 57th St (between 5th and 6th aves) ☎759-2424. Manhattan branches of the prestigious Italian bookstore chain and publisher, specializing in European publications, with a selection of foreign newspapers and magazines.

SPIRITUALITY

C.G. Jung Center Bookstore, 28 E 39th St ☎697-6433. Jungian thought.

Christian Publications Bookstore, 315 W 43rd St (between 8th and 9th aves) ☎582-4311. New Christian titles, as well as classics, greeting cards, Christian merchandise; Spanish books as well.

East West Books, 78 5th Ave (between 13th and 14th sts) ☎243-5994. Bookstore with a mind, body and spirit slant. Eastern Religions, New Age and health and healing.

J. Levine Jewish Books and Judaica, 5 W 30th St (between 5th and 6th aves) ☎695-6888. The ultimate Jewish bookstore.

Logos Bookstore, 1575 York (between 83rd and 84th sts) ☎517-7292. Christian books and gifts.

Paraclete Book Center, 146 E 74th St (at Lexington) ☎535-4050. Catholic scholarly books.

Quest, 240 E 53rd St ☎758-5521. New Age books.

West Side Judaica, 2412 Broadway (between 88th and 89th sts) ☎362-7846. Books about Judaism and funky menorahs for sale on the side.

GAY AND LESBIAN

A Different Light, 151 W 19th St (between 6th and 7th aves) ☎989-4850. Excellent gay/lesbian bookstore, as well as a center for contacts and further information. Has café, and is open until midnight. Frequent fun lectures from authors obsessed with Jacqui Susann and the like.

Oscar Wilde Memorial Bookshop, 15 Christopher St (between Gay and Greenwich aves) ☎255-8097. Aptly located gay and lesbian bookstore – probably the first in the city – with extensive rare book collection, signed and first editions, and framed signed letters from authors including Edward Albee, Gertrude Stein, and Tennessee Williams.

RADICAL/ALTERNATIVE

Blackout, 50 Ave B (between 3rd and 4th sts) ☎777-1967. Anarchist books, magazines and pamphlets as well as a meeting place for the activist community.

Bluestockings, 172 Allen St (at Stanton St) ☎473-9530. New and used titles, authored by or related to women only. Cozy well-stocked shop in what was once a dilapidated crack house.

Ideal Book Store, 547 W 110th, 2nd floor (at Broadway) ☎662-1909. Rumored to have the best philosophy collection in New York. Most books gently used.

Incommunicado, 107 Norfolk St (between Delancy and Rivington sts) ☎473-9530. Located inside *Tonic*, a Lower East Side jazz venue, this independent bookstore sells books by Incommunicado Press as well as 24 other indie presses. Wonderful selection of alternative literature.

Revolution Books, 9 W 19th St ☎691-3345. New York's major left-wing bookshop and contact point. A wide range of political and cultural books, pamphlets, periodicals and information on current action and events.

St Mark's Bookshop, 31 3rd Ave (between 8th and 9th sts) ☎260-7853. Largest and best-known "alternative" bookstore in the city, with a good array of titles on politics, feminism and the environment, literary criticism and journals, as well as more obscure subjects. Good postcards too, and one of the best places to buy radical and art New York magazines. Factory-chic interior. Open until midnight.

MISCELLANEOUS

Audiobook Store, 125 Maiden Lane ☎248-7800. Specializes in fiction and business titles. The biggest books-on-tape selection in New York.

Biography Bookshop, 400 Bleecker (at 11th St) ☎807-8655. Letters, diaries, memoirs.

Dover Books, 180 Varick St ☎255-6399. Go upstairs to the small bookstore, filled to the brim with hard-to-find Dover reproductions.

Kitchen Arts & Letters, 1435 Lexington Ave (at 94th St) ☎876-5550. Cookbooks and books about food, run by a former cookbook editor.

Labyrinth Books, 536 W 112th St ☎865-1588. Largest scholarly bookstore east of the Mississippi.

McGraw-Hill, 1221 6th Ave (at 49th St) ☎512-4100. Specializes in business, technical and scientific books.

Military Bookman, 29 E 93rd St (between Madison and 5th aves) ☎348-1280. Historical aspects of war, as well as fiction and strategy.

See Hear Fanzines, Magazines & Books, 59 E 7th St ☎505-9781. Great zines and small press books, mostly about music and radical culture.

Music

If you're coming from abroad, make a list of must-have **music**: CDs in the US are considerably cheaper than in most European countries, usually retailing at around $12–17 – though as low as $10 for new CDs in certain Village shops. Some savings too can be made on musical instruments, electric guitars in particular. The top music megastores in New York are the British chain HMV, Tower Records and the Virgin Megastore. Specialty pop music stores are clustered in the East and West Villages.

Chains

HMV, 2081 Broadway ☎721-5900. The pleasantest and most fun of the megastores. Also at 86th St and Lexington Ave ☎681-6700; 34th and 6th Ave (Herald Square) ☎629-0900; and 46th St and 5th Ave ☎681-6700.

J&R Music World, 23 Park Row (between Beekman and Anne sts) ☎238-9000. A large Downtown store with a decent selection and good prices. Also at 535 W 116th St near Columbia University ☎222-3673.

Record Explosion, 142 W 34th St (between 6th and 7th aves) ☎714-0450. A smaller chain (but with more Manhattan locations). Check phone book for more locations.

Tower Records at 692 Broadway (at 4th St) ☎505-1500; 1961 Broadway (at 66th St) ☎799-2500 and 725 5th Ave (between 56th and 57th sts) ☎838-8110. Extensive rock, world, jazz and classical sections and a little of everything else. This was the largest store in town until the Virgin Megastore moved in.

Virgin Megastore, 1540 Broadway (at 45th St) ☎921-1020; 52 E 14th St ☎598-4666. Here you can browse endless rows of CDs, get a cappuccino, book a flight on Virgin Atlantic and watch a movie all under one roof, assuming you have occasion to do such a thing. Unfortunately, unlike the London flagship store, they won't let you listen to any CD you want.

Special interest and secondhand

Bleecker Bob's, 118 W 3rd St (at McDougal St) ☎475-9677. Long-established record store specializing in punk and new wave that has sadly of late become something of a tourist rip-off. Best avoid.

Breakbeat Science, 335 E 9th St (betweeen 1st Ave and Ave A). ☎995-2592. British imports reign supreme here. Electronica, techno, trip-hop, etc.

Dance Trax, 91 E 3rd St (at 1st Ave), ☎260-8729. Large collection of underground house music.

Etherea, 66 Ave A (between 4th and 5th sts) ☎358-1126. Specializing in indie rock and electronica; domestic and imports, CDs and vinyl, this is one of the best shops in the city. Good used selection.

Fat Beats, 406 6th Ave, second floor (between 8th and 9th sts) ☎673-3883.

Shops and Markets

Shops and Markets

The name says it all. It's The Source for hip-hop on vinyl in New York City.

Finyl Vinyl, 204 E 6th St (between 2nd Ave and Cooper Square) ☎533-8007. Specializes in records from the 1930s to the 1970s.

Footlight Records, 113 E 12th St (between 3rd and 4th aves) ☎533-1572. The place for show music, film soundtracks and jazz. Everything from Broadway to Big Band, Sinatra to Merman. A must for record collectors.

Generation Records, 210 Thompson St (between Bleecker and W 3rd sts) ☎254-1100. The focus here is on hardcore and punk with some indie. New CDs and vinyl upstairs, used goodies downstairs. It also gets many of the imports the others don't have; plus good bootlegs.

Gryphon Record Shop, 251 W 72nd St (between Broadway and West End), 2nd floor ☎874-1588. Specializes in rare LPs.

House of Oldies, 35 Carmine St (between Bleecker and 6th Ave) ☎243-0500. Just what the name says − oldies but goldies of all kinds. Vinyl only.

Mondo Kim's, 6 St Mark's Place (between 2nd and 3rd aves) ☎598-9985; other location at 144 Bleecker (at LaGuardia St) ☎260-1010. Extensive selection of new and used indie obscurities on CD and vinyl, some real cheap. Esoteric videos upstairs. Staff has a serious attitude problem − and they like it that way.

Moon Ska Records, E 10th St (between 3rd and 4th sts) ☎673-5538. Label headquarters are here and they carry a wide range of things ska related: posters, T-shirts, pins, stickers and of course a broad selection of ska recordings.

Other Music, 15 E 4th St (between Broadway and Lafayette) ☎477-8150. Around the corner from Tower, this is an excellent spot for "alternative" CDs, both old and new, that can be hard to find. Stocking less indie on vinyl than they used to, and now leaning towards experimental and electronica.

Record Mart in the Subway, near the N/R train platform in the Times Square subway station, 1470 Broadway ☎840-0580. An unusual location, which perfumes the subway air with Caribbean and Central and South American music. A knowledgeable staff too; good browsing for the enthusiast. Call for opening times.

Reggae Land, 125 E 7th St (between 1st Ave and Ave A) ☎353-2071. Only reggae here, mainly vinyl, some CDs, good selection of the latest reggae releases.

Second Coming, 235 Sullivan St (between W 3rd and Bleecker sts) ☎228-1313. The place to come to for heavy metal and punk.

Shrine, 441 E 9th St (between 1st Ave and Ave A) ☎529-6646. Collectable rare rock on vinyl. Primarily 1960s and 1970s garage and psychedelic bands you've never heard of.

Sounds, 20 St Mark's Place (between 2nd and 3rd aves) ☎677-2727. New and used CDs; good prices and selection. Cheap new releases. Cash only.

Strange, 445 E 9th St (just off Ave A) ☎505-3025. Specializes in techno/ambient/rave music, with lots of British imports. (You'll pay top dollar for the imports.) Helpful staff.

Temple, 241 Lafayette St (between Spring and Prince sts) ☎343-3595. Located in the lower level of Liquid Sky, the club gear shop. Solid selection of techno and trance; frequented by local DJs.

Throb, 311 E 14th St (between 2nd and 3rd aves) ☎533-2328. Like the name implies, they carry techno, electronica, jungle, hip-hop, etc; but also have a good selection of hardcore records. Turntable is available for previewing selections.

Vinyl Mania, 60 Carmine St (between Bleecker and 6th Ave) ☎924-7223. This is where DJs come for the newest, rarest releases, especially of dance music. Hard-to-find imports too, as well as homemade dance tapes.

Musical instruments and accessories

New York's heaviest concentration of **musical instrument stores** is located on one block of W 48th St between 6th and 7th aves. The best are **Manny's**, at 156 ☎819-0576; **Rudy's Music Stop** at 169 ☎391-1699; **Alex Musical Instruments** at 165 ☎819-0070; and **Sam Ash Music** at 155–160 ☎719-2299, consists of five adjacent buildings, carrying all instruments, recording equipment, music-driven software and sheet music.

A treat for guitar lovers, though harder to get to, is **Mandolin Brothers** at 629 Forest Ave on Staten Island ☎718/981-8585, which has one of the world's best collections of vintage guitars. Their stock is half vintage, half new. Easier to reach is **Guitar Salon**, 45 Grove St (near 7th Ave and Bleecker St, by appointment only) ☎675-3236. Owner Beverly Maher appraised Segovia's guitars before donating them to the Metropolitan Museum in 1987, and sells handmade classical and flamenco guitars.

Drummer's World, at 151 W 46th St ☎840-3057, is a drummer's paradise, and carries ethnic instruments as well as drum kits.

Sheet music

Carl Fischer, 56–62 Cooper Square (at 7th St and 4th Ave) ☎777-0900. A vast resource for sheet music for all different instruments and vocal arrangements.

Colony Record & Radio Center, 1619 Broadway (at 49th St) ☎265-2050. Printed sheet music and hard-to-find records.

Sam Ash Music (see above).

Art supplies

Lee's Art Shop, 220 W 57th St (near Broadway) ☎247-0110. A good art supply store, used by students at the Art Students League down the street.

Pearl Paint Company, 308 Canal St (between Church St and Broadway) ☎431-7932. A likely contender for the title of "World's Largest Art Supply Store."

Housed in a jolly old red-and-white warehouse in the heart of Chinatown, Pearl has five floors of competitively-priced artists' supplies, including fabric paint and airbrushing and silkscreening supplies.

Sam Flax, 425 Park Ave (at 55th St) ☎620-3060; 12 W 20th St ☎620-3038. Another extensively-stocked art store.

Pharmacies and drugstores

There's a **pharmacy** or **drugstore** every few blocks in New York, and during the day it shouldn't be too difficult to find one. If you can't, the Yellow Pages has complete listings of places selling medicines and toiletries, listed under "Pharmacies." Most pharmacies are open roughly Monday to Saturday 9am–6pm, though many are also open on Sunday in busy shopping or residential neighborhoods. Corner **delis** carry some basic necessities; although you will pay more they are great for late-night needs. Some of the better or more specialized pharmacies are listed below, along with a selection of those that stay open longer hours in case of need.

Everywhere

Duane Reade A massive chain of drugstores that has cornered the market on discount medicines, toiletries, cigarettes and basic stationery over much of Manhattan, especially Midtown – and absorbed a lot of local pharmacies in the process. There are a good sixty stores and counting, many of them open 24 hours a day. If you need a pharmacy, this is probably where you'll find yourself.

Love Stores (with their big, juicy heart symbol) are a quintessential New York chain of pharmacies, smaller and more eclectic than Duane Reade, which now threatens their very existence. Still, there are a fair number left, with such evocative names as **Love In The 80's**, at 2336 Broadway (between 84th and 85th sts) ☎799-0900; **First Love**, at 1308 1st Ave and 14th St ☎737-9512; and **True Love**

Shops and Markets

Shops and Markets

at 2600 Broadway (98th St) ☎662-9600. See the phone book for other locations; most are concentrated on the Upper West Side.

Other drugstore chains are **CVS** (the best national chain), **Genovese, McKay, Rite-Aid** (another extensive one), and **Value Drugs**. Check exact locations in the phone book.

Specialty and independent pharmacies

Alexander Pharmacy, 1751 2nd Ave (at 91st St) ☎410-0060. Open seven days.

Bigelow Pharmacy, 414 6th Ave (between 8th and 9th sts) ☎473-7324. Established in 1882, this is the oldest apothecary in the country – and that's exactly how it looks, with the original Victorian shopfittings still in place. Specializes in homeopathic remedies. Open seven days a week.

Caswell-Massey Ltd, 518 Lexington Ave (at 48th St) ☎755-2254. The oldest pharmacy in America, and a national chain, selling a shaving cream created for George Washington and a cologne blended for his wife, as well as more mainstream items.

Edward's Drug Store, 225 E 57th St (between 2nd and 3rd aves) ☎753-2830. General pharmacy, closed on Sunday.

Ewa, 80 Mulberry St ☎964-2017. Herbal Chinese remedies: snakeskin, shark's teeth and the like.

Freeda Vitamins and Pharmacy, 36 E 41st St (between 5th and Madison aves) ☎685-4980.

Kaufmans, 557 Lexington Ave (at 50th St) ☎755-2266. Open till midnight. Will deliver for the cost of a two-way cab ride.

Kiehl's, 109 3rd Ave (between 13th and 14th sts) ☎677-3171. An exclusive pharmacy, decorated with the family collection of aviation and motorcycle memorabilia, which sells its own range of natural ingredient-based classic creams, oils, etc. If you're too strapped to buy, try to accumulate some free samples.

L'Occitane, 1046 Madison Ave ☎639-9185; 198 Columbus Ave ☎362-5146; 146 Spring St ☎343-0109. The perfumes of Provence at more reasonable prices than you'll find in France. Bath and beauty products.

Star Pharmacy, 1540 1st Ave (at 80th St) ☎737-4324. Open seven days.

Westerly Pharmacy, 911 8th Ave (at 55th St) ☎247-1096.

Windsor Pharmacy, 1419 6th Ave (at 58th St) ☎247-1538. Open until midnight seven days a week.

Antiques

You'd have to be pretty crazy – or very rich – to come to New York to buy **antiques**: prices are outrageous by European (and most American) standards. New York is, however, the premier antique source in the country, excellent for browsing, with museum-quality pieces available as well as lots of interesting, fairly priced stuff at the junkier end of the market. Sections of the city with a concentration of antique shops are the East Village and West Village, SoHo, Chelsea, Lower Broadway and the Upper East Side. Recently Lafayette St, from SoHo to just above Houston St, has become a prime spot for finding early twentieth-century American design. A handful of indoor and outdoor junk shops on E Houston (between Lafayette and the Bowery) have eclectic furniture from various funky eras, and even masonry for sale.

The Village and around

American Folk Art Gallery, 374 Bleecker (between Hudson and Perry sts) ☎366-6566. American country painted furniture and hooked rugs, from 1790 to the 1920s.

Carl Victor, 55 E 13th St ☎673-8740. This breathtaking shop carries antique lighting, marble fireplaces and more.

Kitschen, 380 Bleecker (between Perry and Charles sts) ☎727-0430. Fun vintage housewares.

Susan Parrish, 390 Bleecker (between Perry and W 11th sts) ☎645-5020. Americana and Indian art.

SoHo

Chameleon, 231 Lafayette St ☎343-9197. Interesting collection of antique lighting fixtures dating from the nineteenth century up to the 1960s. Many from New York residences.

Cobweb, 116 W Houston St (between Sullivan and Thompson sts) ☎505-1558. Tiled tables, iron beds and cabinets from southern Europe, Egypt, Morocco, Indonesia and Argentina.

Elan, 345 Lafayette St (between Bleecker and 2nd sts) ☎529-2724. Twentieth-century furniture, specializing in Art Nouveau and Art Deco.

Historical Materialism, 125 Crosby St ☎431-3424. Eclectic decorative antiques and unique objects from the 1870s to the 1920s.

280 Modern, 280 Lafayette St ☎941-5825. Tribal art pre-1920s and American design from 1920s to 1970s.

Urban Archeology, 285 Lafayette St ☎431-6969. Large-scale accessories and furniture, mainly American turn-of-the-century, often rented out for film sets. Great place for browsing.

Chelsea

Annex Antiques Fair and Flea Market, on 6th Ave between 25th and 26th. The biggest antiques fair in the city – with several hundred dealers of furniture, rugs, collectibles, photos and more – is the hub of a major antiques neighborhood. Admission $1. Open every Sat and Sun, year round. Look one block north, between 26th and 27th sts, for another large weekend flea market, and on Sun you'll find more spillover on 26th St and on 24th St between 6th Ave and Broadway. And in a parking lot on 7th Ave between 25th and 26th sts, there's the junk-sale Chelsea Flea Market, where the pickings aren't quite as good.

Chelsea Antiques Building, 110 W 25th St (between 6th and 7th aves) ☎929-0909. Better quality, better condition, and higher prices than above listings. 150 dealers on 12 floors of exceptional estate treasures and collectibles. Open Mon–Fri 10am–6pm, Sat–Sun 8.30am–6pm.

The Garage, 112 W 25th St (between 6th and 7th aves). Just a block away from the Annex Antiques Fair is this market located in a parking garage. In the basement level and first floor are 150 dealers – check out the great vintage eyeglass frames.

Metropolitan Arts and Antiques Pavilion, 110 W 19th St (between 6th and 7th aves) ☎463-0200. Open a few times a month for special-interest auctions and fairs ranging from vintage fashion to antique toys.

The Showplace, 40 W 25th St (between 6th Ave and Broadway) ☎633-6063. Indoor market of over 100 dealers of antiques and collectibles plus an espresso bar. Mon–Fri 9am–6pm, Sat & Sun 8.30am–5.30pm.

The Upper East Side

Rival kingpin auction houses Sotheby's and Christie's are both located up here. Although they are great fun to visit, keep in mind that if you're not a serious buyer you're likely to get a snotty and short-fused reception (possibly even if you are, although they tend to start fawning in a hurry once you make your intentions known).

American Hurrah, 766 Madison Ave ☎535-1930. Aged Americana mainly. A wonderful selection of quilts, rugs and samplers.

Christie's, 20 Rockefeller Plaza (49th St between 5th and 6th aves) ☎636-2000; *www.christies.com*. The premier British auction house, recently moved. You can attend an auction even if you don't bid, but expect a clipped reception regardless. Busy times are fall and spring. For schedule of auctions or catalogue, call ☎1-800/395-6300. Catalogues $20–75.

Shops and Markets

Shops and Markets

Seating is first-come, first-served; for evening auctions make reservations. Also Christie's East at 219 E 67th St ☎606-0400.

56th Street Art & Antiques Center, 160 E 56th St ☎755-4252. Three levels of antique furniture, paintings, objets d'art and more.

Manhattan Art and Antiques Center, 1050 2nd Ave (at 55th St) ☎355-4400. Around 70 dealers, spread over three floors, stocking a vast assortment of goodies – everything from American quilts to Oriental ceramics, with an emphasis on small items.

Newel Art Galleries, 425 E 53rd St (east of 1st Ave) ☎758-1970. Dazzle your eyes browsing this six-floor collection of one-of-a-kind big pieces – many for rent.

Sotheby's, York Ave and 72nd St. Mon–Sat 10am–5pm, Sun 1–5pm, closed summer. ☎606-7000; www.sothebys.com. The premier US auction house and rival of Christie's. Come in for a copy of *Preview Magazine*, which gives the auction schedule for 2–3 months – but watch out for snippy staff with a short fuse. Previews are 3–5 days beforehand; reservations are required for some evening auctions. Watch for more affordable Arcade Auctions. Catalogues $15–40.

Electronic equipment and cameras: bargains for overseas visitors

Given even a reasonable exchange rate, **electronic goods** of almost any description are extremely cheap in America when prices are compared to those in Europe. If you're into that sort of thing, the place for risky discount shopping is 6th and 7th aves a little north of Times Square in the 50s, where there are any number of stores selling cameras, stereo equipment, radios and the like; for **cameras**, anywhere in Midtown from 30th and 50th sts between Park and 7th aves is the patch. You'll be offered different prices depending on whether you buy

the equipment with or without a guarantee (ask for the price with guarantee to prevent any misunderstanding), and it's no use going into a shop without an *exact* idea of the model you want. Be on your guard for fake equipment (usually easily spotted) or inferior products that have had the labels of better makes carefully and illegally applied. Yes, it's a jungle out there.

Don't be tempted by American **TVs or videos** – they won't work on British or most European systems – and make sure that anything you buy is **dual voltage** if you want it to work in a country with 240 volts, like Britain. Provided the voltage matches and the machine is pulse/tone dial switchable (and you change the plug for a BT one), most **phones and answering machines** will work in the UK – though neither we nor the shops will guarantee that.

Computers, computer peripherals and software are also particularly cheap, but again you may be faced with the voltage compatibility problem, though most quality equipment comes with a voltage adapter. Peripherals (like CD-ROM players, laptop computers and modems), usually have an external power supply which adapts current. One problem that's impossible to overcome is that a bulky machine is hard for customs officials to miss – legally, you are obliged to pay both import duty and VAT when bringing most of the items mentioned above into European Union countries (see box opposite). And, though cameras and laptop computers are easily concealed, their serial numbers indicate their place of origin. Don't say we didn't warn you.

Tactics

The best advice initially is to get a ballpark figure on the item you desire by checking the newspapers. Look in the "Science" section in Tuesday's *NY Times*, and ads in the *Village Voice*. *Consumer Reports Magazine* is an excellent and reliable source, which rates a variety of products every month, and also prepares yearly buying guides; you can find these at newsstands and at public libraries.

Then shop around as widely as possible, since prices vary hugely. Extremely hard-nosed bargaining is the order of the day, and you should be prepared for rudeness followed by a rapid drop in price when you walk out on someone's "best offer." Remember too that you'll get a better price for cash than if you use a credit or charge card.

Another bargain strip is Canal St between Essex and Ludlow. Take the F train to the E Broadway stop. On this small block there are two main electronics shops: compare the prices. Bring cash. You cannot return merchandise, but they will exchange it. Save your receipt for showing the manufacturer if repairing defective merchandise. Don't be dismayed by the small space each has – the local warehouse will (usually) ship your request to the store within minutes.

ABC Trading Corporation, 31 Canal St ☎ 228-5080. Sun–Fri 10am–6pm.

Pro Electronics, 28 Canal St ☎ 227-4088. Seven days a week, 10am–7pm. Specializes in multi-systems, VCRs and TVs.

Traditional retailers

B&H Photo and Video, 119 W 17th St ☎ 807-7474. For specialty equipment; knowledgeable sales help will take the time to guide you through a buying decision. Closed Sat.

Bang & Olufsen, 952 Madison Ave (at 75th St) ☎ 879-6161. Incredibly good, high-quality audio and some video, in sleek modern Danish design.

CompUSA, 420 5th Ave ☎ 764-6224. This superstore runs a computer camp for kids, offers training for adults, and carries the largest inventory in the city.

DataVision, 445 5th Ave ☎ 689-1111; 10 E 40th St ☎ 685-6445. Superstore filled with computer and video equipment.

Grand Central Camera and Computer, 420 Lexington Ave (at 44th St) ☎ 986-2270. Huge selection, and the staff speaks several languages.

Shops and Markets

Harvey Electronics, 2 W 45th St (at 5th Ave) ☎ 575-5000. Top-of-the-line equipment, sold by experts.

J&R Music and Computer World, 15–23 Park Row (between Beekman and Anne sts) ☎ 238-9000. In this store down by City Hall, you'll find a good selection with good prices for stereo and computer equipment.

Nobody Beats the Wiz ☎ 677-4111; 726 Broadway (at Waverly Place) and six other locations. The Wiz, as it's popularly known, is one of the largest (though never the cheapest) stores. However, their motto, "Nobody Beats The Wiz," promises a matched price for any item you saw for less elsewhere (bring in a flyer as proof). It's a convenient place to shop, and a good place to benchmark prices.

Miscellaneous

The things listed below don't fit easily into any of the previous categories. They're either offbeat shops, interesting to visit simply in and of themselves, or they sell useful items that are cheaper in New York than in most other countries.

ABC Carpet and Home, 888 Broadway (at 19th St) ☎ 473-3000. Six floors of antiques and country furniture, knick-knacks, linens and carpets, of course. The grandiose, museum-like set-up is half the fun. Wander to garner decorating ideas.

Body Worship, 102 E 7th (between 1st Ave and Ave A) ☎ 614-0124. Fetish

Shops and Markets

fashion and erotica, as attested by the shapely phallic doorhandle. Get your latex and corsets here. Some of their window displays qualify as art.

Condomania, 351 Bleecker St (at W 10th St) ☎691-9442. A store for the AIDS-conscious 1990s. Condoms in all shapes, sizes, colors and flavors. Some for jokes but most to use.

Enchanted Forest, 85 Mercer St (between Spring and Broome sts) ☎925-6677. Truly lives up to its name: a veritable magic jungle with a plank bridge and a whimsical collection of toys, books, gems and folk art. Perfect for big (and little) kids.

Hammacher Schlemmer, 147 E 57th St (between Lexington and 3rd aves) ☎421-9000. Established in 1848, and probably New York's longest-running trivia store. Unique items, both practical and whimsical. Claims to be the first store to sell the pop-up toaster.

J&R Tobacco Corp, 11 E 45th St (between 5th and Madison aves) ☎983-4160. Self-proclaimed largest cigar store in the world, with an enormous – and affordably priced – range including all the best-known (and some not so known) brands.

Kate's Paperie, 561 Broadway (between Prince and Spring sts) ☎941-9816. Any kind of paper you could imagine or want. 22,000 square feet of paper in stock from 30 different countries, including great handmade and exotic paper. If you can't find something – ask. They'll even custom-make paper for you. A smaller shop is located at 8 W 13th St (between 5th and 6th aves).

Little Rickie, 49 1/2 1st Ave (at 3rd St) ☎505-6467. A selection of kitsch: "Church of Elvis" fridge magnets, plastic nativity scenes for the dashboard, etc.

Maxilla & Mandible, 451 Columbus Ave (between 81st and 82nd sts) ☎724-6173. Animal and human bones for collectors, scientists or the curious. Worth a visit even if you're not in the market for a perfectly preserved male skeleton.

Merrimack Publishing Corp, 85 5th Ave (at 16th St) ☎989-5162. Victorian repro

toys, decorations, greetings cards, etc, as well as all manner of useless and trivial items – wind-up toys, yo-yos and the like.

New York Yankees Clubhouse Shop, 393 5th Ave (between 36th and 37th sts) ☎685-4693. In case you want that "NY" logo on all your clothing. Another location at 110 E 59th St (between Park and Lexington aves) ☎758-7844.

Our Name is Mud, 1566 2nd Ave (between 81st and 82nd sts) ☎570-6868; 59 Greenwich Ave ☎647-7899; 506 Amsterdam Ave between (64th and 65th sts) ☎579-5575. You can buy beautiful handmade pottery here, even an unfinished vessel to paint with your own personal design.

Pink Pussycat Boutique, 167 W 4th St (between 6th and 7th aves) ☎243-0077. All manner of sex toys and paraphernalia. Somewhat of a Village institution.

The Sharper Image, inside Pier 17 at South Street Seaport ☎693-0477; 900 Madison Ave ☎794-4974; 4 W 57th St (between 5th and 6th aves) ☎265-2550. Expensive novelty items for yuppies – talking alarm clocks, massage devices and the sort of stuff you find in little catalogues that drop out of Sunday newspaper supplements. Classy meets bratty here, but the latest techno-gizmos always impress.

So What!, 153 Prince St (just west of W Broadway) ☎505-7615. Everything that sparkles, glimmers and shines is here and probably selling for less than three bucks. Boas, tiaras, body glitter, hair dye, fake tattoos and accessories galore.

Village Chess Shop, 230 Thompson St (between W 3rd and Bleecker St) ☎475-8130. Every kind of chess set for every kind of pocket. Usually packed with people playing. Open till midnight.

Markets

New York's **markets** are a treat – though not as much of an institution or as grand as European outdoor markets. However, they take the cake as far as the rest of the United States is concerned. Produce is always top-quality, there's a lot of organic food available, and bargains are common.

Greenmarkets

Several days each week, long before sunrise, hundreds of farmers from Long Island, the Hudson Valley and parts of Pennsylvania and New Jersey set out in their trucks transporting fresh-picked bounty to New York City, where they are joined by bakers, cheesemakers and others at **greenmarkets**. These are run by the city authorities, roughly one to four days a week between June and December. Usually you'll find apple cider, jams and preserves, flowers and plants, maple syrup, fresh meat and fish, pretzels, cakes and breads, herbs, honey – just about any and everything that's produced in the rural regions around the city – not to mention occasional live worm composts and baby dairy goats.

Shops and Markets

Where to find greenmarkets

MANHATTAN

Bowling Green at Broadway and Battery Place Thurs, year round.

World Trade Center at Church and Fulton sts Tues, June–Dec, and Thurs, year round.

City Hall at Chambers and Centre sts Tues and Fri, year round.

Washington Market Park at Greenwich and Reade sts Wed, year round.

Federal Plaza at Broadway and Thomas sts Fri, year round.

Lafayette St at Lafayette and Spring sts Thurs, July–Oct.

Tompkins Square at 7th St and Ave A Sun, year round.

St Mark's Church at E 10th St and 2nd Ave Tues, June–Dec.

Abingdon Square at W 12th St and 8th Ave Sat, May–Dec.

Union Square at E 17th St Broadway Mon, Wed, Fri and Sat, year round.

Sheffield Plaza at W 57th and 9th Ave Wed and Sat, year round.

Verdi Square at 72nd St and Broadway Sat, June–Dec.

I.S. 44 at W 77th St and Columbus Ave Sun, year round.

W 97th St between Amsterdam and Columbus aves Fri, June–Dec.

W 144th St and Lenox Ave Tues, July–Oct.

W 175th St at Broadway Thurs, July–Dec.

BRONX

Lincoln Hospital at E 149th St and Park Ave Tues and Fri, July–Oct.

Poe Park, E 192nd St and Grand Concourse Tues, July–Nov.

BROOKLYN

Albee Square at Fulton St and DeKalb Ave Wed, July–Oct.

Bedford-Stuyvesant at Nostrand and DeKalb aves Sat, July–Oct.

Borough Hall at Court and Remsen sts Tues and Sat, year round.

Grand Army Plaza at entrance to Prospect Park Sat, year round.

McCarren Park at Lorimer and Driggs aves Sat, Jun–Nov.

Williamsburg at Havemeyer St and Broadway Thurs, July–Oct.

Windsor Terrace at Prospect Park W and 15th St Wed, year round.

QUEENS

Jackson Heights at Junction Blvd and 34th Ave Wed, July–Oct.

STATEN ISLAND

St George at St Mark's and Hyatt sts Sat, June–Nov.

Shops and Markets

Most greenmarkets are open 8am–5pm, but some start as late as 10am and end as early as 1pm. To find the one nearest to you, call ☎477-3220, or see the box overleaf.

Flea markets and craft fairs

New York **flea markets** are outstanding for funky and old clothes, collectibles, lingerie, jewelry, crafts; there's also any number of odd places – parking lots, playgrounds, or maybe just an extra-wide bit of sidewalk – where people set up to sell their wares. In spring and summer especially you can make a mesmerizing Saturday of neighborhood market-strolling.

DOWNTOWN MANHATTAN
Essex St Covered Market, on Essex St between Rivington and Delancey. Mon–Fri 9am–6pm. In an old municipal building you'll find a kosher fish market along with Latino groceries and a Chinese greenmarket, reflecting the diverse neighborhood. Also jewelry and clothes.

SoHo Antiques and Collectibles Fair, Broadway and Grand St, Sat & Sun 9am–5pm. Collectibles and crafts.

SoHo Flea Market, 503 Broadway (between Spring and Broome sts), Sat, Sun & holidays, 10am–6pm. Not as established version of Tower Market – in fact, can be very slow.

Tower Market, Broadway between W 4th and W 3rd sts, Sat & Sun 10am–7pm. House music, jewelry, clothes, woven goods from South America, New Age paraphernalia and the like.

MIDTOWN MANHATTAN
Annex Antiques Fair and Flea Market, 6th Ave at 26th St, Sat & Sun 10am–6pm. Surrounded by antique shops, this is the fastest growing fair in New York with 600 vendors. Four other locations in the surrounding two blocks. Admission $1. (See p.479 for more detailed information.)

Fifth Avenue Pavilion, 5th Ave and 42nd St, Mon–Fri 11am–7pm, Sat & Sun noon–6pm. Was under a tent, now has a small, crowded building to house 25 vendors – a mix of world crafts and NY souvenirs.

Grand Central Crafts Market, main waiting room, off 42nd St and Park Ave entrance. Christmas and spring seasons, with the best of New York shops displaying their wares. At other times, check out this beautifully renovated space, often used for offbeat art exhibits.

UPTOWN MANHATTAN
Antique Flea and Farmers Market, PS 183, E 67th St between 1st and York Ave, Sat 6am–6pm. Usually about 150 indoor and outdoor stalls of fresh food, odd antiques and needlework.

Columbus Circle Market, 58th St and 8th Ave, in front of the Coliseum. Seven days a week, 11am–7pm. Over twenty stalls in a convenient location – lots of jewelry and a small homemade food area.

Green Flea I.S. 44 Flea Market, Columbus Ave at 77th St. Every Sun 10am–6pm. One of the best and largest markets in the city; antiques and collectibles, new merchandise and a farmer's market.

Malcolm Shabazz Harlem Market, 116th St between Lenox and 5th aves. Daily 8am–9pm. Bazaar-like market, its entrance marked by colorful fake minarets. A dazzling array of West African cloth, clothes, jewelry, masks, Ashanti dolls and beads. Also sells leather bags, music and Black Pride T-shirts.

Chapter 25

Directory

AIRLINES Toll-free phone numbers of foreign airlines include: Air India ☎1-800/223-7776; Air New Zealand ☎1-800/262-1234; British Airways ☎1-800/247-9297; El Al ☎1-800/223-6700; Japan Air Lines ☎1-800/525-3663; Korean Airlines ☎1-800/438-5000; Kuwait Airways ☎1-800/458-9248; Qantas Airways ☎1-800/227-4500; Virgin Atlantic Airways ☎1-800/862-8621. For the toll-free numbers of the major US and Canadian airlines, see p.10.

BRING . . . your credit card – you'll be considered barely human without it.

BUY . . . Good things to take home, especially with a decent exchange rate, include all American-style gear, such as baseball caps, basketball shoes, American Levis, and any kind of trainers. CDs are significantly cheaper, as is almost any photographic or electronic equipment; for the latter, however, make sure the voltages match or can be converted (see overleaf, and read our warnings on p.480).

CONSULATES Australia, 150 E 42nd St (☎351-6500); Canada, 1251 6th Ave at 50th St (☎596-1628); Denmark, 1 Dag Hammerskjöld Plaza (☎223-4545); Ireland, 345 Park Ave at 51st St (☎319-2555); Netherlands, 1 Rockefeller Plaza (entrance at 14 W 49th St between 5th and 6th aves) (☎246-1429); Sweden, 1 Dag Hammerskjöld Plaza (☎583-2550); UK, 845 3rd Ave between 51st and 52nd sts (☎745-0200).

CONTRACEPTION Condoms are available in all pharmacies and delis. If you're on the pill it's obviously best to bring a supply with you; should you run out, or need advice on other aspects of contraception, abortion or related matters, contact Planned Parenthood, Margaret Sanger Center, 26 Bleecker St at Mott (☎274-7200) or the Women's Healthline (☎230-1111).

DATES Written the other way around to Europe. For example, 4.1.99 is not the 4th of January but the 1st of April.

DOGS Dog shit on the sidewalk is much less of a problem than it was, thanks to "pooper scooper" laws that make it illegal not to clear up after your mutt. This is firmly enforced, and wherever you go in the city you'll see conscientious dog owners scraping up after their pets with makeshift cardboard shovels and newspaper, then dumping the evidence in the nearest litter bin. So you might want to think twice before doing your New York friend a favor and walking the dog.

DRUGS While drug use of all kinds is pretty prevalent throughout New York, possession of any "controlled substance" is completely illegal. Should you be found in possession of a small amount of marijuana, you probably won't go to jail – but can expect a hefty fine and, as with most run-ins with the law, the possibility of deportation. The days are gone when you could safely score a "dime bag" of wacky weed in Washington Square Park (David Lee Roth

Directory

learned the hard way); and the guy on the corner wooing you with urgent whispers of "smoke, smoke – sens, sens" is, quite possibly, an undercover cop. Due to periodic crackdowns, buying anything from street dealers is an iffy business, so now resourceful New Yorkers, being true to form, simply have it delivered (but don't expect anyone to tell you by whom).

ELECTRIC CURRENT 110V AC with two-pronged plugs. Unless they're dual voltage, all British appliances will need a voltage converter as well as a plug adapter. Be warned, some converters may not be able to handle certain high-wattage items, especially those with heated elements.

EMERGENCIES For Police, Fire or Ambulance dial ☎911.

FLOORS In the United States, the ground floor is known as the first floor, the first floor the second . . . so if someone you know lives on the third floor you only have to walk up two flights of stairs. Many older buildings (and some newer ones) count floors 11, 12, 14 . . . skipping the 13th floor out of superstition.

HOMELESSNESS Partly due simply to the lack of affordable accommodation, partly to a policy a few years back of releasing long-term mental patients into the community without any real provision of community care, you will be struck by the number of people living on the streets in New York – a population that is ever-growing.

ID Carry some at all times, as there are any number of occasions on which you may be asked to show it. Two pieces of ID are preferable and one should have a photo – passport and credit card are the best bets. Almost every bar and restaurant (serving alcohol) in New York will ask for proof of age (21 and over).

JAYWALKING This is how New Yorkers cross the streets – ie when they can, regardless of what the light might say, or if there's a light there at all. However, you should be aware that Mayor Giuliani recently announced a "get tough" policy

on jaywalking, along with other, so-called "quality of life" crimes.

LAUNDRY Hotels do it but charge the earth. You're much better off going to an ordinary laundromat or dry cleaners, both of which you'll find plenty of in the Yellow Pages under "Laundries." Some budget hotels, YMCAs and hostels also have coin-operated washers and dryers.

LEFT LUGGAGE The most likely place to dump your stuff is Grand Central Station (42nd St and Park Ave ☎340-2555), where the luggage/lost and found department is located by Track 100, on the lower level, open Mon–Fri 7am–11pm, Sat & Sun 10am–11pm, and charges $2 per item per calendar day. Photo ID required.

LIBRARIES The real heavyweight is the central reference section of the New York Public Library on 5th Ave at 42nd St (see p.141). However, as the name suggests, while this is a great place to work and its stock of books is one of the best in America and indeed the world, you can't actually take books home at the end of the day. To do this you need to go to a branch of the NYC Public Library (for a full list ask in the reference library) and produce proof of residence in the city. Across the board, library hours have been reduced drastically due to budget cuts. Not a problem for the visitor, but for the city's 9-to-5ers it's a definite bone of contention.

LOST PROPERTY Things lost on buses or on the subway: NYC Transit Authority, at the 34th St/8th Ave Station at the north end on the lower level subway mezzanine (Mon–Wed & Fri 8am–noon, Thurs 11am–6.30pm ☎712-4500). Things lost on Amtrak: Penn Station (Mon–Fri 7.30am–4pm ☎630-7389). Things lost in a cab: Taxi & Limousine Commission Lost Property Information Dept, 40 Rector St between Washington St and the West Side Highway (Mon–Fri 9am–5pm except national holidays ☎302-8294).

MEASUREMENTS AND SIZES The US has yet to go metric and measurements of length are in inches, feet, yards and miles, with weight measured in ounces, pounds and tons. Liquid measures are slightly more confusing in that an imperial pint is roughly equivalent to 1.25 American pints, and an American gallon thus only equal to about four-fifths of an imperial one. Add to this the fact that milk and orange juice are sold in quarts, while Coke and its equivalents are sold in litres. Clothing and shoe sizes are easier: women's garment sizes are always two figures less than they would be in Britain. Thus, a British size 12 will be a size 10 in the States, a size 14 a size 12. To calculate shoe sizes in America, simply add 2 to your British size – thus, if you're normally size 8 you'll need a size 9 shoe in New York. See p.457 for more.

NOTICE BOARDS For contacts, casual work, articles for sale, etc, it's hard to beat the notice board just inside the doorway of the *Village Voice* office at 36 Cooper Square (just south of the Astor Place subway stop). Otherwise there are numerous notice boards up at Columbia University, in the Loeb Student Center of NYU on Washington Square, and in the groovier coffee shops, health food stores and restaurants in the East Village.

PUBLIC HOLIDAYS You'll find all banks, most offices, some stores and certain museums closed on the following days: January 1; Martin Luther King's Birthday (third Mon in Jan); Presidents' Day (third Mon in Feb); Memorial Day (last Mon in May); Independence Day (July 4 or, if it falls on a weekend, the following Mon); Labor Day (first Mon in Sept); Columbus Day (second Mon in Oct); Veterans Day (Nov 11); Thanksgiving (the third or last Thurs in Nov); Christmas Day (Dec 25). Also, New York's numerous parades mean that on certain days – Washington's Birthday, St Patrick's Day, Gay Pride Day, Easter Sunday and Columbus Day – much of 5th Ave is closed to traffic altogether.

RATS AND ROACHES You'll find both types of pest all around the city, in bigger versions than most anywhere else. Don't worry, though – they may be more afraid of you than you are of them.

STREET NAMES/STREET SIGNS New York likes to honor its favorite sons – or daughters – by renaming thoroughfares after them. Just recently the West Side Highway was rechristened the Joe Di Maggio highway in honor of the late Yankee Clipper. So don't panic when you're strolling up 6th Ave only to find yourself on the Avenue of the Americas. And don't expect street signs to be pointing, necessarily, in the right direction.

SWIMMING POOLS See p.430.

TAX Within New York City you'll pay an 8.25 percent sales tax on top of marked prices on just about everything but the very barest of essentials, a measure brought in to help alleviate the city's 1975 economic crisis, and one which stuck. The tax on clothing is to be lifted in the near future; in anticipation of which there are, from time to time "No Tax Weeks," when you buy items up to, say, $1000, without any tax.

TERMINALS AND TRANSIT INFORMATION Grand Central Terminal, 42nd St and Park Ave (Metro-North commuter trains ☎532-4900); Pennsylvania Station, 33rd St and 8th Ave (Amtrak ☎1-800/USA-RAIL or 582-6875); New Jersey Transit (☎973/762-5100); Long Island Railroad (LIRR ☎718/217-5477); PATH trains (☎1-800/234-7284); Port Authority Bus Terminal, 41st St, and 8th Ave and George Washington Bridge Bus Terminal, W 178th St (between Broadway and Fort Washington) both ☎564-8484; Greyhound (☎1-800/231-2222); Peter Pan Trailways (☎1-800/343-9999); Bonanza (☎1-800/556-3815).

TIME Five hours behind Britain and Ireland, fourteen to sixteen hours behind East Coast Australia (variations for Daylight Savings Time), sixteen to eighteen hours behind New Zealand (variations for Daylight Savings Time), three hours ahead of West Coast North

Directory

Directory

America. Also, when New Yorkers are telling you the time they'll say "after" for "past" and, sometimes, "of" instead of "to" (as in "a quarter of six" meaning "five forty-five").

TIPPING It won't take long before you realize that tipping, in a restaurant, bar, taxi cab, hotel lobby and even in some posh washrooms is a part of life in the States – in restaurants in particular, it's unthinkable not to leave the minimum (15 percent of the bill or double the tax) even if you hated the service.

TOILETS Several years ago, the city temporarily waived its ruling against paying public toilets to test a run of self-cleaning 25¢ sidewalk stalls. These proved immensely popular, so naturally they were removed, although if the city ever gets around to repealing the offending law, they'll be back. For now, the only one that remains is in City Hall park across from the Municipal Building, and it's such an unusual sight that you'll see people taking each other's picture going in and out. If you're anywhere else in the city, however, you have to resort to bravely flouting signs like "Restrooms for patrons only." Otherwise check out the lobbies of any of the swanky hotels in Midtown; the Trump Tower, where there are public loos on the Garden level; the New York Public Library at 42nd St and 5th Ave; and the Lincoln Center's Avery Fisher Hall and Library, both of which have several bathrooms. Starbucks, Barnes & Noble Superstores, and Macy's and Bloomingdale's department stores also have accessible and clean restrooms.

TRAVEL AGENTS Council Travel, America's principal student/youth travel organization, has an office at 205 E 42nd St (☎822-2700) and deals in airline and other tickets, inclusive tours, car rental, international student cards, guidebooks and work camps. Other agents worth trying are STA Travel, 10 Downing St (☎627-3111), and Nouvelles Frontières, 12 E 33rd St (☎779-0600). Bear in mind that Greyhound passes, etc, are better value if you purchase them before you leave home.

TURKISH BATHS Tenth Street Turkish Baths, 268 E 10th St (between 1st Ave and Ave A) ☎674-9250. Manhattan's longest-established bath, where you can use the steam rooms and pool for $20; a half-hour massage is $30 extra ($45 for a full hour). No appointment necessary.

WORSHIP There are regular services and masses at the following churches and synagogues. Anglican (Episcopal): Cathedral of St John the Divine, 1047 Amsterdam Ave at 112th St (☎316-7400); St Bartholomew's, 109 E 50th St (☎751-1616); Trinity Church, Broadway and Wall St (☎602-0800). Catholic: St Patrick's Cathedral, 5th Ave between 50th and 51st sts (☎753-2261). Jewish (Reform): Temple Emanu-el, 5th Ave at 65th St (☎744-1400); Central Synagogue, Lexington Ave at 55th St (☎838-5122). Jewish (Conservative): Park Avenue Synagogue, 87th St at Madison Ave (☎369-2600). Unitarian: Church of All Souls, Lexington Ave at 80th St (☎535-5530).

Part 4

Contexts

The historical framework

To Europe she was America, to America she was the gateway of the earth. But to tell the story of New York would be to write a social history of the world.

H.G. Wells

Early days and colonial rule

In the earliest times, the area that today is New York City was populated by Native Americans. Each tribe had its own territory and lived a settled existence in villages of bark huts, gaining a livelihood from crop planting, hunting, trapping and fishing. In the New York area the Algonquin tribe was the most populous. Survivors of this and other tribes still live on Long Island's **Shinnecock reservation** and remnants of their native cultures can be seen at the upstate Turtle Center for the Native American Indian.

Native American life, as it had existed for several thousand years, was to end with the arrival of European explorers. In 1524 **Giovanni da Verrazano**, an Italian in the service of the French King Francis I, arrived, following in the footsteps of Christopher Columbus 32 years earlier. On his ship, the *Dauphane*, Verrazano had set out to find the legendary Northwest Passage to the Pacific; instead he discovered Manhattan. "We found a very agreeable situation located within two small prominent hills, in the midst of which flowed to the sea a very great river, which was

deep within the mouth; and from the sea to the hills, with the rising of the tide, which we found at eight feet, any laden ship might have passed." Verrazano returned, "leaving the said land with much regret because of its commodiousness and beauty, thinking it was not without some properties of value," to woo the court with tales of fertile lands and friendly natives, but oddly enough it was nearly a century before the powers of Europe were tempted to follow him.

In 1609 **Henry Hudson**, an Englishman employed by the **Dutch East India Company**, landed at Manhattan and sailed his ship, the *Half-Moone*, upriver as far as Albany. Hudson found that the route did not lead to the Northwest Passage he had been commissioned to discover – but in charting its course for the first time he gave his name to the mighty river. "This is a very good land to fall with," noted the ship's mate, "and a pleasant land to see." In a series of skirmishes Hudson's men gave the native people a taste of what to expect from future adventurers. Chastised by the British for exploring new territory for the Dutch, Hudson embarked on another expedition, this time under the British flag. He arrived in Hudson Bay, the temperature falling and the mutinous crew doubting his ability as a navigator; he, his son and several others were set adrift in a small boat on the icy waters where, presumably, they froze to death.

The British fear that the Dutch had gained the upper hand in the newly discovered land proved justified, for they had the commercial advantage and wasted no time in making the most of it. In the next few years the Dutch established a trading post at the most northerly point Hudson had reached, **Fort Nassau**. In 1624, four years after the Pilgrim Fathers had sailed to Massachusetts, thirty families left Holland to become New York's first European settlers, most sailing up to Fort Nassau but a handful – eight families in all – staying behind on a small island they called Nut Island because of the many walnut trees there: today's Governor's Island. Slowly the community grew as more settlers arrived, and the little island became crowded; the decision was made to move to the limitless spaces across the water, and **the settlement of Manhattan**, taken from the Algonquin Indian word *Manna-Hata* meaning "Island of the Hills," began.

The Dutch gave their new outpost the name **New Amsterdam** and in 1626 **Peter Minuit** was sent out to govern the small community of just over three hundred. Among his first, and certainly more politically adroit, moves was to buy the whole of Manhattan Island from the Indians for trinkets worth 60 guilders (about $25 today); of course the other side of the anecdote is that the Indians Minuit dealt with didn't even come from Manhattan, let alone own it. As the colony slowly grew, a string of governors succeeded Minuit, the most famous of them **Peter Stuyvesant** – "Peg Leg Pete," a seasoned colonialist from the Dutch West Indies who'd lost his leg in a scrap with the Portuguese. Under his leadership New Amsterdam doubled in size and population, protected from British settlers to the north by an encircling wall (**Wall Street** today follows its course) and defended by a rough-hewn fort on what is now the site of the Customs House. Stuyvesant also built himself a farm (a *bowerie* in Dutch) nearby, that gave its name to the **Bowery**.

Meanwhile the **British** were steadily and stealthily building up their presence to the north. Though initially preoccupied by Civil War at home, they maintained their claim that all of America's East Coast, from New England to Virginia, was theirs, and in 1664 sent Colonel Richard Nicholls to claim the lands around the Hudson that King Charles II had granted to his brother, the Duke of York. To reinforce his sovereignty Charles sent along four warships and landed troops on Nut Island and Long Island. The Dutch settlers had by then had enough of Stuyvesant's increasingly dictatorial rule, especially the high taxation demanded by the nominal owners of the colony, the Dutch West India Company, and so refused to defend Dutch rule against the British. Captain Nicholls's men took New Amsterdam, renamed it **New York** in honor of the duke and settled down to a hundred-odd years of British rule, interrupted only briefly in 1673 when the Dutch once more managed to gain the upper hand.

During this period not all was plain sailing. When King James II was forced to abdicate and flee Britain in 1689, a German merchant called **James Leisler** led a revolt against British rule. Unfortunately for Leisler it mustered little sympathy, and he was hanged for treason. Also, by now

black slaves constituted a major part of New York's population, and though laws denied them weapons and the right of assembly, in 1712 a number of slaves set fire to a building near Maiden Lane and killed nine people who attempted to stop the blaze. When soldiers arrived, six of the incendiaries committed suicide and twenty-one others were captured and executed. In other areas primitive civil rights were slowly being established: in 1734 **John Peter Zenger**, publisher of the *New York Weekly Journal*, was tried and acquitted of libeling the British government, establishing freedom for the press that would later result in the First Amendment to the Constitution.

Revolution

By the 1750s the city had reached a population of 16,000, spread roughly as far north as Chambers Street. As the new community became more confident, it realized that it could exist independently of the government in Britain. But in 1763 the **Treaty of Paris** concluded the Seven Years' War with France, and sovereignty over most of explored North America was conceded to England. British rule was thus consolidated and the government decided to try throwing its weight about. Within a year, discontent over British rule escalated with the passage of the punitive **Sugar, Stamp and Colonial Currency Acts**, which allowed the British to collect taxes to pay for their local army. Further resentment erupted over the **Quartering Act**, which permitted British troops to requisition private dwellings and inns, their rent to be paid by the colonies themselves. Ill feeling steadily mounted and skirmishes between soldiers and the insurrectionist **Sons of Liberty** culminated in January 1770 with the killing of a colonist and the wounding of several others. **The Boston Massacre**, in which British troops fired upon taunting protestors, occurred a few weeks later and helped foster revolutionary sentiment.

In a way, New York's role during the **War of Independence** was not crucial, for all the battles fought in and around the city were generally won by the side that lost the war. But New York was the site of the first military engagements between the British and American forces after the **Declaration of Independence** was proclaimed to cheering crowds outside the site of today's **City Hall Park**. These crowds then went off to tear down the statue of George III that stood on the Bowling Green. The British, driven from Boston the previous winter, resolved that New York should be the place where they would reassert their authority over the rebels, and in June and July of 1776 some two hundred ships under the command of **Lord Howe** arrived in New York Harbor. The troops made camp on Staten Island while the commander of the American forces, **George Washington**, consolidated his men, in the hope that the mouth of the harbor was sufficiently well defended to stop British ships from entering it and encircling his troops. But Howe decided to make his assault on the city by land: on August 22, 1776 he landed 15,000 men, mainly Hessian mercenaries, on the southwest corner of Brooklyn. His plan was to occupy Brooklyn and launch an attack on Manhattan from there. In the **Battle of Long Island**, Howe's men penetrated the American forward lines at a number of points, the most important engagement taking place at what is today Prospect Park.

The Americans fell back to their positions and as the British made preparations to attack, Washington could see that his garrison would be easily defeated. On the night of August 29, under cover of rain and fog, he evacuated his men safely to Manhattan from the ferry slip beneath where the Brooklyn Bridge now stands, preserving the bulk of his forces. A few days later Howe's army set out in boats from Green Point and Newtown Creek in Brooklyn to land at what is now the 34th Street heliport site. The defenders of the city retreated north to make a stand at Harlem Heights, but were pushed back again to eventual defeat at the **Battle of White Plains** in Westchester County (the Bronx), where Washington lost 1400 of his 4000 men. More tragic still was the defense of **Fort Washington**, perched on a rocky cliff 230 feet above the Hudson, near today's George Washington Bridge. Here, rather than evacuate the troops, the local commander made a decision to stand and fight. It was a fatal mistake: they were trapped by the Hudson to the west, and upwards of 3000 men were killed or taken prisoner. Gathering more forces, Washington retreated, and for the next seven years New York was occupied by the British as a garrison town. During this period many of the remaining inhabitants and most of the prisoners taken by the British slowly starved to death.

Lord Cornwallis's **surrender** to the Americans in October 1783 marked the end of the War of Independence, and a month later New York was finally freed. Washington, the man who had held the American army together by sheer willpower, was there to celebrate, riding in triumphal procession down Canal Street and saying farewell to his officers at **Fraunces Tavern**, a building that still stands at the end of Pearl Street. It was a tearful occasion for men who had fought through the worst of the war years together: "I am not only retiring from all public employments," Washington declared, "but am retiring within myself."

But that was not to be. New York was now the fledgling nation's **capital** and, as Benjamin Franklin et al framed the Constitution and the role of president of the United States, it became increasingly clear that there was only one candidate for the position. On April 30, 1789, Washington took the oath of president at the site of the **Federal Hall National Memorial** on Wall Street. The federal government was transferred to the District of Columbia a year later.

Immigration and civil war

In 1790 the first official census of Manhattan put the population at around 33,000: business and trade were on the increase, with the market under a buttonwood tree on Wall Street being a forerunner to the New York Stock Exchange. A few years later, in 1807, **Robert Fulton** launched the *Clermont*, a steamboat that managed to splutter its way up the Hudson River from New York to Albany, pioneering trade with upstate areas. A year before his death in 1814 Fulton also started a ferry service between Manhattan and Brooklyn, and the dock at which it moored became a focus of trade and eventually a maritime center, taking its name from the inventor.

But it was the opening of the **Erie Canal** in 1825 that really allowed New York to develop as a port. The Great Lakes were suddenly opened to New York, and with them the rest of the country; goods manufactured in the city could be sent easily and cheaply to the American heartland. It was because of this transportation network, and the mass of **cheap labor** that flooded in throughout the nineteenth and early twentieth centuries, that New York – and to an extent the nation – became wealthy. The first waves of **immigrants**, mainly **German** and **Irish**, began to arrive in the mid-nineteenth century, the latter forced out by the potato famine of 1846, the former by the failed revolution of 1848–49, which had left many German liberals, laborers, intellectuals and businessmen dispossessed. The city could not handle people arriving in such great numbers and epidemics of yellow fever and cholera were common, exacerbated by poor water supplies, unsanitary conditions and the poverty of most of the newcomers. Despite this, in the 1880s large-scale **Italian** immigration began, mainly of laborers and peasants from southern Italy and Sicily, while at the same time refugees from **eastern Europe** started to arrive – many of them Jewish. The two communities shared a home on the **Lower East Side**, which became one of the worst slum areas of its day. On the eve of the Civil War the majority of New York's 750,000 population were immigrants; in 1890 one in four of the city's inhabitants was Irish.

During this period life for the well-off was fairly pleasant and development in the city proceeded apace. Despite a great fire in 1835 that destroyed most of the business district Downtown, trade boomed and was celebrated in the opening of the **World's Fair** of 1835 at the Crystal Palace on the site of Bryant Park – an iron and glass building that fared no better than its London namesake, burning down in 1858. In the same year work began on clearing the shantytowns in the center of the island to make way for a new, landscaped open space – a marvelous design by Frederick Law Olmsted and Calvert Vaux that became **Central Park**.

Two years later the **Civil War** broke out, caused by growing differences between the northern and southern states, notably on the issues of slavery and trade. New York sided with the Union (north) against the Confederates (south), but had few experiences of the hand-to-hand fighting that ravaged the rest of the country. It did, however, form a focus for much of the radical thinking behind the war, particularly with **Abraham Lincoln**'s influential "Might makes Right" speech from the **Cooper Union Building** in 1860. In 1863 a **conscription law** was passed that allowed the rich to buy themselves out of military service. Not surprisingly this was deeply unpopular, and New Yorkers rioted, burning buildings and looting shops: more than a thousand people were killed in these **Draft Riots**. A sad addendum to the war was the assassination of Lincoln in 1865: when his body lay in state in New York's City Hall, 120,000 people filed past to pay last respects.

The late nineteenth century

The end of the Civil War saw much of the country devastated but New York intact, and it was fairly predictable that the city would soon become the wealthiest and most influential in the nation. Broadway developed into the main thoroughfare, with grand hotels, restaurants and shops catering to the rich; newspaper editors **William Cullen Bryant** and **Horace Greeley** respectively founded the *Evening Post* and the *Tribune*; and the city became a magnet for writers and intellectuals, with **Washington Irving** and **James Fenimore Cooper** among notable residents. By dint of its skilled immigrant workers, its facilities for marketing goods and the wealth to build factories, New York was also the greatest business, commercial and manufacturing center in the country. **Cornelius Vanderbilt** controlled a vast shipping and railroad empire, and **J.P. Morgan**, the banking and investment wizard, was instrumental in organizing financial mergers that led to the formation of a prototype corporate business.

But even bigger in a way was a character who was not a businessman but a politician: **William Marcy "Boss" Tweed**. From lowly origins Tweed worked his way up the Democratic Party ladder to the position of alderman at the age of 21, eventually becoming chairman of the party's State Committee. Surrounded by his own men – the **Tweed Ring** – and aided by a paid-off mayor, "Boss" Tweed took total control of the city's government and finances. Anyone in a position to challenge his money-making schemes was bought off with cash extorted from contractors eager to carry out municipal services; in this way $160 million found its way into Tweed's and his friends' pockets. Tweed stayed in power by organizing the speedy naturalization of immigrant aliens, who, in repayment, were expected to vote Tweed's way. For his part, Tweed gave generously to the poor, who knew he was swindling the rich but saw him as a Robin Hood figure. As a contemporary observer remarked, "The government of the rich by the manipulation of the poor is a new phenomenon in the world." Tweed's swindles grew in audacity and greed until a determined campaign by **George Jones**, editor of the *New York Times*, and **Thomas Nast**, whose vicious portrayals of Tweed and his henchmen appeared in *Harper's Weekly*, brought him down. The people who kept Tweed in power may not have been able to read or write, but they could understand a cartoon – and Tweed's heyday was finally over. A committee was established to investigate corruption in City Hall and Tweed found himself in court. Despite a temporary escape to Spain he was returned to the US, and died in Ludlow Street jail – ironically a building he had commissioned as Chief of Works.

The latter part of the nineteenth century was in many ways the city's golden age: elevated railways (the **Els**) sprung up to transport people quickly and cheaply around the city; **Thomas Edison** lit the streets with his new electric light bulb, powered by the first electricity plant on Pearl Street; and in 1883, to the wonderment of New Yorkers, the **Brooklyn Bridge** was unveiled. Brooklyn, Staten Island, Queens and the part of Westchester known as the Bronx, along with Manhattan, were officially **incorporated** into New York City in 1898. All this commercial expansion stimulated the city's cultural growth; **Walt Whitman** eulogized the city in his poems and **Henry James** recorded its manners and mores in novels like *Washington Square*. **Richard Morris Hunt** built palaces for the wealthy robber barons along Fifth Avenue, who plundered Europe to assemble art collections to furnish them – collections that would eventually find their way into the newly opened **Metropolitan Museum**. For the "Four Hundred," the wealthy elite that reveled in and owned the city, New York in the "gay nineties" was a constant string of lavish balls and dinners that vied with each other until opulence became obscenity. At one banquet the millionaire guests arrived on horseback and ate their meals in the saddle; afterwards the horses were fed gourmet-prepared fodder.

Turn-of-the-century development

At the same time, the emigration of Europe's impoverished peoples continued unabated, and in 1884 new immigrants from the Orient settled in what became known as **Chinatown**; the following year saw a huge influx of southern Italians to the city. As the Vanderbilts, Astors and Rockefellers lorded it over the mansions Uptown, overcrowded tenements led to terrible living standards for the poor. Working conditions were little better, and were compassionately described by police reporter and photographer **Jacob Riis**, whose book *How the Other Half Lives* detailed

the long working hours, exploitation and child labor that allowed the rich to get richer.

More Jewish immigrants arrived to cram the Lower East Side, and in 1898 the population of New York amounted to more than three million – the largest city in the world. Twelve years earlier Augustus Bartholdi's **Statue of Liberty** was completed, holding a symbolic torch to guide the huddled masses; now pressure grew to limit immigration, but still people flooded in. **Ellis Island**, the depot that processed arrivals, was handling two thousand people a day, leading to a total of ten million by 1929, when laws were passed to curtail immigration. By the turn of the century, around half of the city's people were foreign-born, and a quarter of the population was made up of German and Irish migrants, most of them living in slums. The section of Manhattan bounded by the East River, East 14th Street and Third Avenue, the Bowery and Catherine Street was probably the most densely populated area on earth, inhabited by an "underclass" who lived under worse conditions and paid more rent than the inhabitants of any other big city in the world. By stark contrast, in 1900, J.P. Morgan's United States Steel Company became the first billion-dollar corporation.

The early 1900s saw some of this wealth going into adventurous new architecture. SoHo had already utilized the **cast-iron building** to mass-produce classical facades, and the **Flatiron Building** of 1902 announced the arrival of what was to become the city's trademark – the skyscraper. On the arts front **Stephen Crane**, **Theodore Dreiser** and **Edith Wharton** used New York as the subject for their writing, **George M. Cohan** was the Bright Young Man of Broadway, and in 1913 the **Armory Exhibition** of modernist painting by Picasso, Duchamp and others caused a sensation. Skyscrapers pushed ever higher, and in 1913 a building that many consider the *ne plus ultra* of the genre, the **Woolworth Building**, was completed. Also that year, **Grand Central Terminal** opened, celebrating New York as the gateway to the continent.

The first two decades of the century saw a further wave of immigration. In that period one-third of all the Jews in Eastern Europe arrived in New York, and upwards of 1.5 million of them settled in New York City, primarily in the Lower East Side. Despite advances in public building, caused by the outcry that followed Jacob Riis's reports, the area could not cope with a population density of

640,000 per square mile, and the poverty and inhuman conditions continued to worsen. Many people worked for the growing garment industry in sweatshops in the Hester Street area, which were notoriously exploitative. Most of the garment manufacturers, for example, charged women workers for their needles and the hire of lockers, and handed out stiff fines for spoilage of fabrics. Workers began to strike to demand better wages and working conditions, but the strikes of 1910–11 achieved only limited success, and it took disaster to rouse public and civic conscience. On March 25, 1911, just before the **Triangle Shirtwaist Factory** at Washington Place was about to finish work for the day, a fire broke out. The workers were trapped on the tenth floor and 146 of them died (125 were women), many by leaping from the blazing building. Within months the state had passed 56 factory reform measures, and unionization spread through the city.

The war years and the Depression: 1914–45

With America's entry into World War I in 1917, New York benefited from wartime trade and commerce. Perhaps surprisingly, there was little conflict between the various European communities crammed into the city. Although Germans comprised roughly one-fifth of the city's population, there were few of the attacks on their lives or property that occurred elsewhere in the country.

The postwar years saw one law and one character dominating the New York scene: the law was **Prohibition**, passed in 1920 in an attempt to sober up the nation; the character was **Jimmy Walker**, elected mayor in 1925. Walker led a far from sober lifestyle, "No civilized man," he said, "goes to bed the same day he wakes up," and it was during his flamboyant career that the Jazz Age came to the city. In speakeasies all over town the bootleg liquor flowed and writers as diverse as **Damon Runyon**, **F. Scott Fitzgerald** and **Ernest Hemingway** portrayed the excitement of the times. Musicians such as **George Gershwin** and **Benny Goodman** packed nightclubs with their new sound, and the **Harlem Renaissance** soared to prominence with writers like **Langston Hughes** and **Zora Neale Hurston**, and music from **Duke Ellington**, **Billie Holiday** and the **Apollo Theater**.

With the **Wall Street** crash of 1929 (see Chapter 2, "The Financial District"), however, the party came to an abrupt end. The Depression began and Mayor Walker was sent packing, along with the torrent of civic corruption and malpractice that the changing times had uncovered. By 1932 approximately one in four New Yorkers was unemployed, and shantytowns, known as "Hoovervilles" (after then President Hoover who was widely blamed for the Depression), had sprung up in Central Park to house the jobless and homeless. Yet during this period three of New York's most opulent – and most beautiful – skyscrapers were built: the **Chrysler Building** in 1930, the **Empire State** in 1931 (though it was to stand near-empty for years) and in 1932 **Rockefeller Center** – all very impressive, but of little immediate help to those in Hooverville, Harlem or other depressed parts of the city. It fell to **Fiorello LaGuardia**, Jimmy Walker's successor as mayor, to take over the running of the crisis-strewn city. He did so with stringent taxation and anti-corruption programs, along with social spending, that won him the approval of the people in the street: Walker's good living had gotten the city into trouble, reasoned voters; hard-headed, straight-talking LaGuardia would undo the damage. Moreover President Roosevelt's **New Deal** supplied funds for roads, housing and parks, the latter undertaken by the controversial Parks Commissioner **Robert Moses**. Under LaGuardia and Moses, the most extensive public housing program in the country was undertaken; the Triborough, Whitestone and Henry Hudson bridges were completed; fifty miles of new expressway and five thousand acres of new parks were opened; and, in 1939, Mayor LaGuardia opened the airport that still carries his name.

LaGuardia was in office for three terms (twelve years), taking the city into the **war years**. The country's entry into World War II in 1941 had few direct effects on New York City: lights were blacked out at night in case of bomb attacks, two hundred Japanese were interned on Ellis Island and guards were placed on bridges and tunnels. But, more importantly, behind the scenes experiments taking place at Columbia University split the uranium atom, giving a name to the **Manhattan Project** – the creation of the first atomic weapon.

The postwar years

The city maintained its preeminent position in the fields of finance, art and communications, both in

America and the world, its intellectual and creative community swollen by refugees escaping the Nazi threat to Europe. When the **United Nations Organization** was seeking a permanent home, New York was the obvious choice: lured by Rockefeller-donated land, the UN began the building of the Secretariat in 1947.

The building of the UN complex, along with the boost in the economy that followed the war, brought about the development of midtown Manhattan. First off in the race to fill the once-residential Park Avenue with offices was the **Lever House** of 1952, quickly followed by skyscrapers like the **Seagram Building** that give the area its distinctive look. Downtown, the **Stuyvesant Town** and **Peter Cooper Village** housing projects went ahead, along with many others all over the city. As ever, there were plentiful scandals over the financing of the construction, most famously concerning the **Manhattan Urban Renewal Project** on the Upper East Side.

A further scandal, this time concerning organized crime, ousted Mayor **William O'Dwyer** in 1950: he was replaced by a series of uneventful characters who did little to stop the gradual **decline** that had begun in the early 1950s as the growth of suburbs led to a general stagnation among the country's urban centers. New York was one of the hardest hit: immigration from Puerto Rico and elsewhere in Latin America once more crammed East Harlem and the Lower East Side, and the nationwide trend of black migration from poorer rural areas was also magnified here. Both groups were forced into the ghetto area of Harlem, unable to get a slice of the city's wealth. Racial disturbances and riots occurred in what had for two hundred years been one of the more liberal of American cities. One response to the problem was a general exodus of the white middle classes – the **Great White Flight** as the media gleefully labeled it – out of New York. Between 1950 and 1970 more than a million families left the city. Things went from bad to worse during the 1960s with **race riots** in Harlem, Bedford-Stuyvesant and East Harlem.

The **World's Fair** of 1964 was a white elephant to boost the city's international profile, but on the streets the call for civil liberties for blacks and protest against US involvement in Vietnam were, if anything, stronger than in the rest of the country. What little new building went up during this period seemed willfully to destroy much of the best of earlier traditions: a new, uninspired

Madison Square Garden was built on the site of the old grandly Neoclassical **Pennsylvania Station**, and the **Singer Building** in the Financial District was demolished for an ugly skyscraper. In Harlem municipal investment stopped altogether and the community stagnated.

The 1970s and 1980s

Manhattan reached **crisis point** in 1975. By now the city was spending more than it received in taxes – billions of dollars more. In part, this could be attributed to the effects of the White Flight: companies closed their headquarters in the city when offered lucrative relocation deals elsewhere, and their white-collar employees were usually glad to go with them, thus doubly eroding the city's tax base. Even after municipal securities were sold, New York ran up a debt of millions of dollars. Essential services, long shaky due to underfunding, were ready to collapse. Ironically, the mayor who oversaw this fiasco, **Abraham Beame**, was an accountant.

Three things saved the city: the **Municipal Assistance Corporation** (aka the **Big Mac**), which was formed to borrow the money the city could no longer get its hands on and save it from bankruptcy; the election of **Edward I. Koch** as mayor in 1978; and, in a roundabout way, the plummeting of the dollar on the world currency market following the oil price rises of the 1970s. This last effect, combined with cheap transatlantic airfares, brought European tourists into the city en masse for the first time, and with them came money for the city's hotels and service industries. Tough-talking Koch helped reassure jumpy corporations that staying in New York was all right for business, and gained the reluctant appreciation of New Yorkers for his pugnacious defense of the city. His brash opinions and indifferent swagger managed to offend liberal groups, but win the critical electoral support of wealthy Upper East Siders, and the more conservative outer borough ethnic groups. Mayor Koch, cheerfully saying "Isn't it terrible?" about whatever he could not immediately put right, and asking "How am I doing?" each time he scored a success, gained the appreciation of New Yorkers, ever eager to look to their civic leaders for help or blame.

The slow reversal of fortunes coincided with the completion of two face-saving building projects: though, like the Empire State Building, it long remained half empty, the **World Trade Center** was a gesture of confidence by the Port Authority of New York and New Jersey which financed it; and in 1977 the **Citicorp Center** added modernity and prestige to its environs on Lexington Avenue. Despite the fact that the city was no longer facing bankruptcy, it was still suffering from a massive nationwide recession, and the city turned to its nightlife for relief. Starting in the mid-1970s, singles bars sprang up all over the city, gay bars proliferated in the Village, and Disco was King. **Studio 54** was an internationally known hotspot, attracting the likes of Mick Jagger, Diana Ross and Elton John; drugs and illicit sex were the main events off the dance floor.

In the 1980s the real estate and stock markets boomed and another era of Big Money was ushered in; fortunes were made and lost overnight and big Wall Street names, like **Michael Milken**, were thrown in jail for insider trading. A spate of building gave the city yet more fabulous architecture, notably **Battery Park City** Downtown, and master builder **Donald Trump** provided glitzy housing for the super-wealthy (and plastered his name on everything he could get his hands on). President Ronald Reagan's trickle-down theory of economic recovery, however, proved to be an illusion – the welfare rolls in the city, and throughout the country, swelled and the number of homeless people was staggering; taking shelter in doorways and begging on street corners, even in the previously unaffected neighborhoods of the Upper East Side.

The stock market crash in 1987 started yet another downturn, and the popularity of Mayor Koch waned. Many middle-class constituents considered Koch to have only rich property-owners and developers' interests at heart; he also alienated a number of minorities – particularly blacks – with off-the-cuff statements that he was unable to bluff his way out of. And although he was not directly implicated, the scandals in his administration took their political toll, beginning with the suicide of his friend and supporter Queens borough president **Donald Manes** (who committed suicide when an investigation into the city's various debt-collecting agencies was announced), and continuing with the indictment for bribery (though she was acquitted) of another prominent friend, former Arts Commissioner, **Bess Myerson**.

The 1990s

In 1989, Koch lost the Democratic nomination for the mayoral elections to **David Dinkins**, a 61-year-old, black ex-marine and borough president of Manhattan. In a toughly fought general election, Dinkins beat Republican Rudolph Giuliani, a hard-nosed US attorney (whose role as leader of the prosecution in a police corruption case was made into the film *Prince of the City*). But even before the votes were counted, pundits were forecasting that the condition of the city was beyond any mayoral healing.

By the end of the 1980s New York was slipping hard and fast into a **massive recession**: in 1989 the city's budget deficit ran at $500 million; of the 92 companies that had made the city their base in 1980, only 53 were left, the others having moved to cheaper pastures; and one in four New Yorkers was officially classed as poor – a figure unequaled since the Depression. The first black to hold the office, David Dinkins oversaw his first year as mayor reasonably well: the city's **Board of Estimate** had been declared unconstitutional by the Supreme Court (it violated the one person, one vote principle), and was abolished and replaced by a beefier City Council. Dinkins used his powers to quell racial unrest that had seemed about to explode in the spring, and skillfully passed a complex budget through the Council.

Dinkins's – and to some extent the city's – downward slide can be traced to events during the first week of the US Open tennis tournament in summer 1990. On his way to the match, Brian Watkins, a tennis fan from Utah, was stabbed to death in a subway station by a group of muggers while trying to protect his mother. Instead of holding a Koch-style "What is this city coming to?" press conference, Dinkins issued a statement saying that the media were exaggerating the importance of the murder – and then boarded a police helicopter to fly to the tennis event. Predictably, the press latched onto this immediately and Dinkins fell swiftly from popular favor, becoming known as the man "to whom everything sticks but praise."

From that summer on, the city's fortunes went into free fall. The unions went on the offensive when it was learned the city intended to lay off 15,000 workers; crime – especially related to the sale of crack (a cheap, cocaine-derived stimulant) – escalated; businesses failed. By the end of the year the city's budget deficit had reached $1.5 billion and city creditors were threatening to remove support for municipal borrowing unless the figure was reduced drastically.

Throughout 1991 the effects of these financial problems on the city's ordinary people became more and more apparent: homelessness increased as city aid was cut back, some public schools became no-go zones with armed police and metal detectors at the gates (fewer than half of high school kids in the city graduated, a far smaller proportion than elsewhere in the United States), and a garbage workers' strike in May left piles of rubbish rotting on the streets. Once again, New York seemed to have hit rock bottom, and this time there was no obvious solution. Unlike in 1976, the state government refused to bail the city out with aid or loans; and, as far as the federal government was concerned, the coffers ran out for New York long ago.

Worse yet, a number of serious racial incidents and riots throughout his term contradicted Dinkins' coining of the phrase "gorgeous mosaic" for the city's multicultural make-up, and seemed to prove that the mayor's race alone was not enough to diffuse tensions. In the 1993 mayoral elections, David Dinkins narrowly lost to the brash Republican prosecutor **Rudolph Giuliani**. New York, traditionally a firmly Democratic city, wanted a change and with Giuliani – the city's first Republican mayor in 28 years – they got it.

Recent years

Though it might have been coincidental, Giuliani's first term helped usher in a dramatic upswing in New York's prosperity. A *New York Times* article described 1995 as "the best year in recent memory for New York City." Even the pope came to town and called New York "the capital of the world." The city's reputation flourished, with remarkable decreases in crime statistics and a revitalized economy that helped spur the tourism industry to some of its best years ever.

Giuliani emerged as a very proactive mayor, riding the coattails of the movement to downsize government that has swept America recently. Though the long-term effects of city agency reorganization and major cutbacks, and so-called "work-fare" welfare reforms still aren't known, thus far the mayor has been happy to take credit for reducing crime and the bloated city bureaucracy. Giuliani tends to make political friends and

enemies in equal measure – and with equal energy. His most famous faux pas (at least as far as his party was concerned) came when he actively supported long-time Democratic New York State governor Mario Cuomo over his own party's eventual winner **George Pataki** in the 1994 gubernatorial elections, a move calculated to appease his more liberal city constituents. A red-faced Giuliani had to kowtow to Republicans so that New York City did not get its snout pushed out of the trough by State spending authorities. In 1996, Giuliani's constant battles with Police Commissioner Bratton, whose policies of community policing and crackdowns on petty, as well as major, crime were widely considered responsible for the lower crime rates, forced the popular "Top Cop" into resigning. Many said that the notoriously egotistical Giuliani simply didn't like Bratton sharing the spotlight.

A bitter fight over rent control (it was salvaged, but with vacancy clauses that allow for rent increases) in 1997, along with continued concern about serious overcrowding in the public school system and cutbacks in health and welfare programs seemed to turn the tide against the mayor. However, Giuliani won reelection easily in fall 1997 to a second term, with barely a challenge mounted by his Democratic opponent, Ruth Messinger.

Giuliani's second term has been characterized by the continued growth of the city's economy, and more civic "improvements" such as the cleaning up of previously crime-ridden neighborhoods like Times Square, the renovation of Grand Central Terminal, new hotels and office buildings being built, and the influx of chain stores into Harlem, all of which have greatly boosted tourism and thus the city's coffers. But they have also raised protests that the mayor will do anything to attract national chains to the city, often at the expense of local business and local workers. In addition, several high profile incidents such as the Abner Louima torture case involving shocking allegations of police brutality have led to charges of indifference at the top and a disregard for minority rights. Numerous reports recently have confirmed what many blacks and Hispanics have been claiming for several years now: that under the Giuliani administration, cops have been encouraged to use racial profiling and unconstitutional "wide net" techniques (stopping and frisking people at will in certain neighborhoods)

ARCHITECTURAL CHRONOLOGY

1625	First permanent **Dutch settlement** on Manhattan.	No buildings remain of the period. **Wall Street** marks the settlement's defensive northern boundary in 1653.
Late 18th c.	New York under **British colonial rule**.	**St Paul's Chapel** (1766) built in Georgian style.
1812	British blockade of Manhattan.	**City Hall** built.
1825	Opening of **Erie Canal** increases New York's wealth.	**Fulton Street** dock and market area built. Greek Revival rowhouses popular – eg **Schermerhorn Row, Colonnade Row, St Mark's Place, Chelsea**. Of much Federal-style building, few examples remain: The **Abigail Adams Smith House**, the **Morris–Jumel Mansion** and **Gracie Mansion** the most notable.
1830–50	First wave of **immigration**, principally German and Irish.	The **Lower East Side** developed. **Trinity Church** built (1846) in English Gothic style, **Federal Hall** (1842) in Greek Revival.
1850–1900	**More immigrants** (mostly Irish and Germans, later Italians and East European Jews) settle in Manhattan. **Industrial development** brings extreme wealth to individuals. The **Civil War** (1861–65) has little effect on the city.	Cast-iron architecture enables buildings to mimic grand classical designs cheaply. Highly popular in SoHo, eg the **Haughwout Building** (1859). Large, elaborate mansions built along Fifth Avenue for America's new millionaires. **Central Park** opens (1876). The **Brooklyn Bridge** (1883) links Gothic with industrial strength; **St Patrick's Cathedral** (1879) and **Grace Church** (1846) show it at its most delicate. **Statue of Liberty** is unveiled (1886).
Early 20th c.		The **Flatiron Building** (1902) is the first skyscraper. Much civic architecture in the Beaux Arts Neoclassical style: **Grand Central Terminal** (1919), **New York Public Library** (1911), **US Customs House** (1907), **General Post Office** (1913) and the **Municipal Building** (1914) are the finest examples. The **Woolworth Building** (1913) becomes Manhattan's "Cathedral of Commerce."
1915		The **Equitable Building** fills every square inch of its site on Broadway, causing the first zoning ordinances to ensure a degree of setback and allow light to reach the streets.
1920	**Prohibition** law passed. Economic confidence of the 1920s brings the **Jazz Age**.	Art Deco influences show in the **American Standard Building** (1927) and the **Fuller Building** (1929).
1929	**Wall Street Crash**. America enters the **Great Depression**.	Many of the lavish buildings commissioned and begun in the 1920s reach completion. Skyscrapers combine the monumental with the decorative: **Chrysler Building** (1930), **Empire State Building** (1930), **Waldorf Astoria Hotel** (1931) and the **General Electric Building** (1931). **Rockefeller Center**, the first exponent of the idea of a city-within-a-city, is built throughout the decade. The **McGraw-Hill Building** (1931) is self-consciously modern.
1930s	The **New Deal** and WPA schemes attempt to reduce unemployment.	Little new building other than housing projects. WPA murals decorate buildings around town, notably in the **New York Public Library** and **County Courthouse**.

1941	America enters **World War II**.	New zoning regulations encourage the development of the setback skyscraper: but little is built during the war years.
1950s	**United Nations Organization** established.	The **UN Secretariat** (1950) introduces the glass curtain wall to Manhattan. Similar Corbusier-influenced buildings include the **Lever House** (1952) and, most impressively, the **Seagram Building** (1958), whose plaza causes the zoning regulations to be changed in an attempt to encourage similar public spaces. The **Guggenheim Museum** (1959) opens.
1960s	**Protest movement** stages demonstrations against US involvement in Vietnam.	Much early-1960s building pallidly imitates the glass box skyscraper. The **Pan Am** (1963) building attempts something different, but more successful is the **Ford Foundation** (1967). In the hands of lesser architects, the plaza becomes a liability. New **Madison Square Garden** (1968) is built on the site of the old Penn Station. The minimalist **Verrazano-Narrows Bridge** (1964) links Brooklyn to Staten Island.
1970s	Mayor Abraham Beame presides over **New York's decline**. City financing reaches **crisis point** as businesses leave Manhattan.	The **World Trade Center Towers** (1970) add a soaring landmark to the lower Manhattan skyline. **The Rockefeller Center Extensions** (1973–74) clone the glass-box skyscraper. Virtually no new corporate development until the **Citicorp Center** (1977) adds new textures and profile to the city's skyline. Its popular atrium is adopted by later buildings.
Late 1970s	Investment in the city increases.	**Ed Koch elected mayor** (1978). **One UN Plaza** adapts the glass curtain wall to skilled ends (1975).
1980s	**Corporate wealth returns** to Manhattan.	The **IBM Building** (1982) shows the conservative side of modern architecture; postmodernist designs like the **AT&T Building** (1983) and **Federal Reserve Plaza** (1985) mix historical styles in the same building. **Statue of Liberty** restoration completed. The mixed-use **Battery Park City** opens to wide acclaim.
1986	Wall Street **crashes**; Dow Jones index plunges 500 points in a day.	Real Estate market takes a dive. **Equitable Building** on Seventh Avenue opens.
1989	**Ed Koch** loses Democratic nomination to **David Dinkins**, who goes on to become NYC's first black mayor.	**Rockefeller Center** sold to international conglomerate partially owned by Japanese. **RCA Building** renamed **General Electric Building**.
1990	Major **recession** hits New York.	**Ellis Island Museum of Immigration** opens to public.
1991	NYC's **budget deficit** reaches record proportions.	**Guggenheim Museum** reopens with new extension.
1993	A car bomb explodes at the **World Trade Center**, killing five people and wounding many more. Republican **Rudolph Giuliani** beats Dinkins in mayoral race.	Famed **Ed Sullivan Theater** is given complete overhaul and turned into *David Letterman Show* studio.

ARCHITECTURAL CHRONOLOGY CONTINUED

1996	**NY Yankees** win first World series in almost 20 years.	**SoHo Grand** opens – the first Downtown hotel to be built for decades.
1997	**Murder rates** drop for fourth consecutive year. **Rent Control/Rent Stabilization** laws amended; **Giuliani reelected** to second term. **MetroCard** introduced on subways and buses.	Redevelopment of **Times Square**; **New Victory Theater** opens on 42nd Street; opening of Battery Park City's **Museum of Jewish Heritage**.
1998	**100th anniversary** of the incorporation of New York City. **NY Yankees** win the World Series again. Due to **unlimited-ride Metropasses**, ridership on subways is at all time high of eight million people a day.	Legislation is passed to create **waterfront park** along the Hudson River from Battery Park City to 72nd Street. The grandly renovated **Grand Central Terminal** opens, dedicated by John Kennedy Jr. in honor of his mother, Jacqueline Kennedy Onassis, who helped raise money for the restoration. A new **stadium** is unveiled in Flushing Meadow for US Open tennis tournament.
1999	Speculation abounds about Hillary Rodham Clinton running for Senate in New York in 2001 and the Clintons relocating to Manhattan.	The new **Conde Nast** skyscraper is completed in Times Square. Upscale shops and restaurants open in the renovated **Grand Central Terminal**.
2000		The new **Hayden Planetarium** is scheduled to open in early spring at the American Museum of Natural History.

in order to catch criminals. These widespread allegations of police corruption and abuse of power have cast real doubts on Giuliani's leadership methods, as has his steadfast refusal to sit down with minority group leaders to discuss these problems. His popularity, once amazingly high in this heavily Democratic city, has dwindled significantly.

Currently, the possibility (looking more and more likely every day) of a Senate race in 2001 between the mayor and Hillary Rodham Clinton (who will be, at that point, the former First Lady) has already heated up the rhetoric out of City Hall and promises to keep the media very, very busy. What it means for New York, other than diverting attention away from the real issues, has yet to be seen.

Twentieth-century American art

This is no more than a brief introduction to a handful of American painters; for more detailed appraisals, both of the century's major movements and specific painters, see "Books."

Twentieth-century American art begins with **The Eight**, otherwise known as the **Ashcan School**, a group of artists who were painting in New York in the first decade of this century. Led by Robert Henri, many of them worked as illustrators for city newspapers, and they tried to depict modern American urban life – principally in New York City – as honestly and realistically as possible, in much the same way as earlier painters had depicted nature. Their exhibitions, in 1908 and 1910, were, however, badly received, and most of their work was scorned for representing subjects not seen as fit for painting. Paralleling the work of the Ashcan School was that of the group that met at the **Photo-Secession Gallery** of the photographer Alfred Stieglitz on Fifth Avenue. They were more individual, less concerned with social themes than expressing their own individual styles, but were equally unappreciated. Art, for Americans, even for American critics, was something that came from Europe, and in the early years of the twentieth century attempts to Americanize it were regarded with suspicion.

Change came with the **Armory Show** of 1913: an exhibition, set up by the remaining Ashcan artists (members of the new Association of American Painters and Sculptors), to bring more than 1800 European works together and show them to the American public for the first time. The whole of the French nineteenth century was represented at the show, together with Cubist and Expressionist painters, and, from New York, the work of the Ashcan painters and the Stieglitz circle. It was visited by over 85,000 people in its month-long run in New York, and plenty more caught it as it toured America. The immediate effect was uproar. Americans panned the European paintings, partly because they resented their influence but also since they weren't quite sure how to react; the indigenous American artists were criticized for being afraid to adopt a native style; and the press fanned the flames by playing up to public anxieties about the subversive nature of modern art. But there was a positive effect: the modern art of both Europe and America became known all over the continent, particularly abstract painting. From now on American artists were free to develop their own approach.

The paintings that followed were, however, far from abstract in style. The Great Crash of 1929 and subsequent Depression led to the school of **Social Realism** and paintings like **Thomas Hart Benton**'s *America Today* sequence (now in the Equitable Center at 757 7th Ave): a vast mural that covered, in realistic style, every aspect of contemporary American life. The New Deal and the resultant **Federal Art Project** of the WPA supported many artists through the lean years of the 1930s by commissioning them to decorate public buildings, and it became widely acknowledged that not only were work, workers and public life fit subjects for art, but also that artists had some responsibility to push for social change. Artists like **Edward Hopper** and **Charles Burchfield** sought to re-create, in as precise a way as possible, American contemporary life, making the particular (in Hopper's case empty streets, lone buildings, solitary figures in diners) "epic and universal." Yet while Hopper and Burchfield can be called great artists in their own right, much of the work of the time, particularly that commissioned as public works, was inevitably dull and conformist, and it wasn't long before movements were afoot to inject new life into American painting. It was the beginning of abstraction.

With these ideas so, the center of the visual art world gradually began to shift. The founding of the **Museum of Modern Art**, and also of the **Guggenheim Museum** some years later, combined with the arrival of many European artists throughout the 1930s (Gropius, Hans Hofmann, the Surrealists) to make New York a serious rival to Paris in terms of influence. **Hans Hofmann** in particular was to have considerable influence on New York painters, both through his art school and his own boldly Expressionistic works. Also, the many American artists who had lived abroad came back armed with a set of European experiences which they could couple with their native spirit to produce a new, indigenous and wholly original style. First and most prominent of these was **Arshile Gorky**, a European-born painter who had imbibed the influences of Cézanne and Picasso – and, more so, the Surrealists. His technique, however, was different: not cold and dispassionate like the Europeans but expressive, his paintings textured and more vital. **Stuart Davis**, too, once a prominent member of the Ashcan School, was an important figure, his paintings using everyday objects as subject matter but jumbling them into abstract form – as in works like *Lucky Strike*, which hangs in the Museum of Modern Art. Another artist experimenting with abstract forms was **Georgia O'Keeffe** – who was married to the early twentieth-century photographer Alfred Stieglitz – is best known for her lonely Southwestern landscapes, stark death-white cattle skulls and depictions of blossoming flowers. These she magnified so they became no more than unidentified shapes, in their curves and ovular forms curiously erotic and suggestive of fertility and growth. The Whitney Museum holds a good stock of her work.

The **Abstract Expressionists** – or **The New York School** as they came to be known – were a fairly loose movement, and one that splits broadly into two groups: the first created abstractions with increasing gusto and seemingly endless supplies of paint, while the rest employed a more ordered approach to their work. Best known among the first group is **Jackson Pollock**, a farmer's son from Wyoming who had studied under Thomas Hart Benton in New York and in the 1930s was painting Cubist works reminiscent of Picasso. Pollock considered the American art scene to be still under the thumb of Europe, and he deliberately set about creating canvases that bore little relation to anything that had gone before. For a start his paintings were huge, and it was difficult to tell where they ended; in fact Pollock would simply determine the edge of a composition by cutting the canvas wherever he happened to feel was appropriate at the time – a large-scale approach that was much imitated and in part determined by the large factory spaces and lofts where American artists worked. Also, it was a reaction against bourgeois (and therefore essentially European) notions of what a painting should be: the average Abstract Expressionist painting simply couldn't be contained in the normal collector's home, and as such was at the time impossible to classify. Often Pollock would paint on the floor, adding layers of paint apparently at random, building up a dense composition that said more about the action of painting than any specific subject matter: hence the term "action painting," which is invariably used to describe this technique. As a contemporary critic said: with Pollock the canvas became "an arena in which to act – rather than as a space in which to reproduce...."

Similar to Pollock in technique, but less abstract in subject matter, was the Dutch-born artist **Willem de Kooning**, whose *Women* series clearly attempts to be figurative – as do a number of his other paintings, especially the earlier ones, many of which are in the Museum of Modern Art. Where he and Pollock are alike is in their exuberant use of paint and color, painted, splashed, dripped or scraped on to the canvas with a palette knife. **Franz Kline** was also of this "gestural" school, though he cut down on color and instead covered his canvas with giant black shapes against a stark white background: bold images reminiscent of Chinese ideograms and Oriental calligraphy. **Robert Motherwell**, who some have called the leading light of the Abstract Expressionist movement (in so far as it had one), created a similar effect in his *Elegies to the Spanish Republic*, only here his symbols are drawn from Europe and not the East – and unlike

Abstract Expressionist paintings they gain their inspiration from actual events. Again, for his work the Whitney and MoMA are good sources.

Foremost among the second group of Abstract Expressionists was **Mark Rothko**, a Russian-born artist whose work is easy to recognize by its broad rectangles of color against a single-hued background. Rothko's paintings are more controlled than Pollock's, less concerned with exuding their own painterliness than with expressing, as Rothko put it, "a single tragic idea." Some have called his work mystic, religious even, and his paintings are imbued with a deep melancholy, their fuzzy-edged blocks of color radiating light and, in spite of an increasingly lightened palette, a potent sense of despair. Rothko, a deeply unhappy man, committed suicide in 1970, and it was left to one of his closest friends, **Adolf Gottlieb**, to carry on where he left off. With his "pictographs" Gottlieb spontaneously explored deep psychological states, covering his canvases with "Native" American signs. He also used a unique set of symbols of cosmos and chaos – disks of color above a blotchy earth – as in his *Frozen Sounds* series of the early 1950s, currently in the Whitney collection.

The Abstract Expressionists gave native American art stature worldwide and helped consolidate New York's position as center of the art world. But other painters weren't content to follow the emotional painting of Pollock and Rothko et al, and toned down the technique of excessive and frenzied brushwork into impersonal representations of shapes within clearly defined borders – **Kenneth Noland's** *Target* and the geometric (and later three-dimensional) shapes of **Frank Stella** being good examples. **Ad Reinhardt**, too, honed down his style until he was using only different shades of the same color, taking this to its logical extreme by ultimately covering canvases with differing densities of black.

Barnett Newman is harder to classify, though he is usually associated with the Abstract Expressionists, not least because of the similarities to Rothko of his bold "fields" of color. But his controlled use of one striking tone, painted with only tiny variations in shade, and cut (horizontally or vertically) by a single contrasting strip, give him more in common with the trends in art that followed. **Helen Frankenthaler** (and later **Morris Louis**) took this one stage further with pictures like *Mountains and Sea*, which by staining the canvas rather than painting it lends blank

areas the same importance as colored ones, making the painting seem as if it were created by a single stroke. With these two artists, color was the most important aspect of painting, and the canvas and the color were absorbed as one. In his mature period Louis began – in the words of a contemporary critic – "to think, feel and conceive almost exclusively in terms of open color." And as if in rejection of any other method, he destroyed most of his work of the previous two decades.

With the 1960s came **minimalism** and **Pop Art**. The former produced works composed of industrial materials and fabricated for urban and site-specific landscapes, the medium's physical properties emphasized above all else, including the oeuvre of **Richard Serra**. **Louise Nevelson**, born in Kiev in 1899 and raised in Maine, had come to the Art Students League in Manhattan in 1929 and over a number of decades gained recognition for her grid-and-pillar installations, many of them stark black aluminum sculptures, some now on permanent display along upper Park Avenue and at Louise Nevelson Plaza in the Financial District. Pop Art turned to America's popular media for subject – its films, TV, advertisements and magazines – and depicted it in heightened tones and colors. **Jasper Johns**'s *Flag* bridges the gap, cunningly transforming the Stars and Stripes into little more than a collection of painted shapes, but most Pop Art was more concerned with monumentalizing the tackier side of American culture: **Andy Warhol** did it with Marilyn Monroe and Campbell's Soup; **Claes Oldenburg** by re-creating everyday objects (notably food) in soft fabrics and blowing them up to giant size; **Robert Rauschenberg** by making collages or "assemblages" of ordinary objects; **Roy Lichtenstein** by imitating the screen process of newspapers and cartoon strips; and **Ed Kienholz** through realistic tableaux of the sad, shabby or just plain weird aspects of modern life. But what Pop Art really did was to make art accessible and fun. With it the commonplace became acceptable material for the twentieth-century artist, and as such paved the way for what was to follow. **Graffiti** has since been elevated to the status of art form, and New York painters like **Keith Haring** (who died of AIDS in 1990) and **Kenny Scharf** were celebrities in their own right, regularly called in to decorate Manhattan nightclubs. Haring's last finished work was an altar – complete with his trademark cartoonish stick figures – installed in the Cathedral of St John the Divine.

On the whole, New York's artistic star has waned over recent years, eclipsed by the art scene in London. However, there have been more than a few standouts in the last twenty years, in a variety of styles and mediums. There has been a return to straight figurative depictions, either supra-realistically as in the poignant acetate figures of **Duane Hanson**, or in the more conventional nude studies of **Philip Pearlstein**. The expansive re-creations of Polaroid close-ups by **Chuck Close** took realism to a fantastic level as he replicated the photos segment by segment at enormous scale. After a collapsed spinal artery left him paralyzed from the shoulders down in 1988, his artistry took on a new level as he explored more impressionistic interpretations of his old technique – astonishing the art world once more with his inventive methods. In the 1970s and 1980s, **Cindy Sherman** and **Nan Goldin** took photographic portraiture and atmospheric documentary photography into new territory – the former with her sexually provocative, chameleon-like self-representations in the guises of B-movie characters, the latter in a poignant record of her friends-cum-adoptive family, many of them transvestites now dead from AIDS. **Susan Rothenberg**, a conceptual and atmospheric Impressionist artist with her roots in 1960s New York, is well regarded for her canvases of Southwestern desert landscapes.

One of the best-known artists of the last twenty years has been **Jean-Michel Basquiat**, if only for his well-publicized affair with Madonna, who owns several of his paintings. Basquiat began his career in the mid-Eighties as part of a two-man graffiti team called SAMO ("Same Old Shit"), and was marketed by the city's art dealers as a wild street kid – even though his family background was in fact comfortably middle-class. Sadly, their prophecy turned out to be a self-fulfilling one: Basquiat was a confirmed heroin user and died in 1989. The 1990s failed to generate a New York artist as famous internationally as Basquiat or his mixed-media artist colleague **Julian Schnabel**, who directed a 1996 movie about Basquiat's life. One fairly big name on the scene has been **Jeff Koons**, who picked up the Pop Art mantle where Warhol and others left off, and who is perhaps an even greater self-promoter. Perhaps fortunately, the city's artistic scene in the 1990s was significantly less trend-obsessed than it had been during the previous decade.

Books

Since the number of books about or set in New York is so vast, what follows is necessarily selective – use it as a launchpad for further sleuthing. Publishers are given in the order British/American if they are different for each country; where a book is published only in one country, it is designated UK or US; o/p indicates a book out of print, UP indicates University Press.

Essays and impressions

Ron Alexander *Metropolitan Diary: The Best Selections from the New York Times Column* (William Morrow & Co, US). Every *New York Times* reader's favorite column, now available every day of the week. Indulge your eavesdropping fantasies with these observations, anecdotes and quotes from ordinary New Yorkers overheard on movie lines and in buses, restaurants, bars and elevators, to name just a few of the places where New Yorkers listen to each other's conversations. These vignettes are often hilarious, sometimes infuriating, but oh so quintessentially New York.

Djuna Barnes *New York* (Sun & Moon Press, US). This collection of newspaper stories – from 1913 to 1919 – looks mostly at out-of-the-way characters and places. Highly evocative of the times – a period in New York, and the world over, of great flux. See especially the piece on the "floating hotel for girls."

Anatole Broyard *Kafka Was the Rage* (Vintage, US). This new and highly readable account of "bohemian" 1940s Greenwich Village is occasionally misogynistic and somewhat self-congratulatory in parts. But Broyard's style and his descriptions of City College's radical/intellectual scene are gripping.

Jerome Charyn *Metropolis* (Abacus/Avon). A native of the Bronx, Charyn dives into the New York of the 1980s from every angle and comes up with a book that's still sharp, sensitive and refreshingly real. See also "New York in Fiction," p.510.

William Corbett *New York Literary Lights* (Graywolf Press, US). An informative introduction to New York's literary history, with thumbnail profiles of writers, publishers and other figures of the literary scene; along with descriptions of their hangouts, neighborhoods and favorite publications. The concise, alphabetically arranged entries make it easy to look something up or just browse; you may be surprised at some of the writers who called the city home (Ayn Rand and Mark Twain, to name two) and hopefully you'll be inspired to begin your own New York reading binge.

Daniel Drennan *The New York Diaries* (Ballantine, US). Camp, comic takes on the urban rituals that make up life in New York.

Josh Alan Friedman *Tales of Times Square* (Feral House). Chronicles activities on and around the square between 1978 and 1984, pornography's golden age. Its no-nonsense style of narration documents a culture under siege of impresarios, pimps and 25-cent thrills.

Frederico Garcia Lorca *Poet in New York* (Penguin/Grove Weidenfeld, o/p). The Andalusian poet and dramatist spent nine months in the city around the time of the Wall Street Crash. This collection of over thirty poems reveals his feelings on the brutality, loneliness, greed, corruption, racism and mistreatment of the poor.

Phillip Lopate (ed.) *Writing New York* (Library of America, US). A massive literary anthology taking in both fiction and non-fiction writings on the city, and with selections from everyone from Washington Irving to Tom Wolfe.

Joseph Mitchell *Up in the Old Hotel* (Random House, US). Mitchell's collected essays (he calls them stories), all of which appeared in the *New Yorker*, are works of a sober if manipulative genius. Mitchell depicts characters and situations with a reporter's precision and near-perfect style – he is the definitive chronicler of NYC street life.

Jan Morris *Manhattan '45* (Penguin/Oxford UP). Morris's best piece of writing on Manhattan, reconstructing New York as it greeted returning GIs in 1945. Effortlessly written, fascinatingly anecdotal, marvelously warm about the city. See also *The Great Port* (Oxford UP).

Georges Perec and Robert Bober *Ellis Island* (New Press, US). A brilliant, moving, original account of the "island of tears": part history, meditation and interviews. Some of the stories are heartbreaking (between 1892 and 1924 there were 3000 suicides on the island), and the pictures are even more so.

Guy Trebay *In the Place to Be: Guy Trebay's New York* (Temple University Press, US). Collected columns by one of the more notable *Village Voice* writers. They celebrate populations on the margins, which, as the warm columns show, are the very fabric and spirit of the city – and hence not "marginal" at all.

History, politics and society

Herbert Asbury *The Gangs of New York* (Paragon House, US). First published in 1928, this fascinating account of the seamier side of New York is essential reading. Full of historical detail, anecdotes and character sketches of crooks, the book describes New York mischief in all its incarnations and locales.

Edwin G. Burrows and Mike Wallace *Gotham: A History of New York City to 1898* (Oxford UP). Enormous and encyclopedic in its detail, this is a serious history of the development of New York, with chapters on everything from its role in the Revolution to reform movements to its racial make-up in the 1820s. Surprisingly readable, though best in small doses, it contains fascinating insights into early influences on the city and into sundry things like name origins – especially fun for someone familiar with New York.

Robert A Caro *The Power Broker: Robert Moses and the Fall of New York* (Vintage, US). Despite its imposing length, this brilliant and searing critique of New York City's most powerful twentieth-century figure is one of the most important books ever written about the city and its environs. Caro's book brings to light the megalomania and manipulation responsible for the creation of the nation's largest urban infrastructure.

George Chauncey *Gay New York: The Making of the Gay Male World 1890–1940* (HarperCollins/Flamingo). Definitive, revealing account of the city's gay subculture, superbly researched. Though academic in approach, it's a highly readable chronicle of a much-neglected facet of New York's character.

Anne Douglas *Terrible Honesty: Mongrel Manhattan in the 1920s* (Picador/Farrar, Straus & Giroux). The media and artistic culture of the Roaring Twenties, a fluke that was a casualty of the Depression.

Kenneth T. Jackson (ed) *The Enyclopedia of New York* (Yale University Press). Massive, engrossing and utterly comprehensive guide to just about everything in the city. Much dry detail, but packed with incidental wonders: did you know, for example, that there are more (dead) people in Calvary Cemetery, Queens, than there are (living) people in the whole borough? Or that Truman Capote's real name was Streckford Persons?

John A. Kouwenhoven *Columbia Historical Portrait of New York* (Doubleday, US). Interpreting the evolution of the city in visual terms (with illuminating captions accompanying the illustrations), this opus is monumental, fascinating and definitive.

George J. Lankevich *American Metropolis* (NYU Press, US). Written in a direct, readable style, this is the concise alternative to *Gotham* (see above).

David Levering Lewis *When Harlem was in Vogue* (Penguin, US). Much-needed account of the Harlem Renaissance, a brief flowering of the arts in the 1920s and 1930s. Just reissued, with a new introduction, this detailed but readable history traces the movement to its untimely end, a suffocation by the dual forces of Depression and racism. Lewis also edited the *Portable Harlem Renaissance Reader* (Penguin), an anthology of the writing of the time.

Legs McNeil and Gillian McCain *Please Kill Me* (Abacus/Penguin). An oral history of punk music in New York, artfully constructed by juxtaposing snippets of interviews as if the various protagonists (artists, financiers, impresarios) were in a conversation. Sometimes hilarious, often quite bleak.

Luc Sante *Low Life: Lures and Snares of Old New York* (Vintage, US). This chronicle of the seamy side between 1840 and 1919 is a pioneering work. Full of outrageous details usually left out of conventional history, it reconstructs the day-to-day life of the urban poor, criminals and prostitutes with a shocking clarity. Sante's prose is poetic and nuanced, his evocations of the seedier neighborhoods, their dives and pleasure-palaces, quite vivid.

Art, architecture and photography

Lorraine Diehl *The Late Great Pennsylvania Station* (Four Walls Eight Windows, US). The anatomy of a travesty. How could a railroad palace, modeled after the Baths of Caracalla in Rome, stand for only fifty years before being destroyed? The pictures alone warrant the price.

Horst Hamann *New York Vertical* (Te Neues). This beautiful book pays homage to the New York skyscraper, right down to its own vertical shape. It's filled with dazzling black-and-white vertical shots of Manhattan, from famous skyscrapers to unusual views of streets and neighborhoods, all taken by Hamann and accompanied by witty quotes from the famous and the obscure. Available in two different versions — one affordable, one not.

H. Klotz (ed) *New York Architecture 1970–1990* (Prestel/Rizzoli). Extremely well-illustrated account of the shift from modernism to postmodernism and beyond.

Museum of the City of New York *Our Town: Images and Stories from the Museum of the City of New York* (Abrams, US). A lovely collection of paintings, photographs, artifacts and prints from the Museum's collection, reproduced here to commemorate its 75th anniversary in 1997. New York is explored from early days to contemporary times, with informative captions that place the images in context and essays by Oscar Hijuelos and Louis Auchincloss, among others.

Jacob Riis *How the Other Half Lives* (Dover/Hill & Wang). Republished photojournalism reporting on life in the Lower East Side at the end of the nineteenth century. Its original publication awakened many to the plight of New York's poor.

Stern, Gilmartin, Mellins/Stern, Gilmartin, Massengale/Stern, Mellins, Fishman *New York 1900/1930/1960* (Rizzoli, US). These three exhaustive tomes, subtitled "Metropolitan Architecture and Urbanism," contain all you'd ever want or need to know about architecture and the organization of the city. The facts are dazzling and numbing, the photos nostalgia-inducing.

N. White and E. Willensky (eds) *AIA Guide to New York* (Macmillan/Harcourt Brace). Perhaps even more than the above, the definitive contemporary guide to the city's architecture, far more interesting than it sounds, and useful as an on-site reference.

Gerard R. Wolfe *New York: A Guide to the Metropolis* (McGraw-Hill, US). Set up as a walking tour, this is a little more academic — and less opinionated — than others, but it does include some good stuff on the outer boroughs. Also informed historical background.

Other guides

Richard Alleman *The Movie Lover's Guide to New York* (HarperCollins, US). More than two hundred listings of corners of the city with cinematic associations. Interestingly written, painstakingly researched and indispensable to anyone with even a remote interest in either New York or film history.

Joann Biondi and James Kaskins *Hippocrene USA Guide to Black New York* (Hippocrene, US). Borough-by-borough gazetteer of historic sites, cultural spots, music and food of special African-American interest. Somewhat out-of-date but the only one of its kind.

Judi Culbertson and Tom Randall *Permanent New Yorkers* (Chelsea Green, US). This unique guide to the cemeteries of New York includes the final resting-places of such notables as Herman Melville, Duke Ellington, Billie Holliday, Horace Greeley, Mae West, Judy Garland and 350 others.

Federal Writer's Project *The WPA Guide to New York City* (New Press, US). Originally written in 1939, the fruit of a project designed by the WPA to employ out-of-work writers during the Depression. Recently reissued, this detailed guide offers a fascinating look at life in New York City when the Dodgers played at Ebbetts Field, a trolley ride cost five cents and a room at the *Plaza* was $7.50. It leads you to all the great sights and architecture of the city, a surprising majority of which still stands, and serves as both a guidebook and a reminder of what once was.

Alfred Gingold and Helen Rogan *The Cool Parents Guide to All of New York* (City & Co., US). A terrific resource for people traveling with kids, it covers everything from museums and kid-oriented theater to parks, sports, festivals and other special events, all in a down-to-earth conversational style (it's obviously written by cool parents).

Daniel Hurewitz *Stepping Out: 9 Walks through New York City's Gay and Lesbian Past* (Henry Holt & Co, US). An inspiring book, full of fascinating tidbits of gay-lore and avowedly trashy. The book takes you on walking tours through every corner of the city, pointing out the signs and highlights of gay life and gay culture in a conversational, anecdotal style.

Ed Levine *New York Eats* (St Martins Press, US) Covering all five boroughs – with a small section on that trendiest of Manhattan "suburbs," the Hamptons – each chapter covers a different type of food, from smoked fish to spices, from pizza to pastries, and Levine tells you where to find the best of each, arranged by neighborhood. He rates and reviews the best butchers, bakeries, gourmet takeout, greengrocers, delis and ethnic restaurants, and includes fascinating behind-the-scenes notes on each place. One of the best books ever written about New York food.

Andrew Roth *Infamous Manhattan* (Carol Publishing Group, US). A vivid and engrossing history of New York crime, revealing the sites of Mafia hits, celebrity murders, nineteenth-century brothels, and other wicked spots, including a particularly fascinating guide to restaurants with dubious, infamous or gory pasts. As a walking tour guide it can't be beaten, but the stories and anecdotes of 350 years of Manhattan misdeeds are just as absorbing from an armchair. The most accurate and entertaining book on the subject yet published.

New York in fiction

Martin Amis *Money* (Penguin/Viking Penguin). Following the wayward movements of degenerate film director John Self between London and New York, a weirdly scatological novel that's a striking evocation of 1980s excess.

Paul Auster *The New York Trilogy: City of Glass, Ghosts* and *The Locked Room* (Faber/Viking Penguin). Three Borgesian investigations into the mystery, madness and murders of contemporary NYC. Using the conventions of the crime thriller, Auster unfolds a disturbed and disturbing picture of the city.

James Baldwin *Another Country* (Penguin/Vintage). Baldwin's best-known novel, tracking the feverish search for meaningful relationships among a group of 1960s New York bohemians. The so-called liberated era in the city has never

been more vividly documented – nor its knee-jerk racism.

Jennifer Belle *Going Down* (Virago/Berkley). A brilliant first novel that chronicles the "descent" of an NYU student into working as a call girl. Full of surprising turns of phrase and some deadpan black humor.

Thomas Beller *Seduction Theory* (Abacus/Warner Books). Tales of youthful angst and yearning all set in New York City. Intelligent, penetrating and vaguely melancholic.

Lawrence Block *When the Sacred Ginmill Closes* (Phoenix/Avon). Tough to choose between this and *Dance at the Slaughterhouse*, or any of his other Matthew Scudder suspense novels. However, Block may be at his best here, with expert details of Hell's Kitchen, downtown Manhattan and far-flung parts of Brooklyn woven into this dark mystery.

William Boyd *Stars and Bars* (Penguin/Viking Penguin). Set partly in New York, part in the deep South, a well-observed novel that tells despairingly and hilariously of the unbridgeable gap between the British and Americans. Full of ringing home truths for the first-time visitor to the States.

Claude Brown *Manchild in the Promised Land* (Signet, US). Gripping autobiographical fiction set on the hard streets of Harlem and published in the mid-1960s; not as famous as *Invisible Man*, but still worth the trip.

Truman Capote *Breakfast at Tiffany's* (Penguin/Random House). Far sadder and racier than the movie, this novel is a rhapsody to New York in the early 1940s, tracking the dissolute youthful residents of an Uptown apartment building and their movements about town.

Caleb Carr *The Alienist* (Warner/Bantam). This thriller, set in 1896, evokes Old New York to perfection. The heavy-handed psycho-babble grates at times, but the story line (the pursuit of one of the first serial killers) is worth it. Best for its descriptions of New York's "in places" (and down-and-out locales), as well as saliva-inducing details of meals at long-gone restaurants.

Jerome Charyn *War Cries over Avenue C* (Abacus/Viking Penguin, o/p). Alphabet City is the derelict backdrop for this novel of gang warfare among the Vietnam-crazed coke barons of New York City. An offbeat tale of conspiracy and suspense. A later work, *Paradise Man* (Abacus), is the violent story of a New York hit man.

E.L. Doctorow *Ragtime* (Picador/Bantam). America, and particularly New York, before World War I: Doctorow cleverly weaves together fact and fiction, historical figures and invented characters, to create what ranks as a biting indictment of the country and its racism. See also *World's Fair*, a beautiful evocation of a Bronx boyhood in the 1930s.

Ralph Ellison *Invisible Man* (Penguin/Random House). The definitive if sometimes long-winded novel of what it's like to be black and American, using Harlem and the 1950s race riots as a backdrop.

Jack Finney *Time and Again* (Scribner, US). Equal parts love story, mystery and fantasy, this is really a glowing tribute to the city itself. Part of a secret government experiment in time travel, Simon Morley is transported back to 1880s New York and finds himself falling in love and being torn between his two lives, present and past. Atmospheric and moving, the richly evoked details of old New York and the surprising plot make this a must.

Oscar Hijuelos *Our House in the Last World* (Serpent's Tail/Pocket Books). A warmly evocative novel of immigrant Cuban life in New York from before the war to the present day.

Chester Himes *The Crazy Kill* (Alison & Busby/Random House). Himes writes violent, fast-moving and funny thrillers set in Harlem, of which this is just one.

Andrew Holleran *Dancer from the Dance* (Penguin/NAL-Dutton). Enjoyable account of the embryonic gay disco scene of the early 1970s. Interesting location detail of Manhattan haunts and Fire Island, but suffers from over-exaltation of the central character.

Henry James *Washington Square* (Penguin/Viking Penguin). Skillful and engrossing examination of the mores and strict social expectations of New York genteel society in the late nineteenth century.

Joyce Johnson *Minor Characters* (Picador/Pocket Books). Women were never a prominent feature of the Beat generation; its literature examined a male world through strictly male eyes. This book, written by the woman who lived for a short time with Jack Kerouac, redresses the balance superbly. And there's no better novel available on the Beats in New York. See also her *In the Night Café* (Flamingo), a novel that charts – again in part autobiographically – the relationship between a young woman and a struggling New York artist in the 1960s.

Joseph Koenig *Little Odessa* (Penguin/Ballantine). An ingenious, twisting thriller set in Manhattan and Brooklyn's Russian community in Brighton Beach. A readable, exciting novel, and a good contemporary view of New York City.

David Levering Lewis (ed) *The Portable Harlem Renaissance Reader* (Penguin). Though clunky and chunky as some anthologies tend to be, this offers a good introduction to a pivotal period in African-American arts and letters. Contains selections from essays, memoirs, poetry and fiction.

Mary McCarthy *The Group* (Penguin/Avon). Eight Vassar graduates making their way in the New York of the Thirties. Sad, funny and satirical.

Jay McInerney *Bright Lights, Big City* (Flamingo/Vintage). A trendy, "voice of a generation" book when it came out in the Eighties, it made first-time novelist McInerney a mint. It follows a struggling New York writer in his job as a fact-checker at an important literary magazine (clearly the *New Yorker* to those in the know), and from one cocaine-sozzled nightclub to another. Amusing now, as it vividly captures the times.

Henry Miller *Crazy Cock* (HarperCollins/Grove Weidenfeld, o/p). Semiautobiographical work of love, sex and angst in Greenwich Village in the 1920s. The more easily available trilogy of *Sexus, Plexus* and *Nexus* (HarperCollins/Grove) and the famous *Tropics* duo (*...of Cancer, ...of Capricorn*) contain generous slices of 1920s Manhattan sandwiched between the bohemian life in 1930s Paris.

Dorothy Parker *Complete Stories* (Penguin). Parker's stories are, at times, surprisingly moving. She depicts New York in all its glories, excesses and pretensions with perfect, searing wit. "The Lovely Leave" and "The Game," which focus, as many of the stories do, on the lives of women, are especially worthwhile.

Ann Petry *The Street* (Virago/Houghton Mifflin). The story of a black woman's struggle to rise from the slums of Harlem in the 1940s. Convincingly bleak.

Judith Rossner *Looking for Mr Goodbar* (Cape/Pocket Books). A disquieting book, tracing the life – and eventual demise – of a female teacher in search of love in volatile and permissive 1970s New York. Good on evoking the feel of the city, but on the whole a depressing read.

Henry Roth *Call It Sleep* (Penguin/Avon). Roth's novel traces – presumably autobiographically – the awakening of a small immigrant child to the realities of life among the slums of the Jewish Lower East Side. Read more for the evocations of childhood than the social comment.

Paul Rudnick *Social Disease* (Penguin/Ballantine). Hilarious, often incredible send-up of Manhattan night owls. Very New York, *very* funny.

Damon Runyon *First to Last* and *On Broadway* (Penguin); also *Guys and Dolls* (River City). Collections of short stories drawn from the chatter of *Lindy's Bar* on Broadway and since made into the successful musical *Guys 'n' Dolls*.

J.D. Salinger *The Catcher in the Rye* (Penguin/Bantam). Salinger's gripping novel of adolescence, following Holden Caulfield's sardonic journey of discovery through the streets of New York. A classic.

Sarah Schulman *The Sophie Horowitz Story* (Naiad Press, US) and *After Delores* (Plume, US, o/p). Lesbian detective stories set in contemporary New York: dry, downbeat and very funny. See also *Girls, Visions and Everything* (Seal Press, US), a stylish and, again, humorous study of the lives of Lower East Side lesbians.

Hubert Selby Jr. *Last Exit to Brooklyn* (Paladin/Grove Weidenfeld). When first published in Britain in 1966 this novel was tried on charges of obscenity and even now it's a disturbing read, evoking the sex, the immorality, the drugs and the violence of downtown Brooklyn in the 1960s with fearsome clarity. An important book, but to use the words of David Shepherd at the obscenity trial, you will not be unscathed.

Betty Smith *A Tree Grows in Brooklyn* (Pan/HarperCollins). Something of a classic, and rightly so, in which a courageous Irish girl learns about family, life and sex against a vivid prewar Brooklyn backdrop. Totally absorbing.

Rex Stout *The Doorbell Rang* (Fontana/Bantam). Stout's Nero Wolfe is perhaps the most intrinsically "New York" of all the literary detectives based in the city, a larger-than-life character who, with the help of his dashing assistant, Archie Goodwin, solves crimes – in this story and others – from the comfort of his sumptuous midtown Manhattan brownstone. Compulsive reading, and wonderfully evocative of the city in the 1940s and 1950s.

Kay Thompson *Eloise* (Simon & Schuster, US). Renowned children's book that works just as well for adults. It details a day in the life of our heroine Eloise, who lives at the *Plaza Hotel* with her nanny.

Edith Wharton *Old New York* (Virago/Scribners). A collection of short novels on the manners and mores of New York in the mid-nineteenth century, written with Jamesian clarity and precision. Virago/Scribner also publish her *Hudson River Bracketed* and *The Mother's Recompense*, both of which center around the lives of women in nineteenth-century New York.

New York on film

With its dashing skyline and its rugged facades, its mean streets and its swanky avenues, its electric energy and its no-quarter attitude, New York City is a natural-born **movie star**. From the silent era with its cautionary tales of young lovers ground down by the metropolis, through the smoky location-shot noirs of the 1940s, right through to the Lower East Side indies of the 1980s and 1990s, New York – a perfect setting for glitzy romances and nihilistic thrillers alike – has probably been the most filmed city on earth, or at least the one most instantly recognizable from the movies. And the city's visual pizzazz is matched by the vitality of its filmmaking, fostered by a tough, eccentric and independent spirit that has created mavericks like John Cassavetes and Jim Jarmusch, Shirley Clarke, Spike Lee and Martin Scorsese as well as directors like Woody Allen and Sidney Lumet who hate to film anywhere else.

What follows is a selection not just of the best New York movies but the most *New York* of New York movies – movies that capture the city's atmosphere, its pulse and its style; movies that celebrate its diversity or revel in its misfortunes; and movies that, if nothing else, give you a pretty good idea of what you're going to get before you get there.

Ten great New York movies

Breakfast at Tiffany's (Blake Edwards, 1961). This most charming and cherished of New York movie romances stars Audrey Hepburn as party girl Holly Golightly flitting through the glittering playground of the Upper East Side. Hepburn and George Peppard run up and down each other's fire-escapes and skip down Fifth Avenue taking in the New York Public Library and that jewelry store.

Do the Right Thing (Spike Lee, 1989). Set over 24 hours on the hottest day of the year in Brooklyn's Bed-Stuy section – a day on which the melting pot is reaching boiling point – Spike Lee's colorful, stylish masterpiece moves from comedy to tragedy to compose an epic song of New York that just looks better every time you see it.

King Kong (Merian C. Cooper and Ernest B. Schoedsack, 1933). Though half of it takes place on the tropical island from which the eponymous thirty-foot ape is kidnapped, *King Kong* paints a vivid picture of Depression-era Manhattan upon which Kong wreaks havoc, and gives us the city's most indelible movie image: King Kong straddling the Empire State Building and swatting at passing planes.

Lonesome (Paul Fejos, 1928). This recently rediscovered silent classic follows two lonely working-class New Yorkers through one eventful summer Saturday, culminating in an ebullient afternoon at a breathtakingly crowded Coney Island. For full effect, see this visually expressive masterpiece with the witty, thundering live accompaniment of the Alloy Orchestra.

Manhattan (Woody Allen, 1979). A black-and-white masterpiece of middle-class intellectuals' self-absorptions, lifestyles and romances, cued by a Gershwin soundtrack in what is probably the greatest eulogy to the city ever made.

On the Town (Gene Kelly, Stanley Donen, 1949). Three sailors get 24 hours' shore leave in NYC and fight over whether to do the sights or chase the girls. This exhilarating, landmark musical with Gene Kelly, Frank Sinatra, and Ann Miller flashing her gams in the Museum of Natural History was the first to take the musical out of the studios and onto the streets.

On the Waterfront (Elia Kazan, 1954). Few images of New York are as indelible as Marlon

Brando's rooftop pigeon coop at dawn and those misty views of the New York harbor (actually shot just over the river in Hoboken), in this unforgettable story of long-suffering longshoremen and union racketeering.

Shadows (John Cassavetes, 1960). Cassavetes later headed West, but his debut is a New York movie par excellence: a New Wave melody about jazz musicians, young love and racial prejudice, shot with a bebop verve and a jazzy passion in Central Park, Greenwich Village, and even the MoMA sculpture garden.

The Sweet Smell of Success (Alexander Mackendrick, 1957). Broadway as a nest of vipers. Gossip columnist Burt Lancaster and sleazy press agent Tony Curtis eat each other's tails in this jazzy, cynical study of showbiz corruption. Shot on location, and mostly at night, in steely black and white, Times Square and the Great White Way never looked so alluring.

Taxi Driver (Martin Scorsese, 1976). A long night's journey into day by the great chronicler of the dark side of the city – and New York's greatest filmmaker. Scorsese's New York is hallucinatorily seductive and thoroughly repellent in this superbly unsettling study of obsessive outsider Travis Bickle (Robert De Niro).

New York in the 1990s

All Over Me (Alex Sichel, 1997). A beautifully acted coming-of-age tale about a heavyset teenager who is patently but unspokenly in love with her baby-doll best friend. Set during a humid Hell's Kitchen summer, this doomed romance is played out in cramped tenement bedrooms and sweltering neighborhood bars and set to a pounding riot grrrl score.

Bad Lieutenant (Abel Ferrara, 1992). Nearly every movie by Ferrara from *Driller Killer* to *The Funeral* deserves a place in a list of great New York movies, but this, above all, seems his own personal *Manhattan*: a journey through the circles of Hell with Harvey Keitel as a depraved Dante.

Celebrity (Woody Allen, 1998). Woody reimagines *La Dolce Vita* in 90s Manhattan in this cameo-crammed tale of New York glamour and glitz notable mainly for Leonardo di Caprio's turn as a bratty movie star, Kenneth Branagh's turn as Woody Allen, and Šven Nykvist's rich, luminous black-and-white cinematography.

The Cruise (Bennett Miller, 1998). A documentary portrait of a true New York eccentric, Timothy "Speed" Levitch, a Dostoyevskian character with a baroque flair for language and an encyclopedic knowledge of local history, who takes puzzled tourists on guided "cruises" around the city on which he rails against the tyranny of the grid plan and rhapsodizes about "the lascivious voyeurism of the tour bus."

Eyes Wide Shut, (Stanley Kubrick, 1999). Kubrick's much-hyped priapic folly plays out in a New York netherworld of the rich and decadent. Upscale doctor Tom Cruise prowls Greenwich Village – stunningly re-created by its reclusive director on Pinewood sets – and finds himself an unwelcome guest at a masked orgy in a Long Island mansion.

Jungle Fever (Spike Lee, 1991). Interracial romance in the 1990s seems as taboo as it ever was, and Harlem and Bensonhurst worlds apart, in Lee's ambitious, pessimistic and angry urban love story. With a career-making turn from Samuel L. Jackson as the crack-addicted Gator.

Kids (Larry Clark, 1995). The best New York summer movie since *Do the Right Thing*, and just as controversial. An overhyped but affecting portrait of a group of amoral, though supposedly typical, teenagers hanging out on the Upper East Side, in Washington Square Park, and in the Carmine Street swimming pool on one muggy, mad day.

Little Odessa (James Gray, 1995). Tim Roth plays the prodigal son returning to Brooklyn in this somber, beautifully shot story of the Russian Mafia in Brighton Beach and Coney Island. One of a spate of New York ethnic gangster films made in the 1990s, which, among others, portrayed Irish mobsters (*State of Grace*), Jewish hoodlums (*Amongst Friends*) and African-American gang-bangers (*New Jack City*).

Metropolitan (Whit Stillman, 1990). Away from all the racism, the crime and the homelessness, a group of debutantes and rich young men socialize on the Upper East Side one Christmas, tackling head-on such pressing issues as where to buy a good tuxedo, and behaving as if the 1980s, or the 1880s for that matter, had never ended.

Night Falls on Manhattan (Sidney Lumet, 1996). Gotham's great cinematic chronicler of police corruption delivers another swinging blow in the Giuliani era in this underrated drama about

Harlem drug dealers, bent cops and the District Attorney's office. Stars Andy Garcia as an idealistic D.A. and Ian Holm as his veteran cop pop.

A Price Above Rubies (Boaz Yakin, 1998). Set among the ultra-orthodox Hasidic community of Borough Park in Brooklyn, this film offers tantalizing glimpses of a little-seen world, but its risible story of the rebellion of one young wife (Renée Zellwegger) against patriarchal oppression offers little in the way of enlightenment.

Ransom (Ron Howard, 1996). The haves and the have-nots battle it out on the Upper East Side in this ludicrous Mel Gibson thriller about a millionaire airline magnate whose son is kidnapped by underworld thugs at the Bethesda Fountain in Central Park.

The Saint of Fort Washington (Tim Hunter, 1992). Nearly invisible on film, the plight of the city's homeless is portrayed in this heartfelt and sentimental tale of a schizophrenic (Matt Dillon) and a Vietnam vet (Danny Glover) who meet at the Fort Washington shelter in Washington Heights.

Six Degrees of Separation (Fred Schepisi, 1993). Brilliant, enthralling adaptation of John Guare's acclaimed play uses the story of a young black man (Will Smith) who turns up at a rich Upper East Side apartment claiming to be the son of Sidney Poitier as a springboard for an examination of the great social and racial divides of the city.

Smoke (Wayne Wang, 1995). A clever, beguiling film scripted by novelist Paul Auster, which connects a handful of stories revolving around Harvey Keitel's Brooklyn cigar store. Deals with the "beautiful mosaic" in a somewhat self-satisfied way, but, as a fairy tale about how we might all be able to get along, it's just fine.

Unmade Beds (Nicholas Barker, 1998). This poignant, occasionally hilarious, and beautifully stylized documentary about four single New Yorkers looking for love in the personal columns, visualizes the city as one endless Edward Hopper painting, full of lonely souls biding time in rented rooms.

New York past

The Age of Innocence (Martin Scorsese, 1993). The upper echelons of New York society in the 1870s brought gloriously to life. Though Scorsese, by necessity, restricts most of the action to drawing rooms and ballrooms, look out for the breathtaking matte-shot of a then undeveloped Upper East Side.

The Crowd (King Vidor, 1928). "You've got to be good in that town if you want to beat the crowd." A young couple try to make it in the big city but are swallowed up and spat out by the capitalist machine. A bleak vision of New York in the 1920s, and one of the great silent films.

The Docks of New York (Josef von Sternberg, 1928). Opening with dramatic shots of New York's shoreline during its heyday as a great port, this story of a couple of sailors' shore leave in waterfront flophouses and gin-soaked bars is a far cry from *On the Town*; an ugly world beautifully filmed.

The Godfather Part II (Francis Ford Coppola, 1974). Flashing back to the early life of Vito Corleone, Coppola's great sequel re-created the Italian immigrant experience at the turn of the century, portraying Corleone quarantined at Ellis Island and growing up tough on the meticulously re-created streets of Little Italy.

Hallelujah, I'm a Bum (Lewis Milestone, 1933). Set during the Depression, this eccentric musical comedy (written in rhyming dialogue) imagines Central Park as a benign haven for the homeless. Die-hard hobo Al Jolson travels north to spend the summer *en plein air* in New York but when he falls in love with a girl he meets in the park he has to take a job on Wall Street.

Hester Street (Joan Micklin Silver, 1975). Young, tradition-bound Russian-Jewish immigrant joins her husband in turn-of-the-century Lower East Side to find he's cast off old world ways. Simple but appealing tale with splendid period feeling. The tenements and markets of 1896 Hester Street were convincingly re-created on the quaint back-streets of the West Village.

The Last Days of Disco (Whit Stillman, 1998). About the most unlikely setting for Stillman's brand of square WASPy talkfests would be the bombastic glittery bacchanals that were Studio 54 in its late-'70s heydey, which is what makes this far more enjoyable than the same season's overly literal and melodramatic **54** (Mark Christopher, 1998).

Little Fugitive (Morris Engel and Ruth Orkin, 1953). A Brooklyn seven-year-old, tricked into believing he has killed his older brother, takes flight to Coney Island where he spends a day and a night indulging in all its previously forbidden pleasures. This beautifully photographed time capsule of 1950s Brooklyn influenced both the American indie scene and the French New Wave.

Radio Days (Woody Allen, 1987). Woody contrasts reminiscences of his loud, vulgar family in 1940s Rockaway with reveries of the golden days of radio, and the glamour of Times Square, with the same kind of cynical nostalgia with which, in *Bullets Over Broadway* (1994), he spins a yarn about gangsters and theater people in the 1920s.

Speedy (Ted Wilde, 1928). This silent Harold Lloyd comedy shot on location in the city is a priceless time capsule of New York in the 1920s, featuring a horse-drawn trolley chase through the Lower East Side, a visit to Yankee Stadium and an unforgettably exuberant trip to Coney Island.

Summer of Sam (Spike Lee, 1999). The dark summer of 1977 – the summer of the "Son of Sam" killings, a blistering heatwave, power blackouts, looting, arson and the birth of punk – provides the perfect backdrop for Lee's sprawling tale of paranoia and betrayal in an Italian-American enclave of the Bronx.

New York comedy and romance

An Affair to Remember (Leo McCarey, 1957). After a romance at sea, Cary Grant and Deborah Kerr dock in New York and plan to meet six months hence at the top of the Empire State Building if they can free themselves from prior engagements, and if playboy Grant can make it as a painter in Greenwich Village. A weepy romance canonized by *Sleepless in Seattle*, whose romantic denouement also hinged on an Empire State Building meeting.

Annie Hall (Woody Allen, 1977). Oscar-winning autobiographical comic romance, which flits from reminiscences of Alvy Singer's childhood living beneath the Coney Island *Cyclone*, to life and love in uptown Manhattan (enlivened by endless cocktail parties and trips to see *The Sorrow and the Pity* at the Thalia), is a valentine both to ex-lover co-star Diane Keaton and to the city. Simultaneously clever, bourgeois and very winning.

Antz (Eric Darnell and Lawrence Guterman, 1998). It's only at the punch line of this animated insect odyssey – about a nebbishy hero (voiced by Woody Allen) living in too-close proximity to a few million other schlubs and lorded over by corrupt officials – that you realize that this is not just an allegory for New York, but that its whole magnificently rendered universe is merely an ant hill beside a trash can in Central Park

Big (Penny Marshall, 1988). Tom Hanks grows up far too soon and has to move from New Jersey to the Big City while still at Junior High. A natural at a Madison Avenue toy firm where he finds work as a computer clerk, he impresses his boss with his unbridled enthusiasm for the F.A.O. Schwarz toy store, and relocates from a hellish Times Square dive to a to-die-for SoHo loft while trying to find a cure for the secret of his precocious yuppie success.

Crossing Delancey (Joan Micklin Silver, 1989). Lovely story of a Jewish woman (Amy Irving) who lives Uptown but visits her grandmother south of Delancey each week. The grandmother and the local yenta hitch her up with a nice young pickle vendor when all she wants is a nasty famous novelist. An engaging view of contemporary life in the Jewish Lower East Side and the yuppie Upper West.

The Daytrippers (Greg Mottola, 1996). This sleeper hit follows a hilariously dysfunctional Long Island family on a Manhattan odyssey in search of their eldest daughter's errant husband, taking them from Park Avenue publishing houses to a startling denouement at a rooftop SoHo party.

Desperately Seeking Susan (Susan Seidelman, 1985). Bored New Jersey housewife Rosanna Arquette arrives in Manhattan on a mission: to find Madonna, or rather Susan, the mysterious subject of a number of cryptic personal ads. Infected with East Village élan, Arquette is transformed into a grungy Madonna clone and finds happiness in this charming paean to the joys of Downtown.

Living Out Loud (Richard LaGravenese, 1998). A lovely, quirky portrait of loneliness in New York. Holly Hunter stars as a rich divorcee suddenly alone in a fabulous Fifth Avenue apartment who finds unlikely companionship with Danny DeVito, her elevator operator, and Queen Latifah, a singer in an Uptown jazz club.

Men in Black (Barry Sonnenfeld, 1997). One of the most wittily imaginative Manhattan movies in years portrays the city as a haven for a brave new wave of immigration, with Tommy Lee Jones and Will Smith keeping watch for extraterrestrials and the future of the universe hanging in the balance in a MacDougal Street jewelry store.

Miracle on 34th Street (George Seaton, 1947). The perfect antidote to all the nightmares and mean streets of New York films, *Miracle* opens during Macy's annual Christmas parade, where a kindly old gentleman with a white beard offers to replace the store's inebriated Santa.

The Seven Year Itch (Billy Wilder, 1955). When his wife and kid vacate humid Manhattan, Mitty-like pulp editor Tom Ewell is left guiltily leching over the innocent TV-toothpaste temptress upstairs – Marilyn Monroe, at her most wistfully comic. The sight of her pushing down her billowing skirt as she stands on a subway grating (at Lexington Ave and 52nd St) is one of the era's and the city's most resonant movie images.

Stranger than Paradise (Jim Jarmusch, 1984). Only the first third of this, the original slacker indie, is set in New York, but its portrayal of Lower East Side lethargy is hilariously spot-on and permeates the rest of the film in which a couple of hipster fish venture out of water in Ohio and Florida. The film's Downtown credentials – John Lurie is a jazz saxophonist with the Lounge Lizards, Richard Edson used to drum for Sonic Youth, and Jarmusch himself is an East Village celebrity – are impeccable.

New York nightmares

The Addiction (Abel Ferrara, 1995). A simple trip home from the college library turns into a living nightmare for Lili Taylor when she is bitten by a vampiric street-walker on Bleecker Street and transformed into a blood junkie cruising the East Village for fresh kill.

After Hours (Martin Scorsese, 1985). Yuppie computer programmer Griffin Dunne inadvertently ends upon a nightlong odyssey into the Hades of downtown New York, a journey that goes from bad to worse to awful as he encounters every kook south of 14th Street.

Escape from New York (John Carpenter, 1981). In the not too distant future (1997, in fact), society has given up trying to solve the problems of Manhattan and has walled it up as a lawless maximum-security prison from which Kurt Russell has to rescue the hijacked US president.

Jacob's Ladder (Adrian Lyne, 1990). Tim Robbins gets off the subway in Brooklyn but discovers himself locked inside a deserted station . . . and then his troubles begin as his Vietnam-induced hallucinations turn Manhattan into one hell of a house of horrors.

The Lost Weekend (Billy Wilder, 1945). Alcoholic Ray Milland is left alone in the city with no money and a desperate thirst. The film's most famous scene is his long trek up Third Avenue (shot on location) trying to hawk his typewriter to buy booze, only to find all the pawn shops closed for Yom Kippur.

Marathon Man (John Schlesinger, 1976). Innocent, bookish Dustin Hoffman runs for his life all over Manhattan after being dragged into a conspiracy involving old Nazis and being tortured with dental instruments. Shot memorably around the Central Park Reservoir and Zoo, Columbia University, the Diamond District and Spanish Harlem.

The Out-of-Towners (Arthur Hiller, 1969). If you have any problems getting into town from the airport take solace from the fact that they can be nothing compared to those endured by Jack Lemmon and Sandy Dennis – for whom everything that can go wrong does go wrong – in Neil Simon's frantic comedy. Recently remade with Steve Martin and Goldie Hawn (but stick with the original).

Rosemary's Baby (Roman Polanski, 1968). Mia Farrow and John Cassavetes move into their dream New York apartment in the Dakota Building (72nd and Central Park West, where John Lennon lived and died) and think their problems stop with nosy neighbors and thin walls until Farrow gets pregnant and hell, literally, breaks loose. Arguably the most terrifying film ever set in the city.

The Siege (Edward Zwick, 1998). Zwick's paranoid, controversial film speculates on what would happen if a series of major terrorist attacks by Arab militants in New York City were to lead to the declaration of martial law and the sealing off of Brooklyn. The results are muddle-headed but the images of troops marching over the Brooklyn Bridge are indelible.

The Taking of Pelham One Two Three (Joseph Sargent, 1974). Just when you thought it was safe to get back on the subway. A gang of mercenary hoods hijacks a train on its way through Midtown and threatens to start killing the passengers at the rate of one a minute if their million-dollar ransom is not paid within the hour.

Wolfen (Michael Wadleigh, 1981). The sins of New York's founding fathers and venal property developers return to haunt the city in the form of vicious wolves in this beautiful and serious horror movie from the director of *Woodstock*(!), one of the very few films that touch on the city's Native American history, and one of the first to use the Steadicam to intelligent effect.

The mean streets

The Cool World (Shirley Clarke, 1964). A 1960s *Boyz'n'the Hood*, this radical, documentary-type study of a Harlem teenager who longs to be a gun-toting gang member proved Clarke to be the political conscience of New York's streets; as had *The Connection* (1962), her portrait of a group of addicts awaiting their pusher, and *Portrait of Jason* (1967), her record of the monologue of an aging black hustler.

Dead End (William Wyler, 1937). Highly entertaining, stage-derived tragedy of the Lower East Side's teeming poor, starring Humphrey Bogart as a mother-obsessed small-time gangster, and a pack of lippy adolescents who earned their own movie series as The Dead End Kids.

Fort Apache, The Bronx (Daniel Petrie, 1981). A film to confirm people's worst fears about the Bronx. Paul Newman stars as veteran cop based in the city's most crime-infested and corrupt precinct. Tense, entertaining and totally unbelievable.

The French Connection (William Friedkin, 1971). Plenty of heady Brooklyn atmosphere in this sensational Oscar-winning cop thriller starring Gene Hackman, whose classic car-and-subway chase takes place under the Bensonhurst Elevated Railroad.

Kiss of Death (Henry Hathaway, 1947; Barbet Schroeder, 1995). The 1947 **Kiss**, with squealing ex-con Victor Mature battling giggling psycho Richard Widmark, was one of the very first films to be shot entirely on real New York locations. Schroeder's remake retells the story in the brighter, tackier Queens of the 1990s, with squealing ex-con David Caruso battling dumb ox Nicolas Cage.

Madigan (Don Siegel, 1968). Opens with a jazzy montage of Manhattan skyscrapers and affluent avenues, then plunges rogue cop Richard Widmark into the mean streets of Spanish Harlem. *Madigan* is a vivid study of the inevitability of police corruption with Henry Fonda as the police commissioner struggling to live within the law.

Mean Streets (Martin Scorsese, 1973). Scorsese's brilliant breakthrough film breathlessly follows small-time hood Harvey Keitel and his volatile, harum-scarum buddy Robert de Niro around a vividly portrayed Little Italy before reaching its violent climax.

Midnight Cowboy (John Schlesinger, 1969) The odd love story between Jon Voight's bumpkin hustler and Dustin Hoffman's touching urban creep Ratso Rizzo plays out against both the seediest and swankiest of New York locations.

Naked City (Jules Dassin, 1948). A crime story that views the city with a documentarist's eye. Shot on actual locations, it follows a police manhunt for a ruthless killer all over town toward an unforgettable chase through the Lower East Side and a shoot-out on the Williamsburg Bridge.

Prince of the City (Sidney Lumet, 1981). Lumet is a die-hard New York director, and his crime films, including *Serpico, Dog Day Afternoon, Q&A* and *Twelve Angry Men* are all superb New York movies, but this is his New York epic. A corrupt narcotics detective turns federal informer to assuage his guilt, and Lumet takes us from drug busts in Harlem, to the cops' suburban homes on Long Island, to federal agents' swanky pads overlooking Central Park.

Superfly (Gordon Parks Jr, 1972). Propelled by its ecstatic Curtis Mayfield score, this Blaxploitation classic about one smooth-looking drug dealer's ultimate score is best seen today for its mind-boggling fashion excess and its almost documentary-like look at the Harlem bars, streets, clubs and diners of twenty years ago.

New York song and dance

Fame (Alan Parker, 1980). Set in Manhattan's High School for the Performing Arts, the film that spawned the TV series may be a gawky musical, but in its haphazard, sentimental, ungainly way it still manages to capture some of the city's agony and ecstasy.

42nd Street (Lloyd Bacon, 1933). One of the best films ever made about Broadway – though the film rarely ventures outside the theater. Starring Ruby Keeler as the young chorus girl who has to replace the ailing leading lady: she goes on stage an unknown and, well, you know the rest.

A Great Day in Harlem (Jean Bach, 1994). A unique jazz documentary that spins many tales around the famous Art Kane photograph for which the cream of New York's jazz world assemble on the steps of a Harlem brownstone one August morning in 1958. Using home-movie footage of the event and present-day interviews, Bach creates a wonderful portrait of a golden age.

Guys and Dolls (Joseph L. Mankiewicz, 1955). *The* great Broadway musical shot entirely on soundstages and giving as unlikely a picture of Times Square hoodlums (all colorfully suited sweetie-pies) as was ever seen. And a singing and dancing Marlon Brando to boot!

Hair (Milos Forman, 1979). Film version of the counterculture musical turns Central Park into a hippie paradise for the hirsute Treat Williams and his fellow Aquarians. Choreography (including dancing police horses) by Twyla Tharp.

It's Always Fair Weather (Gene Kelly, Stanley Donen, 1955). *On the Town* gone sour. A trio of wartime buddies vow to reunite in the Apple ten years hence, only to discover that they loathe one other and their own lives. Smart, cynical, satirical musical with a bunch of terrific numbers, including a back-alley trash-can dance.

New York, New York (Martin Scorsese, 1977). Scorsese's homage to the grand musicals of postwar Hollywood, reimagined for the post-Vietnam era. His grand folly opens on V-J day in Times Square with sax player Robert de Niro picking up Liza Minnelli in a dance hall, and follows their career and romance together through the Big Band era. Unusually for Scorsese, but befitting the film, the eponymous city was stylishly re-created on studio soundstages.

Saturday Night Fever (John Badham, 1977). What everybody remembers is the tacky glamour of flared white pants-suits and mirror-balled discos, but *Saturday Night Fever* is actually a touching and believable portrayal of working-class youth in the 1970s (Travolta works in a paint store when he's not strutting the dance floor), Italian-American Brooklyn, and the road to Manhattan.

Sweet Charity (Bob Fosse, 1969). Shirley MacLaine's lovable prostitute Charity hoofs around Manhattan getting the short end of the stick at every turn. Mugged in Central Park *by her boyfriend,* Charity blithely wanders the city dancing on rooftops and in swank Uptown clubs, and ends up back in the Park rescued by a merry band of escapees from *Hair.*

West Side Story (Robert Wise, Jerome Robbins, 1961). Sex, singing and Shakespeare in a hyper-cinematic Oscar-winning musical (via Broadway) about rival street gangs. Lincoln Center now stands where the Sharks and the Jets once rumbled and interracial romance ended in tragedy.

Yankee Doodle Dandy (Michael Curtiz, 1932). James Cagney's Oscar-winning performance as showbiz renaissance man George M. Cohan is a big-spirited biopic with music. Of its kind, probably the best ever.

A glossary of New York terms and people

New York has a **jargon** all its own – some of it unintelligible to non-natives. Though the selection below is by no means a dictionary of New York, it is basic to an understanding of the city and this *Guide*. Also included are some important architecture terms, and lastly, a roll call of prominent New Yorkers, past and present.

New York terms and acronyms

Avenue of the Americas Little-used name for Sixth Avenue.

Bag lady Homeless woman who carries her possessions around in a bag.

Big Apple New York City. Possibly from the slang of jazz musicians who referred to anything large as a "big apple" – and, for them, New York was the biggest apple of all.

Bridge and tunnel A derogatory term used by Manhattanites for people from the Outer Boroughs, Long Island or New Jersey – who have to take bridges or tunnels to get to Manhattan.

The City Local shorthand for Manhattan.

Condo Short for condominium, an individually owned apartment within a building.

Co-op The most popular form of apartment ownership in the city. A co-op differs from a condo in that you buy shares in the building in which the apartment is sited, rather than the apartment itself.

CUNY City University of New York.

Gotham Another name for New York City, introduced in these parts by Washington Irving, and popularized in *Batman* comics.

Gridlock Traffic freeze – when cars get trapped in intersections, preventing traffic on the cross streets from passing through.

Historic District An official designation by the Landmarks Commission that protects a particular building or site of historical/architectural value from future tampering, reconstructing or bulldozing.

Lex Conversational shorthand for Lexington Avenue.

MTA (Metropolitan Transit Authority) Runs the city's buses and subway lines; the IND (Independent), BMT (Brooklyn-Manhattan Transit) and IRT (Interborough Rapid Transit).

NYU New York University.

On line Unlike people in the rest of the country, New Yorkers wait on line, not in line (for movies, etc).

Outer Boroughs Local term for the boroughs of New York City other than Manhattan (in other words, the Bronx, Brooklyn, Queens or Staten Island).

PATH (Port Authority Trans Hudson) The agency that operates the commuter train, also known as the PATH, between Manhattan and New Jersey.

Port Authority Conversational shorthand for the Port Authority Bus Terminal on Eighth Avenue and 41st Street.

Robber barons Late nineteenth-century magnates who made their vast fortunes in banking, railroads and steel, among other things, often at the expense of their workers.

Skyscraper The word comes from the highest sail on a sailing ship, and hence refers to any high building.

SRO Single-room occupancy hotel – most often seedy spaces lived in long term by those on welfare.

Stoop Open platform, with steps leading up to it, at the entrance to an apartment house.

Straphangers Slang for people who ride the subways and buses, which used to have plastic straps riders could hold on to, to keep from falling (now they have poles). There is also a Straphangers' Association, which acts as an advocate for mass transit riders throughout the city.

SUNY State University of New York.

Tenement Large, often slummy, building divided into small apartments.

Tri-State area All-encompassing term for New York, New Jersey and Connecticut.

WPA (Works Project Administration) Agency begun by President Roosevelt in 1935 to create employment. In addition to construction work, the WPA art projects produced many murals in public buildings and a renowned set of guidebooks to the country.

Zoning ordinances Series of building regulations. The first, passed in 1915, stated that the floor space of a building could not be more than twelve times the area of its site, discouraging giant monoliths and leading to the setback or wedding cake style of skyscraper. A later ordinance allowed developers to build higher provided they supplied a public space at the foot of the building. Hence the **plaza**.

Architecture terms

Art Deco Style of decoration popular in the 1930s, characterized by geometrical shapes and patterns.

Art Nouveau Art, architecture and design of the 1890s typified by stylized flower and plant forms.

Beaux Arts Style of Neoclassical architecture taught at the Ecole des Beaux Arts in Paris at the end of the last century and widely adopted in New York City.

Brownstone Originally a nineteenth-century terraced house with a facade of brownstone (a kind of sandstone); now often any townhouse.

Colonial Style of Neoclassical architecture popular in the eighteenth century.

Federal Hybrid of French and Roman domestic architecture common in the late eighteenth century and early nineteenth century.

Greek Revival Style of architecture that mimicked that of classical Greece. Highly popular for major banks and larger houses in the early nineteenth century.

New York people

ABZUG Bella (1920–98) Congresswoman and liberal crusader, easily recognizable by the large hats she was fond of wearing. Outspoken and insistent on issues ranging from women's rights to civil liberties to the war in Vietnam, she was a ground-breaking female politician with a loyal (mostly female) following. Unfortunately, her support was not broad-based enough for higher office; several high profile runs for the senate and New York mayor in the 1970s resulted in severe financial debt and a loss of political influence.

ALLEN Woody Writer, director, comedian. Many people's clichéd idea of the neurotic Jewish Manhattanite. His clever, crafted films, particularly *Annie Hall, Manhattan, Hannah and Her Sisters,* and *Crimes and Misdemeanors,* comment on, and have become part of, the New York myth. His fall from grace in 1993, accused of child abuse by Mia Farrow after he left her for his adopted daughter, caused the biggest storm of publicity seen in the city in years.

ASTOR John Jacob (1822–90) Robber baron, slum landlord and, when he died, the richest man in the world. Astor made his packet from exacting exorbitant rents from those living in abject squalor in his many tenement buildings. By all accounts, a real bastard.

BEECHER Henry Ward (1813–87) Revivalist preacher famed for his support of women's suffrage, the abolition of slavery – and as the victim of a scandalous accusation of adultery that rocked nineteenth-century New York. His sister, Harriet Beecher Stowe, wrote the best-selling novel *Uncle Tom's Cabin,* which contributed greatly to the anti-slavery cause.

BRESLIN Jimmy Bitter, often brilliant columnist for *New York Newsday.* Once ran for mayor on a Secessionist ticket (declaring New York City independent from the State) with Norman Mailer as running mate.

BRYANT William Cullen (1794–1878) Poet, newspaper editor and main proponent of Central Park and the Metropolitan Museum. The small park that bears his name at 42nd Street and Fifth Avenue has been expertly cleaned up and is now a fitting memorial to this nineteenth-century hero.

BURR Aaron (1756–1836) Fascinating politician whose action-packed career included a stint as vice-president, a trial and acquittal for treason, and, most famously, the murder of Alexander Hamilton (q.v.) in a duel. His house, the Morris-Jumel Mansion, still stands.

CARNEGIE Andrew (1835–1919) Émigré Scottish industrialist who spent most of his life amassing a vast fortune and his final years giving it all away. Unlike most of his wealthy contemporaries he was not an ostentatious man, as his house, now the Cooper-Hewitt Museum, shows.

CHISHOLM Shirley In 1968 she became the first black woman elected to Congress, from her home district in Brooklyn.

CUOMO Mario Former governor of New York State and once a suggested contender for the Democratic Party presidential nomination. A liberal politician, Cuomo has increasingly taken a backseat to his son Andrew – a rising star in the Democratic Party.

DINKINS David First black mayor of New York City, elected in 1989 after a hard, mud-slinging mayoral battle against Republican Rudolph Giuliani. His term in office left him seeming ineffectual and weak: "Everything sticks to him but praise," said a pundit.

FRICK Henry Clay (1849–1919) One of the robber barons, Frick's single contribution to civilization was to use his inestimable wealth to collect some of the finest art treasures of Europe, now on show at his home on Fifth Avenue.

GARVEY Marcus (1887–1940) Activist who did much to raise the consciousness of blacks in the early part of the century (and is now a Rasta myth). When he started to become a political threat to the white government he was thrown in prison for fraud; pardoned but deported, he spent his last years in London.

GINSBERG Allen (1926–97) Revered beatnik poet, activist and hero of the Lower East Side.

GIULIANI Rudolph Mayor. Former US district attorney who has carried his bulldog ways of prosecuting crimes to the mayor's office. Often derided for his zealous "quality of life" laws, he has helped reduce crime and attract business to the city, but is criticized for his arrogant tactics and for giving too much power to the police.

GOULD Jay (1836–92) Robber baron extraordinaire. Gould made his fortune with a telegraph network during the Civil War, and went on to manipulate the stock market and make millions more. His most spectacular swindle cornered the gold market, netted him $11 million in a fortnight and provoked the "Black Friday" crash of 1869.

GREELEY Horace (1811–72) Campaigning founder-editor of the *New Yorker* magazine and *Tribune* newspaper who coined the phrase, "Go West, young man!," but never did himself. An advocate of women's rights, union rights, the abolition of slavery and other worthy, liberal matters.

HAMILL Pete Newspaper editor, writer, broadcaster and expert on Manhattan and – especially – the Outer Boroughs. One of the best no-bullshit commentators around today.

HAMILTON Alexander (1755–1804) Brilliant Revolutionary propagandist, soldier, political thinker (drafted sections of the Constitution) and statesman (first Secretary to the Treasury). Shot and killed in a duel by Aaron Burr (q.v.). His house, Hamilton Grange, is preserved at the edge of Harlem.

HARING Keith (1958–90) Big-name artist who used crude animal forms for decoration and art. His early death of AIDS prematurely removed one of America's most promising artists and designers.

HELMSLEY Harry (1904–97) Property-owning tycoon who, like Donald Trump (q.v.), had a penchant for slapping his name on all that fell into his grasp. Hence many old hotels are now Helmsley Hotels.

HELMSLEY Leona Widow of Harry, self-styled "Queen of New York" and major-domo of the *Helmsley Palace Hotel*. To the delight of many, the shit hit the fan for Leona in 1989, when she was found guilty of million-dollar tax evasion.

IRVING Washington (1783–1859) Satirist, biographer, short story writer (*The Legend of Sleepy Hollow*, *Rip Van Winkle*) and diplomat. His house, just outside the city near Tarrytown, is worth a visit.

JOHNSON Philip Architect. Disciple of Ludwig Mies Van der Rohe, high priest of the International Style glass-box skyscraper, he designed the Seagram Building on Park Avenue, the AT&T Building on Third Avenue and the Federal Reserve Plaza on Liberty Street, among others.

KOCH Ed The most popular mayor of New York since Fiorello LaGuardia (q.v.). Elected by a slender majority in 1978, Koch won New Yorkers over by his straight-talking, no-bullshit approach. After three terms in office, he lost the Democratic nomination in 1989 to David Dinkins (q.v.) following scandals involving other city officials and his insensitive handling of black issues.

LAGUARDIA Fiorello (1882–1947) NYC mayor who replaced Jimmy Walker and who gained great popularity with his honest and down-to-earth administration, focusing on anti-corruption programs and social spending for the poor.

MORGAN J. Pierpont (1837–1913) Top industrialist and financier who used a little of his spare cash to build the Morgan Library on Third Avenue. He created a financial empire that was bigger than the Gettys' and that enabled him to buy out both Andrew Carnegie and Henry Frick.

MOSES Robert (1889–1981) Moses is perhaps more than anyone else responsible for the way the city looks today. Holder of all the key planning and building posts from the 1930s to the 1960s, his philosophy of urban development was to tear down whatever was old, build anew and create ordered public spaces with a lot of concrete (paved plazas were a particular favorite).

OLMSTED Fredrick (1822–1903) Landscape designer and writer. Central Park, Riverside Park and many others were the fruits of his partnership with architect Calvert Vaux.

ONASSIS Jaqueline Kennedy (1929–94). The former First Lady spent most of her later years in the city, working as an editor for Doubleday. Long a byword in style and grace, by the time of her death she had regained much of the public favor lost after her unpopular marriage to the Greek shipping magnate.

O'NEILL Eugene (1888–1953) NYC's (and America's) most influential playwright. Many of the characters from plays like *Mourning Becomes Electra, The Iceman Cometh* and *Long Day's Journey into Night* are based on his drinking companions in *The Golden Swan* bar.

PARKER Dorothy (1893–1967) Playwright, essayist and acid wit. A founding member of the Round Table group at the *Algonquin Hotel*, she was one of the few respected women in the New York literary world.

PATAKI George Governor of New York State, who surprisingly ousted Mario Cuomo (q.v) and has had standing feuds with Mayor Giuliani, his fellow Republican who did not back him in 1994.

ROCKEFELLER JR John D. (1874–1960) Unlike his tightfisted dad (founder of the fortune), Rockefeller Junior gave away tidy sums for philanthropic ventures in New York. The Cloisters Museum, The Museum of Modern Art, Lincoln Center, Riverside Church and most famously Rockefeller Center were mostly his doing.

ROCKEFELLER Nelson (1908–79) Politician son of John D. Jr. Elected governor of New York State in 1958, he held on to the post until 1974, when he turned to greater things and sought the Republican Party presidential nomination. He didn't get it, but before his death served briefly as vice-president under Gerald Ford.

SEINFELD Jerry Comedian of the moment, whose long-running and immensely popular TV series (though filmed in LA) captured New Yorkers' neuroses better than anyone this side of Woody Allen.

SHARPTON JR Al (The Reverend) Ordained minister, political activist and perennial candidate for office, Sharpton is known for always putting himself in the center of a publicity storm, particularly if it involves police corruption or racial incidents. Loud-mouthed and confrontational, he enjoys a lot of support from minority groups in the city.

SIMON Neil Playwright. With a record of Broadway/film hits as big as his bank balance (*Brighton Beach Memoirs, Plaza Suite*), Simon can lay claim to being the most popular playwright today.

STEINBRENNER George Controversial baseball team owner/entrepreneur. Known as "The Boss," Steinbrenner runs the beloved NY Yankees, often with an iron fist, though generous pockets.

STEINEM Gloria Feminist/activist and writer. From early feminist consciousness-raising to the founding of *Ms* magazine and the publication of numerous influential essays and books (such as *Outrageous Acts and Everyday Rebellions*), Steinem has been a steady, vocal crusader for women's rights in New York and elsewhere.

TRUMP Donald Property tycoon. When you shell out $70 for your shoebox hotel room, reflect that "The Donald" sits on top of a real estate empire worth, at its peak, $1.3 billion. His creations include the glammed-out Trump Tower on Fifth Avenue, Trump Plaza near Bloomingdale's and Trump's Casino in Atlantic City, NJ. Much despised by New Yorkers for embodying nouveau riche excess and greed.

TWEED William Marcy "Boss" (1823–78) Head of the NY Democratic Party machine whose corrupt practices netted him city funds to the tune of $200 million and gave Democratic Party headquarters Tammany Hall its bad name.

WARHOL Andy (1926–87) Artist and media hound. Instigator of Pop Art, The Velvet

Underground, The Factory, *Interview* magazine and *Empire* – a 24-hour movie of the Empire State Building (no commentary, no gorillas, nothing but the building). Died, oddly enough, after a routine gallstone operation.

WHITE Stanford (1853–1906) Partner of the architectural firm McKim, Mead and White, which designed such Neoclassical landmarks as the General Post Office, Washington Square Arch, the Municipal Building and parts of Columbia University.

Index

M

Stay in touch with us!

ROUGH*NEWS* **is Rough Guides' free newsletter.
In four issues a year we give you news, travel
issues, music reviews, readers' letters and the
latest dispatches from authors on the road.**

I would like to receive ROUGH*NEWS*: please put me on your free mailing list.

NAME . . . .

ADDRESS . . . .

Please clip or photocopy and send to: Rough Guides, 62–70 Shorts Gardens, London WC2H 9AB,
England or Rough Guides, 375 Hudson Street, New York, NY 10014, USA.

ROUGH GUIDES: Travel

Amsterdam
Andalucia
Australia

Austria
Bali & Lombok
Barcelona
Belgium &
  Luxembourg
Belize
Berlin
Brazil
Britain
Brittany &
  Normandy
Bulgaria
California
Canada
Central America
Chile
China
Corfu & the
  Ionian Islands
Corsica
Costa Rica
Crete
Cuba
Cyprus
Czech & Slovak
  Republics

Dodecanese
Dominican
  Republic
Egypt
England
Europe
Florida
France
French Hotels &
  Restaurants 1999
Germany
Goa
Greece
Greek Islands
Guatemala
Hawaii
Holland
Hong Kong
  & Macau
Hungary
India
Indonesia
Ireland
Israel & the
  Palestinian
  Territories
Italy
Jamaica
Japan
Jordan

Kenya
Laos
London
London
  Restaurants
Los Angeles
Malaysia,
  Singapore &
  Brunei
Mallorca &
  Menorca
Maya World
Mexico
Morocco
Moscow
Nepal
New England
New York
New Zealand
Norway
Pacific Northwest
Paris
Peru
Poland
Portugal
Prague
Provence & the
  Côte d'Azur
The Pyrenees
Romania

St Petersburg
San Francisco
Sardinia
Scandinavia
Scotland
Scottish Highlands
  & Islands
Sicily
Singapore

South Africa
Southern India
Southwest USA
Spain
Sweden
Syria
Thailand
Trinidad & Tobago
Tunisia
Turkey
Tuscany & Umbria
USA
Venice
Vienna
Vietnam
Wales
Washington DC
West Africa
Zimbabwe &
  Botswana

AVAILABLE AT ALL GOOD BOOKSHOPS

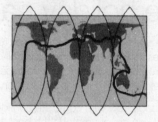

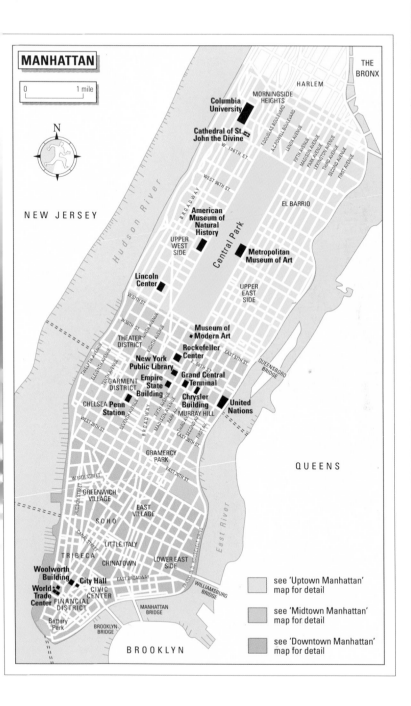

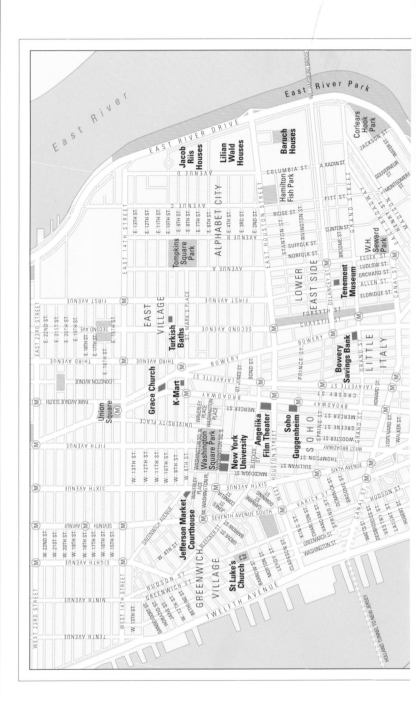

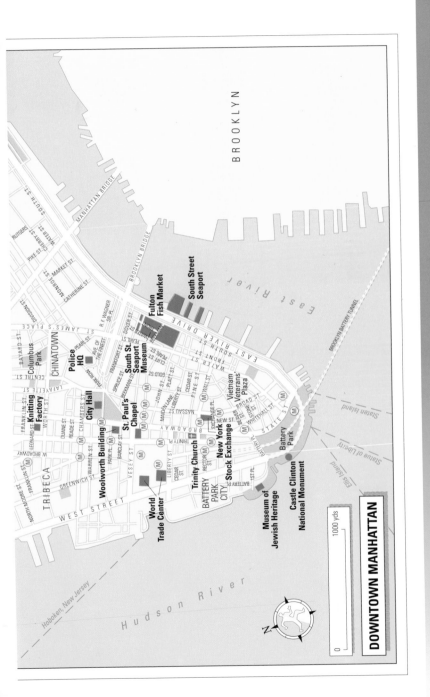

DOWNTOWN MANHATTAN

0   1000 yds

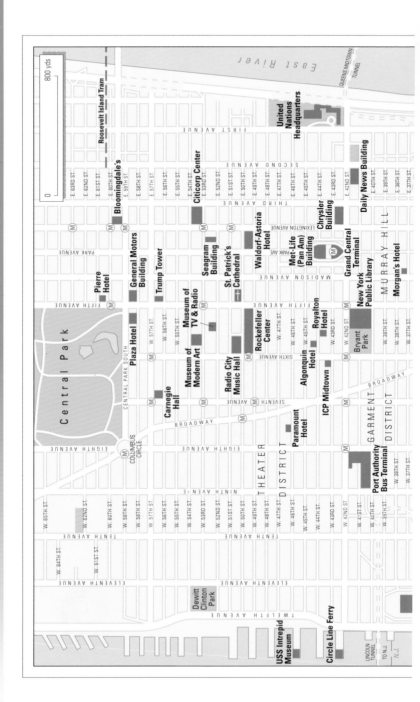

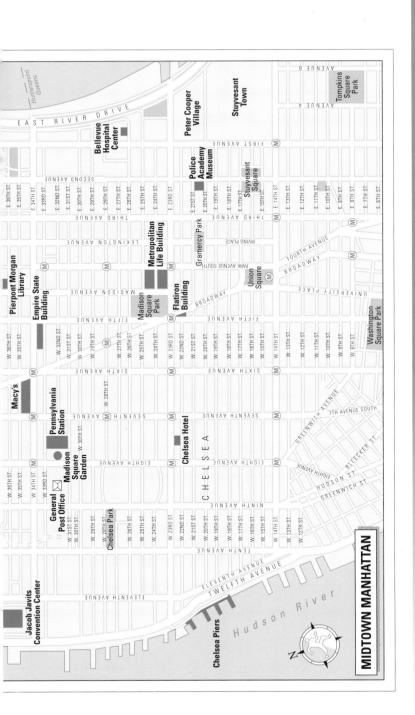

MIDTOWN MANHATTAN

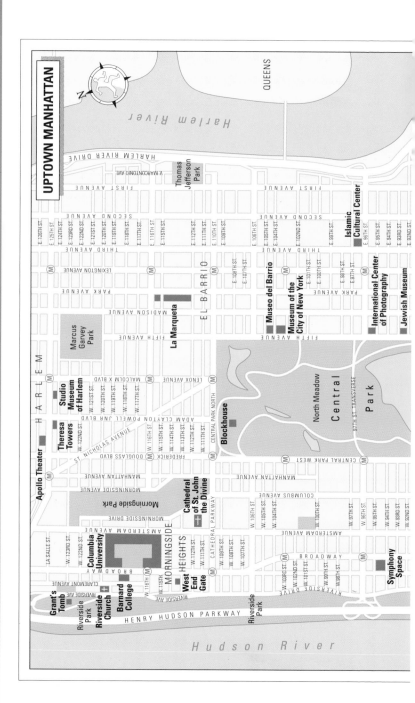

UPTOWN MANHATTAN

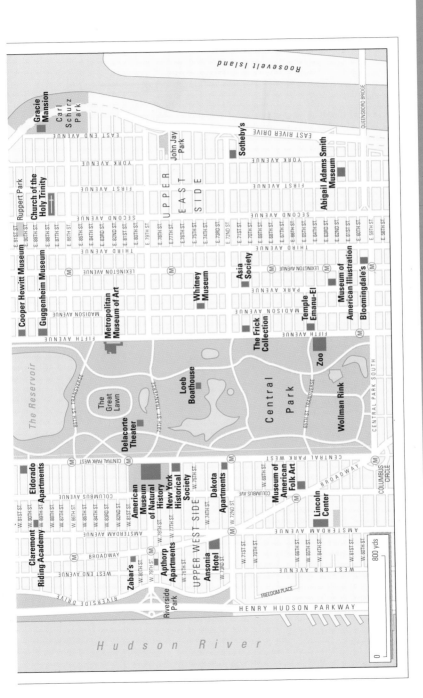

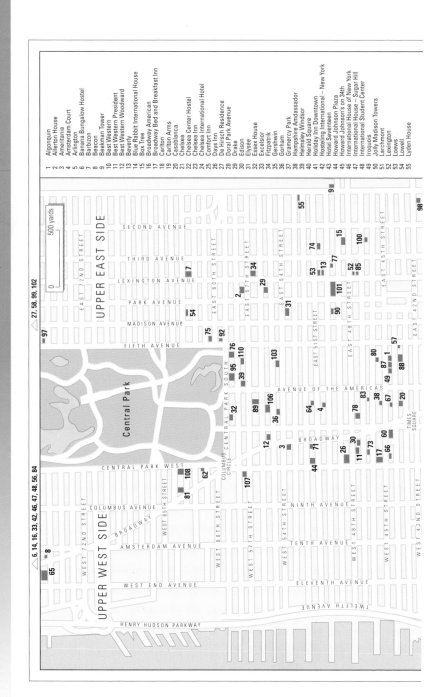

1 Algonquin
2 Allerton House
3 Ameritania
4 Amsterdam Court
5 Arlington
6 Banana Bungalow Hostel
7 Barbizon
8 Beacon
9 Beekman Tower
10 Best Western
11 Best Western President
12 Best Western Woodward
13 Beverly
14 Blue Rabbit International House
15 Box Tree
16 Broadway American
17 Broadway Bed and Breakfast Inn
18 Carlton
19 Carlton Arms
20 Casablanca
21 Chelsea
22 Chelsea Center Hostel
23 Chelsea Inn
24 Chelsea International Hotel
25 Comfort Inn
26 Days Inn
27 De Hirsch Residence
28 Doral Park Avenue
29 Drake
30 Edison
31 Elysée
32 Essex House
33 Excelsior
34 Fitzpatrick
35 Gershwin
36 Gorham
37 Gramercy Park
38 Hampshire Amdassador
39 Helmsley Windsor
40 Herald Square
41 Holiday Inn Downtown
42 Hosteling International – New York
43 Hotel Seventeen
44 Howard Johnson Plaza
45 Howard Johnson's on 34th
46 International House of New York
47 International House – Sugar Hill
48 International Student Center
49 Iroquois
50 Jolly Madison Towers
51 Larchmont
52 Lexington
53 Loews
54 Lowell
55 Lyden House

500 yards

0

UPPER EAST SIDE

△ 27, 58, 99, 102

△ 6, 14, 16, 33, 42, 46, 47, 48, 56, 84

UPPER WEST SIDE

Central Park

TIMES SQUARE

SECOND AVENUE
THIRD AVENUE
LEXINGTON AVENUE
PARK AVENUE
MADISON AVENUE
FIFTH AVENUE
CENTRAL PARK WEST
COLUMBUS AVENUE
AMSTERDAM AVENUE
WEST END AVENUE
ELEVENTH AVENUE
TWELFTH AVENUE
HENRY HUDSON PARKWAY

AVENUE OF THE AMERICAS
BROADWAY
SEVENTH AVENUE
EIGHTH AVENUE
NINTH AVENUE
TENTH AVENUE

EAST 72ND STREET
EAST 60TH STREET
EAST 57TH STREET
EAST 54TH STREET
EAST 51ST STREET
EAST 48TH STREET
EAST 45TH STREET
EAST 42ND STREET

WEST 72ND STREET
WEST 65TH STREET
WEST 60TH STREET
WEST 57TH STREET
WEST 54TH STREET
WEST 48TH STREET
WEST 45TH STREET
WEST 42ND STREET

CENTRAL PARK SOUTH
COLUMBUS CIRCLE

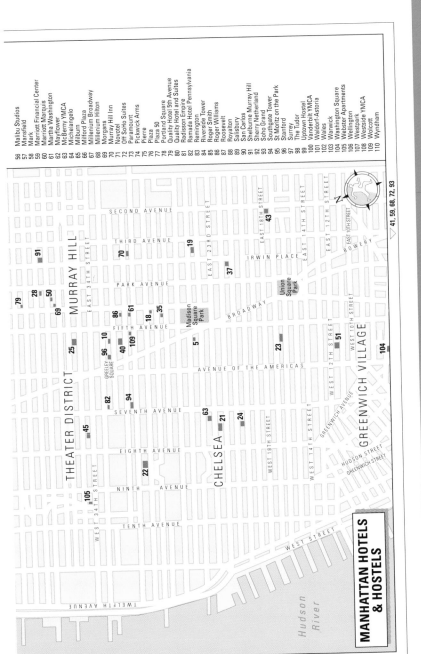

56 Malibu Studios
57 Mansfield
58 Mark
59 Marriott Financial Center
60 Marriott Marquis
61 Martha Washington
62 Mayflower
63 McBerny YMCA
64 Michelangelo
65 Milburn
66 Milford Plaza
67 Millenium Broadway
68 Millenium Hilton
69 Morgans
70 Murray Hill Inn
71 Novotel
72 Off SoHo Suites
73 Paramount
74 Pickwick Arms
75 Pierre
76 Plaza
77 Plaza 50
78 Portland Square
79 Quality Hotel 5th Avenue
80 Quality Hotel and Suites
81 Radisson Empire
82 Ramada Hotel Pennsylvania
83 Remington
84 Riverside Tower
85 Roger Smith
86 Roger Williams
87 Roosevelt
88 Royalton
89 Salisbury
90 San Carlos
91 Shelburne Murray Hill
92 Sherry Netherland
93 Soho Grand
94 Southgate Tower
95 St Moritz on the Park
96 Stanford
97 Surrey
98 The Tudor
99 Uptown Hostel
100 Vanderbilt YMCA
101 Waldorf-Astoria
102 Wales
103 Warwick
104 Washington Square
105 Webster Apartments
106 Wellington
107 Westpark
108 Westside YMCA
109 Wolcott
110 Wyndham

MANHATTAN HOTELS
& HOSTELS

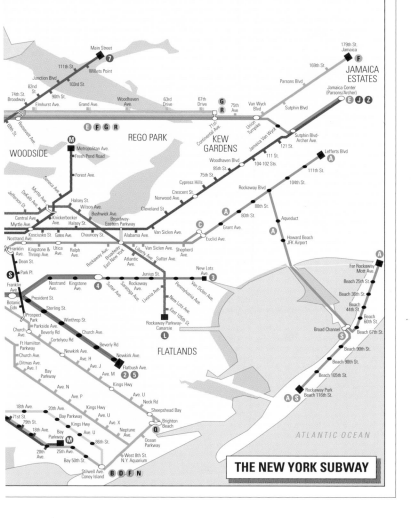

How to Use This Map

Transit Authority services operate 24 hours a day, but not all routes operate at all times. Train identification letters or numbers next to the station names on this map show the basic, seven-day-a-week service, from 6AM to midnight.

- ■ Terminal
- ▬ Local Stop
- ● Express Stop
- ○ All trains stops
- ⚇ Express and Local Stop (Free Transfer)

JAMAICA ESTATES

REGO PARK

KEW GARDENS

WOODSIDE

FLATLANDS

ATLANTIC OCEAN

THE NEW YORK SUBWAY

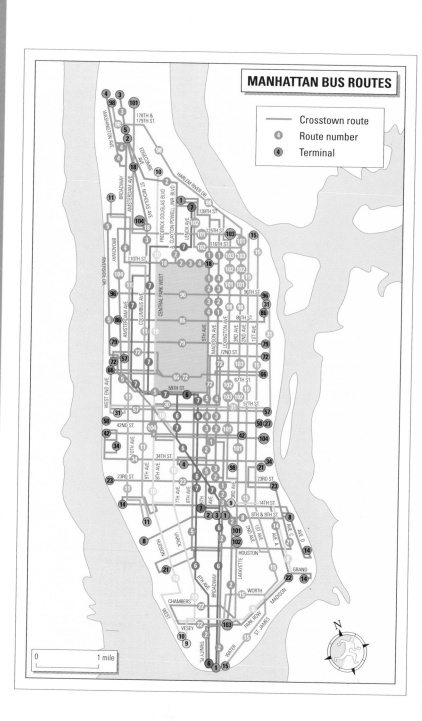

MANHATTAN BUS ROUTES

Crosstown route

④ Route number

④ Terminal